# THE COLLECTED PLAYS
## OF
## TERENCE RATTIGAN

# THE
# COLLECTED PLAYS
# OF
# TERENCE RATTIGAN

VOLUME TWO

The Later Plays 1953–1977

# CONTENTS

PREFACE
(This Preface appeared in Volume Three of
the Hamish Hamilton edition of 1964)


## AUNT EDNA v. RATTIGAN
### An Action for Libel

*Extract from the cross-examination of the defendant.*

COUNSEL FOR PLAINTIFF. You admit, then—and it has taken us nearly two days
to reach this admission—that it is you and you alone who are responsible for the distorted and perverted image of Aunt Edna that has been
trumpeted throughout this country, and abroad?

MYSELF. I don't think you can trumpet an image, Sir Robert, either here or
abroad.

COUNSEL FOR PLAINTIFF. Never mind about niceties of language, sir. Did you
or did you not write, in a preface to the second volume of your collected
plays, and published by Hamish Hamilton Limited in 1953, this description of my client? (*To usher.*) Would you hand him this book, please?
Exhibit A. Now, Mr. Rattigan, perhaps you would care to read out the
passages I have marked?

MYSELF. (*Reading.*) 'She is a nice respectable, middle-class, middle-aged
maiden lady, with time on her hands and the money to help her pass it.'

JUDGE. Keep your voice up, please.

MYSELF. I'm sorry, My Lord, but it has been a long and trying ordeal—

JUDGE. Continue, Sir Robert.

COUNSEL FOR PLAINTIFF. Read the next marked passage.

MYSELF. (*Reading.*) 'She is, in short, a hopeless lowbrow.'

JUDGE. He is mumbling again. Was the phrase: 'a hopeless lowbrow'?

COUNSEL FOR PLAINTIFF. Yes, My Lord. 'A hopeless lowbrow.'

JUDGE. 'A hopeless lowbrow.' Thank you. I have it. Continue.

COUNSEL FOR PLAINTIFF. Mr. Rattigan, when you composed the two phrases
that you have just read out, did you mean them as true?

MYSELF. I suppose so.

COUNSEL FOR PLAINTIFF. There can be no room for supposition in a libel action as serious as this. Did you or did you not mean them as true?

MYSELF. I meant them as true.

COUNSEL FOR PLAINTIFF. Think carefully, please, before you answer the next
question. Is there in fact any truth whatever in either of them?

MYSELF. No. Not in 1964.

JUDGE. I heard 'No'. I did not catch what followed.

COUNSEL FOR PLAINTIFF. I think he said 'not in 1964', My Lord.

JUDGE. I see. How can something be false in 1964 and not false when he wrote the passage in 1953?

COUNSEL FOR PLAINTIFF. I propose to follow that line, My Lord.

JUDGE. You are under no obligation to do so, Sir Robert. It was just a passing thought that struck me.

COUNSEL FOR PLAINTIFF. It struck me too, My Lord—with some force. Now, Mr. Rattigan, what you are saying, in effect, is that the description you gave of Aunt Edna in 1953 is wholly false?

MYSELF. Well, not *wholly* false, Sir Robert. Some things I said about her were true. For instance, that she has lived since the time of Sophocles and, if the bomb doesn't fall, is immortal—

COUNSEL FOR PLAINTIFF. Never mind about the bomb—

MYSELF. But I do—

COUNSEL FOR PLAINTIFF. Indeed? One would hardly gather so from your plays.

MYSELF. That's because I believe that plays should be mainly about people and not mainly about things. I wrote an article on that theme in the *New Statesman* in 1949 and had the compliment paid me of being pummelled on successive weeks by Benn Levy, James Bridie, Peter Ustinov, Sean O'Casey, Ted Willis, Christopher Fry and finally Bernard Shaw. Despite that I have always firmly stuck to that belief—

JUDGE. Is any of this relevant, Sir Robert?

COUNSEL FOR PLAINTIFF. No, My Lord—but the irrelevance was not mine but the witness's.

JUDGE. True. Proceed.

COUNSEL FOR PLAINTIFF. Now, Mr. Rattigan, you admitted at the beginning of your examination-in-chief to having created this lady in 1953?

MYSELF. I did.

COUNSEL FOR PLAINTIFF. And yet you are now saying that in all *material* particulars—we will forget, don't you think, that whimsy about her having lived since the time of Sophocles and possibly being immortal—in all *material* particulars, Mr. Rattigan, the description you gave of the lady at that time was totally false?

MYSELF. Yes.

COUNSEL FOR PLAINTIFF. Then we can establish that, in creating this lady eleven years ago, you told a whole series of outrageous lies?

MYSELF. Yes, I suppose I did. But they didn't seem like outrageous lies to me at the time.

COUNSEL FOR PLAINTIFF. Explain, please.

MYSELF. I wrote the passage before the advent of Osborne—

JUDGE. What is Osborne?

COUNSEL FOR PLAINTIFF. Osborne is a playwright, My Lord, who, in 1955, wrote a play called *Look Back in Anger*, and thereby initiated what has been called the Theatre of Revolt. Now, Mr. Rattigan—

JUDGE. Revolt against what?

COUNSEL FOR PLAINTIFF. The establishment. Now, Mr. Rattigan—

JUDGE. What is the establishment?

COUNSEL FOR PLAINTIFF. It has never been clearly defined, My Lord. The *status quo*, the class structure, authority in any form, the existing order, the—

JUDGE. Not *me?*

COUNSEL FOR PLAINTIFF. Oh no, My Lord. What an idea!

JUDGE. Against whom is this revolt directed, then?

COUNSEL FOR PLAINTIFF. Many people, My Lord. The defendant, for obvious reasons. Also unhappily the plaintiff.

JUDGE. Why the plaintiff?

COUNSEL FOR PLAINTIFF. Because, mainly on account of the false statements issued about her by the defendant, the new playwrights see her as their enemy—

PLAINTIFF. (*From the well of the court.*) I certainly am not their enemy. I go to the Royal Court very often—

USHER. Quiet, please—

PLAINTIFF. —and some plays of revolt I like very much indeed, when they're good plays.

USHER. Quiet, please—

PLAINTIFF. And that's why I've brought this case. I will not be labelled a hopeless lowbrow and the rest of it. It's a disgrace—that's what it is! A disgrace!

*Some applause from the public galleries, instantly quelled by the Judge.*

JUDGE. (*To Counsel.*) If you cannot keep your client in order, Sir Robert, I fear I must order her removal from this court.

COUNSEL FOR PLAINTIFF. I am extremely sorry, My Lord, and I will do so— but she has been very overwrought by this long case and is perhaps a little disturbed now at hearing her creator's belated, cynical and barefaced attempts to deny that he ever meant what in fact he wrote in plain English about her eleven years ago.

JUDGE. She is not the only person in this court to be disturbed at that, Sir Robert.

COUNSEL FOR PLAINTIFF. I don't doubt it, My Lord.

JUDGE. However, your client has already had her say in the witness box— and a very forthright say, it was, I thought.

COUNSEL FOR PLAINTIFF. She is a very forthright lady, My Lord.

JUDGE. So it appears. But now she must keep quiet. You may continue your cross-examination. I have here: the witness: 'They did not seem like outrageous lies to me at the time. I wrote the passage before the advent of Osborne.'

COUNSEL FOR PLAINTIFF. Thank you, My Lord. I have the same note. Now, Mr. Rattigan, the lady you created before the advent of Osborne and the lady you see sitting over there today, you would now have us believe, are two entirely different ladies?

MYSELF. Oh no. They are exactly the same lady. It's the theatrical situation that is different, and has now made her seem different too.

COUNSEL FOR PLAINTIFF. How, pray, can a theatrical situation make a lady seem different?

MYSELF. Well, I suppose because she has risen to meet that situation.

COUNSEL FOR PLAINTIFF. And in 1953, you didn't believe that she would?

MYSELF. Oh no. I always believed she would. Since Sophocles—

COUNSEL FOR PLAINTIFF. Ah. Sophocles—

MYSELF. Since Euripides she has always risen to meet any new theatrical situation. Look how she embraced the Elizabethan dramatists at their bawdiest and bloodiest, most morose and most obscure. Then we know how she fumed and fretted when the Puritans closed the theatres and how gladly she rushed to those candle-lit sexual frolics known as Restoration Drama which she now justifies because of its style and wit, but which she went to then, and I suspect does now, for no more impelling reason than to get herself some good, dirty, elegant, belly-laughs—

A VOICE. (*From the well of the court.*) It's a lie!

JUDGE. Sir Robert—

COUNSEL FOR PLAINTIFF. It was not my client, My Lord. As you see she has stuffed a handkerchief over her mouth. Only her suffused complexion is betraying her feelings.

JUDGE. Who was it, then?

COUNSEL FOR PLAINTIFF. Probably a critic, My Lord. Some admirer of the verbal graces of Congreve, Wycherley, and Dryden, no doubt—

JUDGE. He or she must stifle his or her indignation as I do mine. Continue.

MYSELF. I except Dryden—

COUNSEL FOR PLAINTIFF. Oh. You except Dryden?

MYSELF. Yes. Now, when we come to the theatre of Sheridan and Goldsmith—

COUNSEL FOR PLAINTIFF. But I don't think we do come to the theatre of Sheridan and Goldsmith, Mr. Rattigan, because we appear to be straying very far from the point—

COUNSEL FOR DEFENDANT. (*Rising.*) I think my learned friend should allow my client to finish his answer, My Lord—

JUDGE. Well, Sir Charles, it was a very wide question, I grant, but if, in reply, we are going to get a whole history of the British theatre, we might well be here all night.

MYSELF. Perhaps I had better jump to the nineteen-thirties, My Lord.

JUDGE. You could not, perhaps, jump further?

MYSELF. Not and make my point, My Lord.

JUDGE. Is it a point that you believe will help your case?

MYSELF. I don't believe anything will help my case.

JUDGE. Quite so. But you still wish to make your point?

MYSELF. Yes. I do.

JUDGE. Very well, then. But please be succinct.

MYSELF. What is succinct?

JUDGE. That is my part, sir. Kindly play your own. You know perfectly well what succinct is. Don't forget, Rattigan, I have your record before me, and it includes, I notice, an extremely expensive education—

COUNSEL FOR DEFENDANT. (*Rising.*) With the utmost possible respect, My Lord, such information, if given to the jury at this stage, could not have anything but a highly prejudicial effect, and I must most emphatically protest. The phrase 'expensive education' is, again with respect, anyway quite inaccurate—

JUDGE. Harrow and Trinity College, Oxford?

COUNSEL FOR DEFENDANT. Since your Lordship has seen fit to reveal such damaging facts from the defendant's past record, your well-known sense of fairness will no doubt permit me to point out that my client could not have gone to either of those educational centres unless he had secured valuable scholarships to both.

JUDGE. *Could* not, Sir Charles?

COUNSEL FOR DEFENDANT. Could *not*, My Lord.

JUDGE. I presume he obtained first-class honours?

COUNSEL FOR DEFENDANT. No, My Lord. He did not sit for his examinations.

JUDGE. *He did not sit for his examinations?*

COUNSEL FOR DEFENDANT. No, My Lord.

JUDGE. But how come this, Sir Charles? Was he sent down for riotous and licentious behaviour?

COUNSEL FOR DEFENDANT. Certainly not, My Lord. He *came* down from Oxford of his own volition in order to begin his career as a practising dramatist.

JUDGE. It was not, perhaps, in order to escape the stigma of a 'third'?

COUNSEL FOR DEFENDANT. If your Lordship would refer to a certain document before you—that is the one—you will find it to be a letter written by his ex-tutor at Oxford who, as you see, most confidently asserts that he might well have got a first if he had continued his studies.

JUDGE. (*After studying the document.*) The gentleman in question admits to being ninety-four, and writes an extremely shaky hand.

COUNSEL FOR DEFENDANT. There are contemporaries of the defendant's who are prepared to swear—

COUNSEL FOR PLAINTIFF. (*Rising.*) Hearsay, My Lord.

JUDGE. Agreed, Sir Robert. Now, Sir Charles, coming back to the question of income—forgive me for a few seconds longer, Sir Robert, but this is of moment to Sir Charles' somewhat surprising interruption—of what income did the defendant's father and mother dispose?

COUNSEL FOR DEFENDANT. Roughly a thousand pounds a year, My Lord.

JUDGE. Ah. And that, by modern standards, would be roughly in the neighbourhood of three thousand pounds—

COUNSEL FOR DEFENDANT. True, My Lord. I cannot deny it, and the facts thereby qualify my client as having been born into the middle or professional classes. Damaging as that is, my client has—I trust your

Lordship will agree—never made any secret of it. You have heard him admit it all, openly, in this very court, and the admission, I submit, does him honour. But the phrase: 'expensive education', which your Lordship saw fit to use a moment ago, can only imply, today, for a practising playwright that he was born, decidedly, on the wrong side of the fence—

JUDGE. Your point is taken, Sir Charles.

COUNSEL FOR DEFENDANT. —and could be most injurious to his reputation—

JUDGE. Your point is taken, Sir Charles. I shall endeavour to redress the balance in my summing-up. I shall even point out that, for a time, during his apprenticeship for the theatre, the defendant lived on an allowance of two pounds a week only—

COUNSEL FOR DEFENDANT. (*Sitting.*) Thank you, My Lord.

JUDGE. Which, of course, by today's standards, means six pounds a week—and with board and lodging to boot, and, with loving parents, no worry about where the next meal was coming from—

COUNSEL FOR DEFENDANT. (*Rising.*) My Lord—

JUDGE. *You* have raised the issue, Sir Charles. I must later present it to the jury fairly and squarely. They must see both sides of the picture—

COUNSEL FOR DEFENDANT. With respect, My Lord, there is only one side of a picture. The side that has been painted on.

JUDGE. Will you please resume your seat, Sir Charles? (*To me.*) Now, sir, do you now admit that you do know the meaning of the word 'succinct'?

MYSELF. Yes, My Lord.

JUDGE. (*To Counsel for Defendant.*) You see, Sir Charles? (*To me.*) Then jump to the nineteen-thirties, and make it snappy.

MYSELF. Yes, My Lord. Well, the image I gave to Aunt Edna in 1953 applied—I want to be quite honest—far more truthfully to the nineteen-thirties than to the nineteen-sixties. In fact, in writing the passage in question, I was guilty of looking back rather than of looking forward.

COUNSEL FOR PLAINTIFF. You are, of course, a playwright of the thir-ties?

MYSELF. No, Sir Robert. I am not.

COUNSEL FOR PLAINTIFF. But you are very often so described.

MYSELF. Yes, but inaccurately. Out of the twenty or so plays I have so far written, only two were produced in the thirties.

COUNSEL FOR PLAINTIFF. I have before me several critical assessments, made by men of the highest standing in their calling, who refer to you, and refer to you constantly, as a playwright of the thirties. I must warn you to be particularly careful on this point. You are saying that all these eminent critics are lying?

MYSELF. Heaven forbid. That would be most unwise. I merely say that they appear to have been factually misinformed.

COUNSEL FOR PLAINTIFF. And they have been 'factually misinformed' when they link your name with that of Noël Coward's?

MYSELF. Noël Coward is a great friend of mine and I admire him very much but he is twelve years older than I and he had his first play performed sixteen years before mine.

JUDGE. Perhaps he will now cease to be a great friend of yours.

*Laughter in court, in which His Lordship was seen to join.*

MYSELF. Facts are facts, My Lord.

JUDGE. Then pray stick to them. You testified just now that the image you gave to Aunt Edna in 1953 was truer of the thirties than the sixties. If you are not a playwright of the thirties how comes it that in so *imagining* her—to coin a word—you should have chanced upon a period with which you now say you have little or no connection?

MYSELF. I didn't say quite that, My Lord. I have a strong connection with the thirties. Most of my early playgoing, which, at that time, was almost obsessional, was done in that era. But then I must point out that the so-called theatre of the thirties continued unbroken through the forties and early fifties—in fact more 'French Window' drama was produced through the war and for some years after it than in the thirties

JUDGE. What is 'French Window drama'?

COUNSEL FOR PLAINTIFF. I was anticipating that question, My Lord. It is a port-manteau phrase to cover a species of complacent middle-class theatre, either comedy or drama, and utterly devoid of either intellectual or so-ciological content—

MYSELF. Ibsen had french windows—

JUDGE. Silence, sir! Speak when you are spoken to. Continue, Sir Robert. Why 'French Window'?

COUNSEL FOR PLAINTIFF. Because in such plays french windows were exten-sively employed for entrances—usually for young couples in tennis clothes who after depositing their rackets, often went straight into a pro-posal scene on a sofa, seat facing squarely to the audience and with its back to the fireplace; but it was also useful for the entrance, at the end of Act One, for characters, often pseudonymized in the programme as 'The Stranger', who would ultimately reveal themselves as the Devil or God or someone's long-lost husband. French windows were often use-ful, too, for the heroine's frantic final exit to plunge herself into the mill-race—

MYSELF. Ibsen again!

COUNSEL FOR PLAINTIFF AND JUDGE. (*Simultaneously.*) Will you be quiet, sir!

JUDGE. (*To Counsel.*) Have you anything to add to your definition of French Window drama, Sir Robert?

COUNSEL FOR PLAINTIFF. Only this, My Lord. It was a totally effete and de-generate school of drama, aimed solely to flatter and please the rich, idle, mindless, stalls' public—and its plays were often so ill-conceived as to dare to begin the action with a maid crossing an empty stage to answer a telephone—

MYSELF. I used to queue for a one and sixpenny seat, to see Gertrude Lawrence and Marie Tempest—and a maid answering a telephone is less clumsy an exposition than a character in a spotlight addressing the audience—

COUNSEL FOR PLAINTIFF. I did not elicit that admission, My Lord. The defendant, as you heard, volunteered it. I trust the jury heard it too. May I proceed, My Lord?

JUDGE. It would be as well. We all seem to have got somewhat lost. Yon have a very talkative witness, Sir Robert, of a rather hysterical disposition, it would seem, and apt to fly off at tangents at the slightest provocation. You have my sympathy. It would seem impossible to keep him to the point.

COUNSEL FOR PLAINTIFF. If your Lordship would refer to some other documents on your desk—

JUDGE. Ah yes. I find one here. (*Reading.*) 'He has an incurably second-rate mind.' Another. 'His plays are empty of all intellectual content whatever.' And yet another: 'The trouble with Mr. Rattigan is that he just cannot think.' Yes, Sir Robert, that might explain your difficulty.

COUNSEL FOR DEFENDANT. (*Rising.*) May I remind your Lordship of the defendant's various youthful academic distinctions—

JUDGE. You have already done so, Sir Charles. But evidence of the defendant's mental qualities in 1925 and 1930 are not evidence of the defendant's mental qualities in 1964. Minds have been known to deteriorate—

COUNSEL FOR DEFENDANT. Also to improve—

JUDGE. Not, I think, in this case. Continue, Sir Robert, and kindly bring your cross-examination back, as soon as possible, to the vital point at issue—the defendant's publication of certain statements in 1953 about the plaintiff. Meanwhile I suppose we must hear him out about the thirties—

COUNSEL FOR PLAINTIFF. (*To me.*) You were saying that when you made these false and damaging statements about Aunt Edna in 1953 you were thinking back rather than forward, and that the so-called theatre of the thirties had continued unbroken throughout the forties and early fifties. Therefore you gave to Aunt Edna a 1934 image rather than a 1964 image. Is that correct?

MYSELF. Yes. But I object to your definition of the thirties' drama as 'totally effete and degenerate'.

COUNSEL FOR PLAINTIFF. Indeed? What is your own definition?

MYSELF. It was a theatre designed principally, I grant, to entertain; but then I don't think that entertainment *per se* is necessarily an unworthy objective of drama.

COUNSEL FOR PLAINTIFF. You don't, Mr. Rattigan?

MYSELF. No, I don't, After all even Shakespeare called a play *As You Like It*, and he was right because they did, and still do.

JUDGE. What has Shakespeare to do with the drama of the thirties?

COUNSEL FOR PLAINTIFF. I have really no idea, My Lord. (*To me.*) Kindly *try* to stick to the point, Mr. Rattigan—

MYSELF. I *was* trying. *As You Like It* was an example of the theatre of entertainment and escapism, entirely sans social significance

JUDGE. *Sans?*

COUNSEL FOR PLAINTIFF. A reference to a word used in a famous speech in the play in question. It means 'without'.

JUDGE. Why did he not say 'without'?

COUNSEL FOR PLAINTIFF. No doubt he was trying to dazzle us with his erudition. (*Laughter.*) Back to the drama of the thirties, please, Mr. Rattigan.

MYSELF. Well, admittedly it contained much that was ill-written, stupid and bad—but so does the theatre of today—and the ill-written, stupid and bad play does not now, and did not then, entertain. But it also contained much that was good. To select just a few examples, it contained the later and best plays of Somerset Maugham, the earlier and best plays of J. B. Priestley, the Tyrone Guthrie seasons at the Old Vic, John Gielgud's *Hamlet* at the New, the same actor's season at the Queen's which included the best production of a Chekhov play ever seen in this country—

COUNSEL FOR PLAINTIFF. Are you leaving out the visit of the Moscow Arts Theatre in 1958; and *Uncle Vanya* at the National Theatre?

MYSELF. —the best production, I repeat, of a Chekhov play ever seen in this country. There was also a memorable production of *Romeo and Juliet* with John Gielgud and Laurence Olivier alternating the parts of Romeo and Mercutio, and I can only say I would love to see today some theatrical venture that might generate the same atomic excitement which that did—

JUDGE. Atomic? He has gone out of his period, hasn't he?

COUNSEL FOR PLAINTIFF. Yes, My Lord. (*To me.*) Pray stick to your period.

MYSELF. Yes, sir. Well, it was a period that began in slump and political crisis, continued after 1933 under the gathering clouds of an increasingly certain world cataclysm, and, if we may continue into the forties and early fifties—

JUDGE. We certainly may—

MYSELF. —up, in fact, to the date in question, 1953, we find, not unnaturally, an increasingly escapist and trivial theatre—with some exceptions, of course, such as the triumphant Olivier-Richardson Old Vic Seasons and various worthy classical revivals—but the five years of war and the seven years of poverty and austerity that followed, provided an atmosphere hardly conducive to a theatre that would force audiences to face uncomfortable facts. It needed increasing affluence and a growing sense of security from war—gained by what Churchill called 'The balance of terror'—to do that—

*Disturbance in the public gallery. A man in clerical dress shouted a slogan which was interpreted as either 'Better Red than Dead' or 'Better Dead than Red'. He was ejected. Simultaneously a group of Chinese law students struck up a chant of 'Ban the bomb! For the time being anyway.' They too were ejected.*

COUNSEL FOR PLAINTIFF. (*After the disturbance.*) You might wish to retract that observation, Mr. Rattigan, and I shall give you that opportunity now. Otherwise, I shall, of course, base my address to the jury largely on what you have just said. Do you, sir, now wish to repeat that statement about affluence, the growing sense of security from war, and the balance of terror?

MYSELF. Yes.

COUNSEL FOR PLAINTIFF. Earlier you said that you 'minded about the bomb'?

MYSELF. I mind about death too.

COUNSEL FOR PLAINTIFF. Quite so. But do you actually wish to go on record as saying that the later fifties and early sixties have been a period of growing security from war?

MYSELF. My God—compared to the thirties—with a major international crisis every other week-end—

JUDGE. There is no need for profanity as well.

MYSELF. I'm sorry, but compared to the thirties you might almost say of to-day:

'Uncertainties now crown themselves assured
And peace proclaims olives of endless age.'

JUDGE. What was that?

COUNSEL FOR PLAINTIFF. Another quotation from Shakespeare, My Lord.

JUDGE. He seems addicted to them.

COUNSEL FOR DEFENDANT. (*Rising.*) Your Lordship will remember that in examination-in-chief my client constantly adduced Shakespeare as an example of an essentially noncommitted and escapist dramatist, more concerned with people than with things, accepting the establishment of the period, and seemingly unaware of the profound social changes that were going on around him and which would result, not long after his death, in a violent revolution.

JUDGE. I remember it all well, Sir Charles, and have made a note upon it. (*To Counsel.*) Has he finished with this question of the thirties, forties and early fifties?

COUNSEL FOR PLAINTIFF. Have you, Mr. Rattigan?

MYSELF. Well, there is just one thing, though, I'd like to add—

JUDGE. Oh my God—

COUNSEL FOR PLAINTIFF. My Lord?

JUDGE. I said nothing. Continue.

MYSELF. Just this. Labels are no doubt useful to the theatrical historian—labels such as 'French Window School', 'Kitchen Sink School', 'Sociological School', 'Fry-Eliot School', 'Brechtian Epic School', 'Manchester School', 'Shavian School', 'Ibsenite School', 'Chekhovian School'—even 'Coward-Rattigan School'—but the theatre remains the theatre. What is good, of any school, is good. What is bad, of any school, is bad. Fashion is ephemeral. The theatre is immortal. I have said my say.

COUNSEL FOR PLAINTIFF. Don't get down, sir. Officer—Officer—catch him. Pray put him back in the witness box at once—

JUDGE. Must you, Sir Robert?

COUNSEL FOR PLAINTIFF. For only a very few more moments, My Lord. I will not try your patience much longer, I promise you—nor my own. But I have a duty to the plaintiff. The defendant has admitted that he lied about her abominably in his previous preface, and it is plainly my task, in this, to discover from him what he now considers to be the truth.

JUDGE. Very well, if you so wish it. But pray be very brief.

COUNSEL FOR PLAINTIFF. Now, Mr. Rattigan, will you look again at those passages marked in red? Thank you. 'A nice, respectable, middle-class, middle-aged, maiden lady.' You have that passage to hand? Good. We will take the words as they come. 'Nice'?

MYSELF. Well, you heard her in the box—

COUNSEL FOR PLAINTIFF. Impertinence will get you nowhere. Do you substitute 'nasty'?

MYSELF. No.

COUNSEL FOR PLAINTIFF. What do you substitute?

MYSELF. Either nice or nasty.

COUNSEL FOR PLAINTIFF. An illuminating reply. 'Respectable'?

MYSELF. Not necessarily.

COUNSEL FOR PLAINTIFF. Now we are getting somewhere. 'Middle-class'?

MYSELF. Not necessarily.

COUNSEL FOR PLAINTIFF. Lower-class?

MYSELF. Only sometimes.

COUNSEL FOR PLAINTIFF. Upper-class?

MYSELF. Less often.

COUNSEL FOR PLAINTIFF. What do you substitute then?

MYSELF. Classless. She is part of our classless society.

COUNSEL FOR PLAINTIFF. Do you really believe that we have a classless society, Mr. Rattigan?

MYSELF. No, but if we had one I expect she would welcome it.

COUNSEL FOR PLAINTIFF. I see. How does she vote?

MYSELF. Conservative, perhaps, more likely Labour, but most likely Liberal.

COUNSEL FOR PLAINTIFF. Now we are really progressing. 'Middle-aged'?

MYSELF. She had a rejuvenation treatment in 1955.

COUNSEL FOR PLAINTIFF. 'Maiden lady'?

MYSELF. Not necessarily. In fact, judging by some of the plays she has seen and relished since that time I would say very unlikely.

COUNSEL FOR PLAINTIFF. What would you substitute?

MYSELF. A lady of some sexual experience, either practised or imagined.

COUNSEL FOR PLAINTIFF. Good. We now have a nice or nasty, respectable or unrespectable, classless, rejuvenated, most-likely—Liberal—voting lady, of some sexual experience, either practised or imagined. The passage about 'time on her hands and the money to help her pass it'?

MYSELF. After her rejuvenation treatment such money as she has is no doubt earned, and such time as she has on her hands is only enough to go to the theatre.

COUNSEL FOR PLAINTIFF. Quite so. *Now* we come to the very crux and kernel of the whole case—to wit—your vilification of my client as 'a hopeless lowbrow'—

PLAINTIFF. (*From the well of the court.*) It's a disgrace—that's what it is—a positive disgrace! I go to Osborne and Wesker and just because I sometimes go to *his* plays too—not always, mind you—not that Variation thing about the tart and the gigolo—oh no. Nothing would get me to that—but the others in this volume I did go to, I grant—still that doesn't make me a *lowbrow!* That's the lowbrow, in the witness box. My creator! Some creator! I tell you all—I'm no f . . . . . g lowbrow!

JUDGE. Sir Robert, your client, apart from making another unwarranted interruption, has just uttered an expletive which, though perfectly permissible nowadays, I expect, on the stage—which is doubtless where she learnt it—is still not quite seemly in a court of law. I am not going to ask you what it means. I know what it means. Alas, only too well. However I fear I must now order her bodily removal from this court. Officer—pray see to it.

*The plaintiff was ejected, amid loud cries of protest from the public gallery, and some slogans, amongst which could be recognized: 'Down with the reactionary backward-looking school of bourgeois uncommitted theatre!' and 'Up with Mother Courage!' To the latter slogan the lady appeared to take offence, uttering another expletive of a violent nature before the doors closed behind her. The disturbance subsided quickly.*

JUDGE. That was disgraceful, Sir Robert. This court is rapidly becoming a place of public entertainment—

A MAN FROM THE PUBLIC GALLERY. Down with public entertainment! Down with the reactionary backward-looking school of bourgeois—

*Before he had completed his slogan he was ejected.*

JUDGE. Dear me! I had no idea that this case would arouse feelings so strong—

COUNSEL FOR PLAINTIFF. It is hardly to be wondered at, My Lord. A lady with whom many hundreds of thousands of devoted playgoers identify themselves has been most grossly libelled—

COUNSEL FOR DEFENDANT. (*Rising.*) That will surely be for the jury to decide, My Lord.

JUDGE. It will, indeed, Sir Charles—and very shortly too, I trust. I understand you are calling no other evidence?

COUNSEL FOR DEFENDANT. No, My Lord. The many eminent witnesses we hoped to present have all, it seems, gone abroad—

COUNSEL FOR PLAINTIFF. In rather a hurry, I gather?

COUNSEL FOR DEFENDANT. My learned friend's imputation is unworthy.

COUNSEL FOR PLAINTIFF. But factual. May I proceed? (*Counsel sat.*) Mr. Rattigan, we are dealing with the word 'lowbrow', are we not?

MYSELF. Yes.

COUNSEL FOR PLAINTIFF. What word do you wish to substitute for that? (*The Defendant showed some signs of hesitation.*) Come, come, sir. She must have some kind of brow, and there are only three, are there not—high, middle and low?

MYSELF. I don't know.

COUNSEL FOR PLAINTIFF. You don't know? What other brows are there besides these three?

MYSELF. I don't know. I just don't know. I can't think.

JUDGE. Perhaps a glass of water?

COUNSEL FOR PLAINTIFF. It is growing late, My Lord.

JUDGE. True, Proceed.

COUNSEL FOR PLAINTIFF. Is she a *high* brow, Mr. Rattigan?

MYSELF. Good heavens, no.

COUNSEL FOR PLAINTIFF. Why 'good heavens, no'? You heard her say that she goes to Osborne and Wesker.

MYSELF. But they're not *highbrow*. Their strength as dramatists lies in their feelings and in their gift for expressing those feelings—

COUNSEL FOR PLAINTIFF. Pinter, Ionesco, Beckett? She told us, in the box, that she has sometimes enjoyed those authors. Aren't they highbrow?

MYSELF. They are mystifying.

COUNSEL FOR PLAINTIFF. Isn't that highbrow?

MYSELF. No. Aunt Edna enjoys being mystified, but she loathes being baffled. All those three authors have a strong theatrical gift, which can always be identified as the gift for stirring emotions in an audience, whether to tears or to laughter or to pure theatrical excitement. The three gentlemen named may well be highbrows themselves. That I would hardly know. I do know that their plays are not.

COUNSEL FOR PLAINTIFF. What plays, then, do you consider highbrow, Mr. Rattigan?

MYSELF. Can I have that glass of water?

JUDGE AND COUNSEL FOR PLAINTIFF. (*Together.*) No.

MYSELF. Oh dear! A highbrow play? A real *play*—not something to be read in the study? I'm terribly sorry. I can't think of one. I can think of many advanced plays, and many experimental plays—

COUNSEL FOR PLAINTIFF. Do you consider such plays as highbrow?

MYSELF. Not necessarily, I'm afraid. Definitely not if they have appealed to an ordinary, paying audience. Strictly speaking, a highbrow play would appeal only to an audience of highbrows, and I can't think of such a play. I'm sorry, Sir Robert, but I can't, I really can't.

*The witness again showed signs of distress.*

COUNSEL FOR PLAINTIFF. May I perhaps help you, Mr. Rattigan, and cite an example from your favourite dramatist? What about *Lear*?

MYSELF. Oh no. It's a great work of art, the most stupendous achievement ever accomplished by any dramatist, written on more levels of thought and symbolism than Ibsen ever dreamt of. But it's not *highbrow*. There's always one level on which even the most moronic of Elizabethan groundlings could have appreciated it, and on which Aunt Edna still does—the straight level of narrative, with the engrossing sense of something very mystifying going on around and above that level. Nobody can fully understand *Lear*. Nobody can fail to be held by it.

COUNSEL FOR PLAINTIFF. So now we have my client as a 'moronic groundling'?

MYSELF. I didn't mean that. I'm so sorry. I'm terribly tired and confused—

COUNSEL FOR PLAINTIFF. What *did* you mean, then?

MYSELF. Just that Aunt Edna is a part of a majority audience for which true theatre exists, and always has existed; while highbrow theatre, if there were such a thing, would exist only for a minority audience, which is a euphemism for a small audience, which is a euphemism for a half-empty house, which is a euphemism for a play that might have filled a cellar in Islington for ten or twenty performances, which is a euphemism for a play that should have been read and not acted, which is a euphemism for a flop. Once more I have said my say.

COUNSEL FOR PLAINTIFF. No, sir. Once more you have not. Aunt Edna is neither high nor low brow. She must therefore be middle.

MYSELF. No.

COUNSEL FOR PLAINTIFF. No?

MYSELF. Not in its modern connotation. That means Annigoni and *Punch*. I know. It's always being said about myself. There are painters she prefers to Annigoni, and she reads the *New Statesman* as well as *Punch*.

COUNSEL FOR PLAINTIFF. So, if she is not high, nor low, nor middle brow, what is she? (*The witness again showed hesitation.*) Answer me, pray. What is she, sir?

MYSELF. No brow at all.

JUDGE. Speak up, please.

MYSELF. No brow at all. Or rather an elastic brow. A brow that can stretch from the National Theatre to the Whitehall, from Plautus in the original—if Sir Laurence does it—to A *Funny Thing Happened On The Way To The Forum*. She is brow*less*, Sir Robert. Brow*less!*

COUNSEL FOR PLAINTIFF. There is no need to shout.

MYSELF. I am at the end of my tether—

COUNSEL FOR PLAINTIFF. So are we. A last question, and I have done. You have now entirely reversed the image of Aunt Edna that you gave to the world in 1953. And yet you said earlier in today's testimony that the Aunt Edna of 1953 and the Aunt Edna of 1964—and here I quote your exact words—'are exactly the same lady'. How came you, Mr. Rattigan, to utter such a palpable falsehood?

MYSELF. It is not a palpable falsehood. It is the truth, Sir Robert. Please believe me. Please! I know this lady. I made her—

COUNSEL FOR PLAINTIFF. In your image, it would seem—

MYSELF. If you like. I don't care what I say now. Everything is lost, I see that
   clearly. But Aunt Edna is the same lady, because Aunt Edna doesn't
   change. In the light of what I have been saying about her that must sound
   ridiculous—

JUDGE. It does.

MYSELF. It's only Aunt Edna's *image* that changes, and changes constantly from
   generation to generation. When I come to write my next preface, if I
   do, her image may well have changed completely again. But she herself
   remains the same, she always has and she always will. *She knows what
   she likes*, and there is nothing she likes better than *a nice change!* She is
   liking one at the moment, but that doesn't and cannot change *her!*

COUNSEL FOR PLAINTIFF. You are shouting again.

MYSELF. I know and I'm going to shout louder. Aunt Edna remains Aunt
   Edna, with only two basic demands of the theatre—first, that it excite
   her to laugh or to cry or to wonder what is going to happen next; and,
   second, that she can suspend her disbelief willingly and without effort.
   It's only Aunt Edna's *emotions* that a playwright can hope to excite, because we know for sure that she does bring those to the theatre. But we
   can't hope to excite her intellect because, if she has one at all, which is
   unlikely, she will almost certainly have left it behind in her rooms, or
   forgotten it on the bus, or checked it in at the theatre cloakroom. You
   may ask me: 'What about plays of rhetoric?' or 'What about plays of wit?'
   I would answer by repeating that both, too, are aimed at the plaintiff's
   emotions, not at her intellect. Laughter, tears, excitement. That is all she
   demands. She is bored by propaganda, enraged at being 'alienated',
   loathes placards coming down and telling her what is going to happen
   next, hates a lot of philosophical talk on the stage with nothing happening
   at all, enjoys poetry only when it is dramatic and fine prose only when
   there is action to go with it. Her greatest joy is still and always will be
   for a good strong meaty plot told by good strong meaty characters—

COUNSEL FOR PLAINTIFF. You are growing very shrill. Have you finished?

MYSELF. No. She is unchanging and unchangeable, immortal and everlast-
   ing, and all she ever brings to the theatre is her undying love for it. Long
   live Aunt Edna! Long live the theatre! For the two are one and the same—

JUDGE. What has become of the witness, Sir Robert? I don't appear to see
   him any longer.

COUNSEL FOR PLAINTIFF. He would seem to have fainted, My Lord.

JUDGE. Ah. Yes, that would explain it. Well, I think this would be a convenient time to adjourn, don't you?

*His Lordship rose.*

# THE SLEEPING PRINCE

First published 1954
by Hamish Hamilton Ltd

TO
HUGH BEAUMONT
With affection, admiration and gratitude

THE SLEEPING PRINCE
An occasional fairy tale

*Concerning (in strict order of precedence) the following personages*:

His Majesty King Nicholas VIII of Carpathia

His Royal Highness, The Grand Duke Charles, Prince Regent of
Carpathia

Her Imperial and Royal Highness, The Grand Duchess Charles

Her Royal Highness, The Archduchess Ferdinand of Styria

Her Royal Highness, The Princess Louisa of Styria

Count Trigorinsky (*Major-Domo to The Grand Duke*)

The Countess von und zu Meissenbronn
(*Lady in Waiting to The Grand Duchess*)

The Hon. Peter Northbrook
(*attached to The Grand Duke's Suite*)

The Baroness Brunheim
(*Lady in Waiting to The Grand Duchess*)

Baron Schwartz (*Butler to The Grand Duke*)

Freiherr von Braun (*Personal Footman to The Grand Duke*)

Ur de Grune (*Personal Footman to The Grand Duke*)

Miss Mary Morgan, whose stage name (to avoid confusion)
is Elaine Dagenham

## ACT I

SCENE 1: WEDNESDAY, JUNE 21ST, 1911, ABOUT ELEVEN-THIRTY P.M.
SCENE 2: THURSDAY, JUNE 22ND, 1911, ABOUT EIGHT A.M.

## ACT II

SCENE 1: THURSDAY, JUNE 22ND, 1911, ABOUT SEVEN P.M.
SCENE 2: FRIDAY, JUNE 23RD, 1911, ABOUT ONE A.M.
SCENE 3: FRIDAY, JUNE 23RD, 1911, ABOUT TEN A.M.

The scene throughout is a room in the Carpathian Legation in London.

*The Sleeping Prince* was first produced at the Phoenix Theatre, London, on November 5th, 1953, with the following cast:

| | |
|---|---|
| PETER NORTHBROOK | Richard Wattis |
| MARY | Vivien Leigh |
| THE MAJOR-DOMO | Paul Hardwick |
| THE REGENT | Laurence Olivier |
| THE KING | Jeremy Spenser |
| THE GRAND DUCHESS | Martha Hunt |
| THE COUNTESS | Rosamund Greenwood |
| THE BARONESS | Daphne Newton |
| THE ARCHDUCHESS | Elaine Inescort |
| THE PRINCESS | Nicola Delman |
| FOOTMEN | Peter Barkworth |
| | Angus Mackay |
| | Terence Owen |

The play directed by LAURENCE OLIVIER

Setting and costumes by ROGER FURSE
Words and music for *The Coconut Girl* by VIVIAN ELLIS

# ACT I

## SCENE 1

SCENE: *A reception room in a foreign Legation in Belgrave Square. The time is about eleven-thirty on the evening of Wednesday, June 2lst, 1911.*

*We are looking at a very elegantly furnished octagonal room of which five walls are visible—the 'fourth' wall in this case being, in fact, the sixth, seventh and eighth. Taking up the entire central wall, backstage, is a pair of massive double doors. In the two walls R., and L., of it are set two smaller doors. Downstage R., are large windows, curtained at the moment.*

*At the rise of the curtain the stage is empty, but all the lights are on. After a moment the double doors are thrown open and* TWO FOOTMEN, *dressed in a distinctive livery, enter and stand on either side of the battants. Behind them enters* MARY MORGAN, *and behind her* PETER NORTHBROOK. MARY, *whose stage name (to avoid confusion) is* ELAINE DAGENHAM, *stands stock still looking about her in wonder. She is dressed in a very simple white evening dress, is young and considered very alluring. When she speaks it is with a fairly pronounced American accent.* PETER *is about forty and is something in the Foreign Office. He is wearing tails.*

MARY. (*Looking around in awe.*) Gosh!

*The* TWO FOOTMEN *go out and close the doors.*

This is the first time I've ever seen the inside of an Embassy.

PETER. Legation.

MARY. Same thing, isn't it?

PETER. Not quite. There are only nine Embassies in London at the present time.

MARY. (*Slightly disappointed.*) Oh, you mean they don't rate Carpathia as all that important?

PETER. Not yet.

MARY. It looks enormous on the map.

PETER. Maps can be misleading. Don't misunderstand me, Miss—er—Dagenham. I'm not, in any way, trying to belittle Carpathia. I've never been there, but I gather there is quite a lot to be said for the country. Its trains run on time—and its army, after France, Russia and Germany, is the best in Europe. What is more—

MARY. Pardon me. May I sit down?

PETER. Of course.

MARY *settles herself gingerly on end of sofa, with evident pleasure.*

MARY. This is really something, isn't it?

PETER. Something?

MARY. This room and everything.

PETER. (*Looking round.*) Yes. Personally I find the decorations a little vulgar.

MARY. Then give me vulgarity. Do you live here?

PETER. No. I am merely temporarily attached to the Grand Duke's suite. There are, of course, similar appointments made for all the Royal visitors to the Coronation, but in view of the recent adherence of Carpathia to the Entente Cordiale and the great importance attached by the Foreign Secretary to that adherence, a rather special appointment has been made in the case of the Grand Duke. You see, I am actually the head of the Balkan Department at the Foreign Office.

MARY. (*Uninterested.*) You don't say! Who's coming to this supper?—apart from His Majesty, I mean.

PETER. (*Startled.*) His Majesty?

MARY. The Grand Duke.

PETER. Oh. My dear, you quite startled me. Look, Miss Dagenham, as I gather you're a citizen of the United States, I think perhaps—before the Grand Duke arrives—you should learn the correct form of address. Otherwise, who knows, there may be a few petits moments d'embarras.

MARY. (*Murmuring.*) Now, I should just hate that.

PETER. The Grand Duke is not King of Carpathia, but Regent.

MARY. Same—

PETER. (*Interrupting.*) No, it is not the same thing. The Grand Duke, who was a prince of Hungary, married the late Queen of Carpathia, and while she was alive had the title and form of Prince Consort. On her death their son, Nicolas—a minor—became King, and the Grand Duke was appointed Prince Regent. The correct form of address is therefore Your Royal Highness.

MARY. I thought his wife was alive.

PETER. She is. But it's his wife—en secondes noces.

MARY. What's that mean?

PETER. (*After due thought.*) His second wife.

MARY. Why isn't she queen?

PETER. Oh, for heaven's sake. It's perfectly simple—

MARY. Not to me—

PETER. Look, Miss Dagenham, I really don't think you need bother your very pretty little head—

MARY. Thank you.

PETER. —with abstruse questions of primogeniture and Salic Laws and things. Just remember that your host tonight—The Grand Duke Charles—is addressed as Your Royal Highness, or Sir, that his wife, the Grand Duchess Charles, is addressed as Your Imperial and Royal Highness, or Ma'am—

MARY. Hi, wait a moment. That's a lot to remember. Imperial and Royal? Why all that?

PETER. That is far too complicated to explain. It all goes back to the Holy Roman Empire. She is a niece of the Emperor Franz Joseph.

MARY. No wisecracks about Austria then?

PETER. I sincerely trust no wisecracks about anything, Miss Dagenham—of diplomatic moment, that is. In these troubled times the lightest remark can have terrible repercussions—

MARY. Gee! I can see the history books now. The war of Dagenham's Remark.

PETER. If you *should* meet the young King—

MARY. Oh gosh! *Another* one?

PETER. He is addressed as Your Majesty, Sire, or Sir. Now have you got all that straight?

MARY. Gee. I don't think so. Altogether far too much plot in far too little time—

PETER. (*Puzzled.*) Plot? (*He smiles politely.*) Oh yes, of course. A stage term. Oh, and one other point. In conversation with Royalty only speak when you are directly addressed.

MARY. You mean wait for the cue before speaking the line?

PETER. I suppose you could put it like that.

MARY. Oh, God, I'm shaking. It's worse than a first night. Do you think we've come to the right place? Where, are the other guests?

PETER. I don't know. I was told eleven-thirty. It's after that now.

MARY. But why am I asked anyway—do you know?

PETER. Well, after all you met him the other night, didn't you, when he came to your show.

MARY. Sure, but so did the ten other principals, and I was right at the end of the line.

PETER. It seemed to me that he paid you rather particular attention that night.

MARY. Well, now you mention it, it did strike me, I admit, that I was a couple of yeses and a no up on Laura Cardus, who was standing next to me. But I can assure you our dialogue wasn't so brilliant that he must have felt he simply had to have that female Oscar Wilde to set his supper table on a roar tonight. Are you sure he hasn't mixed me up with Maisie?

PETER. Maisie?

MARY. Maisie Springfield, the leading lady. She's met him before, in Paris. She's always telling us.

PETER. No. I'm quite sure he means you.

MARY. But why—when I've only got that little bit in the second act?

PETER. Perhaps that was just the little bit he liked.

*Pause. She paces the room.*

MARY. You know, this silence is getting me down. Apart from the other guests, where the heck is my host?

PETER. I don't know. Earlier he was due to have dinner with the Foreign Secretary.

MARY. What does he want supper for then?

PETER. The appetite of these Balkan royalties is often quite prodigious.
*There is a sound at the door.*

MARY. (*In a frantic whisper.*) Oh God! Here they come. I only hope to heaven I know some of them. I hope there are about a hundred guests, then I can get lost—

*The door at the back opens—the* BARON TRIGORINSKY—*major-domo to the Regent—appears. He bows to* MARY, *who has risen nervously, then imperiously beckons to the open door.* TWO FOOTMEN *appear, and enter, carrying a small table which they place in the centre of the room. A table-cloth is placed on it, under the supervision of the* MAJOR-DOMO, *and then another, evidently grander,* FOOTMAN *appears bearing a tray. The tray is held by one of the other* FOOTMEN, *while the* FOOTMAN-IN-CHIEF *begins to lay the table.* MARY *has her eyes riveted to the proceedings. As soon as it becomes apparent that only two places are being laid* MARY *tries to catch the attention of* PETER *who is, rather studiedly, staring at a picture.*

MARY. (*Under her breath.*) Hey!

PETER *takes no notice.*

(Louder.) Hey!

PETER *turns.* MARY *points frantically to the supper table.*

Two places—

PETER. (*Out of the corner of his mouth.*) Pas devant—

MARY. What?

PETER. (*As before.*) Not in front of—(He indicates the footmen.)

MARY. (*Frantically.*) Yes—but two places—

PETER. (*Peremptorily.*) Sh!

*There is a pause while* MARY *watches the setting of the table with agonized eyes. The places having been laid, the procession of* FOOTMEN *and* MAJOR-DOMO *forms up and retires, in slow dignified march. At the door the* MAJOR-DOMO *turns and bows. Then he too retires, closing the great doors.* MARY *makes a swoop on her wrap, which is on a chair, and moves to the door.*

PETER. (*Barring her way.*) Please. I beg you, Miss Dagenham, control yourself. There's no need for panic—

MARY. Isn't there just? This is a plot, isn't it—supper for two? You knew all about it—

PETER. Well, I suppose I have to confess that I did have an idea—when I received the Grand Duke's instructions regarding yourself—

MARY. (*Angrily.*) You know, there's a word for what *you* are, and it's not head of the Balkan Department.

PETER. Miss Dagenham—I implore you not to leap to conclusions—

MARY. I don't have to do any leaping to this conclusion. I can just walk straight there. And I can walk straight out—

PETER. But why this panic at a harmless little tête à tête supper?

MARY. Listen. Where do you think I've been all my life? I know all about these harmless little tête à tête suppers. I've had to fight my way out of quite a few. Champagne and 'I hope you like caviare and something cold to follow because we don't really want the servants around do we? It's so much more fun serving ourselves don't you think?' And then after supper—'you must be tired after your show, Miss Dagenham, why don't you put your feet up on this nice sofa?' Oh yes. I know every gambit.

PETER. Aren't you confusing this Legation with a private room at Romano's?

MARY. Well, where's the difference, except that here there's a longer run from the sofa to the door and there's no evidence that Grand Dukes can't move just as fast as the next man? No, seriously, I'm off. Make any excuse you like. My aunt's ill, or something.

PETER. Your aunt, Miss Dagenham?

MARY. I'm awfully sorry, really I am—but I just don't know why he should have to go and pick on me. I'm just about the only girl in the show who'd say no to a deal of this sort. I'm really funny that way—and get worried about myself, sometimes. Maybe I shouldn't be in musical comedy. It seems to give people the wrong ideas. Maybe I should have stuck to Shakespeare, except that seemed to give people worse ones. Well, goodbye.

*She moves towards the door.* PETER *bars her way.*

PETER. (*Pleadingly.*) Please, please, please. Do you want to get me and the whole Foreign Office into the most terrible trouble?

MARY. Since you ask, yes.

PETER. (*Coaxingly.*) Now you don't mean that, Miss Dagenham. You know you don't. I'm sure you don't want to insult the Grand Duke, or to do the Entente a disservice. So why don't you just have a little supper with him? It'll be a very good one, and he's a most charming conversationalist. After supper—well—all you have to say is—'Well good night, Sir—it's been a most delightful evening, and now I must go home.'

MARY. Yes—as an exit line that's swell, but can you personally guarantee the exit? This is a Balkan Grand Duke—for heaven's sake—

PETER. Educated at Eton.

MARY. That's what I mean. No. I'm off.

PETER. (*Frantically.*) Wait a moment, please, Miss Dagenham. Supposing I do guarantee your exit, as you call it? Supposing I give you time for supper and then come in with a message from a hospital where your aunt has been taken after an accident—

MARY. (*Doubtfully.*) Well—that's possible, I suppose. Not more than half an hour, though—

PETER. But surely that isn't enough?

MARY. It's far too much.

*The* REGENT *enters, preceded by the* MAJOR-DOMO, *and* MARY *freezes into silence. He is in evening dress, with orders, and carries a brief-ease. He advances on* MARY *with outstretched hand.*

REGENT. How do you do? So good of you to come at such short notice.

MARY. That's all right—Your Royal Highness.

REGENT. I must apologize for being late. The crowds are already gathering in the streets and my motor was held up. (*He turns to Peter.*) Northbrook, I expect you are looking forward to your night's rest. We have a very full day before us.

PETER. We have indeed, Sir.

REGENT. The carriage leaves the Legation for the Abbey at nine o'clock. If you are here at eight-twenty?

PETER. Yes, Sir.

REGENT. Good night.

PETER. Good night, Your Royal Highness.

*Evidently conversant with, the etiquette demanded at the Carpathian court, he bows and backs skilfully to the door, where he bows again, and goes out.* MARY *watches the manoeuvre in awe and admiration. The* MAJOR-DOMO *whisks* MARY'S *wrap from her shoulders, takes it into the bedroom L., and returns immediately.*

REGENT. Serve supper.

*The* MAJOR-DOMO *bows, and backs out.*

Were you surprised to get my invitation?

MARY. I'll say I was. In fact I was so surprised I thought you couldn't possibly mean me.

REGENT. (*Reassuringly.*) But of course I meant you. I had your name most carefully marked down on my programme. In matters of this kind, I assure you, I am most methodical.

MARY. Oh. Yes. I can see you'd need to be.

REGENT. Who did you think I meant—if not you?

MARY. Well—Maisie Springfield.

REGENT. Oh no. I have already met her, in Paris, some time ago.

MARY. I know. That's why I thought—

REGENT. (*Jovially.*) Oh no, no, no. Maisie Springfield. She is quite what I would call—old hat.

MARY. Oh. Would you? And I'm what you would call—new hat?

REGENT. (*Laughing politely.*) Excellent, Miss—er—Miss—

MARY. You haven't got your programme handy?

REGENT. (*Laughing again.*) Capital. Most amusing.

MARY. Dagenham, Elaine Dagenham.

*The* MAJOR-DOMO *enters, followed by the* THREE FOOTMEN, *manoeuvring a dumb-waiter.*

REGENT. Of course. How stupid of me.

MARY. That's just my stage name. My real name's Mary Morgan.

REGENT. You like caviare, I hope?

MARY. (*Resignedly.*) Oh yes.

REGENT. I ordered a cold supper because then we can serve ourselves and that's so much more fun, don't you agree?

MARY. (*Resignedly again.*) Oh yes. Much more fun.

REGENT. That is a charming dress.

MARY. It's very old, I'm afraid.

*She makes a move to sit, but is stopped by a shocked hiss from the* MAJOR-DOMO. *The* REGENT *is still standing inspecting a bottle.*

REGENT. Do you like vodka?

MARY. I've never tried it. I don't know whether—

REGENT. (*Pouring some into two glasses.*) Oh, you must. This is very special.

*He hands her one.*

    Well, cheerio.

MARY. Cheerio.

*The* REGENT *throws his off at a gulp.* MARY *sips hers and makes a wry face.*

REGENT. No, no. Not to sip, like that. You will make yourself, as you say, tiddly. Like this—and then it has no dangerous effect.

*He has poured himself another, and throws it back again.* MARY *closes her eyes and bravely gulps hers. She stands quite still for a moment, with eyes closed, and then opens them in quiet amazement.*

MARY. I see what you mean. (*He fills her glass.*) Oh no, no more, please—

REGENT. One more will not hurt a fly.

MARY. Possibly. But there's a saying about being as drunk as a fly, you know.

*The* REGENT *laughs delightedly.*

REGENT. Oh, but that is really quite excellent. I can see you have a witty little tongue, Miss Dagenham.

MARY. Have I?

REGENT. Hurt a fly—drunk as a fly. I must remember that.

MARY. I really shouldn't bother, Your Royal Highness.

REGENT. (*Toasting again.*) Well—cheerio.

MARY. (*With some trepidation.*) Cheerio.

*Both drink. This time* MARY *splutters.*

REGENT. What's the matter?

MARY. That time I burnt my witty little tongue.

REGENT. Oh, that is very sad.

*He surveys her appraisingly. They are still standing facing each other.*

    I am quite delighted you're here, Miss—er—Dagenham. Quite delighted. I hope you are too?

MARY. Oh yes. Enraptured.

REGENT. Now will you sit here?

*He indicates a place for her.* MARY *looks questioningly at the* MAJOR-DOMO *and receives a very slight nod. She sits. The* REGENT *signs to the* FOOTMEN, *who go in procession to the door.* MARY *watches them leave with regretful resignation. The* MAJOR-DOMO *backs out. Once again* MARY *watches him with a mixture of awe and trepidation at the thought of having to do it herself.*

    Champagne?

MARY. (*Resignedly.*) Yes.

REGENT. There, now we are to ourselves.

MARY. (*Resignedly again.*) Yes.

*The* REGENT *pours out two glasses and holds his out to clink with hers, giving her what he plainly conceives to be a seductive smile.* MARY'S *answering smile is resigned again.*

REGENT. (*Briskly.*) Good. Well, now, you will forgive me if I don't join you for the moment. I have already had dinner, and have one or two matters of business to attend to.

*Holding his glass he walks briskly to the other end of the room and picks up the briefcase with which he entered. He takes out a document and studies it— first putting on a pair of spectacles.* MARY *looks extremely taken aback. Then she shrugs her shoulders and begins her supper, looking at her host between mouthfuls. He now appears completely oblivious of her. There is a long silence.*

MARY. (*At length, brightly.*) Turned quite warm all of a sudden, hasn't it?

*The* REGENT *appears not to hear.* MARY *makes a little gesture of annoyance at herself.*

(*Muttering.*) Wasn't addressed—

*She goes on with her food, still studying the back of the* REGENT'S *head, which is bent in concentrated thought over a document. He reaches out and picks up a telephone.*

REGENT. (*Into receiver, in a low but perfectly audible voice.*) Give me the Minister. . . . Very well. Then wake him. . . . Karnof? Were you asleep? . . . I make no apologies. We are in the middle of a major crisis. I had an hour alone with Sir Edward and there is no question but that the arrest of Wolffstein has stirred up an international hornets' nest. I have an aide-memoire—what? . . . For heaven's sake, my dear fellow, don't talk Carpathian. You know I can't understand it properly. . . . That's better. . . . Yes, we can speak freely, there's no one here. . . .

MARY *raises her eyebrows slightly.*

I explained the entire situation to Sir Edward. I told him that if I hadn't had Wolffstein arrested there would have had to have been a general election. Wolffstein would certainly have come to power, and the French alliance would have been revoked. Within a year we would have been allied to Germany, and Sir Edward did not need to be told that if that happened Wilhelm would at once force the issue with the Entente Powers on Morocco. . . . Yes. Well, of course, he talked about the grave effect on public opinion, and I agree, it does not look too good to put the Leader of the Opposition in gaol on a charge of treason, but what else could I do? Sir Edward requests that the trial be held in public, which makes it rather awkward. It means we shall have to get some evidence, and you know how difficult that is in these cases. . . . Yes, he's a good man. I'll give him to Wolffstein as defending counsel. He'll certainly help us. . . .

*During this,* MARY, *having finished her caviare, has decided to help herself to the next course. She is now at the dumbwaiter, putting some chicken salad on a plate, and plainly listening to the conversation at the same time.*

But what has chiefly disturbed Sir Edward is the fact that those stupid Americans have protested. . . .

MARY, *on her way back to the table with her plate, stops short and glares at him.* Oh, some nonsense about political freedom, and democratic rights. You know what children the Americans are in matters of this kind. Their diplomacy always makes me think of the Minotaur Legend reversed—you know—the bull chasing Theseus through the Labyrinth. . . . Yes. A steam traction engine in Hampton Court maze. . . . (*He chuckles.*) Excellent.

MARY *resumes her seat and puts her plate down with an angry clatter. The* REGENT *looks up, smiles his seductive smile, rather absently, and raises his glass.* MARY'S *answering smile is none too cordial, but the* REGENT *is far too preoccupied to notice.*

Oh no. The British, of course, will be more sensible. They'll wait until after the trial, and then protest. . . .

MARY'S *glance at the* REGENT *is now ferocious.*

. . . Yes, unhappily the American protest has been published in all our newspapers, and there have been a few riots tonight I hear. . . . No. The situation is well under control, but oh, Herr Gott! When will those idiotic Americans grow up? . . . Yes. We will talk tomorrow. Good night.

*He rings off, sits for a moment deep in thought, and then appears to pull himself out of his reverie. He gets up and strolls over to the table.*

REGENT. (*Heartily.*) Well, well, well. And how is everything?

MARY. (*Glaring.*) Just dandy.

REGENT. Ah, I see you have already served yourself. How remiss of me.

MARY. Oh, not at all. I prefer it that way.

REGENT. Splendid.

*The* REGENT *fills the two glasses and raises his.*

Cheerio.

MARY. Mud in your eye!

*The* REGENT *splutters into his drink.*

REGENT. What a priceless expression! Wherever did you learn it?

MARY. In America.

REGENT. (*Absently.*) Really? Have you been there?

MARY. I was born there. I am American.

REGENT. (*Looking at the telephone, deep in thought.*) Are you, indeed?

MARY. Yes, Your Royal Highness, that's what I am and—

REGENT. Will you excuse me? I've thought of another telephone call I must make.

MARY. Oh—that's quite all right. I just adore my own company.

*The* REGENT *walks briskly to the telephone, and picks up the receiver.*

REGENT. (*Into telephone.*) Connect me with the French Ambassador. . . . Oh yes, of course. He'll be at the reception. Well, I shall try later. . . .

*He rings off, then takes up his aide-memoire, puts on his spectacles and begins to study it closely.* MARY *crossly pours herself some more champagne, then raises her glass.*

MARY. (*Firmly.*) To President Taft.

*There is no reply.*

I said—to President Taft.

*Again there is no reply.* MARY *gets to her feet and drinks a lonely toast to her President. Then she resumes her seat.*

(*Muttering to herself.*) O.K. So I wasn't addressed. So who cares?

*There is another silence.* MARY *gets up with a sigh and goes and inspects the dumbwaiter. We can see that her various toasts have had a certain effect.*

(*Muttering to herself.*) Bull in a labyrinth? Who the heck's Theseus anyway?

*She helps herself to a sweet and goes back to her seat. The* REGENT *has not moved, except occasionally to turn over a page.*

(*Muttering to herself.*) Protest? I should darn well think they should protest. Arresting people like that. Disgraceful.

*She takes up the bottle.*

(*Still muttering.*) Won't you have some more champagne, Miss Dagenham? . . . Well, I don't know, Your Royal Highness. Do you really think I ought? . . . Well, perhaps just a sip—just up to there. Whoa!

*She has poured herself a glass. The* REGENT *has looked up.*

REGENT. I beg your pardon? You said something?

MARY. (*Confused.*) No, no. Just playing a little game over here—all by myself.

REGENT. Good. (*Raising his glass.*) Cheerio!

MARY. (*Raising hers.*) Chin, Chin!

*The door is suddenly thrown open imperiously and a boy* (NICOLAS) *of about sixteen in pyjamas and dressing-gown enters, looking very grim. He takes in Mary quickly, and then turns to glare at the* REGENT.

NICOLAS. Why was I not informed of Wolffstein's arrest?

REGENT. (*Quietly.*) Go back to bed, Nicky. We'll talk about it in the morning.

NICOLAS. No, father. We'll talk about it now. Why was I not informed of Wolffstein's arrest? Why was I left to learn it from the London *Evening Standard?*

REGENT. (*Patiently.*) There was no need to inform you.

NICOLAS. No need to inform the King?

MARY *who, still tucking into the trifle, has been watching this exchange with interest, now rises quickly, knocking over a glass as she does so. Both* NICOLAS *and the* REGENT *glance at her.*

REGENT. (*Perfunctorily.*) May I present Miss Elaine Dagenham.

MARY *approaches Nicolas and takes his outstretched hand.*

NICOLAS. (*Equally perfunctory, but with royalty's well-trained smile.*) Good evening. It's delightful to meet you. Won't you sit down?

*He turns back to the* REGENT, *switching the smile off with rapidity.*

When the Leader of His Majesty's Opposition is thrown into prison on a trumped-up charge, His Majesty himself is apparently the last person to learn about it.

MARY, *who was only half-way through her curtsy when* NICOLAS *turned from her, shrugs her shoulders philosophically and returns to her trifle, her eyes on father and son.*

REGENT. (*Pacifically.*) Your right to be informed I perfectly concede, Nicky, and it was only because your step-mother told me before she went out that you had gone to your bedroom with your Meccano set, and had left orders not to be disturbed, that I omitted to do so.

NICOLAS. That is mere evasion. By whose orders was Wolffstein arrested?

REGENT. By mine, of course.

NICOLAS. He must be released immediately.

REGENT. (*Quietly.*) It seems to be my duty to point out to your Majesty that it is only your right to information that I concede; not your right to give me orders. You will have to wait another eighteen months for that.

NICOLAS. Oh? I wonder if you should count on that?

REGENT. (*Wearily.*) I know exactly what that threat implies, Nicky, and so, I've no doubt, do my secret police.

NICOLAS. I don't understand what you mean by that. But it may happen that the people's anger at misgovernment, and at being dragged into a war on behalf of British imperialism and French greed, may perhaps take a drastic course—and sooner than you expect—

REGENT. Yes. You may be a real King very soon, Nicky, but for the moment I am still the ruler of Carpathia and of yourself. (*Sternly.*) Go to your room.

NICOLAS *stands undecided.*

Go to your room at once.

NICOLAS *goes slowly to the door.*

NICOLAS. Where is Uncle Wilhelm now? At Potsdam?

REGENT. I don't know, but the Crown Prince is much more easily reached. He is staying at Buckingham Palace, and the number is Westminster 832.

NICOLAS *turns abruptly to go through the door, and then remembers his manners. He turns and bows to* MARY.

NICOLAS. (*With his royal smile.*) Good night, Miss Dagenham. It has been a great pleasure.

MARY. (*Struggling to her feet.*) Good night, Your Majesty.

NICOLAS *goes out. The* REGENT *goes quickly to the telephone.*

REGENT. (*Into receiver, quietly.*) Colonel Hoffman. . . . Hoffman—go to the King's bedroom, see if he's there, and lock him in. Better put a guard on as well. If he's not there, find him, wherever he is, and never leave him. Also—most important—put no telephone calls through to him—outward or inward until further notice.

*He rings off, sighs, stretches himself, then goes over to the table.*

It was most unfortunate that you should have been a witness to one of our little family quarrels. I'm so sorry to have embarrassed you.

MARY. (*With wide eyes.*) But he's your son, isn't he?

REGENT. Yes.

MARY. Your real son? Not a step-son, or anything?

REGENT. No.

MARY. Your only son?

REGENT. Yes.

MARY. (*Appalled.*) Well!

*Pause.*

Do you know—a moment ago I was good and mad at you—

REGENT. Good and mad? What is that expression?

MARY. It doesn't matter, because I'm not any more. Now I just feel terribly sorry for you. Oh, you poor, poor man!

REGENT. My dear Miss Dagenham, you really must not let Nicky's rather emotional tendencies mislead you too much. He is merely expressing his loyalty to an old and long-established Carpathian Royal tradition—that a son must of necessity oppose his father's policy. There was exactly the same tradition in English Royal circles until quite recently.

MARY. But not plots—and secret police.

REGENT. Ah yes, but you see we're not a constitutional monarchy.

MARY. (*With great firmness.*) Ah. Now that's just the point. You should be.

REGENT. (*Politely.*) You think so, Miss Dagenham?

MARY. I most certainly do think so. Putting people in prison for no reason, cooking up evidence—yes, I heard you—going against the popular will—it's all absolutely disgraceful, and if you want to know, I think the American State Department was absolutely right to protest. Incidentally, as I told you just now, only I don't think you heard me, I'm an American myself.

REGENT. Are you indeed, Miss Dagenham?

MARY. Yes, Your Royal Highness, that's what I am—an American citizen, and proud of it.

REGENT. (*Politely.*) So you should be.

MARY. The Rights of Man—Government of the People—for the (*the flow is interrupted by a slight hiccup*) and the rest of it. Oh, and habeas corpus—which is English really, but it's American too—

REGENT. Yes. I have heard of it.

MARY. (*Severely.*) And that means that you just don't go about arresting people because you don't agree with their political opinions. Poor Mr.—what's his name—Wolffstein! He's probably got a wife—and a family—and—oh, it's dreadful. I honestly don't know how you could do a thing like that. How could you?

REGENT. (*Quietly.*) Because, in this case, I believe that the end justifies the means.

MARY. Ah. Now, I could give an answer to that, if I'd had a little less to drink. (*She ponders a moment. Triumphantly.*) I know. If the means are bad the end cannot be good. (*Surprised.*) Who said that?

REGENT. You did, I think.

MARY. Did I? Imagine!

REGENT. But in this case, you see, the end is world peace. Is that not an end good in itself?

*Pause.*

MARY. (*At length.*) Difficult, isn't it?

REGENT. Very.

MARY. Look, I tell you. Why don't you just persuade this Mr. Wolffstein to alter his policy?

REGENT. (*Smiling.*) He is a very obstinate man, he is half-German, and is in the pay of the Kaiser.

MARY. Then get public opinion on your side.

REGENT. A third of my people can't read or write and two-thirds are of German stock.

*Another pause.*

MARY. Yes. It really is tough! Gosh!

*There is a ring at the telephone.*

REGENT. (*Rising.*) Excuse me.

MARY. Oh, darn it! Just when we were getting to be comfortable. And I might have got a solution to the whole problem in a minute—

REGENT. (*At telephone.*) Yes? . . . I see. Very well.

*He rings off.*

(*Quietly.*) My wife has returned from St. James's Palace earlier than expected and is coming up for a moment.

MARY. Oh. (*Suddenly realizing and jumping up.*) Your wife! Oh, heavens! You'll want me to hide then, won't you? Now where? (*Pointing.*) In there? Or is there a cupboard?

REGENT. (*Quietly.*) My dear—I see you have a very strong sense of the dramatic. I hate to disappoint you—but darting into cupboards—though it might be amusing for both of us—is really not necessary. Besides—as always happens, I notice, on the stage—you'd be bound to leave something behind—like a glove or a fan—and we would both look foolish. No. Just sit there, (*he pushes her gently into a seat*) and calm yourself. Now before you meet my wife I must warn you that she is a little vague and can be very deaf—on occasions—

*The* GRAND DUCHESS *comes in. She is a woman of about the same age as the* REGENT, *at the moment very resplendently dressed, having been at an official ball, beautiful and extremely regal. She is followed by a rather mousy-looking Lady in Waiting* (COUNTESS VON UND ZU MEISSENBRONN). *She comes up to the* REGENT, *without glancing either at the supper table or at* MARY *though both are in her line of vision, and kisses him on the cheek.*

GRAND DUCHESS. My dear! Such boredom! The decorations, hideous—and the music a catastrophe. My carriage was ordered for one, but that strange little Turk drove us home—that one that May Herzogovina once lost her head about—do you remember?

*She sits down in the chair just vacated by* MARY *who stands only a few feet away from her, but still, apparently, invisible. The* REGENT *is waiting for an interruption in the flow to present* MARY.

My dear, at dinner Olga Bosnia—who looked ridiculous, but I shall come back to that—had an accident with her ice—it was chocolate, I think, and it slid across the table into poor Rosie Schlumberger-Lippe-Gildenstern's lap—too killing—how we all roared—but that idiotic Olga laughed loudest of all and then had to say: 'It was lucky it wasn't a bombe surprise.' Well—my dear, you can imagine! Such a silence you never heard. Afterwards she said she had quite forgotten that poor old Prince Schlumberger-Lippe-Gildenstern had been so brutally assassinated and anyway it wasn't a bomb, she said, it was a grenade, as if that made any difference. Now I must tell you how she was dressed—(*Breaking off.*) Maud! Where is that—

*The Lady in Waiting comes from behind the chair.*

Oh, there you are, dear. I didn't see you. Give me a glass of that champagne I see over there. (*She points to the supper table.*) She had on a—

REGENT. (*Deftly interrupting.*) My dear, might I present Miss Elaine Dagenham.

MARY, *very nervously, comes forward and takes the outstretched hand.*

GRAND DUCHESS. (*With a gracious smile.*) Ah yes, my dear, of course, I remember you well.

MARY. I'm quite sure you don't, Your Royal and—Your Imperial and Royal Highness.

GRAND DUCHESS. (*To* REGENT.) What does she say?

REGENT. (*In a perfectly normal voice.*) She says she is deeply flattered and compliments you on your wonderful memory.

GRAND DUCHESS. (*To* MARY.) Thank you, my dear. (*To* REGENT.) Sweetly pretty. She should use more mascara. When one is young one should use a lot of mascara and when one is old one should use much more.

*The Lady in Waiting has brought her her glass of champagne.*

(*After a sip.*) Olga Bosnia—in baby pink, my dear, from head to foot. Ridiculous. She looked like one of those revolting cakes that one gets when one has tea with dear Irene Bessarabia—and which she says melt in one's mouth and in fact squirt all over the place. Tiara—over one eye, and false, of course—as we all know—incidentally May Herzogovina says she bought the original in a pawnshop in Salonika and that that was false too—but May is not strictly truthful, I'm afraid. (*Turning abruptly to* MARY.) And what do you do, my dear?

MARY. I'm in *The Coconut Girl* at the Gaiety.

GRAND DUCHESS. (*Looking inquiringly at the* REGENT.) Yes?

REGENT. She says she is an actress.

GRAND DUCHESS. An actress? How interesting. Madame Bernhardt has stayed with us, you know. Personally I do not find her so good in *Magda* as Mademoiselle Duse. You agree, no?

MARY. (*Baffled.*) No.

GRAND DUCHESS. You don't agree? That is interesting. You know Lucien Guitry too?

MARY. No, Ma'am.

GRAND DUCHESS, Only Madame Bernhardt. You are quite right to be loyal to your friends, my dear. Loyalty is a quality that we do not see enough nowadays. Très bien, (*She pats* MARY *with her fan.*) I saw her in *Phèdre* not long ago. You, of course, must have seen her in it countless times— so close to her as you are—mais, ma chère—entre nous—I found the play quite irritating—so much love—most tedious. I never know why people want to write about love when there are so many more pleasant subjects to choose from. (*To* REGENT.) Well, my dear, I must go to bed. Which uniform are you wearing tomorrow?

REGENT. Royal Guards.

GRAND DUCHESS. Now let me see—what colour? (*After a thought.*) Yes, that's all right. We won't clash. Good night, my dear.

REGENT. Good night, my dear.

*They kiss each other on the cheek.*

GRAND DUCHESS. Maud! Where is that idio—

COUNTESS. Here, Ma'am.

GRAND DUCHESS. Oh yes. Run ahead, dear, and find my book. You know what it is, don't you? *The Life and Trial of Doctor Crippen.* I shall want you to read to me for twenty minutes

COUNTESS. Yes, Ma'am.

GRAND DUCHESS. Maud—you look very pinched. What is the matter with you?

COUNTESS. I have a slight cold.

GRAND DUCHESS. (*Solicitously.*) Oh, poor thing! I'm so very, very sorry. I must make you one of my syrups.

COUNTESS. Oh. So kind of you, Ma'am.

*From her expression we see she has experienced one of the Grand Duchess's syrups before. She curtsies and backs out.*

GRAND DUCHESS. (*The gracious smile hardly off her face.*) Idiotic creature, always catching cold. I really can't think how. As far as I know, her life is quite blameless. Anyway—with a face like that—

*She turns graciously to* MARY.

Good night, my dear. So delightful—

MARY. Good night, Ma'am.

GRAND DUCHESS. —and just a touch more on the cheeks too, I think.

MARY. Yes, Ma'am.

*The* GRAND DUCHESS *smiles her farewell and goes to the door, where she turns, looking severe.*

GRAND DUCHESS. Don't make mischief between me and Madame Bernhardt, now—or I shall be cross.

*She goes out.*

MARY. A *little* vague? Well? Say, listen—didn't she mind *at all* about you and me?

*Pause. The* REGENT *lights a cigarette.*

REGENT. (*Slowly.*) My dear, I proposed to my wife because I needed to reinforce the Austrian Trade Agreement. She accepted me because the emperor told her to. For ten years we have been utterly and completely devoted to each other, with never a single unkind word spoken on either side. Why should she mind?

*Pause.*

MARY. (*At length.*) I think it's dreadful.

REGENT. (*Puzzled.*) Something else is dreadful?

MARY. I find your life quite shocking—and you know why?

REGENT. Why?

MARY. Because there's no love in it.

*The* REGENT *opens his mouth to reply.*

(*Interrupting, scornfully.*) Oh yes, Maisie Springfields by the bushel load, I've no doubt. I meant, real love.

*There is a ring at the telephone.*

(*Angrily.*) Oh. Not again!

REGENT. Excuse me

*He goes to the telephone.*

(*Into receiver.*) Yes. . . . (*Gravely.*) I see. . . . How many casualties? . . . Not so serious, then. . . . My dear fellow, there's no need to panic. The new Chief of Police is a good man and I trust him. . . . No.

*He rings off, looking distracted.* MARY *is watching him closely. The* REGENT *comes out of his reverie, and catches her eye. He smiles his automatic seductive smile—as he does so surreptitiously looking at his watch.*

(*Heartily.*) Well, my dear?

MARY. Well?

REGENT. My dear, wouldn't you be more comfortable on the sofa? You could put your feet up there and rest.

*Pause.*

MARY. I think I'll stay here, thank you.

REGENT. Very well. Just as you please.

*He studies her as she sits in the chair, evidently calculating possible lines of attack. Then he takes a footstool, and sits beside her. There is a pause, during which there is just the faintest suggestion of a yawn from the* REGENT—*out of sight of* MARY. *Then he lays his hand gently on her knee.* MARY *watches the hand cautiously.*

My dear—it was so good of you to come and see me tonight.

*The hand creeps higher.*

MARY. (*Her voice at a rather nervous pitch.*) You said that before.

REGENT. Did I?

*His hand gets to the vicinity of her waist. The posture now seems rather cramped for the* REGENT, *and he plainly suffers from a momentary twinge of rheuma-*

*tism, for he withdraws his hand and twitches his shoulders with an expression of discomfort. Then he methodically places the stool in a more convenient position and lays his hand once more on her waist.*

That is a beautiful dress.

MARY. You said that before too.

REGENT. (*Amorously.*) What does it matter? What are words— (*He is interrupted by a slight fit of coughing.*) Excuse me. (*Amorously again.*) What are words, where deeds can say so much more?

*This is plainly his accustomed cue for action. With a fairly practised, if not exactly lissom swing, he slips his arm round her waist and heaves himself, with just the faintest giving at the knees, on to the arm of the chair. He is bending his head forward tenderly for the embrace when* MARY *jabs him hard in the stomach with her elbow and jumps out of the chair.*

MARY. Say, that's just terrible.

REGENT. (*Holding his stomach.*) What is terrible?

MARY. That performance of yours.

REGENT. (*Rising, aggrieved.*) I fear I do not altogether understand you, Miss Dagenham.

MARY. Now, don't come the Grand Duke on me. There's no need for that. You made a pass. I turned it down. That's all that's happened. We can still be friendly.

*There is a pause, then the* REGENT *abruptly turns and goes to the table.*

REGENT. Excuse me.

*He picks up the vodka bottle, and pours himself a drink, throwing it straight back.*

MARY. Say—listen—I could do with a small one too.

*The* REGENT, *without replying, pours another glass and takes it to her.*

I need it for my heart. It's still pounding away down here—

REGENT. (*Stiffly.*) I'm so sorry.

MARY. Oh, it's not your fault. In fact if I'd known that that was all that was going to happen, I wouldn't have been nervous at all. (*Raising her glass.*) Well—long life and good health to Your Royal Highness.

REGENT. (*Automatically.*) Cheerio.

MARY. (*Naughtily.*) And better luck next time.

*She hands the glass back, empty.*

Say—there is something to that stuff, you know. Sure it has no effect— drunk that way?

REGENT. After three of them, you might experience a certain euphoria. I think you have had enough.

MARY. O.K. I admit I was feeling a bit muzzy a moment ago, but your rendition of the balcony scene just now sobered me up.

*Pause. The* REGENT *looks impatiently at his watch.*

REGENT. How is your heart, now?

MARY. Fine. Right back to normal. I'll tell you why I was so nervous, Your Royal Highness. You see—I thought I was going to have a real struggle

with myself tonight. I should have explained to you early on that I don't
do this sort of thing as a rule, you know, on account of I'm a well-known
eccentric—and that's what I usually do explain right at the beginning of
supper, because I think it's fair—but this time we didn't seem to have
much chit-chat together before the curtain went up and so I never somehow got the cue. So then when it did go up I thought, here we go,
girl—this is it. He's a Grand Duke with Balkan fire in his veins, and there's
going to be a flood of turgid intoxicating love talk. And then I thought—
well—the court musicians will be playing Tzigane music just outside the
door, and the lights will be discreetly dimmed, and there will be a strange
seductive perfume in the air—and well—I just thought, well, you'd better
watch out, girl, I thought. You'd just better watch out. (*With a sigh.*) Oh
well!

*She yawns and stretches herself.*

    (*Interestedly.*) Tell me, do they all fall as easily as that—the Maisies and
the others?

REGENT. (*With controlled anger.*) Before your insults grow too great to be
borne, Miss Dagenham, I am ringing for your car. He rings the bell.

MARY. O.K. That's a deal, except I haven't got a car.

REGENT. (*Angrily.*) A cab, then.

MARY. Sure—but—I live way out in Brixton.

REGENT. I shall naturally arrange for you to be escorted to your home.

MARY. Oh well, I can do the tip. I guess I'll get my wrap then.

*He strides across the room and opens the door L.*

    Thank you.

*She goes to the door, and then appears to remember something.*

    Oh, sorry.

*She turns round and proceeds to walk gingerly backwards through the door.*

    (*Triumphantly, having reached her objective.*) Pretty good, huh?

*The* REGENT *impatiently closes the door and stands for a moment, scowling. The*
MAJOR-DOMO *comes in and bows.*

REGENT. (*Savagely.*) Why am I deserted? Why is there no one to answer a
bell?

MAJOR-DOMO. With respect, Your Royal Highness yourself gave orders that
the attendants were to be moved from the door.

REGENT. See that a taxi is fetched at once, and tell the A.D.C. on duty he is
to escort Miss Dagenham to a place called Brixton.

MAJOR-DOMO. As your Royal Highness commands.

*The* MAJOR-DOMO *bows. The* REGENT *turns from him abruptly. The* MAJOR-DOMO
*begins to back out.*

REGENT. Wait. One of my personal servants plays the violin. Who is that?

MAJOR-DOMO. I think it is Franz, Your Royal Highness—one of the under-
valets.

REGENT. Does he play it well?

MAJOR-DOMO. I am tone deaf, Your Royal Highness.

REGENT. Where is he now?

MAJOR-DOMO. In bed, sir.

REGENT. Fetch him out of it. Tell him I may need him to play his confounded fiddle outside this door—(*Pointing to dumbwaiter.*) And take this away.

*The* MAJOR-DOMO *pulls the dumb-waiter towards the door.*

Wait. Not directly outside the door. That would seem too obvious. Let me see, now. About ten paces down the passage.

MAJOR-DOMO. (*Nodding.*) Just outside the Minister's bedroom?

REGENT. Yes. Station him there at once, but don't let him begin until I ring. I will probably not need him at all.

MAJOR-DOMO. And the taxi—Your Royal Highness?

REGENT. (*Angrily.*) Use your own judgment.

*The* MAJOR-DOMO *bows low and backs out. The* REGENT *looks round the room. Then he goes quickly into his bedroom, returning immediately with a scent spray, which he uses, with savage concentration, all over the room. Then he begins to switch out lamps. He has only done two when* MARY *comes in, and the illumination is not noticeably less.*

MARY. Say—Your Royal Highness—that's some bedroom you've got in there. Yours?

REGENT. No. It's the room they prepared for the Grand Duchess, but she prefers a room on the garden side.

MARY. I see. Well—this is my exit, I guess.

*The* REGENT *crosses the room slowly and takes her hand tenderly.* MARY *is going into her curtsy, but the* REGENT *lifts her gently up.*

REGENT. Please. This is not, quite yet, good-bye. Give me just one minute to tell you how deeply distressed I feel at what has happened between us.

MARY. (*Murmuring.*) Listen—I'm the one that should be sorry—

REGENT. (*Pleadingly.*) Please, please. Let me try and explain a little about something that is in my mind at the moment. Won't you sit down—just for a second?

MARY. The taxi isn't ticking up, is it?

REGENT. No. They will tell us when it arrives.

*She sits on the edge of the settee, which is the nearest seat to her. The* REGENT *walks slowly round the room.*

It is simply this, my dear. I have behaved to you tonight like a cad and a boor and you must accept my most heartfelt apologies. But in my defence let me say this—I have many things to disturb me at this moment—you know some of them. And just now I learnt that there are terrible riots tonight all over my country—tomorrow I may have to declare martial law—

*Unseen by* MARY, *he turns out a lamp in the corner of the room.*

—and—well—you remember what Shakespeare said, 'It is hard to sleep well with a crown on your head'—

MARY. Not quite that, but the meaning's clear.

REGENT. I am so bitterly, my dear, so heartbrokenly unhappy that you should leave me now, at my darkest hour, with harsh, cruel hating thoughts. I am a very lonely person—

*He approaches* MARY *with a glass of vodka. She takes it absently. He has carefully placed the footstool a few feet from her. He now sits on it, with another very slight twinge of rheumatism. Then he stares at her with studied, but now serious, amorousness.*

REGENT. You cannot possibly understand, with your happy childish soul, what it would mean to me if I could only find someone like yourself to share my life. (*He glances surreptitiously at his watch.*) If only I hadn't spoiled everything just now. Ah, what fools these human beings be!

MARY. (*Murmuring.*) Mortals. (*She absently throws the drink back.*) Hey! I didn't ask for that.

REGENT. You are right about my life. It is quite without love. I am growing into middle age—

MARY. Oh no—

REGENT. Almost into middle age—My life has fallen into the sere and yellow leaf—

MARY. (*Mildly surprised.*) Well, now! You got that one right.

REGENT. Yes. Here am I, having reached the age of fort—thirty-nine, and I have never known what it is to love or be loved. It is like the legend of the Sleeping Princess. Only here it is the Prince that sleeps—and awaits the kiss of the beautiful young maiden that will bring him back to life.

*Pause.*

MARY. (*At length.*) You mean you want me to kiss you?

REGENT. You are so literal. (*With a deep sigh.*) It is love that I need. The ennobling love of a pure young woman—her bright faith in me as I am and as I might yet be—her glowing self-sacrifice to my little weaknesses and desires—for love is sacrifice, is it not? Yes. There is the mystic kiss that might bring this sleeping Prince to life—

*Pause. The* REGENT, *who has plainly been embarrassing even himself with this dialogue, turns to see how it has been going down.* MARY *is sitting back, relaxed, and apparently content—her eyes half-closed.*

MARY. (*At length, noticing the pause.*) O.K. I got you.

*The* REGENT *slides the footstool close to the settee, and tenderly takes* MARY'S *hand. Reaching behind him he presses a bell push on the table.*

REGENT. Do you know what your hair reminds me of? Summer corn, kissed by the wind into enchantingly exciting furrows. Your eyes—

*He stops—listening. A violin, playing a Tzigane melody, can be heard. The* REGENT *nods approvingly.*

MARY. Say—where's that music coming from?

REGENT. One of my servants, a Hungarian, always plays at this hour. He is lamenting his lost love.

MARY. (*Disturbed.*) Oh, poor darling. (*With a deep sigh.*) Oh, isn't life awful?

(*Evidently rising above the awfulness of life.*) You were saying about my eyes—

*She has her feet up on the settee.*

REGENT. Twin pools—of gladness and joy—in which any man would be glad to drown himself—

MARY. (*Sleepily.*) You mean—in both?

REGENT. (*A shade crossly.*) In either.

MARY. Anyway I like twin pools. That's good. Twin pools. Go on.

REGENT. Your chin—

MARY. You left out my nose.

REGENT. Of course. What can one say of perfection?

MARY *is now firmly, and a trifle somnolently, lying full length on the settee. The* REGENT *has both arms round her waist.*

MARY. (*Dreamily.*) That's O.K. Now go back to my chin.

REGENT. This is what I think of your chin.

*Far more expertly than the last time—his position, of course, is easier for him— he slides on to the settee, and kisses her chin. She does not resist. Then he kisses her mouth and she responds.*

REGENT. My darling—oh, my darling!

MARY. (*Emerging from the embrace.*) That poor Hungarian! Oh, I do hope he gets his love back.

*She keeps time sleepily with her hand.*

REGENT. Don't think of *his* love. Think of ours.

*He kisses her again.*

MARY. (*Dreamily, fingering his hair.*) Gosh! Your hair's pretty.

REGENT. (*Tenderly.*) Do you think so?

MARY. You put the wrong stuff on it, though. What do you use?

REGENT. A little pomade.

MARY. Now, that's where you're wrong. You should use Pinaud's Lilac.

REGENT. I shall remember. (*A shade impatiently.*) I asked you, my darling, to remember our love—

MARY. (*Dreamily.*) Your eyebrows are pretty too—

REGENT. (*Interrupting imperiously again.*) What a universe of joy and pain lies in that little word!

*There is a pause while* MARY *stares thoughtfully at the face so close to hers. The Tzigane music seems to come closer. It is certainly louder. One wonders if the* MAJOR-DOMO *has his eye to the keyhole.*

MARY. (*Suddenly.*) All right. You asked for it.

*She draws his head down and gives him a passionate kiss. It is prolonged. There is a discreet knock at the door, unnoticed. Then one less discreet. Finally an agitated-looking* PETER *comes in. The embrace continues.* PETER *coughs. The* REGENT *jumps to his feet.*

PETER. If your Royal Highness will forgive this intrusion.

REGENT. (*Furiously.*) This is intolerable!

PETER. With deepest respect, sir, my message is so important that I had no choice but to intrude.

REGENT. Revolution?

PETER. No, sir. Miss Dagenham's aunt has been in a motor accident and the hospital is calling for her most urgently—

MARY. (*From the settee whence she has not stirred.*) What? (*She turns her head and looks at* PETER, *and remembrance comes back.*) Oh, go away, you silly man!

PETER. (*Approaching her.*) But your aunt—Miss Dagenham—you realize how very serious her condition—

MARY. It's her own fault. She's no right to be out in an automobile as late as this, at ninety-three—

PETER. (*Protestingly.*) But Miss Dagenham—

REGENT. (*Roaring.*) Miss Dagenham asked you to go away—and I command you to go away!

PETER. (*Beginning to back away.*) Your Royal Highness—

REGENT. I am most seriously displeased at this breach of etiquette, Mr. Northbrook, and shall no doubt find opportunity of expressing my displeasure in certain quarters.

PETER. Your Royal Highness—

REGENT. Go.

PETER *disappears hastily backwards through the door.* MARY, *from the settee, makes a carefree gesture of dismissal. The* REGENT, *behind the settee, looks at his watch, and nods, evidently quite satisfied with the performance.*
     (*With an amorous gesture.*) Come, my darling—

MARY. Where to? (*After thinking it out.*) Oh. I know where you mean.
*She swings her legs round to a sitting position.*
     I've got euphoria like mad.
*Still sitting, she looks up, a little hazily, at the* REGENT, *who is still holding his amorous gesture and seductive expression.*
     (*Sharply.*) Listen, before I go one step further, I must utter a solemn warning.

REGENT. Utter it, my beloved.

MARY. If I *do* go one step further, you know what's going to happen? I'm going to fall in love with you. I always, always do.

REGENT. (*Gently.*) Always?

MARY. Both times. (*Darkly.*) So you just watch out, that's all. You just watch out.

REGENT. But why? Isn't your loving me exactly what I crave for?

MARY. Not unless you're even crazier than you look—swaying about there, with that star thing twinkling all over the place and your hair all mussed—

REGENT. (*Resuming the gesture.*) Come, my dear.

MARY. One step further?

REGENT. (*Imperiously.*) Come.

MARY. (*Sighing.*) You poor man. You poor, poor man. All right. You're for it, then. (*She gets up with difficulty.*) All right, one step further.

*She takes it—with catastrophic results. Her knees seem quietly to collapse under her, and with a resigned sigh, she crumples slowly to the floor, ending, at length, in a comfortable position on her back, staring at the ceiling. The* REGENT, *alarmed, starts forward.*

Oh, what lovely cherubs on the ceiling!

*The* REGENT *is bending over her.*

MARY. Good night, my darling. Good night. See you in the morning.

*She turns over into a dormant position. The* REGENT *gets to his knees, and examines her. Then he climbs to his feet and strides angrily to the bell. He rings it. The* MAJOR-DOMO *appears instantly. The* REGENT *nods in the direction of the recumbent* MARY. *The* MAJOR-DOMO *goes over, his face impassive, and looks down at her. The* REGENT *makes a sign of removal. The* MAJOR-DOMO, *nods inquiringly at the other bedroom. The* REGENT *shrugs his shoulders impatiently and goes towards his own door. The Tzigane melody is continuing.*

REGENT. (*Shouting.*) Stop that infernal din! Herr Gott noch mal! How do you expect a man to get any sleep

*He goes into his room, angrily slamming the door. The* MAJOR-DOMO *has gathered* MARY *into his arms, and is carrying her towards the other door as the* CURTAIN *falls.*

## SCENE 2

SCENE: *The same. About eight-thirty the following morning. The* MAJOR-DOMO *is supervising the preparation of the breakfast table by the* TWO FOOTMEN. *After a moment* PETER *enters. He is in full dress Diplomatic uniform. The* MAJOR-DOMO *greets him with a bow and then, out of sight of the* FOOTMEN, *makes a slight movement of the head, indicating his wish to speak with him.* PETER *goes over to him and there begins a whispered colloquy, of which no sound is ever audible, but the purport of which is fairly plain owing to the number of glances both parties continually make towards the door of the bedroom L., originally prepared for the* GRAND DUCHESS. PETER'S *face is grave and deeply disturbed; the other's impassive. At length he nods, and goes hesitantly towards the door L. He knocks grave and deeply disturbed; the other's impassive. At length gently. Then again, less gently. Finally, after an exchange of glances with the* MAJOR-DOMO *he opens the door and looks inside. He closes it again immediately, and nods to the* MAJOR-DOMO. *The inaudible colloquy begins again. The* FOOTMEN, *during this, are standing, rock-like, staring impassively ahead. The colloquy proceeds.*

PETER. (*At length.*) I'd better go and ask.

*He goes to the other door R. and knocks.*

REGENT. (*Off.*) Yes? Who?

PETER. Northbrook, sir.

REGENT. (*Off.*) Come in.

PETER *goes into the bedroom, and we hear the murmur of his discreetly lowered voice followed by a sudden short, enraged bellow from the* REGENT. PETER *reappears hastily at the door, behind first, and closes the door.*

PETER. (*Harassed.*) One place.

*The* MAJOR-DOMO *nods, and makes the necessary signal to the* FOOTMEN. *They proceed to lay a single place. While they are doing so, under the* MAJOR-DOMO'S *vigilant eye, the bedroom door L. is suddenly opened and* MARY *appears, blinking in the daylight. Her hair is tousled, and she is swathed in a large bed-cover, on which the Royal Arms of Carpathia are boldly displayed. Unseen by either* PETER *or the* MAJOR-DOMO *she goes slowly towards the breakfast table, walking rather as if every step she takes is jarring a very tender head, and picks up a glass of iced water that has just been placed there. She finishes it in a single gulp. She then takes up a full carafe from the table, about turns, and moves back towards the bedroom as gingerly as she had come.* PETER *turns round and sees her.*

(*Starting forward.*) Miss Dagenham—I must have a word with you, please—

*She disappears into the room.* PETER *turns to the* MAJOR-DOMO *and raises his eyebrows inquiringly. The* MAJOR-DOMO *almost imperceptibly shrugs his shoulders.* (*All the* MAJOR-DOMO'S *gestures are almost imperceptible.*) *The* FOOTMEN *leave followed by the* MAJOR-DOMO. PETER *is striding about the room looking worried as the main door is opened by a* FOOTMAN *and* NICOLAS *comes in. He is dressed in a plain blue suit.* PETER, *on seeing him, bows.*

NICOLAS. Good morning, Mr. Northbrook.

PETER. Good morning, Sir.

NICOLAS. My father has sent for me. Am I to go in?

PETER. I think, perhaps, better not, Sir. His valets are with him, and he is having a little trouble with his top boots. He should be out in a moment—

NICOLAS *throws himself into a chair, and picks up a morning paper.*

NICOLAS. (*After a moment, impatiently.*) Coronation. Coronation. Coronation. Nothing about the rest of the world. Nothing about my own country, where there is practically civil war—

PETER. You are surely exaggerating, Sir. I understand the situation in Carpathia is well under control—

NICOLAS. (*Muttering.*) The wrong control. That's the trouble. (*Looking up at* PETER.) Yes. Report that remark to the Foreign Office. I don't care.

PETER. Your Majesty does me an injustice.

NICOLAS. Only in the sense that you would be reporting nothing that they did not know already.

PETER. (*Chattily.*) Splendid weather for the Coronation, isn't it, Sir? I understand you are seeing the procession from a window in the Ritz Hotel. You should have an exceptionally good view. A pity that you cannot go to the Abbey, but, of course, protocol forbids it. Who is accompanying Your Majesty?

NICOLAS. My gaoler, of course.

PETER. Your gaoler, Sir?

NICOLAS. Colonel Hoffman.

PETER *smiles mirthlessly. The* REGENT *comes out. He is wearing a dressing-gown, under which we see top boots.*

REGENT. Nicky, I trust you have not forgotten that you are entertaining your Aunt Maria and Cousin Louisa at seven this evening.

NICOLAS. (*Gloomily.*) No, father.

REGENT. And as you won't be seeing your little cousin again for some time, and as we will probably want to make an official announcement soon, it might be as well if you gave her some slight indication of your feelings for her.

NICOLAS. (*Boldly.*) May the indication be as slight as the feelings?

REGENT. (*Sharply.*) Nicky! Don't be ridiculous! You know you find little Louisa very attractive. You told me so yourself.

NICOLAS. I said I liked the way she looked when she was skating, that's all. Is that such a strong basis for marriage? I mean what do I do in the summer? Anyway, I find her most unintelligent and snobbish.

REGENT. Nonsense. You're devoted to her, and she to you. It's only that you're sulking because of Wolffstein's arrest.

NICOLAS. That issue is far too important for mere sulking, father. You have granted me my right to information. What has happened in my country since last night?

REGENT. The riots are still continuing. As they appear to be well organized, I have had no option but to order certain further arrests.

NICOLAS. (*Sharply.*) Further arrests?

REGENT. I have the list on me, I think. (*He takes out a piece of paper from his dressing-gown pocket.*) Yes. Here it is.

NICOLAS *snatches it, and hastily runs his eye down it.*
    Any friends of yours there?

NICOLAS. (*Blandly.*) I am not allowed to have politicians for friends, father. You know that.

*He hands the list back, plainly rather relieved, and goes to the door.*

REGENT. (*Pacifically.*) Nicky, I have arranged for Harrods to send you a new Meccano set.

NICOLAS. (*Turning eagerly.*) What number?

REGENT. Number four.

NICOLAS. (*With a childish wail.*) Oh, but I've got number four. It's number five I want. Oh, father—really!

*He goes out.*

REGENT. (*Explosively.*) That idiot Hoffman! He swore it was number four. The consequences of such a blunder could be serious—

PETER. I shall see that the mistake is rectified immediately, Sir.

REGENT. (*Nodding and scrutinizing his list of ringleaders.*) Now I wonder who it is I've left off this list? There was some name he was looking for, and was relieved to find not there.

*He studies the list a moment, with a puzzled frown.*

(*At length.*) Verflucht!

*He puts the list back in his pocket and attends to his breakfast.*

Well? You have got rid of her?

PETER. Er—not yet, sir. There has been so little time.

REGENT. (*Alarmed.*) You mean she is still there? (PETER *nods.*) She might come out at any moment?

PETER. She has already been out.

REGENT. (*Muttering.*) Is there a lock on this side of the door?

PETER. (*Examining the door.*) I'm afraid not!

REGENT. Um Gottes willen! (*He gulps his coffee hastily.*)

PETER. (*Diffidently.*) Do I gather, Sir, that the evening was not an unqualified success?

*The* REGENT *looks up at him ferociously.*

REGENT. Northbrook, this Foreign Office parlance of yours I begin to find— irritating. (*Fiercely.*) The evening was an unqualified nightmare.

PETER. Oh, I'm so sorry, Sir. What went wrong?

REGENT. (*Angrily.*) Everything went wrong—but chiefly the girl—

PETER. (*With a snigger.*) I thought the trouble was rather the reverse.

REGENT. That is not humorous. This is not a humorous matter, Northbrook. I have only one evening in London, one single evening, in which I can hope to arrange for myself a little relaxation. And what happens? Out of the whole of this vast teeming city—teeming with beautiful willing women—the most beautiful, if not always the most willing on earth — you find me what? A little American ninnycompoop—

PETER. With respect, Sir—either ninny by itself or nincompoop.

REGENT. Ninnycompoop will serve. She fully deserves a new word. The mind of a backward child, the muscles of a boxer and an approach to life of such stomach-turning sentimentality that I found myself, Northbrook, I found myself, last night, uttering phrases which—had any single one of them been overheard—would have made me the laughing-stock of Europe. And—to crown it all—and at the crucial moment—she is rendered insensible by an amount of vodka which, in Carpathia, you would add to the bread and milk of a four-year-old as a mild tonic. I am not pleased with your part in the affair, Northbrook. I am distinctly not pleased.

PETER. But, again, with respect, Sir, my part in the affair was limited to carrying out your orders—

REGENT. (*Pointing an accusing finger.*) And who was it who said to me, 'Why do you not invite this little actress to supper?' Who?

PETER. Ah. But it was your initial interest in the lady, Sir, that inspired me to that remark. I was not to know how unsuitable a guest she would turn out to be.

REGENT. British diplomacy at its most hypocritical. Herr Gott, how maddening! To think that Lucy Maidenhead has been telephoning me every day since my arrival begging me, imploring me to spare her just a few brief moments of my time.

PETER. If I might remind Your Royal Highness, I think I heard you remark the other day that you found Lady Maidenhead—'old hat'.

REGENT. I have no doubt at all that I did. Nevertheless, my dear Northbrook, there is an old Russian saying 'better an old hat than a bare head'. Telephone to Lady Maidenhead and ask her to join me tonight here for supper.

PETER. But, Sir—the Foreign Office Ball—

REGENT. I shall make an acte de présence and leave in good time. Say about twelve-thirty.

PETER. Very well, Sir. Do you know her telephone number?

REGENT. Mayfair 822—no 382—no. (*He stops.*) Ah, how the years run by! There was a time when those little numerals would have leaped to my lips. (*He sighs.*) Hoffman keeps my private list of numbers in his safe.

PETER *goes to the door.*

PETER. Tonight, Sir, Coronation Night—she may well have an engagement.

REGENT. (*Quietly confident.*) She will break it.

PETER *bows and backs out. The* REGENT *finishes his coffee and rises, stretching himself luxuriously. He goes over to a cigarette box, for the moment apparently oblivious of his danger. The door L. opens and* MARY *comes out. She is now dressed again in the evening dress we saw her in the night before, and looks fresh and happy. She sees the* REGENT *who is in the process of lighting a cigarette with his back to her, creeps up to him and puts her hand over his eyes.*

MARY. (*Gaily.*) Guess who?

REGENT. (*Muttering simultaneously.*) Herr Gott!

*He turns and summons up a smile.*

Good morning, my dear. And how are you?

MARY. Well, I admit I did feel a little frail at first, but now, after a bath in that Albert Hall of a bathroom, I feel wonderful—real wonderful. Oh, darling— (*She throws her arms round his neck.*) I'm so happy.

*The* REGENT, *smiling a set smile, releases himself.*

What's the matter?

REGENT. Someone might come in.

MARY. Sure. This room is Grand Central Station. I found that out last night. Who cares?

REGENT. (*Crossly.*) But this is the morning. It's different.

MARY. What's so different about it? Unless maybe it's you.

REGENT. I assure you, my dear, I am exactly the same person—

MARY. You're not acting exactly the same way.

REGENT. But this is the morning—

MARY. You keep saying that. I remember from last night the way you tend to repeat yourself.

*The* REGENT *turns, embarrassed, from her steady stare.*

(*Quietly.*) Now, tell me, darling, is it only late at night that you're such a very lonely person that you feel the need to share your life with a pure young woman whose ennobling love and bright faith and glowing self-sacrifice might bring you back to life? Comes the morning and all the universe of pain and joy that lies in that little word 'love' just—

REGENT. (*Interrupting, after wincing at each word.*) Please! Please! I beg you. There are certain phrases which should never be quoted out of context.

MARY. But the context's the same, isn't it?

*The* REGENT *opens his mouth to reply.*

MARY. Yes, I know. It's the morning. Can I have some coffee?

REGENT. There's no cup.

MARY. I'll have yours.

*She pours herself some coffee.*

(*Sunnily.*) Well, my darling Grand Duke, it may be morning for you, but it's still dream-time for me. On this Coronation Day, 1911, I've woken up to find myself madly and romantically and joyously in love with you. So there you are.

*Pause.*

REGENT. (*At a loss.*) My dear—I am overwhelmed, but I feel it my duty to—

MARY. (*Interrupting.*) No, don't go into another long speech. It'll probably be utter nonsense, like most of your long speeches last night.

*The* REGENT *looks surprised.*

There's no need to raise those pretty eyebrows, my darling. Because, you see, some of the things you said—even though they sounded like Marie Corelli going further than her furthest—were pretty darn true. You do need love in your life. In fact I've never met anyone who needs it more. (*Brightly.*) Well, dear, now you've got it, and good luck to you.

*She raises her coffee cup in a toast.*

REGENT. (*Automatically.*) Cheerio.

MARY. And I'm not going to apologize too much because I gave you very fair warning last night—

REGENT. Excuse me—but that warning covered only a certain contingency.

MARY. (*Surprised.*) Sure. Why?

REGENT. Let me hasten to assure you that no such contingency took place.

MARY. No?

REGENT. No.

MARY. Well, what did happen then? I can remember everything up to the time I said: 'O.K. I'll take the fatal step.'

REGENT. (*Shortly.*) You took it. It proved fatal, certainly, but not in the usually accepted sense.

MARY. My legs betrayed me?

REGENT. They were all that did.

MARY. Pass-out, huh? Do you know I haven't done that since an applejack party when I was fifteen?

REGENT. Have you not?

MARY. Well, imagine me passing out on you!

REGENT. Imagine.

MARY. Oh, you poor man. You poor, poor Regent, you. Oh. darling, I am so very, very sorry.

REGENT. (*Stiffly.*) That is—O.K.

MARY. (*Tenderly.*) Learning my language, huh?

*She gently slips her arms around his neck.*

> (*Softly.*) Never mind, my darling. We have years and years and years ahead of us, haven't we?

*The REGENT releases himself gently.*

REGENT. Alas, my dear, that is what is so terrible. Most unhappily I must return to Carpathia tomorrow.

MARY. Tomorrow? That's tough, I admit. (*She goes back to her coffee.*) Oh well. The minute my show comes off, I'll be right over. That's a promise.

REGENT. Splendid.

MARY. (*With a sigh.*) Oh dear! (*Looking meditatively out of the window.*) Oh well! It's a lovely day and it's wonderful to think we're going to spend some of it together. Aren't we?

*Pause.*

REGENT. (*Carefully.*) Well, now, you see, dear Miss Dagenham—

MARY. Miss Dagenham? It was beloved, last night.

REGENT. Well, you see, beloved—in ten minutes' time I have to leave for the Abbey. The ceremony and the procession will last four or five hours. I am meeting the Prime Minister at four and the French Ambassador at five-thirty. At six-thirty I have a reception here, and at seven-thirty I go to Dorchester House for a moment, and from there to the Russian Embassy. At nine I am dining with the Bulgarian Crown Prince and at ten I go to the ball at the Foreign Office where, of course, I must remain for the rest of the evening. (*Triumphantly.*) So, you see, it appears, alas, that there can be no chance whatever—

MARY. I tell you what. I'll walk with you from Dorchester House to the Russian Embassy. How's that?

REGENT. Alas, my dear. There is a certain protocol that has to be—

MARY. What's protocol?

REGENT. (*Floundering.*) Well—a certain question of formality—carriages— precedence—(*Raising his voice.*) It is impossible for me to walk with you through crowded streets from Dorchester House to the Russian Embassy.

MARY. (*Brightly.*) We could walk through the park.

REGENT. (*Sharply.*) No. (*Recovering his poise.*) Alas, my dear, such things are not possible—

MARY. Don't go on saying 'alas' in that phoney way, or I might begin to think you're really glad to get away from me—and then—I warn you—I shall be a fiend. A remorseless fiend—

PETER *comes in.*

MARY. Here we go. Grand Central. (*To* PETER.) Good morning.

PETER. Good morning, Miss Dagenham. (*Tactfully.*) What a pleasant surprise—

MARY. I don't know what's a surprise about it. How's poor old auntie this morning?

PETER *laughs mirthlessly and exchanges a glance with the* REGENT *who silently indicates that he is going to leave* PETER *to cope with the situation.*

REGENT. My dear—I must go and get ready. So—alas—I mean, I'm afraid— we must say our little adieus—

MARY. Oh no. Not till the last possible second. Not till you actually leave this building. And it won't be adieu. It'll be au revoir.

REGENT. (*With a sigh.*) Yes. Well—

*He goes quickly to the door.* MARY *continues placidly drinking her coffee. There is a shocked hiss from* PETER *at this breach of etiquette.*

PETER. Miss Dagenham!

MARY. Oh gosh! Do we have to go through all that again?

*She rises and drops him a very graceful curtsy.*

　　Your Royal Highness.

REGENT. (*Helplessly.*) Pray be seated, Miss Dagenham.

*He goes into his room.* MARY *goes back to her breakfast.*

MARY. (*Feeling her knees.*) A little hard on the knee muscles these Royal circles. Say listen—could you find me an old raincoat or something?

PETER. An old raincoat?

MARY. Sure. I've paid two pounds for a seat on the balcony of the Haymarket theatre, and I can't turn up in an evening dress. with Maisie and the whole gang there.

PETER. Very well. I shall see if I can find you an old mackintosh—but such things are not so easy to come by as you may think, in Belgrave Square. Let me see now. Perhaps one of the kitchen staff—

*He goes out.*

*A barrel organ is playing in the street outside, a jaunty little tune which is plainly recognizable to* MARY. *She begins to sing absent-mindedly to herself:*

MARY. They call me The Coconut Girl;

　　　　No mediocre nut girl.

*She gets up to put her cup down and slips into a dance routine of the period, singing the while.*

　　　　Two shies a penny,

　　　　And I've been offered many

　　　　A ruby or a pearl.

　　　　You may be coconut shy

Do say you'll give me a try.

Walk up, walk up, commoner or earl

Ev'ry bloke likes a joke with the coconut girl.

*During the last few steps of the routine* NICOLAS *has come in unobserved by* MARY. *She now turns and sees him.*

MARY. Oh, it's you. I mean it's Your Majesty.

*She does a curtsy.*

NICOLAS. Good morning, Miss Dagenham. What is that dance?

MARY. (*Flustered.*) Well, it's a new routine. You wouldn't understand what that means—but it's something I have to practise. Your Majesty is probably wondering why I'm still wearing the same dress as last night. The fact is I had a stupid accident with my latch key and so a bed had to be found for me in the Legation.

NICOLAS. (*With perfect, if slightly bored, politeness.*) Of course. What could be more natural? Where is my father?

MARY. In there, getting ready.

NICOLAS. (*Eagerly.*) Has he just gone in?

MARY. A moment ago.

NICOLAS. Miss Dagenham, may I ask you to do a small favour for me?

MARY. I should be delighted.

NICOLAS. Will you ring up a certain telephone number—this one—

*He hands her a piece of paper.*

MARY. What could be easier?

*She picks up the receiver.*

(*Into telephone.*) Hullo . . . Gerrard 245, please.

NICOLAS. (*Eagerly.*) Ask for the Ambassador.

MARY *nods.*

MARY. (*Into receiver.*) Hullo. Give me the Ambassador, please. . . . Well, it's not me, it's the King of Carpathia—

NICOLAS. (*Grabbing the receiver.*) You shouldn't have said that. There are spies everywhere.

MARY. Oh. Are there?

NICOLAS. (*Into receiver, speaking in a quick low voice.*) Euer Exzellenz! Ich werde ständigt beobachtet. Sie sind der Einzige durch den ich eine Nachricht senden kann. Dies ist an General Ravinof weiterzuleiten. 'In Anbetracht der letzten Entwicklungen fällt die Entscheidung auf Datum eins. Datum eins.' Jawohl. Auf Wiedersehen.

*He rings off, carefully putting the receiver down, so that no ring shall be audible. Then he goes quickly to the door.*

(*To* MARY.) I shall not soon forget your kindness in this matter, Miss Dagenham.

MARY. Think nothing of it.

*He goes out.* MARY *picks up the receiver.*

I want another number, please. Brixton 937 . . . Brixton. Yes. . . . Hullo,

Fanny. . . . Hiya. Were you worried about me? . . . Well, it's a long story. . . . No, darling, that'd be a short story. This is a long one. . . . Listen, don't tell the gang a thing, will you? . . .

*The* REGENT *comes out of his bedroom. He is dressed for the Coronation in a very grandiose uniform, with many trimmings.* MARY *does not see him.*

Sure I'm coming. I wouldn't miss it for the world. Besides he'll be in the procession. . . . Oh, he's the cutest little Grand Duke in the world. . . . No. Not really handsome, just kind of cute. . . . Oh no. Not at all like the Grand Dukes you see on the stage. . . . No sense of humour, no charm, not much manners, but for all that I love him so much I could eat him. Chew him up. . . . Yes, darling. I'll tell you all about it later. Don't forget now—not a word. Bye.

*She rings off. The* REGENT *who has been standing by the door now walks forward.*

REGENT. (*Very angrily.*) But I have a very good sense of humour.

MARY. (*Soothingly.*) Yes, darling. Of course you have—only it's a kind of Balkan one. Just as good as Anglo-Saxon, I'm sure, but different. Anyway you shouldn't listen to private telephone conversations—

REGENT. Here.

*Brusquely he hands her a small jewel-box.*

MARY. What's this?

REGENT. A small parting gift. I was going to present it to you with a few appropriate words. but now you have driven them clean out of my head.

MARY. (*Taking out a brooch.*) Say, this is beautiful—with your crest and everything.

REGENT. (*Brusquely.*) It is nothing.

MARY. I'm not looking a gift horse, but I'll bet there are quite a few of these being worn round Europe, huh? Say—not Maisie Springfield—

REGENT. No. She got a snuff-box.

MARY. Gee. I guess this rates higher than hers, then.

REGENT. It was a Fabergé snuff-box—in gold and diamonds.

MARY. Oh. (*With a shrug.*) Oh well, I can't complain. After all she really earned hers. Here. Pin it on please.

*He does so. She looks down, suddenly rather sad, at the top of his head.*

So this is where I wake up, is it?

REGENT. I fear so, my dear.

MARY. (*Staring at him.*) Pity. Well—all I can say is that for a good-bye scene you've got quite the wrong costume on.

REGENT. What is the matter with it?

MARY. Nothing. Nothing at all. That's the trouble.

REGENT. It makes me look—cute?

MARY. I'll say.

REGENT. Almost like a Grand Duke on the stage?

MARY. Almost.

*The* REGENT *smiles and glances briefly at his watch.*

Yes. O.K. That's my cue. Good-bye.

*He moves towards her to give her a tender kiss.*

REGENT. It has been wonderful knowing you. If only it could have lasted longer.

MARY *starts suddenly to giggle, and steps back.*

REGENT. What is the matter? Have I said anything wrong?

MARY. No. You spoke the line beautifully. It was your medals. They were tickling me.

REGENT. (*Angrily.*) Why are you always saying such things? You seem to enjoy disconcerting me—and that is one thing I cannot bear—to be disconcerted—

PETER *comes in, carrying a mackintosh. The* REGENT *strides angrily to the door.* (*To* PETER.) I am spending two minutes with the Minister. Join us in the hall.

*He turns and bows to* MARY.

Good-bye again.

MARY. (*Curtsying.*) Your Royal Highness.

*The* REGENT *goes out.* PETER *comes forward with the mackintosh.*

PETER. This is all I could find, I'm afraid. It belongs to a scullery maid.

MARY. It'll do very well.

*He helps her into it. It is old and rather shabby.* MARY *goes to her bag, takes out a handkerchief and blows her nose.*

(*With a sigh.*) Oh dear! Life's rather sad sometimes, isn't it?

PETER. Sometimes.

MARY. I'll never get a taxi or anything now. I'll have to walk. Oh well—

*She is moving towards the door when it is opened by a* FOOTMAN, *and the* GRAND DUCHESS *comes in—in full regalia.* MARY *turns tail and flees through the door L.*

GRAND DUCHESS. Who was that? Mr. Northbrook, who was that creature? Was it an anarchist?

PETER. No, Ma'am.

GRAND DUCHESS. Well, who was it?

PETER. A young lady, Ma'am, called Miss Elaine Dagenham.

GRAND DUCHESS. Fetch her to me.

*She sits down, while* PETER *goes to the door L. and beckons.* MARY *comes timidly in. The* GRAND DUCHESS *makes a gesture for her to come up to her chair.* MARY *does so. She curtsies and the* GRAND DUCHESS *holds out her hand.*

Good morning, my dear. So delightful to see you again. Why are you dressed up as a revolutionary? Is this a new game? If it is you should have let me know. I love games.

MARY. It isn't a game, Ma'am—

GRAND DUCHESS. Well, take that thing off. It looks most unbecoming,

MARY *takes off the mackintosh, revealing her evening dress of which the* GRAND DUCHESS *seems utterly oblivious.*

And please sit down.

MARY *sits on the edge of a chair.*
> I am going to have a cigarette. So soothing before a long ordeal. Will
> you join me?

MARY. No thank you, Ma'am.

PETER *offers the* GRAND DUCHESS *a cigarette from a box and lights it for her.*
> (*Acutely conscious of her attire.*) Your Imperial and Royal Highness is prob-
> ably wondering why I'm still dressed as I was last night. The fact is, I
> had a stupid accident with my latch key—

GRAND DUCHESS. (*To* PETER.) What does she say?

PETER. She says she had an accident with her latch key—

GRAND DUCHESS. Latch key? What is a latch key?

PETER. Well, Ma'am, it's—

GRAND DUCHESS. It doesn't matter. I'm sure it's something very dull. (*Still to*
PETER.) Such irritating news, Mr. Northbrook, this morning. Maud von
and zu Meissenbronn—my Chief Lady in Waiting—claims she cannot
leave her bed, so I have no option but to take the Baroness Brunheim to
the Abbey, which means we shall all be very squashed in the carriage. So
maddening of Maud—this morning of all mornings.

PETER. I trust that there is nothing seriously wrong with her?

GRAND DUCHESS. Nothing at all. Last night she had a slight head cold, so I
dosed her with one of my syrups. This morning she announces the cold
has left her head and descended to her stomach. Imagine—(*To* MARY.) Je
ne sais pas pourquoi mais les maladies des autres m'embêtent toujours,
surtout si elles sont imaginaires, comme celles de la Comtesse—Vous
trouvez ça aussi?

*Pause.*

MARY. (*At length.*) Excuse me, Ma'am, I didn't quite catch what you said.

GRAND DUCHESS. (*To* PETER.) Yes?

PETER. I don't think Miss Dagenham speaks French, Ma'am.

GRAND DUCHESS. Doesn't speak French? Ridiculous. She lives with Madame
Bernhardt in Paris. (*To* MARY.) N'est-ce pas, ma petite? Je suis sûre que
vous parlez le français mieux qu'une Française, et surtout d'une voix d'or.

MARY. (*At length.*) Oui.

GRAND DUCHESS. (*To* PETER.) You see. (*To* MARY.) Au sujet des maladies des
autres, c'est La Rochefoucauld, n'est-ce pas, qui a dit: 'dans l'adversité
de nos meilleurs amis, nous trouvons quelque chose qui ne nous déplait
pas'?

MARY. (*At length.*) Oui.

GRAND DUCHESS. Eh bien, je vous assure que dans les adversités de Maud, je
ne trouve jamais rien qui ne me déplait pas infiniment.

*She laughs.* MARY, *taking the cue, laughs too. The* GRAND DUCHESS *turns and gives
her half-finished cigarette to* PETER, *who takes it and puts it out.*
> (*To* PETER.) Most intelligent, reading La Rochefoucauld. Mr. Northbrook,
> please tell Baroness Brunheim to bring me my jewel-box.

PETER *bows and goes.* MARY *stares at the* GRAND DUCHESS, *like a rabbit at a snake. She breathes a sigh of relief as the* GRAND DUCHESS *resumes her conversation in English.*

My dear, I hear there are great multitudes in the streets, and all being so enthusiastic and loyal that even the soldiers have turned their backs to the people, and are facing the procession. Most gratifying. Isn't that an evening dress you are wearing?

MARY. (*Helplessly.*) Yes, Ma'am. I was trying to explain—

GRAND DUCHESS. Stand up and let me see it. Walk across here, please.

MARY *stands up, while the* GRAND DUCHESS *inspects.*

Excellent. Most suitable. Now what was I saying?

MARY. About the crowds being so loyal, Ma'am.

GRAND DUCHESS. Oh yes. Such a change from the last Coronation I attended—the Bessarabias. My dear—only the merest trickle of people in the streets, revolver shots going off like kettle-drums and the sky black with infernal machines. Happily no fatalities—except in the crowd—but it all left a very bad impression. And the service far too long and the singing really not at all good. Not good at all.

BARONESS BRUNHEIM, *a plumpish lady of middle age, dressed for the Abbey, enters, carrying, with* PETER, *a large, jewel-case.*

GRAND DUCHESS. Ah, Lottie, put it there. Thank you, Mr. Northbrook. (PETER *goes out.*)

*The* GRAND DUCHESS *stands up.* MARY *follows suit. The* GRAND DUCHESS *approaches* MARY *with the jewel-box. She takes out a 'choker' of pearls.*

Just stand still, dear.

*The* GRAND DUCHESS *fastens it on* MARY'S *neck, and stands back to survey the result.*

Yes. That is very possible. We need this, too, of course.

MARY. (*Frantically.*) What's happening, Ma'am? Is this a game, Ma'am?

GRAND DUCHESS. What did you say, my dear?

MARY. (*To* BARONESS.) Ask Ma'am is this a game.

BARONESS. (*To* GRAND DUCHESS.) She wants to know, is this a game?

*A broad diamond collar is put round* MARY'S *neck.*

GRAND DUCHESS. (*To* BARONESS.) Lottie, my dear, put your cape on her, would you?

MARY. Please tell me, what is happening?

BARONESS BRUNHEIM *takes her fur cape off and puts it round* MARY'S *shoulders.*

GRAND DUCHESS. Better and better. (*Turning to* BARONESS BRUNHEIM.) Lottie, will you be very disappointed—

BARONESS. (*With a beaming smile.*) Oh, but that is perfectly all right. Ma'am. As you know—with my trouble—I always have been a little nervous of long ceremonies.

GRAND DUCHESS. Good. That is settled, then. Arrange your veil on her, and lend her your gloves.

MARY. (*Bewildered.*) Please tell me, Ma'am? What's going on?

BARONESS BRUNHEIM *is arranging a veil on* MARY'S *head.*

GRAND DUCHESS. I am appointing you my Lady in Waiting for the day, my dear, and taking you to the Abbey.

MARY. But, Ma'am, you can't. I mean, someone will recognize me, and I shall be arrested—

GRAND DUCHESS. (*In icy tones.*) *Arrest my Lady in Waiting?* My dear child! Such an imbecility!

MARY. (*In a frenzy.*) But what do I do? Where do I sit?

GRAND DUCHESS. (*Impatiently.*) Just do what I do, and sit next to me. You still look a little bare. I know. You need an order.

*The* REGENT *enters.*

REGENT. It is time—that we—

*He is suddenly transfixed by the sight of the now nearly transformed* MARY.

MARY. Hullo.

GRAND DUCHESS. My dear, such fun! How you will roar! We are taking Miss Dagenham to the Abbey.

*Pause.*

REGENT. (*At length.*) Oh? Are we?

GRAND DUCHESS. I need an order for her, my dear. (*To* BARONESS BRUNHEIM.) What is that one you are wearing, Lottie? The Purple Pillow? No, that would hardly suit. I know—that nice mauve one—what is it called?— you know the one I mean, my dear, the one you gave to the Foreign Secretary the other day. So fetching. Give her that, Lottie—in that bureau there—the centre drawer. Hand it to the Regent.

BARONESS BRUNHEIM *goes to the bureau in question and brings out a case.* (*During this, looking at* MARY.) We will now be most comfortable in the carriage. For those hips, I suppose you do those new Swedish exercises. Most ingenious, I hear—like everything Swedish.

BARONESS BRUNHEIM *hands the case to the Regent, who stands, speechless, staring at it.*

REGENT. You realize, no doubt, that this order is only given for a very special personal service to the head of the State.

GRAND DUCHESS. (*Impatiently.*) Such hair-splitting! No doubt she will do you one, one day.

*The* REGENT *dazedly opens the case and takes out a mauve ribbon.*

REGENT. (*To* MARY.) Take your cape off.

*She does so.*

   Kneel down.

MARY *kneels.*

   I hereby invest you with the Royal Carpathian Order of Perseverance— second class.

*He fastens the order to her dress. She then stands up.*

GRAND DUCHESS. (*At door.*) Come, my dears.

MARY *unfastens her brooch quickly.*

MARY. And I hereby return you this.

*She hands him the brooch.*

> After all, we're not parting quite yet—are we, my darling?

*She curtsies to him. The* REGENT, *his face expressionless, goes to the door and joins the* GRAND DUCHESS. MARY *shrugs her shoulders, happily, and follows them.*

CURTAIN

# ACT II

## SCENE 1

SCENE: *The same. The time is about seven o'clock of the same day. The* GRAND DUCHESS *is reclining on the settee with her feet up, and beside her a large box of chocolates, into which she is occasionally dipping.* MARY *is sitting on a stool, close to her, engaged in reading aloud. Both ladies are wearing the clothes in which they had been to the Abbey that morning.*

MARY. (*Reading.*) At this juncture the prisoner asked for a glass of water which was given to him by a warder. Mr. Muir (resuming his cross-examination). Now, Dr. Crippen, kindly tell the jury why it was that you pawned your wife's jewels. Dr. Crippen. Because I needed some new dental instruments. Was that an urgent matter? No. Then why were you in such a hurry to pawn your wife's ear-rings and marquise rings?

GRAND DUCHESS. There are photographs of these jewels, are there not?

MARY. Yes, Ma'am.

*She hands the book to the* GRAND DUCHESS *who inspects the photographs carefully.*

GRAND DUCHESS. Most disappointing. Plainly not the motive. (*Handing the book back.*) Go on, dear, I want to get on to the summing up. So many holes in the evidence—such fun.

MARY. (*Reading.*) Dr. Crippen. I don't know. Mr. Muir. Was the money so raised to enable you to flee the country? No. But you did flee the country? Yes. Under a false name? Yes. Having shaved off your moustache? Yes. Taking Miss le Neve with you? Yes. Disguised as a boy? Yes. Posing as your son? I cannot deny it.

*The* REGENT *comes out of his bedroom. He is wearing a different uniform.* MARY *stops reading and stares at him with open admiration, then remembering herself, stands up hastily, still staring.*

GRAND DUCHESS. My dear—so much noise and confusion downstairs. The Minister is giving a reception for some wretchedly dull people, and when, to cap the horror, they announced the arrival of that dreadful Archduchess Ferdinand and her idiotic daughter, I simply flew up here—

REGENT. But, my dear, I wanted you to be particularly polite to Maria and Louisa this afternoon. It is most important.

GRAND DUCHESS. Important? For what reason?

REGENT. (*Patiently.*) I have told you many times of our plans for Louisa and Nicky.

GRAND DUCHESS. So you have. So you have. I keep forgetting. (*After a moment's cogitation.*) Yes. Most suitable, I suppose. Most suitable. A pity she is such a horrid little brat and has such dreadful parents, but I agree that in every other way the match is ideal. (*She gets up.*) Very well, my dear. I shall not shirk my duty.

REGENT. Why don't you receive them here? and I shall send Nicky up to join you. Where is he?

GRAND DUCHESS. Now where is Nicky? I saw him somewhere, I know. Oh yes. He was in the garden, kicking something.

REGENT. (*Alarmed.*) Kicking? Kicking what?

GRAND DUCHESS. (*To* MARY.) What was it the King was kicking, dear?

MARY. A football.

GRAND DUCHESS. Yes, that's what it was. A football. Dear Miss Dagenham. She has been such a help to me all day, Charles. I can hardly tell you how good she has been.

REGENT. I'm so glad.

GRAND DUCHESS. Reads most prettily, too. Of course with such a dramatic training one would expect that. And so intelligent and erudite, Charles. Do you know that there is hardly a French author whom she has not read. To every name I give her she just answers 'Oui'. So modest and charming. And looked most handsome at the Abbey I thought—didn't you, my dear?

REGENT. Most handsome.

GRAND DUCHESS. I am happy to tell you that I have succeeded in wringing a promise from her to pay us a long visit to Carpathia. Isn't that good?

REGENT. Quite splendid. Well, I must collect Maria and—(*He turns to the door.*) My dear, we mustn't be selfish and keep Miss Dagenham too long. (*He looks at his watch.*) I fear she will have to leave us very soon for her theatre.

*He goes out.*

GRAND DUCHESS. Theatre? What theatre? Are you giving something tonight, my dear? I had no idea.

MARY. Yes, Ma'am.

GRAND DUCHESS. But how exciting! What are you giving?

MARY. (*In a small voice.*) *The Coconut Girl.*

GRAND DUCHESS. I didn't quite catch that, my dear. Speak a little more clearly. What is the name of your role?

MARY. Fifi.

GRAND DUCHESS. *Fifi?* Ah yes. Of course, I know it well. By Sardou, I think.

MARY. (*Accustomed to this by now.*) Er, no, Ma'am.

GRAND DUCHESS. Who is it by then?

MARY. (*With resignation.*) Al Fleischberg, Buddy Maxwell and Joe Zink.

GRAND DUCHESS. (*After a moment's reflection.*) I do not think I know these authors.

MARY. They are American, Ma'am.

GRAND DUCHESS. American? Tiens! They have theatre in America too?

MARY. Oh yes, Ma'am.

GRAND DUCHESS. How strange! And this Fifi, of these authors, you are giving it tonight as a special performance?

MARY. No, Ma'am. It's already been running for over a year.

GRAND DUCHESS. A year! My dear, such a role, so many times—how dreadfully tired you must be. Please sit down. I remember once at Furstenstein we gave *King Lear* to the villagers and foresters, and we were so successful that dear Daisy insisted we should give it again the next night for the gamekeepers and huntsmen. But, my dear. So exhausted were we all that we had to cancel the performance, although the money had been paid and the seats engaged. Only the man who acted Lear wanted to do it again, but as he was a professional actor there was, of course, no effort for him to remember his words, like the rest of us. You know *King Lear?*

MARY. Not well, Ma'am.

GRAND DUCHESS. A most delightful little play. Quite touching and very little love. I acted the part of Kent—we had not enough men as usual—but everyone was most kind, and said I made a very handsome boy. I was quite word perfect and made only one mistake—when I was talking to Princess Schlumberger-Lippe-Gildenstern about her poor husband— such a worry to us all—and, my dear, I quite forgot to go on to the stage for the scene where I am put in the stocks. However, the Duke of Stirling who was acting the steward most ingeniously saved the situation by saying some of my words as well as his, omitting the fight and sitting in the stocks himself. So quick-witted and nothing was noticed—but of course, the majority of our audience only spoke German, and we were acting, naturally, in English—

*The doors are opened by the* FOOTMEN, *and the* MAJOR-DOMO *begins to enter.*

GRAND DUCHESS. (*Hastily.*) What time must you leave for your theatre?

MARY. In about twenty minutes.

GRAND DUCHESS. Stay with me through this.

MAJOR-DOMO. Her Royal Highness the Archduchess Ferdinand of Styria: Her Royal Highness the Princess Louisa.

*The* ARCHDUCHESS *is large and red-faced. Her daughter—a girl of about fifteen— is an angry-looking child in pigtails. The two* DUCHESSES, *grand and arch, meet with a loving kiss, on both cheeks. The girl curtsies and is rewarded with a quick kiss on the forehead.*

GRAND DUCHESS. Dear Maria! So delightful. And how handsome little Louisa has become.

ARCHDUCHESS. (*A shade truculently.*) Did you not think her handsome before?

GRAND DUCHESS. My dear, there are degrees in these things. Shall we sit down? This is Miss Dagenham, the actress. You have heard of her, of course.

ARCHDUCHESS. Of course. Many times.

LOUISA. (*Suspiciously.*) What are you acting in?

GRAND DUCHESS. At the moment she is giving the Fifi of Fleischberg, Maxwell and Zink.

LOUISA. I've never heard of it.

GRAND DUCHESS. (*Sharply.*) Then you should have done. (*To* MARY, *who stands behind her chair.*) Give the Princess a chocolate, dear.

MARY *goes to* LOUISA'S *chair and proffers her a chocolate.* LOUISA *takes one.* MARY *is about to move away, but* LOUISA *summons her imperiously back, and takes two more.*

GRAND DUCHESS. And how is your dear husband?

ARCHDUCHESS. Ah, Ferdinand is very well.

GRAND DUCHESS. (*To* MARY, *noticing* LOUISA'S *grabbing of the chocolates.*) Bring the chocolates here, dear.

MARY *brings the chocolates to the* GRAND DUCHESS.

(*To* ARCHDUCHESS.) Would you care—?

*The* ARCHDUCHESS *shakes her head and the* GRAND DUCHESS *firmly places the lid on the box and puts it beside her.*

The same irrepressible high spirits?

ARCHDUCHESS. My dear—the other day, at a restaurant in Paris—how you would have roared. He sat down at the table with his hat on his head, and when the maître d'hôtel came up and said, 'May I take Your Royal Highness' hat,' he said, 'Yes, and you can take your soup too.' And with that he poured his soup into his hat and handed it to the maître d'hôtel. My dear—the man's face—it was a study.

*She laughs uproariously. Even* LOUISA *cracks a smile. Only the* GRAND DUCHESS *is stony faced.*

GRAND DUCHESS. You know my little affliction. Excuse me. (*To* MARY.) Yes, dear?

MARY. The Archduchess's husband—

GRAND DUCHESS. The Archduke Ferdinand, dear. Such a witty man. Go on.

MARY. (*In a low voice—she has learnt the trick*). The Archduke Ferdinand sat down at a table in a restaurant in Paris with his hat on his head. When the head waiter asked him for his hat he said: 'You can have the hat and the soup too.' So then he poured the soup into the hat and handed it to the head waiter—whose face, the Archduchess said, was a study.

GRAND DUCHESS. (*At length, to the* ARCHDUCHESS.) Incomparable.

ARCHDUCHESS. You remember when he went to the Serbian Legation in a false beard?

GRAND DUCHESS. (*To* MARY.) Yes?

MARY. (*In her interpreting voice.*) The Archduchess asks if you remember when the Archduke went to the Serbian Legation in a false beard.

GRAND DUCHESS. (*To the* ARCHDUCHESS.) Vividly.

ARCHDUCHESS. And half of it fell off in the soup.

*She laughs again. The* GRAND DUCHESS *glances inquiringly at* MARY.

MARY. And half of the false beard fell off in the soup.

GRAND DUCHESS. (*At length.*) Irresistible. And whose hat did he put that in? I forget now.

ARCHDUCHESS. No, no. He didn't put it in anyone's hat. He called the head butler over and said, 'I think you have given me hare soup.' Understand? Hare soup? HAIR and HARE.

MARY *bends forward to repeat but the* GRAND DUCHESS *waves her back.*

GRAND DUCHESS. Thank you, dear. I heard that.

*The* MAJOR-DOMO *enters.*

MAJOR-DOMO. His Majesty.

NICOLAS *comes in. He is looking regal, in a uniform, with orders.* MARIA *and* LOUISA, *both rather unwillingly, it seems, get up.*

NICOLAS. How are you. Aunt Maria?

ARCHDUCHESS. Very well, thank you, Nicky. He kisses her and she bobs.

NICOLAS. And Cousin Louisa?

*He kisses* LOUISA, *whose bob is more perfunctory, than her mother's.*

NICOLAS. Won't you sit down?

GRAND DUCHESS. My dear, I know how eager you are to talk to dear little Louisa, and I must not be selfish and keep your Aunt Maria any longer from the reception downstairs. (*To the* ARCHDUCHESS.) So, my dear, shall I deliver you back into the hands of our Minister, who I know is furious with me already for stealing you?

ARCHDUCHESS. There will be a chaperon of course?

GRAND DUCHESS. Miss Dagenham will stay.

MARY. But, Ma'am, I should be going

NICOLAS *touches her sleeve in a quick, pathetic, pleading gesture.*

GRAND DUCHESS. Did you say something, dear?

MARY. Nothing, Ma'am.

GRAND DUCHESS. (*To* ARCHDUCHESS.) I wonder if dear Ferdinand does not nurture some strange fascination for soup. I notice so many of his most brilliant escapades are connected with it. Ah, but of course, I was forgetting the famous incident with the lemon meringue at Homburg—

*The doors are closed behind the two ladies. There is a pause.* NICOLAS *is plainly diffident and embarrassed.* LOUISA *just looks sullen.*

NICOLAS. (*At length, to* LOUISA.) Won't you sit down?

LOUISA. No, thank you.

*She kicks listlessly at the settee. Pause.*

NICOLAS. Shall we talk in English, oder sollen wir Deutsch sprechen? Ou français, si vous préférez.

LOUISA. That is just boasting. I speak seven languages.

NICOLAS. (*Politely.*) Very clever. (*After a pause.*) I speak eight.

LOUISA. You are older, and Carpathian hardly counts.

NICOLAS. (*Hotly.*) Why not? What is the matter with my native tongue?

LOUISA. A patois.

NICOLAS. (*Furious.*) Patois be—

MARY. (*Restrainingly.*) Sir.

NICOLAS. (*Murmuring.*) Yes. (*After another pause.*) Are you going to the ball tonight?

LOUISA. That is just boasting too. You know I can't go. I don't know why they let you go.

NICOLAS. I go to balls in my own country.

LOUISA. (*In tones of faint scorn.*) Do they have balls in Carpathia? I thought it was all lederhosen, bare knees and slapping each other.

NICOLAS *takes a breath to reply in kind.* MARY *quickly touches him restrainingly on the arm.* NICOLAS *nods.* LOUISA *has discovered a magazine in which she appears deeply interested. She sits down.*

I've sat down. You did ask me to. Anyway I think such things are stupid.

NICOLAS. I agree.

*He goes up and sits next to her.*

(*Dutifully.*) Cousin Louisa—(*He stops uncertainly.*)

LOUISA. (*Deep in the magazine.*) Cousin Nicolas? (*After a further silence from* NICOLAS, *she looks at him over the edge of her magazine.*) There's really no need to say what you are going to say, unless you particularly want to. I'll tell my mother you said it, and you can tell your father I made the right answer. It's not for eighteen months, anyway—is it?

NICOLAS. No.

LOUISA. (*Back to her magazine.*) So that's all right.

NICOLAS. (*After a pause.*) I find that rather sensible.

LOUISA. I am sensible.

*There is a long pause, while* LOUISA *buries herself deeper in her magazine.* MARY, *plainly shocked at what she has heard, looks at the clock.*

MARY. Look—I wonder whether you two really need a chaperon?

NICOLAS. Don't go, please, unless you have to.

MARY. Well, Your Majesty—

NICOLAS. I heard you went to the Coronation with my stepmother? What did you think of it?

MARY. The greatest experience of my life—that's all.

NICOLAS. You must come to mine.

MARY. I should like to very much, Sir, always provided you haven't put your father in some deep dungeon by then.

NICOLAS. That is a good joke, Miss Dagenham.

MARY. Is it such a joke? I'm remembering a little telephone conversation from this morning.

NICOLAS. (*Defensively.*) I was talking to the German Ambassador about an invitation to a shooting party.

MARY. Shooting party may be right. I happen to speak German, you know. I was born in Milwaukee.

LOUISA. (*From her chair.*) What are you two talking about?

NICOLAS. You wouldn't be interested.

LOUISA. I might be. What was it?

NICOLAS. Miss Dagenham was telling me about where she was born.

LOUISA. (*Into her magazine.*) No. I wouldn't be.

NICOLAS. (*To* MARY.) All right. If you speak German give me an English translation of what I said.

MARY. Let's see. For relay to General Ravinof. In view of recent developments, date one. Right?

NICOLAS. You've told father, of course?

MARY. No.

NICOLAS. But you're going to?

MARY. No.

NICOLAS. Why not?

MARY. Never mind. Just take it I won't.

LOUISA *has got up and has wandered over to the door L.*

LOUISA. What is this room?

NICOLAS. A bedroom.

LOUISA. I think I will read in here. I cannot concentrate when there is talking.

*She goes out.*

NICOLAS. Odious girl.

MARY. Agreed.

*She laughs.* NICOLAS *joins her.*

NICOLAS. It is good of you not to give me away to father. I am grateful.

MARY. I have one proviso, though. A serious one, and on this you must give me your Kingly oath, or whatever it is. You don't intend him any harm?

NICOLAS. (*Carefully.*) If he agrees to the changed situation, he may remain in Carpathia without let or hindrance, and with all due rights and honours.

MARY. And if he disagrees?

NICOLAS. (*After a pause.*) He must live outside Carpathia.

MARY. Exile, in fact?

NICOLAS. Well—

MARY. (*Warmly.*) But, Nicky, for heaven's sake, the guy's your pa!

NICOLAS *turns, with regal dignity, to stare at her.*

Excuse me. I'm an American and I get mixed up sometimes.

NICOLAS. (*Slowly.*) No, but it is interesting. It bears out so much of what I have heard concerning your nation's strongly emotional tendencies towards parent worship. The fact, Miss Dagenham, that the guy is my father is of very minor importance. The essential fact is that he is Regent, and that his policy is leading my country into war.

MARY. That's what you think, I know. Anyway it's what your Uncle Wilhelm thinks. Your father thinks different. But you're only sixteen while he's— well, he told me forty—but I'll make a rough guess at forty-five. Isn't there just a chance that he might know better than you?

NICOLAS. Now there is surely another American characteristic, no? The idea that the old are wise simply because they are not young, and that the young are children until they are twenty-one, and sometimes, I believe, much longer.

MARY. (*Hotly.*) Well, maybe it's just because we're kinder and more clear-sighted than other people. We know that the most precious thing in life is childhood, and we don't see why we should take it away from people too soon. Anyway, you mustn't argue with me on that subject. I'm prejudiced. I've never grown up, I admit, and I've never wanted to either, and if I think it's wrong for boys of sixteen to plot dirty tricks on their fathers, and try and shove them off into limbo, and then justify themselves by talking like they were George Bernard Shaw, well it's only me, see— and don't you go blaming my country just because of it.

NICOLAS *smiles. There is a pause.*

NICOLAS. Miss Dagenham, may I pay you a compliment?

MARY. (*Suspiciously.*) There'll be a catch to this, I'll bet.

NICOLAS. (*Simply.*) Oh no.

MARY. Go ahead, then.

NICOLAS. (*Simply.*) I think I like you much the best of all my father's mistresses.

*Pause.*

MARY. (*At length.*) Oh—er—well—er—Anyway, I thank Your Majesty for the compliment. (*She curtsies.*)

LOUISA *emerges from the bedroom.*

LOUISA. I've found some cards. Let's play a game.

NICOLAS. Wouldn't you rather read your nice magazine?

LOUISA. I've finished it. (*She is shuffling a pack of cards.*) Let's play poker.

NICOLAS. I don't remember it well.

LOUISA. It's easy.

NICOLAS *sits down on the settee beside* LOUISA. *She shuffles.*

NICOLAS. What shall we play for?

LOUISA. Those chocolates. We'll each have twenty. (*With an imperious gesture.*) Miss Dagenham—

MARY. (*Loyally.*) They belong to the Grand Duchess—Ma'am. (*The salutation plainly sticks in her throat.*)

LOUISA *glares murderously at her.*

LOUISA. (*Viciously, after a pause.*) I've never heard of Fifi. I don't believe there is such a play. (*To* NICOLAS.) We'll play for money and remember what we lose.

MARY. (*To* NICOLAS, *after a slight pause.*) Shall I help Your Majesty with your cards?

NICOLAS. Thank you. Most kind.

MARY *perches on the settee behind* NICOLAS. LOUISA *deals five cards to each.*

LOUISA. How many cards?

MARY. Three.

LOUISA *gives him three.*

LOUISA. I'm taking four.

MARY. (*Whispering.*) That means she's only got an ace or a king.

LOUISA. It doesn't mean anything of the kind. Now, you bet.

NICOLAS. (*After whispered advice.*) Sixpence.

LOUISA. I'll raise you a shilling.

NICOLAS. (*After further whispered advice.*) I'll raise you two shillings.

LOUISA. (*After due thought.*) I'll raise you a hundred pounds.

NICOLAS. You haven't got a hundred pounds.

LOUISA. I can get it. All right then. (*She thinks.*) I'll raise you a thousand Styrian marks.

MARY. (*Mildly.*) Ma'am, I wonder whether you should—

LOUISA. Silence, please. Speak only when you are addressed. A thousand Styrian marks.

MARY *nods quietly, with pursed lips, and whispers to* NICOLAS.

NICOLAS. (*At length.*) Fifty thousand Carpathian crowns.

LOUISA. A hundred thousand Styrian marks.

NICOLAS. (*Without consultation.*) Two hundred thousand Carpathian crowns.

LOUISA. Five hundred thousand Styrian marks.

NICOLAS. Nine hundred thousand . . .

MARY *is frantically trying to restrain* NICOLAS.

MARY. Sir—I beg you—

LOUISA. (*Bouncing triumphantly on the settee.*) Yes, but he said it! He said it! A million Styrian marks.

MARY. I think we'd better see her. Say see you.

NICOLAS. See you.

LOUISA *triumphantly lays down her cards.*

MARY. But that's only two pairs.

LOUISA. Well?

MARY. We have four queens.

LOUISA. Two pairs is better.

MARY. No, it isn't. The King wins.

LOUISA. (*Loudly.*) He doesn't. He doesn't. In Styria two pairs is better.

NICOLAS. Miss Dagenham is American and this is an American game.

LOUISA. It isn't. It's a Styrian game.

NICOLAS. (*Raising his voice.*) It's an American game. Anyone knows that. Billy the Kid invented it.

LOUISA. (*Screaming.*) My uncle invented it. It's a Styrian game.

MARY. (*Pacifically.*) Really, Ma'am, I think it really is an American game, you know, and in our rules two pairs are definitely less than fours.

LOUISA. (*Leaning forward, viciously.*) Shall I tell you what you are? You're both of you dirty cheats!

*She hurls the cards in* NICOLAS' *face and gets up.*

NICOLAS. (*Rising, furious.*) I will not be so insulted, nor will Miss Dagenham.
*He catches* LOUISA *by the hair.*
    Take that back at once.
LOUISA. (*Screaming.*) I won't. I won't. I won't. Dirty cheats, dirty cheats, dirty
    cheats. Ow! You're hurting. Stop it. Dirty cheats!
*The* REGENT *walks in, a benign smile on his face. The smile is wiped off his face
at what he sees.*
REGENT. (*Angrily.*) Nicolas! What are you doing?
NICOLAS *reluctantly lets her go. She flies to the* REGENT *for protection.*
LOUISA. Uncle Charles, I have to protest. Nicolas pulled my hair, Miss
    Dagenham was insolent, and both of them have obtained money from
    me at poker by what I can only call sharp practice.
REGENT. My dear Louisa, I am sure there is some little mistake—
LOUISA. (*With dignity.*) There is no mistake whatever. As for the money it
    will be paid in full, of course, by my father, although what observation
    he may have to make concerning the transaction I cannot say. I am now
    going to look for my mother. (*With a curtsy to* NICOLAS.) Your Majesty.
*She goes out. The* REGENT *looks from one to the other, grimly.*
REGENT. (*At length, to* NICOLAS.) How much?
NICOLAS. (*Muttering.*) A million.
REGENT. (*Appalled.*) A million?
MARY. (*Reassuringly.*) Oh, not pounds. Only Styrian marks. (*Murmuring.*)
    They're about three and a half to the dollar, aren't they? I don't know
    what that makes them to the pound. Let me see now—
REGENT. (*To* NICOLAS.) This conduct is utterly appalling—worse even, and
    this is saying much, than I might have expected from you.
MARY. It was entirely her fault.
REGENT. (*Coldly.*) Miss Dagenham, is it not time you were at your theatre?
MARY. Not quite. Listen. I was here for the whole interview. The King did
    his best—and his best was a good deal better than mine would have been,
    let me tell you, considering the acute provocation he suffered from that
    little—(*Restraining herself.*) Princess.
REGENT. I see you have found a champion, Nicolas. I wonder if Miss
    Dagenham can help you in another even more serious matter in which
    she is as deeply involved as yourself. The telephone operator reports that
    you talked to the German Ambassador this morning. That is so?
NICOLAS. (*Tense.*) Yes.
REGENT. After Miss Dagenham had obtained you the number?
NICOLAS. She didn't know what the number was.
REGENT. You passed some message, didn't you?
NICOLAS. Yes.
REGENT. About your forthcoming coup d'état.
NICOLAS. That exists only in your and your secret police's imagination, fa-
    ther.

REGENT. (*Quietly menacing.*) What exactly was the message?

NICOLAS. Your operator will tell you.

REGENT. She doesn't speak German.

NICOLAS. I know. I found that out.

*Pause.*

REGENT. (*Quietly.*) Will you tell me that message, Nicky?

NICOLAS. Isn't it nice it was such a fine day for the Coronation?

*Another pause.*

REGENT. You will go to your room. Colonel Hoffman will visit you there later.

NICOLAS *shrugs his shoulders philosophically.*

And, of course, there is no question whatever of your going to the ball tonight. I prefer not to keep company with traitors.

NICOLAS *goes to the door, turns and bows to* MARY.

NICOLAS. Miss Dagenham, I say this with sincerity. It has been a real pleasure.

*He goes out. After he has gone there is a long pause, while the* REGENT *stands deep in thought. Finally he sits down wearily.*

REGENT. (*More to himself than to* MARY.) What am I to do with such a boy?

MARY *has been staring at him with her wontedly fond gaze. She now comes behind his chair, puts her hand on his shoulder, and looks down at him.*

MARY. If you were asking me that question seriously, my darling, I'd answer you. But as you're not, I'll just take off all my finery—and slip quietly out of your life for ever.

*She begins to take off the veil.*

REGENT. (*Angrily.*) I am asking you—although, Herr Gott, I know what the answer's going to be. Something about his not having enough love in his life, I suppose?

MARY. (*Lightly.*) Not such a bad guess.

REGENT. (*Even more angrily.*) And Wolffstein, whom he's conspiring with, and the other more dangerous one to whom he sent the message today, and Kaiser Wilhelm who's only waiting for me to be eliminated and Nicky made King in order to start his war, and all those poor dupes of my fellow countrymen who are shooting at my policemen this evening, I suppose, all of them need more love in their lives, too?

MARY. I shouldn't be at all surprised.

*She has taken off her pearls. She looks longingly at them, and then, averting her eyes, puts them on the table out of sight.*

REGENT. (*At length.*) Herr Gott. Kreuz donner wetter noch mal! Such sentimental idiocy!

MARY. Why do you always swear in German?

REGENT. Because the Germans have the best oaths. (*Muttering unhappily.*) And the best machine-guns.

MARY. Yes, I suppose 'Cross thunder weather yet again' wouldn't sound nearly so fierce. (*She has taken off her diamonds now, and is holding them up to*

*the light.*) I often wondered what it was about diamonds. Now I know.
(*With a sigh.*) Oh, well!

*She averts her gaze again and slips the necklace on to the table.*

REGENT. (*Suddenly and sharply.*) What?

MARY. I said I wondered what it was about diamonds—

REGENT. Before that. You translated—do you speak German?

MARY. Oh yes.

REGENT. (*Excited.*) Then you heard his message?

MARY. Oh yes. But I'm not going to tell you what it was, so don't excite yourself
too much.

*The* REGENT *has jumped up, and now stares at her menacingly.*

MARY. Gosh, you're pretty when you look fierce.

REGENT. Miss Dagenham, you are in possession of some very dangerous information, and I must warn you—

MARY. Now you can't put the thumbscrews on me, darling, and you know
it.

*Pause.*

REGENT. Oh my dear, dear child, if only you would understand—

MARY. And you can't wheedle me either.

*Pause. They stare at each other.*

REGENT. (*Suddenly.*) Himmel heilige bimbaum!

MARY. Well done. That's the best yet.

REGENT. (*Pleadingly*). The peace of the entire world depends—

MARY. Oh yes, I know. The *end* couldn't be better, but telling tales out of
school and getting other people into trouble makes bad *means*.

REGENT. But Herr Gott noch mal! The world isn't a nursery. It's a jungle.
When you are surrounded by ravening lions, do you refuse to use violence because it is bad means?

MARY. Well, Daniel did all right, didn't he?

*The* REGENT *opens his mouth to deliver an expletive.*

Now don't swear any more, my darling, or you'll run out of oaths. I'm
not going to tell you, and that's flat. But I will tell you I think your treatment of your son just now was not only bad means, but bad policy.

REGENT. (*Scornfully.*) Good policy, I suppose, would be to kiss the little
schweinhund on both cheeks, and say let bygones be bygones, dear child,
come to the ball?

MARY. The words right out of my mouth. When one line of attack fails, switch
to another. You should be an expert on those tactics. Remember last
night.

*The* REGENT *is about to swear again.* MARY *puts her hand over his mouth.*

MARY. Now, now. Just ask yourself this question, my darling. Who is Nicky
more likely to tell his plot to—nasty old Colonel Hoffman, giving him
what for in his room, or his dream prince of a gorgeous father giving
him a strawberry ice at a ball?

REGENT. (*Furiously.*) Do not call me by these names! It is grotesque!

MARY. One day I may call you by other names but for the moment, my darling, you'll have to excuse the language of love.

*She peels off her white gloves, and is now divested of all ornaments except her order.*

Well, I'm ready for my good-bye kiss.

*The* REGENT *walks over to her, and brusquely kisses her on the cheek.*

Is that all I get?

REGENT. The way I am feeling at the moment, it is considerably too much.

*He rings a bell. The door is instantly opened. The* MAJOR-DOMO *appears.*

Tell His Majesty to come and see me.

*The* MAJOR-DOMO *bows and goes out.*

MARY. What about my parting present?

*The* REGENT *stares at her malevolently, then silently crosses the room, takes a box from the table, and hands it to her.*

Oh, no, no. Pin it on, please.

*The* REGENT *takes the brooch out of the case and pins it on.*

Now say what you said to me this morning.

REGENT. If I do you will only laugh, because my epaulettes are scratching you or something and I shall be disconcerted again.

MARY. Take the risk.

REGENT. (*Murmuring.*) It has been wonderful knowing you. If only it could have lasted longer.

MARY. Thank you, my darling.

*She kisses him gently on the mouth. He responds. They disengage as the door begins to open.*

MAJOR-DOMO. (*Announcing.*) His Majesty.

NICOLAS *comes in, and stands silently by the door, staring defiantly at his father.*

REGENT. (*Quietly.*) Nicky. Sit down, Nicky—this German Embassy affair has made me most unhappy. I have always known that you and I did not see eye to eye on policy, but that my own son should conspire against me has been a most bitter shock.

NICOLAS. I don't see why it should be. You told me last night that your secret police—

REGENT. I was joking, of course. (*He sits down in an attitude of despair.*) Ah, Nicky, Nicky! I don't know whether you realize how easy it is to break a father's heart.

MARY, *watching this exchange interestedly in the background, surreptitiously shows him an attitude more indicative of heartbreak. He adopts it.*

NICOLAS. (*At length.*) If you mean your heart, father, I don't.

REGENT. Ah, perhaps that is because I don't wear my heart on my sleeve, Nicky. Some people prefer to keep their feelings bottled up, and I, it may be—

MARY. (*In an apologetic murmur.*) Er—sorry to interrupt—but have you seen an old raincoat lying around anywhere?

REGENT. (*Bewildered.*) Old raincoat?

MARY. Yes. Oh, I remember. Here it is. I don't want to be seen going through the stage door in an evening dress, you see. It looks too silly. So sorry. Go on.

*She puts the raincoat on, while the* REGENT *sits trying to recover his flow of thought. He suddenly rises.*

REGENT. Anyway, Nicky, I don't want to say any more about it tonight. I have decided to let bygones be bygones. In spite of everything you may come to the ball.

NICOLAS. Thank you, father, but I don't think I want to. I think I'd rather go to bed—

MARY. (*Shocked.*) Oh, but you must go, Sir. I mean, just think—the greatest ball of the season—wonderful dresses, beautiful uniforms, the decorations alone costing five thousand pounds—invitations harder to get than—

NICOLAS. No. I would have liked to, but step-mother says she's not going because she's tired, and I won't know anyone, and I won't have anyone to dance with.

REGENT. (*Crossly.*) Well, then, invite someone to dance with.

NICOLAS. Invite someone?

REGENT. Yes. I can easily arrange it.

NICOLAS. You mean—anyone?

REGENT. Yes, anyone.

NICOLAS. All right, then.

*He turns to* MARY *who is on the point of slipping unobserved from the room, her raincoat gathered round her.*

Miss Dagenham, will you accompany me to the ball at the Foreign Office tonight?

*There is a long pause, while* MARY *looks over* NICOLAS' *head at the* REGENT'S *face.*

MARY. (*At length.*) I shall be most happy to obey Your Majesty's Command.

NICOLAS. Oh, that is good.

*She glances once more at the* REGENT, *whose face is expressionless, and wanders back to the table on which she has left her borrowed jewels, picks them up, and shows them to* NICOLAS.

MARY. (*To* NICOLAS.) Do you think your step-mother will mind?

NICOLAS. (*Excitedly.*) Oh no, of course not. She'll just say what fun. And I'll borrow one of her tiaras for you, too.

MARY. Oh, well—if they're going to see me leave the theatre in a tiara, they can damn well see me arrive in an evening dress. (*She takes her raincoat off.*)

NICOLAS. I think I shall find you another order. The one you are wearing is not first class.

MARY. No? Oh well—I wasn't going to say anything, mind you, but if you feel that—

NICOLAS. Then, I shall come in person to collect you at your theatre at eleven o'clock?

MARY. Yes, that'll be nice.

*She crosses over to the silent and grim-faced* REGENT, *unfastens her brooch and hands it to him. Then she backs gracefully to the door.*

(*In a small voice.*) Well—see you later, then.

*She goes out.*

CURTAIN

SCENE 2

SCENE: *The same. It is about twelve-thirty of the same night. The little table has been laid for a discreet supper for two. The* REGENT *is inspecting a bottle of champagne. Satisfied, he puts it back in its ice-bucket, and pours himself a vodka which he drinks. The door is opened and* PETER *comes in.*

PETER. I have to report, Sir, that His Majesty has returned.

REGENT. Alone?

PETER. I fear not, Sir.

REGENT. (*Alarmed.*) She is here—in the Legation?

PETER *nods.*

Where are they?

PETER. In the stewards' room.

REGENT. The stewards' room? What are they doing in the stewards' room?

PETER. There is a gramophone there. She is teaching him an American dance called The Fox Trot.

REGENT. Herr Gott noch mal!

PETER. Exactly, Sir.

REGENT. But how did they travel from the ball? Why was his carriage sent away? What conveyance did they use?

PETER. (*At length, in a shocked murmur.*) A bus.

REGENT. A bus? A public bus?

PETER. A number fifty-seven.

REGENT. But, in the name of Saint Francis, why?

PETER. It appears that His Majesty expressed a wish to travel in that manner.

*Pause.*

REGENT. The girl's influence, I have no doubt.

PETER. Nor indeed, Sir, have I.

REGENT. This may mean a scandal, Northbrook.

PETER. I need hardly tell Your Royal Highness that all possible steps will be taken to dissuade the more responsible journals from reporting the occurrence. I cannot, of course, answer for the halfpenny press.

REGENT. Why did they leave the ball so soon, in any case?

PETER. I understand that Miss Dagenham, when dancing a two-step with His Majesty, decided to—er—alter the tempo.

REGENT. You mean—a one-step?

PETER *nods.*

At the Foreign Office?

PETER. I'm afraid so, Sir.

REGENT. They were asked to leave the floor, of course?

PETER. (*Reassuringly.*) Oh no, Sir. His Majesty, of course, was known. It was merely suggested to them that they should—well—alter the tempo back again. However, the King thereupon expressed himself insulted and there were unfortunate words.

REGENT. Verflucht! I should never have let them out of my sight for a moment.

PETER. (*Reprovingly.*) No, Sir.

*Pause.*

REGENT. (*Distractedly.*) Lucy Maidenhead is late.

PETER. Only a few minutes, Sir.

REGENT. Her unpunctuality used to be one of her most irritating characteristics. I had hoped she might have grown out of it, by now. She has had, after all, time.

PETER. I can venture to reassure Your Royal Highness that Lady Maidenhead hardly looks a day older than she did ten years ago. In fact I think I can say that she seems to have found the secret of perpetual youth.

REGENT. I am most glad to hear it. (*Murmuring*) She must need it by now.

PETER. (*Concerned.*) Oh dear! Is Your Royal Highness not feeling quite so enthusiastic about this reunion as you did this morning? Should I meet the lady downstairs and make your excuses?

REGENT. No, no. Of course not. I am most looking, forward to seeing Lucy again. Dear Lucy. Dear, enchanting, witty, grown-up Lucy—

*The words die on his lips as the door is opened, unguarded for the moment by footmen, and* MARY *walks in. She is looking very splendid and glittering in her tiara, orders and jewels.*

MARY. Hullo,

REGENT. Hullo.

MARY. Oo! Supper. How lovely.

*She comes forward and inspects the table.*

Oh, darling, how thoughtful of you.

REGENT. (*At length.*) Not at all.

MARY. I'll just nip down and say good night to Nicky, and then I'll be right back.

*She goes out. The* REGENT *gives* PETER *a gloomy glance. There is a pause.*

PETER. (*Encouragingly.*) Come, come, Sir. All that is needed is a little firmness. You should tell her straight out that the supper is not for her, and that you are expecting another guest.

REGENT. That is your considered suggestion for surmounting this crisis, Northbrook?

PETER. Yes, Sir, It is.

REGENT. (*Savagely.*) Then I can only say that I now fully understand why the Foreign Office always makes such a mess of its relations with the State Department. Northbrook—we are not here dealing with a civilized adult—but an unruly child. (*Roaring.*) Do you think I am anxious to have supper for three?

PETER. I'm sorry, Sir. I had not, I agree, considered that aspect. (*After reflection.*) The best policy, then, would appear to be for me to intercept Lady Maidenhead on arrival, and escort her to one of the downstairs rooms. There I can arrange to have another table laid—

REGENT. (*Plaintively.*) Two suppers I am to eat?

PETER. I'm afraid I see no alternative.

REGENT. (*Gloomily.*) But how am I to leave this one? That is the crux, Northbrook.

PETER. A few moments after Lady Maidenhead arrives I shall come up and announce that the Minister urgently requires your presence in the Chancery, and that your business will last for at least an hour. You then say good-bye to Miss Dagenham—I shall be here, Sir—no harm will come to you—and leave Miss Dagenham for me to escort to her home.

*There is a pause while the* REGENT *considers the scheme.*

REGENT. 'At least an hour' is hopeless. You had better say all night. Only so will your plan have the faintest chance of success.

MARY *comes back again.*

MARY. (*Brightly.*) Well, here I am. What a sweet little boy that is.

REGENT. (*To* PETER.) You may leave us, Northbrook.

PETER. Very well, Sir.

*After a meaning exchange of glances,* PETER *backs out of the room.*

MARY. Say! He doesn't do that half as well as me.

REGENT. Who is a sweet little boy? My son?

MARY. Yes. Far too grown-up for his age, of course, but I expect that's just the fault of his upbringing.

*She picks up the bottle of vodka.*

     (*To* REGENT.) Vodka?

REGENT. Thank you.

*She pours him a very generous measure.*

     Stop. That is too much.

MARY. Oh, you can take that all right, surely.

*She pours herself out a thimbleful, while the* REGENT *is gulping his.*

     Hey. That's too quick. I wanted to give you a toast. You'll have to have another now.

REGENT. (*As she pours.*) Not so much, please. (*He snatches the glass away.*)

MARY. Say, you don't want to spoil my illusions of you, do you?

REGENT. What are your illusions of me?

MARY. Well, your capacity for vodka is certainly one of them.

*Reluctantly he hands the glass back. She pours some more vodka into it. Then she raises her own glass containing its infinitesimal portion.*

Here's to more love in everybody's life.

REGENT. (*Muttering.*) Cheerio.

*He throws his gargantuan drink back, without visible effect.* MARY *downs hers.*

MARY. (*Very businesslike.*) Well, now, I have a little document here that I think will interest you. The writing's bad, because I did it on the top of a bus, so I'll read it to you. Incidentally that poor little creature has never been on top of a bus in his life. Imagine. It was a bigger thrill for him than going to the ball was for me, and that's saying something. Now. (*Reading.*) Manifesto to my faithful subjects. I, Nicolas VIII, King, do hereby renounce and reject utterly the overtures lately made to me by certain persons that I should assume the powers of government before the appointed time, and I do hereby solemnly adjure all citizens of the realm to unite loyally and whole-heartedly under the Regency of my father, the Grand Duke Charles, for the settled peace of the Kingdom. Signed— Nicolas.

*The* REGENT *snatches the document.*

REGENT. But it isn't signed Nicolas at all.

MARY. No. Not yet, but it will be. There's got to be a little give and take in this life, you know, darling. You have something to sign too.

*She takes a crumpled piece of paper from her bag.*

These are Nicky's conditions.

REGENT. (*Furiously.*) Conditions?

MARY. Oh, they're very simple ones. I took them down just as he said them. This is a bit of a scrawl too. We were sitting on the stairs leading to the ballroom and people kept treading on us. Incidentally, did you know that a one-step at a Court Ball is about as popular as a fan dance at a church fete? Idiotic. (*Reading.*) One. Martial law must not be declared. Two. The King must be allowed to purchase a new motor bicycle and to ride it anywhere in his dominion without let or hindrance. Three. There must be a general amnesty of all political prisoners, Parliament must be dissolved forthwith, and a general election called. Four. The marriage between the King and the Princess Louisa will definitely not take place. That's all.

*There is a pause. The* REGENT, *with a grim expression, absently pours himself another vodka.*

MARY. (*Approvingly.*) Quite right, my darling. That'll help you to see it all in the best possible light.

REGENT. (*At length.*) Herr Gott kreuz donner-wetter noch mal!

MARY. Funny. That's just what I thought you'd say.

REGENT. You two have been having a fine joke at my expense this evening—

MARY. (*Hurt.*) That isn't true, darling. I've worked, as hard as I know, for you tonight, not against you. I've got all the details of his plot now, you know, and I really think it would have succeeded. Or may succeed yet, if you're foolish enough not to sign this bit of paper.

REGENT. What does it matter either way? Declaring a general election now will put the German party in power as surely as his coup d'état.

MARY. Oh, I don't know. After all you might win. You know that's the funny thing about general elections. You never can tell who's going to win. Now if you could only beat Mr. Wolffstein constitutionally

REGENT. (*Scornfully.*) Beat Mr. Wolffstein constitutionally! Beat Mr. Wolffstein—constitutionally—

*His voice trails away as an idea seems to come to him. He snatches the manifesto from her and begins to read it.*

MARY. Yes. And wouldn't that take the wax out of the Kaiser's moustache?

REGENT. (*Abruptly, flourishing the manifesto.*) Did you phrase this?

MARY. (*Innocently.*) I think so. Why?

REGENT. (*Glowering at her.*) Herr Gott! How could you have so deceived me?

MARY. Deceived you, darling? What are you talking about?

REGENT. (*Angrily.*) A brilliant intriguante.

MARY. I don't know what that is, but I do hope it's not as rude as it sounds.

REGENT. (*Confidently.*) Of course you do not realize just what you are making the boy sign?

MARY. Yes, dear. A manifesto.

REGENT. (*Excitedly.*) A confession. An abject confession by my son that the leaders of the German party had been plotting with him to overthrow me, and what is much more, important, to destroy the Constitution. (*Quoting.*) 'The overtures lately made to me by certain persons.' Ausgezeichnet! (*He chuckles.*) Don't you see what I can do now?

MARY *shakes her head.*

My dear child, do you not see? Now it is I and not Wolffstein who can go to the country as the champion of freedom, of the Constitution and of democracy. (*Happily.*) You know, with this in my hands, it might even not be necessary to rig a single election.

MARY. I should just hope not indeed. Oh, but darling, how clever of you to see all that in that! (*She points to the document.*) Have another vodka.

REGENT. (*Absently.*) What? No, I have had enough.

MARY. Oh, just a little one.

*She pours him another drink. The* REGENT, *deep in thought, throws it back.* Don't you want to eat?

REGENT. No, I'm not hungry. Of course the timing of events will have to be most carefully considered. (*He sits down.*) I hold the initiative now. I must not lose it.

MARY. Oh, but I'm sure that with your fine brain and your great flair for politics and your wonderful grasp of a situation, you wouldn't ever lose a thing like an initiative—

*She rests her head tenderly on his knee. The posture is a little uncomfortable, so she adjusts the stool and resumes the attitude.*

Oh, I do envy you, darling.

REGENT. Envy me?

MARY. For being blessed with so much. Rank, position, wealth, looks—oh such wonderful, wonderful looks—youth.

REGENT. You are flattering.

MARY. Oh no. After all late thirties is still young. And above all virility and strength of character. Oh yes. You have so much to be thankful for. So much. (*After a slight pause.*) Wouldn't you be more comfortable with your feet up?

*She points to the settee.*

REGENT. (*Still abstracted.*) No, thank you.

MARY. Another vodka?

REGENT. No, thank you. (*Suddenly leaping up.*) Herr Gott, I have it.

MARY. (*Startled.*) What?

REGENT. I shall release Wolffstein. Tomorrow night on my return I shall release them all, unconditionally. That will confuse them utterly. They will think I have done it from weakness.

MARY. Wonderful.

REGENT. Yes, but here lies the real clou of the plan. The very next day while they are off-guard, rejoicing in their apparent victory, I shall suddenly dissolve Parliament, call an immediate general election and publish in every newspaper in the Kingdom the King's manifesto—with appropriate editorial comment—I shall have of course to work hard there—these editors are such dummkopfs—but happily I compose such things without great difficulty—

*The REGENT in his excitement is striding up and down. MARY has poured another vodka which she hands him. He takes it absently and throws it back.*

The effect in the country will be immense. Immense.

MARY. (*With breathless admiration.*) Brilliant. Quite, quite brilliant. And all out of that little piece of paper in your hand.

REGENT. Yes, I am most happy with this thought of mine. Most happy.

*He sits down, rather heavily, on the settee.*

MARY. And so you should be, my darling. I can see you haven't earned the title of the Fox of the Balkans for nothing.

*She sits down next to him and, unseen by him, presses the bell on the table.*

REGENT. Am I called so?

MARY. Didn't you know?

REGENT. (*Pleased.*) The Fox of the Balkans. Hm!

MARY. And those eyebrows make you look rather like a fox too. A beautiful, sleek, dangerous animal—

*The* REGENT *rests his head on the back of the settee, and pats her cheek affection-
ately. The music of a violin playing, this time, a waltz, can be heard from
outside the room.* MARY *rests her head lovingly on his chest.*
  But such a lonely one.
REGENT. (*With a sigh.*) Oh, my child. It is my lot to be lonely.
MARY. Must it always be?
REGENT. Ah yes. It must. It must. (*He strokes her hair.*) Dear child—if only
  you could understand—(He suddenly sits bolt upright.) Where's that
  music coming from?
MARY. It's that Hungarian again, I expect. You told me he played every night.
REGENT. Yes, but—(*He stares at her suspiciously.*)
MARY. Never mind, my darling. Go on about being lonely.
*She pushes him gently back, and resumes her own position on his chest.*
  Have you never loved?
REGENT. I have never allowed myself to love. Love is the enemy of all the
  cold, hard virtues that a man must have to rule a country such as mine.
MARY. Who says so?
REGENT. Caesar Augustus was the first.
MARY. And what happened to him?
REGENT. He became the Ruler of the World.
MARY. Poor lamb.
REGENT. You think he needed love in his life?
MARY. I'll bet like crazy he did.
REGENT. As much as I?
MARY. I don't know. That's hard to judge. (*Gently.*) You see I wasn't there to
  provide it for him.
*Pause.*
REGENT. (*Gently.*) Do you wish to catch your fox in a net?
MARY. Oh, but it would be such a very soft little net—made of the very fin-
  est-spun cobwebs.
*She raises her head to look at him. He pulls her to him and kisses her.*
REGENT. (*At length.*) Ah, but even a net of the very spinest-fun—the sfinest-
  pun—(*He sits up, surprised.*) Herr Gott! I am drunk.
MARY. (*Concerned.*) Oh no you're not, are you, darling? Look, just get up and
  see if you can walk all right. Walk to that door, for instance.
*She points vaguely towards the door of his bedroom. The* REGENT *gets up and
walks fairly steadily to the indicated objective.*
  There you see. All right, come back.
*He comes back to the settee.*
  Now go on with what you were saying.
REGENT. What do words matter when deeds can say so much more ?
MARY. Oh, not again, darling. Can't you think of anything else to say? (*There
  is a pause.*)
REGENT. (*At length feelingly.*) Draga kis galambon gyere ide, maradj itten,
  szeress engem ahogy en szeretlek teged.

MARY. Oh, excuse me, darling, I didn't quite catch what you said. (*There is another pause.*)

REGENT. (*At length.*) I love you.

MARY. And I love you. Oh gosh, Your Royal Highness, how I love you—

*She kisses him and he responds. The music grows louder. Suddenly* PETER *walks in.*

PETER. (*Briskly.*) Sir, you are most urgently required in the Chancery—

REGENT. (*Jumping up.*) Northbrook! These constant intrusions of yours are beyond all bounds. How—dare you!

PETER. But Your Royal Highness—(*Meaningly.*) The Minister has arrived, if you see what I mean—

REGENT. Will you please not argue with me? Leave the room at once—and think yourself lucky I am not telephoning to the Foreign Secretary immediately—

PETER *backs out hastily. The* REGENT *comes back to the settee.* MARY, *looking at his disconcerted face, laughs.*

*The* REGENT *looks even more disconcerted for the moment and then begins to laugh too. Suddenly they both stop laughing and are staring at each other as the* CURTAIN *falls.*


## SCENE 3

SCENE: *The same, the following morning. The* MAJOR-DOMO *and a* FOOTMAN *are standing in the room as* PETER *enters. He is still in diplomatic uniform and indeed, from his agitated manner, it would seem doubtful if he has taken it off since the night before. He approaches the* MAJOR-DOMO *and begins to whisper an evident question, or series of questions. The* MAJOR-DOMO *whispers his replies, each one of which seems to disturb* PETER *deeply. They occasionally glance at the door R.*

*The door of the* REGENT'S *bedroom opens and* NICOLAS *comes out. He is dressed in a plain suit. He looks rather bewildered. The* MAJOR-DOMO *backs out.*

NICOLAS. Mr. Northbrook, is my father quite well, this morning?

PETER. I gather so, Sir.

NICOLAS. (*In a stunned voice.*) He has just—embraced me.

PETER. Well—surely he has done that often before?

NICOLAS. In public, of course. But this was in private, Mr. Northbrook, in his bedroom with only his valets to see it. And he called me his darling son.

PETER. How nice.

NICOLAS. It is most suspicious. He was asking, too, the most extraordinary, not to say embarrassing, questions. Was I not sometimes very lonely, had he always been a good father to me, did I not feel the lack of love in my life? (*Assuming from* PETER'S *blank expression that he has not heard.*) Mr. Northbrook, my father asked if I did not feel the lack of love in my life?

PETER. Yes, Sir. I heard you.

NICOLAS. You are not surprised? You have heard something already perhaps. Was the excitement yesterday too much for him? Is there cause for concern?

PETER. No, Sir. At least not regarding his health.

NICOLAS. (*Darkly.*) I strongly suspect some Foreign Office hocus-pocus in all this.

PETER. (*Stiffly.*) The Foreign Office, Sir, never resorts to hocus-pocus. You are doubtless thinking of the Quai d'Orsay.

*The* REGENT *comes out of his bedroom. He is wearing a dressing-gown, and is plainly in a sunny mood.*

REGENT. (*To* PETER.) Ah good morning, Northbrook. Punctual as usual, I see. Splendid. Herr Gott! How handsome you look in that uniform of yours. I had meant to tell you that last night, but it somehow slipped my mind.

*He pours himself a cup of coffee.*

(*To* NICOLAS.) Nicky—my darling boy—

NICOLAS. Yes, father?

REGENT. Nothing. Just my darling boy. (*He smiles affectionately at him.*) You had better get ready. We leave in ten minutes.

NICOLAS. Yes, father.

REGENT. Give me a kiss, Nicky.

NICOLAS. (*Appalled.*) Another kiss?

REGENT. Why not?

NICOLAS. One can overdo such things.

REGENT. Nonsense. Fathers should kiss their sons.

NICOLAS. When they are children, but not when—

REGENT. (*Sharply.*) Nicky! Come and give me a kiss, this instant.

NICOLAS *walks over and awkwardly pecks his father's cheek. Then he shrugs his shoulders at* PETER, *behind his father's back, and goes out. The* REGENT *leans back in his chair, beaming at* PETER.

REGENT. Well, well, Northbrook. Well, well, well.

PETER. Well, well, indeed, Sir.

REGENT. A wonderful morning, is it not?

PETER. Yes, Sir. Wonderful. I have here a letter for Your Royal Highness of a somewhat private nature.

*He hands the* REGENT *a letter.*

REGENT. Who is it from?

PETER. Lady Maidenhead.

REGENT. Oh. (*He opens the letter, and his face darkens slightly as he reads.*) Dear, dear! Oh well. (*He tears the letter up. Thoughtfully.*) You know, Northbrook, what I think is the trouble with Lady Maidenhead?

PETER. (*Politely.*) She has not enough love in her life?

REGENT. Too much. One should keep a balance in these things. (*He finishes his coffee and rises.*) Now, Northbrook, I have one or two commissions for you—to be performed after we leave.

PETER. I shall be honoured.

REGENT. First a laissez-passer must be obtained for a journey to Carpathia in a few days' time, and made out in the name of Miss Mary Morgan.

PETER. (*Alarmed.*) Miss who?

REGENT. Citizeness of the United States, profession, actress—stage name, Elaine Dagenham.

PETER. (*Almost relieved.*) Oh. I was beginning to wonder, Sir.

REGENT. Second—for the journey itself, a special coach must be attached to the Orient Express for the accommodation of Miss Morgan and her staff.

PETER. Her staff?

REGENT. Well, her habilleuse, or whatever—

PETER. Yes, Sir. The expense of course to be charged to Your Royal Highness?

REGENT. (*Crossly.*) I should have supposed that the British Government might afford so trifling an outlay, in view of the importance of Miss Dagenham's mission.

PETER. (*Politely.*) I shall naturally apply to the Chancellor of the Exchequer in person, Sir, but I am just a shade on the doubtful side whether—

REGENT. (*Impatiently.*) No matter, no matter. Enough of this cheese-paring. Special servants must, of course, be engaged for the journey, and I shall send one of my own chefs to board the train at Ostend. Flowers, bowers of flowers, in the saloons and bedrooms, of course—roses, I believe, are her favourites—and champagne, vodka, caviare—you will attend to these petty details, yourself, will you not?

PETER. (*With a sigh.*) I shall be overjoyed, Sir.

REGENT. Now, one other little matter. She may require a few dresses, furs and personal ornaments for the journey. You will see to it that in that respect she is given carte blanche.

PETER. (*After a slight pause.*) Carte quite blanche, Sir?

REGENT. As blanche as she cares to make it. I have, you see, Northbrook—in your idiom—got it bad.

PETER. (*With a sigh.*) You have indeed, Sir.

REGENT. It is a strange phenomenon. I do not yet quite know how it has happened to me. For forty-three years I have tried—(*Excitedly.*) There, you see, Northbrook! I now even state my age correctly. Herr Gott noch mal! There is something in this falling in love that frightens me.

PETER. I am not surprised, Sir. I have myself always studiously avoided the ailment.

REGENT. Take care, Northbrook. Take care. There is a nemesis for such as you—and it may well, one day, take some such form as a Circassian trapeze artist in a music hall at Casablanca. And when it does, Northbrook—when it does—you too will awake from the long grey sleep of Prudence to the magnificent scarlet dawn of Folly. (*He seems extremely taken aback at what he has just said.*) Um Gottes willen! That was myself speaking?

PETER. It was, Sir.

REGENT. (*After a pause, with a deep sigh.*) Oh well, I suppose it cannot be helped.

*Shrugging his shoulders philosophically he goes into his bedroom. After a slight pause,* NICOLAS *furtively puts his head round the door.*

NICOLAS. My father is here?

PETER. Just gone into his room, Sir.

NICOLAS *comes quickly over to* PETER *and hands him a small case.*

NICOLAS. Thank heavens! I want you, if you see Miss Dagenham, to say good-bye to her for me, and give her this small parting present, Also this photograph.

PETER. Most certainly, Sir.

NICOLAS. (*Hurriedly.*) Tell her I enjoyed myself last night more than I ever have before in my life, and thank her most gratefully.

PETER. I shall indeed, Sir.

NICOLAS *goes quickly to the door, where he stops.*

NICOLAS. Has he kissed you too?

PETER. Not yet, Sir.

NICOLAS. I should not be too confident, Mr. Northbrook. Do you know that I have never been so frightened of him in my whole life as this morning. It is all most disconcerting—

*He goes out.* PETER, *left alone, prudently picks up the scraps of Lady Maidenhead's letter, places them in a saucer and puts a match to them.* MARY *comes out of the door L. She has on the same evening dress, stripped now of all ornaments.*

MARY. Playing with fire?

PETER. What? Oh, good morning, Miss Dagenham.

MARY. Good morning.

PETER. Yes, I am.

MARY. That's a sport you should leave to me. (*At the window, looking out.*) Oh, what a lovely morning!

PETER. Yes. Isn't it? I have to present these to you, with His Majesty's compliments, and his thanks for last night, which he claims was the pleasantest evening he has ever spent in his life. (*He hands her* NICOLAS' *presents.*)

MARY. Gee! (*Looking at the photograph.*) Gee! Signed, too. How sweet of him. (*She opens the case.*) Oh, a brooch with the Royal Arms. Wouldn't you have known it?

*The doors are opened by* FOOTMEN *and the* GRAND DUCHESS *comes in, followed by her* TWO LADIES IN WAITING. *All are dressed in travelling clothes.*

GRAND DUCHESS. Good morning, Mr. Northbrook.

PETER. (*With a bow.*) Your Imperial and Royal Highness.

GRAND DUCHESS. And Miss Dagenham. So delightful. How are you this morning?

MARY. (*Murmuring.*) Very well, thank you, Ma'am.

GRAND DUCHESS. (*Sitting.*) My dear—such a night. Not a wink of sleep. Some dreadful drunkard fiddling in the corridor for hours and hours. And the night before too, but not so long. I didn't dare go out to stop him, in case it was an anarchist, or a republican or something. One never knows nowadays, and even a violin, they tell me, can be a most dangerous weapon. So disturbing. My dear, why do you always wear white?

MARY. Well—I suppose because I think it suits me, Ma'am.

GRAND DUCHESS. But not all the time, dear. You are imitating the divine Sarah, no doubt, but even she, I am told, changes her dress occasionally. (*Turning.*) Maud. (*Crossly.*) Where is that—

MAUD. (*Hastily—she has wandered a little way of to blow her nose.*) Here, Ma'am.

GRAND DUCHESS. (*Amazed.*) Your cold has come back again, Maud?

MAUD. It appears to have, Ma'am.

GRAND DUCHESS. I cannot possibly see how it could have done. Are you sure you are not imagining it?

MAUD. Quite sure, Ma'am.

GRAND DUCHESS. Then there is no alternative but for me to prepare you one of my hot plasters—

MAUD. (*Involuntarily.*) Oh no, Ma'am.

GRAND DUCHESS. (*To* MARY.) Most tedious. All those ingredients—and boiling everything—but happily it can all be done on the train.

MAUD. Oh!

GRAND DUCHESS. Did you say something, Maud?

MAUD. Most good of you, Ma'am. It's just that it sometimes seems to burn a little.

GRAND DUCHESS. Burn? Of course it burns. That is its point, my dear. It burns the cold clean out of the body. Now what was it I called you for, dear? I remember. The present for Miss Dagenham.

MAUD. Yes, Ma'am. I have it here.

*She hands the* GRAND DUCHESS *a small jewel-case.*

GRAND DUCHESS. Good. (*To* MARY.) Come here, dear.

MARY *approaches.*

GRAND DUCHESS. Here is a little brooch for you, with the Carpathian Arms on it.

MARY. Ma'am, I am overwhelmed.

GRAND DUCHESS. And I have a photograph for you, too.

MAUD *hands her the photograph.*

Let me see. Yes, I have signed it. (*She hands it to* MARY.) It goes best in a simple frame—nothing elaborate—I loathe elaborate frames—just plain gold—or even silver—not below eye-level because, as you see, I am looking down and it would spoil the effect. And not too much light from above.

MARY. No, Ma'am. Thank you very much indeed.

GRAND DUCHESS. (*Extending her cheek.*) You may kiss me.

MARY *kisses her on the cheek and curtsies at the same time—no mean feat.*

GRAND DUCHESS. You already have a photograph, have you not, Mr. Northbrook?

PETER. Most proudly displayed, Ma'am.

GRAND DUCHESS. (*Sharply.*) Not on the same table as Olga Bosnia, I trust.

PETER. No, Ma'am. I was most particular in obeying your instructions on that point.

*The* REGENT *comes in, dressed, too, in travelling clothes.*

GRAND DUCHESS. My dear, (*pointing to* MARY) look who has come to see us off.

REGENT. How delightful.

*The* GRAND DUCHESS *has risen and is going to the door.*

GRAND DUCHESS. So good of her to be here so early.

REGENT. Yes, indeed.

GRAND DUCHESS. You will be at the station, Mr. Northbrook?

PETER. Of course, Ma'am.

GRAND DUCHESS. Who else will be there, officially?

PETER. The Prime Minister, I believe.

GRAND DUCHESS. Oh, and that dear witty Mrs. Asquith. How delightful! (*Turning at door and looking at* MARY.) Yes. I do think just a little more variety in your costume, dear. Nothing outrée, of course. Simply from time to time, an ordinary little day dress. Such fun it has been. Good-bye.

MARY. (*In a curtsy.*) Good-bye, Ma'am.

*The* GRAND DUCHESS *smiles graciously, gives the Royal gesture of farewell, and goes, followed by her* LADIES IN WAITING. *There is a pause.*

PETER. (*With a smirk.*) As I am plainly de trop, I shall await Your Royal Highness in the hall.

*The* REGENT *nods.*

(*To* MARY.) I won't say good-bye, Miss Dagenham, as I understand I shall be seeing a lot of you in the next few days, what with special passports and other things.

MARY. (*Surprised.*) Special passports?

REGENT. (*Angrily to* PETER.) Herr Gott! Northbrook. That was intended to be a surprise, and now you have utterly ruined it.

PETER. Oh. I'm so sorry, Sir, but how was I to know that last night—you didn't—

REGENT. (*Thundering.*) Go, before you make things worse.

PETER. Your Royal Highness—

*He backs hastily out of the room. The* REGENT *turns to* MARY. *She comes forward slowly.*

MARY. Good morning.

REGENT. Good morning.

*They embrace fervently.*

My dear, I have been making such a spectacle of myself today. Behaving like a schoolboy and—this is so surprising—loving it. I see now suddenly the truth of all that you have been saying to me about the joys of childishness. It is exhilarating.

MARY. (*A little sadly.*) Yes, it is, isn't it? Oh dear! So this morning it's for me to be the grown-up one, is it?

REGENT. How? Grown-up?

MARY. Darling—listen—you don't need to send Peter Northbrook out for a special passport. My own is quite good enough to take me to Carpathia when I come there. And what's more, my darling, I've found out the name of a good cheap pension to stay at—the Villa Malmaison—only just outside the city—

REGENT. But what nonsense is this? Pension? Do you not realize what I am preparing for you on your arrival?

MARY. (*Sadly.*) No. Tell me, please. I'd love to hear.

REGENT. The Sonia Residenz, an enchanting house in the late Renaissance style—quite little—you will only need ten or fifteen servants—with a few hundred acres of park and a most beautiful garden, on a lake, with the mountains close by. It was built by a sixteenth-century ancestor of mine—for his favourite mistress—

MARY. And has been used by his twentieth-century descendant before now, huh?

REGENT. Well—(*He makes a gesture.*) But never for long.

MARY. I know, my darling. (*She kisses him on the cheek.*) That's just what I mean.

REGENT. (*Explosively, pulling her round to face him.*) But Herr Gott noch mal! For not one of the others have I felt any small part of what I now feel for you.

MARY. (*Gently.*) Yes. And for how long will you feel it, darling?

REGENT. For life.

MARY. (*Briskly.*) Good. And so will I. You can be quite, quite sure of that. So that when my show comes off and I come out to your country and take a room at the Villa Malmaison and drop you a line to say that I'm there—we can go over together to the Sonia Residenz, and I can tell you what I want done to it—because if I'm to stay in it for the rest of my time on earth, I'll need quite a lot done, won't I?

*Pause. The* REGENT *is looking angry and perplexed.*

REGENT. When will this show of yours come off?

MARY. Oh, I'd give it another six months.

REGENT. Six months! Donner wetter, girl! Do you not realize what can happen in the world in the course of six months?

MARY. (*With resigned acceptance of the facts.*) Yes, darling, only too well. Go on, now, or you'll miss your train.

REGENT. You cannot possibly come before?

MARY. No. But thank you, my darling, so much—so very, very much, for asking me.

*Pause.*

REGENT. This is good-bye, then?

MARY. Au revoir.

REGENT. Au revoir, of course.

MARY. Of course.

*There is a pause. A violin can be heard playing outside.*

REGENT. That verdammte music! Did you order it?

MARY. No.

REGENT. Northbrook!

MARY. Maybe. May I have my parting present, now, please?

*There is a pause. The* REGENT, *at length, shrugs his shoulders, goes to the desk and picks up a case. He hands it to her in silence. She takes it out of its case and makes a slight scratch with her nail.*

REGENT. What are you doing?

MARY. Just so I'll know which one it is.

*The* REGENT *pins it on.* MARY *looks sadly at the top of his head.*

   Poor darling! Do you feel terribly disconcerted?

REGENT. Yes, I do.

MARY. (*She kisses him.*) Now go quickly, or I'll cry and that wouldn't be right.

*The* REGENT *goes to the door and turns to look at her for a long time.*

REGENT. Um Gottes willen! I am nearly crying myself, and that is something I have not done since I was a child.

MARY. Childishness isn't all fun, is it?

REGENT. No. (*He stares at her again.*)

MARY. Anyway, my darling, whatever happens, always remember this. Coming out of a heavenly dream can be a little sad, I grant, but that doesn't make the dream any the less heavenly, does it? Which is another way of saying, thank you, Your Royal Highness, from my heart.

*She curtsies.*

REGENT. (*After a pause.*) From my heart, too, Miss Dagenham. I believe I have as much right to that word as yourself. Perhaps more. Who knows?

*He turns quickly and goes out.*

MARY *takes a handkerchief from her bag, and blows her nose. Then, as if having forgotten something, she runs quickly to the door.*

MARY. (*Calling.*) Oh darling, I forgot to ask. Send me a photograph, please.

REGENT. (*Off.*) Mein Gott! What a thing to ask!

MARY. (*Calling.*) Address it to the theatre.

*She turns away, when another thought strikes her.*

   (*Calling.*) And sign it.

REGENT. (*Off, his voice coming now very faintly.*) Himmel heilige bimbaum!

*She waits at the door a moment then comes back into the room and wanders over to a corner where she finds her mackintosh. She puts it on.*

*Sadly she goes to the desk where she gathers up the three identical brooch-cases, and places them, one by one, in her handbag. Her two Orders of Perseverance, first and second class, follow the brooches in and the handbag is closed. Then she gathers up the two photographs and walks towards the door. Halfway there she stops, turns and looks round the room with a slight smile. Then she firmly pulls up the collar of her mackintosh and walks out.*

CURTAIN

# SEPARATE TABLES

First published 1955
by Hamish Hamilton Ltd

TO
MY MOTHER

*Separate Tables* was first produced at the St. James's Theatre, London, on September 22nd, 1954, with the following cast:

## TABLE BY THE WINDOW
*Characters in order of speaking:*

| | |
|---|---|
| MABEL | Marion Fawcett |
| LADY MATHESON | Jane Eccles |
| MRS. RAILTON-BELL | Phyllis Neilson-Terry |
| MISS MEACHAM | May Hallatt |
| DOREEN | Priscilla Morgan |
| MR. FOWLER | Aubrey Mather |
| MRS. SHANKLAND | Margaret Leighton |
| MISS COOPER | Beryl Measor |
| MR. MALCOLM | Eric Portman |
| CHARLES STRATTON | Basil Henson |
| JEAN TANNER | Patricia Raine |

## TABLE NUMBER SEVEN
*Characters in order of speaking:*

| | |
|---|---|
| JEAN STRATTON | Patricia Raine |
| CHARLES STRATTON | Basil Henson |
| MAJOR POLLOCK | Eric Portman |
| MR. FOWLER | Aubrey Mather |
| MISS COOPER | Beryl Measor |
| MRS. RAILTON-BELL | Phyllis Neilson-Terry |
| MISS RAILTON-BELL | Margaret Leighton |
| LADY MATHESON | Jane Eccles |
| MISS MEACHAM | May Hallatt |
| MABEL | Marion Fawcett |
| DOREEN | Priscilla Morgan |

The plays directed by PETER GLENVILLE

Decor by MICHAEL WEIGHT

The action of both plays takes place in the Lounge and Dining-room of the Beauregard Private Hotel, near Bournemouth.

# TABLE BY THE WINDOW

*A play in three scenes*

Characters
(*in order of speaking*)

MABEL
LADY MATHESON
MRS. RAILTON-BELL
MISS MEACHAM
DOREEN
MR. FOWLER
MRS. SHANKLAND
MISS COOPER
MR. MALCOLM
CHARLES STRATTON
JEAN TANNER


*Time: Winter*

SCENE 1: DINING-ROOM. DINNER.
SCENE 2: LOUNGE. AFTER DINNER.
SCENE 3: DINING-ROOM. BREAKFAST.

## SCENE 1

SCENE: *The dining-room of the Beauregard Private Hotel, near Bournemouth. It is small, rather bare and quite unpretentious. A door at back leads into the lounge, a swing door upstage R. into the kitchen, and another downstage R. into the hall and the rest of the hotel. Windows L. are curtained at the moment, for it is a winter evening, about seven o'clock, and the guests are at dinner.*

*Each sits at a small separate table, except for a young couple,* CHARLES STRATTON *and* JEAN TANNER, *who, as mere transients, occupy a table together in a corner of the room, not garnished, as are the other tables, with the bottles of medicine and favourite pickles and other idiosyncratic personal accessories of the permanent residents. Surprisingly, for they are an attractive-looking pair,* CHARLES *and* JEAN *are paying no attention to each other at all, and each is avidly reading a book propped up on the flower vase between them.*

*Prominently placed, and indeed a rather prominent-looking person altogether, is* MRS. RAILTON-BELL. *All the ladies (except* JEAN *who wears slacks) always change "into something" for dinner, but* MRS. RAILTON-BELL *always changes into something much grander than the others. All the ladies (except* JEAN) *wear fur stoles, but* MRS. RAILTON-BELL *wears silver foxes. All the ladies (except* JEAN) *wear some small items of jewellery, but* MRS. RAILTON-BELL'S *are far less small than the others.*

MISS MEACHAM *sits near her, reading (very close to her unspectacled eyes) a copy of 'Racing Up To Date'. Although much the same age as* MRS. RAILTON-BELL *(about sixty-five) she is dressed in a far more sprightly fashion, but has not succeeded in looking any younger.*

LADY MATHESON, *a Civil Servant's widow, living on an annuity and therefore the poorest of all the residents, sits close by, a grey-faced, mousy, impeccably dressed woman, rather younger than the other two.* MR. FOWLER, *ex-public-school master, seventyish, quiet, and impassive-looking, sits further away.*

*The table by the window is unoccupied-as is another towards the centre of the room and close to* MRS. RAILTON-BELL.

*Two waitresses, one middle-aged* (MABEL) *the other young* (DOREEN), *serve the various tables.* MABEL *is taciturn, gloomy and dependable.* DOREEN *is flighty, talkative and undependable. At the moment only* MABEL *is visible. She is serving* LADY MATHESON.

MABEL. Were you medaillon or goulash?

LADY MATHESON. (*Correctly accenting.*) Medaillon.

MABEL. Sorry. I thought you were goulash.

*She stumps with the unwanted goulash to the kitchen door.*

LADY MATHESON. It was probably my fault.

MABEL. (*Gloomily.*) I dare say.

*She passes on to* MISS MEACHAM.

Now, you *were* goulash, weren't you, Miss Meacham?

MISS MEACHAM. (*Deep in her book.*) What? Oh yes, Mabel. Thank you.

MABEL. (*Serving her.*) And what to follow—the mousse angelic, or the turnover?

MISS MEACHAM. Which do you think?

MABEL. Turnover.

MISS MEACHAM. Turnover, then.

MABEL *drifts away.*

MRS. RAILTON-BELL. I think cook's acquiring a little lighter touch with her pastry, don't you think?

MISS MEACHAM. Not judging by the tarts we had at tea yesterday. Cannonballs.

MRS. RAILTON-BELL. Did you think so? I quite liked them. I much preferred them to those pink cakes on Tuesday.

MISS MEACHAM. I didn't mind the pink cakes. The tarts gave me the collywobbles. I had the most terrible dreams.

MRS. RAILTON-BELL. (*With a faint smile.*) I thought you were always having dreams.

MISS MEACHAM. Oh, these weren't my proper dreams. Not the ones I make myself dream. These were just horrible, pointless nightmares. Cosh boys and things. (*After a slight pause.*) I talked to Louis XV on Thursday night.

MRS. RAILTON-BELL. (*Plainly humouring her.*) Did you indeed, dear?

MISS MEACHAM. The goulash's rather good. I think you made a mistake.

*She goes back to her book. There is a silence for a few moments while* MISS MEACHAM *peruses her 'Racing Up To Date' with myopic concentration.*

MRS. RAILTON-BELL. Think you've found a winner for tomorrow, Miss Meacham?

MISS MEACHAM. Well, according to this form book, Marston Lad is worth a bob or two each way.

MRS. RAILTON-BELL. I never bet nowadays. (*After a meditative pause.*) When my husband was alive he used sometimes to put as much as five pounds on a horse for me.

MISS MEACHAM. (*Looking up.*) I used to bet in ponies when my father was alive, and I had an allowance.

*She goes back to her 'Racing Up To Date'.*

MRS. RAILTON-BELL. (*Suddenly irritable.*) Why don't you get spectacles?

MISS MEACHAM *lowers her book.*

MISS MEACHAM. Because I don't need them.

*She goes back to her book again.* DOREEN, *the other waitress, has come in and is now hovering over* MR. FOWLER.

DOREEN. Sorry, Mr. Fowler, the goulash's off.

MR. FOWLER *looks up abstractedly.*

MR. FOWLER. What? Oh. What about the cold pie?

DOREEN. I shouldn't have that, if I were you. I saw what went into it. If I were you I'd have the tongue—

MR. FOWLER. All right. Whatever you say.

DOREEN disappears into the kitchen.

MRS. RAILTON-BELL. (*To* LADY MATHESON, *meaningly.*) She won't last.

LADY MATHESON. I'm afraid not.

MRS. RAILTON-BELL. Still, it's disgraceful that the goulash's off, and two people not even in yet.

LADY MATHESON. I know.

MRS. RAILTON-BELL. Of course Mr. Malcolm's never on time, (*she indicates the table by the window*) and really deserves it. (*In another confidential whisper.*) Anyway, after those long sessions at the Feathers I often wonder if he ever really knows what he's eating. But the new lady (*she indicates the other unoccupied table*)—I mean, my dear, what will she think?

LADY MATHESON. I saw her arrive.

MRS. RAILTON-BELL. Did you?

LADY MATHESON. Did you?

MRS. RAILTON-BELL. (*Slightly annoyed.*) I was in the lounge, but I didn't—excuse me—think it quite the thing to peer out of the window at her—

LADY MATHESON. (*Firmly.*) I happened to be in the hall.

MISS MEACHAM. I met her on the stairs.

MRS. RAILTON-BELL. Really, dear?

MISS MEACHAM. (*Still absorbed in her book.*) She's called Mrs. Shankland. She comes from London, she arrived by train, she has four suitcases and a hatbox and she's staying two weeks.

MRS. RAILTON-BELL. (*Unwillingly impressed.*) Four suitcases?

MISS MEACHAM. And a hatbox.

LADY MATHESON. She was awfully smartly dressed. Nothing flashy—very good taste—but—well—Mayfair, if you know what I mean.

MRS. RAILTON-BELL. Really? (*Changing the subject from this unwelcome topic.*) It was quite nice out this afternoon, didn't you think, dear—I mean, for December?

LADY MATHESON. I didn't go out, I'm afraid. There was a Sibelius concert on the Home—

MRS. RAILTON-BELL. You and your music. Did you go out, Mr. Fowler?

MR. FOWLER. What? No, I didn't. I was waiting for a telephone call.

MRS. RAILTON-BELL. I was the only brave one then? Fancy.

*She breaks off abruptly as the door from the hall opens and* MRS. SHANKLAND (ANNE), *the new arrival, comes in. She is about forty, and, as she stands just inside the room looking around rather timidly, she seems entirely out of place in such an environment. Not that her clothes are unsuitable, although they are smart, nor that her coiffure is too stylish, although it is stylish, but that she has brought on with her an air of Belgravia and the smarter London restaurants. She stands now as if waiting for a head waiter to guide her to*

*her table. None of the other guests glance at her.* MABEL, *who is serving* MISS
MEACHAM *with her turnover, turns and sees her.*

MABEL. You're the new one, aren't you?

ANNE. Yes.

MABEL. You're here.

*She points to the table in the centre.*

ANNE. Oh. Thank you.

*She goes to the table and sits down. Dead silence still reigns.* MABEL *hands her a
menu and, while she is studying it, eyes begin to cast quick, furtive glances
in her direction.*

MABEL. The brown windsor or the petite marmite?

ANNE. I don't think I'll have any soup, thank you. I'll try the goulash.

MABEL. That's right. We've got a portion left.

MR. FOWLER *glares furiously at* MABEL *as she goes past him to the kitchen, but
decides not to make a scene. Eyes are lowered again as* ANNE *looks curiously
round the room. The silence continues until it is at length broken by* MRS.
RAILTON-BELL, *speaking now in a rather louder and more self-consciously well-
bred voice than before.*

MRS. RAILTON-BELL. (*To* LADY MATHESON.) I was saying about the weather in
December—

LADY MATHESON. Oh yes?

MRS. RAILTON-BELL. It can be so treacherous, especially here, on the south coast.
This afternoon, for instance, even though the sun was quite bright, I put
on a fur coat—my warmest one too—the Persian Lamb.

LADY MATHESON. Very sensible of you.

*The two young people rise abruptly and make for the lounge door, each carrying
their book. They have still, as far as we can see, not addressed a word to each
other.* MRS. RAILTON-BELL *eyes them with disdain.*

MRS. RAILTON-BELL. Trousers at dinner!

LADY MATHESON. I know.

MRS. RAILTON-BELL. And *he* never changes either. I wonder Miss Cooper
doesn't say something. You'd think they'd teach them better manners at
Oxford.

LADY MATHESON. Yes, you would. (*After a slight pause.*) My husband was at
Oxford.

MRS. RAILTON-BELL. (*Gently.*) Yes, dear. You've told me so before. Mine only
went to Birmingham because, of the wonderful engineering course they
have there. He hated it, of course.

MISS COOPER *has come in and is crossing the room towards* ANNE. *She is youngish, with a rather masculine appearance and a quiet manner.*

MISS COOPER. Good evening, Mrs. Railton-Bell.

MRS. RAILTON-BELL. Good evening, Miss Cooper.

MISS COOPER. Good evening, Lady Matheson.

LADY MATHESON. Good evening.

MISS MEACHAM *does not look up.* MISS COOPER *continues her journey towards*
    ANNE'S *table.*

MISS COOPER. Is everything all right, Mrs. Shankland?

ANNE. Yes, thank you.

MISS COOPER. I'm so sorry I wasn't here to show you your table. I had a tel-
    ephone call from London. Are you being looked after all right?

ANNE. Yes, thank you.

MABEL *has brought her dish and now places it before her.*

MISS COOPER. (*Sharply.*) No soup?

ANNE. No. I don't care for it. It's bad for the figure.

MISS COOPER. I shouldn't have thought you'd have to worry about that, Mrs.
    Shankland.

ANNE. Oh, I do. I work at modelling, you know.

MISS COOPER. And now you're down here for a little rest?

ANNE. Yes. That's right.

MISS COOPER. I hope you find your room quite comfortable.

ANNE. I'm sure I shall.

MISS COOPER. If there's anything you want please don't hesitate to ask me.

ANNE. I won't.

MISS COOPER *flashes her a cordial smile, extinguished instantly as she turns away.*
    *She glances at the empty table by the window, and summons* MABEL *with a*
    *gesture.*

MISS COOPER. Mabel, go to Mr. Malcolm's room and tell him—

MABEL. I've been. He's not there.

MISS COOPER. Oh. Have they kept something hot for him?

MABEL. Yes, but cook says if he's not in in five minutes he'll have to have
    cold.

MISS COOPER. Oh, well, I don't expect he'll be more than that.

MABEL *looks unconvinced.* MISS COOPER *goes towards the hall door.* MR. FOWLER,
    *rising from his table, intercepts her.*

MR. FOWLER. Did I hear you say something about a telephone call?

MISS COOPER. I'm afraid it wasn't from your guest, Mr. Fowler. It was from
    Major Pollock. He wanted to leave a new forwarding address.

MRS. RAILTON-BELL. Ringing up from London? That's very extravagant—for
    the Major—

MISS COOPER. (*With a faint smile.*) He was calling from a friend's house, I
    gather. He's coming back next Tuesday he says.

MISS MEACHAM. (*Through her book.*) Oh God! That old bore!

MR. FOWLER. I can't understand Philip not ringing up. How can he expect to
    be met at the station if we don't know what train—

MISS COOPER. Have you tried ringing him?

MR. FOWLER. Yes. Twice. No answer either time. Perhaps I'd better try
    again—

*He goes through the change in his pocket.*

MISS COOPER. It's a little late, Mr. Fowler. There's only one train left from London—

MR. FOWLER. (*On his way to the door.*) Please don't worry about the room,
Miss Cooper. If anything's gone wrong—which I don't believe, mind
you—I'll pay for it, I promise you.

MISS COOPER. That won't be necessary, Mr. Fowler. But I *would* rather like to
know—if you don't mind—as soon as possible—

MR. FOWLER *goes.* MISS COOPER *takes up the vase from his table.*

MRS. RAILTON-BELL. (*Sympathetically.*) It's too bad, Miss Cooper. This is the
third time, isn't it?

MISS COOPER. I expect he'll turn up. Just forgotten to phone, that's all. You
know what these Bohemian young people are like.

*She goes out.*

MRS. RAILTON-BELL. (*To* LADY MATHESON.) I don't as it happens. I don't care
for Bohemians. (*In her confidential whisper.*) We have one too many here,
I should have thought. (*With her head she indicates the table by the window.*) And I'm beginning to doubt the very existence of Mr. Fowler's
famous young painter friend.

LADY MATHESON. I know he exists. Mr. Fowler showed me an article on him
in *Picture Post.* He was the head boy of Mr. Fowler's house at Tonbridge,
I gather. So proud of him, Mr. Fowler is—it's really quite touching to
hear him go on

MRS. RAILTON-BELL. Well, I think it's a disgrace that he keeps on letting him
down like this—

MISS MEACHAM *suddenly closes her book.*

MISS MEACHAM. Nonsense.

MRS. RAILTON-BELL. (*Startled.*) What, dear?

MISS MEACHAM. It's not a disgrace at all. Why should we old has-beens expect the young to show us consideration? We've had our life. They've
still got theirs to live. Seeing us can only remind them of death, and old
people's diseases. I've got two of the prettiest nieces you ever saw. You've
seen their photographs in my room. But they never come near me, and
I wouldn't like it if they did. God knows I don't want to remind them of
what they've got to become.

*She goes into the lounge, holding her book.*

MRS. RAILTON-BELL. (*In her confidential whisper to* LADY MATHESON.) I'm getting a little worried about Miss Meacham.

LADY MATHESON. She's certainly getting more and more—unusual, every day.

MRS. RAILTON-BELL. These dream-games of hers. Well, I suppose they're harmless—but I really don't know what a psychiatrist would say. The human
mind, you know—it's a very delicate piece of machinery—as my husband used to say—and—one never knows. Well—(*She rises majestically.*)
Shall I see you in the lounge, or have you a date with the Third Programme?

LADY MATHESON. No. There's nothing worth hearing on tonight.

MRS. RAILTON-BELL. Good. A toute à l'heure, then.

*She sweeps regally into the lounge.* LADY MATHESON *is now on her sweet.* ANNE *has finished toying with her goulash. Deep silence reigns.* MABEL *comes in.*

MABEL. (*To* ANNE.) I've brought you the turnover. It's better than the other.

ANNE. Oh. Thank you so much.

MABEL *replaces her dishes and goes out. Once more silence reigns. The door is pushed open rather violently and* JOHN MALCOLM *comes in. He is in the early forties, of rather rugged appearance, untidily dressed, and with unruly hair. When he speaks it will be with a slight north country accent. He looks quickly at his watch, and then at the kitchen door. Then he walks towards the table by the window. To reach it he has to pass* ANNE. *She has seen him before he sees her, and is now staring at him, remotely, with no change of expression. Conscious of the stare he looks in her direction and then stops dead, his back to the audience. After a moment he walks on to his own table and takes his seat, which is facing hers. He stares at the table-cloth.* DOREEN *comes in.*

DOREEN. Oh. You in at last? Thank heavens. I thought we'd never get off. Where you been? The Feathers?

JOHN. Yes.

DOREEN. Thought so. The goulash's off. You'll have to have medaillon.

JOHN. (*Still staring at the table-cloth.*) That's all right.

DOREEN. Brown windsor, like usual?

JOHN. Yes.

DOREEN *goes. There is silence between the three. Finally* LADY MATHESON *finishes, gets up, and goes out into the lounge, as* DOREEN *comes in with* JOHN'S soup.

DOREEN. There you are. Tuck into that. Not but what I wouldn't expect you've had enough liquid tonight already.

*She goes out.* JOHN *crumbles a piece of bread, and then slowly lifts his eyes from the table-cloth to gaze at the other guest.*

JOHN. (*At length.*) Is this coincidence?

ANNE. Of course.

JOHN. What are you doing here?

ANNE. A rest-cure.

JOHN. Why this place—of all places?

ANNE. It was recommended to me.

JOHN. Who by?

ANNE. A man I met at a party somewhere.

JOHN. He didn't tell you I was here?

ANNE. He did say something about a journalist—called John Malcolm. Is that you?

JOHN. Yes.

ANNE. John Malcolm. Oh yes, of course. Your Christian names.

JOHN. (*Savagely.*) Why, for the love of God, didn't you go to the Royal Bath or the Norfolk or the Branksome Towers, or any of the grand hotels—why?

*He stops as* DOREEN *comes in.*

DOREEN. What you having after, 'cause cook's got to leave it out? Turnover is best.

JOHN. All right.

DOREEN. Finished your soup?

JOHN. Yes, thank you.

DOREEN. You haven't touched it. I said too much liquid—

*She takes the soup into the kitchen.*

ANNE. I couldn't afford a grand hotel.

JOHN. He pays you alimony, doesn't he?

ANNE. Seven fifty a year. I don't find it very easy. You see. I'm not getting work these days—

JOHN. I thought he was a rich man.

ANNE. Michael? Oh no. His antique shop lost a lot of money.

JOHN. He gets his name in the papers a lot.

ANNE. Oh yes. Quite a social figure-first nights and all that.

JOHN. How long exactly were you married to him?

ANNE. Three years and six months.

JOHN. Beating me by three months? I saw the headlines of the case. They were quite juicy—but not as juicy as ours—you'll admit. It was cruelty again, wasn't it?

ANNE. Yes.

JOHN. Did *he* try to kill you too?

ANNE. (*Quietly.*) No.

DOREEN *comes in with* JOHN's *second course.*

DOREEN. There you are. Usual veg? (JOHN *nods.* DOREEN *helps him.*) You look a bit down in the dumps tonight. Anything the matter?

JOHN. No.

DOREEN. All right. Don't take long, will you? My friend's waiting—

*She goes out.* JOHN *makes no attempt to touch his food.*

JOHN. How did he show *his* cruelty?

ANNE. In a lot of ways. Small ways. They can all be summed up by saying that he doesn't really like women.

JOHN. Why did he marry you?

ANNE. He wanted a wife.

JOHN. And you wanted a husband? (*She nods.*) As wide a contrast as possible from your first, I suppose. Still, couldn't you have done a bit better for yourself?

ANNE. I suppose so. But he was gentle and kind and made me laugh and I was fond of him. I went into it with my eyes well open. I thought I could make it work. I was wrong. (JOHN *laughs suddenly.*) What's the joke?

JOHN. A nice poser for a woman's magazine. Girls, which husband would you choose? One who loves you too little—or one who loves you too much? (*After a pause.*) Third time lucky perhaps.

ANNE. Perhaps.

*Pause.*

JOHN. How long are you staying here?

ANNE. I booked for two weeks.

JOHN. I'll go to London.

ANNE. No. If you feel like that, then I'll go to another hotel.

JOHN. That might be easier.

*Pause.*

ANNE. John—I don't see why—

JOHN. Do you think these old women don't notice anything? They spend their whole days gossiping. It would take them less than a day to nose out the whole story and wouldn't they have a time with it? They're suspicious enough of me as it is. They know I write in the *New Outlook* under the name of Cato—and how they found that out I'll never know, because none of them would sully their dainty fingers by even touching such a bolshie rag.

ANNE. I read it every week.

JOHN. Turning left-wing in your old age?

ANNE. (*Quietly.*) My old age?

JOHN. How old are you now?

ANNE. Well—let's just say eight years older than when I last saw you.

JOHN. Yes. You don't look it.

ANNE. Thank you. But I feel it.

*Pause.*

JOHN. Why didn't you come to see me in prison yourself?

ANNE. I wanted to. I was stopped.

JOHN. Who by?

ANNE. My mother and father.

JOHN. I suppose they told you I might try to strangle you in front of the warder. I nearly did try to strangle your solicitor.

ANNE. They thought it would make it easier for you if I kept away.

JOHN. A very well-bred, Christian thought. My dear ex-in-laws. How are they?

ANNE. My father's dead. My mother lives in a place rather like this, in Kensington.

*Pause.* JOHN *is gazing at her intently.*

JOHN. (*At length.*) Then you'll go tomorrow, will you?

ANNE. Yes.

JOHN. Thank you. (*Stiffly.*) I'm sorry to have to put you to so much inconvenience.

ANNE. That's all right.

*He gets up abruptly from his table and walks up to hers.* ANNE *rises quickly.*

JOHN. Well, what do we do—shake hands?

ANNE. I'm very glad to see you again, John.

*She kisses him gently on the cheek.*

JOHN. It may seem boorish of me not to be able to say the same, Anne. But then I am a boor, as you know. In fact, you must still have a scar on the side of your head to prove it to you.

ANNE. It's gone now.

JOHN. Gone? After five stitches and a week in hospital?

ANNE. Eight years will cure most scars.

JOHN. Most, I suppose. Not all, though. Well, good night.

*He goes towards the hall door. Before he reaches it* MISS COOPER *comes in.*

MISS COOPER. Mrs. Shankland—(*seeing* JOHN) Oh, good evening, Mr. Malcolm.

JOHN. Good evening.

*He makes to move past her.*

MISS COOPER. Did you want something? Is there anything I can do for you?

JOHN. I've finished, thank you. I'm going out.

MISS COOPER. Oh. (*With a hint of anxiety.*) It's a horrible night, you know. It's started to pour—

JOHN. It doesn't matter—

*He goes into the hall.*

MISS COOPER. (*Following him.*) I'll have to open the door for you. I've already locked up. Excuse me, Mrs. Shankland—

*She follows him out.* ANNE, *left alone, sits down again. She looks thoughtfully at herself in a hand-mirror for a long time.* MISS COOPER *comes back.*

Coffee is served in the lounge, Mrs. Shankland. I thought when you've finished your dinner, you might like me to take you in there and introduce you to some of your fellow-guests. People are sometimes so odd about not talking to newcomers, I don't know why, and I hate any of my guests to feel lonely. (*Conversationally.*) Loneliness is a terrible thing, don't you agree?

ANNE. Yes, I do agree. A terrible thing.

*She gets up from the table.*

MISS COOPER. Oh. Have you finished? Good. Then let's go in, shall we? The lounge is through here.

*She leads the way to the lounge door.*

ANNE. Thank you.


THE LIGHTS FADE


SCENE 2


SCENE: *The lounge, about two hours later. The dining-room door is upstage R. and the door leading to the hall is at back. French windows L. are curtained and we can hear the rain beating against them. There is a fireplace downstage R. with an electric fire burning.*

CHARLES *and* JEAN *are the only two residents in the room. They sit side by side on a sofa, still reading intently. Both are making an occasional note.*

CHARLES. (*Breaking a long silence, into his book.*) There's going to be a storm.

JEAN. Hell. I hate spray.

CHARLES. (*After another silence.*) Where are they all?

JEAN. The new one's gone up to her room. So has old Dream-girl. The Bournemouth Belle and Minnie Mouse are in the television room. Karl Marx is out boozing. Mr. Chips is still ringing up his painter friend.

CHARLES. He won't come.

JEAN. Of course he won't. (*She closes her book and stretches herself.*) I've finished my Stubbs. How are you doing with your anatomy?

CHARLES. I'd do better if you'd shut up.

JEAN. (*Going to the window.*) I didn't start the small talk. You did. Does your father know about me?

CHARLES. (*Making a note.*) Yes.

JEAN. What did you tell him?

CHARLES. What?

*She pushes his book against his lap, preventing him from reading.*

JEAN. What did you tell him?

CHARLES. Don't do that, Jean. I'm in the middle of the trickiest duct in the whole human body.

JEAN. What did you tell him?

CHARLES. (*Angrily.*) Oh, for God's sake—that we were in love with each other and were going to get married.

*He pulls the book back and furrows his brows over it again.*

JEAN. You told him a dirty lie, then, didn't you—I mean about us going to get married?

CHARLES. What? Oh yes. I had to put it like that. Otherwise he wouldn't have understood. Now shut up for God's sake.

JEAN. You'd better stop now. If you go on much longer you know you won't sleep and it'll make you old before your time.

*He allows her to take the book from him.*

CHARLES. I suppose you're right. Don't lose the place. (*He stretches.*) My God—to be old before one's time. What a fate! I wonder if all old people are as miserable as these.

JEAN. They're not miserable. Look at old Dream-girl. She's as happy as a sandgirl communing with her spirits and waiting for the racing results. The Bournemouth Belle's quite happy. too, queening it around here in her silver fox, and with her daughter to look after her.

CHARLES. Has she got a daughter?

JEAN. Don't you listen to anything? She never stops trilling away about her dear Sibyl, and how they're really more like good pals than mother and daughter, and how dear Sibyl can't live without her

CHARLES. You mean the daughter lives with her here? My God, what a fate! I haven't seen her—

JEAN. She's escaped for a couple of weeks, I gather, to an aunt. Anyway, the Bournemouth Belle's too self-centred an old brute to be anything but happy. Minnie Mouse *is* a bit grey and depressed, I grant. But she's got her music, and Mr. Chips has got his ex-pupils, even if he doesn't ever see them. As for Karl Marx—well—

CHARLES. Now you can't say Karl Marx isn't miserable. I've never seen a more miserable-looking wreck—

JEAN. Oh, I don't know. He's got his booze and his articles in the *New Outlook* and his vague air of a murky past, and his hints of former glories. (*With seriousness.*) No, Charles. Do you know who I think is the only one in this hotel who really is miserable?

CHARLES. Miss Cooper?

JEAN. (*Scornfully.*) Miss Cooper? No. She's as gay as a bee pinning up her notices in the bathroom and being generally managerial. No. I meant the new one.

CHARLES. Mrs. Shankland? But you've only met her for a second an hour ago.

JEAN. A woman can't fool another woman with a pretty dress and a gay manner and a bright smile. She's been through some form of hell, that creature. Anyway, what's she doing down here? Dressed like that and looking like that she ought to be at the Royal Bath, or somewhere— (*Darkly.*) Besides—she's not wearing a wedding ring.

CHARLES. Really, Jean, you're getting as bad as the old girls. Perhaps it's got broken or something.

JEAN. She's divorced—that I'm sure of.

CHARLES. Well, all right. So she's divorced. Does that make her a tragic figure? I should have thought, according to your ideas on marriage, it ought to make her a happy one.

JEAN. My ideas on marriage are only for us, Charles—because I'm going to have a career and you're going to be a famous surgeon and don't want hordes of children cluttering up your consulting-room. But most people aren't as sensible as we are. They get married and are miserable when it goes wrong. Thank heavens that can't happen to us. We're too integrated. At least I am, I know, and I hope you are too—

CHARLES. Come and give me a kiss and I'll show you how integrated I am.

JEAN. I'd only put lipstick on your collar and the old girls will notice.

CHARLES. Sometimes, Jean darling, I'm not sure I wouldn't like to see you, just ever so slightly, disintegrate.

*He strides over and kisses her. She appears quite to enjoy the embrace. There is the sound of voices in the hall.*

CHARLES. Oh blast!

JEAN. (*Levelly.*) Wipe your mouth.

CHARLES. Damn it all, even the old girls know the facts of life.

JEAN. They may know them, but they don't like them.

MRS. RAILTON-BELL *and* LADY MATHESON *come in.*

MRS. RAILTON-BELL. Yes, wasn't he splendid? He completely floored that horrid socialist—(*Coldly.*) Hullo. Finished your work?

CHARLES. ⎱ (*Together.*) Yes.
JEAN.  ⎰ Yes we have. Just going to bed.

MRS. RAILTON-BELL. Good night.

CHARLES. ⎱ (*Together.*) Good night, Mrs. Railton-Bell.
JEAN.  ⎰ Good night, Lady Matheson.

*They go out.*

MRS. RAILTON-BELL. They've been making love.

LADY MATHESON. How do you know?

MRS. RAILTON-BELL. The look in their eyes. And just as I came in he was putting a handkerchief away with lipstick marks on it.

LADY MATHESON. Well, perhaps they *are* in love. I always thought there must be something.

MRS. RAILTON-BELL. But they're supposed to have come here just to work. Old friends, and all that. That's what they told Miss Cooper. If they're in love, why don't they say so? I hate anything furtive. What were we saying?

*They take their (evidently usual) seats by the fire.*

LADY MATHESON. About the man on television being so good.

MRS. RAILTON-BELL. Oh yes. Now what was it he said that was so true—

*The french windows are opened from the outside and the curtains are blown violently inwards.*

Good gracious!

*After a moment's battling with the bellying curtains,* JOHN *emerges. He is wearing a drenched raincoat.*

Please close that at once. There's the most terrible draught.

JOHN. A draught? Oh yes.

*He disappears behind the curtains again.* MRS. RAILTON-BELL *exchanges a speaking glance with* LADY MATHESON *and frames the word 'drunk' with her lips.*

LADY MATHESON. Yes. Now what was it he said? So telling. Something about the national cake.

JOHN'S *struggles to close the french windows are concluded. He emerges again and, still in his mackintosh, walks over to a chair by the fire, where he warms his hands. The two ladies look at him, and* MRS. RAILTON-BELL *decides to ignore his presence.*

MRS. RAILTON-BELL. Yes. I remember now. It was in that wonderful answer he gave about levelling up rather than levelling down. He said, don't you remember, that whereas the Socialists were only concerned about cutting the national cake into exactly equal slices, the Conservatives were trying to increase the size of the cake.

*She glances at* JOHN *to see if this has registered. Still holding his hands to the fire he does not appear to have heard.*

MRS. RAILTON-BELL. And then he said that every wage increase meant a smaller cake for cutting—

JOHN. (*Abruptly.*) Who said this?

MRS. RAILTON-BELL. Sir Roger Williamson, on television.

JOHN. I might have guessed it.

MRS. RAILTON-BELL. (*Bristling.*) I gather you don't agree with what he said, Mr. Malcolm?

JOHN. Of course I don't agree. You know damn well I don't agree. That's not the point. They've got some clever people in that party. Why do they have to put an old ass like that on television—with a falsetto voice, a face like an angry walrus and the mind of a backward child of eight?

MRS. RAILTON-BELL. That was not our impression of Sir Roger.

JOHN *does not reply. He seems, for the moment, to be lost in reverie.*

JOHN. Poor old Roger. I suppose he needs the dough to make a little back on what he spends on all those girl friends of his.

MRS. RAILTON-BELL. (*After a moment's appalled silence.*) Do I understand that you are personally acquainted with Sir Roger, Mr. Malcolm?

JOHN *turns and looks at her as if, for the moment, he, had been oblivious of her presence.*

JOHN. No. Never met him.

MRS. RAILTON-BELL. Then may I ask by what right—

JOHN. No right. I just hear things, that's all.

MRS. RAILTON-BELL. Some very libellous things, if I may say so.

JOHN. Yes, the greater the truth the greater the libel is the phrase, isn't it? What else did Sir Roger say? Did he mention the go-slow in the docks?

MRS. RAILTON-BELL. Yes. As a matter of fact he did. He said that the dock workers seemed to have no sense of national responsibility—

JOHN. There's no body of men in England with more.

MRS. RAILTON-BELL. That's no doubt something else that you have *heard*, Mr. Malcolm.

JOHN. No. That's something I *know*. I used to be a docker myself.

*Pause.*

MRS. RAILTON-BELL. (*At length.*) I am not, if I may say so, at all surprised to hear it.

JOHN. And I am not surprised you're not surprised, Mrs. Railton-Bell. (*He burps gently.*) Excuse me. Too much whisky.

*He sits down, still in his mackintosh.* MRS. RAILTON-BELL *and* LADY MATHESON *exchange a glance,* JOHN *intercepts it.*

Keeps the cold out, you know. I gather you two ladies read the *New Outlook?*

MRS. RAILTON-BELL. I certainly never do any such thing. I wouldn't soil my hands—

JOHN. That's just what I thought. Do you. Lady Matheson?

LADY MATHESON. I have glanced at it on occasions, yes. (*Hastily.*) Not for the political side, of course, but it has very good music criticism.

JOHN. So it was you who found out I was Cato, was it? Smart of you. How did you guess?

LADY MATHESON. (*Confused.*) If you must know, you left some typescript lying about on that table over there. I picked it up, not knowing what it was, and read just the opening paragraph, no more, but it was enough for me to recognize it in print a week or so later.

JOHN. I see. My fault then. No ill-feelings—on this side anyway. (*He burps again.*) Excuse me. What was the article on?

LADY MATHESON. Dividends and wages.

JOHN. Did you read it all?

LADY MATHESON. Yes, I did.

JOHN. What did you think of it?

LADY MATHESON. (*With unusual spirit.*) Since you ask I thought it was monstrous—utterly monstrous. I very nearly wrote you a letter about it.

JOHN. I wish you had. I enjoy controversy. You must have taken it a bit personally, I'm afraid.

LADY MATHESON. And how else could I take it? Do you realize that I have to live on a little less than half of what the average dock worker makes a year? My husband was in the Civil Service and died before the pension scheme came into force. Still, the sum he left me seemed perfectly adequate at the time. And now—

JOHN. I know. You can't afford to have your wireless repaired—and you live by it. You had to move into a small back room when they raised the hotel prices last year. You can only afford one cinema a week, in the front rows. I bet you don't even buy the *New Outlook*—you borrow it. In short by any reasonable standards you're well below the poverty line, and, as the poor have always had my passionate sympathy, Lady Matheson, you have mine.

LADY MATHESON. Thank you, but I can do very well without it.

JOHN. I wonder if you can. You're the unlucky victims of our revolution—you and Miss Meacham and Mr. Fowler and the others. You should appeal to our humane instincts, Lady Matheson.

LADY MATHESON. By voting for your side, I suppose.

JOHN. That would be the most practical way, I agree.

LADY MATHESON. (*Staunchly.*) Never. Never till I die.

MRS. RAILTON-BELL. Tell me, why didn't you mention *me* just now, when you were talking of victims?

JOHN. Because you're not one, and won't be, either, until our capital levy gets at that tidy little nest-egg of yours.

MRS. RAILTON-BELL. (*Utterly outraged. To* LADY MATHESON.) I think we should go, Gladys, and leave Mr. Malcolm down here to sleep it off.

*The two ladies rise.*

JOHN. Oh, are you leaving, ladies? I mustn't forget my manners, must I?

*He gets out of the chair, with slight difficulty.*

I've enjoyed our little chat. Don't forget, next election—vote Labour.

MRS. RAILTON-BELL. It's our own fault, Gladys. We should never have allowed ourselves to be drawn into an argument with a drunken red.

*She has plainly intended this as an exit line, but her exit is delayed because* LADY

MATHESON *is feverishly searching the room for something.*
(*Impatiently.*) Come along, Gladys.

LADY MATHESON. I've left my reading glasses somewhere.

MISS COOPER *comes in with a tray on which is a coffee-pot and a cup.*

MISS COOPER. (*Brightly.*) Here you are, Mrs. Railton-Bell. I'm not too late, I hope.

MRS. RAILTON-BELL. (*With heavy meaning.*) Thank you, Miss Cooper, but I'm not having my coffee tonight. (*Impatiently, to* LADY MATHESON.) Can't you find them, dear?

LADY MATHESON. I'll just have another look in my chair.

*She goes to her chair.* MISS COOPER *meanwhile has quickly taken in the scene. She puts the tray down and she stares coldly at* JOHN.

MISS COOPER. (*In a very managerial voice.*) Mr. Malcolm, did you come in through the french windows?

JOHN. (*Humbly.*) Yes, I did.

MISS COOPER. You know that there's a hotel rule against that?

JOHN. I'd forgotten it. I'm very sorry.

MISS COOPER. There's mud all over the floor, (*advancing on his chair*) and you've been sitting in this chair with your wet mackintosh on. Oh really!

JOHN. I'm very sorry.

MISS COOPER. I must ask you if you would be so kind as to take your mackintosh off and hang it up in the proper place. Also to wipe your shoes on the mat provided for that purpose.

JOHN. Yes. I'm very sorry.

*He goes past* MRS. RAILTON-BELL *and out into the hall.* LADY MATHESON *is still looking in her chair.*

MISS COOPER. (*Anxiously.*) Has there been a little bother?

MRS. RAILTON-BELL. A little bother is a distinct understatement.

MISS COOPER. Oh dear! What was it?

MRS. RAILTON-BELL. I would prefer not to discuss it now. (*Very impatiently.*) For heaven's sake come along, Gladys. That dreadful man may be back at any moment.

LADY MATHESON. (*Triumphantly.*) Ah, I've got them. They were underneath the chair.

MRS. RAILTON-BELL. I can't think why you didn't look there in the first place.

LADY MATHESON. Well, I was sitting in Mr. Fowler's chair after dinner, you see, as the new lady was sitting in mine, quite inadvertently, I'm sure, and I thought—

MRS. RAILTON-BELL. It doesn't matter, dear. Go along now. Quick.

*She shoos her through the door and turns to* MISS COOPER.

I should like to see you tomorrow morning after breakfast, Miss Cooper. Good night.

MISS COOPER. Good night, Mrs. Railton-Bell.

MRS. RAILTON-BELL *goes out.* MISS COOPER *sighs and goes over to the chair in which*

JOHN *has sat. She takes the cushion out and places it near the fire.* MR. FOWLER *comes in, and goes over to the writing-desk.*

MR. FOWLER. Ah, there you are, Miss Cooper. I've come for some notepaper.

MISS COOPER. Any luck, Mr. Fowler?

MR. FOWLER. I'm afraid not. I shall try again, of course. I'm quite sure there's been some mistake—a telegram wrongly addressed, or something.

MISS COOPER. I expect so.

MR. FOWLER. I don't want anyone to wait up, but as I can hear the front-door bell from my room, I wonder if you'd mind if I answer it myself tonight?

MISS COOPER. That's quite all right, Mr. Fowler, but you're surely not still expecting him, are you?

MR. FOWLER. He might have hired a car, you know. He's a very extravagant boy. You know what these artists are. Well, good night.

MISS COOPER. Good night, Mr. Fowler.

MR. FOWLER *goes out.* MISS COOPER *wanders over to inspect the muddy footprints on the carpet. She is on her knees as* JOHN *comes back. He sits down moodily, in silence.* MISS COOPER *methodically finishes scraping up pieces of dried mud, walks to the waste-paper basket and throws them in. Then she goes to* MRS. RAILTON-BELL'S *unwanted coffee and pours a cup, black, with two lumps of sugar. Silently she hands it to him. He takes it, looking up at her, and sips it. She sits on the arm of his chair and leans her head affectionately on his shoulder.*

(*Gently.*) Are you very drunk?

JOHN. No.

MISS COOPER. How many?

JOHN. As many as I could afford. It wasn't a lot.

*Pause. She takes his hand.*

MISS COOPER. Something's the matter, isn't it?

JOHN. Nothing much.

MISS COOPER. Want to tell me?

JOHN. I can't tell you.

MISS COOPER. (*Cheerfully.*) That's all right. What did you say to the old women?

JOHN. Too much. Far too damn much. Oh God!

*He puts the coffee down, gets up and walks away from her. She watches him anxiously.*

I may have to leave.

MISS COOPER. (*Sharply.*) You can't leave.

JOHN. I may have to.

MISS COOPER. You won't have to. I'll see to that. But was it so bad?

JOHN. (*Bitterly.*) Not very bad, I suppose. Just an ordinary show-off, a rather sordid little piece of alcoholic self-assertion. Taking it out on two old women, telling them what a brilliant political thinker I am, hinting at what a great man I once was. I even gave away that I used to work in the docks.

MISS COOPER. Oh Lord!

JOHN. And that I knew Roger Williamson. I think I covered that up, though. I hope I did.

MISS COOPER. I hope you did too, otherwise old Railton-Bell will be on to it like a bloodhound. Anything else?

JOHN. I don't know. I can't think now. I'll remember it all in the morning. (*Miserably.*) Oh, Pat. I'm so sorry.

*He puts his arm round her affectionately.*

MISS COOPER. That's all right. I'll cover up for you. Finish your coffee.

*He obediently takes the cup up again.*

JOHN. Why do I do these things? I used to know how to behave.

MISS COOPER. (*Kissing him gently on the cheek.*) I'd do them too, in your place.

JOHN. Don't over-dramatize me. I do that enough myself. I'd probably have been nothing.

MISS COOPER. What about that newspaper cutting about yourself you showed me which prophesied—?

JOHN. One political tipster napping an outsider. If nothing happens his tip is forgotten. If, by a fluke, it does, he can say: 'Look how clever I was twenty years ago—'

MISS COOPER. But before you were even thirty you'd been made a junior Minister.

JOHN. (*Brusquely rising.*) Yes, yes, yes. It doesn't matter. The world is full of promising young men who haven't, in middle age, fulfilled their promise. There's nothing to that. Nothing at all.

*He has turned away from her and is staring at the floor.*

MISS COOPER. (*Quietly.*) I wish you'd tell me what's happened.

JOHN. I can't. I've told you I can't. But it's not important.

MISS COOPER. Important enough for quite a few whiskies.

JOHN. A lot of things are important enough for that. The day I heard Willy Barker had been made a Cabinet Minister I had a bottle.

*Pause.*

MISS COOPER. Couldn't you *ever* get back?

JOHN *laughs sharply.*

JOHN. God, what a field day for the Tory press that would be! John Malcolm Ramsden has decided to stand as a Labour Independent for his old constituency. It will be recalled that Mr. Ramsden, who was a junior Minister in the 1945 Administration, went to prison for six months in 1946 on the triple charge of assaulting a police officer in the course of his duty, of being drunk and disorderly and of causing grievous bodily harm to his wife. The headline—Gaol-Bird Stands Again. No thank you. I'll stay John Malcolm—journalist, middle-aged soak and has-been, the terror of the older lady residents of the Hotel Beauregard, Bournemouth. That's vastly preferable, I assure you.

*He has turned away from her again. She goes up to him quietly and puts her arms on his shoulders.*

MISS COOPER. John, dear, I don't want to know what it is, but let me help you, if I can.

*He turns round and gazes at her.*

JOHN. (*Simply.*) Do you know, Pat, that I love you very sincerely?

MISS COOPER. (*With a smile.*) Sincerely? That sounds a little like what a brother says to a sister.

JOHN. (*With an answering smile.*) You have surely reason enough to know that my feelings for you can transcend the fraternal.

MISS COOPER. Yes. But for all that—and don't think I'm not grateful for all that—not really quite enough reason.

*They are drawing together when there is a sound outside the hall door and they move apart, not in alarm, and as if from long practice.* ANNE *comes in.*

MISS COOPER. (*Brightly.*) Oh, hullo, Mrs. Shankland. They told me you'd gone up some time ago.

ANNE. I had, but not to bed. I was reading.

MISS COOPER. That's a comfy armchair, in there, isn't it?

ANNE. Very.

*She stands, uncertainly, just inside the door, looking at* JOHN *who, after a brief glance, has turned slightly away from her.*

MISS COOPER. Was there anything you wanted, Mrs. Shankland?

ANNE. (*Diffidently.*) No. I just wanted a word or two with—Mr. Malcolm.

MISS COOPER. (*Brightly again.*) Oh really? Had you two met before?

ANNE. Yes. A long time ago.

MISS COOPER. Oh.

*She glances at* JOHN, *evidently disturbed at the danger to his anonymity inherent in this situation, but she gets no answering look.*

Oh well. I'll leave you two alone, then. If you want anything, I shall be up for quite a time yet.

*She goes out, closing the door.* ANNE *gazes steadily at her ex-husband, but he is still looking away from her.*

ANNE. I didn't want to go away without our saying something to each other, John. I hope you don't mind?

JOHN. Mind? Why should I mind?

ANNE. Your rushing out of dinner like a whirlwind made it look as if you hated the very sight of me.

JOHN. (*Slowly, looking at her fully for the first time.*) The very sight of you, Anne, is perhaps the one thing about you that I don't hate.

ANNE. (*With a slight, nervous laugh.*) Oh dear. That's not very nice to hear.

JOHN. Don't you enjoy being complimented on your looks any more? Has your narcissism vanished?

ANNE. No. I suppose not. But I don't enjoy being hated by you.

JOHN. Don't you? You used to.

ANNE. You've got me wrong, John. You always did, you know.

JOHN. (*Quietly.*) I don't think so, Anne. If I had I wouldn't have found you so predictable.

ANNE. You always used to say I was predictable. I remember that was one of the things that used to irritate me most. It's such an easy thing to say, and so impossible to disprove.

JOHN. Yes, yes, yes. I've no doubt. Go to bed, Anne, and disappear quietly tomorrow. It's better, really it is.

ANNE. No, John. Let me stay just a little longer. May I sit down?

JOHN. Is that a way of reminding me of my bad manners? I know I shouldn't sit while you're standing

ANNE. (*Laughing gently.*) You're so bristly. Even bristlier now than before. (*She sits down.*) Your manners were always very good.

JOHN. You used to tick me off about them often enough.

ANNE. Well—only sometimes—when we had silly conventional people at the flat who didn't understand you as I did.

JOHN. (*With a faint smile.*) I think if I'd been given time, I could have predicted that answer.

ANNE. (*With an answering smile.*) Oh dear! Tell me, did you always find me so predictable—even at the very beginning?

JOHN. Yes.

ANNE. Why did you marry me, then?

JOHN. If it pleases your vanity to hear my answer once again, you shall. Because my love for you at that time was so desperate, my craving for you was so violent, that I could refuse you nothing that you asked—not even a marriage that every prompting of reason told me must be disastrous.

ANNE. Why did it so necessarily have to be disastrous?

JOHN. Because of class mainly.

ANNE. Class? Oh, that's nonsense, John. It's just inverted snobbery.

JOHN. No. I don't think so. The gulf between Kensington Gore and the Hull Docks is still fairly wide. I was one of a family of eight, as I must have told you many a time, and my views of a wife's duties must have been at least a little coloured by watching my mother sacrifice her health, strength and comfort and eventually her life to looking after us children, and to keeping the old man out of trouble. I'm not saying my demands on a wife would have been pitched as high as that. But they would, I think, at least have included the proper running of a home and the begetting of children.

ANNE. (*Hotly.*) About children, I did make it perfectly clear before our marriage—

JOHN. Yes. You made it perfectly clear. A famous model mustn't gamble her figure merely for posterity. I accepted the bargain, Anne, the whole bargain. I have no complaint.

ANNE. (*Angrily.*) You have, John. You know you have. Your real complaint is still the same as it always was—that I didn't love you when we got married—

JOHN. Oh God! Do we have to go into that again?

ANNE. Yes, we do, it needs clearing up. You admitted just now that I was the

one who wanted the marriage. All right. If that's true—which it is—what
could have been the motive, except love? Oh yes. I know. You were an
under-secretary at the time, but, let's face it, there were even grander figures that I might have—

JOHN. (*Interrupting.*) I know, Anne dear. I remember it all in detail. A baronet, an Australian millionaire, and that film producer.

ANNE. Well, then?

JOHN. (*Quietly.*) You married me because you were frightened. You were going to be thirty. You'd realized suddenly that you couldn't go on for the
rest of your life gazing joyously at yourself in the mirror, because the time
would come when what you saw in the mirror would no longer give you
joy. And you couldn't go on treading happily on the faces of all the men
who wanted you, because the time would come when there wouldn't be
so many faces to tread on.

ANNE. Eloquent, John, but unconvincing. If so, why not a baronet, or a millionaire? Why Mrs. Ramsden?

JOHN. Because the others couldn't pay you the full price.

ANNE. What price?

JOHN. The price you so reluctantly put on yourself when you settled for giving yourself to the highest bidder in marriage.

ANNE. You mean, a title wasn't enough?

JOHN. No.

ANNE. Nor a million?

JOHN. Nor a million.

ANNE. What was the price then?

JOHN. Enslavement.

ANNE. John, really. How ridiculous you are. I seem to remember this accu-
sation from the old days—

JOHN. I've no doubt you do.

ANNE. If all I wanted to do was to make my husband a slave, why should I
specially have chosen you and not the others?

JOHN. Because where would your fun have been in enslaving the sort of man
who was already the slave of his own head gardener? You wanted bigger
game. Wilder game. None of your tame baronets and Australian mil-
lionaires, too well-mannered to protest when you denied them their
conjugal rights, and too well-brought-up not to take your headaches at
bedtime as just headaches at bedtime. 'Poor old girl! Bad show! So sorry.
Better in the morning, I hope. Feeling a bit tired myself, anyway.' No,
Anne, dear. What enjoyment would there have been for you in using
your weapons on that sort of a husband? But to turn them on a genuine, live, roaring savage from the slums of Hull, to make him grovel at
the vague and distant promise of delights that were his anyway by right,
or goad him to such a frenzy of drink and rage by a locked door that
he'd kick it in and hit you with his fist so hard that you'd knock yourself
unconscious against a wall—that must really have been fun.

ANNE. (*At length.*) Goodness, John, how you do go on.

JOHN. Yes. I do. You must forgive me. It's a foible, perhaps, of disappointed politicians. Besides, tonight I'm rather drunker than usual.

ANNE. (*With a hint of eagerness.*) Because of seeing me?

JOHN. Yes.

ANNE. I'm sorry.

JOHN. No you're not.

ANNE *laughs, quite gaily now, and with far more confidence.*

ANNE. You haven't changed much, have you?

JOHN. Haven't I?

ANNE. The same old John pouring out the same old cascade of truths, half-truths and distortions, all beaten up together, to make a neat, consistent story. *Your* story. Human nature isn't quite as simple as you make it, John. You've left out the most important fact of all.

JOHN. What's that?

ANNE. That you're the only person in the world I've ever been really fond of. You notice how tactfully I leave out the word love. Give me a cigarette. (*He pulls a packet from his pocket.*) Oh, not *still* those awful cork-tipped things. I'll have one of my own. Hand me my bag.

*A faint note of authority has crept back into her voice.* JOHN *obediently hands her her bag and she takes out a gold cigarette-case.*

Do you dispute that?

JOHN. I might observe that your fondness for me was sometimes shown in rather surprising ways—

ANNE. Well, I wasn't prepared to be your doormat. I had to fight back sometimes, didn't I?

JOHN. I suppose so. It was your choice of weapons that was unfair.

ANNE. I didn't have any others. You had the brains and the eloquence and the ability to make me feel cheap—which, incidentally, you've done again tonight.

JOHN. Have I? I'm sorry.

ANNE. Anyway, isn't it a principle of war that you always play on the opponent's weakness?

JOHN. A principle of war, not necessarily of marriage.

ANNE. Marriage is a kind of war.

JOHN. It is for you.

ANNE. (*With a smile.*) For you too, John. Be fair now.

JOHN. And the weakness you played on was my overpowering love for you?

ANNE. You can put it that way, if you like. There are less pretty-sounding ways.

JOHN *remains silent, looking at her as she smokes her cigarette, through a holder—now plainly quite confident of herself.*

Besides you and I never could have agreed on *that* aspect of married life.

JOHN. No. We couldn't.

ANNE. Why are you staring at me?

JOHN. You know very well why.

ANNE. (*Contentedly.*) Well, don't. It makes me embarrassed.

JOHN. I'm sorry.

ANNE. You really think I haven't changed much—to look at, I mean?

JOHN. (*Not looking at her.*) Not at all.

ANNE. Just a clever make-up, I expect.

JOHN. I don't think so.

ANNE. If you'd wanted an obedient little hausfrau, why didn't you marry
   one—like that manageress I caught you canoodling with a moment ago?
   That *was* a canoodle, wasn't it?

JOHN. A canoodle is what you would call it—yes.

ANNE. Why haven't you married her?

JOHN. Because I'm not in love with her.

ANNE. Does that matter?

JOHN. I'm old-fashioned enough to think it does.

ANNE. Couldn't you—as they say—learn to love her? After all she's your type.

JOHN. I have still only one type in the whole world, Anne. God knows it
   does little for my pride to have to admit that to you, but I never was
   very good at lying about myself. (*Looking at her again.*) Only one type.
   The prototype.

ANNE. (*Quietly.*) I'm glad.

JOHN. I've no doubt you are. Tell me, does a compliment still give you that
   little jab in the solar plexus that you used to describe to me?

ANNE. Yes, it does. More so than ever, now that I'm forty. There—I've admitted it.

JOHN. I'd worked it out anyway.

*They both laugh quietly. He picks up her cigarette-case.*

   That's a nice little affair. Who gave you that? Your second?

ANNE. Yes.

JOHN. He had good taste.

ANNE. In jewels.

JOHN. You ought to have made a go of it with that man. He sounds much
   more your form.

ANNE. He wasn't a man. He was a mouse.

JOHN. Didn't he pay you enough compliments?

ANNE. Too many and none of them meant.

JOHN. No solar plexus?

ANNE. No.

*She takes his hand suddenly in an intimate friendly gesture.*

   John, I'm in a bad way, you know.

JOHN. I'm sorry.

ANNE. Some of the things you used to tell me might happen to me *are* happening.

JOHN. Such as?

ANNE. Loneliness—for one.

JOHN. No friends?

ANNE. Not many. I haven't the gift.

JOHN. There's no gift. To make people love you is a gift, and you have it—

ANNE (*Bitterly.*) Had it—

JOHN. Have it.

ANNE. Yet I hate being alone. Oh God, how I hate it. This place, for instance, gives me the creeps.

JOHN. (*Innocently.*) Why did you come here, then?

*For the briefest instant she looks startled, but recovers at once.*

ANNE. I suppose I didn't realize what it would be like. Oh God! What a life. I can just see myself in a few years' time at one of those separate tables—

JOHN. Is there no one on the horizon?

ANNE. No one that I'd want. And time is slipping. God, it goes fast, doesn't it?

JOHN. I haven't found it to, these last eight years.

ANNE. Poor John. I'm so sorry. (*She squeezes his hand.*) But it's such a wonderful fluke our meeting again like this, that we really shouldn't waste it. We must see some more of each other now. After all when fate plays as astounding a trick as this on us, it must mean something, mustn't it? Don't send me away tomorrow. Let me stay on a little while.

JOHN *makes no reply. He is staring at her.*

(*Gently.*) I won't be a nuisance.

JOHN *still does not answer. He is still staring at her.*

I won't, John. Really I won't.

JOHN. (*At length, murmuring thickly.*) You won't be a nuisance.

*He embraces her suddenly and violently. She responds. After a moment she begins to say something.*

(*Savagely.*) Don't speak. For God's sake, don't speak. You'll kill this moment.

ANNE. Darling John, even at the risk of 'killing your moment' I think I really *must* say something. I think I must remind you that we are in a public lounge, and inform you that Miss Cooper has been good enough to give me what appears to be a very isolated room, the number of which is— (*she pulls a key from her pocket*)—nineteen. Give me one of those horrid cork-tipped things of yours. I'm right out of mine.

*He takes a packet and brusquely thrusts them at her. She takes a cigarette. He tenders a lighter to her. His hand is trembling.*

Oh—what a shaky hand!

*She holds it still and lights her cigarette.* JOHN *thrusts his hand back into his coat pocket and keeps it there. She gets up, gathers her bag in silence, smooths her dress, makes some adjustment to her hair, and turns to him.*

How do I look? All right?

JOHN. (*Murmuring.*) All right.

ANNE. (*Happily blowing him a kiss.*) Darling John.

JOHN. (*Not returning the gesture.*) Darling Anne.

ANNE. Half an hour?

*She goes towards the door. Before she gets there* MISS COOPER *can be heard calling* 'Mrs. Shankland' *from the hall.* ANNE *stops and smiles at* JOHN.

ANNE. You see?

*The door opens and* MISS COOPER *comes in.*

MISS COOPER. Oh, Mrs. Shankland—you're wanted on the telephone—a London call.

ANNE. Oh? Where is the telephone?

MISS COOPER. I'll show you. It's just through here.

*The two women go out. Left alone* JOHN *sits down suddenly, as if his knees had weakened. He rests his head on his hands. He is in that attitude when* MISS COOPER *comes back. She looks at him for a moment before she speaks.*

That's her, isn't it?

JOHN. What?

MISS COOPER. Mrs. Shankland. That's the one, isn't it?

JOHN. Yes.

MISS COOPER. She looks exactly the way you described her. Carved in ice, you said once, I remember.

JOHN. Did I?

MISS COOPER. What's going to happen now, John?

*He looks up at her without replying. There is a pause.*

(*Quietly, at length.*) I see. Well—I always knew you were still in love with her and always would be. You never made any bones about that—

JOHN. (*Pleadingly.*) Pat, dearest—

MISS COOPER. No. You don't need to say anything. I understand. So you'll be going away, will you?

JOHN. I don't know. Oh God, I don't know.

MISS COOPER. I expect you will. She looks as if she'd got some will-power, that girl. If she's taken that much trouble to run you to earth down here, she won't let you go so easily—

JOHN. She hasn't run me to earth. It was a coincidence her coming down here.

MISS COOPER. Coincidence? Do you really believe that?

JOHN. Yes.

MISS COOPER. All right, then. I'm not saying anything.

JOHN. Say It.

MISS COOPER. No, I won't.

*He jumps up and fiercely grabs her by the arms.*

JOHN. (*Fiercely.*) Say it. Say it, damn you.

MISS COOPER. (*Quietly.*) Don't knock *me* about, John. I'm not her, you know.

*He relaxes his grip.*

MISS COOPER. All right. I'll say it. If it was coincidence, why is she talking to the editor of the *New Outlook* on the telephone now?

JOHN. What?

MISS COOPER. His name's Wilder, isn't it?

JOHN. Yes.

MISS COOPER. Terminus number?

JOHN. Yes.

MISS COOPER. And he knows who you really are, doesn't he, and where you live?

JOHN. Yes.

MISS COOPER. And he goes around the West End quite a bit, I'd imagine—cocktail parties and things?

JOHN *has sat down again, this time without replying.*

Mind you, it could be a different Mr. Wilder, I suppose. If there's one coincidence—why not another?

ANNE *comes back. She looks happy and unruffled.*

ANNE. (*To* MISS COOPER.) Thank you so much, Miss Cooper. I'm going to bed now. I've put down a call for 8.30 with hot water and lemon. I hope that's all right?

MISS COOPER. Quite all right, Mrs. Shankland.

ANNE. Well, good night. Good night, Mr. Malcolm.

JOHN *gets up suddenly from his chair.*

JOHN. Stay here, Anne. Pat, you go.

MISS COOPER. (*Urgently.*) Not now, John. Leave it till the morning.

JOHN. It's got to be now.

*He holds the door open for her.*

Leave us alone, Pat, please.

MISS COOPER *goes out quietly.* JOHN *closes the door after her and turns to face* ANNE.

When fate plays as astounding a trick as this it must mean something, Anne, mustn't it?

ANNE. Yes, that's what I said.

JOHN. (*Harshly.*) What did you tell Wilder?

ANNE *opens her mouth to speak.*

No, no. There's no need to lie any more. I'll quote you, shall I? My dear, our little plot's gone off quite wonderfully. Thank you so much for your help. Ten minutes alone with him was all I needed to have him grovelling. My dear, it was too funny, but after only one kiss his hand was shaking so much he couldn't even light my cigarette. You should have seen it. You'd have died laughing. Oh yes. He's at my feet again, all right, and I can tread on his face just any time I like from now on.

*He has advanced on her slowly and stands facing her. She stands her ground, but looks a little scared.*

ANNE. (*Sincerely.*) John, please, don't be so angry with me. It's not as if I'd done anything so terrible. I had to see you again. I was desperate to see you again, and this was the only way I could think of—

JOHN. The only way *you* could think of, of course. You wouldn't have thought of writing me a letter, or ringing me up, or telling me the truth in there? (*He points to the dining-room.*) Oh no. You had to have your conquest, you had to have your unconditional surrender, and if you could do it by lying and cheating so much the better. It makes the greater triumph.

ANNE. That's not true. Really it isn't. Oh yes, I should have told you, John. Of course I should have told you, but you see even now I've still got a little pride left—

JOHN. And so have I, Anne, thank God. So have I.

*He puts his hands on her arms and pulls her close to him, staring at her face.*

Yes, I can see the make-up now all right. Yes, Anne, I can see little lines there that weren't there before and it won't be very long now before this face will begin to decay and then there'll be nothing left to drive a man to—

*He has slipped his hands on to her throat.*

ANNE. (*Quietly.*) Why don't you?

*He stands looking down at her for a moment and then pushes her violently away. She falls from the chair on which she has been sitting, and in her fall knocks over an occasional table.* JOHN *goes to the french windows, pulls them open, and runs out. The wind blows the curtains into the room. She gets up from the floor and stands quite still, her face expressionless. There is a mirror over the fireplace and she stares at herself for a long time. She turns quickly away and begins to sob, quietly at first, and then more violently until, as she makes her way blindly to the hall door, it is uncontrollable.* MISS COOPER *comes in before* ANNE *has reached the door.* ANNE. *seeing her barring the way, runs back into the room, still sobbing.* MISS COOPER *deliberately closes the windows, before turning to* ANNE. *Then she approaches her and puts her hand on her shoulder.*

MISS COOPER. Come to my room, won't you. Mrs. Shankland? There's a fire there and a nice comfortable chair and I've even got a little sherry, I think. We'll be quite cosy there and no one can disturb us.

*She begins to move her towards the door.*

You see, someone might come in here and we don't want that, do we? Come along now, Mrs. Shankland, Come along—

*She is leading her towards the door as*

THE LIGHTS FADE

## SCENE 3

SCENE: *The dining-room, the following morning.* MISS MEACHAM *sits at her table, poring over the sporting page of a morning paper. The two undergraduates are at their table reading. The other tables have been occupied, except for the table by the window, and* ANNE'S. MISS COOPER *comes in from the lounge.*

MISS COOPER. (*Talking into the lounge.*) Yes, Mrs. Railton-Bell, I promise I will.

*The murmur of* MRS. RAILTON-BELL'S *voice can be heard off.*

Yes, utterly disgraceful, I quite agree. I shall speak to him most severely.
*She closes the door with a faint sigh.*

(*Brightly, to the two undergraduates.*) Good morning, Miss Tanner. Good morning, Mr. Stratton.

*They reply with a polite murmur and plunge back into their books.*

Good morning, Miss Meacham. It looks as if we're going to have a nice dry day at last.

MISS MEACHAM. Is it going to be dry at Newbury?—that's the point. Walled Garden's a dog on heavy going.

MISS COOPER. Ah, now there you have me, Miss Meacham.

MABEL *comes in.*

MABEL. Miss Cooper, Mr. Malcolm wasn't in his room when I took his tea up, and his bed hadn't been slept in.

MISS COOPER. (*With a reassuring smile.*) Yes, I know, Mabel.

MABEL. You know?

MISS COOPER. I should have told you, of course, but I'm afraid I clean forgot. He had to go to London unexpectedly last night.

MABEL. He won't be in to breakfast, then?

MISS COOPER. I don't suppose so.

*The* UNDERGRADUATES *go into the lounge.*

MABEL. That's something anyway. It's nearly ten, now. What about the new lady? She's not down yet.

MISS COOPER. Yes, she's down, Mabel, but I don't think she's having breakfast.

MABEL. Not having breakfast?

MISS COOPER, She has to be very careful of her figure, you see.

MABEL. (*With puzzled gloom.*) Can't see what good a figure's going to be to you, when you're dead of starvation.

*She goes into the kitchen.*

MISS MEACHAM. She's leaving, isn't she, the new one?

MISS COOPER. Yes. She is. How did you know?

MISS MEACHAM. I heard her ask for her bags to be brought down. I knew she'd never stick it.

MISS COOPER. (*Coldly.*) *Stick* it, Miss Meacham?

MISS MEACHAM. Oh, I don't mean the hotel. Best for the price in Bournemouth. I've always said so. I meant the life. All this—(*She indicates the empty tables.*) She's not an 'alone' type.

MISS COOPER. Is any type an 'alone' type, Miss Meacham?

MISS MEACHAM. Oh yes. They're rare, of course, but *you* are for one, I'd say.

MISS COOPER. Am I?

MISS MEACHAM. Oh, I'm not saying you won't fall in love one day, and get married, or something silly like that. I'm only saying that if you don't you'll be all right. You're self-sufficient.

MISS COOPER. (*A shade wearily, but polite.*) I'm glad you think so, Miss Meacham. Perhaps even a little gladder than you realize.

MISS MEACHAM. What do you mean by that?

MISS COOPER. I've no idea. I'm a bit tired this morning. I had very little sleep last night.

MISS MEACHAM. Well—I don't suppose you *are* glad, really. Probably you haven't had to face up to it yet. I faced up to it very early on—long before I was an old wreck—while I was still young and pretty and had money and position and could choose from quite a few. (*Reminiscently.*) Quite a few. Well, I didn't choose any of them, and I've never regretted it—not for an instant. People have always scared me a bit, you see. They're so complicated. I suppose that's why I prefer the dead ones. Any trouble from them and you switch them off like a television set.

*She rises.*

No, what I've always said is—being alone, that's the real blessed state— if you've the character for it. Not Mrs. What's-her-name from Mayfair, though. I could tell that at a glance. A couple of weeks here and she'd have her head in the gas oven. It's pork for lunch, isn't it?

MISS COOPER. Yes, Miss Meacham.

MISS MEACHAM. I loathe pork. Ah well. I'd have a bit on Walled Garden, dear, if I were you. He's past the post if the going's on top.

*She goes out.* MISS COOPER, *left alone, slumps wearily into the chair* MISS MEACHAM *has vacated. She washes out* MISS MEACHAM'S *cup and pours some coffee out for herself. She sips it, and then lets her head fall wearily forward on to her chest, in an attitude of utter exhaustion. After a moment* JOHN *comes in slowly from the hall. After a look round he walks up to her quietly.*

JOHN. (*In a low voice.*) Pat. I must see you a moment.

MISS COOPER *opens her eyes and looks up at him. She jumps to her feet as she takes him in.*

MISS COOPER. Are you all right?

JOHN. Yes. I'm all right.

MISS COOPER. Where did you go?

JOHN. I don't know. I walked a long way.

MISS COOPER. Were you out all night?

JOHN. No. I sat in a shelter for a time. Pat, I've got to have some money. I'm broke to the wide. I spent my whole week's cheque in the Feathers last night—

MISS COOPER. How much do you want?

JOHN. Enough to get me on a train and keep me some place for a few days. Three or four pounds, I suppose. Can you let me have it, Pat?

MISS COOPER. You won't need it, John. She's going.

JOHN. Are you sure?

MISS COOPER. Yes.

JOHN. Where is she now?

MISS COOPER. In my office. It's all right. She won't come in here.

*She feels his clothes.*

Did you get very wet?

JOHN. Yes, I suppose so. It's dried off now.

MISS COOPER. You'd better sit down and have some breakfast. Your hands are like ice. (*She rings a bell.*)

JOHN. I don't want anything to eat. Just some tea.

MISS COOPER. All right. Now sit down. Straighten your tie a bit, and turn your collar down. That's better. Now you look quite respectable.

*She pulls out a chair for* JOHN *to sit down at his table.* DOREEN *comes in.*

DOREEN. Yes, miss? (*Seeing* JOHN.) Oh, you back? I suppose you think you can have breakfast at this time?

MISS COOPER. Just some tea, Doreen—that's all.

DOREEN. Okey doke.

*She goes into the kitchen.*

MISS COOPER. She'll have to go, that girl. (*She turns to* JOHN.) Well, that was a fine way to behave, dashing out into the night, and scaring us out of our wits—

JOHN. Us?

MISS COOPER. Oh yes. She was scared too. I stopped her from calling the police.

JOHN. So you talked, did you?

MISS COOPER. Most of the night. She was a bit hysterical and needed quieting. I didn't want to get a doctor.

JOHN. Did I—Pat, tell me the truth—did I hurt her?

MISS COOPER. Her throat? No.

JOHN. She fell though, didn't she? I seem to remember pushing her, and her falling and hitting her head—or perhaps I'm confusing it with—

MISS COOPER. (*Firmly.*) She's as right as rain. There isn't a mark on her of any kind.

JOHN. (*Murmuring.*) Thank God.

DOREEN *comes in with a pot of tea and a plate.*

DOREEN. I brought you some digestive biscuits. I know you like them.

JOHN. Thank you. Thank you, Doreen, very much.

DOREEN. Had a tumble or something? You've got mud all over your arm.

JOHN. What? Oh yes. So I have. Yes, I remember now. I fell down last night in the dark.

DOREEN. Give it to me after and I'll get it off.

*She goes out.*

MISS COOPER. I should have seen that. I'm sorry.

JOHN. It's all right. They'll just think I was drunk. How is she this morning?

MISS COOPER. A bit shaky. Quieter, though. Did you know she took drugs?

JOHN. Drugs? What sort of drugs?

MISS COOPER. Oh, just those things that make you sleep. Only she takes about three times the proper dose and takes them in the day too.

JOHN. How long has this been going on?

MISS COOPER. About a year, I gather.

JOHN. The damn little fool. Why does she do it?

MISS COOPER. (*Shrugging.*) Why do you go to the Feathers?

*Pause.*

Yes—there's not all that much to choose between you, I'd say. When you're together you slash each other to pieces, and when you're apart you slash yourselves to pieces. All told, it's quite a problem.

*Pause.*

JOHN. Why didn't she tell me about this last night?

MISS COOPER. Because she's what she is, that's why. If she'd shown you she was unhappy she'd have had to show you how much she needed you and that she'd never do—not her—not in a million years. Of course that's why she lied about coming down here. I've got rather a bad conscience about that, you know. I should never have told you. Just a flash of jealousy, I suppose. I'm sorry.

JOHN. What time is she leaving?

MISS COOPER. She's only waiting now to get some news of you. I was just going to start ringing up the hospitals. She asked me to do that.

JOHN. I see. Well, when I've finished this I'll slip out somewhere. You can tell her that I'm all right. Then when she's gone you can give me a ring.

MISS COOPER. You don't think you might tell her that yourself?

*Pause.*

JOHN. No.

MISS COOPER. It's your business, of course, but I think if I were in your place, I'd want to.

JOHN. (*Savagely.*) You don't know what it's like to be in my place. You can't even guess.

MISS COOPER. (*Quietly.*) I think I can. Gosh, I'm tired. I shouldn't be sitting here gossiping with you. I've got work to do. You'd better let me tell her you're here.

JOHN. No, Pat, don't. Give me one good reason why I should ever see her again. Just one reason—

MISS COOPER. All right. Just one then. And God knows it's not for me to say it. Because you love her and because she needs your help.

*Pause.*

JOHN. (*Suspiciously.*) What went on between you two last night? How did she win you over?

MISS COOPER. She didn't win me over, for heaven's sake. Feeling the way I do, do you think she could? Anyway, to do her justice she didn't even try. She didn't give me an act and I could see her as she is, all right. I think all you've ever told me about her is probably true. She *is* vain and spoiled and selfish and deceitful. Of course, with you being in love with her, you look at all those faults like in a kind of distorting mirror, so that they seem like monstrous sins and drive you to—well—the sort of thing that happened last night. Well, I just see them as ordinary human faults, that's all—the sort of faults a lot of people have—mostly women. I grant, but some men too. I don't like them but they don't stop me feeling sorry for a woman who's unhappy and desperate and ill and needing help more than anyone I have ever known. Well? Shall I call her in?

JOHN. No. Pat. No. Don't interfere in this. Just let her go back to London and her own life, and leave me to live the rest of mine in peace.

MISS COOPER. (*Quietly.*) That'd be fine, John, if you'd just tell me a little something first. Exactly what kind of peace *are* you living in down here?

JOHN. A kind of peace, anyway.

MISS COOPER. Is it? Is it even really living?

*He makes no reply.*

Is it, John? Be honest, now. Oh, I know there's your work and your pals at the Feathers and—well—me—but is it even living?

*Pause.*

JOHN. (*Shortly, at length.*) It'll do.

MISS COOPER. (*With a faint laugh.*) Thank you. I'm glad you didn't hand me one of those tactful tarradiddles. I *did* try—you know—when we first began—you and I—all that time ago—I *did* try to help you to get back into some sort of life. As a matter of fact I tried very hard—

JOHN. I know you did.

MISS COOPER. It didn't take me long, though, to see I hadn't a hope.

JOHN. Don't blame me for that, Pat. Circumstances, as they say, outside my control—

MISS COOPER. Outside your control? Yes. That's right. (*Quite brightly.*) When you think of it it seems really rather a pity you two ever met, doesn't it?

JOHN. Yes. A great pity.

MISS COOPER. (*Brightly.*) If you hadn't, she'd have been a millionairess, and you'd have been Prime Minister, and I'd have married Mr. Hopkins from the bank, and then we'd have all been happy. I'm going into my office now and I'm going to tell her you're here. I'll have a word with Mr. Fowler first, about a room he didn't take up, so if you want to skedaddle, you can. The door's through there and the street's outside, and down the street is the Feathers. It's a bit early, but I've no doubt they'll open for you.

*She goes into the lounge.*

(*As she goes.*) Oh, Mr. Fowler, I'm so sorry to bother you, but I just want to have a word—

*The door closes behind her. Left alone* JOHN *stands in evident doubt and irresolution. Then he sits down at his table.* DOREEN *comes in.*

DOREEN. Have you finished?

JOHN. Not quite, Doreen.

DOREEN. Make up your mind.

*She begins to clear some things from the other tables.* ANNE *comes in from the lounge.* JOHN *doesn't look at her.*

Oh, hullo, Mrs. Shankland. You're a bit late for breakfast, I'm afraid. I expect you didn't know. There's some coffee left, though, or tea if you'd rather, and I can get you some biscuits. Is that all right?

ANNE. Thank you. That's very kind. Coffee please. Not tea.

DOREEN. Righty-oh.

*She goes into the kitchen.*

ANNE. (*Standing by* JOHN'S *table, pleadingly.*) John. (*He doesn't look up.*) John—

JOHN. (*Quietly.*) You'd better sit at your table. She'll be back in a moment.

ANNE. Yes. Yes, I will.

*She sits down at her table. He remains at his.*

I was desperately worried about you.

JOHN. You needn't have been. I was quite all right. How are you now?

ANNE. All right too. (*After a pause.*) I'm going this morning, you know.

JOHN. So I heard.

ANNE. I won't bother you again. Ever again. I just wanted to say I'm sorry I had to lie to you—

JOHN. Thank you, Anne.

ANNE. I don't know why I did. Not for the reasons you gave, I think, though they may be right too, I admit. I don't seem to know very much about myself any more. I'm sorry, John.

JOHN. That's all right.

ANNE. I *am* an awful liar. I always have been—ever since school. I don't know why but I'd rather lie than tell the truth even about the simplest things. (*With a wan smile.*) It was nearly always about my lying that we used to quarrel in the old days—do you remember?

JOHN. Yes. I remember.

ANNE *lowers her head quickly as the tears come suddenly.*

ANNE. Oh, John. I don't know what's going to happen to me—

DOREEN *comes in with a tray.* ANNE *turns her head quickly away from her.* DOREEN *goes to* JOHN'S *table first, and puts down a plate of biscuits.*

DOREEN. Thought you might like some more. I know your appetite.

*She goes to* ANNE' S *table with some biscuits.* ANNE *has managed to wipe her eyes unseen.*

DOREEN. Here you are, Mrs. Shankland.

ANNE. Thank you.

DOREEN. Coffee's just coming.

DOREEN *goes out, having noticed nothing.*

ANNE. (*Smiling again.*) Narrow escape. I'm sorry. I'm in a rather weak state this morning.

JOHN. How much money exactly does Shankland give you, Anne?

ANNE. I've told you—seven fifty. (*She meets his eyes. At length, murmuring shamefacedly.*) Fifteen hundred.

JOHN. Can't you live quite happily on that?

ANNE. How can *I* live happily on anything now?

JOHN. But you don't need to be alone in London. You may not have many friends, but you have hundreds of acquaintances, and surely you can go out and enjoy yourself—

ANNE. You can be more alone in London than in this place, John. Here at least you can talk from table to table. In London it's the phone and usually no answer.

*Pause.*

JOHN. You must give up those drugs. Anne.

ANNE. She told you?

JOHN. They won't help, you know.

ANNE. I know they won't.

JOHN. Throw them all into the dustbin. They're no good, those things.

ANNE. I won't do that. I can't. I'm not strong enough. But I'll cut them down if I can.

JOHN. Try.

ANNE. I *will* try. I promise.

*Pause.*

JOHN. Tell me, Anne. When you say you need me, is it me you really mean, or just my love? Because if it's my love you must know now that you have that. You have that for life.

ANNE. It's you, John.

JOHN. But why? Why, for heaven's sake?

ANNE. I suppose because you're all the things I'm not. You're honest and true and sincere and dependable and—(*She breaks off and tries to smile.*) Oh dear, this is just becoming a boring catalogue of your virtues. Too embarrassing. I'm sorry, and that damn waitress will come in and catch me crying again.

JOHN. (*Slowly.*) I may have had some of those virtues once, Anne. I'm not at all sure that I have them now, so I don't know if I'd be able to satisfy your need. I do know though that you can never satisfy mine.

ANNE. How can you know?

JOHN. Experience.

ANNE. Supposing I'd learnt something from the last eight years?

JOHN. It's not a lesson that can be learnt.

ANNE. I could still try.

JOHN. So could I. Anne. So could I. And we'd both fail.

ANNE. How can you be so sure?

,JOHN. Because our two needs for each other are like two chemicals that are harmless by themselves, but when brought together in a test-tube can make an explosive as deadly as dynamite.

ANNE. (*Shrugging.*) I could take the risk. After all, there are worse deaths, aren't there? (*She looks round the room at the empty tables.*) Slower and more painful and more frightening. So frightening, John. So frightening. (*She lowers her head as once more the tears come.*) I'm an awful coward you see. I never have been able to face anything alone—the blitzes in the war, being ill, having operations, all that. And now I can't even face—just getting old.

JOHN *gets up quietly from his table and walks to hers. She has her head lowered and a handkerchief to her eyes, so that it is only when she has recovered herself a little that she finds him sitting there. She looks at him without saying anything. He takes her hand.*

JOHN. (*Gently.*) You realize, don't you, that we haven't very much hope together?

ANNE *nods, and holds his hand tight in hers.*

ANNE. Have we all that much apart?

DOREEN *comes in with* ANNE'S *coffee. They release their hands.*

DOREEN. (*Seeing them.*) Oh. (*To* JOHN.) Do you want your tea over there?

JOHN. Yes, please.

*She brings his cup over, and gives* ANNE *her coffee.*

　　Thank you.

DOREEN. Do you two want to sit at the same table from now on? You can, if you like.

JOHN. Yes. I think we do.

DOREEN. Oh. I'll make up a double for you for lunch then. It's just so long as we know—

*She goes into the kitchen.* JOHN *once again takes* ANNE'S *hand.*

CURTAIN

# TABLE NUMBER SEVEN

*A play in two scenes*

*Characters*
*(in order of speaking)*

JEAN STRATTON
CHARLES STRATTON
MAJOR POLLOCK
MR. FOWLER
MISS COOPER
MRS. RAILTON-BELL
MISS RAILTON-BELL
LADY MATHESON
MISS MEACHAM MABEL
DOREEN


SCENE 1: LOUNGE. AFTER TEA.
SCENE 2: DINING-ROOM. DINNER.

SCENE: *The lounge of the Beauregard Private Hotel. It is, perhaps, eighteen months or so since the events of the preceding play, but apart from a rearrangement of the chairs to accord with the summer season, and a set of new covers on those chairs, there has been little alteration.*

CHARLES STRATTON, *in flannels and sports-shirt, lies on the sofa, reading some large medical treatise. Through the french windows, which are open,* JEAN STRATTON (*nee* JEAN TANNER) *appears pulling a pram.*

JEAN. (*To the unseen baby.*) Tum along now. Tum along. Tum and see Daddy— Daddy will give you a little tiss and then beddy-byes—

CHARLES' *face shows his annoyance at the interruption to his studies.*

CHARLES. Bed-time, already?

JEAN. After six. How are you getting along?

CHARLES. Miles behind. Endless interruptions. It was idiotic to come back to this place. I should have remembered what it was like from the last time. We could have borrowed David's cottage—

JEAN. Nasty air in the Thames Valley. Not good for baby. Bournemouth air much better, (*to baby*) isn't it, my little lammykins? He says, Yes Mummy, lovely air, lovely sun, makes baby teep like an ickle top—

CHARLES. He doesn't say anything of the sort. All he ever appears to say is 'goo'. I'm getting a bit worried.

JEAN. Don't be silly, darling. What do you expect him to do at five months? Quote T. S. Eliot?

CHARLES. I think all this 'tum along' stuff you smother him in is bad for him. It's very dangerous, too, you know. It can lead to arrested development later on—

JEAN. (*Complacently.*) What nonsense you do talk.

*She has now sat on the sofa beside him and kisses him fondly. He turns from the caress a trifle brusquely.*

JEAN. Give me a proper kiss.

CHARLES. (*Murmuring.*) A kiss, but not a tiss.

*He kisses her with a little more warmth, then breaks off.*

JEAN. Go on.

CHARLES. No.

JEAN. Why not?

CHARLES. It's too early.

JEAN. You're so horribly coarse-grained sometimes that I wonder why I love you so much. But I do, you know, that's the awful thing. I've been thinking all the afternoon how much I loved you. Funny how it seems sort of to have crept up on me like this— Did it creep up on you too, or did you lie in your teeth before we got married?

CHARLES. I lied in my teeth. Now take baby up to beddy-byes, dear, and leave Daddy to his worky-perky—or Daddy won't ever become a docky-wocky.

*There is the sound of a loud jovial voice in the garden.*

MAJOR POLLOCK. (*Off.*) Hullo, 'ullo, Miss Meacham. Working out the form, eh? Got any tips for tomorrow?

MISS MEACHAM. (*Off.*) Let me see.

CHARLES. Oh God! Here's the Major. Go on, darling, for heaven's sake. If he sees the baby we're lost. He'll talk for hours about infant welfare in Polynesia or something.

JEAN. All right. (*To baby.*) Tum along then— (*She meets* CHARLES' *eyes. Firmly.*) Come along, then, Vincent Michael Charles. It is time for your bath and subsequently for your bed. Better?

MISS MEACHAM. (*Off.*) Red Robin in the three-thirty.

CHARLES. Much.

*He blows her a kiss as she goes out into the hall with the pram, from which emerges a faint wail.*

JEAN. (*As she goes.*) Oh. Did Mummy bring him out of 'ovely garden into nasty dark pace. Naughty Mummy.

*Her voice subsides.* CHARLES *returns to his book.*

MAJOR POLLOCK. (*Off.*) Red Robin in the three-thirty? I'll remember that. Not that I can afford much these days, you know. Not like the old days when one would ring up the hall porter at White's, and get him to put on a couple of ponies. Lovely day, what?

MISS MEACHAM. (*Off.*) Not bad.

MAJOR POLLOCK *comes in. He is in the middle fifties, with a clipped military moustache and extremely neat clothes. In fact both in dress and appearance he is almost too exact a replica of the retired major to be entirely true.*

MAJOR POLLOCK. Hullo, Stratton. Still at it?

CHARLES. (*With only the most perfunctory look-up from his book.*) Yes, Major.

MAJOR POLLOCK. Don't know how you do it. Really don't. Most praiseworthy effort, I think.

CHARLES. Thank you, Major.

*Pause. The* MAJOR *sits.*

MAJOR POLLOCK. Of course when I was at Sandhurst—oh so sorry—mustn't disturb you, must I?

CHARLES. (*Politely lowering his book.*) That's all right, Major. When you were at Sandhurst?

MAJOR POLLOCK. Well, I was going to say that I was a bit like you. Off duty, while most of the other young fellers were gallivanting about in town, I used to be up in my room, or in the library there, cramming away like mad. Military history—great battles of the world—Clausewitz—that sort of stuff. I could have told you quite a lot about Clausewitz once.

CHARLES. Oh. And you can't now?

MAJOR POLLOCK. No. Afraid not. Everything goes, you know. Everything goes.

Still I didn't regret all those hours of study at the time. I did jolly well at Sandhurst.

CHARLES. Did you get the Sword of Honour?

MAJOR POLLOCK. What? No. Came quite close to it, though. Passed out pretty high. Pretty high. Not that it did me much good later on—except that they made me battalion adjutant because I was good at paper work. Could have been brigade major, as it happens. Turned it down because I thought if trouble came—well—you know—miles behind the line— away from one's own chaps. I suppose it was a bit foolish. I'd probably have been a general now, on full pay. Promotion was always a bit tight in the Black Watch. Should have chosen another regiment, I suppose.

CHARLES. (*Plainly hoping to terminate the conversation.*) Yes.

MAJOR POLLOCK. Go on my boy. Go on. So sorry. I talk too much. That's usually the trouble with old retired majors, what.

CHARLES. Not at all, sir. But I will go on, if you don't mind. I've rather a lot to do.

*There is a pause.* CHARLES *continues reading. The* MAJOR *gets up and, taking infinite pains not to make a sound, tiptoes to a table where he picks up a magazine, and tiptoeing back, sits down again.* CHARLES *has plainly been aware of the* MAJOR'S *tactfully silent passage.* MR. FOWLER *comes through the french windows, holding a letter.*

MR. FOWLER. Oh, hullo, Major. I've just had the most charming letter—

MAJOR POLLOCK. (*Putting his fingers to his lips, and indicating* CHARLES.) Sh!

CHARLES *gets up resignedly and goes to the door.*

Oh, I say. I do hope we're not driving you away.

CHARLES. No, that's quite all right. I can always concentrate much better in my room.

MAJOR POLLOCK. But you've got the baby up there. haven't you?

CHARLES. Yes, but it's a very quiet baby. It hasn't learnt to talk yet.

*He goes out.*

MAJOR POLLOCK. Well, Fowler, who's your letter from? An old flame?

MR. FOWLER. (*Chuckling happily.*) Old flame? I haven't got any old flames. I leave that to you galloping majors.

MAJOR POLLOCK. Well, I used to do all right once, I must say. In the regiment they used to call me Bucko Pollock. Regency buck—you see. Still, those days are past and gone. *Eheu fugaces, Postume, Postume.*

MR. FOWLER. (*Correcting his accent.*) *Eheu fugaces, Postume, Postume.* Didn't they teach you the new pronunciation at Wellington?

MAJOR POLLOCK. No. The old.

MR. FOWLER. When were you there?

MAJOR POLLOCK. Now let's think. It must have been nineteen eighteen I went up—

MR. FOWLER. But they were using the new pronunciation then, I know. Our head classics master was an old Wellingtonian, and I remember distinctly his telling me—

MAJOR POLLOCK. Well, perhaps they did and I've forgotten it. Never was much of a hand at Greek.

MR. FOWLER. (*Shocked.*) Latin. Horace.

MAJOR POLLOCK. Horace, of course. Stupid of me. (*Plainly changing the subject.*) Well, who is your letter from?

MR. FOWLER. It's a boy who used to be in my house and I haven't heard from for well over ten years. Brilliant boy he was, and done very well since. I can't think how he knew I was down here. Very good of him, I must say.

MAJOR POLLOCK. What happened to that other ex-pupil of yours—the painter feller?

MR. FOWLER. Oh. I still read about him in the newspapers occasionally. But I'm afraid I don't get much personal news of him. We've—rather lost touch, lately.

MISS COOPER *comes in with a newspaper under her arm.*

MISS COOPER. Good afternoon, Major, we've managed to get your copy of the *West Hampshire Weekly News.*

MAJOR POLLOCK. (*Eagerly.*) Good afternoon, Miss Cooper.

MISS COOPER. (*Handing him the newspaper.*) Joe had to go to three places before he could find one.

MAJOR POLLOCK. Thank you very much.

MISS COOPER. What was the urgency?

MAJOR POLLOCK. Oh—I just wanted to have a look at it, you know. I've never read it—strange to say—although I've been here—what is it—four years?

MISS COOPER. I'm not surprised. There's never anything in it except parking offences and cattle shows.

*The* MAJOR *opens the paper, turning away from her.*

MAJOR POLLOCK. Well, thanks anyway.

MR. FOWLER. I've had a charming letter, Miss Cooper, from someone I haven't seen or heard from in over ten years.

MISS COOPER. (*Brightly.*) How nice. I'm so glad.

MR. FOWLER. I'm going to write to him and ask him if he'd care to come down for a day or two. Of course he probably won't—but just in case he does, will that room be vacant?

MISS COOPER. Not at the moment, I'm afraid, Mr. Fowler. We have so many casuals. But at the end of September—

MR. FOWLER. Good. I'll ask him for then.

*During this interchange between* MISS COOPER *and* MR. FOWLER, MAJOR POLLOCK, *unseen by them, has turned the pages of his paper over quickly, as if he was searching for something. Suddenly his eye is evidently caught by what he reads, and he folds the paper back with a sharp sound.* MR. FOWLER *looks up at him.*

MR. FOWLER. You were with the Highland Division at Alamein, weren't you, Major?

*There is no immediate reply. When the* MAJOR *does look up his eyes are glassy and staring.*

MAJOR POLLOCK. What? No. No I wasn't. Not with the Highland Division.

MR. FOWLER. I thought you were.

MAJOR POLLOCK. (*Almost fiercely.*) I never said so.

MR. FOWLER. I just wondered because this boy—Macleod his name is—James, I think, or John—anyway he was known at school as Curly—he says in this letter he was with the Highland Division. I just wondered if you'd run into him at all.

MAJOR POLLOCK. Macleod? No. No, I don't think so.

MR. FOWLER. Well, of course, it would have been very unlikely if you had. It was just possible, though.

*He goes to the door.* MISS COOPER *has been straightening cushions and tidying up.* MAJOR POLLOCK *sits down, holding his paper, and staring blankly into space.*

(*To himself.*) Curly Macleod. He once elided a whole word in his Greek Iambics—

*He chuckles to himself and goes out.* MAJOR POLLOCK *looks down again at his paper, and, as* MISS COOPER *straightens herself from her labours, pretends to be reading it casually.*

MAJOR POLLOCK. Yes. Pretty dull, I grant you.

MISS COOPER. What?

MAJOR POLLOCK. This paper. I don't suppose it's much read, is it?

MISS COOPER. Only by locals, I suppose. Farmers, estate agents—those sort of people.

MAJOR POLLOCK. I've never heard of anyone in the hotel reading it—have you?

MISS COOPER. Oh yes. Mrs. Railton-Bell takes it every week.

MAJOR POLLOCK. Does she? Whatever for?

MISS COOPER. I don't know, I'm sure. There's not a lot that goes on in the world—even in West Hampshire—that she likes to miss. And she can afford fourpence for the information, I suppose.

MAJOR POLLOCK. (*Laughing jovially.*) Yes, I suppose so. Funny, though—I've never seen her reading it.

MISS COOPER. Oh, she gets a lot of things sent in to her that she never reads. Most of the stuff on that table over there is hers—

MAJOR POLLOCK. Yes. Yes, I know. She'd have had hers this morning then, I suppose?

MISS COOPER. Yes. I suppose so.

MAJOR POLLOCK. Oh. Dash it all. Here I've gone and spent fourpence for nothing. I mean I could have borrowed hers, couldn't I?

*He laughs heartily.* MISS COOPER *smiles politely and having finished her tidying up, goes to the door.*

MISS COOPER. I know you don't like venison, Major, so I've ordered you a chop for lunch tomorrow. Only I must ask you to be discreet about it, if you don't mind.

MAJOR POLLOCK. Yes, of course. Of course. Thank you so much, Miss Cooper.

MISS COOPER *goes out.* MAJOR POLLOCK *opens the paper quickly and stares at it for some time, reading avidly. Then he suddenly rips out the whole page, crum-*

*pling it up and thrusting it into his pocket. Then he goes quickly to the ta-*
*ble, and, after a feverish search, finds the 'West Hampshire Weekly News'.*
*He has turned it over to find the evidently offending page when* MRS. RAILTON-
BELL *walks into the room from the hall, followed by her daughter* SIBYL. *The*
*latter is a timid-looking, wizened creature in the thirties, bespectacled, dowdy*
*and without make-up.*

MRS. RAILTON-BELL. (*As she enters.*) Well, if that's what you meant, you should
have said so, dear. I wish you'd learn to express yourself a little bit better— Good afternoon, Major Pollock.

MAJOR POLLOCK. Good afternoon, Mrs. Railton-Bell. (*Jovially to* SIBYL.) Afternoon, Miss R.B.

*He is holding the paper, unable to hide it, or put it back on the table. He sees*
*that* MRS. RAILTON-BELL *has noticed it.*

I'm so sorry. I was just glancing through your *West Hampshire News*. I
wonder if you'd let me borrow it for a few moments. There's something
in it I want to see.

MRS. RAILTON-BELL. Very well, Major. Only please return it.

MAJOR POLLOCK. Of course.

*He goes to the door.* MRS. RAILTON-BELL *has moved to her seat. As she does so she*
*picks up the other copy of the 'West Hampshire Weekly News' from the floor,*
*where* MAJOR POLLOCK *has dropped it.*

MRS. RAILTON-BELL. What's this? Here's another copy—

MAJOR POLLOCK. (*Feigning astonishment.*) Of the *West Hampshire Weekly News?*

MRS. RAILTON-BELL. Yes.

MAJOR POLLOCK. Well I'm dashed.

MRS. RAILTON-BELL. It was on the floor over here.

MAJOR POLLOCK. Must be one of the casuals, I suppose.

MRS. RAILTON-BELL. You'd better take it, anyway, and leave me mine.

MAJOR POLLOCK. (*Doubtfully.*) You don't think, whoever owns it, might—

MRS. RAILTON-BELL. If it's been thrown down on the floor, it's plainly been
read. I'd like mine back, if you don't mind, please, Major.

MAJOR POLLOCK. (*Conceding defeat.*) Righty-oh. I'll put it back with the others.

*He does so, and takes the other copy from* MRS. RAILTON-BELL.

Think I'll just go out for a little stroll.

SIBYL. (*Shyly.*) You don't happen to want company, do you, Major Pollock? I
haven't had my walk yet.

MAJOR POLLOCK. (*Embarrassed.*) Well, Miss R.B.—jolly nice suggestion and
all that—the only thing is I'm going to call on a friend—you see—and—

SIBYL. (*More embarrassed than he.*) Oh yes, yes. Of course. I'm so sorry.

MAJOR POLLOCK. No, no. I'm the one who's sorry. Well, cheeriebye till dinner.

*He goes out.*

MRS. RAILTON-BELL. I wish he wouldn't use that revolting expression. It's so
common. But then he is common—

SIBYL. Oh no, Mummy. Do you think so? He was in a very good regiment.

MRS. RAILTON-BELL. You can be in the Horse Guards and still be common, dear. (*Gently.*) Sibyl, my dearest, do you mind awfully if your tactless old mother whispers something in your ear?

SIBYL. (*Resigned.*) No.

MRS. RAILTON-BELL. I didn't think it was *terribly* wise of you to lay yourself open to that snub just now.

SIBYL. It wasn't a snub, Mummy. I'm sure he really *was* going to see a friend—

MRS. RAILTON-BELL *smiles understandingly and sympathetically, shaking her head ever so slightly.*

Well, I often *do* go for walks with the Major.

MRS. RAILTON-BELL. I know you do, dear. What is more quite a lot of people have noticed it.

*Pause.* SIBYL *stares at her mother.*

SIBYL. (*At length.*) You don't mean—you can't mean—(*She jumps up and holds her cheeks with a sudden gesture.*) Oh no. How can people be so awful!

MRS. RAILTON-BELL. It's not being particularly awful when an unattached girl is noticed constantly seeking the company of an attractive older man.

SIBYL. (*Still holding her cheeks.*) They think I chase him. Is that it? They think I run after him, they think I want—they think—no it *is* awful. It *is*. It *is*. It *is*.

MRS. RAILTON-BELL. (*Sharply.*) Quieten yourself my dear. Don't get into one of your *states*, now.

SIBYL. It's all right, Mummy. I'm not in a state. It's just—well—it's just so dreadful that people should believe such a thing is even possible. I hate that side of life. I hate it.

MRS. RAILTON-BELL. (*Soothingly.*) I know you do, dear. But it exists, all the same, and one has to be very careful in this world not to give people the wrong impression. Quieter now?

SIBYL. Yes. Mummy.

MRS. RAILTON-BELL. Good. You must try not to let these things upset you so much, dear.

SIBYL. I only go for walks with the Major because I like hearing him talk. I like all his stories about London and the war and the regiment—and—well—he's seen so much of life and I haven't—

MRS. RAILTON-BELL. I don't know what you mean by that, dear, I'm sure.

SIBYL. I only meant— (*She checks herself.*) I'm sorry.

MRS. RAILTON-BELL. (*Relentlessly pursuing her prey.*) Of course I realize that you must occasionally miss some of the gaieties of life—the balls and the cocktail parties and things—that a few other lucky young people can enjoy. I can assure you, dearest, if I could possibly afford it, you'd have them. But I do do my best, you know.

SIBYL. I know you do, Mummy.

MRS. RAILTON-BELL. There was Rome last year, and our Scandinavian cruise the year before—

SIBYL. I know, Mummy. I know. Don't think I'm not grateful. Please. It's
  only— (*She stops.*)

MRS. RAILTON-BELL. (*Gentle prompting.*) Only what, dear?

SIBYL. If only I could *do* something. After all, I'm thirty-three—

MRS. RAILTON-BELL. Now, my dear. We've been over this so often. Dearest
  child, you'd never stand any job for more than a few weeks. Remember
  Jones & Jones?

SIBYL. But that was because I had to work in a basement, and I used to feel
  stifled and faint. But there must be something else.

MRS. RAILTON-BELL. (*Gently patting her hand.*) You're not a very strong child,
  dear. You must get that into your head. Your nervous system isn't nearly
  as sound as it should be.

SIBYL. You mean my *states?* But I haven't had one of those for a long time—

MRS. RAILTON-BELL. No, dear—you've been doing very well. Very well, indeed. But there's quite a big difference between not having hysterical fits
  and being strong enough to take on a job. (*Concluding the topic decisively.*) Hand me that newspaper, would you, dear?

SIBYL. Which one?

MRS. RAILTON-BELL. The *West Hampshire Weekly News.* I want to see what the
  Major was so interested in.

SIBYL *hands her the paper.* MRS. RAILTON-BELL *fumbles in her pockets.*
  Oh, dear me, what a silly billy! I've gone and left my glasses and my book
  in the shelter at the end of Ragusa Road. Oh dear, I do hope they're not
  stolen. I expect they're bound to be. Now—doesn't that show how de-
  pendent I am on you, my dear? If you hadn't had that headache you'd
  have been with me this afternoon, and then you'd never have allowed
  me to—

SIBYL. I'll go and look for them.

MRS. RAILTON-BELL. Oh, would you, dear? That really is so kind of you. I hate
  you to fetch and carry for me, as you know—but my old legs are just a
  wee bit tired—it was the far end of the shelter, facing the sea.

SIBYL. Where we usually sit? I know.

*She goes out.* MRS. RAILTON-BELL *opens the paper and scanning it very close to
  her eyes, she turns the pages to what she plainly knows, from past experience,
  to be the interesting section. Suddenly she stops moving the paper across her
  eyes. We do not see her face but the paper itself begins to shake slightly as she
  reads.* LADY MATHESON *comes in.*

LADY MATHESON. Oh, hullo dear. It's nearly time for the newsreel.

MRS. RAILTON-BELL. (*In a strained voice.*) Gladys, have you got your glasses?

LADY MATHESON. Yes, I think so. (*She feels in her pocket.*) Yes, here they are.

MRS. RAILTON-BELL. Then read this out to me.

*She hands her the paper and points.*

LADY MATHESON. (*Unsuspecting.*) Where, dear? Lorry driver loses licence?

MRS. RAILTON-BELL. No, no. Ex-officer bound over.

LADY MATHESON. (*Brightly.*) Oh yes. (*Reading.*) 'Ex-officer bound over. Offence in cinema.' (*Looking up.*) In cinema? Oh dear—do we really want to hear this?

MRS. RAILTON-BELL. (*Grimly.*) Yes, we do. Go on.

LADY MATHESON. (*Reading, resignedly.*) 'On Thursday last, before the Bournemouth Magistrates, David Angus Pollock, 55, giving his address as (*she starts violently*) the Beauregard Hotel, Morgan Crescent—' (*In a feverish whisper.*) Major Pollock? Oh!

MRS. RAILTON-BELL. Go on.

LADY MATHESON. (*Reading.*) 'Morgan Crescent—pleaded guilty to a charge of insulting behaviour in a Bournemouth cinema.' Oh! Oh! 'On the complaint of a Mrs. Osborn, 43 (*breathlessly*) of 4 Studland Road.' He must have been drinking—

MRS. RAILTON-BELL. He's a teetotaller.

LADY MATHESON. Perhaps just that one night.

MRS. RAILTON-BELL. No. Read on.

LADY MATHESON. 'Mrs. Osborn, giving evidence, stated that Pollock, sitting next to her, persistently nudged her in the arm, and later attempted to take other liberties. She subsequently vacated her seat and complained to an usherette. Inspector Franklin, giving evidence, said that in response to a telephone call from the cinema manager, Pollock had been kept under observation by police officers from three fifty-three p.m. until seven-ten p.m. by which time he had been observed to change his seat no less than five times, always choosing a seat next to a female person. There had, he admitted, been no further complaints, but that was not unusual in cases of this kind. On leaving the cinema Pollock was arrested and after being charged and cautioned stated: "You have made a terrible mistake. You have the wrong man. I was only in the place half an hour. I am a colonel in the Scots Guards." Later he made a statement. Appearing on behalf of the defendant, Mr. William Crowther, solicitor, stated that his client had had a momentary aberration. He was extremely sorry and ashamed of himself and would undertake never to behave in so stupid and improper a manner in future. He asked that his client's blameless record should be taken into account. He had enlisted in the army in 1925 and in 1939 was granted a commission as second lieutenant in the Royal Army Service Corps. During the war, he had held a responsible position in charge of an Army Supply Depot in the Orkney Islands, and had been discharged in 1946 with the rank of full lieutenant. Pollock was not called. The Chairman of the Bench, giving judgment, said: "You have behaved disgustingly, but because this appears to be your first offence we propose to deal leniently with you." The defendant was bound over for twelve months.'

*She lowers the paper, disturbed and flustered to the core of her being.*

Oh dear. Oh dear. Oh dear.

MRS. RAILTON-BELL. (*Perfectly composed but excited.*) Thursday. It must have happened on Wednesday. Do you remember—he missed dinner that night?

LADY MATHESON. Did he? Yes, so he did. Oh dear. It's all too frightful! I can hardly believe it. Persistently. It's so dreadful.

MRS. RAILTON-BELL. On the Thursday he was terribly nervous and depressed. I remember now. And then on the Friday, suddenly as bright as a button. Of course he must have read the papers and thought he'd got away with it. What a stroke of luck that I get this weekly one sent to me.

LADY MATHESON. Luck, dear? Is it luck?

MRS. RAILTON-BELL. Of course it's luck. Otherwise we'd never have known.

LADY MATHESON. Wouldn't that have been better?

MRS. RAILTON-BELL. Gladys! What *are* you saying?

LADY MATHESON. I don't know, oh dear. I'm so fussed and confused. No, of course, it wouldn't have been better. One has to know these things, I suppose—although sometimes I wonder why.

MRS. RAILTON-BELL. Because if there's a liar and a fraudulent crook and a—I can't bring myself to say it—wandering around among us unsuspected, there could be—well—there could be the most terrible repercussions.

LADY MATHESON. Well, he's been wandering around among us for four years now and there haven't been any repercussions yet. (*With a faint sigh.*) I suppose we're too old.

MRS. RAILTON-BELL. (*Coldly.*) I have a daughter, you know.

LADY MATHESON. Oh. Poor Sibyl. Yes. And she's such a friend of his, isn't she? Oh dear.

MRS. RAILTON-BELL. Exactly.

LADY MATHESON. (*After a moment's troubled reflection.*) Maud, dear—it's not my business, I know, and of course you have a mother's duty to protect your child, that of course I do see—and yet—well—she's such a strange girl—so excitable and shy—and so ungrownup in so many ways—

MRS. RAILTON-BELL. Come to the point, Gladys.

LADY MATHESON. Yes, I will. It's this. I don't think you ought to tell her this.

MRS. RAILTON-BELL. Not *tell* her?

LADY MATHESON. Well, not all of it. Not the details. Say he's a fraud, if you like, but not—please, Maud—not about the cinema. (*Suddenly distressed by the thought herself.*) Oh dear! I don't know how I shall ever look him in the face again.

MRS. RAILTON-BELL. You won't have to, dear. (*She has risen purposefully from her chair.*) I'm going to see Miss Cooper now, and insist that he leaves this hotel before dinner tonight.

LADY MATHESON. Oh dear. I wonder if you should?

MRS. RAILTON-BELL. Gladys, what *has* come over you this evening? Of course I should.

LADY MATHESON. But you know what Miss Cooper is—so independent and stubborn sometimes. She might not agree.

MRS. RAILTON-BELL. Of course she'll agree. She *has* to agree if we all insist.

LADY MATHESON. But we don't *all*. I mean it's just the two of us. Shouldn't we consult the others first? (*Suddenly realizing the implication.*) Oh gracious! Of course that means we'll have to tell them all, doesn't it?

MRS. RAILTON-BELL. (*Delighted.*) An excellent idea, Gladys. Where's Mr. Fowler?

LADY MATHESON. In his room, I think.

MRS. RAILTON-BELL. And the young people? Shall we have them? They count as regulars by now, I suppose. Yes. We'll have them too.

LADY MATHESON. Oh dear. I hate telling tales.

MRS. RAILTON-BELL. Telling tales? (*She points dramatically to the 'West Hampshire Weekly News'.*) The tale is told already, Gladys—to the world.

LADY MATHESON. Well, strictly speaking—only to West Hampshire.

MRS. RAILTON-BELL. Don't quibble, Gladys. (*At the french windows.*) Miss Meacham's in the garden. I really don't think we need bother about Miss Meacham. She's so odd and unpredictable—and getting odder and more unpredictable every day. Here comes Sibyl. Go up and get the others down, dear. I'll deal with her.

LADY MATHESON. Maud, you won't—

SIBYL *comes in.*

You'll remember what I said, won't you?

MRS. RAILTON-BELL. Yes, of course. Go on, dear.

LADY MATHESON *goes out.*

(*To* SIBYL.) Clever girl. You found them, did you, darling?

*She takes the book and the glasses from* SIBYL. *There is a pause.*

(*At length.*) Sibyl dear. I think you'd better go to your room if you don't mind.

SIBYL. Why, Mummy?

MRS. RAILTON-BELL. We're holding a meeting of the regulars down here to discuss a very urgent matter that has just cropped up.

SIBYL. Oh, but how exciting. Can't I stay? After all, I'm a regular, too—

MRS. RAILTON-BELL. I know, dear, but I doubt if the subject of the meeting is quite suitable for you.

SIBYL. Why, Mummy? What is it?

MRS. RAILTON-BELL. Oh dear! You're such an inquisitive child. Very well, then. I'll tell you this much—but only this much. We are going to discuss whether or not we think that Miss Cooper should be told to ask Major Pollock to leave this hotel at once and never come back.

SIBYL. (*Aghast.*) What? But I don't understand. Why, Mummy? (MRS. RAILTON-BELL *does not reply.*) Mummy, tell me, why?

MRS. RAILTON-BELL. I can't tell you, dear. It might upset you too much.

SIBYL. But I must know, Mummy. I must. What has he done?

MRS. RAILTON-BELL. (*After only the slightest hesitation.*) You really *insist* I should tell you?

SIBYL. Yes, I do.

MRS. RAILTON-BELL. Even after my strong warning?

SIBYL. Yes.

MRS. RAILTON-BELL. (*With a sigh.*) Very well, then, dear. I have no option, I suppose.

*With a quick gesture she hands the paper to* SIBYL.

Read that. Middle column. Half-way down. Ex-officer bound over.

SIBYL *reads.* MRS. RAILTON-BELL *watches her. Suddenly* SIBYL *sits, her eyes staring, but her face blank.* LADY MATHESON *comes in. She sees* SIBYL, *instantly.*

LADY MATHESON. (*Shocked.*) Oh, Maud, you haven't—

MRS. RAILTON-BELL. I did my best, my dear, but she insisted. She absolutely insisted. (*Solicitously bending over her daughter's chair.*) I'm so sorry, my dear. It must be the most dreadful shock for you. It was for us too, as you can imagine. Are you all right?

SIBYL *takes her spectacles off and folding the paper meticulously, lays it down on the arm of her chair. She makes no reply.*

(*Slightly more sharply.*) Are you all right, Sibyl?

SIBYL. (*Barely audible.*) Yes, Mummy.

JEAN *comes in, looking rather annoyed.*

JEAN. What is it, Mrs. Railton-Bell? I can only stay a moment. I must get back to the baby.

MRS. RAILTON-BELL. I won't keep you long, I promise you. Take a seat. (*Turning to* SIBYL, *sharply.*) Sibyl, what have you done?

CHARLES *comes in.*

(*She takes* SIBYL'S *glasses from her hand.*) Look, you've broken your glasses.

SIBYL. (*Murmuring.*) How stupid.

CHARLES. Hullo, you've cut your hand, haven't you?

SIBYL. No.

CHARLES. Yes, you have. Let's see.

*With a rather professional air he picks up her limp hand and examines it.*

Nothing much. No splinters. Here, you'd better have this. It's quite clean.

*He takes a clean handkerchief from his breast pocket and ties it neatly round her hand.*

Iodine and a bit of plaster later.

MR. FOWLER *has come in.*

MRS. RAILTON-BELL. Ah, Mr. Fowler, good. Would you take a seat, and then we can begin. The two young people are in a hurry. I'm afraid I have very grave news for you all.

CHARLES. The boiler's gone wrong again?

MRS. RAILTON-BELL. No. I only wish it were something so trivial.

CHARLES. I don't consider shaving in cold, brown water trivial.

MRS. RAILTON-BELL. Please, Mr. Stratton.

MR. FOWLER. (*Anxiously.*) They're raising the prices again?

MRS. RAILTON-BELL. No. My news is graver even than that.

MR. FOWLER. I don't know what could be graver than that.

MRS. RAILTON-BELL. The news I have to give you, Mr Fowler.

CHARLES. Look, Mrs. Railton-Bell, must we play twenty questions? Can't you just tell us what it is?

MRS. RAILTON-BELL. (*Angrily.*) My hesitation is only because the matter is so painful and so embarrassing for me that I find it difficult to choose my words. However, if you want it baldly, you shall have it. (*After a dramatic pause.*) Major Pollock—who is not a major at all but a lieutenant promoted from the ranks in the R.A.S.C.—

CHARLES. (*Excitedly.*) No. You don't say! I knew it, you know. I always knew Sandhurst and the Black Watch was a phoney. Didn't I say so, Jean?

JEAN. Yes, you did, but I said it first—that night he made the boob about serviettes.

MR. FOWLER. (*Chipping in quickly.*) I must admit I've always slightly suspected the public-school education. I mean only today he made the most shocking mistake in quoting Horace—quite appalling.

MRS. RAILTON-BELL. (*Raising her voice.*) Please, please, ladies and gentlemen. This is not the point. The dreadful, the really ghastly revelation is still to come.

*She gains silence, and once again pauses dramatically.*

He was found guilty—

LADY MATHESON. Pleaded guilty—

MRS. RAILTON-BELL. Please. Gladys. He was found or pleaded guilty—I don't really see that it matters which—to behaving insultingly to no less than six respectable women in a Bournemouth cinema.

*There is an aghast silence.*

CHARLES. (*At length.*) Good God! What a performance.

LADY MATHESON. Really, Maud, I must correct that. I must. We only know one was respectable—the one who complained—and even she seemed a little odd in her behaviour. Why didn't she just say straight out to the Major: 'I do wish you'd stop doing whatever it is that you are doing'? That's what I'd have done. About the other five we don't know anything at all. We don't even know if he nudged them or anything.

MRS. RAILTON-BELL. Of course he nudged them. He was in that cinema for an immoral purpose—he admitted it. And he was seen to change his seat five times—always choosing one next to female persons.

CHARLES. That could make ten nudges, really, couldn't it? If he had the chance of using both elbows.

JEAN. Eleven, with the original one. Or twelve, supposing—

MRS. RAILTON-BELL. Really, we seem to be losing the essential point in a welter of trivialities. The point is surely that the Major—the so-called Major— has pleaded guilty to a criminal offence of a disgusting nature, and I want to know what action we regular residents propose to take.

MR. FOWLER. What action do you propose, Mrs. Railton-Bell?

MRS. RAILTON-BELL. I propose, on your behalf, to go to Miss Cooper and demand that he leaves the hotel forthwith.

CHARLES. No.

MRS. RAILTON-BELL. You disagree, Mr. Stratton?

CHARLES. Yes, I do. Please don't think I'm making light of this business, Mrs. Railton-Bell. To me what he's done, if he's done it, seems ugly and repulsive. I've always had an intense dislike of the more furtive forms of sexual expression. So emotionally I'm entirely on your side. But logically I'm not.

MRS. RAILTON-BELL. (*Cuttingly.*) Are you making a speech, Mr. Stratton? If so, perhaps you'd like to stand over there and address us.

CHARLES. No. I'm all right where I am, thank you. I'm not making a speech either. I'm just saying that my dislike of the Major's offence is emotional and not logical. My lack of understanding of it is probably a shortcoming in me. The Major presumably understands my form of lovemaking. I *should* therefore understand his. But I don't. So I am plainly in a state of prejudice against him, and must be very wary of any moral judgments I may pass in this matter. It's only fair to approach it from the purely logical standpoint of practical Christian ethics, and ask myself the question: 'What harm has the man done?' Well, apart from possibly slightly bruising the arm of a certain lady, whose motives in complaining—I agree with Lady Matheson—are extremely questionable—apart from that, and apart from telling us a few rather pathetic lies about his past life, which most of us do anyway from time to time, I really can't see he's done anything to justify us chucking him out into the street.

JEAN. (*Hotly.*) I don't agree at all. I feel disgusted at what he's done too, but I think I'm quite right to feel disgusted. I don't consider myself prejudiced at all, and I think that people who behave like that are a public menace and deserve anything they get.

CHARLES. Your vehemence is highly suspect. I must have you psycho-analysed.

JEAN. It's absolutely logical, Charles. Supposing next time it's a daughter—

CHARLES. (*Wearily.*) I know. I know. And supposing in twenty or thirty years' time she sits next to a Major Pollock in a cinema—

JEAN. Exactly. (*He laughs.*) It's not funny, Charles. How would you feel—

CHARLES. Very ashamed of her if she didn't use her elbows back, very hard, and in the right place.

JEAN. Charles, I think that's an absolutely monstrous—

MRS. RAILTON-BELL. Please, please, please. This is not a private argument between the two of you. I take it, Mr. Stratton, you are against any action regarding this matter? (CHARLES *nods.*) Of any kind at all?

CHARLES *shakes his head.*

Not even a protest?

CHARLES. I might give him a reproving glance at dinner.

MRS. RAILTON-BELL. (*Turning from him in disgust.*) You, Mrs. Stratton, I gather, agree with me that I should see Miss Cooper.

JEAN. (*Firmly.*) Yes.

CHARLES. (*Murmuring to her.*) Book-burner.

JEAN. (*Furiously.*) What's book-burning got to do with it?

CHARLES. A lot.

MRS. RAILTON-BELL. (*Imperiously.*) Quiet please. (*Turning to* MR. FOWLER.) Mr. Fowler? What do you think?

MR. FOWLER. (*Confused.*) Well, it's difficult. Very difficult. I can't say I see it like Stratton. That's the modern viewpoint, I know—nothing is really wrong that doesn't do actual and assessible harm to another human being. But he's not correct when he calls that Christianity. Christianity, surely, goes much further than that. Certain acts are wrong because they are, in themselves and by themselves, impure and immoral, and it seems to me that this terrible wave of vice and sexual excess which seems to have flooded this country since the war might well, in part, be due to the decline of the old standards, emotional and illogical though they may well seem to the younger generation. Tolerance is not necessarily a good, you know. Tolerance of evil may itself be an evil. After all it was Aristotle, wasn't it, who said—

MISS MEACHAM *appears from the garden.*

MISS MEACHAM. Oh really—you've all gone on far too long about it. And when you start quoting Aristotle, well, personally, I'm going to my room.

MRS. RAILTON-BELL. You heard, Miss Meacham?

MISS MEACHAM. I couldn't help hearing. I didn't want to. I was doing my system and you need to concentrate like billy-oh on that, but I had my chair against the wall to catch the sun, and I wasn't going to move into the cold just for you people.

MRS. RAILTON-BELL. Well, as you know the facts, I suppose we should canvass your opinion. What is it?

MISS MEACHAM. I haven't any.

MRS. RAILTON-BELL. You must have *some* opinion?

MISS MEACHAM. Why should I? I've been out of the world for far longer than any of you and what do I know about morals and ethics? Only what I read in novels, and as I only read thrillers, that isn't worth much. In Peter Cheyney the hero does far worse things to his girls than the Major's done, and no one seems to mind.

MRS. RAILTON-BELL. I don't think that it's quite the point what Peter Cheyney's heroes do to his girls, Miss Meacham. We want your views on Major Pollock.

MISS MEACHAM. Do you? Well, my views on Major Pollock have always been that he's a crashing old bore, and a wicked old fraud. Now I hear he's a dirty old man, too, well, I'm not at all surprised, and quite between these four walls, I don't give a damn.

*She goes out. There is a pause, and then* MRS. RAILTON-BELL *turns to* MR. FOWLER.

MRS. RAILTON-BELL. Well. Mr. Fowler, I take it you are on the side of action?

*Pause.*

MR. FOWLER. I once had to recommend a boy for expulsion. Only once, in the whole of the fifteen years I was a housemaster. I was deeply unhappy about it. Deeply. And yet events proved me right. He was no good. He became a thief and a blackmailer, and—oh—horrible things happened to him. Horrible. (*After a moment's pause.*) Poor boy. He *had* a way with him—

MRS. RAILTON-BELL. (*Impatiently.*) Are you in favour of action, Mr. Fowler?

MR. FOWLER. (*Unhappily.*) Yes, I suppose so. Yes, I am.

MRS. RAILTON-BELL. (*To* LADY MATHESON.) And you, Gladys?

*As* LADY MATHESON *hesitates.*

You don't need to make a speech like the others, dear. Just say yes or no.

*Pause.*

LADY MATHESON. (*At length.*) Oh dear!

MRS. RAILTON-BELL. Now don't shilly-shally. Gladys. You know perfectly well what you feel about all this dreadful vice that's going on all over the country. You've told me often how people like that should be locked up—

LADY MATHESON. (*At length.*) Oh dear!

MRS. RAILTON-BELL. (*Really impatient.*) Oh, for heaven's sake, make up your mind. Gladys. Are you on the side of Mr. Stratton with his defence of vice, or are you on the side of the Christian virtues like Mr. Fowler, Mrs. Stratton and myself?

CHARLES. (*Quietly.*) I have never in my life heard a question more disgracefully begged. Senator McCarthy could use your talents. Mrs. Railton-Bell.

MRS. RAILTON-BELL. Will you keep quiet! Well, Gladys, which is it to be?

LADY MATHESON. I'm on your side, of course. It's only—

MRS. RAILTON-BELL. (*To* CHARLES.) Well, Mr. Stratton—apart from Miss Meacham, who must be said to be neutral, the count appears now to be five to one against you.

CHARLES. *Five* to one?

MRS. RAILTON-BELL. My daughter, of course, agrees with me.

CHARLES. How do you know?

MRS. RAILTON-BELL. I know her feelings in this matter.

CHARLES. May we hear them from herself?

SIBYL, *during the whole of this discussion, has not stirred in her chair. Her two hands, one bound with a handkerchief, have rested motionless in her lap, and she has been staring at the wall opposite her.*

Miss Railton-Bell—could we hear your views?

*There is no reply.*

MRS. RAILTON-BELL. Mr. Stratton is asking you a question, dear.

SIBYL. Yes, Mummy?

CHARLES. Could we hear your views?

SIBYL. My views?

MRS. RAILTON-BELL. (*Clearly, as to a child.*) On Major Pollock, dear. What action should we take about him?

SIBYL *seems puzzled and makes no reply.*

(*To the others, in an aside.*) It's the shock. (*To* SIBYL *again.*) You know what you've just read in that paper, dear? What do you think of it?

SIBYL. (*In a whisper.*) It made me sick.

MRS. RAILTON-BELL. Of course it did, dear. That's how we all feel.

SIBYL. (*Her voice growing louder in a crescendo.*) It made me sick. It made me sick. It made me sick. It made me sick.

MRS. RAILTON-BELL. (*Going quickly to her and embracing her.*) Yes, dear. Yes. Don't fuss now, don't fuss. It's all right.

SIBYL. (*Burying her face in her mother's arms.*) I don't feel well, Mummy. Can I go and lie down?

MRS. RAILTON-BELL. Of course you can, dear. We can go into the writing-room. Such a nice comfy sofa, and there's never anyone there. (*She leads her to the hall door.*) And don't fret any more, my dear. Try and forget the whole nasty business. Make believe it never happened—that there never was such a person as Major Pollock. That's the way.

*They disappear together into the hall.*

LADY MATHESON. She should never have told her like that. It was such a mistake.

CHARLES. (*Angrily.*) I agree. If that girl doesn't end as a mental case it won't be the fault of her mother.

LADY MATHESON. (*Loyally.*) Mr. Stratton—I must say I consider that a quite outrageous way of twisting my remark. I used the word 'mistake', and you have no right—

CHARLES. No, I haven't. I'm sorry. The comment was purely my own.

JEAN. It was *your* fault for asking her views.

CHARLES. She was sitting there quite peacefully, apparently listening. I wasn't to know she was in a state of high suppressed hysteria. I might, admittedly, have guessed, but anyway, I had an idiotic but well-meaning hope that I might get her—just this once—just this once in the whole of her life—to disagree publicly with her mother. It could save her soul if she ever did.

MR. FOWLER. I didn't realize that modern psychiatry recognized so old-fashioned and sentimental a term as soul, Mr. Stratton.

CHARLES. Very well, for soul read mind, and one day when you have a spare ten minutes explain to me the difference.

MR. FOWLER. I will.

CHARLES. (*Getting up.*) Not now, I'm afraid. It might muddle my anatomical studies. (*To* JEAN.) Are you coming?

JEAN *gets up, rather reluctantly.*

JEAN. I don't know what's the matter with you, this evening, Charles. You're behaving like an arrogant pompous boor.

CHARLES. You must forgive me. I suppose it's just that I'm feeling a little light-headed at finding myself, on an issue of common humanity, in a minority of one. The sin of spiritual pride, that's called—isn't it, Mr. Fowler?

*He goes out.* JEAN *comes back from the door.*

JEAN. (*To the other two.*) He's been overworking, you know. He'll be quite different about all this tomorrow. (*Confidently.*) I'll see to that.

MRS. RAILTON-BELL *comes in.*

MRS. RAILTON-BELL. She's quite all right, now. She always recovers from these little states very quickly. She's resting in the writing-room.

LADY MATHESON. Oh good.

JEAN. I was just apologizing for my husband's behaviour, Mrs. Railton-Bell.

MRS. RAILTON-BELL. Thank you, my dear—but what I always say is—we're all of us entitled to our own opinions, however odd and dangerous and distasteful they may sometimes be. (*Briskly.*) Now. Shall we all go and see Miss Cooper in a body, or would you rather I acted as your spokesman?

*It is plain which course she would prefer. After a pause, they begin to murmur diffidently.*

LADY MATHESON. I think, perhaps, if you went, dear—

MR. FOWLER. I don't think a deputation is a good idea—

JEAN. You be our spokesman.

MRS. RAILTON-BELL. Very well.

*She picks up the copy of the newspaper and goes to the door.*

I hope you all understand it's a duty I hardly relish.

*She goes out.*

MR. FOWLER. (*To* LADY MATHESON.) I would hardly call that a strictly accurate self-appraisal, would you?

LADY MATHESON. (*Doubtfully.*) Well—after all—doing a duty can seem a pleasure, to some people, can't it? It never has done to me, I agree, but then I'm—well—so weak and silly about these things

JEAN. (*At the door.*) It would be a pleasure to me in this case. Horrid old man! (*To herself as she goes.*) I hope the baby's not been crying

*She goes out.*

MR. FOWLER. A ruthless young girl, that, I would say.

LADY MATHESON. So many young people are these days, don't you think?

MR. FOWLER. (*Meaningly.*) Not only young people.

LADY MATHESON. (*Unhappily.*) Yes—well. (*With a sigh.*) Oh dear! What a dreadful affair. It's made me quite miserable.

MR. FOWLER. I feel a little unhappy about it all myself. (*He sighs and gets up.*) The trouble about being on the side of right, as one sees it, is that one sometimes finds oneself in the company of such very questionable allies. Let's go and take our minds off it all with television.

LADY MATHESON. (*Getting up.*) Yes. Good idea. The newsreel will be nearly over now—but I think that dear Philip Harben is on, after. Such a pity I'll never have the chance of following any of his recipes.

MR. FOWLER. (*As they go out.*) I agree. One suffers the tortures of Tantalus, and yet the pleasure is intense. Isn't that what is today called masochism?

*They go out. The room is empty for a moment, and then* MAJOR POLLOCK *tenta-*

*tively appears at the open french windows. He peers cautiously into the room, and, satisfying himself that it is empty, comes in. He goes quickly to the table on which are* MRS. RAILTON-BELL'S *journals. He sees at once that the 'West Hampshire Weekly News' is no longer where he left it. Frantically he rummages through the pile, and then begins to search the room. He is standing, in doubt, by the fireplace, when the door opens quietly and* SIBYL *comes in. As she sees him she stands stock still. He does not move either.*

MAJOR POLLOCK. (*At length, with pathetic jauntiness.*) Evening, Miss R.B. And how's the world with you, eh?

SIBYL. Were you looking for Mummy's paper?

MAJOR POLLOCK. What? No, of course not. I've got the other copy—

SIBYL. Don't pretend any more, please. She's read it, you see.

MAJOR POLLOCK. Oh.

*There is a long pause. The* MAJOR'S *shoulders droop, and he holds the table for support.*

MAJOR POLLOCK. Did she show it to you?

SIBYL. Yes.

MAJOR POLLOCK. Oh.

SIBYL. And to all the others.

MAJOR POLLOCK. Miss Cooper too?

SIBYL. Mummy's gone to tell her.

*The* MAJOR *nods, hopelessly.*

MAJOR POLLOCK. (*At length.*) Well—that's it, then, isn't it?

SIBYL. Yes.

MAJOR POLLOCK. Oh God—

*He sits down, staring at the floor. She looks at him steadily.*

SIBYL. (*Passionately.*) Why did you do it? Why did you do it?

MAJOR POLLOCK. I don't know. I wish I could answer that. Why does anyone do anything they shouldn't? Why do some people drink too much, and other people smoke fifty cigarettes a day? Because they can't stop it, I suppose.

SIBYL. Then this wasn't—the first time?

MAJOR POLLOCK. (*Quietly.*) No.

SIBYL. It's horrible.

MAJOR POLLOCK. Yes, of course it is. I'm not trying to defend it. You wouldn't guess, I know, but ever since school I've always been scared to death of women. Of everyone, in a way, I suppose; but mostly of women. I had a bad time at school—which wasn't Wellington, of course—just a Council school. Boys hate other boys to be timid and shy, and they gave it to me good and proper. My father despised me, too. He was a sergeant-major in the Black Watch. He made me join the Army, but I was always a bitter disappointment to him. He died before I got my commission. I only got that by a wangle. It wasn't difficult at the beginning of the war. But it meant everything to me, all the same. Being saluted, being called sir—I thought I'm someone, now, a real person. Perhaps some woman might even— (*He stops.*) But it didn't work. It never has worked. I'm made in a certain way, and I can't change it. It has to be the dark, you see, and strangers, because—

SIBYL. (*Holding her hands to her ears.*) Stop, stop. I don't want to hear it. It makes me ill.

MAJOR POLLOCK. (*Quietly.*) Yes. It would, of course. I should have known that. It was only that you'd asked me about why I did such things, and I wanted to talk to someone about it. I never have, you see, not in the whole of my life. (*He gets up and gently touches her sleeve.*) I'm sorry to have upset you, of all people.

*He goes to a table and collects two books.*

SIBYL. Why me, so especially? Why not the others?

MAJOR POLLOCK. Oh, I don't give a hang about the others. They'll all take it in their various ways, I suppose—but it won't mean much more to them than another bit of gossip to snort or snigger about. But it'll be different for you, Sibyl, and that makes me unhappy.

SIBYL. That's the first time you've ever called me Sibyl.

MAJOR POLLOCK. Is it? Well, there's not much point in all that Miss R.B. stuff now, is there?

SIBYL. What makes me so different from the others?

*The* MAJOR *has gathered another book from a corner of the room, and a pipe. He turns now and looks at her.*

MAJOR POLLOCK. Your being so scared of—well—shall we call it life? It sounds more respectable than the word which I know you hate. You and I are awfully alike, you know. That's why I suppose we've drifted so much together in this place.

SIBYL. How can you say we're alike? I don't— (*She stops, unable to continue.*)

MAJOR POLLOCK. I know you don't. You're not even tempted and never will be. You're very lucky. Or are you? Who's to say, really? All I meant was that we're both of us frightened of people, and yet we've somehow managed to forget our fright when we've been in each other's company. Speaking for myself, I'm grateful and always will be. Of course I can't expect you to feel the same way now.

SIBYL. What are you doing?

MAJOR POLLOCK. Getting my things together. Have you seen a pouch anywhere?

SIBYL. It's here.

*She goes to a table and collects it. He takes it from her.*

MAJOR POLLOCK. (*With a wry smile.*) Old Wellingtonian colours.

SIBYL. Why have you told so many awful lies?

MAJOR POLLOCK. I don't like myself as I am, I suppose, so I've had to invent another person. It's not so harmful, really. We've all got daydreams. Mine have gone a step further than most people's—that's all. Quite often I've even managed to believe in the Major myself. (*He starts.*) Is that someone in the hall?

SIBYL. (*Listening.*) No, I don't think so. Where will you go?

MAJOR POLLOCK. I don't know. There's a chap in London might put me up for a day or two. Only I don't so awfully want to go there—

SIBYL. Why not?

MAJOR POLLOCK. (*After a slight pause.*) Well—you see—it's rather a case of birds of a feather.

SIBYL. Don't go to him. You mustn't go to him.

MAJOR POLLOCK. I don't know where else.

SIBYL. Another hotel.

MAJOR POLLOCK. It can't be Bournemouth or anywhere near here. It'll have to be London, and I don't know anywhere there I can afford—

SIBYL. I'll lend you some money.

MAJOR POLLOCK. You certainly won't.

SIBYL. I will. I have some savings certificates. You can have those. I can get more too, if you need it.

MAJOR POLLOCK. (*Holding her hand, gently.*) No, Sybil. No. Thank you—but no.

SIBYL. But you'll go to this man.

MAJOR POLLOCK. No, I won't. I'll find somewhere else.

SIBYL. Where?

MAJOR POLLOCK, Don't worry. I'll be all right.

MISS COOPER *comes in, and closes the door behind her.*

MISS COOPER. (*Brightly.*) There you are, Major Pollock. Can I see you in my office a moment?

MAJOR POLLOCK. We don't need to talk in your office, Miss Cooper. I know what you have to say. I'm leaving at once.

MISS COOPER. I see. That's your own choice, is it?

MAJOR POLLOCK. Of course.

MISS COOPER. Because I would like to make it perfectly plain to you that there's no question whatever of my requiring you to leave this hotel. If you want to stay on here you're at perfect liberty to do so. It's entirely a matter for you.

*Pause.*

MAJOR POLLOCK. I see. That's good of you. But of course, I have to go.

MISS COOPER. I quite understand that you'd want to. I shan't charge the usual week's notice. When will you be going? Before dinner?

MAJOR POLLOCK. Of course.

MISS COOPER. Do you want me to help you find some place to stay until you can get settled?

MAJOR POLLOCK. I can hardly expect that, Miss Cooper.

MISS COOPER. Why on earth not? There are two hotels in London run by the Beauregard group. One is in West Kensington and the other in St. John's Wood. They're both about the same price. Which would you prefer?

MAJOR POLLOCK. (*After a pause.*) West Kensington, I think.

MISS COOPER. I've got their card here somewhere. Yes, there's one here.

*She goes to the mantelpiece and takes a card from a small holder. She hands it to him.*

Would you like me to ring them up for you?

MAJOR POLLOCK. Thank you, but I think perhaps I'd better ring them myself. In case of—further trouble, I don't want to involve you more than I need. May I use the phone in your office?

MISS COOPER. Certainly.

MAJOR POLLOCK. I'll pay for the call of course.

*He goes to the door and looks to see if anyone is about in the hall.*

Sibyl, if I don't have a chance of seeing you again, I'll write and say goodbye.

*He goes out.* MISS COOPER *turns to* SIBYL.

MISS COOPER. Your mother's gone up to dress for dinner, Miss Railton-Bell. She told me I'd find you in the writing-room lying down and I was to tell you that you can have your meal upstairs tonight, if you'd rather.

SIBYL. That's all right.

MISS COOPER. (*Sympathetically.*) How are you feeling now?

SIBYL. (*Brusquely.*) All right.

MISS COOPER *approaches her.*

MISS COOPER. (*Quietly.*) Is there anything I can do to help you?

SIBYL. (*Angrily.*) No. Nothing;. And please don't say things like that. You'll make me feel bad again, and I'll make a fool of myself. I feel well now. He's going and that's good. I despise him.

MISS COOPER. Do you? I wonder if you should.

SIBYL. He's a vile, wicked man, and he's done a horrible beastly thing. It's not the first time, either. He admits that.

MISS COOPER. I didn't think it was.

SIBYL. And yet you told him he could stay on in the hotel if he wanted to? That's wicked too.

MISS COOPER. Then I suppose I *am* wicked too. (*She puts her hand on her arm.*) Sibyl, dear—

SIBYL. Why is everyone calling me Sibyl this evening? Please stop. You'll only make me cry.

MISS COOPER. I don't mean to do that. I just mean to help you.

SIBYL *breaks down suddenly, but now quietly and without hysteria.* MISS COOPER *holds her.*

That's better. Much better.

SIBYL. It's so horrible.

MISS COOPER. I know it is. I'm very sorry for you.

SIBYL. He says we're alike—he and I.

MISS COOPER. Does he?

SIBYL. He says we're both scared of life and people and sex. There—I've said the word. He says I hate *saying* it even, and he's right. I do. What's the matter with me? There must be something the matter with me.

MISS COOPER. Nothing very much, I should say. Shall we sit down?

*She gently propels her on to the sofa and sits beside her.*

SIBYL. I'm a freak, aren't I?

MISS COOPER. (*In matter-of-fact tones.*) I never know what that word means. If you mean you're different from other people, then, I suppose, you are a freak. But all human beings are a bit different from each other, aren't they? What a dull world it would be if they weren't.

SIBYL. I'd like to be ordinary.

MISS COOPER. I wouldn't know about that, dear. You see, I've never met an ordinary person. To me all people are extraordinary. I meet all sorts here, you know, in my job, and the one thing I've learnt in five years is that the word normal, applied to any human being, is utterly meaningless. In a sort of a way it's an insult to our Maker, don't you think, to suppose that He could possibly work to any set pattern.

SIBYL. I don't think Mummy would agree with you.

MISS COOPER. I'm fairly sure she wouldn't. Tell me—when did your father die?

SIBYL. When I was seven.

MISS COOPER. Did you go to school?

SIBYL. No. Mummy said I was too delicate. I had a governess some of the time, but most of the time Mummy taught me herself.

MISS COOPER. Yes. I see. And you've never really been away from her, have you?

SIBYL. Only when I had a job, for a bit. (*Proudly.*) I was a sales-girl in a big shop in London—Jones & Jones. I sold lampshades. But I got ill, though, and had to leave.

MISS COOPER. (*Brightly.*) What bad luck. Well, you must try again, some day, mustn't you?

SIBYL. Mummy says no.

MISS COOPER. Mummy says no. Well, then, you must just try and get Mummy to say yes, don't you think?

SIBYL. I don't know how.

MISS COOPER. I'll tell you how. By running off and getting a job on your own. She'll say yes quick enough then.

*She pats* SIBYL'S *knee sympathetically and gets up.*

I have my menus to do. (*She goes towards the door.*)

SIBYL. (*Urgently.*) Will he be all right, do you think?

MISS COOPER. The Major? I don't know. I hope so.

SIBYL. In spite of what he's done, I don't want anything bad to happen to him. I want him to be happy. Is it a nice hotel—this one in West Kensington?

MISS COOPER. Very nice.

SIBYL. Do you think he'll find a friend there? He told me just now that he'd always be grateful to me for making him forget how frightened he was of people.

MISS COOPER. He's helped you too, hasn't he?

SIBYL. Yes.

MISS COOPER. (*After a pause.*) I hope he'll find a friend in the new hotel.

SIBYL. So do I. Oh God, so do I.

*The* MAJOR *comes in.*

MAJOR POLLOCK. (*Quickly, to* MISS COOPER.) It's all right. I've fixed it. It might please you to know that I said *Mr. Pollock*, and didn't have to mention your name or this hotel. I must dash upstairs and pack now.

*He turns to* SIBYL *and holds out his hand.*

   Good-bye, Sibyl.

SIBYL *takes his hand, after a second's hesitation.*

SIBYL. Good-bye.

*She drops his hand and runs quickly to the door.*

SIBYL. (*Without looking back.*) God bless you.

*She goes out.*

MAJOR POLLOCK. Very upset? (MISS COOPER *nods.*) That's the part I've hated most, you know. It's funny. She's rather an odd one—almost a case— she's got a child's mind and hardly makes sense sometimes—and yet she means quite a lot to me.

MISS COOPER. I think you mean quite a lot to her too.

MAJOR POLLOCK. I did, I think. Not now, of course. It was the gallant ex-soldier she was fond of—not— (*He stops.*) I told her the whole story about myself. I thought it right. There's just a chance she might understand it all a bit better one day. I'm afraid, though, she'll never get over it.

MISS COOPER. No. I don't suppose she will.

MAJOR POLLOCK. One's apt to excuse oneself sometimes by saying: Well, af-ter all, what I do doesn't do anybody much harm. But one does, you see. That's not a thought I like. Could you have a squint in the hall and see if anyone's around?

MISS COOPER *half-opens the door.*

MISS COOPER. Miss Meacham's at the telephone.

MAJOR POLLOCK. Damn.

MISS COOPER. What train are you catching?

MAJOR POLLOCK. Seven forty-five.

MISS COOPER. You've got time.

MAJOR POLLOCK. I've got a tremendous lot of packing to do. Four years, you know. Hellish business. I'm dreading the first few days in a new place. I mean dreading, you know—literally trembling with funk at the thought of meeting new people. The trouble is I'll probably be forced by sheer terror to take refuge in all that Major stuff again.

MISS COOPER. Try not to.

MAJOR POLLOCK. Oh, I'll try all right. I'll try. I only hope I'll succeed.

*He goes cautiously to the door and turns.*

   Still there. Damn. (*Coming back.*) Thank you for being so kind. God knows why you have been. I don't deserve it—but I'm grateful. Very grateful.

MISS COOPER. That's all right.

MAJOR POLLOCK. You're an odd fish, you know, if you don't mind my saying so. A good deal more goes on behind that calm managerial front of yours than anyone would imagine. Has something bad ever happened to you?

MISS COOPER. Yes.

MAJOR POLLOCK. Very bad?

MISS COOPER. I've got over it.

MAJOR POLLOCK. What was it?

MISS COOPER. I loved a man who loved somebody else.

MAJOR POLLOCK. Still love him?

MISS COOPER. Oh yes. I always will.

MAJOR POLLOCK. Any hope?

MISS COOPER. (*Cheerfully.*) No. None at all.

MAJOR POLLOCK. Why so cheerful about it?

MISS COOPER. Because there's no point in being anything else. I've settled for the situation, you see, and it's surprising how cheerful one can be when one gives up hope. I've still got the memory, you see, which is a very pleasant one—all things considered.

MAJOR POLLOCK. (*Nodding.*) I see. Quite the philosopher, what? (*To himself.*) I must give up saying what. Well, Meacham or no Meacham, I'm going to make a dash for it, or I'll miss that train.

*He turns back to the door.*

MISS COOPER. Why don't you stay?

MAJOR POLLOCK. (*Turning, incredulously.*) Stay? In the hotel, you mean?

MISS COOPER. You say you dread the new hotel.

MAJOR POLLOCK. I dread this one a damn sight more, now.

MISS COOPER. Yes, I expect you do. But at least you couldn't be forced by terror into any more Major stuff, could you?

*Pause.*

MAJOR POLLOCK. I might be forced into something a good deal more—conclusive—cleaning my old service revolver, perhaps—you know the form—make a nasty mess on one of your carpets and an ugly scandal in your hotel.

MISS COOPER. (*Lightly.*) I'd take the risk, if you would.

MAJOR POLLOCK. My dear Miss Cooper, I'm far too much of a coward to stay on here now. Far too much.

MISS COOPER. I see. Pity. I just thought it would be so nice if you could prove to yourself that you weren't.

*Pause.*

MAJOR POLLOCK. (*At length.*) You're thinking of her too, of course, aren't you?

MISS COOPER. Yes.

MAJOR POLLOCK. Reinstate the gallant ex-soldier in her eyes?

MISS COOPER. That's right.

MAJOR POLLOCK. Make her think she's helped me find my soul and all that.

MISS COOPER. Yes.

*Another pause.*

MAJOR POLLOCK. (*With an eventual sigh.*) Not a hope. Not a hope in the whole, wide, blinking world. I know my form, you see.

MISS COOPER. I wonder if you do.

MAJOR POLLOCK. (*Sadly.*) Oh I do. I do, only too well. Thanks for trying, anyway.

*He looks cautiously out into the hall.*

    Coast's clear.

*He turns round and looks at her for a long time. She stares back steadily at him.* (*At length.*) There's a nine-something train, isn't there?

MISS COOPER. Nine thirty-two.

*There is another pause as he looks at her in doubt. Then he gives a shamefaced smile.*

MAJOR POLLOCK. I expect I'll still catch the seven forty-five.

*He goes out.*


THE LIGHTS FADE


## SCENE 2


SCENE: *The dining-room. As at the beginning of the first play, dinner is in full swing. The table by the window is now occupied by a pair of young 'casuals'— much interested in each other, and totally oblivious of everyone else. One table is unoccupied and unlaid; otherwise all the tables are occupied by the usual owners.*

    *As the lights come on, conversation is general—which means, more precisely, that the two casuals are murmuring together, the* STRATTONS *are arguing,* LADY MATHESON *and* MR. FOWLER *are talking between tables, and* MRS. RAILTON-BELL *is talking to* SIBYL. MABEL *is hovering over* MISS MEACHAM *who is absorbed in 'Racing Up To Date'.*

MABEL. (*Heard above the background.*) Were you the fricassee or the Cambridge steak?

MISS MEACHAM. What? Oh, it doesn't matter. Both are uneatable.

MABEL. What about the cold chicken, then?

MISS MEACHAM. *Cold* chicken? But we haven't had it hot yet.

MABEL. If I were you I'd have the fricassee. It's all right. It's rabbit.

MISS MEACHAM. The fricassee then.

MR. FOWLER. Any cheese. Mabel?

MABEL. Afraid not.

MR. FOWLER. There's never any cheese.

MABEL *serves* MISS MEACHAM *and stumps out to the kitchen.* MRS. RAILTON-BELL *leans across to* LADY MATHESON.

MRS. RAILTON-BELL. I believe there's a new game on television tonight.

LADY MATHESON. Yes, I know, dear. I read all about it in the *Radio Times*. It sounds quite fascinating—I shall certainly see it next week.

MRS. RAILTON-BELL. Why not tonight, dear?

LADY MATHESON. I feel too tired. I'm going to go to bed directly after dinner.

MRS. RAILTON-BELL. Of course. (*Lowering her voice.*) What a really nerve-racking day it's been, hasn't it? I don't suppose any of us will ever forget it. Ever. I feel utterly shattered, myself. (*To* SIBYL.) Pass the sauce, dear.

LADY MATHESON *nods.* MRS. RAILTON-BELL *takes a sip of wine. The* MAJOR *has walked quietly into the dining-room.* MRS. RAILTON-BELL *turns and stares unbelievingly at him as he walks slowly to his table and sits down. The conversation in the dining-room has frozen into a dead silence, for even the casuals seem affected by the electric atmosphere—though oblivious of the cause—and have ceased talking. The silence is broken by* DOREEN *entering the dining-room and seeing him.*

DOREEN. (*Calling through the kitchen door.*) Mabel—Number Seven's in. You said he was out.

MABEL. (*Off.*) Well, that's what Joe said. Joe said he was leaving before dinner.

DOREEN. Sorry, Major. There's been a muddle. I'll lay your table right away.

*She goes back into the kitchen. The silence remains unbroken, until* DOREEN *returns with a tray and begins quickly to lay the* MAJOR'S *table.*

What would you like? The fricassee's nice.

MAJOR POLLOCK. I'll have that. Thank you.

DOREEN. Soup first?

MAJOR POLLOCK. No, thank you.

DOREEN. (*Finally laying the table.*) There we are. All cosy now. Fricassee you said?

MAJOR POLLOCK. That's right.

*She goes into the kitchen.* SIBYL *is staring at the* MAJOR, *but he does not meet her eyes. He is looking down at his table, as is everyone else, aware of his presence, save* SIBYL *and* MRS. RAILTON-BELL *who is glaring furiously in turn at him and at the others. The silence is broken suddenly by a rather nervously high-pitched greeting from* CHARLES.

CHARLES. (*To the* MAJOR.) Hullo.

MAJOR POLLOCK. (*Murmuring.*) Hullo.

CHARLES. Clouding over a bit, isn't it? I'm afraid we may get rain later.

JEAN *is furiously glaring at her husband.* MRS. RAILTON-BELL *has turned fully round in her chair in an attempt to paralyse him into silence.*

MAJOR POLLOCK. Yes. I'm afraid we may.

MISS MEACHAM. We need it. This hard going's murder on form. (*To* MAJOR POLLOCK.) You know Newmarket, don't you?

MAJOR POLLOCK. No, I don't.

MISS MEACHAM. But I remember your saying— (*She gets it.*) Oh, I see. Well, it's a very tricky course in hard going. Still, if they get some rain up there tomorrow, I think I'll be able to give you a winner on Tuesday.

MAJOR POLLOCK. Thank you. Thank you very much. The only thing is, I may not be here on Tuesday.

MISS MEACHAM. Oh, really? All right. Leave me your address then and I'll wire it to you. I'll need the money for the wire, though.

MAJOR POLLOCK. Thank you. That's very kind of you.

MISS MEACHAM. You won't think it so kind of me, if it loses.

*She goes back to her 'Racing Up To Date'.*

MISS COOPER *comes in.*

MISS COOPER. (*Brightly.*) Good evening, Mrs. Railton-Bell. Good evening, Lady Matheson. Good evening, Mr. Pollock.

*The 'Mr.' is barely distinguishable from 'Major', and her voice is as brightly 'managerial' to him as to the others.*

I hear they didn't lay your table tonight. I'm so sorry.

MAJOR POLLOCK. Quite all right.

MISS COOPER. I'd advise the fricassee, if I were you. It's really awfully nice.

MAJOR POLLOCK. I've ordered it.

MISS COOPER. Good, I'm so glad. (*She passes on.*) Good evening, Mr. and Mrs. Stratton. Everything all right? (*They nod and smile.*) Splendid.

*She bows rather less warmly to 'the casuals' and goes out.* MRS. RAILTON-BELL *pretends to feel an imaginary draught.*

MRS. RAILTON-BELL. (*To* LADY MATHESON.) It's very cold in here suddenly, don't you think, dear?

LADY MATHESON *nods, nervously.*

I think I'll turn my chair round a bit, and get out of the draught.

*She does so, turning her back neatly on the* MAJOR. MR. FOWLER *gets up quietly from his table and walks to the door. To do this he has to pass the* MAJOR. *A step or so past him he hesitates and then looks back, nods and smiles.*

MR. FOWLER. Good evening.

MAJOR POLLOCK. Good evening.

MRS. RAILTON-BELL *has had to twist her head sharply round in order to allow her eyes to confirm this shameful betrayal.*

MR. FOWLER. Hampshire did pretty well today, did you see? Three hundred and eighty-odd for five.

MAJOR POLLOCK. Very good.

MR. FOWLER. I wish they had more bowling. Well—

*He smiles vaguely and goes on into the lounge. There is an audible and outraged 'Well!' from* MRS. RAILTON-BELL. *Silence falls again. Suddenly and by an accident the* MAJOR'S *and* LADY MATHESON'S *eyes meet. Automatically she inclines her head and gives him a slight smile. He returns the salute.*

LADY MATHESON. (*To* MAJOR POLLOCK.) Good evening.

MRS. RAILTON-BELL. (*In a whisper.*) Gladys!

LADY MATHESON, *who has genuinely acted from instinct, looks startled. Then she apparently decides to be as well hanged for a sheep as a lamb.*

LADY MATHESON. (*Suddenly very bold, and in a loud voice.*) I advise the apple charlotte. It's very good.

MAJOR POLLOCK. Thank you. I'll have that.

*She is instantly conscience-stricken at what she has done and hangs her head over her apple charlotte, eating feverishly. She refuses to look at* MRS. RAILTON-BELL, *who is staring at her with wide, unbelieving and furious eyes.* MRS. RAILTON-BELL, *getting no response from* LADY MATHESON, *deliberately folds her napkin and rises.*

MRS. RAILTON-BELL. (*Quietly.*) Come, Sibyl.

SIBYL. (*Equally quietly.*) I haven't finished yet, Mummy.

MRS. RAILTON-BELL. (*Looking puzzled at this unaccustomed response.*) It doesn't matter, dear. Come into the lounge.

SIBYL *makes no move to rise. She stares up at her mother. There is a pause.*

SIBYL. No, Mummy.

*Pause.*

MRS. RAILTON-BELL. (*Sharply.*) Sibyl, come with me at once—

SIBYL. (*With quiet firmness.*) No, Mummy. I'm going to stay in the dining-room, and finish my dinner.

MRS. RAILTON-BELL *hesitates, plainly meditating various courses of action. Finally she decides on the only really possible course left to her—the dignified exit. Before she has got to the door* SIBYL *has spoken to the* MAJOR.

There's a new moon tonight, you know. We must all go and look at it afterwards.

MAJOR POLLOCK. Yes. We must.

DOREEN *has bustled in with the* MAJOR'S *dish as* MRS. RAILTON-BELL, *her world crumbling, goes into the lounge.* DOREEN *serves* MAJOR POLLOCK.

DOREEN. Sorry it's been so long. You're a bit late, you see.

MAJOR POLLOCK. Yes. My fault.

DOREEN. What's the matter with you tonight? You always say 'mea culpa'.

*She beats her breast in imitation of an obvious* MAJOR *bon mot.*

MAJOR POLLOCK. Do I? Well—they both mean the same, don't they?

DOREEN. I suppose *so.* (*Finishing the serving.*) There you are. Now what about breakfast?

MAJOR POLLOCK. Breakfast?

DOREEN. Joe got it wrong about your going, didn't he?

*There is a pause.* SIBYL *is looking steadily at the* MAJOR, *who now raises his eyes from his plate and meets her glance.*

MAJOR POLLOCK. (*Quietly, at length.*) Yes, he did.

DOREEN. That's good. Breakfast usual time, then?

MAJOR POLLOCK. Yes, Doreen. Breakfast usual time.

DOREEN *goes into the kitchen.* MAJOR POLLOCK *begins to eat his fricassee.* SIBYL *continues to eat her sweet. A decorous silence, broken only by the renewed murmur of 'the casuals', reigns once more, and the dining-room of the Beauregard Private Hotel no longer gives any sign of the battle that has just been fought and won between its four, bare walls.*

CURTAIN

# VARIATION ON A THEME

First published 1958
by Hamish Hamilton Ltd

Dedicated, with deep gratitude and affection, to
MARGARET LEIGHTON
for whom this play was most eagerly written and
by whom it was most brilliantly played.

*Characters:*

ROSE
HETTIE
RON
KURT
FIONA
MONA
ADRIAN
SAM


ACT I
SCENE 1: APRIL
SCENE 2: JUNE

ACT II
SCENE 1: AUGUST
SCENE 2: NOVEMBER

The action of the play takes place at the Château Auguste, Cannes.

*Variation on a Theme* was first produced at the Globe Theatre, London, on May 8th, 1958, with the following cast:

| | |
|---|---|
| ROSE | Margaret Leighton |
| HETTIE | Jean Anderson |
| RON | Jeremy Brett |
| KURT | George Pravda |
| FIONA | Felicity Ross |
| MONA | Mavis Villiers |
| ADRIAN | Lawrence Dalzell |
| SAM | Michael Goodliffe |

The play directed by JOHN GIELGUD

# ACT I

## SCENE 1

SCENE: A *terrace of a villa in the south of France.*

*What we see of the building shows its age, which is about eighty years, and its ancestry, which is grand-ducal. The terrace is broad and furnished with very comfortable-looking modern garden furniture.*

*The villa is in process of being done up for its present occupier; a tarpaulin covers some part of the outer wall, and the drawing-room, whose french windows give access to the terrace and into a part of which we may see, has its furniture covered in dust-sheets.*

*Steps L. and R. lead respectively to drive and front door, and garden and swimming-pool (both unseen).*

*It is just after sunrise. A woman of about sixty* (HETTIE) *is snoozing, fully dressed, on a day bed with a blanket over her.* ROSE *comes up the steps L. She is in the middle thirties, beautiful and dressed (now in a dinner dress) with a style and elegance that has little to do with current fashion, and which one feels she has carefully studied to suit her personality.*

*Not seeing* HETTIE *she goes to a tray of drinks that is on a table backstage, and pours herself out a drink. At the sound of the soda water siphoning into the glass* HETTIE *wakes.*

HETTIE. This is a hell of a time to come home.

ROSE. (*Turning, startled.*) Hettie—I told you not to wait up.

HETTIE. I know you did. I wasn't. My room was too damned hot and there was a blasted convocation of politic mosquitoes in there—

ROSE. There aren't any mosquitoes up here.

HETTIE. That's what you think. When you rename this place you should call it The Villa Moustique—

ROSE. (*Angrily.*) I hate you waiting up for me like this, Hettie. You do it every night I go out. It's not what I'm paying you for.

HETTIE. No. I suppose it isn't. What are you drinking?

ROSE. All right, all right. An orange squash and soda.

HETTIE. Let's see.

*She goes over to* ROSE, *takes the drink from her hand and sniffs it suspiciously. Then she hands it back to her.*

How many drinks did you have at the Casino?

ROSE. One.

HETTIE. Like hell—

ROSE. I had one brandy, and Lord knows I needed that. Let me tell you what happened—

*She suddenly looks contrite and with a quick movement kisses* HETTIE *on the cheek.*
I'm sorry, Hettie.

HETTIE. What about?

ROSE. That thing I just said about paying you.

HETTIE. Well, you do pay me, so why shouldn't you say so?

ROSE. Do you want me to answer that?

HETTIE. I'm a paid companion. Who cares? I don't. I'd only care if I were unpaid. Which I might be soon, the way things are going. How much did you lose down at the Casino tonight?

ROSE. Nothing. Well—four and a half thousand—

HETTIE. (*Quickly.*) Pounds?

ROSE. No, francs, for heaven's sake. When have I ever lost four and a half thousand pounds?

HETTIE. Not—let me see—since last Thursday.

ROSE. That was an exception. I just got carried away watching that fat man with all those big white plaques, and it wasn't four and a half. It was two. I'll get that back, don't worry. No, tonight was awful.

HETTIE. Four pounds ten awful?

ROSE. It was the way it happened. That's why I needed that brandy. (*Accusingly.*) Hettie, do you realize you sent me out tonight without any money?

HETTIE. Oh God, did I? Sorry. Still, as you were with Kurt I thought—

ROSE. I ditched Kurt at Cannes—

HETTIE. Ditched fifty million?

ROSE. (*Smiling.*) Don't worry. Not for good. Only he bored me so much tonight, I could have screamed in his face. In fact I rather think I did. Well, anyway, I told him I had a migraine and as he wanted to go on trying to bust the Greek syndicate, I got clean away.

HETTIE. So you migrained Kurt? That was quite an achievement. So then?

ROSE So then—as it was still quite early—

HETTIE *looks at her watch.*
(*Impatiently.*) Listen, the doctor didn't say I had to be in bed by twelve every night of my life—

HETTIE. (*Quietly.*) He did, you know.

ROSE. Well, anyway, it didn't seem late and I wanted a little more gambling so I stopped off at Juan. Well, there was practically no one there—only one table of chemmy left—but no seat and there was a bank that had gone a couple of times—a terrible woman with a squint was running it—so I walked up and said banco. I got an eight—and—

HETTIE. (*Simultaneously, with* ROSE.) She had a nine.

ROSE. That's right. So I opened my bag with that bright smile I keep for losing bets—and well—nothing. Not one blasted franc.

HETTIE. But they must have known who you were.

ROSE. If they did they concealed it pretty well. Anyway, I haven't been to Juan for ages. There was the longest and iciest pause in world history while I fumbled away in my bag—with that smile becoming glassier every second—producing bric-a-brac—

HETTIE. Look, love, there's bric-a-brac and bric-a-brac. Surely that cigarette-case—

ROSE. Have some sense, Hettie. Did you want me to throw a cigarette-case on to the table and say: 'This is genuine Fabergé, given me by my second husband—the Marquis de Beaupré; oh, and by the way, these pearls were given me by my very last husband, Michael Bradford—that's the film star, and these emeralds by the gentleman I'm walking out with at the moment—Kurt Mast—you know—the financier?

HETTIE. You didn't need to do any of that, but you could surely have told them who you were.

ROSE. And who am I? You tell me.

HETTIE. They'd have recognized the name.

ROSE. Which one?

HETTIE. The one you were born with, idiot. The one the papers call you by.

ROSE. Supposing they hadn't. Anyway, you know I loathe it. I don't know why the papers use it all the time. My right name is Bradford and will be until it is or isn't Mast. Anyway, I challenge anyone to face a woman with a squint that one owes four and a half thousand francs to and say, 'Madame, I happen to be-' (*She stops and turns to the drink tray.*) I'm going to have a drink.

*As* HETTIE *looks at her.*

He only said 'not too much'. He didn't say 'nothing at all'.

HETTIE. I know. I heard him.

*Watching* ROSE *pouring out a brandy.*

Only I doubt if he recommended brandy at five-thirty in the morning.

ROSE. He doesn't know a damn thing—that silly little doctor. I'm going to try another one.

HETTIE. Why not? You only need one more for game.

*After a pause.*

You don't even like saying it, do you?

ROSE. What?

HETTIE. Your name.

ROSE. I've told you. It isn't my name.

HETTIE. Well—so what *did* you do to this woman with the squint?

ROSE. I faced her with a frank and honest gaze—only it was a bit difficult not knowing which eye to try to be frank and honest into—and said I'm afraid, Madam, I've come out without any money and shall have to give you a cheque. Faultless French, a winning, apologetic smile, sincere charm oozing—but no damn good. Pandemonium. The usual little character with the usual spade beard summoned out of the office and I'd have been off to the clink, I suppose—if it hadn't been for this young man—

HETTIE. Ah. Now we come to the point.

ROSE. Oh no. No point.

HETTIE. Sure?

ROSE. Quite Sure.

HETTIE. Why?

ROSE. A pompadour to here. (*She indicates a lofty hair style.*)

HETTIE. Hell, these days that could mean he's the Olympic welter-weight champion.

ROSE. This one's a ballet dancer.

HETTIE. So?

ROSE. So he's also got a friend. Nice and quiet, but very firm, and very wary. The boy's hell, anyway, I may say. The show-off of the world. Apparently he knew who I was because I met him in Sophie—what's-her-name's dressing-room one evening. He was flattering about the white Balenciaga I was wearing that night. Have you got four five on you, Hettie?

HETTIE. No. I'll have to go upstairs to the safe. Why?

ROSE. Because they're coming up to collect it.

HETTIE. When? Tomorrow?

ROSE. No. Tonight. I mean this morning. They wanted to play another shoe. As soon as that's finished

HETTIE. (*Angrily.*) Rose—for God's sake! Honestly, sometimes I think you really *are* round the bend—

ROSE. Well, I've got to pay them back, haven't I, and they live in Monte—

HETTIE. Is there a postal strike on?

ROSE. Well, they so obviously wanted to be asked. The boy anyway. He's heard about the new house—

HETTIE. (*Looking at the shrouded sitting-room.*) A lot you'll have to show him, won't you? Rose—honestly! You'll be kept up at least another hour—and just to impress a chorus boy with an unfinished mosquito-ridden, draughty old villa—

ROSE. Ah. But built by the Grand Duke Auguste. And he's not a chorus boy. He dances Spectre de la Rose and the Blue Bird. And the friend's very grand indeed. A famous choreographer. He did the dances for that musical we saw in New York the night we sailed. (*Impatiently.*) All right, Hettie, I'll sleep all day tomorrow.

HETTIE. You won't. You've got that lunch party.

ROSE. Oh yes. Well, in the afternoon—

HETTIE. Tea with Mona and cocktails with the Johnsons—

ROSE. Oh well. What the hell!

HETTIE. As you say. What the hell. I'll meet them, give them the money and a drink, and show them over the ruins. You go to bed.

ROSE. No point. I wouldn't sleep anyway.

HETTIE. Take something.

ROSE. I took two last night. I don't want to become a junkie like Mona—

HETTIE. What stops you sleeping? Is it— (*She puts her hand on her lung.*)

ROSE. Oh, no. I don't feel that at all these days.

HETTIE. Then what—?

ROSE. (*Lightly.*) God knows. Remorse, I suppose, for a life of guilt and shame. (*Seeing* HETTIE'S *eyes on her.*) I just don't sleep well. Lots of people don't sleep well. (*She looks over the side of the terrace.*) Why does a sunrise on this coast always look like a cheap water-colour? Pale and mean and sort of fetid?

HETTIE. (*Shrugging.*) Because that's exactly what this coast is. I suppose.

ROSE. That's just fashionable talk, Hettie. This coast is all right. It's corny and vulgar, but it's fun—like Blackpool or Atlantic City. You mustn't take the people's pleasures away from us. (*She turns to listen.*) That's the car. They've found the house all right.

HETTIE. Not so hard considering you can practically see it from Marseilles.

ROSE. (*Leaning over railings L. and calling.*) Hullo. I'm on the terrace. (*She turns to* HETTIE.) A pale blue Thunderbird.

HETTIE. You amaze me.

RON *comes on. He is about twenty-six, dressed in sports clothes, with an elaborate 'Tony Curtis' hair style.*

ROSE. I'm glad you made it. Where's your friend?

RON. He went back to Monte. He asked me to make his apologies, but he was feeling most tired.

*He speaks with a very indeterminate accent, vaguely French, vaguely Russian and basically English Midlands.*

ROSE. But I thought you came over to Juan together. How did he get back?

RON. Oh—taxi.

ROSE. (*Rather wickedly.*) Then that beautiful blue object down there is yours, is it?

RON. No. Not really. But he is a rich choreographer and can afford a taxi, and I am only a poor dancer and cannot.

ROSE. Oh, I see. (*Preparing to introduce* HETTIE.) By the way, I'm absolutely terrible about names, and yours is rather difficult.

RON. Anton Valov.

ROSE. Oh yes, of course. Monsieur Valov—Lady Henrietta Crichton-Parry.

HETTIE. ⎫
RON.   ⎬ (*Murmuring.*) How do you do?

HETTIE. Can I get you a drink?

RON. (*Who has plainly been impressed by the title.*) Oh, but Lady Henrietta— can't I—

HETTIE. No. Getting drinks is part of my duties. The pleasantest part. What's it to be?

RON. Have you any vin rosé?

HETTIE. Of course.

RON. (*To* ROSE.) This is a magnificent view. The best I have ever seen, I think— except possibly for Mabel Penrhyn's at Cap Ferrat.

ROSE. Who's Mabel Penrhyn?

RON. The Countess of Penrhyn. You do not know her? That surprises me. Everybody knows her.

ROSE. Ah, but then, you see, I don't know everybody. And she has a good view?

RON. Magnificent. But of course I am seeing this at dawn which is a great privilege. I think dawn in the south of France surpasses any sight of the kind anywhere else in the world. (*With a wide gesture.*) The colour. It is magnificent, is it not? Oh. Excuse me.

HETTIE *has approached with his vin rosé and his expansive gesture has nearly knocked it out of her hand.*

HETTIE. That's quite all right.

RON. Yes. The mystery and magic of the Riviera dawn never fails—does it?

HETTIE *and* ROSE *have exchanged a glance.*

ROSE. (*At length.*) No. (*She turns to* HETTIE.) Hettie, dear, would you get Monsieur Valov the money I owe him?

RON. (*With a gesture of apparent embarrassment.*) Oh no—please.

ROSE. (*Showing her irritation.*) You don't want it back?

RON. At your convenience.

ROSE. This is my convenience. (*To* HETTIE.) And get me a brandy and soda on the way—would you, dear?

HETTIE. (*As she goes.*) No. You can damn well dig your own grave.

*She goes out into the sitting-room.* ROSE *smiles, looks at the drink tray, decides against it and sits down.*

RON. (*Trying to keep the awe out of his voice.*) Lady Henrietta Crichton-Parry— she must be a daughter of the Duke of Ayrshire, is she not?

ROSE. Yes. That's right.

RON. And she has been working for you long?

ROSE. Two years.

RON. Tiens. C'est amusant, ça!

ROSE. Qu'est ce qui est amusant?

RON. (*Switching quickly. His accent was not as good as hers.*) A duke's daughter working as a housekeeper—

ROSE. Social secretary.

RON. Well—whatever it is called—I thought the family was well off.

ROSE. (*Her voice gradually acquiring an edge to it.*) I suppose they were once. So was she. Unhappily they had death duties and she had an infallible system at roulette. She needed a job quickly and was lucky to get this one. I was lucky to get her. I think that exhausts the subject, don't you?

*Pause.*

RON. (*Playfully.*) Dear Madame la Marquise de Beaupré is a little angry with me, I think. She must not be. She must remember that a humble ballet dancer must always be curious about the ways and manners of the great world.

*There is another pause.*

ROSE. (*At length.*) Look, Monsieur Valov—just three points. First, I'm not angry with you at all. Only perhaps a little tired and I'm sorry if I showed it just now. Secondly, regarding Madame la Marquise de Beaupré. I'm afraid you're two whole husbands out.

RON. Oh, my God! Mrs. Michael Bradford. Of course. I am so sorry.

ROSE. That's all right. It's hard to keep pace, I know. Now the last point. You may be a bit offended by this, but please, please try not to be. All my life I've been irritated to death by phoney accents. Now, would you mind really dreadfully if you dropped that one of yours and reverted to your native Birmingham?

*Pause.*

RON. I beg your pardon.

ROSE. It is Birmingham, isn't it? I'm very rarely wrong.

RON. (*Stiffly still with accent.*) I am afraid I do not understand—

ROSE. You see, I spent the first twenty years of my life in Frogmore Road, off Five Towns Avenue, and I can spot a Brum accent a mile away. I expect you can with me too. We never really lose it, do we? I'd guess you come from somewhere much more posh than Frogmore Road. Say the North Side. Am I right?

RON *stares at her, still acting polite bewilderment.* HETTIE *comes in with some notes in her hand.*

What have you been doing? Reading my old love letters?

HETTIE. That's a show-off—pretending to your guest that the people who loved you could actually write. No. There are more interesting things in that safe than love letters.

ROSE. Such as?

HETTIE. Accounts.

ROSE. (*Yawning.*) Oh. Those.

HETTIE. (*To* RON.) It *was* four thousand five, wasn't it?

RON. (*Still with accent.*) No. Four thousand, three fifty. See, I will give you change.

HETTIE *glances at him. He does not meet her gaze. She shrugs sadly.* RON *gives* HETTIE *some coins and takes the notes from her.*

HETTIE. An honest man—on this coast! Fancy. Well, I'm to bed. (*To* RON.) Please don't keep her up too long, Monsieur Valov. You have an invalid on your hands.

RON. (*Still with accent.*) Oh, I am most sorry to hear that. What is the trouble?

HETTIE. Consumption.

ROSE. (*Angrily.*) Oh really, Hettie—you live in a Victorian dream world. (*To* RON.) I have a slight lung condition, Monsieur Valov, which is in process of being cured by an antibiotic called streptomycin—

HETTIE. Which makes her pass out every time they give it her—

ROSE. A little allergy, which is perfectly natural. They're giving me a lovely new pill now—

HETTIE. Which she washes down with gulps of brandy she's been strictly forbidden even to sniff.

ROSE. Oh, go to bed, Hettie. I'm quite sure you're boring Monsieur Valov, as much as you're boring me.

HETTIE. Well, good night. Good *dawn*, I mean.

*She goes out. There is a pause.* ROSE *goes to the drink tray.*

ROSE. Let me replenish.

RON *walks slowly over to her, with his empty glass. She takes the bottle which* HETTIE *has opened and fills his glass. Then she pours out a brandy and soda for herself.*

RON. (*Pointing to her glass.*) 'Ere—you didn't oughter-'ve done that, did yer, girl?

ROSE. (*Answering in similar Birmingham accent.*) You're bloomin' right—I didn't oughter—but I done it, see.

*She laughs softly—pleased with him for the first time.*

(*Touching his sleeve and reverting to leer normal accent.*) Thank you and sorry. But mostly thank you.

RON. You got the district wrong. Acacia Avenue.

ROSE. Off Leamington Road? Oh, that's real posh. Did you ever go to the Warwick Arms?

RON. You bet I did. I didn't drink then, mind you. I was training for the ballet. But I used to pop in there quite often on Saturday nights.

*He now speaks with his natural voice which still has a trace of the Midlands.*

ROSE. That's when they had 'Harry's Hotspurs' playing in the lounge. Oh no—of course that'd be before your time.

RON. No, they were still there in '52. Bloody awful they were, too.

ROSE. Were they? I used to think they were wonderful. In fact my idea of heaven was to get someone to take me there Saturday night, give me a 'gin and It' and let me listen to 'It's a Lovely Day Tomorrow', by special request of Miss Rose Fish.

RON. When did you leave Brum?

ROSE. The year the war ended.

RON. (*Admiringly*) You've come quite a way in that time, haven't you?

ROSE. Quite a way. So have you.

RON. Oh, I haven't started. I haven't got anywhere yet. But I will, you know. All those geezers that read palms and crystals and things—they all say I've got it.

ROSE. What? Talent?

RON. No. Money. It's the same thing, isn't it?

ROSE. Yes. I suppose so. (*The topic seems to bore her. She turns brusquely to the gramophone.*) What sort of music do you like, Mr.—what is your real name?

RON. Vale. Ron Vale.

ROSE. But why did you change it? It's a good name. Surely this Anton Valov stuff is dated now, isn't it?

RON. Not in France. They're old-fashioned here. Anywhere else in the world Ronald Vale would be great. But here—oh yes, they've heard of the Royal Ballet all right, and they think Fonteyn and Soames and Ashton are fine, but to them ballet still really means Diaghilev and Fokine and Karsavina and the full Russian chi-chi. Besides, it pays down here to have a bit of mystery about one's nationality—

ROSE. Pays? In what way?

RON. Oh, a lot of ways. *You'd* be surprised.

ROSE. I don't think I would. What music?

RON. (*Coming to the gramophone.*) Oh, anything. Not ballet.

ROSE. Rock 'n' roll? Classical? Something romantic?

RON. Something romantic.

*Suddenly, and with great assurance, he throws his arms around her and tries to kiss her. Quite gently, but with expertise matching his assurance, she pushes him away.*

ROSE. We'll have what's on.

*She switches on the machine. After a moment we hear the overture to 'Traviata'.* Damn. That's not my choice. It must be Fiona's.

RON. Fiona?

ROSE. My daughter. She's sixteen and like you, she has a taste for romantic music. I'm afraid I haven't.

*She switches the gramophone off. She is looking among records when* RON *walks brusquely up to her and turns her round to face him.*

RON. I know just what you're thinking.

ROSE. Do you?

RON. You're thinking—this one isn't on the level. You're thinking of Sam—

ROSE. Sam?

RON. Sam Duveen. The choreographer. (*As she still looks blank.*) The chap I was at the Casino with.

ROSE. (*Quietly.*) Oh. Well, do you know, Mr. Vale, I wasn't thinking of Sam Duveen. I really wasn't. Now what record shall we have?

RON. (*Turning her round again.*) Oh yes, I know. That's the impression I give. It's not my fault. All right—I could wear my hair differently, but why should I?

ROSE. Why indeed?

RON. It's being in the ballet too. You girls never give us the benefit of the doubt, do you? (*Fiercely.*) Sam Duveen's just a good friend of mine and that's that—

ROSE. You really mustn't disturb yourself like this, Mr. Vale. All I know, or indeed care, about your friend Sam Duveen is that he did some very good dances for a musical I once saw and that he has a very nice pale blue Thunderbird. Now please help me choose.

RON. (*Darkly.*) There's a crack in that, too—I know. All right—so he lets me drive his car. All right, so I live in his villa at Monte. All right, if you like, so for all I know he may be—but that doesn't make *me*, does it?

ROSE, *failing advice from* RON, *has finally chosen a record and put it on.*

ROSE. This is harmless. It's called 'Background Music for Talking'. Go on, please.

*She sits down far away from him. He follows her.*

RON. I can't help what he feels about me, can I?

ROSE. (*Quietly.*) Since you ask me, Mr. Vale, I have to answer that I should think you probably can. Now let's talk about something else.

RON. Do you believe what I've just been saying?

ROSE. I'm not very clear about what you've just been saying.

RON. Do you believe I go for women?

ROSE. (*After a pause.*) I believe it quite probable that you go for those women who go for you.

RON. (*Desperately.*) Well—do you believe I go for you?

ROSE. In view of my last answer, I can't quite see that the question applies.

RON. (*Smiling appreciatively.*) God, you're good. You're not just good, you're great. I'm beginning to see—

*There is the sound of a car.*

ROSE. Oh damn!

RON. Who'd come visiting at this time?

ROSE. (*Urgently.*) Turn that light out.

RON. (*Struggling with a table lamp.*) Where's the switch?

KURT. (*Off, calling.*) Rose? You up?

ROSE. It's loo late. (*Calling, wearily.*) Come on up, Kurt.

RON. (*Looking over railings.*) God. What a car! And a chauffeur. At six in the morning, yet!

ROSE. (*Shrugging.*) He's got six chauffeurs yet.

RON. This is Kurt Mast, isn't it?

ROSE *nods.*

Wow! This is the life all right—

KURT MAST *appears on the terrace. He is in the late thirties, and rather handsome in an unsmiling, uncharming way. His clothes (lounge suit now) are made in London and he speaks English well without a strong accent, but his English vocabulary and phrasing, learnt mainly by contact with American Occupation troops after the war, is sometimes incongruously inelegant.*

*Taking no notice of* RON *he walks straight up to* ROSE *and kisses her.*

KURT. Migraine better?

ROSE. Not really. (*Pointing to* RON.) This is—

KURT, *without looking at* RON, *goes to the gramophone and turns it off. Then he goes back to* ROSE.

KURT. You should be hitting the hay with the aspirin and the supponeryls. It's damn fool stuff sitting up like this.

ROSE. I suppose so. May I introduce—

KURT. I was on my way up to the villa and from the road I see the light on this terrace, and I see you moving about so I said, Jeez, this dame, when will she learn some sense? I'll go in and tell her where she is getting off.

So now I am telling you. It was two thirty-five when you left me. What in hell are you doing for three and a half hours?

ROSE. For some of the time I have been talking to Mr. Anton Valov here. Mr. Valov—Mr. Mast.

*At last* KURT *turns and glances at* RON, *who smiles warmly at him.* KURT *does not return the smile, but nods in greeting.*

KURT. How do you do?

*They shake hands.*

You are Russian?

RON. No. English.

KURT. (*Approvingly.*) Fine, fine. (*He turns abruptly back to* ROSE.) Baby, oh baby, did I carve up that Greek syndicate tonight. I am telling you I carved them in slices. (*He makes the appropriate gesture.*) We will eat them tomorrow night with a thick mushroom sauce at the Château de Madrid. (*Holding her hands.*) We must be there at a quarter to nine.

ROSE. It rather depends how I feel.

KURT. (*With a glint of steel.*) You will feel well tomorrow. No migraine tomorrow. So I will call for you at seven-thirty and be punctual, please. Her Highness must not be kept waiting.

ROSE. Lottie? She's been kept waiting all her life. For a free meal she'd wait until the Mediterranean froze over.

KURT. (*After a pause.*) Tomorrow night I am not keeping the Princess waiting.

ROSE. Quite right. You mustn't ever lose your reputation for exquisite manners.

KURT. (*After another pause.*) Your migraine must be good and bad tonight, I think. You said things, too, at the Casino, I am remembering. (*With a jovial laugh.*) It's no good, baby. If ever you want Kurt out of your life, you'll need more than wisecracks. But you don't want Kurt out of your life, do you, my baby? And you won't ever, will you?

*He puts his arms around her.*

ROSE. Something tells me that just at the moment we're not being awfully entertaining to Mr. Valov. (*She breaks free and turns to* RON.) Can I get you another drink?

RON. No, thank you. (*Diffidently.*) I was thinking that perhaps I'd better—

ROSE. (*Firmly.*) Certainly not. I won't hear of your going. You must forgive Kurt's vocabulary, Mr. Valov. He learnt his English in the American Zone. Most Americans, I know, speak far better English than we do, but Kurt doesn't seem to have met them, which, as he was very actively engaged in the black market at the time, is hardly surprising. Now, please let me get you just one more glass of rosé.

RON. Thank you.

*She takes his glass and goes to the drink tray.*

ROSE. Kurt?

KURT. Are you crazy?

ROSE. I thought perhaps a coca-cola.

KURT. No, thank you.

*He is staring at* RON, *taking him in for the first time. He seems puzzled.*

KURT. It is late, isn't it, Mr. Valov, for you to be out visiting?

ROSE. (*From the drink tray.*) Mr. Valov could easily say the same of you, couldn't he? Here, Mr. Valov.

*She hands* RON *his drink.* KURT *looks from one to the other, then enlightenment suddenly dawns.*

KURT. I got it. He's a journalist.

ROSE. (*Quickly silencing* RON.) How did you guess so quickly?

KURT. They are not fooling me. Nowadays they dress so as not to look like journalists, but I can always spot them. You are interviewing Miss Fish?

RON. Well

ROSE. Yes—he's interviewing me.

KURT. It is smart to catch her at this hour. You would not be catching her in the day. What paper?

ROSE. The *Daily Mail.*

KURT. An excellent paper. You will please to say nothing about the American Zone and the black market, remembering please that Miss Fish likes her little funny jokes, but you may say you met me, and that the wedding is to be on December 17th in Düsseldorf—which is my birthday—

RON. (*Entering more into the* spirit.) Is it indeed? I see. Thank you.

KURT. You will also want to know why I am quarrelling with the *Daily Express* and Mr. Sefton Delmer. I will tell you. I am not making fusses about the expression 'Gutter Tycoon' or his joke about 'Back Street boy makes bad', because I am not ashamed I come from the working class, and I am not objecting to the story that I was buying war junk from the Americans in 'forty-five and selling it back to them in the Korean War at ten times the money. So is only good business. No, sir. Financiers are always goddam villains and so are Germans always goddam villains, and German financiers are the goddamdest villains in the world, especially one who is beginning in a cellar in Düsseldorf with fifty Occupation pfennigs in his pocket and is ending in the Schloss Guldheim with fifty million West German marks—so I am not caring a tinker's nickel what the Press is saying about me. But 'neo-Nazi'—now that I am not taking. Jeez, I am not taking that. You can quote this. Kurt Mast is a social democrat.

ROSE. Is that the way you voted in the last election, Kurt?

KURT. In the last election I was not voting at all. I wasn't even voting for Adenauer. By God, I wasn't. By sincere conviction am I a social democrat. (*To* RON.) You got that straight, bud?

RON. Yes. Quite straight.

KURT. Neo-Nazi! Where are they getting such stuff from? That's criminal talk. O.K. So that's all, I guess. Any questions?

RON. No. I don't think so.

KURT. You're a smart kid. Working at six in the morning. That's the way I made it—maybe that's the way you'll make it. O.K. I am not interrupt-ing you and Miss Fish any more. (*He turns to* ROSE.) Good night, baby.

*He tries to kiss her on the lips, but she offers her cheek, which he is forced to accept.*

Sleep well. Take those pills. They're good—non-toxic—the latest. I had them flown over specially. (*He pats her familiarly on the behind.*) No migraine tomorrow. Seven-thirty sharp, if you please.

*He turns abruptly and goes out. There is a pause.*

ROSE. (*At length.*) I'm sorry.

RON. I enjoyed it.

ROSE. He's scared of journalists. I knew it would get rid of him pretty quick.

RON. Is that the way to talk about the man you're going to marry?

ROSE. It's the way to talk about Kurt Mast.

RON. You'll get a good settlement, I hope.

ROSE. Are you kidding? I'm settling for half the Ruhr.

RON *laughs and raises his glass.*

RON. Well— Congratulations.

ROSE. I think you really mean that.

*Pause.*

RON. Well, if you don't like this tycoon, why not get yourself another?

ROSE. When you get to know tycoons as well as I do, which one day I'm quite sure you will—(*mischievously*) female ones, I mean for you, of course—you'll find that they don't usually come complete with good figures and handsome faces. Kurt is a pretty rare specimen.

RON *gets up and walks gracefully past* ROSE, *the object of the journey being to replace his glass on the tray, and of the exercise, to impress* ROSE *with his fig-ure.*

RON. My God—do you think *that's* a good figure?

ROSE. (*Watching him, amused.*) Only by tycoon standards. Not by ballet, of course. Pour yourself another rosé.

RON. No. I mustn't disobey instructions and keep you up. Before I go though, do tell me one thing. How did all this start?

ROSE. All what?

RON. You know. This. (*He waves his hand to indicate the villa.*) Lords, Mar-quises, film stars and tycoons. Who was the very first?

*There is a pause while* ROSE *coolly measures the degree of his impertinence. Then she decides to answer him.*

ROSE. A solicitor called Peter Hawkins—of Cartwright & Hawkins, twenty-three Commerce Square, and he lived in Edgbaston. In 1943 he was my boss and I married him. He died two years later and left me a little money. With that I came down here and met—people—

RON. You say he was your boss? But you were on the stage, weren't you?

ROSE. I certainly wasn't. Where did that story start? I was a respectable girl I'll have you know. I was a typist.

RON. (*Laughing.*) You were what?

ROSE. What's the joke?

RON. (*Still laughing.*) You—a typist! I'm just picturing it—you bent over a typewriter, with the bracelets jangling—and the pearls getting all caught up in the machinery—

ROSE. (*Acidly.*) I didn't have pearls or bracelets then, you know.

RON. Listen. I'll swallow most things. Old gullible Ron—they call me. But this is too much. You a typist! But that, no!

ROSE, *after an angry glance at him, disappears quickly into the sitting-room, emerging in a second with a portable typewriter, and a sheet of typing paper. She sets the typewriter up on a table, opens it up and with plainly practised dexterity inserts the sheet of paper. Then she sits down—her back towards us—savagely pulls off her bracelets, and flexes her fingers.*

ROSE. All right. Now dictate something.

RON. Dictate? What?

ROSE. (*Speaking very deliberately.*) Dictate anything you like, but at roughly this speed. You don't need to go slower. All right. Go ahead.

*Pause.*

RON. Dear Mrs. Bradford, dear Marquise de Beaupré, dear Lady—hell, what was it?—Huntercombe—dear Mrs. Hawkins—and I've quite likely left out one—dear Miss Fish—anyway—this is a message for you from Ron Vale.

ROSE, *appearing to take no notice of the words, types with quiet, evidently highly practised and methodical speed. As he pauses for inspiration she stops and looks down at the typewriter.*

Ever since I came into Sophie's dressing-room that night and saw you standing there in that white dress I have not been able to think of anything else. You are just about the most beautiful thing I ever saw in all my born—

ROSE. (*Quietly.*) Too fast.

RON. The most beautiful thing I ever saw in all my born days—and to meet you tonight, and talk to you, and be asked up to this house has been just about the greatest thrill of my life.

*He stops for a moment.*

I want to say I am sorry I tried my phoney accent on you, but that was only because I was shy, and wanted to impress—as per usual, I am afraid.

*He stops again.*

Thank you for letting me come up here tonight and I would like to point out while I have the chance that it is a hell of a way from here to Monte Carlo—especially driving at this time in the morning after a few drinks. That is all, I think—except I still do not bloody well believe you were ever a typist.

*He has gone faster at the end, and it is a few seconds before* ROSE *completes her methodical typing. Then she pulls out the sheet from the machine, turns and hands it to him. He stares at her for a moment, searching in her face for an answer to his unspoken question, but she turns and lights a cigarette.*

ROSE. Correct?

RON. (*Glancing at the page.*) A hundred per. All right. I take it back. You *were* a typist.

ROSE. And a very good one, too.

*She comes and takes the page out of his hand, reading it. He looks down at the top of her head, uncertain and puzzled.*

RON. (*At length.*) Well?

ROSE. (*Not looking up.*) Well what?

RON. (*Brusquely, daring all.*) Well, am I staying or going?

*Pause.* ROSE *still is scrutinizing the paper.*

ROSE. I did make a mistake. I spelt 'born' wrong—

RON *angrily snatches the paper from her hand.*

RON. I'm keeping this as a souvenir. I hope you don't mind. (*He folds the paper and puts it in his pocket.*) Good night and thank you for your hospitality.

*He bows with rather ludicrous formality and goes towards the steps.*

ROSE. Mr. Vale—

*He stops and turns.*

RON. My name is Ron.

ROSE. Please don't be angry with me, Ron. I'd hate that because I'm really very grateful to you for the compliment you've just paid me. Please say you're not angry.

RON. (*Shortly.*) That's all right. I quite realize I'm not Kurt Mast. I quite realize I haven't got anything to offer—

ROSE. (*Sincerely.*) But really you have a lot to offer. An awful lot. I know there are many, many women in the world who must find you devastatingly attractive—

RON. But you're not one of them, eh?

ROSE. Well, you see, I've never in all my life found any man devastatingly attractive. Just as well, or I might have been devastated, and that would never have done— Dear Ron, you do see that I'm not really an awfully nice or rewarding person and in a few minutes, when you're bowling along the Monte Carlo road in your pretty blue Thunderbird. congratulate yourself on being well out of what would have been an utterly pointless little adventure. Good night.

*She goes to him and shakes his hand.*

Incidentally, next time you're this way, please do come up—have a drink and meet some of my friends—

RON, *angrily, pushes her away from him.*

RON. You think that's all I'm after, don't you—to get where I can come up here when I like, have a drink and meet your smart, rich friends? That's what you think, isn't it?

ROSE, *looking at him with some sympathy and understanding, does not reply.*

RON. (*Roughly.*) Isn't it?

ROSE. That one I don't answer, Ron.

RON. (*Violently.*) Well, it isn't bloody true, see. Do you know what I'm after? Just one thing. I'm after you.

ROSE *continues to look at him. He angrily stubs out a cigarette.*

　　Well, I'm off.

ROSE. (*Quietly.*) *How* old are you, Ron?

RON. (*Turning.*) Twenty-six.

ROSE *nods.*

　　Listen—put *that* thought right out of your head. I've never gone for the young ones anyway. I prefer older women, and I always say that when two people have a real *rapport* the question of disparity of age just doesn't arise—

ROSE *throws her head back and laughs with real enjoyment.*

　　(*Bewildered.*) What's the joke?

ROSE. Just that it might have been myself talking to my second husband in our walking-out days. I used that word *rapport* too. Only my prospective victim was in the late fifties, and, as of now, I can still put money on my own age on a roulette table. Only just, I grant, but then you're in the dernière douzaine, too. No, Ron, I don't think it's age that's the problem between us—

RON, *prepared for one last try, walks towards her and takes her hand.*

RON. (*Tenderly.*) What is it that's the problem between us?

*Pause.*

ROSE. (*With sudden and genuine misery.*) Oh, I don't know. Just me, I suppose. Just me and what I am.

RON. Forget it.

ROSE. You be me and try to forget it!

*A thought strikes her and she laughs.*

　　Come to think of it you *are* me. At least—me nine years younger. That's funny—you being me—that's awfully funny. Ron minus Acacia Avenue equals Rose minus Frogmore Road. So cancel out Birmingham on either side and what have you got? You've got Ron equals Rose. Rose equals Ron. If you really do like me at all you're a narcissist, Ron.

RON. (*His face close to hers.*) I'm not listening. I'm just looking. Christ—you're beautiful. Given half a chance I could go for you the way I've never gone for anyone before.

*He draws her towards him. This time she does not try to evade him, nor resists when he kisses her. Eventually she disengages herself gently and pats his cheek.*

ROSE. You'd better put your car in the garage. Otherwise there'll be too much speculation among the servants. Some we can hardly avoid—

*He kisses her on the forehead with a brief, triumphant smile. Then he turns quickly and walks to the steps, goes down them and disappears towards the drive. We hear the car's engine being started up.*

ROSE, *meanwhile, has looked after him, her expression troubled. Then she wanders to the drink tray. She, is pouring herself out a brandy and soda as* FIONA, *her daughter, appears suddenly in the french windows. She is in a bathing-*

*dress, and carries a towel and a portable record-player. She stops at sight of her mother, then walks towards the steps R.* ROSE *sees her.*

Fiona. You're up very early.

FIONA. No, not really. I always have a bathe before breakfast and I have my breakfast at seven.

ROSE. Is that so? I didn't know.

FIONA. I don't want to waste the sun, you see.

ROSE. Yes. You're quite right. (*She kisses her on the cheek.*) Good morning.

FIONA. Good morning, Mummy.

ROSE. What did you do last night?

FIONA. Oh, I had dinner up here with Hettie, and then I went down to the Ciel et Enfer.

ROSE. Ciel et Enfer? What's that? A night club?

FIONA. No. It's just a café. Upstairs is just ordinary—that's Ciel. Downstairs is much more fun. That's Enfer—and it's where all the interesting people go. Jean-Louis took me down on his Vespa.

ROSE. Jean-Louis? That's the boy who's writing the novel?

FIONA. Yes. Hettie made a terrible boob. She went and asked him if it was existentialist.

ROSE. What was so wrong about that?

FIONA. (*Genuinely shocked.*) Mummy—existentialism's had it years ago.

ROSE. Has it? I didn't know.

FIONA. It's as old-fashioned as Angry Young Men, or James Deanery.

ROSE. Is it really? What's his novel about then?

FIONA. Oh, about a lot of young people who have love affairs with each other and don't much enjoy it, but go on doing it because there isn't any point in doing anything else.

ROSE. It sounds fascinating.

FIONA. Oh, it is. It's an advance on straightforward 'Je m'en foutisme' you see. The two main characters actually fall in love—I mean, real nineteenth-century love—not being able to do without each other and all that—and die together in a suicide pact.

ROSE. That sounds very romantic.

FIONA. That's his school—neo-romantic. It's the very latest St. Germain. Well—

*She moves towards the steps R.* ROSE *looks at her.*

ROSE. Are you doing anything tomorrow night, Fiona?

FIONA. (*A shade suspiciously.*) No, Mummy. Why?

ROSE. (*Nervously.*) I wondered if you'd like, perhaps, to have an evening with me. Just the two of us.

FIONA. (*After a pause, without enthusiasm.*) Yes, Mummy. That'd be fun.

ROSE. I've seen so little of you since you arrived. We could go and have dinner somewhere up in the mountains, perhaps, and afterwards you could take me to this Ciel et Enfer.

FIONA. (*After a pause.*) You wouldn't like it at all.

ROSE. How do you know I wouldn't?

FIONA. I just know, that's all. It's not for you, Mummy. Not Enfer, anyway.

ROSE. You mean everyone there is very young?

FIONA. No. There are some quite old people there. There's a painter and his
    wife there every night and they're both well over forty. It's just—well—
    (*She pauses.*) Anyway, you'd be dressed all wrong.

ROSE. I could wear slacks and do my hair in a fringe—

FIONA *smiles—not rudely—but conclusively.* ROSE *turns away from her abruptly.*
    Don't use the spring-board. It needs repairing.

FIONA. No, Mummy.

*She goes out.* ROSE *goes to the railings to watch her.* RON *comes slowly up on to
the terrace, sees* ROSE'S *back but does not go immediately to her, as his supposed ardour might seem to demand. Instead he looks up at the façade of the
house, and then down at the view. Finally he joins* ROSE *at the railings, and
slips an arm possessively around her waist.*

RON. Your daughter?

ROSE *nods.*

    Is she with you all the time?

ROSE. She was at boarding-school in England until a month ago. Her choice.
    I don't go to England much. But I see as much of her as I can.

RON. Was her father the solicitor?

ROSE *nods.*

    Skinny little mite. She doesn't look a bit like you.

ROSE. (*Simply.*) I don't know about that. I only know I love the way she looks.
    (*Calling, suddenly.*) I said not the spring-board, Fiona.

RON *ducks quickly out of sight.*

FIONA. (*Calling, off.*) It's all right, Mummy. I was only trying it.

RON. Did she see me?

ROSE. (*Listlessly.*) Maybe. I don't know. It doesn't matter anyway.

RON. She wouldn't think anything of it?

ROSE. Oh yes. Something. But not very much.

RON. You mean—she wouldn't be shocked?

ROSE. (*With a hard laugh.*) That's straight from Acacia Avenue—that ques-
    tion. (*She turns from gazing at her daughter and looks at* RON.) No, she
    wouldn't be shocked. If anything she'd be pleased. At least I'd be living
    up to my reputation, which is just about the only thing she enjoys about
    me. No, I'm afraid I don't shock my daughter, Ron. I just bore her. I
    bore her to death.

RON. (*Uncomfortably.*) Do you mind?

ROSE. Yes.

*She turns back to the railings and gazes down at the swimming-pool.*

RON. Have you got any others?

ROSE. No. She's the lot. (*With a smile.*) I ought to have done better with four
    husbands—oughtn't I?—but things went a bit wrong after her.

RON. See much of her?

ROSE. As much as I can. The main reason I got this house was because she adores the sun. (*Calling.*) That's enough, darling. Don't tire yourself out.

FIONA. (*Off.*) All right—Mummy.

ROSE *turns from watching* FIONA.

ROSE. (*At length.*) Well, do you want me to show you your room?

RON. Yes, please.

ROSE *nods and goes slowly towards the sitting-room,* RON *following. He stops at a vase.*

Red roses. (*Pointing to another vase.*) Red roses. (*At another.*) Red roses. I guess you like red roses.

ROSE. Red's my lucky colour, and Rose is my name. It's a kind of superstition.

*She takes both his hands, lowers her head and speaks quickly and very quietly.*

Listen, Monte Carlo isn't so far. I honestly do think—for both our sakes—

RON. (*Roughly.*) Why are you so scared?

*He takes her by the shoulders and pushes her back to look into her eyes.*

ROSE. Me, scared? Really, Ron—you go too far.

RON. But you are, you know. Why?

*The strains of the overture to 'Traviata' can be heard coming from the swimming-pool.* ROSE *goes quickly to the railings.*

(*Calling.*) Not so loud, Fiona. You'll wake everyone up.

FIONA. (*Off.*) All right, Mummy.

*The record continues more softly.*

RON. Why are you scared?

ROSE *turns and looks at him.*

ROSE. I rather wish I knew.

*She goes to a vase, takes out a rose and puts it in his buttonhole, Then she kisses him lightly, takes a step back and looks at him.*

RON. (*Holding her hand.*) Well—shall we go?

*There is a pause.* ROSE *looks at him, then smiles.*

ROSE. (*At, length, lightly.*) Why not?

*Holding his hand she leads the way towards the french windows of the sitting-room.* FIONA *has turned up the volume of her record-player, and the strains of 'Traviata' are now again quite loud.*

CURTAIN

SCENE: *The same, two months later.*

*The time is about eleven at night. The lights are on in the sitting-room, from which the dust sheets have now been removed, and a canasta four is in session there. The table is out of sight, but the players can occasionally be seen at the window as they move about.*

*On the terrace are* FIONA *and* HETTIE. FIONA *is listening to a recording machine, prominently placed.* HETTIE *is knitting.*

FIONA'S VOICE. (*From the machine.*) —and so—all around us—ruin, shame, lies. So I dreamt, at moments, of meeting a man noble enough not to demand a mere reckoning of me, but to love me—Marguerite Gautier—to love the woman that I really am. This man might have been the Duke; but he is old, and old age cannot console me for the hell my life has fallen into. My heart has a need—a need that an older man cannot satisfy. Then—dear Armand—I met you—young, ardent, happy. In a minute—like some mad creature, I built a whole future on your love. I dreamt of the country, of purity and I remembered my childhood—for whatever I may now have become, there was a time when, once, I was a child. Ah, but I was dreaming of what cannot be. Now—dear Armand—you know everything.

FIONA *switches it off.*

FIONA. That's terrible, isn't it?

HETTIE. I'm prejudiced. I heard Bernhardt.

FIONA. You couldn't have.

HETTIE. Why the hell not? I was seven and she was a hundred and eight and it was in French and I didn't understand a damn word, but I still heard Bernhardt. You should do Juliet, dear—not this. Juliet's your age group.

FIONA. Yes, and she's the age group of every other girl trying to get into R.A.D.A. this year. Gosh, the number of potion scenes that must be spouted at those poor examiners every year! Makes one almost sorry for them. No, this is my lady.

HETTIE. Why?

FIONA. I don't know. I suppose because she's sold her soul to the devil.

HETTIE. Does that specially commend a part? Are we going to see you playing Faust some time?

FIONA. Oh, I don't love her only because she's wicked, but because she's honest and warm and brave and true and—oh, I don't know. I just love her, and I feel for her like mad, and I'm going to convey that feeling to the examiners even if I have to work on that machine all summer. I ought really to try and meet someone like that, I suppose, and study them at close quarters—but of course they don't exist nowadays.

HETTIE. Don't they?

FIONA. You mean Mona, or that Italian countess in there? Or that strip-tease girl Mummy brought up the other afternoon?

HETTIE *says nothing.*

Oh no, Hettie. They're just awful and sad and dull. I mean, there's no point in selling your soul to the devil these days—because the devil's got nothing to give you in return anyway. Of course in *her* day (*she points to the machine*) it was different. In yours too, I expect.

HETTIE. Possibly. I don't know. You see, I made no deal with Lucifer. In fact he never even made me an offer.

FIONA. But I bet it was fun, though, wasn't it—for the girls who did? Homburg and Aix-les-Bains, and enormous places in Scotland with sixty servants, and Vienna with the waltzes and special trains to Moscow to stay with a grand duke and—well—even this place. (*She looks up at the façade with distaste.*) Yes, even this place would have had a point then, I suppose.

HETTIE. Hasn't it now?

FIONA. No, of course it hasn't. Just a lot of unused bedrooms. What does luxury mean, Hettie? Only being able to live a life that no one else can afford. Look at Mona. With all her millions, does she ever take a special train anywhere? No. She goes on a tourist flight because there usually isn't a first class, and gets lunch trays spilt over her like everyone else. She's got a bigger television set than most people, I agree—but that'll be out of date in a few years' time. And, anyway, is a twenty-four-inch screen really worth selling your soul to the devil for—when your hairdresser probably gets a clearer picture on his seventeen?

HETTIE. (*Mildly.*) I didn't know you were so firmly right wing, Fiona.

FIONA. I'm not right wing. I'm on the side of the hairdresser. I think equality's a very good thing. (*Wistfully.*) Only—it—well—does rather take the romance out of life. Oh, well, I'm going to have a swim.

*She goes to the railings R. where her bathing-dress has been hanging out to dry.*

Oh Lord! Mummy's down there.

HETTIE. Where?

FIONA. By the pool. (*She puts the bathing-dress back.*) I'll have my swim later.

HETTIE. Why? Who's she with?

FIONA. No one. She's just sitting there.

HETTIE *looks up at* FIONA.

Well, if I go down I'll have to talk to her.

HETTIE *continues to look.*

I want a swim, not a conversation.

*The french windows are opened and* MONA *appears. She is an American lady of great wealth, indomitable gaiety and uncertain age.*

HETTIE. Hullo, Mona. We were just talking about you.

MONA. That's no subject for children. Where the hell's Rose? The Antoninis are going—

HETTIE. She's down by the pool.

MONA. Doing what, for God's sake?

FIONA. Nothing. Just sitting there, musing. Musing on her vanished youth.

MONA. That's enough from you, young lady. One day your youth will vanish and we'll see how you like that.

FIONA. Gosh. I wish it would this minute. I hate the beastly thing. I want to be at least forty-five and be able to say 'foolish boy' to all my lovers.

MONA. (*To* HETTIE.) She's got lovers, already?

HETTIE. Only in dreams. They all look like Armand Duval.

MONA. Who's he? A dish?

HETTIE. A dish of the period.

MONA *stares at her questioningly.*

He's dead, Mona. Don't worry. Anyway, another girl got him. I'll cope with the Antoninis.

*She goes inside.*

MONA. You were kind about me?

FIONA. (*At the gramophone.*) Very sympathetic.

MONA. (*At the railings R.*) What's she doing down there? Really?

FIONA. (*Indifferently.*) I don't know. She's taken to doing that rather a lot lately.

*She has put a record of 'The Sleeping Princess' on the gramophone. It now begins to play.*

MONA. She hasn't even got a drink.

FIONA. Oh, that's out altogether now. The last doctor's put her on a very strict regime. He even says she might have to leave the south of France altogether and go to Switzerland, or somewhere.

MONA. Switzerland? That shouldn't happen to a dog.

*A young man* (ADRIAN) *momentarily appears at the french windows, holding cards.*

ADRIAN. Mona, for God's sake—are you quitting just because I've got four canastas for once?

MONA. All right, Adrian. just coming.

ADRIAN *disappears.*

(*To herself.*) He's hell, that one. He'll have to go.

*She suddenly takes in Fiona's age group, and adopts another tone.*

What I meant, Fiona, was—

FIONA. (*Indifferently.*) That's all right, Mona. I realized from the way he was behaving at dinner that quite soon he'd have to go.

MONA. Cute little child. So innocent and fresh, and unsullied and doesn't miss a goddam trick.

FIONA. (*Sententiously.*) You mustn't confuse innocence with ignorance, Mona.

MONA. I'll confuse what I like with what I like, see. As an adult that's my right.

*She smiles at* FIONA *and goes into the house.* FIONA, *listening to the music, does a couple of very ill-executed ballet steps. Then she picks up the recording machine, which is plainly quite a weight.* RON *appears on the steps L. He is dressed and coiffured a shade more soberly than when we last saw him, but this so-*

*briety hardly extends, at the moment, to himself. He has plainly had quite a few drinks.*

FIONA. Hullo, Ron. I didn't know you were coming. Help me with this.

RON. (*Doing so.*) What is it?

FIONA. It's a recording machine. Mummy bought it for me to practise on— but I don't want her to know I've been using it, or she'll want to hear it, and then she'll be *kind*. Know what I mean?

RON. Who better?

FIONA. Thanks.

RON. This music for my benefit?

FIONA. No, but as you're here, you can jolly well do some work for your living. (*She gets into a ballet position.*) Come on.

RON. (*At drink table, pouring himself a drink.*) No. Not tonight.

FIONA. Come on.

RON. I'm not in the mood. (*He knocks a glass over on the tray.*)

FIONA. You're drunk, that's what.

RON. I certainly am not.

FIONA. All right, then. Go on. Prove it.

RON *puts his cigarette down and goes up to* FIONA. *He stands behind her, also adopting a ballet pose.* FIONA, *in her eagerness, begins a movement.*

RON. No. Wait for the music. One, two, three—now, Arabesque.

FIONA *executes a very clumsy arabesque.*

    Another.

FIONA *does another, giggling with delight.*

    All right. Now. Allez-oops.

*He lifts her on to his shoulder with practised ease. Still giggling, she clutches first at his neck. Then she removes her hands precariously and waves her arms triumphantly in the air.*

FIONA. No hands.

RON, *holding her firmly, executes a few turns, to the accompaniment of shrieks of delight from* FIONA. *Then he stops and lifts her to the ground, finishing the movement with a balletic flourish—on his knees, his left hand on his heart, his right directed towards* FIONA *in earnest homage.*

    Gosh! Oh, gosh. ballet's fun. Ron, do you think I could change my mind about R.A.D.A. and be a ballet dancer?

RON. (*Taking up his cigarette.*) No. You're too old. You have to start at about ten.

FIONA. Is that when you started?

RON. No. I started at eight.

FIONA. At eight. Gosh! You must have been keen.

RON. Yes, I was, then.

FIONA. Come on, Ron. Just once more.

RON. No.

FIONA. (*Behind his chair, wheedling him.*) Come on—

HETTIE *Comes out, and stops short at sight of* RON. *He does not get up.*

RON. (*With a shade of defiance.*) Good evening, Hettie.

HETTIE. (*With a shade of alarm.*) Rose didn't ask you over tonight?

RON. No. Can't say she did. Just thought I'd drop by.

HETTIE. Without telephoning?

RON. Wanted to surprise her. Where is she?

HETTIE. (*Quickly.*) No idea.

*She glances quickly and warningly at* FIONA. *The exchange is not lost on* RON.
    She's gone out somewhere.

RON. When will she be back?

HETTIE. I don't know.

RON. (*Nodding at the house.*) There are people in there.

HETTIE. Only Mona and Adrian.

RON. (*Getting up.*) Dear old Mona. I'll get a welcome from her at least.

*He gets up and with slightly self-conscious effrontery walks past* HETTIE *into the
    house.*
    (*As he goes in.*) Hullo, Mona.

MONA. (*Off.*) Why, Ron. This is wonderful. Come and join us in a hand—

HETTIE. (*Angrily, muttering.*) The nerve. (*To* FIONA, *sternly.*) Fiona, I don't like
    you having anything to do with that character.

FIONA. Why not?

HETTIE. Because he's a bad boy.

FIONA. Do you think so? I think he's rather a sad boy—trying hard to be a
    bad boy. Anyway, why shouldn't I be polite to Mummy's friends?

HETTIE. (*For once nonplussed.*) Your mother just happens to admire him as a
    dancer—

FIONA. Really? I didn't think she'd ever seen him dance. I have. He's good
    virtuoso—that's all. He hasn't the feeling to put him right up top. Pity,
    because he's got the technique. Is that what Mummy thinks?

HETTIE. (*After a pause.*) Lord, sixteen's an awkward age, isn't it? Still, it's not
    too old for spanking. You'd better go to bed before I get too tempted.

FIONA. No. I'm going up to the top of the hill. Only for ten minutes—but I
    want to rehearse that speech again.

HETTIE. Why not in your room?

FIONA. There's a statue of the Grand Duke Auguste up there. I speak the lines
    to him. He kind of inspires me. He's got the right period clothes, too.

*She goes out* L. HETTIE *calls over the railings R.*

HETTIE. Rose.

ROSE. (*Off.*) Yes?

HETTIE. Come up. There's a crisis.

ROSE. (*Off.*) Have we run out of vodka?

HETTIE. A lot worse than that. Come up quick. What in hell do you do down
    there anyway?

ROSE. (*Off, nearer.*) Cogitate.

HETTIE. Can't you cogitate when you haven't got guests? I had to say good-
    bye to the Antoninis for you.

ROSE *appears, in evening dress.*

ROSE. What a social disaster! I'll never be able to show my face in Cannes society again.

*She begins to cough, and sits down. She seems exhausted by her climb from the pool.*

(*Between coughs.*) How much did they cheat at canasta tonight?

HETTIE. I don't know. I wasn't watching them.

*She is, however, watching* ROSE, *as she coughs into a handkerchief. She pours out a glass of water and takes it to her.*

ROSE. Thanks. It's those damn steps. I think I'll have a lift put in. (*Recovering herself.*) Well, all right. Give me the crisis. It's about Ron, isn't it?

HETTIE. How do you know?

ROSE. You've got your Ron face on.

HETTIE. Have I got a Ron face?

ROSE. Like a disapproving Victorian governess. (*Cheerfully.*) Well, what's he done this time? Smashed up the new car?

HETTIE. (*With sudden and surprising virulence.*) I wish to God he had, and him with it.

ROSE. (*Gently.*) Now, now, Hettie. That's dangerous talk.

HETTIE. Oh no. He won't last.

ROSE. He might, you know. He just might.

*She has taken a cigarette and now lights it.* HETTIE *looks at her.*

This is allowed. Ten a day. My seventh. Well, go on. I can take it. What's he done?

HETTIE. Only turned up in this house tonight, uninvited and blotto.

ROSE. (*With quick eagerness.*) He's here?

HETTIE. (*Pointing to the sitting-room.*) Playing canasta with Mona.

*Pause.*

ROSE. Fancy him coming for once without being asked.

HETTIE. Fancy.

ROSE *has wandered to the sitting-room window and looks through it.*

ROSE. The cashmere jacket's rather a success, don't you think?

HETTIE. Great.

ROSE. The hair's fine, now, too, isn't it?

HETTIE. Fine.

ROSE *turns from the window and makes a moue at* HETTIE.

ROSE. Oh well, better anyway.

*Until now she has plainly enjoyed the implications of* HETTIE'S *news. Now her voice becomes hard and firm.*

All right. You'd better ring Kurt and tell him not to come up here for me. I'll meet him down at Maxim's at twelve-thirty.

HETTIE. I can't. He's dining at St. Tropez. I don't know where, and anyway he's probably on his way by now.

ROSE. Yes, of course. (*She looks at her watch.*) Well, I've got plenty of time. Get Ron out here, will you?

HETTIE. Away from Mona?

ROSE. Yes.

HETTIE *turns.* ROSE *suddenly runs after her and catches her arm.*

Why that voice? Are you trying to make mischief?

HETTIE. Yes.

ROSE. All right. Give it to me. What do you know?

HETTIE. Only what you know. That he went to Mona's party on Thursday without letting you know, and the tobacco shares that Mona's last husband left her are paying pretty well this year. Better than an actor's alimony which he defaults on every month anyway—plus the odd present from Kurt. If you want to keep a Ron, you should have husbands that die, like Mona's.

*Pause.*

ROSE. Please don't hate him so much, Hettie. For my sake, don't hate him so much.

HETTIE. For your sake, I'd do a lot of things. That no.

ROSE *turns away with a shrug.*

ROSE. (*Smiling.*) I happen to know he tried to call me Thursday—

HETTIE. Who do you happen to know it from?

*Pause.*

ROSE. Go and get him—there's a dear. Play his cards for him. Mona won't mind.

HETTIE *nods and goes into the sitting-room.* ROSE *turns eagerly at first to face the french windows and then as* RON'S *shadow appears, hastily turns away from the house, as if gazing unconcernedly at the view.* RON *goes up to her and kisses her on the back of the neck. She takes his hand.*

RON. Had you really gone out, or was that old bitch lying as usual?

ROSE. She was lying as usual. I was in the garden.

RON. Alone?

ROSE. Yes.

RON. Thinking of me?

ROSE. Amongst other things.

*She turns and kisses him on the lips. On neither side is the embrace very passionate; affectionate on hers, and on his rather balletically romantic. Then* ROSE *pushes him away and looks at his jacket appraisingly.*

ROSE. Yes. It's very good. Suits you wonderfully.

RON. Bit too much on the shoulders. They can't cut in France. I'm taking it back. I don't want to look like a spiv, do I?

ROSE. No.

RON *goes to the drink tray and pours himself a drink.* ROSE *watches him.*

RON. Want one?

ROSE. No. I'm off it. Doctor's orders.

RON. Good girl.

ROSE. (*A shade timidly.*) Do you think you should. Ron? You've had a few tonight, haven't you?

RON. (*With, sudden ferocity.*) Don't mother me. I hate being mothered— (*He downs his glass of rosé.*)

ROSE I was only thinking of your dancing.

RON. I know exactly what you were thinking of.

ROSE. (*After a pause.*) It really *was* your performance on the stage I was worrying about, Ron.

*Pause.* RON, *without replying, pours himself out another rosé. Then he turns and flashes* ROSE *a beaming smile.*

RON. This stuff's like water, you know. Couldn't hurt a fly.

ROSE. Ron, dear, I'm terribly sorry, but I'm afraid I'll have to ask you to leave in a minute.

RON. Leave?

ROSE. I've got Kurt coming up quite soon and I'm going out with him.

RON. I see.

ROSE. He goes on his yacht tomorrow for a two months' trip. This is his last night in Cannes and I can't put him off tonight. I really can't. Any other night—but not this.

RON. I see.

ROSE. You should have phoned.

RON. Wouldn't have made much difference if I had, would it? —except it might have saved me some petrol.

ROSE. (*Unhappily.*) I'm sorry, Ron.

RON. I wanted like hell to see you tonight.

ROSE. (*Tenderly.*) Did you, Ron? Well—tomorrow—

RON. I wanted tonight. Anyway, I've got my suitcase in the car and I need a bed.

ROSE. (*After a pause.*) You've had a row with Sam?

RON. It was bound to come, wasn't it?

ROSE. Was it about me?

RON. Well, indirectly. I think it was really about the new car—

ROSE. Indirectly, I suppose that might have been about me.

RON. It showed up his—that was the trouble—and he just couldn't bear it. He just couldn't. Anyway. I'm glad it's over. He's done three of our ballets this season, and I've had the lead in two of them—not the last one—oh no—that came after you, so I didn't get that one—that little creep Michel Brun got that—but anyway people in the company were beginning to talk and I was being made to feel a bit—I don't know—cheap.

ROSE. (*Laughing quietly.*) Oh, but that's the last thing you ever ought to feel, Ron.

RON *looks at her, then walks quickly up to her and takes her hand.*

RON. (*Fiercely.*) Listen, Saturday night, you said something to me—remember?

ROSE. I said a lot of things to you.

RON. One thing in particular.

ROSE. (*After a pause.*) I said I was very fond of you.

RON. Was that true?

*Pause.*

ROSE. (*Quietly.*) Yes, Ron. Quite true.

RON. So you're very fond of me. So why are you always needling me, sending me up, taking the mickey out of me? Why? Why? (*Shaking her.*) Why do you needle me?

ROSE. It's not you I needle, Ron. It's myself.

RON. That's another thing. You talk in a lot of bloody riddles to me—all the time—sometimes like you were just talking to yourself just to make yourself laugh. Ce n'est pas très chic, ça, je t'assure.

ROSE. (*With an affectionate smile.*) Non, chéri. Je suis de ton avis. C'est une habitude abominable. Je te demande pardon.

RON. Did you ever take French lessons?

ROSE. (*Laughing.*) Yes. From records, in Edgbaston. My first husband bought them for me. I thought they might come in handy some time. They did. When he died and left me two thousand I came down here and captured myself a French husband. Is that another thing you're going to hold against me—that I speak French better than you?

RON. It doesn't help. It doesn't help that you do everything better than me—

ROSE. Give yourself time, Ron. Remember you're only just starting.

MONA *appears at the window.*

MONA. Hi. How long are you going to monopolize this guy? I've got fifty dollars to get back yet—

ROSE. I told Hettie to take his hand.

MONA. Hell, I don't play with Hettie. She's too goddam good.

RON. All right, Mona. I'll be with you in a second.

MONA, *sensing an atmosphere, turns to the window.*

MONA. You better.

*She disappears.*

RON. What time's Kurt coming for you?

ROSE. Twelve.

RON. O.K. You tip me the wink when you hear the car, and I'll nip upstairs. End room?

ROSE. No.

RON. (*Turning on his way to the door.*) No?

ROSE. No. I don't want you in this house tonight. I'll get Hettie to book you a room at the Carlton. Tomorrow you can come up here.

RON, *without saying anything, or even appearing to have heard, goes to the drink tray and pours himself a rosé.*

(*Looking at her watch.*) And don't play more than one hand with Mona. Try and get out by ten to twelve—

RON *looks at her, clicks his heels and salutes.*

RON. Yes, Ma'am. Very good, Ma'am.

ROSE. (*Ignoring the pantomime.*) And as I may not see you to say good night,

I'd like to say it now. Also to thank you for coming all this way to see me.

*She goes to him and kisses him, as before, with warmth but without passion.*

RON. (*Bowing now and clicking his heels*). Your ladyship's most bloody humble and bloodiest possible obedient servant.

*He turns to the sitting-room, stumbling as he does so.*

ROSE. (*Quickly.*) Ron.

*He turns.*

You *did* try and phone me Thursday, didn't you?

RON. Thursday?

ROSE. The night of Mona's party.

RON. Oh. Yes, of course I did. I told you. My phone was out of order.

ROSE. (*Quickly.*) You said *mine* was.

*Pause.*

RON. (*Shrugging.*) Yours—mine. Anybody caring?

ROSE. Nobody that matters much.

RON. (*Feeling he may have gone too far.*) Now, Rose, my dearest Rose—you can't possibly think—

ROSE. Go back to your canasta, Ron. Only one hand. Double the stakes, if you like. I'll pay your losses.

*Pause.* RON *stares at her, half angry, half frightened.*

RON. Your Majesty's generosity knows no bounds.

*He gives her an elaborate bow, as to a ballet queen, and then makes an exit into the sitting-room in full ballet style—hoping, evidently, to make Rose laugh. She does not. The moment he has gone, she goes quickly to the drink tray and, with slightly feverish hands, pours herself a brandy. She is squirting soda into the glass as* HETTIE *comes in.*

ROSE. (*Raising her glass.*) Caught red-handed. This isn't the last either. Back to the régime tomorrow.

HETTIE. What's upset you?

ROSE. Who knows better than you, you wicked old pudding-stirrer.

HETTIE. Scene about Mona?

ROSE. No. But nearly. My God, how nearly. (*To herself, in wonderment.*) Me—jealous! Jealous of Mona! God! You may be right, Hettie. Perhaps I'd better call time.

HETTIE. (*Morosely.*) If it's not too late.

ROSE. Too late? Of course it's not too late. I could give him up tomorrow if I wanted to.

HETTIE. Why don't you want to?

ROSE. (*After a pause.*) Maybe it's just that at my late age I'm getting—a bit bored with always being the loved one. Maybe I'm beginning to feel it's time that I did the loving.

HETTIE. (*Scornfully.*) Loving!

ROSE. (*After a pause.*) Yes. In a way—loving. You mustn't confuse me with Mona.

HETTIE. If you behave like her, how can I avoid it?

ROSE. Fair comment. (*With a smile.*) Oh Lord, how can I explain it? It's not
*that*. anyway. At least not very much—not nearly enough to justify that
nasty word that's trembling on those Victorian lips. I don't give him
cashmere jackets and Lagondas just to get him to bed, Hettie. I think I
can do that without—I really do—and I'm not one to flatter myself on
that score, as you know. No. I give him cashmere jackets and Lagondas
for the simple and honest reason that I enjoy giving him cashmere jackets and Lagondas. It's fun to give. Great fun. I never really knew how
much. You see, I haven't had much practice in it until now.

HETTIE. Have you had a look at the accounts lately—?

ROSE. Don't be so materialistic, Hettie. All right. So the Lagonda was a mistake, and so I'll never be able to pay for it, without selling a couple of
pictures. But that's not all I give him, and enjoy giving him. (*Musingly.*)
He's a bit lost, our Ron, you know. Of course he doesn't realize it. Oh
no— (*Imitating.*) he knows his way through the jungle—knows it like
the back of his hand. Well, I've been through the same jungle myself, in
my time, and quite frankly, Hettie, I don't think the poor little brute
even knows the back of his hand. Yes. It's rather fun hacking a path for
him without his even knowing it.

HETTIE. You must be very happy then to see that the path you've hacked for
him has led straight to a clearing called Mona.

*Pause.* ROSE *gets up and goes to the drink tray.*

ROSE. Yes. All right. One up.

HETTIE. Don't have another brandy. Have a vin rosé.

ROSE. I prefer a woman's drink, thank you. (*She pours herself a brandy and
soda.*) Yes. You're right. He'll have to go. I can't have my heart skipping
a couple of beats at the sound of another woman's name. Not yet, anyway. Not at thirty-five. Not until I have to. Oh yes—he'll have to go, all
right—the poor little beast—

FIONA *comes in L.*

Hullo, darling. I didn't know you'd gone out.

HETTIE. I told her she could. I thought you wouldn't mind.

ROSE. Of course I don't mind. I don't know why you two always behave as if
I was an ogress-mother.

HETTIE. Well—you've been known to fuss.

ROSE. Only about her health. She's very delicate. She doesn't look after herself as she should—

HETTIE. Pardon a slight titter.

ROSE. That's different. I'm tough. When I was her age I was fighting girls in
Frogmore Road twice her size. And beating them. Did you have a nice
time tonight, darling?

FIONA. (*Politely.*) Yes, thank you, Mummy. I'm going to bed now. Good night.
(*She goes towards the french windows.*)

ROSE. (*Timidly, as always with Fiona.*) Fiona—I met David Cranston at Eden Roc this afternoon.

FIONA. (*Excitedly.*) David Cranston? He's down here? Isn't he up at Stratford?

ROSE. He's got a week off.

FIONA. Oh, Mummy, what's he like to talk to? Does he speak right down in his boots like he does on the stage? Is he very good-looking?

ROSE. (*Complacently.*) Well, you'll have a chance of finding out all that to-morrow afternoon, because he's coming up here.

*The effect of the news on* ROSE *is not at all as evidently envisaged by* ROSE. *The smile is wiped* off FIONA'S *face and her eyes narrow suspiciously.*

FIONA. Up here?

ROSE. Yes. And just to meet you. I told him all about you and your ambitions. He was very interested—

FIONA. Oh Mummy, of course he wasn't interested—

ROSE. He was, you know. He even said he'd hear you read a part—

FIONA. (*With some force.*) No.

ROSE. You mustn't be scared, darling.

FIONA. I'm not scared, but I won't let him hear me read. Not up here, where he's your guest and has to be polite.

ROSE. It's a wonderful chance.

FIONA. Of course it is, but I won't do it. I won't. One day I'll read to him on a stage, when I'll just be Fiona Hawkins and one of fifty others and he won't know whose daughter I am. But not until.

ROSE. (*Quietly.*) But he will know whose daughter you are, won't he—as you're going to meet him tomorrow?

FIONA *shakes her head.*

You mean, you don't want even to meet him?

FIONA *shakes her head again, plainly deeply disturbed.*

But he's your favourite of all, isn't he?

FIONA. I once waited in the rain for an hour outside the Haymarket to get his autograph—and then I missed it. But I'm not going to meet him up here. I'm sorry, Mummy. I'll go out tomorrow—

ROSE. But it was entirely for your sake that I asked him, darling—

FIONA. Yes, Mummy. I know that. I'm awfully sorry.

ROSE. (*Growing angry.*) But why, for heaven's sake?

FIONA. I can't explain it. I only know I don't want to meet him if he's coming up here to have a drink with you.

*Pause.*

ROSE. (*Quietly.*) You say some hurting things sometimes, Fiona.

FIONA. If I do, I don't mean them.

ROSE. No. I don't think you do. That doesn't stop them from hurting.

FIONA. I'm sorry, Mummy. May I go to bed now?

ROSE. Yes. You should.

FIONA *walks dutifully over to* ROSE *and plants a filial kiss on her cheek.*

FIONA. Good night, Mummy.

ROSE. Good night, Fiona.

FIONA. Good night, Hettie.

HETTIE. Good night, you little beast.

FIONA. You understand, don't you?

HETTIE. Don't drag me into it. Go on.

FIONA *goes into the house.*

ROSE. Do you understand?

HETTIE. (*Tactfully.*) Not really.

ROSE. You do, I think. What is it? She can't dislike me all that much, can she?

HETTIE. Of course she doesn't dislike you. All she dislikes is being the daughter of Rose Fish.

ROSE. But Rose Fish doesn't shock her. I know it doesn't—

HETTIE. I know, too. But there's a difference between not being shocked by Rose Fish and wanting to be Rose Fish's daughter.

ROSE. (*Shrugging.*) The wages of sin?

HETTIE. Part of them. Not a very important part, I'd say.

ROSE. (*With sudden violence.*) God, Hettie. The most important part. I'd give anything—anything in the world—to break down the defences of that remote, withdrawn little monster, and make her feel something for me. Something. Even shame or hatred. I could cope with that. What I can't cope with is 'Yes, Mummy', 'No Mummy', 'I'm sorry, Mummy', 'May I go to bed, Mummy'. Oh God, Hettie, if only I could get her to *need* me.

HETTIE. The wail of mothers all down the centuries.

ROSE. (*Wiping her eyes quickly.*) This mother happens to be rather a special mother—and means it rather specially—

HETTIE. That's the first time I've ever seen you cry.

ROSE. It's just about the first time I ever have. Damn it! How idiotic! I don't know why she dislikes being the daughter of Rose Fish. If you ask me she's damn lucky to be the daughter of Rose Fish.

HETTIE. I cordially agree.

*There is the sound of a car drawing up, and headlights light up the railings L.*

ROSE. Oh God, Kurt. (*Looking at her watch.*) Quarter of an hour early. Trust him. (*Coolly.*) I'll keep him here for a few minutes. You get Ron out of the house. Book him a room at the Carlton—charge it to me. Tell him to call after his rehearsal tomorrow and come over for supper if he wants to.

HETTIE. He'll want to.

ROSE. And tell him to bring his things. From tomorrow he's staying here. (*Calling into drive.*) Hullo, Kurt. Come on up on the terrace.

HETTIE. I thought you said he had to go.

ROSE. I'll think about that tomorrow. Go on.

HETTIE *goes. After a moment* KURT *appears. He is in a white dinner jacket.*
   You're early.

KURT. I know. The most boring party. Disgusting food, and all trying to play
   me for crazy schemes like I was the biggest sucker in Europe. (*He stops
   and looks at her appraisingly.*) Yes. You are looking good tonight. Very
   good.

*He kisses her slowly and with evident relish. She accepts the embrace compos-
edly.*

ROSE. (*Emerging at length.*) You've ruined my make-up.

KURT. Not *your* make-up, my dear. It can stand up to more than that. It has
   to, I'd guess.

ROSE. Not unless *you're* around—you wolf.

KURT. (*Laughing.*) You are being in good form tonight. That is good. We will
   be having fun tonight, my baby. We will be beating up this old burg
   tonight like it has not been beaten in ions.

ROSE. (*Correcting.*) Aeons.

KURT. Aeons? So? I was reading it today for the first time. It's a good word.
   It means for ever, like the way I love you. Your guests have gone?

ROSE. No. Mona and her boy friend are still here.

KURT. Not the boy friend, my dear. When I was coming in the drive, he was
   leaving it—going like the goddam wind.

ROSE. Oh? He and Mona must have had one of their tiffs. She wasn't with
   him?

KURT. No. Go and say good-bye to her and then we shoot off—(*He turns to
   go back to the car.*)

ROSE. (*Coolly.*) Just a moment, Kurt.

*He turns.*

   You know I hate talking sordid business matters late at night.

KURT. Quite right, my dear. Late at night is most unsuitable.

*He takes out a cheque book and a pen. He deliberately opens it on a table and
poises the pen over a cheque. One feels he enjoys the moment.*

   O.K. Baby. Shoot.

ROSE. I honestly don't know how much we're owing at the moment. I'm afraid
   it's rather a lot. I'll have to ask Hettie—

KURT. (*Beginning to write.*) No need to be asking Hettie. This will be round
   enough for any owings—

ROSE. (*Automatically correcting.*) Debts.

KURT. Debts. As if that word I should know.

*He hands her a cheque. She glances at it.*

ROSE. (*Quietly, handing it back.*) No, I won't need all that. Thanks all the
   same, but make it for half, would you?

KURT. (*Putting his arm around her gleefully.*) My baby, my baby, to whom are
   you saying that? And who is saying it to me? Make it for half! Yes, you
   are being in good form tonight.

ROSE. (*Putting the cheque into her bag.*) I meant it, you know. You're too generous.

KURT. I am a business man. Value for money. For the best goods you must
always be paying the highest prices—

ROSE *turns abruptly to the drink tray and pours herself a brandy.*
Can't you wait until Maxim's?

ROSE. Frankly, no. (*She turns and lifts the glass to him.*) Thank you, Kurt. I'm
very grateful.

KURT. (*Deprecatingly.*) My dear—

ROSE. The gambling's been terrible lately, and a lot of expenses seem to have
come all at once. Decorating this house, and fixing up the pool—

KURT. (*Quietly.*) And buying a Lagonda for Ron Vale—

ROSE *stares at him in silence. He laughs delightedly.*
My dear, when other people are saying they have spies everywhere, they
are using an expression of speaking. But with Kurt Mast it may not be
such nonsense talk.

ROSE *opens her bag and takes out the cheque. She walks over to him. As she reaches
him he pushes her outstretched hand impatiently away from him.*

KURT. Don't be crazy. Do you think I am caring?

ROSE. (*Quietly.*) But you should care, shouldn't you?

KURT. About a Ron Vale? My dearest honey child, I am hearing my baby
has found herself a little ballet boy, and I am saying not my baby, not
my Rose, such things are not for her—a Greek shipowner, yes, but not
a ballet boy. And then I am finding out it is goddam true. But I am also
checking up on this Vale—Valof, and baby. (*He laughs.*) Oh well, I am
saying, if my Rose, who I am always knowing is so generous and so extravagant is wanting to throw money away by giving expensive motor-cars
to such a boy—well, I am not objecting. Not yet, When she is my wife—
another story. Also when I see this Vale I will very likely be pulling him
apart with my hands. But caring? Me? About such a boy. Pfui. My Rose
is still *my* Rose and no one else's and I am knowing it goddam well.

*Pause.* ROSE *tears up the cheque deliberately, and puts the pieces in an ashtray.*
Why so dramatic? Don't you know I will only be writing you another
one later?

ROSE. Yes. You certainly will.

KURT. (*Laughing.*) For double, to punish me?

ROSE. No. For exactly this amount—less the price of a Lagonda.

KURT. I am not knowing the price of a Lagonda.

ROSE. Nor am I exactly, but we'll find out. Now let's go. I'll just get my wrap—

*Her voice fades as* RON *appears at the sitting-room windows. He is drunker than
when last seen.*

RON. I just came to tell you that you don't need to worry about a bed for me
tonight. Mona's going to put me up. (*Turning to* KURT.) Good evening,
Herr Mast. We met once before, do you remember? You thought I was
a journalist.

KURT. Yes. I remember.

RON. You told me you had no objection to the expression 'Gutter tycoon' and I'm glad about that. Very glad, because you see I think it's a very good expression indeed—'Gutter tycoon'. Very good.

ROSE. (*Authoritatively.*) Go and say hullo to Mona and Hettie, would you, Kurt?

KURT *stands for a moment undecided, then turns briskly to the window and goes into the house without looking back.*

Trying to get yourself killed, Ron?

RON. Let him have a go. I'd be only too happy.

ROSE. He doesn't have to do it himself, you know. He's got plenty of thugs around.

RON. Nice class of people you choose for your boy friends, don't you?

ROSE. Yes, I do, don't I? All right. The damage is done now. You'd better go in the End Room.

RON. I've told you. I'm not going in the End Room, or the Carlton, or any other damn place. I'm staying with Mona.

*Pause.*

ROSE. How drunk are you, Ron?

RON. Not so drunk I don't know exactly what I'm doing.

ROSE. You know that if you stay with Mona tonight, you'll never see me again.

RON. Yes, I know that. One law for the bloody rich and another for the bloody poor. You can go off on the town with your gutter tycoon, but I have to be a good little boy and tuck myself up in the Carlton—probably with Hettie locking me in.

ROSE. I'm sorry, Ron, but I'm just telling you the facts. I'm not discussing the justice of them.

RON. All right—so you've told me the facts.

ROSE. And you accept them?

RON. You bet I accept them. I bloody well welcome them.

ROSE. All right. So that's it. (*Smiling at him.*) How do we say good-bye in a situation like this? It's rather difficult to know. Shake hands and wish each other luck?

RON. Fish. God, they knew something when they gave you that name. Do you breathe with gills? Have you any feelings at all? Have you ever given one minute's thought to me in the last two months?

ROSE. Yes, Ron. Quite a few minutes.

RON. I wonder. Have you ever thought what it's been like for me, asked over here a couple of odd evenings a week whenever there're no important people around—because common Ron mustn't meet important people—oh dear no—that'd never do—and then when I'm here shoved around, needled, sent up—everyone talking about people I don't know, and things I don't understand. Do you know why I came over tonight? Do you know?

ROSE. To get a bed, I thought.

RON. I could have got a hundred beds without driving for an hour and a half. I came over to find out what sort of greeting I'd get from my girl if I turned up here out of the blue without letting her know. A kind of test case you could call it. Well. I found out all right. My God, I found out. The paid companion is sent in to bundle me out of the house because the other boy friend—the rich one—has turned up unexpectedly—

ROSE. (*Wearily.*) Oh, really, Ron. You've always known about Kurt—

RON. And has that made it any easier, do you think? Do you think I enjoy living on your immoral earnings?

ROSE. You mean you'd rattler they were moral earnings? Like Mona's tobacco shares?

RON. That's right. Be funny. Make a joke. Needle me. My feelings don't matter a damn, and never have.

*Pause.* ROSE *goes up to him, at length, and gives him an affectionate kiss.*

ROSE. Good-bye, Ron.

HETTIE *comes in and stands in the window.*

HETTIE. (*To* ROSE.) Having any trouble?

ROSE. No. No trouble at all.

*She goes into the house.*

RON. I suppose you're pleased about this.

HETTIE. Delighted.

RON. (*Pouring himself a rosé.*) And so am I. My God, am I delighted? I feel free now, my own master, and it's a good feeling.

HETTIE. I wonder if Mona will appreciate the feeling.

RON. Listen, if you think I'm going to jump out of *this* fryingpan into *that* fire, you're wrong. Dead wrong. When I say free, I mean free.

HETTIE. Going to give back the Lagonda?

RON. Who knows?

HETTIE. I do, I think.

RON. You're not as wise as you like to believe, Hettie. I might surprise you.

HETTIE. You might, but will you?

RON. (*Bravely.*) All right. Send to Monte tomorrow and collect it. There. Or do you want it in writing?

HETTIE. Oh no. Your word, I'm sure, is your bond.

ROSE *comes on to the terrace, now with wrap, talking quite gaily to* MONA. KURT *follows them.*

ROSE. No, it's red, impair and my age tonight. At chemmy, it's bancos. The banks won't run.

MONA. Famous last words. What's it for you, Kurt?

KURT. Baccarat.

ROSE. It's always baccarat for Kurt, and he always wins.

KURT. Because I am lucky in love.

ROSE. It's the other way round, darling.

MONA. I've a good mind to come down with you.

ROSE. Why don't you?

MONA. What about it, Ron?

RON. I've got to be early tonight. I'm dancing tomorrow.

KURT. What are you dancing tomorrow?

RON. The Blue Bird.

KURT. The blue bird? What is that? You have wires and go flying over the stage—like Peter Pansy?

*He flutters his arms in a derisory gesture.*

RON. (*Quietly.*) No. Not like Peter Pansy. The Blue Bird is a virtuoso part, and I'd say just about as difficult to dance well as to make a fortune out of the black market—

ROSE. You won't come then, Mona? (*To* KURT.) All right, darling. Then let's go.

FIONA *comes in in a dressing-gown.*

FIONA. I'm going to have a swim, Mummy.

ROSE. You ought to be asleep, Fiona.

FIONA. Swimming helps me to sleep. I do it every night.

*She moves towards the steps and collects her bathing-suit.*

KURT. I must come to Monte Carlo one night, Mr. Vale, and see you dancing these virtuoso dances that are so difficult—

RON. Don't bother, Herr Mast. Monte Carlo is a long way and from what you told me about yourself the other morning I doubt if you appreciate the fine arts very much. I tell you what. I'll give you an exhibition now. (*Rounding on* FIONA.) Here's my partner.

FIONA. No, Ron. Not now.

RON. Nonsense. (*To* ROSE.) You haven't seen us do this, have you. Rose?

FIONA. No, Ron, please. We haven't any music.

RON. Who wants music

*He gets into ballet position behind her.*

FIONA. No, Ron.

RON. Now don't be scared. What have you got to be scared of? (*He begins to hum the music of 'Swan Lake.'*) Now, Arabesque.

FIONA *obediently performs, plainly not enjoying herself.*

Well done. Now another.

*She does it again.*

Bravo. You have a budding Fonteyn here. Now—allez-oops.

*He lifts* FIONA *on to his shoulder.*

HETTIE. (*Quietly.*) Ron—stop it.

RON. What about that? Isn't she marvellous? Now hold tight, and we'll show them a bit of virtuoso stuff.

HETTIE. No, Ron. Let her down.

RON. (*To* FIONA.) All right? Here we go, then.

*He does a spectacular turn, successful the first time, but in repeating it, trips and falls.* FIONA *screams.* RON *twists his body around so as to fall backwards and break* FIONA'S *fall.*

ROSE. Oh, my God! (*Running to* FIONA'S *side.*) Fiona, are you all right?

FIONA. (*Scrambling to her feet.*) Yes, Mummy. I think so. (*She feels her elbow.*) Bit of a bump here, that's all.

HETTIE. Let's see. (*She examines* FIONA'S *elbow.*)

KURT. (*Also looking at it.*) A bruise tomorrow, maybe. (*To* HETTIE.) The best thing is a hot compress—

FIONA. Oh no. It's not bad at all. Just hurts a bit.

MONA. It's the funny bone, I expect. That always hurts.

RON, *meanwhile, unwatched by anyone, has been lying motionless on the ground. He now gets laboriously to his feet. As he puts his right ankle to the ground it crumples under him and, as he straightens it, we can see that he is in great pain. He nevertheless manages to stand, nonchalantly holding on to a chair.*

RON. I'm sorry, Fiona.

FIONA. That's all right.

RON. I'm a lousy partner. Always have been. Much better alone and that's the truth.

ROSE. (*To* FIONA.) Better go to bed, darling. Hettie'll look after you.

FIONA. Yes, Mummy. (ROSE *kisses her.*) Good night. Good night, everyone. Good night, Ron. It wasn't your fault. I over-balanced—

*She goes out, followed by* HETTIE.

MONA. You've got your car, Ron?

RON. Yes.

MONA. I'll go ahead, then. You know the way?

RON. Like the back of my hand.

ROSE *looks at him for about the first time, and what she sees in his motionless form tells her the truth.*

MONA. (*On her way out.*) Good night, Rose darling. Lovely evening.

ROSE. (*Accepting her kiss, still looking at* RON.) Glad you enjoyed it, Mona.

MONA *goes out.*

KURT. Well, I have much enjoyed your exhibition of this virtuoso dancing, Mr. Vale. And that is as difficult to perform as to make five hundred million marks?

RON. We can all of us come an unexpected cropper, Herr Mast. Let's face it—any of us back-street boys can sometimes make bad.

*Barely perceptibly he staggers, and holds on tightly to the chair.*

ROSE. (*To* KURT.) Darling, go on to Maxim's, will you? I'm a bit worried about Fiona and she might need a doctor or something. I'll use my car. (*As* KURT *is about to protest.*) Order me Lanson '47 and scrambled eggs. I'll be down in ten minutes.

KURT. I would not be liking it to be any longer.

ROSE. It won't be. Don't forget the Lanson '47, or they'll try and palm you off with a non-vintage. And no nonsense about caviar aux blinis. Just scrambled eggs—

KURT. (*At steps.*) Good night, Mr. Vale—and I think I am meaning good-bye, is it not?

RON. (*Wearily.*) Yes, it may be, Herr Mast. God! this is a silly game—but I'll go on playing it if you like. Good-bye is a word that sounds very sweet when it's said to you.

ROSE. (*To* KURT *as he is about to reply.*) Go on, Kurt. He's quite right, it's a silly game.

KURT. He may find, one day—silly or not—it is perhaps not such a game.

*He goes out. The second he is out of sight,* RON *collapses on to his knees.*

ROSE. (*Authoritatively.*) Lie down. Right down. On your back. That's right. (*She examines his ankle.*) Yes. It's broken.

RON. No. It's only a sprain.

ROSE. It's broken.

RON. What do you know about ankles?

ROSE. I was in the A.R.P. in the war. You damn little idiot. You've made it much worse getting up and standing on it.

RON. I wasn't going to give that Nazi bastard a belly laugh by seeing me down and out.

ROSE. Lie there. Don't move it any more whatever you do. I'll get a cushion for it.

*She goes to collect a cushion.* HETTIE *comes in.*

Hettie, ring up Doctor Marton and tell him to come up at once. Ron has broken his ankle.

RON. Sprained.

ROSE. Broken. There's no doubt, I'm afraid.

HETTIE. I'm sorry.

RON. (*Wearily.*) You're not, you old bitch, so why do you say so?

HETTIE. A perfect gentleman. isn't he? Even adversity he wears with a smile—

ROSE. Doctor Marton's number is in my book, Hettie.

HETTIE *goes out.* ROSE, *kneeling beside* RON, *very gingerly lifts his leg a few inches and slips a cushion under his ankle.* RON *groans.*

(*On the ground beside him.*) I'm sorry, darling, but it's better that way.

RON *suddenly grabs* ROSE *and buries his face in her stomach.*

RON. (*Sobbing.*) Oh Rose! Oh my God!

ROSE. (*Stroking his head.*) Does it hurt very much?

RON. It hurt like hell when I was standing on it. It doesn't hurt now.

ROSE. Well, just stay quiet.

RON. (*With another sob.*) Oh God!

ROSE. What is it, darling?

RON. It's so awful.

ROSE. It'll mend all right, Ron.

RON. I'm not talking about the bloody ankle. I'm talking about me. About you and me. You all think I'm a proper bastard, I know, and just out for what I can get, and I dare say you may be right. But that's how I was told when I was a kid—in this world, Ron boy, they said, you got to work it so it's 'F.U., Jack, I'm all right', or you go under—and Christ, Rose, that's true. Look at the people who do go under—even in this bloody Welfare world.

*He raises a tear-stained face and looks up at her. She says nothing, looking down at him, and continuing mechanically to stroke his hair.*

What's so wrong in looking after oneself? You've done it all your life, haven't you?

ROSE. Yes.

RON. Why does everybody think I'm such a bastard because I do it?

ROSE. Perhaps they think the same of me.

RON. They don't. You know that's a lie. (*Sobbing again.*) I can't give you up, you know. It's no good. I can pretend about Mona, but she makes me bloody sick, and Sam, and all the others. It's the same with them. I can't give you up, Rose. Don't send me away.

ROSE *does not reply. There is a pause.* RON *recovers himself a little.*

You think this is just another act, because I don't want to lose my rich girl friend. Yes. I know that's the way your mind works. I don't blame you. So would mine in your place. Yes, all right. That's the way it started. 'Rose Fish? Oh yes. I know her very well. As a matter of fact I'm popping up to the Château Auguste tomorrow—staying all night as it happens. Yes, she's really very nice—not a bit like what the papers say about her—can't trust the papers, can you?—yes, awfully amusing, and terribly beautiful—and, of course—mad about me—'

*He holds her tightly to him again.*

But it isn't like that now, Rose. I don't know just what's happened, but it isn't like that. Christ, I'm jealous of Kurt. Me! Jealous! What a laugh! (*He begins to sob again.*) I don't understand it. I hardly ever see you, when you call me in the mornings, we don't say much to each other, just gossip, your friends treat me like dirt and so do you, only more polite, and yet I can't damn well do without you. I need you in my life.

*He looks up at her again.*

For some bloody silly reason which I can't explain, I need you in my life.

*He is still looking at her, waiting for some answer, when* HETTIE *comes in.*

HETTIE. Doctor Marton's on his way. I've also rung the hospital and got an ambulance.

ROSE. Thank you, Hettie. You've done very well. In a few moments would you ring Maxim's and tell Kurt that I'm not coming down tonight?

HETTIE. Shall I tell him what's happened?

ROSE. No.

HETTIE. Then what *shall* I tell him?

ROSE. Whatever you think best, in the circumstances.

HETTIE. What are the circumstances?

ROSE. I'm needed by Ron.

*She bends her head over* RON'S *in a protective embrace.*

CURTAIN

# ACT II

## SCENE 1

SCENE: *The same, two months later.*

*Five people sit on the terrace, with* ROSE *pouring coffee, and giving the cups to* RON *to hand round.* RON *walks with a stick. The new face is that of* SAM DUVEEN, *a lean athletic-looking man in the middle forties, It is just after lunch.*

ROSE. (*Handing a cup to* RON.) That's for Hettie. You shouldn't be doing this. Go and sit down—

RON. It's all right. He said as long as I don't put any weight on it, it's all right.

ROSE. Fiona, you come and take coffee round, would you?

RON. (*Taking the cup to* HETTIE.) You all behave as if I'd done it yesterday. Dammit, it's been out of plaster since last week.

SAM. Ron's quite right, Mrs. Bradford. The more exercise he gives it, the sooner he'll be dancing again.

RON. I'm not dancing again.

*He sits down.* SAM *looks at him in surprise.*

ROSE. (*Giving a cup to* FIONA.) For Mr. Duveen.

SAM. Not ever?

RON. No. I thought you knew.

SAM. You didn't tell me.

RON. I told everyone else, including the boss. I suppose I was scared to tell you, because I knew what you'd say.

ROSE. And what do you say, Mr. Duveen?

SAM. (*Lightly.*) Nothing at all. Why should I?

ROSE. (*A shade defensively.*) It was his idea, you know. Not mine.

SAM. Oh, I'm quite sure of that.

ROSE. On the other hand I can't say I'm not glad. I didn't particularly relish the thought of being a dancer's wife and trekking all over Europe with him on one-night stands and things—

SAM. (*Politely.*) I quite agree. I don't know any dancer's wife who doesn't want her husband to give up the ballet.

RON. The trouble is it's the worst paid job in the world—and after years of sweating to get to the top you suddenly find you've had it because your muscles don't work so well any more. I ask you—what sort of career is it for anyone that ends at forty—without a pension?

SAM. Yes. It's a bad career, unless you happen to love it.

RON. And I never did. You know that. Remember how I used to shock you?

SAM. You did—but then about ballet I'm easily shockable.

ROSE. Was he good, Mr. Duveen?

SAM. As a technician, yes—but to have been good by the highest standards
he needed to have worked a good deal harder than he did.

RON. Hell, Sam, I worked. I never missed class—

SAM. (*Smiling.*) Only because I told the boss to dock your pay cheque if you
did. Besides, there's more in working at dancing than just not missing
class.

ROSE. (*Brightly.*) Anyway, Mr. Duveen, you don't think the ballet is going to
suffer a mortal blow by losing Ron?

SAM. I think the ballet will survive. (*To* RON.) What are you going to do, then,
Ron?

RON. I'm not quite sure. Rose knows a man who runs a travel agency who
needs some dough and would take a partner. Only it's a ten to six job.

SAM *smiles understandingly.*

A more attractive idea is for Rose and me to get ourselves a small picture
gallery in Paris.

SAM. I didn't know you liked pictures.

RON. I don't know that I do but Rose does, and I'm learning fast. Aren't I,
darling?

ROSE. (*Fondly.*) Frankly, no. Besides, I'm a terrible teacher. Still a picture gallery would be fun. It'd probably be on the rocks after a month, but it'd
be fun. (*She holds* RON'S *hand.*)

HETTIE. (*Getting up, suddenly.*) I'm not speeding the parting guest, but you
said something about Mr. Duveen having the Rolls to take him back,
and I'd better warn Gaston.

ROSE. Yes, that's right.

HETTIE *goes out.*

SAM. It's very kind.

ROSE. Not at all. Taxis down here are appallingly expensive.

RON. Did you sell the Thunderbird?

SAM. No. I've lent it until I get back from New York.

RON. (*Casually.*) To Michel?

SAM. Yes.

ROSE. Is it tonight you're going, Mr. Duveen?

SAM. No, Mrs. Bradford, tomorrow night—from Paris.

RON. Darling, why all this Mr. Duveen, Mrs. Bradford stuff? You've had a
very nice lunch together—and I happen to know—because both of you
have taken me aside separately and said it to me—that you each think
the other's heaven—

ROSE. ⎱ (*Murmuring* ⎰ Ron—really—
SAM. ⎰ *together.*) ⎱ How embarrassing can you get?

RON. Well, you both said exactly the same thing to me. You both said she—
or he—is far nicer than I expected. Anyone denying that?

*There is no answer.*

So why in hell can't you call each other Sam and Rose?

ROSE. (*After a pause.*) We come from a politer generation than yours. We wait for permission before we Christian-name each other. (*Smiling.*) Isn't that right, Sam?

SAM. (*Smiling back.*) It certainly is, Rose. Except that you shouldn't lie by including me in your generation.

HETTIE *comes back with three letters which she hands to* ROSE.

Or, if it comes to that, by excluding Ron's from yours.

ROSE. (*Beginning to open the letters.*) A woman is as old as she feels, isn't she? And I usually feel old enough to be his grandmother. Would you excuse me?

SAM. Of course.

ROSE *reads two of the letters.*

RON. What's the ballet you're doing in New York?

SAM. It's not New York. I'm going on to Hollywood.

RON. What film?

SAM. I don't know. I don't even know who's going to be in it.

RON. (*Smiling.*) But you know the money.

SAM. (*Smiling back.*) Just a vague idea.

RON. Good?

SAM. Best yet. That's still not good—but—better—

ROSE. (*To* HETTIE, *indicating letters.*) That's a firm no. That's a qualified yes. (*Giving* HETTIE *the third letter unopened.*) And that you can throw away.

HETTIE. Shouldn't you at least take a glance at the postmark?

ROSE. (*Glancing at the envelope.*) All right. So he's back. I knew he was about due.

*She hands the letter back to* HETTIE, *making a gesture of tearing it up.* HETTIE *nods and goes out.*

RON. Kurt?

ROSE. Yes.

SAM. Kurt Mast?

ROSE. That's right. My ex-intended.

SAM. (*Nodding.*) I read that interview he gave in Capri—the one where he said that there was no other man in your life but himself and that the marriage in Düsseldorf would take place precisely as planned. I thought that was rather sad.

ROSE. Why sad? It was just a silly lie. I haven't had any contact with Kurt for two months.

SAM. I'm sure.

RON. What's sad, then?

SAM. That he should find it necessary to his pride to tell such a silly lie. This is one story he couldn't buy off—and it was plainly the one that has hurt him the most. He must love you very much—that man.

FIONA, *who has been reading the 'History of Western* Philosophy' *by Bertrand Russell, raises her head for just one quick glance at* SAM. *Apparently he has been the first of the adults to say something that has interested her.*

RON. Who doesn't?

SAM. Who indeed?

ROSE. I don't think you need be too sorry for Kurt, Sam. He can look after himself. After all, he has the means.

SAM. They're a bit material, aren't they—in a crisis like this? Material enough to be immaterial, I'd have thought.

*Pause.*

RON. I should have warned you about Sam, darling. He only really likes people he can feel sorry for, so he tries to find some reason to feel sorry for everyone in the world. Like me, for instance. When we first met he felt sorry for me because I could do six pirouettes dead on the spot and none of the others could. Isn't that true, Sam?

SAM. (*Quietly.*) Yes, Ron. That's completely true.

FIONA *gets up.*

FIONA. Mummy, may I go down to the pool?

ROSE. Isn't it a bit soon after lunch, dear?

FIONA. Oh, that's just an old person's—I mean an older person's superstition. (*Extending her hand.*) Good-bye, Mr. Duveen.

SAM. Good-bye.

ROSE *is looking at the recording machine, which is on a table.*

ROSE. Have you been using this, this morning?

FIONA. (*Casually.*) No, Mummy.

ROSE. (*Sharply.*) Oh God, why do you lie? It's so idiotic. Who else uses this but you?

FIONA. (*Sullenly.*) I was going to use it and then I didn't.

ROSE. You did use it, but you don't want me to hear the result. That's it, isn't it?

FIONA *does not reply.*

All right. I'll respect the injunction. What play did you do?

FIONA. *The Seagull.*

ROSE. One day would you let me hear you reading a part? Any part?

FIONA. Yes, Mummy.

SAM. Is the young lady going to be an actress?

RON. She's mad about it. She's not half bad either. I've heard her.

ROSE. (*Bitterly.*) You're privileged.

RON. What do you think, Sam?

SAM. (*Looking at* FIONA *appraisingly.*) Can I ask you a question? An impertinent question?

FIONA. They're the ones I prefer.

SAM. Do you think acting's going to be fun?

FIONA. (*After a pause.*) No. I think it's going to be hell.

SAM. (*Nodding approvingly.*) Good. You may make an actress.

FIONA. That's a trick question, *that* one. I know it. Still I answered it truthfully.

SAM. I'm sure you did. I can see you've inherited your mother's honesty. Good luck to you, anyway.

FIONA *turns to the steps R. to be stopped by* ROSE.

ROSE. I want you to be ready to come out to dinner tonight, Fiona. I've promised to take you to the de Tocquevilles. Eight o'clock.

FIONA. (*Quickly.*) No, I can't. Not at eight. That's the time I'm going with
Hettie to the station.

*Pause.*

ROSE. You're doing what, Fiona?

FIONA. Hasn't she told you yet?

ROSE. (*Bewildered.*) No.

*She looks round at* RON *who nods quietly.*

(*To* RON.) You knew?

RON. Yes.

ROSE. Where's she going to?

RON. (*Shrugging.*) Back to Scotland, I think.

*Pause.*

ROSE. Why on earth hasn't she said something? Was she thinking of sneaking out of my life without saying a damn word?

SAM *is looking at the view. Both he and* FIONA *are uncomfortable.*

RON. I think the plot was to tell you only when all her bags were at the station and whatever you said to her couldn't make her change her mind.

ROSE. And that plot you encouraged?

RON. I didn't actually discourage it.

ROSE *looks in bewilderment from* RON *to* FIONA. *Both look at her with differing
degrees of sympathy.* SAM *is not looking at anyone.*

ROSE. (*At length.*) All right, Fiona. I won't take you to the de Tocquevilles.
You can see Hettie off.

FIONA. Thank you, Mummy.

*She goes off to the pool.* ROSE *turns to* RON.

ROSE. Ron. Oh, Ron. What is it?

RON *gets up from his chair and limps over to her, putting his arm around her.*
SAM *is still staring at the view.*

RON. You know what it is.

ROSE. Damn her. Damn her. Damn her.

RON. It's best, you know.

ROSE. Without saying a word

RON. (*Sincerely.*) I'm sorry. I'm awfully sorry, my darling. I knew how you'd
feel. I told her what she was going to do to you.

ROSE. You could have got her to stay, couldn't you?

RON. By dying?

ROSE. (*Fiercely.*) Wasn't there anything you could say to her?

RON. Nothing. Nothing in the world. You know how she feels.

*He kisses her tenderly.*

ROSE. (*Defiantly.*) All right. Let her go. Let them all go. (*She turns to* SAM.)
I'm so sorry. A little domestic crisis. Not really important.

SAM *bows politely and understandingly.*

Hettie—my housekeeper—is leaving—after five years—without thinking of even saying good-bye.

SAM. (*Murmuring.*) I'm sorry.

ROSE. I'm not. I agree with Ron. It's for the best. She was always damned
inefficient, anyway. What about our lunch today? A pâté en croute, followed by a vol-au-vent. Does she want to suffocate us with pastry—

HETTIE *comes in.* ROSE *turns quickly away from her.*

HETTIE. The taxi's here for Ron.

*There is a pause.* ROSE, *at length, nerves herself for the ordeal of turning and
looking at* HETTIE.

ROSE. (*Quietly.*) What was that, Hettie?

HETTIE. I said the taxi was here for Ron.

ROSE. Why a taxi?

HETTIE. (*Patiently.*) Because the Rolls is taking Mr. Duveen to Monte, and
Ron, as you know, can't drive his car, and I've far too much to do this
afternoon to drive him to the hospital and wait for an hour for his treatment—

ROSE. Far too much to do? Yes. I suppose you have.

HETTIE, *at the tone of* ROSE'S *voice, turns to* RON, *who nods.*

RON. Yes. She knows.

HETTIE. Good. Now I don't have to tell her.

ROSE. But you can tell me the time of your train.

HETTIE. Eight-thirty-five—the Blue Train minor—the one that takes third-
class compartments—

ROSE. (*Coldly and politely.*) Oh. Then at least I'll have a chance of seeing you
for a moment before you go.

HETTIE. If you want to take it. (*She turns to go.*)

ROSE. Hettie.

HETTIE *turns back.*

Is there any significance in the date?

HETTIE. August the tenth? Yes, of course. I don't like anniversaries but I always remember them.

ROSE. I don't remember them until I'm forced to.

HETTIE. Five years to the day makes things tidier, don't you think?

*She goes out.* RON *hobbles over to* ROSE.

RON. Don't be too angry with her. It's just blind jealousy—that's all. We can't
any of us help our feelings, can we? (*He kisses her.*)

ROSE. No. We can't. (*To* SAM.) Oh dear. Wouldn't this be a nicer world if we
could?

SAM. (*Quoting* HETTIE.) It might 'make things tidier'. Whether a tidier world
would be a nicer world is a different matter.

RON. (*Going up to him.*) Well, good-bye, Sam. I'm glad you came up today.
I'd have hated you to have gone off into the blue with—well—the way
things were—

SAM. (*Shaking hands.*) The way things were wasn't so bad, you know, Ron.

RON. Well, I mean—considering— (*He pauses.*)

SAM. (*Quietly.*) Considering?

RON. (*Shrugging, embarrassed.*) Just considering. Anyway, I'm glad you've seen what I mean about Rose. (*Earnestly.*) That was on the level, wasn't it—what you said to me about her just now?

SAM. (*To* ROSE. *with a smile.*) Ron has all the suspiciousness of extreme immaturity. (*To* RON.) Yes, Ron. What I said to you about Rose just now was entirely on the level.

RON. Good. Well, sorry I've got to dash off, but this masseur geezer's not one to be kept waiting.

SAM. (*Suddenly, with eagerness.*) The part to worry about, Ron, is this muscle here, (*he points to his own foot*) because that's where you get your elevation. (*He remembers suddenly and stops. With a smile.*) But of course a travel agent or a picture dealer doesn't have to worry about elevation, does he?

RON. (*Smiling.*) He doesn't have to worry about anything. Anything in the world. Well, good-bye, and good luck in Hollywood.

SAM. Same to you.

RON. Hope you *can* make the wedding, after all.

SAM. If I'm anywhere near Paris next month I certainly will.

RON. (*Rather shyly.*) Would it be any inducement if I said you could be best man?

SAM. To me it would. I doubt if it would to M.G.M. Still, let's hope I can make it.

*They shake hands, a shade of awkwardness on both sides. Then* RON *turns to* ROSE.

RON. (*Kissing her.*) I'll go to the beach after the treatment. Can you come?

ROSE. No. Not allowed it.

RON. I'd forgotten. Meet you at the de Tocquevilles then.

ROSE. All right.

*He embraces her with sudden warmth.*

RON. I don't care what anybody says. It's just a bloody miracle—and that's a fact.

ROSE. (*Laughing.*) Can a miracle be a fact?

RON. This one can.

*He releases her and hobbles to the door, which* SAM *holds open for him. He looks at* SAM *as if wanting to say something, checks himself and contents himself with a nervous smile and a pat on the arm. He goes out.* ROSE *wanders to the side of the terrace L. to watch him go. She waves and blows a kiss. We hear the sound of the taxi starting.*

ROSE. (*Musingly.*) Do you think a miracle can be a fact?

SAM. (*Quietly.*) No.

ROSE, *waving good-bye to* RON, *turns suddenly and looks at* SAM.

ROSE. I love him more than life, you know.

SAM. More than whose life? Yours or his?

*Pause.* ROSE *offers* SAM *a cigarette. He shakes his head. She takes one herself.*

ROSE. Just a woman's sentimental exaggeration. I'm sorry. I only meant that I love him very much.

SAM. (*Politely lighting her cigarette.*) Yes.

ROSE. (*Defiantly.*) And will for life.

SAM *does not reply.*

Why don't you say yes to that?

SAM. I told you that I don't believe in miracles.

*Pause.*

ROSE. (*Sadly.*) Are you an enemy, after all?

SAM. For an honest and intelligent woman you ask some very unsubtle questions.

ROSE. For an honest and intelligent man you give some very indirect answers. Are you an enemy?

SAM. How can I answer that one except indirectly? I'm a friend of his, and I like and admire you.

ROSE. But?

SAM. (*With a sigh.*) But I'm an enemy.

ROSE. Why?

SAM. (*Gently.*) Wouldn't it be easier for you to answer that yourself? You only need one convenient word.

ROSE. I know. It's too convenient. Ron used it about Hettie and it isn't true of her. I don't think it's true of you either. Why are you an enemy? Because I'm taking him away from the ballet?

SAM. Of course.

ROSE. (*Smiling.*) You said the ballet would survive without Ron.

SAM. I didn't say Ron would survive without the ballet.

ROSE. (*Smiling.*) He told me you'd a one-track mind. Ron doesn't even like the ballet. It's not important to him at all.

SAM. He doesn't think it is. It's too much like work, and when there's a rich lady around—

ROSE. Not so damn rich. After selling this house and the pictures we'll only have about three and a half thousand a year—

SAM. And you to look after him.

ROSE. Yes.

SAM. The combination will be quite enough, I'd say. Travel Agency. Picture Gallery. What a hope. He won't last a week in either. I can see you don't know your Ron as well as I thought.

ROSE. Why is the ballet so important to him?

SAM. Because it's a job he does quite well, and the only one he ever will do, which I believe you really know just as well as I. Anyway, it's the one job he had the guts to teach himself to do when he was a kid. Fighting his father to do it, too—which was good for that thing we laughingly call his soul. Oh yes. He doesn't know it, of course—Ron doesn't know anything about himself—but the ballet's as important to him as—well—as a lifebelt is to a non-swimmer in a rough sea.

ROSE. (*Thoughtfully.*) He could go on with the ballet—I suppose.

SAM *laughs shortly.*

　　(*Rather angrily.*) I could persuade him to, I'm sure.

SAM. (*Quietly.*) Could you persuade him to class by nine in the morning? Could you persuade him off the vin rosé and the night clubs and the week-ends in Rome and the yachts and the late-night parties?

ROSE. Yes. I think I could.

SAM. I called you honest a moment ago.

ROSE. Well, I could try.

SAM. If you did it would only lead to a series of bloody rows, and an even earlier bust-up than will happen anyway. No. Take him off to Paris and the travel agency and/or picture gallery. That's much better—for both of you. I must go.

ROSE. (*Stopping him.*) You seem damn sure this won't last.

SAM. Yes. I am.

ROSE. Why?

SAM. I know my Ron.

ROSE. You don't know me.

SAM, Only what I've read in the Sunday papers and seen today. A lady who's got exactly where she wants by marrying four husbands she didn't love, and now thinks it's time to settle down happily and marry a fifth that she does.

ROSE. At least you grant that.

SAM. I've already said so. It's the duration I don't.

ROSE. How long do you give it?

SAM. The record for loving Ron up to now is, I believe, six months.

ROSE. I won't have much trouble breaking that record.

SAM. No. You're fairly tough, I'd say. You might even double it.

ROSE. Oh, for heaven's sake. I said a lifetime.

SAM. Don't worry. It'll seem a lifetime.

ROSE. What's so damn hard about loving Ron?

SAM. What's hard about loving anyone who can't love back?

ROSE. He can love back. He loves me.

SAM *says nothing.*

　　Anyway he needs me.

SAM. Oh yes. He's always needed people and always will.

ROSE. Fine. That's all I want. Why should I want more?

SAM. (*Slowly.*) Why indeed? But I see you're rather new to this business of being needed by Ron. You don't seem to understand that the Rons of this world always end by hating the people they need. They can't help it. It's compulsive. Of course it probably isn't plain hate. It's love-hate, or hate-love, or some other Freudian jargon—but it's still a pretty good imitation of the real thing. You see—when day after day, night after night—you're being kicked hard and steadily in the teeth, it's not all that important what the character who's doing it feels for you. You can leave that to the psychiatrists to work out. All you can do is to nurse a broken jaw and, in your own good time, get the hell out. I'll give you six months—from the honeymoon. Take a bet?

ROSE. No. I don't want your money.

SAM. Why not? It's as hard earned as yours.

ROSE. (*At length, with anger.*) You seem to think you know an awful lot about Ron—after only six months.

SAM. Six months? Who said—

ROSE. (*Quickly.*) I'm sorry. I thought—

SAM. (*Equally quickly.*) Did you? That's interesting. Oh no. I've taken my kicks in the teeth for longer than six months. In fact for—let's think now—pretty near seven years. But that's all right, you see. The kicks have been only intermittent—with intervals for recovery. I don't see him all that often. And anyway I've learnt to wear a gum-shield.

*Pause.*

ROSE. I don't think I've got you straight, Sam. What's your interest in Ron?

SAM. Father figure.

ROSE. Can you enlarge?

SAM. I met him when he was at the Ballet Rambert in '52. He'd run away from home to join it. His mother was dead, and he hated his father. He wasn't liked by the other kids and in London he lived alone. You feel he needs looking after now, and you're right, but you can imagine how much he needed it then. Well—I provided that need—and have provided it— in the background—off and on—more or less until you came along. I got him this job here—and in spite of commitments, I've usually managed to be around when he's needed me.

ROSE. I see.

*Pause.*

SAM. (*Slowly.*) There are ways and ways of saying 'I see'. You've chosen that way. Who gave you that idea? Ron, I suppose—

ROSE. I don't know. I can't remember. No, I don't think so.

SAM. I bet he did.

ROSE. Perhaps he did. Perhaps he was right to.

SAM. (*Quietly.*) He did, and he wasn't right to. Would you try to get this into your Wolfenden-conscious mind? Feelings can't sometimes be helped, but the expression of them can. They can and they are.

ROSE. That sounds very noble.

SAM. No. Not noble. Difficult and rather humiliating—and well—just generally pretty good hell. But not ignoble.

ROSE. I'm sorry.

SAM. That's all right.

ROSE. I'm sorry you quarrelled.

SAM. So am I.

ROSE. Still, you've made it up now.

SAM. Yes. We'll nod to each other in the Ritz bar.

ROSE. No more than that?

SAM. No.

ROSE. Why not?

SAM. I've had a belly-full. Seven years is a long time. Besides—there's some-one else now.

ROSE. Yes, I'd heard. Pity.

SAM. Not a pity at all.

ROSE. Was it all because of me?

SAM. Is that what he told you?

ROSE. More or less.

SAM. Rather more than less, I imagine. (*Imitating.*) 'Sam's so jealous and pos-sessive, Rose—I can't tell you. Ever since you came into my life he's been like a fiend—and I can't stand it—' Something like that?

ROSE. Something. It was about your being jealous of the new car—because it showed up yours—

SAM *laughs with genuine and affectionate amusement.*

SAM. Oh good. Very good. Real vintage Ron. Jealous of the car. Poor little bastard. (*Quietly, facing her.*) I came over this year to do three ballets. Ron was to have had the lead in all of them. No favouritism. He is their best virtuoso dancer. He did two—could have been better, but all right— and then we were rehearsing the third when you came into his life. After he'd cut two rehearsals I fired him, and got another boy—not too good, but coming along. At least he works. When Ron heard the news he did his best to carve up the new boy, then came home and staged a phoney suicide scene with me, and when that didn't work got into his car and roared off into the night. Up here, to you, I suppose. I didn't follow as I used to, because I'd had it. Had it for keeps. That's the story. Not excit-ing, but—conclusive. (*He looks over the side of the terrace.*) I see the car's waiting. I'd really better be going.

ROSE. (*Absently.*) So soon?

SAM. I've got a lot of packing

ROSE. (*A shade hysterically.*) Everybody's packing.

SAM. (*Extending his hand.*) Well—thank you for a very delightful lunch—

ROSE. (*Taking his hand.*) If you've had it—why are you an enemy?

SAM. (*He smiles.*) As we used to say once in Bomber Command—bang on. Because, I suppose, I haven't really had it. I don't want ever to see him again—that's true—but I still hate the thought of seven years' work— God, what work—utterly wasted—thrown into the ashcan—no return—no return at all. I'm not talking about the ballet, you know. He'd never have been a Nijinsky. He might have made Covent Garden in mi-nor leads in a year or two—but he wasn't ever going to have biographies written about him—even if he'd really worked, which, even without you, wasn't very likely. No. It's him. It's the human being I worked on—and

tried to make a man of— (*He stops.*) Yes. That's an easy laugh, isn't it?
Still, it's true— Anyway, it's stupid to care. What does one Ron Vale
matter in this world, more or less?

*Pause.*

ROSE. (*Hotly.*) You damn fool. Do you think I'd ever let him down?

SAM. Oh no, I don't. I'm sure, after you leave him, he'll have no reason to
complain about the size of his allowance. At least he'll have no reason
to—but if I know Ron—he will. Still, all your friends and the Press and
your sixth husband will all say you've behaved very generously—considering. Of course he won't be able to go back to the ballet, because at
his age you can't give it up even for six months. Besides, he'll have gone
to seed a bit by then, probably off the rosé and on to the brandy, I should
think. Still, in whatever queer bar he finds himself in London or Paris
or New York, I'm sure he'll always be pointed out with some envy as
Rose Fish's fifth—'lucky guy. Doesn't have to work. He was a dancer,
once, they say. Hard to believe now, looking at him. Let's go over and
talk to him. He's fun when he's drunk.'

ROSE. (*Laughing.*) Do you think you can frighten me with a temperance play?

SAM. I know I can't frighten you at all. How could I? What have you got to
be frightened of?

ROSE. (*After a pause.*) Well—walking into that bar and seeing him, perhaps.

SAM. No risk. You wouldn't go to that sort of bar.

ROSE. That's funny—from you.

SAM. I know, but I wouldn't either.

ROSE. You think—you really think—I shouldn't go ahead?

SAM. It doesn't matter a damn what I think. You'll go ahead anyway. You've
earned your right to your bit of fun, and nothing and nobody in the
world is going to stop you having it. Even if it is fun with another human being's life—

ROSE. As Ron would say—a pure case of F.U., Jack, I'm all right.

SAM. Yes. As Ron would say. Well— (*He turns.*)

ROSE. (*Quietly, stopping him.*) I just want to correct a misconception, that's
all. The word 'fun'. I'm going ahead with Ron—but it's not for my fun.
It's because his needing me is—well—the best thing that's ever happened
to me, and without it I wouldn't see much point in going on living. That's
not a woman's exaggeration, Sam. It's the simple truth. I can't explain
why it means so much. Hettie quoted Horace at my head the other day.
Something about expelling Nature with a pitchfork, but it always comes
back. Meaning, I suppose, that since Birmingham I've suppressed my
natural instincts, and now Nature has taken a mean revenge—

SAM. Oh no. Hettie's wrong on that. What you feel for Ron isn't Nature's
revenge on you. It's much more your revenge on Nature.

ROSE. (*Very angry.*) That *sounds* good. Does it *mean* anything?

SAM. Yes, I'd say it does. I'd say it means that just because you've had a real
tough time fighting Nature to get where you are, now you're going to

turn the tables on the old bag by taking a boy nine years younger than you and turning him from a fairly good virtuoso dancer into a male Rose Fish.

*Pause.*

ROSE. (*In a whisper.*) You're brutal.

SAM. I'm not. The truth is.

ROSE. (*Raising her voice.*) It isn't the truth. Remember what he was like when I met him.

SAM. (*Quietly.*) I do. Very well.

ROSE. That side was always in him.

SAM. I know. It just needed bringing out.

ROSE. If it hadn't been me, it'd have been someone else.

SAM. Quite likely. It just happened to be you.

*Pause.*

ROSE. God, I hate you.

SAM. Pity, because I don't hate you. In fact I like you very much.

*Pause.*

ROSE. (*Pitifully.*) Oh God—Sam—please—you don't understand—

HETTIE *comes in.*

HETTIE. (*Ignoring* ROSE, *to* SAM) The chauffeur asked me to tell you that the car is waiting to take you to Monte Carlo.

SAM. Yes, I know. I'm sorry to have kept him.

HETTIE. Oh, that's all right. He's used to waiting.

*She begins to gather a few personal oddments from the terrace.*

SAM. (*Formally to* ROSE.) Well—thank you once again for a delightful lunch.

ROSE. (*In the same tone.*) Not at all. I'm so glad you could come.

SAM. (*Stopping her as she moves towards the stairs.*) No, please don't see me off. Those stairs tire you. I saw that this morning.

ROSE. (*Smiling.*) They do a bit. It's this blasted cough of mine. I hope to see you at the wedding, after all.

SAM. Yes. I'll make it, if I can, I promise you. Good-bye.

ROSE. Good-bye.

SAM *goes out.* HETTIE *is still gathering things.*

HETTIE. (*Her back to* ROSE.) Is *Napoleon's Loves* mine or yours?

ROSE. Yours.

HETTIE. And *Over the Seas to Skye?*

ROSE. Mine.

HETTIE. Yes, of course.

ROSE. Hettie, why are you leaving me?

HETTIE. God, you should know that by now.

ROSE. In a nutshell—once more.

*She sits down in a chair, not looking at* HETTIE, *who now turns and stares at her.*

HETTIE. Because I hate dishonesty and I hate funk.

ROSE. Funk? You haven't said that before.

HETTIE. Trying to have your cake and eat it is a form of funk. You made your bed a long time ago

ROSE. Don't mix your metaphors.

HETTIE. I certainly will. I'll give you a third if you like. Time off for 'Love in a Cottage' was never a clause in your original contract—and it's just plain cheating for you to pretend it was. Well, I hate cheating, I hate dishonesty and I hate funk. At least—from you.

ROSE *makes no reply.*

(*At length.*) All right?

ROSE. (*Quietly, without looking at her.*) All right.

HETTIE *goes out.* ROSE *sits quite motionless, staring ahead of her.* FIONA *comes on from the steps R. Her dishevelled hair shows she has been swimming. Seeing her mother she stops resignedly, preparing to be spoken to. But* ROSE *is utterly oblivious of her.* FIONA *looks at her curiously, shrugs her shoulders and goes into the house.* ROSE *continues to stare into space.*

*The lights fade and when they come on again the sun has set and there is very little light on the terrace.* ROSE *has not changed her attitude.*

HETTIE *comes on from the house. She is dressed for her journey.*

HETTIE. You ought to be changing for your dinner party.

ROSE. (*Not changing her attitude.*) What's the time?

HETTIE. After seven. (*She turns back towards the house.*)

ROSE. Don't go. (*She gets up and goes to the drink tray.*) We'd better at least have a last drink together.

HETTIE. Thanks. I'll have a beer.

ROSE. (*Wearily.*) If you'd been me, Hettie, these last few weeks—how would you have coped with it all?

HETTIE. Oh, I'd have told him to buzz off.

ROSE. If you'd really been me you might not have found that very easy.

HETTIE. No. Damn difficult, I should think. But that's what I'd have done.

ROSE. Supposing he'd refused to buzz off?

HETTIE. Then I'd have buzzed off myself.

ROSE. Supposing he'd have followed?

HETTIE. You're putting his feeling for you a bit high there, aren't you?

ROSE. (*Quietly.*) No. Not at the moment. He needs me with him.

HETTIE. Well, then I'd just have told him that I didn't need him with *me.*

ROSE. Do you think he'd have believed that? You've seen the way I behave when he's anywhere near me—

HETTIE. Yes. Like an idiotic schoolgirl. Well, then—last, but best—I'd just have seen to it that he didn't need me any more. I'd have destroyed this damn need of his—

ROSE. How?

HETTIE. (*Shrugging.*) Give me time. I haven't thought. (*After a moment.*) Well, I imagine what he needs from you is security, protection, permanence—the usual mother business. That right?

ROSE. Yes.

HETTIE. Well, then I'd have done something so brutal and outrageous to him, that I'd have blown all that security stuff up for him right in his face. There wouldn't have been a shred of sonny-boy's mummy-need left.

ROSE. (*Nodding slowly.*) You haven't thought, you said. Give me time, you said. And yet after a few seconds you arrive at exactly the same solution that I've taken the whole damn afternoon to find. You must think an awful lot faster than me, Hettie. But then you're not involved, are you, and emotions, they do say, muddle the brain—

*Her voice, relaxed before, is now tense and strained. She turns to the recording machine, left on a table, where* FIONA *must have used it.*

Show me how this thing works, would you? I've forgotten.

HETTIE, *staring at* ROSE, *puzzled, walks across to the machine, and switches it on. A red light begins to glow.*

HETTIE. Do you want to record or listen?

ROSE. Record.

HETTIE *switches a knob.*

HETTIE. (*Pointing.*) There's the microphone there. You don't have to talk right into it. Just stand about where you are—that should be all right. It's not going on tape yet, but it's live. Just say something, so I can adjust the volume.

ROSE. Hullo, Ron. Hullo, Ron. Hullo, Ron.

HETTIE *adjusts the volume control.*

HETTIE. That's about right. Now when you let that button up you're record-ing. If anything goes wrong, or you can't think what you want to say, press that button down and it stops the tape.

ROSE. I see.

HETTIE. It's quite simple. (*She moves to the door.*)

ROSE. Hettie.

HETTIE *turns.*

Stay, will you?

HETTIE. All right.

ROSE. You'd better work that button. It is just possible that something might go wrong—or I mightn't be able to think what to say.

*Her voice is beginning to show that overwhelming emotion is not far away.*

(*To* HETTIE.) On.

HETTIE *presses the button. The reel of tape begins slowly to revolve.*

Ron, my dear, I'm sorry to have to use this machine to talk to you, but I'm bad at writing letters, as you know, and I thought anyway you might prefer to hear what I've got to say to you in my own voice. I should have said it to you personally I suppose, but quite frankly, I funked it. I've got to try and tell you why I've decided to leave you and go back to Kurt—

*She makes a quick sign to* HETTIE *to stop the tape. Until now her voice has been hard and casual, but she has felt the tears coming. She takes a sip of her drink, then nods to* HETTIE, *who switches the tape on.*

I'm afraid it'll be a big shock for you, darling, when you hear it, and I'm sorry—

*Her voice is again unemotional.*

I've hated doing it, too, because you know how I've felt about you— that's to say until just lately, when I admit I've had to do a tiny bit of acting—because I did fix up things with Kurt when he got back a few days ago. But you mustn't think that my feelings for you haven't been quite sincere—anyway in the beginning. I did love you, you know, Ron. I really did—

*She makes a sign to* HETTIE *and breaks down completely.* HETTIE *watches her from the machine.*

HETTIE. I shouldn't go on with this, if I were you. Why not a letter?

ROSE. With tear-stains all over it—shaking handwriting? No, this is the way. This is the way all right. Just give me a moment. I've got to finish it now— this minute, otherwise there isn't a hope.

*She dries her eyes.* HETTIE *goes back to the machine.*

(*Murmuring.*) I did love you, Ron. I really did.

*She nods to* HETTIE *who switches it on.*

But my trouble has always been that I can't love anyone for very long. And anyway it wouldn't have worked. It really wouldn't. Darling—you know me. Could you really have seen *me* living on in a three-room flat? *Me*, after all I've done to escape from just that sort of life? And, anyway, what girl in her senses would turn down fifty million? Well, that's all, darling. You won't see me again. Not ever. I'm going off somewhere with Kurt for a week or so. After a bit I don't suppose you'll mind. You'd bet- ter go back to the ballet, when your ankle's all right again. After all, it's still money, isn't it? Good-bye, darling. Good-bye, and I suppose I should say—thanks, too—

HETTIE *switches it off, as* ROSE *turns away in tears once more.* HETTIE *goes up to her, and puts her arm round her shoulders.*

ROSE. Why couldn't you have left me in peace?

HETTIE. I'm sorry. Oh God, I'm sorry.

ROSE. You don't need to go now.

HETTIE. (*Pointing to recording machine.*) We can wipe it out. I could be wrong, you know. I'm pretty old. Perhaps I don't know about things the way I think I do.

ROSE. (*Still in tears.*) Ron says it's just jealousy—

HETTIE. (*Quietly.*) It might be only that. Shall we wipe it out? It's very easy—

ROSE. No. (*She recovers herself a little.*) I'm sorry, Hettie, it's just that I've got to blame somebody. It wasn't you, anyway. I'd made up my own mind an hour ago. (*Wiping her eyes.*) I think you *do* know about things. I wish to God you didn't, but you do. Now listen. I'm going out now.

HETTIE. To Kurt?

ROSE. God, no. Not tonight, anyway. Not for an awful lot of nights, if at all. Anyway, I don't know if he'll have me. Did you read that letter?

HETTIE. Yes.

ROSE. Is it—

HETTIE *nods.*

    I'm not going to think about that now. I'll go to an hotel tonight.

HETTIE. Do you want me to come with you?

ROSE. No. You'd better stay here. Ron will be calling from the de Tocquevilles when he finds I'm not there. You'd better tell him to come straight home, as there's an important message here from me. Don't be with him when he hears it.

HETTIE *shakes her head.*

    And Hettie—I know what you feel about him, but he's going to be more unhappy tonight and for a few days to come than he's ever been in his life before. Perhaps than he ever will be. Be kind.

HETTIE *nods.*

    It won't be too easy. He's bound to be pretty bloody—particularly about me. Just remember—the bloodier the better. It might be an idea to get his friend Sam round. He'll need someone pretty close to look after him tonight—say the right things and lend a shoulder to cry on—

HETTIE *nods again.* ROSE *is on the point of tears once more.*

    Oh, Hettie. (*She stops.*)

HETTIE. Yes?

ROSE. (*Trying to smile.*) I was just thinking—if only it could have been me—
*She goes out quickly.*


CURTAIN


SCENE 2


SCENE: *The same, three months later.*

    *It is about eight in the evening. A large cocktail party has only just finished, and the terrace shows signs of it. Through the sitting-room window we can see white-coated servants clearing up. On the terrace a card table has been laid out and at it* KURT *is playing a game of baccarat with* HETTIE *and* MONA. *He is taking the bank and has just finished a hand.*

KURT. Faites vos jeux, Mesdames et Mesdemoiselles. Faites vos jeux—

MONA. Well, this time he must lose.

*She takes a five-thousand-franc note from her bag and puts it in front of her.*

KURT. Five thousand francs premier tableau and—

*He turns to* HETTIE.

HETTIE. Ten.

KURT. Ten francs deuxième tableau.

HETTIE *puts a coin down.* KURT *deals the cards—one to each, one to himself, then another to each, another for himself.* MONA, *on his right, looks at her cards.*

MONA. Card.

HETTIE. (*Looking at hers.*) No.

KURT *turns his cards on the table.*

KURT. (*Gurgling delightedly.*) Et neuf en banque.

*He takes the money from both sides.*

MONA. Hell. How do you do it? Stack the cards?

KURT. Of course. Before the party I am spending hours making up this shoe.

MONA. I wouldn't be surprised.

HETTIE. Well, that cleans me. (*She gets up.*)

KURT. Go on, Hettie. Your credit is good.

HETTIE, Listen—my credit is terrible. Ask the Sporting Club.

MONA. Do you still owe them, Hettie?

HETTIE. Seven fifty thousand.

MONA. But that's nothing. You *did* owe them a fortune once, didn't you?

HETTIE. Yes, once. In the days when they thought an English lady of title couldn't be a crook.

MONA. How much?

HETTIE. Ten million.

MONA. And you've managed to pay all that back?

HETTIE. Over the years—in dribs and drabs.

MONA. Why didn't you ever ask Rose to settle it for you?

HETTIE. Because that's exactly what she would have done. (*Meaningly.*) Of course if someone else had offered—

KURT. A measly two hundred and twenty thousand is all I am winning to-night. Still, it is paying for the party—

KURT, *puffing contentedly at his cigar, is engaged in counting a pile of notes.* HETTIE, *behind* KURT, *makes a gesture at his head, indicating to* MONA *exactly whom she means by someone else.*

MONA. Why don't you pay it, Kurt?

KURT. Pay what?

MONA. What Hettie still owes the Sporting Club.

KURT. How much is that?

MONA. (*Making it sound small.*) Seven fifty thousand.

KURT *laughs politely—as at a joke.* HETTIE *shrugs resignedly.* MONA *smiles.*

Well, it's been a lovely party, but I wish like hell I'd have gone when everyone else did. It might have saved me quite a bit of dough—

KURT. A few more hands. You will be winning. I guarantee.

MONA. O.K.

HETTIE. Aren't you cold out here?

MONA. No. It's still quite warm. (*As* KURT *deals.*) My God, you were lucky with the weather this evening. If you'd had the real November stuff, we'd all have been sardines in there—hell, I haven't put any money up. I'm doubling up. Ten mille. O.K.

KURT *nods.*

How many people, Hettie? (*To* KURT.) Card.

HETTIE. Three hundred plus—

FIONA *comes in, as* KURT *turns his own cards face upwards and grins.*

MONA. Goddam you, Kurt, for a— (*Seeing* FIONA.) Oh hullo, Fiona.

FIONA. Hullo. (*To* HETTIE.) Where's Mummy?

HETTIE. Up in her room. She's not feeling well.

FIONA. Oh. I'm sorry.

KURT *has given* MONA *a card and now turns his.*

KURT. Neuf en banque. On paie partout.

MONA. Only your presence, Fiona, prevents me saying something that's in my mind. All right. Same again.

HETTIE. (*To* FIONA.) Do you want her for anything special?

FIONA. She won't mind if I go before dinner instead of after, will she?

HETTIE. You know damn well she will. You know equally well she won't stop you.

FIONA. (*A shade unhappily for once.*) They've planned something for me at the Ciel et Enfer. A sort of good-bye do.

MONA. (*Laying down her new hand.*) Eight. That's better.

KURT *pays her.*

All right. (*Pointing to her wager.*) That stays.

FIONA. (*Continuing.*) I can't get out of it, Hettie. Really I can't.

HETTIE. (*Sadly, after a pause.*) I think you're being a bit of a rat, Fiona. It could be that this damn coast affects even children.

FIONA. (*Rather near tears.*) If Mummy wants to come to the airport to see me off, she can. I've always said she could, if she wanted to.

HETTIE. Yes, and I know the tone of voice you said it in. Anyway, do you suppose she wants to come to the airport surrounded by a mob of juvenile delinquents on Vespas? You're off to London, and she won't see you till the wedding—and a last meal with her wouldn't have been all that difficult to arrange, I'd have thought

FIONA. (*Her voice rising.*) I couldn't help it, Hettie. I couldn't—

KURT. (*With a shout of triumph.*) Neuf.

MONA. (*Simultaneously.*) Oh, my God! Not again.

FIONA. (*Going to* KURT *to escape* HETTIE.) Are you winning?

KURT. (*Throwing his arm round her waist.*) Oh, my little Fiona. Yes, I am winning a little chicken food. (*He looks up at her.*) Do you know one day you are going to be a very beautiful heart-breaker. Yes, one day, I shall be being very proud of my little stepdaughter of the future.

FIONA. I don't want to break any hearts.

KURT. (*Dealing another hand.*) No?

FIONA. I just want mine broken—by the right person.

KURT. Very unbusinesslike. (*To* MONA.) No cards? (*He turns his cards up.*) Egalité. (*To* FIONA.) What time is your plane?

FIONA. Midnight, (*looking at* HETTIE) but I'm leaving the house before dinner.

KURT. Ah. Then I must be saying good-bye. (*He gets up.*)

FIONA. I'm not going just yet.

KURT. Ah, but I have three angry Swiss bankers waiting for me up at my house—and I have to see them before dinner.

FIONA. Why are they angry?

KURT. Because they are Swiss, because they are bankers, and because they are waiting. No bankers are used to waiting, even for me. (*Kissing her.*) Good-bye, mein liebchen. Will you like your new stepfather?

FIONA. (*With patent insincerity.*) Yes. Very much, I'm sure.

HETTIE. And she speaks from a wide experience of stepfathers, remember.

FIONA. (*Ignoring her.*) Mummy's not really ill, is she?

KURT. Oh no, no. A little tiredness—no more.

FIONA. (*Looking firmly at* HETTIE.) Good. I'll go and see her now. I've got something to ask her.

*She goes out.*

KURT. Three more hands, Mona?

MONA. O.K.

*He deals.*

It really was only tiredness, wasn't it? No card.

KURT. Sure, sure. (*He gives her a card and then another to himself.*) Goddam baccarat! Yes. Only tiredness—after the party—

HETTIE. (*With weary irony.*) You know how people often get a bit tired after a party, Mona, and cough up blood. Nothing to worry about at all—

KURT. (*Banging his cards angrily on the table.*) You will please not be saying such things.

HETTIE. Why won't I?

MONA. Was it so bad?

KURT. Of course it wasn't so bad. Don't listen to this crazy woman. She will be making a drama of everything—

HETTIE. I haven't made much of a drama yet, have I? I haven't said that you're damn lucky it was such a slight attack and that your show-off party this afternoon might quite easily have bumped off your bride-to-be altogether.

KURT. Lady Henrietta—I must be asking you please to remember that in this house you are only a paid employee—

HETTIE. Not by you. I'm paid by a lady who has just been told by her doctors that if she doesn't have complete rest for three months in a sanatorium she'll be dead inside that time. I'm paid to look after that lady—as best I can—and I think in that capacity I've the right to make the comment that a party for over three hundred bods given in her own house, with herself as hostess and having to cope, wasn't the wisest way of following doctors' orders.

KURT. Go away. You are boring me. Mona—another hand.

*He deals the cards.*

(*Explosively.*) Goddam, Hettie, it was she was wanting this party—

HETTIE. Of course it was. When she's in the sanatorium it'll be she who'll be wanting to give the parties there too. It's just that it might have been an idea to discourage her—

MONA. Card. There *were* rather a lot of people, Kurt—

KURT. (*Angrily.*) For a farewell to the Château Auguste one should be having tea and buns for six? (*Taking a card.*) One against baccarat. Mine.

MONA. You're a wizard. Oh hell. Will your bankers still wait?

KURT. Sure they'll wait.

MONA. All right, then. One last hand.

RON *has walked quietly on to the terrace from the drive below. There has been no sound of a car arriving and both* KURT *and* MONA *are unaware of his presence.* HETTIE *sees him first.*

RON. (*Nodding to her pleasantly.*) Hullo, Hettie.

HETTIE. What are you doing here?

RON. I've come by invitation.

HETTIE. Whose invitation?

RON. Mona's. I'm the 'and friend' on her invitation card. Isn't that right, Mona? Hullo, Kurt.

KURT. (*With quiet anger, to* MONA.) This is true?

MONA. Of course not. As if I would—

KURT. (*To* RON.) You will please be leaving here at once—or do you want I shall be calling the police?

RON. Why the police? What's the fuss? I saw Mona in the casino last night, and she asked me to come with her to this party. If you doubt it— (*he produces a card from his pocket*) how is it I've got her invitation card?

MONA. It was a joke, Kurt. I'd had one too many. I never thought for a moment he'd take me seriously—

RON. But I did take you seriously, Mona. Very seriously. I heard this was going to be one of the best parties ever, and I particularly wanted to come.

HETTIE. Then why arrive after it's over?

RON. A good question, Hettie. I remember—you always ask good questions. Because I had a sudden rehearsal, and because I thought that the party— a party as grand and as lavish as this one—would probably go on after nine.

HETTIE. Well, it hasn't. So I don't see there's any particular reason for your staying around, do you?

RON. No. To be quite frank, I don't.

MONA. (*Very hastily.*) I'm leaving anyway, Ron.

RON. Good. You can give me a lift back into Cannes.

HETTIE. How did you get up here?

RON. By bus to the top of the road and walked from there.

KURT. (*Laughing.*) By bus?

RON. Yes. They have them you know, even on this coast.

KURT. And what has happened to the beautiful Lagonda? Sold?

RON. No. Not sold. (*He glances through the windows into the sitting-room.*)

HETTIE. No. She's not in there, Ron.

RON. I know she's not. She's in her bedroom. I saw the light coming up. (*To*

MONA.) Do you mind waiting just a second, darling, while I spend a penny?

*To* HETTIE, *who has made an involuntary move to stop him going into the house.* It's all right, Hettie. I know the way.

HETTIE *still bars the way.*

I won't go upstairs. If you want to check on it, you can stand here and watch the staircase.

HETTIE. I will.

RON *smiles and goes inside.* HETTIE *stations herself where she can see into the house.*

MONA. (*To* KURT.) Oh my God, Kurt—will you ever forgive me? But it wasn't my fault—it really wasn't. How could I know he was even remotely serious?

KURT. You gave him your card.

MONA. He took it. I showed it to him and he took it. At the bar, it was, in the Casino Municipale. That's where his company are dancing this week. (*Angrily.*) Don't think it's a plot, for God's sake. I haven't seen the guy since Rose fired him—I swear it—not until last night when I was playing chemmy and—

KURT. (*To* HETTIE.) What about his Lagonda?

HETTIE. (*Gazing into the house.*) He gave it back.

KURT. That is a damned lie. I would be knowing if he had given it back. It is not here, in the garage.

HETTIE. She wouldn't take it.

KURT. Where is it, then?

HETTIE. In no-man's-land. A garage in Juan. I have the keys and the registration book. No one is paying the garage, yet—but I pay for the petrol when I use it.

KURT. You use the car?

HETTIE. Oh yes,

*She turns from the window, satisfied* RON *is on his way back.*

Well, it seems silly just to let it sit there and rust, doesn't it?

RON *comes back.*

RON. (*Looking at the table.*) Who's been winning?

MONA. Kurt. He cleaned me. Come on, Ron.

RON. Would you like a hand, Kurt?

MONA. Don't be silly, Ron. Come on.

RON. (*Repeating steadily.*) Would you like a hand, Kurt?

KURT. Sure. We'll play for your bus fare.

RON. Oh no. (*He throws down some notes.*) Not what you're used to playing for, I know, but a bit more than my bus fare. There's twenty-five thousand there.

KURT. (*With a smile.*) You are being lucky in love again?

RON. No. Not in the way you mean. That's my week's salary—with extra for dancing the blue bird or Peter Pansy as you called it once—remember. I'll take the bank. (*He deals the cards.*)

KURT. Card.

RON *turns his cards up. It is evidently an eight or nine. He shows no emotion, staring quietly at* KURT. KURT *takes some notes from his pocket and throws them on the table.*

Suivi.

RON *deals the cards again.*

No.

RON *turns his cards up, and takes a card. Again he has won, but again his face shows no expression.* KURT *throws fifty thousand francs on to the table and turns to go.*

RON (*Quietly.*) Quitting, Kurt?

KURT *turns back and goes to the table. He raps his fingers on it in the gesture which means banco.* RON *deals.*

KURT. Card.

RON *gives him one, and then raps his own cards in the gesture which means that he is standing.* KURT *once more pulls out money and throws the notes on to the table.*

Suivi.

MONA. (*To* RON.) For heaven's sake stop now. Ron. Take it in, and let's go. You've got nearly two hundred pounds—

RON. Yes, but if I give it again, I'd have nearly four hundred, wouldn't I?

MONA. Or nothing. More likely nothing.

HETTIE. Mona's right. You should take your money and think yourself damn lucky—

RON. (*Gently.*) But Kurt said suivi, didn't he? Well, now, what shall I do?

ROSE *comes in, dressed as she was, presumably, for the party.*

ROSE. (*As she enters.*) Well, that little do of ours is hardly going to make history—I must say. Only nine o'clock, and not a bod left in the house. Not even the usual pair of drunks lying under the—

*Her voice trails away as she sees* RON, *who has turned from the table to face her.*

(*Her voice a trifle shrill, but apparently controlled.*) Well, Ron. What a surprise.

RON. Hullo, Rose.

ROSE. I didn't see you at the party.

RON. I wasn't at the party. I missed it, I'm afraid.

KURT. Mona asked him, Rose.

MONA. I didn't—I promise I didn't, Rose.

ROSE. (*In control.*) I really don't see that it matters who asked him. He's here, and I see that none of you has thought of giving the poor boy a drink. (*At the drink tray.*) What's it to be, Ron? Still rosé?

RON. No. I don't drink these days.

ROSE. Don't you really? (*She picks up a bottle of brandy.*)

HETTIE. And nor do you, Rose—if you remember.

ROSE. (*Putting back the bottle, after a pause.*) No, nor I do. (*Approaching the table.*) Well, how are you, Ron? You're looking very well. A bit thinner, perhaps—

RON. Yes. I am thinner. Settle a problem for me, will you? I have two hundred thousand francs here—the bank's run three times and Kurt suivied. Shall I give it?

ROSE. No. Take it in.

RON. That settles the problem nicely. All right, Kurt. Here we go. The fourth coup.

*He deals the cards.* KURT *takes his up, very slowly, trying to rattle* RON. *He makes a move to throw his cards face upwards—as if he had an eight or nine— and then holds them, laughing derisively.*

KURT. Card.

RON. So that's the sort of player you are, is it? Real old-fashioned funny stuff. I might have guessed it. (*He turns his cards up.*) Neuf en banque.

ROSE. Well done, Ron. Pay up, Kurt.

KURT *is doing so, trying to appear unconcerned.*

Don't worry, Ron. He won all this and more at the party.

RON. I'm not worrying.

ROSE. Why should you? (*To* KURT.) Darling, shouldn't you be at your meeting?

KURT. Yes, I should. But I think I am waiting just a little longer—just to see our friend here safely out of the house. One is never knowing—with so much money on him—he could be being coshed or something.

RON. I won't have so much money on me.

*He is counting the notes. He removes twenty-five thousand and puts it in his breast pocket.*

Just what I came with—that's all.

*He wheels suddenly on* ROSE *and thrusts out to her the bundle of remaining notes.*

There you are. Take it.

ROSE. What are you talking about?

RON. Three seventy-five thousand. God knows it's not all I owe you—not by a long chalk—but you'll get the rest back one day—every bloody penny—with interest too. Meanwhile—take this to be going on with.

ROSE. Really, Ron. You mustn't be so hysterical.

RON. Take it, damn you. Take it.

*He screws the bills together and throws them at her. The bundle falls to the floor.*

RON. Come on, Mona.

*He turns towards the steps L.*

KURT. Not quite so easily, my friend.

*He bars the way out, and then, as* RON *stops, begins to walk slowly and menacingly towards him. Before he is there,* RON, *with a sudden gesture, has picked up a tumbler and broken it on a table. He holds the jagged edge towards* KURT.

(*Laughing.*) A tough little baby, I see. So much the more amusing—

*He picks up a heavy garden chair with one hand.*

It is good to see I am still being able to do that.

*He brings the other hand to the chair preparatory to using it as a weapon of of-fence.*

Now we shall see.

ROSE. (*Quietly.*) Kurt—if you touch him you'll never see me again as long as you live.

KURT. That is maybe a risk I am taking.

ROSE. It's no risk. It's a certainty. I don't lie when I say things like that.

RON. (*Through his teeth, shivering slightly, his eyes on* KURT.) Only when you say things like I love you more than life.

ROSE. (*Quietly.*) That's right. Only when I say things like I love you more than life.

*She goes to* RON *and gently takes the tumbler from his hand.* KURT, *meanwhile, has lowered the chair.*

(*Pointing to the money.*) Now pick that up.

RON. I'm not going to take it.

ROSE. I didn't say you were. I said pick it up.

*After a pause he stoops and gathers the bills. Then he hands them to her again.*

Put it on the table.

RON *does so.*

If you like to tell me the name of your favourite charity, I'll send it to them in your name. Otherwise I'll send it to mine.

*He stands undecided, staring at her—wanting to say more, dissatisfied with the result of his scene, wanting to begin it again, but not knowing how.* ROSE *smiles suddenly at him.*

(*Gently.*) You silly little boy.

*With a half-sob he turns and runs out L.*

(*Urgently.*) See he's all right, Mona. Stay with him if you can. I know these moods. Anything can happen.

MONA. I'll do my best. I can't say I care for the thought of having a high hysteric on my hands. Still, I'll try.

ROSE. He's not so hard to handle. He just needs a little—looking after, that's all.

MONA. O.K. Well, good night. And sorry, too, I guess. Not really my fault though.

*She follows* RON *out.* ROSE *suddenly collapses into a chair.* HETTIE *approaches her solicitously.*

HETTIE. Back to bed, may be?

ROSE. Certainly not. I've just come from bed and I feel fine. (*She laughs.*) What about that, eh? I bet he's been working that one out for months. Poor little beast. I suppose he meant to do it with just a couple of mille, which would have been just as good as a gesture, and wouldn't have been nearly so expensive. Winning all that money from Kurt must have gone to his head. Think how awful he'll feel in the morning when he remembers what he's given to charity—three seventy-five. Think how many sports jackets he could have bought himself for that.

*She is talking rapidly and a shade hysterically.* HETTIE *is watching her with concern,* KURT *with a certain anger.*

HETTIE. I think a little rest upstairs, don't you?

ROSE. Don't be such a bore, Hettie. (*Pointing to the money.*) Listen, tomorrow when you're clearing up and after we're safely on our way to Switzerland, pop that in an envelope, and leave it for him at his stage door. He's dancing at the Théâtre du Casino Municipale—

KURT. How are you knowing that, my dear?

ROSE. I happened to see it in the local paper.

KURT. Yes. You are always no doubt looking in the local paper to see what is playing in the Théâtre du Casino Municipale.

ROSE. (*After a pause.*) I haven't been down there to see him, you know—if that's what that rather heavy Teutonic irony implied.

KURT. You haven't been down, but you were maybe tempted to go—possibly?

ROSE. Maybe. Possibly. I haven't seen him dance often, and always enjoyed it when I have. He's very good and so is the company—

KURT. And why were you saying to me—don't touch him—don't touch him—but not to him are you saying much? It is all right for him to be pushing broken glass in my face, I am noticing—

ROSE. (*After a faint pause, battling with her anger.*) Women's sympathies are usually with the underdog—Englishwomen especially. We're sentimental, you see.

KURT. Not too sentimental, I am hoping.

ROSE. (*Rising, now angry.*) Kurt, if you're out to make a scene you may get one—with warhead attached. Ron isn't the only hysteric in the world. Given the right mood, I can do all right too, you know. And I've *got* the right mood.

KURT. It is a good thing you are going to this sanatorium. A very good thing—

ROSE. Yes, it is. Go to your conference.

KURT *nods and goes to the steps L.*

KURT. Get them to make something light for me when I come back. Say, about an hour—

ROSE. No.

KURT. No?

ROSE. Unless you want to have supper alone, or with Hettie, if she'll join you. I'm going to bed.

KURT. A moment ago you were saying you are feeling fine—you are not wanting to go to bed—

ROSE. (*Raising her voice.*) I've changed my mind.

KURT. We will have a little supper together in your room.

ROSE. No.

KURT. Why not?

*Pause.*

I am wanting to know why not?

ROSE. (*Wearily.*) Oh because I'm going down to the Théâtre du Casino Municipale, of course—to see Ron and take him out on the town and to beg him to come back to me. Oh Kurt! How can you be so damn stupid. The doctors have forbidden me this coast for the rest of my life, so I can never, never, never see him again—even if I wanted to. And do you think I want to? Do you really think I want to, Kurt? Do you think I enjoyed seeing him tonight?

KURT. It is not just a question of a girl to be seeing someone to be making a man jealous, my dear. There is too a question of feeling. Why are you feeling always so much for this boy?

ROSE. Put that in the past tense, and I might answer you.

KURT. (*Advancing on her angrily.*) I am not putting it in the past tense. I am putting it in the now tense.

ROSE. Present tense.

KURT. (*Shouting.*) Why are you still feeling so much for the boy—right now?

ROSE. (*Shrugging.*) Hangover.

KURT. Hangovers get cured.

ROSE. Yes. In time. So will this.

KURT. Himmel, you have had three months—

ROSE. The textbooks on emotional disorders give six, I believe—for complete recovery. (*She pats his hand.*) Don't worry, Kurt. After the sanatorium I shall have a clean bill of health. Go to your bankers.

KURT *kisses her roughly. She accepts the embrace impassively. Then he turns and goes to the steps L.*

See you tomorrow.

KURT. (*For once rather forlorn.*) Why are you never feeling for me what you are feeling for this gigolo?

ROSE. One day, perhaps I will, Kurt. You may have to lose all your money, first, and pawn my jewels, and cry on my shoulder and need my help. Still, that could happen, I suppose.

KURT. My father was right when he is saying—never get involved with women. They are all crazy idiots, and about life are they knowing from nothing. From nothing.

*He goes out.* ROSE *sits down wearily.*

HETTIE. I hope he doesn't take you too seriously, and let those Swiss bankers get the better of him.

ROSE. Can you see him?

HETTIE. Frankly, I can't.

ROSE *holds out her hand to* HETTIE, *who takes it.*

ROSE. Do I have to marry him, Hettie?

HETTIE. Yes, dear. Quite frankly, you do.

ROSE. Otherwise, no lolly?

HETTIE. No lolly at all.

ROSE. If I sold this damn house—

HETTIE. It's been up for sale for five months. I haven't heard of an offer yet.

ROSE. In the Ron days I was going to live on the income from the sale—do you remember?

HETTIE. I remember.

ROSE. I was on the level, you know. I really did think someone would want to buy it.

HETTIE. You couldn't have given it away. I knew that.

ROSE. So I'd only have had the pictures to sell. And the car.

HETTIE. For what you could get.

ROSE. (*With a faint laugh.*) Yes. Yes, it'd have been love in a cottage, all right. A smaller cottage than I'd even bargained for.

HETTIE. Or than *he'd* bargained for.

ROSE. (*Looking up at her, gently.*) Quite right, Hettie. You must always say things like that. Go on being an antidote, will you?

HETTIE. The strongest in the business. (*She turns away.*) I'm having a beer.

ROSE. (*Murmuring.*) The little twirp. Throwing money in my face, yet. Hm! I bet he's making a lovely story of it now—down in the theatre, with all the chorus boys—

HETTIE. (*At drink tray.*) And girls—

ROSE. Yes. And girls. (*Imitating* RON.) 'I showed her what I thought of her, all right. I showed her she couldn't treat me like a common little pick-up.' (*Excitedly.*) No. Wait a minute. Down at the theatre he uses his accent, doesn't he? (*Imitating, again, with phoney Russian accent.*) 'So. I draw myself up to my full height and I say—Madame—I pray you to accept this insignificant sum and present it, Madame, to any charity. (*Her voice trails away.*) Any charity.' (*With suppressed tears.*) Oh, Hettie—

HETTIE *comes over and takes her hand again.*

What an awful mess I've made of it all.

HETTIE. No dear. He's out of your life.

ROSE. (*Angrily.*) I didn't mean *him*. I meant me. I meant Kurt—I meant my whole damned existence. How the hell did I start it all? I can't even re-member now. I know I loathed home—but a lot of girls do that. I know I read a lot of magazine trash about rich peers marrying humble work-ing girls, and about the glittering, glamorous life of the international set, but a lot of girls do that too. I know I preferred Cannes to Edgbaston, and Florida to the Welfare State, but am I alone in that?

HETTIE. No, dear. I wouldn't say so.

ROSE. Then why is it me who's got to marry Kurt in three months' time?

HETTIE. Poor little multi-millionairess.

*Pause.* ROSE *looks up at her and smiles.*

ROSE. (*Brusquely.*) Quite right, Hettie. Self-pity—maudlin and ridiculous. As you never stopped saying to me once, I've made my bed and a very comfortable bed it's been too, and after Kurt—let me tell you, it's damn well going to be the most comfortable bed in Europe. No one will ever have seen such a bed. It'll have flounces and canopies and solid gold cherubs—and—

*She stops abruptly.* RON *has come back on to the terrace.*

(*Her voice level.*) I thought you went with Mona.

RON. Just to the end of the drive. I waited there till I saw Kurt go.

ROSE. Very wise. What have you come back for? Your money?

RON. (*Murmuring.*) No.

ROSE. It's over there, if you want it.

RON. I don't want it. I want you to have it.

ROSE. Yes. You made that clear just now. What have you come back for then?

RON. To ask you to forgive me.

ROSE. All right. I've forgiven you. Now how are you going to get back to Cannes?

RON. I hadn't thought.

ROSE. Hettie, would you ring up for a taxi? From the Carlton. My account.

HETTIE. Right.

*She goes out.*

RON. (*After a pause, in a low voice.*) Why do you hate me so much?

ROSE. Do I hate you, Ron?

RON. You must. If you don't, then why do you say things like 'have you come back for your money', and 'my account'? They're only meant to hurt, aren't they?

ROSE. Yes, I suppose that's how they must seem.

RON. Surely if either of us is to hate the other, it ought to be me hating you—oughtn't it?

ROSE. Yes. It ought.

RON. Oh God, Rose, how could you do that to me? What did I do to you to make you do that?

ROSE. You did nothing, Ron.

RON. I must have done something. Every night I've tried to think—what could it have been. What the hell could it possibly have been. (*After a pause.*) Was it that pullover I ordered without telling you—?

ROSE. No, Ron. It wasn't the pullover.

RON. Something I said, then. That row we had in the Martinez?

ROSE. No. It wasn't the row in the Martinez.

RON. It must have been something. I think I've been over everything I said or did that week a hundred times—and I still don't know. I still don't know, Rose. Are you sure it wasn't the pullover?

ROSE. I'm sure it wasn't the pullover.

RON. What was it then?

ROSE. I'd just stopped loving you, Ron—that's all.

RON. You wouldn't—like that. Not unless I'd done something really bad. I know that.

ROSE. How do you know?

RON. I know you.

ROSE. Perhaps you don't. Perhaps you never did.

RON. I did, anyway. Knew you like the back of my hand. If I hadn't I wouldn't have felt about you the way I did.

ROSE. How was that, Ron?

RON. Well—happy—and—well, you know—safe—

ROSE. Yes. I know.

RON. No. It must have been something awful I did—

ROSE. (*Explosively.*) Oh God, why can't you grow up? Must you go on through life thinking that everything bad that ever happens to you must always be your own fault? I just stopped loving you. There wasn't any reason. I just stopped loving you. It happens, you know. It happens every day—

HETTIE *comes out of the house.*

HETTIE. The taxi's on its way.

ROSE. Thank you, Hettie.

HETTIE. And Fiona's boy friend's arrived to take her down to the Ciel et Enfer. She's waiting in the hall to say good-bye.

ROSE. (*With sudden violence.*) I'm not going to—

HETTIE. (*Bewildered.*) I thought she'd better not come out here. But if you want—

ROSE. No. I don't want her out here. I just don't want to say good-bye to Fiona. Get it?

HETTIE. Yes.

ROSE. Why should I have my feelings bulldozed by that self-contained little snow-maiden, and be always expected to come up with a happy maternal smile: 'Well, good-bye, Fiona, darling. So glad you've enjoyed your stay. Write to me, won't you, and look after yourself—and remember Mummy will be thinking of you every day—ever; if you never spend one single damn second of the next three months thinking of Mummy.' I'm not going to do it, Hettie. I'm not going to.

HETTIE. Yes. I heard you. What shall I tell her?

ROSE. That I'm very, very tired, and that I'll call her at the airport.

HETTIE. Right.

*She goes out.*

RON. That's funny.

ROSE. What's funny?

RON. My feelings have been bulldozed all right—you can't deny it—but I come up smiling.

ROSE. I haven't noticed you smiling.

RON. That's just a figure of speech. I'm here, aren't I?—apologizing and eating dirt when I ought to be hating you and despising you—the way you do me. (*Angrily.*) Why can't I hate you?

ROSE. Perhaps you haven't tried hard enough.

RON. Tried? Lord, I've tried. I'll go on trying too—never you fear. Only—(*his voice falters*) it doesn't seem much use—I don't know why.

*He turns away from her to hide his emotion.*

ROSE. (*Her voice harsh with anger.*) Don't cry—for God's sake—don't cry.

RON. (*Quickly.*) I wasn't. I'm quite all right. It was only just seeing you after all this time—

ROSE. (*Her voice still harsh.*) I prefer you in your money-throwing, glass-breaking mood—

RON. That was a give-away, wasn't it? You don't do that if you don't care. I was going to be all hard and bright and tough and couldn't care less to-night—the old Ron Vale—the one you met at the Casino that night—remember—and before you came out I wasn't doing too badly either—and then—(*He stops.*)

ROSE. And then?

RON. And then you did come out.

ROSE. (*Still hard.*) And something snapped, as they say in novels—and everything became a blur—

RON. You could put it like that, I suppose. (*Quickly.*) God, you've changed, Rose. You were always a bit hard at times, I'm not denying—but nothing like this. It's not the way I'll be wanting to remember you.

ROSE. But it's the way you should remember me. It might help you to hate me—

RON. (*Sadly.*) No, it won't. I know it won't. I suppose the truth is, if you need somebody enough it doesn't seem to matter that much what they do to you, or what they turn out to be. In spite of everything, you see—and I really am eating dirt now all right—I still want like mad to be in your life—only one of three hundred other guests, if you like, and on sufferance from that German bastard—but just to see you and talk to you now and then. (*Shame-facedly.*) Fine bloody manly attitude that is, isn't it? Still, I can't help it. It's the truth and I thought you'd like to know it.

ROSE. (*Now becoming desperate.*) Why did you think I'd like to know it? Why?

RON. God, if I'd treated another girl the way you treated me, I wouldn't mind knowing she'd forgiven me.

ROSE. I don't want to know it, Ron. I'd far rather think you hadn't forgiven me and never would. I'd far rather think you had some guts.

RON. Well, I haven't and I've admitted it. (*After a pause.*) Maybe I shouldn't have told you then. Only when you've got certain feelings about someone, it's damned hard to stop yourself saying it.

ROSE. (*Facing him squarely.*) It's not hard at all, Ron. It's quite easy. And what feelings are you talking about? Are you trying to suggest—love? That you feel love?

RON. (*Nodding, at length.*) That's about it, I suppose.

ROSE. (*Laughing.*) That's not about it, Ron—it's nowhere within a hundred miles of it. Love means giving, doesn't it—and what have you ever done all your life except take—take anything from motor-cars to other people's love? (*Derisively.*) You feel love? That'll be the day.

RON. It doesn't matter much what you call it, does it? I've told you the truth.

ROSE. You haven't. You're just trying to sneak into my life again—through the servants' entrance, this time—not like that first night when you used the front door and you were oh so cocky and sure of yourself—and convinced no one could ever resist you—not even me—not even me—

RON. Yes. I was a bit cocky then, I grant. Seems I've changed a bit this summer—

ROSE. Oh my God! Isn't there anything in the world I can say to you that will make you angry?

*She turns quickly away.* RON *stares at her, surprised.*

RON. Do you want to make me angry?

ROSE. Of course I don't. I don't give a damn what you feel. Why should I? Why the hell should I?

*Her voice is beginning to betray her.* RON *has taken a few faltering steps towards her, when* HETTIE *appears.*

HETTIE. Taxi's here.

ROSE. (*Murmuring.*) Thank God.

HETTIE *stares at* ROSE'S *face as she stands, her back still to* RON. ROSE *signs her to go away.* HETTIE *turns abruptly and goes out. When* ROSE *faces* RON *again she has partly recovered herself. She picks up the money on the table.*
You'd better take this. You'll be needing it.

RON *shakes his head quickly.* ROSE *throws the money back on to the table.*
I'm afraid it won't be possible for us to meet again, Ron. You see, I'm going away to Switzerland tomorrow and won't be back here any more.

RON. I didn't know. Oh Lord! That's terrible, isn't it?

ROSE. Why terrible?

RON. For me, I meant. We've got a season soon in Paris. Perhaps—

ROSE. (*Quickly.*) Perhaps. (*Brightly.*) How's the dancing going, Ron?

RON. Not bad. I'm going to try for the Garden next year.

ROSE. Good. I hope you make it.

RON. If I do, that might mean we could meet in London too. Or New York. They go there quite a bit.

ROSE. Yes, I know.

RON. (*Quietly.*) I'm not going to let you right out of my life, you know. You say I've got no guts—but about that I have. And I don't mind the servants' entrance. Hell. Why should I? It's where I belong.

ROSE. Why you more than me?

RON. You've made the grade. I haven't.

ROSE. Well, good-bye, Ron.

RON. Can't I stay on just a little bit longer?

ROSE. No. I'm sorry.

RON. I've nothing to do in town, except eat by myself somewhere and go to bed. Can't I stay on just a bit?

ROSE. No, I'm sorry. I've got some people coming in in a minute, you see, and—

RON. (*With a smile.*) And you don't want them to meet common Ron. I see. All right. I'll go quietly. Good-bye. Or rather—be seeing you, Rose.

*He turns to the steps and then turns back.*

(*In genuine bewilderment.*) I wish you'd tell me what it was I did to make you change like that. (*After a pause for thought.*) Listen, was it anything to do with that day when you said I always stayed in the sea too long, and you were waving from the beach and I was on the raft pretending not to notice—?

ROSE'S *expression, not unimpassive until now, suddenly dissolves completely. She puts her hands quickly to her face and turns away, but her tears have been all too visible to* RON. *He stares at her.*

It was that, then?

ROSE, *in tears, does not answer.* RON *walks slowly towards her.*

ROSE. (*As she senses his closeness.*) Go away. Oh, God, please go away.

RON. No. Not when you're like this. Was it that, Rose?

ROSE. (*With a wail.*) No—it wasn't that. Of course it wasn't that—

RON. What's the matter, then?

ROSE. Nothing's the matter. I'm feeling tired—that's all. Get Hettie for me—

RON. No. I won't do that. (*He puts his hands on her shoulders.*)

ROSE. Please go away, Ron. Please.

RON. No. I won't do that either, now.

ROSE. Oh God. Ten more seconds. Ten more seconds, and it was done. Why did you say that about the beach?

*She turns to him, still crying, and holds him to her. Then she lets him raise her head with his hand and kiss her.*

RON. I thought it might really have been that.

ROSE. You damn little fool.

RON. Why have you been pretending to me?

ROSE. I haven't been pretending

RON. (*Still holding her.*) Is there any point in fighting it any more?

ROSE. No. I suppose there isn't. I suppose there isn't.

*She recovers herself.* RON *looks at her frowning and puzzled.*

RON. (*Explosively.*) But why? Why? Why those awful things you said to me on that machine? It wasn't just the money. I know that.

ROSE. How do you know that?

RON. I know my Rose better than most people. Better than Hettie or Kurt. Why? Why?

ROSE. Oh God, you're such a fool.

*She breaks away from him and takes a cigarette.*

Haven't you any idea?

*He shakes his head.*

No. I suppose it would be the very last idea that'd occur to you. It was for you, Ron.

RON. For me? And make me bloody miserable for three months—

ROSE. We weren't thinking so much of months, Ron. More of years. Many, many years. A lifetime, in fact.

RON. You said 'we'. You mean Hettie and you?

ROSE. Yes. Hettie and I.

RON. The interfering old—

ROSE. Don't blame *her*, Ron. It was *my* doing. Mine entirely.

RON. I don't get the idea, Rose.

ROSE. We thought—I thought—and I was right too, mind you—I thought if things hadn't lasted between us, it might have been worse for you than for me.

RON. Why?

ROSE. You might have been left a bit—stranded—

RON. Stranded? Me? Hell, I can take care of myself.

ROSE. Cocky again, eh?

RON. I can, Rose. Really, I can. I mean, look at the way I've looked after myself since you did ditch me. Bloody lonely, I grant, and not sleeping or eating too well either. But doing all right, I tell you. Ask anyone in the Company. As a matter of fact I've been dancing better these last three months than ever before in my life—

ROSE. (*Looking at him.*) I'm glad to hear it.

RON. Oh, my God—what a damn crazy idea! Typical of a woman. And when you think what I've been going through since August. Of course you've been giving gay parties up here.

ROSE. The parties haven't been awfully gay, Ron. At least—not for me.

*Pause.*

RON. Just torturing ourselves for no reason. No reason at all.

*He embraces her again.*

(*At length.*) Going to give up Kurt?

*Pause.*

ROSE. (*Quietly, at length.*) Yes.

RON. And marry me?

ROSE. No.

RON. Oh, yes you are, you know. Why do you think you're not?

ROSE. We haven't the money.

RON. (*Laughing.*) Money! (*He looks up at the house.*)

ROSE. No one will buy it, Ron.

RON. That's all right. We can live in it.

ROSE. (*After a pause.*) Yes. I suppose we can.

RON. And with the money I get from the ballet we can pay for food and things. Or you might perhaps be able to get me something that pays a bit better.

ROSE. No. You must stick to dancing, Ron. Whatever happens, you must stick to that.

RON. Well, anyway—we'll live.

ROSE. Yes.

RON *has wandered to the drink tray.*

RON. We must have a toast on this, don't you think? Or are you really on the level about the wagon?

ROSE. No, of course not. When have you ever known me on the level about the wagon?

RON. Brandy and soda?

ROSE. And not too light on the brandy, either. (*Approaching him.*) I think perhaps we'd better wait a little bit about getting married, Ron.

RON. How long?

ROSE. Oh—only—say a couple of months. Not much longer.

RON. Why?

ROSE. Well—one thing—it might be nice to get married after the winter—

RON. Very charming and sentimental idea, considering who it's from. Have all your marriages been in the spring?

ROSE. (*Smiling.*) This is a very special one.

RON. Granted. (*He raises his glass.*) Well—to the spring.

ROSE. (*Murmuring.*) To the spring.

RON. And to no more practical jokes, that make me wish I'd never been born—even if they *are* for my good.

ROSE. Oh, Ron—

RON. And no more tears either. We've done with that, now.

ROSE. People can cry from just being glad, you know—

RON. (*Stroking her hair.*) Yes, and later tonight it's quite likely I'll be doing that, too. But when we're together from now on—let's try and keep it smiles. Smiles all the way.

ROSE. I'll try. And I'll succeed too. Because it won't be hard at all.

RON. It's funny about us, isn't it? I mean, both of us coming from the same town, both of us knowing exactly what we want—and exactly how we're going to get it, too—and then, suddenly, what have we got? Just what everybody else in the world has got—each other. Whoever it is that fixes things up there has quite a line in practical jokes himself—you've got to grant—

ROSE. (*Smiling tenderly at him.*) Yes, Ron. In the past I haven't always granted the accuracy of your observations on the Universe and its meaning—but oddly enough, that one I do.

*There is a raucous sound from the drive.*

TAXI-DRIVER. (*Off.*) Mais, dites-donc. Qu'est ce qui a? On va attendre toute la nuit, ou quoi?

RON. (*Calling down.*) On vient tout de suite. (*Turning back.*) Shall I send him away, or shall we take it together, and have a night on the town?

ROSE. A night on the town, of course.

RON. (*Doubtfully.*) Good. But you know we can't exactly afford one of *your* sort of nights

ROSE. Why not? Look what we've got, Ron. (*She picks up the money from the table.*) And what's left over after our orgy I'll put on red. Yes. It's red tonight. It'll come up ten times running, and all our troubles will be over. Let's go.

RON. Hadn't you better have a coat? It gets a bit chilly these nights—

ROSE. Yes. I suppose it does. Get me my camel hair, would you? You know the one?

RON *nods.*

It's in my cupboard upstairs.

RON. O.K.

ROSE. And as you go tell Hettie to stop listening at the window and come out.

RON *nods, smiles at her and goes.* ROSE *takes a long gulp from her brandy, and then begins to cough violently.* HETTIE *comes out.*

(*Between coughs.*) There's not a damn thing in the world you can do about it.

HETTIE. Oh yes, there is. I can tell him about the sanatorium.

ROSE. I'll tell him different. It's *me* he'll believe, because he'll want to. You're the enemy.

HETTIE. I'll get the doctors to fight it.

ROSE. (*Shrugging.*) Oh God, Hettie. I've fought doctors all my life, and I've always won.

HETTIE. (*Fiercely.*) I'll get the doctors to tell *him* exactly what a winter in this place must mean for you. That he'll have to believe.

ROSE. Why? He knows that doctors can be wrong. So do you. So do I. They've been wrong about me often enough before. Why not now?

HETTIE. This time you know they're not.

ROSE. I don't think I know anything very much, any more, Hettie. Nor does he. I think you'll find he'll be just as content as I am to put it all on red. That's not such a bad way to gamble, you know. Systems don't always pay off, and who am I saying *that* to?

*She turns and smiles at* HETTIE *tenderly.*

You won't leave me this time, will you? Not, at least, until after the winter—

HETTIE. (*Suddenly losing all her toughness: a broken. bewildered old woman.*) Oh God, Rose. You know there's no gamble in this. You know it as well as I do. It's a certainty.

ROSE *merely smiles.*

But why? Why? Why?

ROSE. (*Echoing what she once said to Ron.*) Why not?

*She looks tenderly at* HETTIE'S *distressed face.*

I've picked up the hand, Hettie. I can't refuse to play the cards, can I?

HETTIE. Of course you can, when playing them must mean— (*She stops.*)

ROSE. (*Gently.*) I lose the game? Would you do that, Hettie? Would you be proud of yourself if you did? Oh no, surely we've got to play the rules, haven't we? I can't claim I don't know them, either. I learnt them at my father's knee. Quite often, in his few sober moments, he used to say to me: 'If there's one thing that's certain in this world, Rose, my girl, it's that you'll come to a bad end.' I believed him, too, and always have. Only, being a bit of a puritan myself, as you know, I'd always imagined an end far more lurid and horrifying than a winter in Cannes with a man I love more than life. More than life? Silly phrase, that—isn't it? Just a woman's exaggeration.

HETTIE *is crying.*

ROSE. Oh, Hettie—please.

RON *comes back with* ROSE'S *coat, brushes past* HETTIE *without looking at her, and helps* ROSE *into the coat.*

Thank you, Ron. I was just talking about you.

RON. (*Embarrassed before* HETTIE.) Nicely?

ROSE. Yes. I think even *your* vanity would be satisfied.

*She hands him the money she has been holding.*

You'd better take this, and cause a sensation at Maxim's by being seen paying for me for once.

RON. That's right. Back to normal. Needling poor old Ron again. Hell, have you forgotten it's my money?

ROSE. You gave it to me.

RON. Yes, but I won it.

ROSE. Yes. You won it—and gave it to me. (*She smiles at his angry face.*) Oh, well, it couldn't matter less, could it? From now on, what's mine is yours, anyway.

*She turns to look at* HETTIE *who is crying. She walks over to her and puts her hands on her shoulders.*

(*With a smile.*) Hettie. Hettie—for heaven's sake. I'm terribly happy.

*She kisses her gently on the cheek and then goes to* RON. *She takes a red rose from a vase and puts it in his buttonhole.*

It's a bit early for Maxim's. Let's have dinner at that new place on the port, and then try a bar that Mona told me about the other day—somewhere on the Rue d'Antibestout ce qu'il y a de plus hellish, I'm sure, but worth a try. It's called the Chien something—

*They begin to go down the steps together.*

RON. Yes. I know it. The Chien Noir—

ROSE Noir? Oh dear. I hope that isn't an omen. Anyway it doesn't matter. I've said rouge and rouge is what I mean. After that—well, I suppose what we could do is—

*They have disappeared.* HETTIE *makes a hopeless gesture after* ROSE, *but she has not looked back.*

CURTAIN

# ROSS

*A DRAMATIC PORTRAIT*

First published 1960
by Hamish Hamilton Ltd


The Author gratefully acknowledges his debt to Captain B. H. Liddell Hart, both for the illumination afforded by his book *T. E. Lawrence—in Arabia and After* and for his help in checking the script.

DEDICATED WITH GRATITUDE TO
ANATOLE DE GRUNWALD
Who brought Lawrence to me and me to Lawrence

Characters
(*in order of appearance*)

FLIGHT LIEUTENANT STOKER
FLIGHT SERGEANT THOMPSON
AIRCRAFTMAN PARSONS
AIRCRAFTMAN EVANS
AIRCRAFTMAN DICKINSON
LAWRENCE
FRANKS (*The lecturer*)
GENERAL ALLENBY
RONALD STORRS
COLONEL BARRINGTON
AUDA ABU TAYI
THE TURKISH MILITARY GOVERNOR,
   DERAA DISTRICT
HAMED
RASHID
A TURKISH CAPTAIN
A TURKISH SERGEANT
A BRITISH CORPORAL
A.D.C.
A PHOTOGRAPHER
AN AUSTRALIAN SOLDIER
FLIGHT LIEUTENANT HIGGINS
GROUP CAPTAIN WOOD

The action of the play begins and ends at a Royal Air Force Depot, near London, on an afternoon, the same night and following morning of a day in winter, 1922. The central passages cover the two years 1916–18 and are set in the Middle East.

*Ross* was first produced at the Haymarket Theatre, London, on May 12th, 1960, with the following cast:

| | |
|---|---|
| FLIGHT LIEUTENANT STOKER | Geoffrey Colvile |
| FLIGHT SERGEANT THOMPSON | Dervis Ward |
| AIRCRAFTMAN PARSONS | Peter Bayliss |
| AIRCRAFTMAN EVANS | John Southworth |
| AIRCRAFTMAN DICKINSON | Gerald Harper |
| AIRCRAFTMAN ROSS | Alec Guinness |
| FRANKS (The lecturer) | James Grout |
| GENERAL ALLENBY | Harry Andrews |
| RONALD STORRS | Anthony Nicholls |
| COLONEL BARRINGTON | Leon Sinden |
| AUDA ABU TAYI | Mark Dignam |
| THE TURKISH MILITARY GOVERNOR, DERAA DISTRICT | Geoffrey Keen |
| HAMED | Robert Arnold |
| RASHID | Charles Laurence |
| A TURKISH CAPTAIN | Basil Hoskins |
| A TURKISH SERGEANT | Raymond Adamson |
| A BRITISH CORPORAL | John Trenaman |
| A.D.C. | Ian Clark |
| A PHOTOGRAPHER | Antony Kenway |
| AN AUSTRALIAN SOLDIER | William Feltham |
| FLIGHT LIEUTENANT HIGGINS | Peter Cellier |
| GROUP CAPTAIN WOOD | John Stuart |

Directed by GLEN BYAM SHAW

Scenery and Costumes by MOTLEY

SCENE: *An office. Behind a desk sits a Flight Lieutenant. He is an earnest, well-meaning young officer with a manner alternately avuncular and fierce.*

*A Flight Sergeant stands in front of him. He is an oldish man, with a harsh rasping voice, that inadequately conceals a soft heart for recruits and a contempt for all officers, including this one.*

F/LT. Next charge.

F/SGT. (*Barking.*) Sir.

*He salutes with guardsmanlike punctiliousness, marches to the door, throws it open and shouts gabblingly and with a familiarity born of long usage.*
    Prisoner and escort, attention, quick march, left right, left right, halt, left turn. Aircraftman Parsons.

PARSONS *is a tough ex-sailor of about thirty-five; of his two escorts,* EVANS *is young and red-haired, and the other,* DICKINSON, *is an ex-officer of the war-time Army, in the ranks of the R.A.F. for economic reasons.*

F/LT. (*Inspecting a charge sheet.*) 352179 A.C.2 Parsons?

PARSONS. Sir.

F/LT. (*Reading from the charge sheet.*) Conduct to the prejudice of good order and Royal Air Force discipline in that on December 16th, 1922, at the 0830 hours colour-hoisting parade the accused broke ranks and swore aloud. (*Looking up.*) What's all this, Parsons?

PARSONS. Slammed my rifle-butt on my toe, sir. Lifted my foot half an inch, sir. May have made a slight sound—but only to myself, of course, sir.

F/LT. (*To* FLIGHT SERGEANT.) Witness present?

F/SGT. I am the only witness, sir. I was drilling B Flight that morning.

F/LT. Was the sound slight?

F/SGT. Rang across the parade ground, sir.

F/LT. And was it—identifiable?

F/SGT. Very, sir.

F/LT. I see. (*To* PARSONS.) You don't dispute the actual word you used?

PARSONS. No, sir.

F/LT. Merely its volume?

PARSONS. Whisper, sir.

F/LT. But it was heard clearly by the Flight Sergeant.

PARSONS. Might have lip-read, sir.

F/LT. It's still swearing on parade, isn't it?

PARSONS. Yes, sir.

F/LT. And that's a serious offence. (*Looking down at the paper on his desk.*)

However, I'm glad to see it's your first. Still, that's not saying much after only ten weeks in the Service. (*To* FLIGHT SERGEANT.) How is he at drill, generally?

F/SGT. He used to be in the Navy, sir.

F/LT. Don't they order arms from the slope in the Navy?

PARSONS. Yes, sir. But they do it proper time.

F/LT. Careful, Parsons.

PARSONS. Sorry, sir. I meant different time.

F/LT. Well, you'll just have to get used to the timing we use here at the Depot—which is, anyway, exactly the same as the Guards. Also to learn to order arms properly without hitting your foot and swearing.

PARSONS. Yes, sir.

F/LT. Think yourself lucky I'm not putting this on your conduct sheet. All right. Accused admonished.

F/SGT. Prisoner and escort right turn, quick march, left right, left right. Halt. A.C.2 Parsons. Dismiss.

PARSONS *and his escort are marched out.*

F/LT. Next.

F/SGT. (*Barking.*) Prisoner and escort, attention, quick march, left right, left right, halt, left turn. Aircraftman Ross.

*Another* AIRCRAFTMAN *has been marched in. The escorts are the same. The accused is a small man of thirty-five with a long face and a sad, shy expression. He speaks in a very gentle voice. His name is now Ross, and will, one day, be Shaw, but in the text he is designated by his first surname.*

F/LT. (*Looking at the charge sheet.*) 352087 A.C.2 Ross?

LAWRENCE. Yes, sir.

F/LT. (*Reading.*) Conduct prejudicial to good order and Royal Air Force discipline in that the accused failed to report to the Guard Room by 2359 hours on December 16th, 1922, on expiry of his late pass issued on that date and did not in fact report until 0017 hours on December 17th, 1922. Period of unauthorized absence—eighteen minutes. (*He looks up at the* FLIGHT SERGEANT.) Witness present?

F/SGT. Guard commander's report, sir.

F/LT. (*Looking at another document.*) Oh yes. Well, Ross. Anything to say?

LAWRENCE. No, sir.

F/LT. You admit the charge?

LAWRENCE. Yes, sir.

F/LT. (*Looking at another document.*) I see you've been on two charges already. Untidy turn-out, three days' confined to camp, dumb insolence to an officer, seven days' confined to camp. So this charge makes the third in the ten weeks you've been in the Air Force. That's bad, Ross. That's very bad indeed. (*Suddenly thumping the desk.*) Ross, I'm speaking to you. I said that's very bad indeed.

LAWRENCE. I'm sorry, sir. I took it as an observation, not as a question. I agree, it's very bad indeed.

F/LT. (*After a pause.*) I've an idea you don't care for authority, Ross?

LAWRENCE. I care for discipline, sir.

F/LT. What's the distinction?

LAWRENCE. Very wide, I believe.

F/LT. Being late on pass is an offence against both authority and discipline, isn't it?

LAWRENCE. Yes sir. The point was academic.

F/LT. (*After a pause.*) What made you join the R.A.F.?

LAWRENCE. I think I had a mental breakdown, sir.

F/LT. (*More hurt than angry.*) That kind of insolence isn't called for, Ross. I'm here not only to judge you but to help you. Will you try and understand that?

LAWRENCE. Yes, sir.

F/LT. All right. Let's start again. Why did you join the R.A.F.?

LAWRENCE. (*Slowly.*) Because I wanted to, because I was destitute, because I enjoy discipline, and because I had a mental breakdown.

*The* FLIGHT LIEUTENANT *stares at him, angrily.*

If you prefer, sir, we can substitute for 'mental'—the word 'spiritual'. I don't happen to like it myself, but at least it avoids the imputation of insolence.

F/LT. (*To* FLIGHT SERGEANT.) Flight?

F/SGT. Sir.

F/LT. What is your report on this airman, in terms of general conduct?

F/SGT. Satisfactory, sir.

F/LT. No signs of being bolshie—or general bloody-mindedness?

F/SGT. No, sir.

F/LT. Drill?

F/SGT. Behind the others, sir, but then he's older and therefore slower. But he tries hard.

F/LT. P/T?

F/SGT. According to the sergeant instructor, sir, he has difficulty in keeping up with the squad, but then his age comes into that too, and his—physical handicaps.

F/LT. Physical handicaps? This is a recruit, Flight Sergeant, passed into the R.A.F. as A.1. What physical handicaps are you talking about?

F/SGT. (*Uneasily.*) Well, sir. I only know that twice after P/T I've seen him being sick into a bucket, and he has some bad marks on his back, sir.

F/LT. (*To* LAWRENCE.) What are these marks?

LAWRENCE. The scars of an accident, sir.

F/LT. A serious accident?

LAWRENCE. At the time it seemed so.

F/LT. And you were passed as A.1?

LAWRENCE. Yes, sir.

F/LT. (*To* FLIGHT SERGEANT.) It seems very mysterious to me. (*To* LAWRENCE.) Where did you go last night?

LAWRENCE. To a place in Buckinghamshire—near Taplow.

F/LT. By bus or train?

LAWRENCE. Motor bicycle.

F/LT. I see. Why were you late?

LAWRENCE. I fell off it.

F/LT. Were you drunk?

LAWRENCE. No, sir. I only drink water, and I'm rather particular about that.

F/LT. How did you fall off?

LAWRENCE. I was going through Denham rather fast, but with a good ten minutes in hand, when a dog ran out into the street and I swerved. A car coming the other way hit me, and I was left with very little bicycle. It became necessary to run, which, as the Flight Sergeant has just told you, I'm not as adept at as some.

F/LT. (*After a pause.*) When I asked you just now if you had anything to say in answer to this charge, you said no.

LAWRENCE. Yes, sir.

F/LT. You didn't think a motorcycle accident might be taken as a possible excuse?

LAWRENCE. No, sir. Only as a reason.

F/LT. Another distinction.

LAWRENCE. Yes, sir. Another wide one.

*Pause.*

F/LT. Ross, I hope you realize that most officers trying your case would, by now, have given you the maximum sentence, or remanded you to the Station Commander with an additional charge of insubordination.

LAWRENCE. Yes, sir.

F/LT. You think it's going to help your case if you impress me with the fact that you're an educated man. But that fact doesn't impress me at all— do you understand?

LAWRENCE. Yes, sir.

F/LT. There are plenty of educated men in the ranks of the R.A.F. nowadays.

*He looks suddenly from* LAWRENCE *to one of his escorts* (DICKINSON).

You—escort—what's your name?

DICKINSON *very smartly steps a pace forward and stamps his foot in parade-ground manner.*

DICKINSON. Dickinson, sir.

F/LT. I know something about you. You were at a public school, weren't you?

DICKINSON. Yes, sir.

F/LT. Weren't you also an officer in the Gunners?

DICKINSON. Yes, sir. Captain. War-time commission, of course.

F/LT. At the front?

DICKINSON. Yes, sir. Passchendaele and the big Hun push in March '18. I got a blighty there.

F/LT. And why did you join the R.A.F.?

DICKINSON. I got a job when I was demobbed, selling motorcars, but found

I preferred Service life, sir. I considered the R.A.F. the Service of the future and, when they turned me down for a commission, I decided to join anyway and work my way up through the ranks.

*His answer has plainly pleased the* FLIGHT LIEUTENANT, *who nods smilingly at him.*

F/LT. I hope you will. All right, Dickinson.

DICKINSON *steps back to his place beside* LAWRENCE *with supreme smartness.*

You see, Ross, this airman is in your flight, and there are many others with similar records in other recruit squads. Where were you at school?

LAWRENCE. Oxford High School, sir.

F/LT. Were you in the war?

LAWRENCE. Yes, sir.

F/LT. In what capacity?

LAWRENCE. Oh—mostly—liaison work.

F/LT. Liaison work? Where?

LAWRENCE (*After a slight hesitation.*) The Middle East.

F/LT. Where in the Middle East?

LAWRENCE. Oh, all kinds of places.

F/LT. You seem very vague about it.

LAWRENCE. It was rather a vague kind of job.

F/LT. (*Angrily.*) For heaven's sake, man, you must have known what you were doing.

LAWRENCE. Not very often, sir.

F/LT. When you talk about mental breakdown you don't happen to mean just plain mad, do you?

LAWRENCE. Not certifiably so, sir.

F/LT. You're in trouble of some kind?

LAWRENCE. (*Quietly.*) Yes, sir.

F/LT. Bad trouble?

LAWRENCE. It seems so, to me.

F/LT. You mean when you tell other people they don't find it so bad?

LAWRENCE. I don't tell other people, sir.

F/LT. No one at all?

LAWRENCE. No one at all.

F/LT. If I sent the Flight Sergeant and the escort out now—would you tell it to me?

LAWRENCE. No, sir.

F/LT. (*After a pause.*) Look here, Ross, I'm not just your Flight Commander. You've got to try and look on me as a sort of Dutch uncle. (*After another pause.*) Well?

LAWRENCE. The untellable—even to a sort of Dutch uncle—can't be told.

*There is a pause. The* FLIGHT LIEUTENANT, *frustrated, looks down at his desk.*

F/LT. Why did you go to this place in Buckinghamshire?

LAWRENCE. To have a meal with some friends.

F/LT. Close friends?

LAWRENCE. Some of them.

F/LT. Give me their names.

LAWRENCE. (*Momentarily nonplussed.*) Their names, sir?

F/LT. (*Barking.*) Yes, their names. (*He has taken up a notebook and pencil.*)

LAWRENCE. But have you the right—?

F/LT. Yes, I have the right. (*Shouting.*) I want these people's names *now.* That's an order, Ross.

LAWRENCE. (*With a faint sigh.*) Very well, sir. Lord and Lady Astor, Mr. and Mrs. George Bernard Shaw, the Archbishop of Canterbury—

*The* FLIGHT LIEUTENANT *has thrown his pencil down.*

F/LT. All right. You now have two charges to answer—the present one and the one I'm putting you on tomorrow to be dealt with by the Group Captain—to wit—gross insubordination to your Flight Commander. On the present charge you get seven days' confined to camp. As for the second—well—I doubt if in future you're going to find much time to relax your troubled soul.

LAWRENCE. No, sir. I don't think it needs that kind of relaxation—

F/LT. (*Shouting.*) That's enough, unless you want a court martial. March him out, Flight.

F/SGT. Prisoner and escort right turn, quick march, left right, left right. Halt. Prisoner and escort, dismiss.

LAWRENCE, DICKINSON *and* EVANS *march out. The* FLIGHT SERGEANT *turns at the door.*

That is the last charge, sir.

F/LT. (*Wearily.*) Thank God for that.

*He collects the charge sheets from his desk and throws them into his 'Out' tray. Then he looks up at the Flight Sergeant.*

How's the Flight coming along generally?

F/SGT. About average, sir.

F/LT. Think you'll make airmen of them?

F/SGT. Of a sort, sir.

F/LT. (*With a sigh.*) I know what you mean. Shocking lot we're getting these days. (*With a change of tone.*) But keep your eye on that chap Dickinson. I like the look of him. He ought to do well.

F/SGT. Yes, sir.

F/LT. (*Feelingly.*) And give that cocky little bastard, Ross, hell.

F/SGT. Yes, sir.

*He salutes magnificently, turns, stamping his feet as if to split his heelbones.*


THE LIGHTS FADE


*In the darkness we hear the sound of a mouth-organ playing, and men's voices singing, softly and sentimentally, a popular song of the period ('The Sheik of Araby').*

SCENE: *Part of a yard in the depot.* PARSONS, EVANS *and* DICKINSON *are prominent among a small group of the other recruits, one of whom is playing a mouthorgan, while others, only intermittently visible, are singing or whistling gently to his accompaniment.* EVANS *is talking to* PARSONS *while* DICKINSON *is sitting apart from the others, hands behind his head, eyes open, musing.*

EVANS. (*Excitedly.*) But he did, Sailor. I promise you he did.

PARSONS. (*Incredulously.*) Archbishop of Canterbury? Rossie say a thing like that? Our Rossie? Oh no—

EVANS. But I was there, Sailor. I was escort. I heard him, clear as a bell. (*Indicating* DICKINSON.) So did you, didn't you, Dickie-bird?

DICKINSON. (*Without moving.*) What?

EVANS. When our officer—this morning said to Rossie 'Look here, my man, I want you to tell me who you went out with last night'—what a bloody nerve to ask such a thing, mind you—did Rossie say Mr. and Mrs. George Bernard Shaw and the Archbishop of Canterbury?

DICKINSON. Yes. Also—Lord and Lady Astor.

EVANS. (*Triumphantly to* PARSONS.) You see. You couldn't have done better yourself, Sailor. (*To* DICKINSON.) Weren't you proud of him, Dickie-bird?

DICKINSON. Not particularly.

PARSONS. Ex-ruddy-officer himself. Can't bear lip to one of his own kind.

DICKINSON. (*Quietly.*) You know that's a bloody lie, Sailor.

PARSONS. Why weren't you proud of him, then?

DICKINSON. (*Without taking his eyes from the sky.*) The Archbishop was enough. With the other names he overdid it.

LAWRENCE *comes in, staggering under the weight of a refuse bin.*

PARSONS. And what do you think you're doing, Rossie, old bean?

LAWRENCE. There are still three left to fill in there.

PARSONS. Yes, Rossie-boy, and left by my own instructions for a very good purpose, which is in case some bloody officer sticks his nose out here and says: 'I see you bleeders have done your fatigue, so you can bleeding well do another.'

LAWRENCE. (*Contrite.*) I'm sorry, Sailor. I should have thought.

PARSONS. (*Kindly.*) Yes, you should, shouldn't you? (*To* EVANS.) Ruddy marvel, isn't it? Reads Greek like it was the *Pink 'Un*, and don't know his bottom from Uxbridge Town Hall. (LAWRENCE *has turned to take the bin back again.*) No, leave it there, for Gawd's sake. We don't want to have to fill it again— (*Helplessly.*) Cripes!

LAWRENCE. (*Flustered.*) I'm sorry.

PARSONS. Never mind. Never mind. (*He suddenly thrusts out his hand.*) Rossie-boy—

LAWRENCE *turns and looks at* PARSONS' *outstretched hand in bewilderment.*

EVANS. (*Explanatorily.*) The Archbishop.

LAWRENCE. (*Still bewildered.*) The Archbishop?

PARSONS. And Mr. and Mrs. George Bernard Shaw, and in spite of what Dickie-bird says—Lord and Lady ruddy Astor—and though you might have added the Dolly Sisters and Gaby Deslys, no one can think of everything at once and I congratulate you, Rossie-boy. B Flight is proud of you.

LAWRENCE. (*Rather overwhelmed, and wincing at the force of* PARSONS' *famous handshake.*) It wasn't much, really—

PARSONS. (*To the others.*) Salute our hero, boys.

*There is a mild and faintly ironic cheer, and a few bars, also ironic, of a triumphal march from the mouth-organist.*

(*Putting his arm around* LAWRENCE'S *shoulder.*) Come and sing, Rossie. (*To the* MOUTH-ORGANIST.) Give us the old Sheik again.

*The mouth-organ starts up.*

LAWRENCE. (*Timidly.*) I'm afraid I don't know the words.

PARSONS. (*Shocked.*) Cor stuff me. You must be the only man in England who don't. (*To* MOUTH-ORGANIST.) Know anything in Latin or Greek?

LAWRENCE. I know Tipperary.

PARSONS. (*To the others, with irony.*) He knows Tipperary. (*To* MOUTH-ORGAN-IST.) Tipperary.

*The* MEN *begin to sing it,* PARSONS' *voice leading the others, but softly, because of fear of discovery.* LAWRENCE'S *voice, rather quavering, can be heard, proving that at least he does know the words. They finish a chorus and* PARSONS *starts 'Pack up your Troubles'.* LAWRENCE, *suddenly and brusquely, breaks away from* PARSONS' *friendly embrace and moves quickly away from the group, his back to them.* PARSONS *looks after him, rather surprised, but says nothing, continuing to sing. The* FLIGHT SERGEANT *comes in past* LAWRENCE *who turns quickly from him. The singing stops abruptly.*

F/SGT. What's the idea of the concert?

PARSONS. We'd nearly finished fatigue, Flight.

F/SGT. Nearly isn't quite, is it? (*Pointing to bin.*) What's that doing here? And how many more is there to fill?

PARSONS. Three, Flight.

F/SGT. Well, if you're smart and do 'em quickly I might find something else for you to do before supper. Jump to it now. Many hands make light work—

PARSONS. Oh. I wish I'd said that. How *do* you think of 'em, Flight?

F/SGT. (*Automatically.*) None of your lip, Parsons, now—unless you want a dose of jankers.

LAWRENCE *attempts to pick up the filled bin.*

No. Not you, Ross. Evans—Dickinson, you take that. Rest of you inside, at the double. Ross, stay here.

EVANS *and* DICKINSON *take the bin from* LAWRENCE, *and disappear, presumably*

*towards the incinerator, in the opposite direction to the others.* LAWRENCE
*and the* FLIGHT SERGEANT *are left alone. The* FLIGHT SERGEANT *stares at*
LAWRENCE *curiously for a moment.*

F/SGT. They been picking on you again, son?

LAWRENCE. No, Flight.

F/SGT. You don't ought to mind 'em so much.

LAWRENCE. I don't mind them, Flight.

F/SGT. Listen, I've got eyes in my head, haven't I?

LAWRENCE *lowers his, in embarrassment.*

LAWRENCE. (*With a smile.*) Flight, I'm sorry, but I'm afraid you've got it wrong.
　　It was just that—suddenly—for the first time in five years I'd remem-
　　bered what it was to feel life worth living.

EVANS *and* DICKINSON *come in,* EVANS *with his hands in his pockets.*

F/SGT. (*Barking.*) Hands out of your pockets, you.

EVANS. Sorry, Flight. Can we go now, Flight?

F/SGT. No. Get a broom and sweep up those leaves over there.

*He points off.* DICKINSON *turns to make himself inconspicuous.*
　　And you, Dickinson.

*The* MEN *murmur 'Yes, Flight' and go off the way they came. The* FLIGHT SER-
　　GEANT *looks at* LAWRENCE, *frowning.*
　　(*At length.*) Yes. You've got it bad, all right, haven't you? Real bad. (*Smil-
　　ing.*) Don't worry, I'm not young 'greaser'. I'm not going to ask you what
　　your trouble is.

LAWRENCE. Young 'greaser'?

F/SGT. Flight Lieutenant Stoker to you. (*In 'officer' accent.*) 'I'm not just here
　　to judge you, you know, my man. I'm here to help you. Look on me as
　　a sort of Dutch uncle, old fruit.' Makes you bloody vomit.

LAWRENCE. It does, rather.

F/SGT. Mind you, I didn't say that and nor did you.

LAWRENCE. No, Flight.

F/SGT. One day, if you want to tell me what's up with you, you can and I'll
　　listen. If you don't, that's all right too. Meanwhile I've got to try and stop
　　young greaser from having you hung, drawn and quartered

*The* MEN *have begun to come out of the building carrying the bins.*
　　All right. At the double. And afterwards you can dismiss. But don't let
　　anyone see you or I'll personally screw all your—

PARSONS. Isn't our Flight Sergeant the best little Flight Sergeant in the world?
　　Say yes, boys, or it'll seem rude.

F/SGT. (*Shouting.*) That's quite enough of that. (*To* LAWRENCE.) All right. I'll
　　do what I can. (*Suddenly roaring.*) But don't ever let me hear you being
　　insubordinate to your Flight Commander like that again, do you hear?

LAWRENCE. Yes, Flight.

F/SGT. (*To the corner, whither* DICKINSON *and* EVANS *have disappeared.*) All right,
　　you two. Fini. But keep out of sight of any bleeding officer, if you please.

*He goes out. After a moment* DICKINSON *and* EVANS *come on.* DICKINSON *puts a broom against a wall and having done that turns and languidly looks at* LAWRENCE, *who has taken out a small notebook in which he is writing, squatting on the ground, with his legs tucked under his body.* EVANS *approaches* LAWRENCE.

EVANS. Rossie?

LAWRENCE. Yes, Taff?

EVANS. (*With acute embarrassment.*) I wouldn't be asking this at all, but I thought perhaps—well—you're not the same as the rest of us and perhaps pay parade doesn't mean to you as much as it means to some of us, and—

LAWRENCE. I'm afraid it does, Taff. Quite as much.

EVANS. (*Overwhelmed with remorse.*) Oh, but, then, please you must not on any account—

LAWRENCE. How much would it have been?

EVANS. Well, it was a ring you see—something I had to buy—you know—to make it up with my girl, you see, and she likes the best, always has—thirty-seven and six.

LAWRENCE. I wish I had it, Taff.

EVANS *looks over at* DICKINSON, *who, almost imperceptibly, shakes his head.*

EVANS. (*With a sigh.*) Oh well.

*He goes sadly out.* LAWRENCE *continues to write in his notebook.*

*Pause.* DICKINSON *walks slowly forward.*

DICKINSON. Why do you sit like that?

LAWRENCE. I always do.

DICKINSON. It's the way the Arabs sit, isn't it?

LAWRENCE. I don't know.

DICKINSON. (*Squatting beside* him.) But you should know—shouldn't you—after all that liaison work you did in the Middle East in the last war?

LAWRENCE. I'm sorry. I wasn't paying attention. Yes, it's the way the Arabs sit.

DICKINSON. Damned uncomfortable it looks. Why are you shivering?

LAWRENCE. I've got a touch of malaria.

DICKINSON. Middle East, I suppose? You're shaking quite badly. You'd better see the M.O.

LAWRENCE. No. I'll have a temperature tonight and tomorrow it'll be gone.

DICKINSON. Yes, but you shouldn't take risks, old chap. After all, we don't want to lose you, do we?

LAWRENCE. I doubt if B Flight would notice.

DICKINSON. I wasn't talking about B Flight. I was talking about the nation.

LAWRENCE *puts down the notebook at last, and stares steadily at* DICKINSON.

Aren't you going to say what on earth do you mean? Aren't you going to try and act it out just a little longer?

*Pause.* LAWRENCE, *staring at him steadily, says nothing.*

I agree, old boy. Useless. At the same time I notice you're not falling into the trap of saying 'How on earth did you find out?' and so confirming what might, after all, be only a wild guess. Secret Agent training, no doubt. Well, it isn't a guess. It *was* until this morning, I grant. As a matter of fact I did see you once, in Paris, in 1919—Peace Conference time—I was just a humble captain, walking down a street and suddenly I was shoved back against some railings by some brawny gendarmes and practically squashed to death by an hysterical crowd because you were leaving your hotel. I couldn't see you well, but I remember you walking shyly—oh so shyly—between two policemen—to your car, head well down under that Arab head-dress and then—at the car—turning to talk to someone so that the crowd grew even more hysterical, and then, when you were in the car, modestly pulling down the blind. Still, I wouldn't necessarily have recognized you, old boy, from that—nor even from the lecture I went to at the Albert Hall which was supposed to be about the Palestine Campaign, but which had your picture on every other slide—very carefully posed, old boy, I hope you don't mind my saying.

*He offers a cigarette to* LAWRENCE, *who shakes his head silently.* DICKINSON *lights one for himself.*

Still think I'm guessing? Look, old chap, it isn't awfully hard—even for a humble airman like me—to find out the telephone number of Cliveden House, to ring up and ask if there'd been a raincoat left behind last night by Colonel Lawrence. 'Colonel Lawrence, sir?' Well-trained, this footman evidently. 'Yes, for heaven's sake—Colonel Lawrence—my dear man—Oh, very well, then, Aircraftman Ross, if you like.' Slight pause. Then 'No, sir. The Colonel left nothing behind last night. In fact I distinctly remember when he left that he had his raincoat strapped on to the back of his motor bicycle.' (*Pause.*) Your hand really is shaking badly. I honestly think you'd better see the M.O., old boy. After all, you can't do punishment drill with malaria.

LAWRENCE. (*In a low voice.*) What do you want from me?

DICKINSON. (*Genially.*) Money.

LAWRENCE. I haven't any.

DICKINSON. (*Murmuring.*) Oh yes. Destitute. I enjoyed that, this morning.

LAWRENCE. It was the truth.

DICKINSON. (*Hurt.*) Don't treat me like a half-wit, old boy. I'm not like the others. I can use the old grey matter, you know. I can tell how much money a man with your name could make for himself if he tried. Your memoirs? God! They'd make you a bloody fortune, and don't tell me you're not writing them, old boy, because I've seen you scribbling away in that notebook when you think no one's looking.

LAWRENCE. What I'm writing is for my friends. It's not for money.

DICKINSON. Jolly noble. Well, a bit of it had better be for money, old boy, because to keep my trap shut about this little masquerade of yours, you're going to have to pay me a hundred quid. That's what I reckon I could get from Fleet Street—

LAWRENCE *shakes his head.*

Listen, I haven't an earthly what you're up to, old boy, and I don't care either. Hiding? Spying? Having fun? Doesn't concern me. But it must be damned important to you that I don't give the story to the papers. So let's not haggle. Seventy-five, and I'll take a cheque.

*Pause.*

LAWRENCE. (*At length.*) No.

DICKINSON. You mean that?

LAWRENCE. Yes.

DICKINSON. (*With a sigh.*) Oh well, I thought you mightn't fork out. You were so damn careless this morning with young greaser, that I felt pretty sure you must have finished whatever it was you came into this thing to do

LAWRENCE. (*Suddenly fierce.*) I haven't finished. I haven't even started.

DICKINSON. What *did* you come into this thing to do?

LAWRENCE. To find peace.

*Pause.* DICKINSON *laughs quietly.*

DICKINSON. Oh yes—the mental and spiritual breakdown—

LAWRENCE. Go and telephone the papers—

DICKINSON. Oh, I'm not ringing them up. This transaction's got to be strictly cash.

LAWRENCE. You'll go and see them?

DICKINSON. Yes.

LAWRENCE. When?

DICKINSON. Tonight.

LAWRENCE. Have you got a late pass?

DICKINSON. No. Just ways of egress and ingress.

LAWRENCE. (*Bitterly.*) I see. Well, have fun tomorrow with the headlines.

DICKINSON. Don't tell me you're frightened of headlines, old boy.

LAWRENCE. I am now. Oh yes, you spotted my enjoyment of that crowd in Paris and this morning too—showing off to the Flight Lieutenant, but forgetting all about the sharp-witted escort who was going to end my life—

DICKINSON. Suicide threat?

LAWRENCE. No. Statement of fact. I mean my life as Aircraftman Ross.

DICKINSON. What does that matter? Lawrence will still be alive.

LAWRENCE. (*With anger.*) Lawrence doesn't exist any more. If you kill Aircraftman Ross you kill me. Can I put it more simply than that?

*Pause.*

DICKINSON. I don't scare very easily, you know.

LAWRENCE. I'm sure you don't. I wish I didn't.

DICKINSON. (*Angrily.*) Why the hell is all this so important to you?

LAWRENCE. Why is a monastery important to the man who takes refuge in it?

DICKINSON. A monastery is for someone who's lost his will to live. (*Angrily.*) All right. The spiritual breakdown. I'll buy it. How did you lose your soul?

LAWRENCE. The way most people lose it, I suppose. By worshipping a false god.

DICKINSON. What god?

LAWRENCE. The will.

DICKINSON. The thing that's up in your head, you mean?

LAWRENCE. The thing that *was* up in my head.

DICKINSON. Isn't that what's made you what you are?

LAWRENCE. Yes.

DICKINSON. I meant Lawrence of Arabia.

LAWRENCE. I meant Ross of Uxbridge.

DICKINSON. (*Hotly.*) Self-pity—that's all it is. There's nothing in the world worse than self-pity—

LAWRENCE. Oh yes there is. Self-knowledge. Why shouldn't a man pity himself if to him he is pitiable? But to know yourself—or rather to be shown yourself—as you really are— (*He breaks off.*) Yes. How stupid those ancient Greeks were. With your public-school education I'm sure you'd understand what I mean. Can I borrow a couple of pounds?

DICKINSON *takes out his wallet and extracts two pound notes from it. Then he walks over to* LAWRENCE *and hands them to him.*

Thank you. That proves it. You're going to do it.

DICKINSON. Good psychology. Yes, I'm going to do it, all right—because I'm damn well not going to be cheated out of money I need by a bit of fake play-acting—

LAWRENCE. Aren't you confusing Ross with Lawrence? Or is Ross a fake too? Perhaps you're right. It doesn't matter much anyway. Fake or not he's been a dreadful failure. Lets the Flight down at drill and P/T, can't tell a dirty joke to save his life and never sees the point of one either, talks la-de-da and spoils any party by trying too hard. Still, just now, with Sailor and Tipperary I thought it was just possible— (*He breaks off.*) No. That was sloppy thinking. Ross dies tomorrow and he'll be better dead. (*He looks dispassionately at his shaking hand, then up at* DICKINSON, *with a quick smile.*) Do you really think the papers will pay you a hundred?

DICKINSON. More, perhaps.

LAWRENCE. Really? You will tell me how much they *do* pay, won't you?

*He turns and goes out.*

THE LIGHTS FADE

*In the darkness we hear the distant sound of the 'Last Post'.*

SCENE: *A hut. Four beds are visible.* PARSONS *lies on one, in his underclothes. He is working out racing results from an evening paper.* EVANS *lies on another, in pyjamas. He is writing a letter.*

PARSONS. Taff—what's six to four on, doubled with a hundred to eight against?

EVANS. Sorry, Sailor, I'm not a racing man. (*Bent over his letter.*) You tell me something.

PARSONS. (*Bent over his calculations.*) What?

EVANS. Another word for love.

PARSONS *looks at him morosely without replying.*
  (*Explosively.*) Love, love, love. Man, you get sick of it. I tell you. (*Waving letter.*) Don't you know another word?

PARSONS. Who's it to?

EVANS. My girl. The one I'm marrying.

PARSONS. That Minister's daughter? (EVANS *nods.*) I don't know another word.

EVANS. But she's different, you know, Sailor. Not at all what you'd imagine. Free-thinking, that's what she is—

PARSONS. (*Muttering.*) Free-doing, too, I hope.

EVANS. You'd be surprised.

DICKINSON *comes in and goes to one of the unoccupied beds.*

PARSONS. Dickie-bird—you'd know. Six to four on doubled with a hundred to eight against in half-crowns?

DICKINSON. Let's see. Two-thirds of twelve and a half—roughly eight and a third. Two over three plus twelve and a half—thirteen and a bit. Twenty-one and a half to one double—two pounds thirteen and threepence.

PARSONS. (*Admiringly.*) Now that's the sort of brainwork I appreciate—not— (*He nods his head disparagingly towards the fourth bed.*) I'll bet you don't read Greek poetry in the lats, Dickie-bird.

DICKINSON. You're damn right, I don't, old boy. The *Police Gazette's* about my level.

LAWRENCE *comes in and goes to the fourth bed, passing* DICKINSON *as he does so.* DICKINSON *is lying on his bed, fully dressed, and does not look at* LAWRENCE, *who begins to take his jacket off with evidently rather uncertain fingers.* LAWRENCE *suddenly seems to remember something. He walks across to* EVANS, *takes two pounds out of his trouser pocket and hands them to him.*

LAWRENCE. Have you got half a crown?

EVANS. But you said you didn't have it.

LAWRENCE. (*Not looking at* DICKINSON.) I managed to raise it.

EVANS. Oh, Ross, you shouldn't have. Will he wait—your man?

LAWRENCE. I'm sure he will.

EVANS. For how long?

LAWRENCE. I should think—for eternity.

EVANS. (*Handing him half a crown.*) Pay day after next you shall have it back. It's a promise. And one day—

LAWRENCE. That's all right.

EVANS. (*Back to his letter.*) Rossie—you'd know. Aren't there any other words for love, except love, in the English? Think of something to surprise her—

LAWRENCE. I'm not an expert.

EVANS. Try.

LAWRENCE. Tenderness, devotion, the communion of two spirits—

EVANS. (*Doubtfully.*) A bit tame.

LAWRENCE. I'm sorry—

PARSONS. (*Who has been staring at* LAWRENCE, *frowning.*) Hey. What's the matter with you?

LAWRENCE. Nothing.

*He goes to his bed.* PARSONS *follows him.*

PARSONS. You're shaking like a ruddy shimmy dancer. The sweats, too. Got a dose of something?

LAWRENCE *does not answer.* DICKINSON *answers for him quietly.*

DICKINSON. Malaria.

PARSONS. Malaria?

LAWRENCE. It's all right, Sailor. It's not catching.

PARSONS. I don't care if it is or it isn't. I'm the senior here and I'm not taking no chances. (*Peremptorily, as* LAWRENCE *continues silently to undress.*) Put your things on again and go and report sick. Don't play 'silly bleeders' now—

*He thrusts* LAWRENCE'S *tunic towards him roughly trying to manoeuvre his arm into the sleeve.*

LAWRENCE. (*Quietly, but in a voice of sudden, unmistakable authority.*) Take your hands off me.

PARSONS. (*Bewildered.*) What you say?

LAWRENCE. I dislike being touched.

*He takes his jacket from* PARSONS, *and hangs it up.*

PARSONS. Listen, Ross. I'm telling you to report sick.

LAWRENCE. (*Still quietly, but with the same authority.*) I'm not going to report sick. I'm going to sleep it off here.

*He lies down on the bed, half-undressed, shivering, and pulls the blanket over him.*

PARSONS. I'm warning you, my lad, if you're not reporting sick tonight, you're doing your bleeding P/T tomorrow morning—malaria or no malaria. Compris?

LAWRENCE. (*Half-asleep.*) Compris.

PARSONS. Enjoy torturing yourself by any chance?

LAWRENCE. It's a fair comment, I suppose. Good night, Sailor. If I make too much noise in the night, wake me up.

PARSONS. I'll keep a boot handy.

*Defeated, he turns to* DICKINSON *who is still lying, fully dressed, on his bed.*
    And what do you think you're doing? Going to sleep like that?
DICKINSON *gives him a lazy wink.*
    What again? (DICKINSON *nods.*) Who is she tonight?
DICKINSON. No she tonight. Business.
PARSONS. Funny time for business.
DICKINSON. It's funny business.
PARSONS. Well, for God's sake don't get caught.
DICKINSON. I won't.
PARSONS. (*Lowering his voice.*) I'll expect the usual half-nicker.
DICKINSON. You might get a whole nicker if things go right.
PARSONS. I'll believe that when I see it.
*The lights go out suddenly.*
EVANS. (*With a wail.*) Oh no. Just when I'd got sort of inspired. I won't re-
    member it tomorrow.
PARSONS. What?
EVANS. A time we were together one night on a beach near Rhyl.
PARSONS. You'll remember it tomorrow.
EVANS. Not the words I was using—
PARSONS. You'll be remembering some other words if you don't put a sock
    in it.
EVANS. But the words were good, Sailor—
PARSONS. Pipe down, you sex-mad Celt. 'Night, all.
EVANS.
DICKINSON.  } 'Night, Sailor.
*After a moment of silence and near darkness,* DICKINSON *quietly gets up from
    his bed and moves on tiptoe towards the door. He stops a second by* LAWRENCE'S
    *bed and looks down. Then he goes on.* LAWRENCE *suddenly flings out his arm
    in a pleading gesture.*
LAWRENCE. (*Murmuring.*) No. No—
DICKINSON *stops and turns back.*
DICKINSON. (*In a whisper.*) Speaking to me, old boy?
*There is no answer, save a faint moan. It is plain that* LAWRENCE *was talking in
    his sleep.*
    Happy dreams—Colonel—
*He tiptoes cautiously to the door, opens it a fraction, peeps out furtively, and then
    quickly slips from sight, closing the door behind him.*

THE LIGHTS DIE TO A COMPLETE BLACK-OUT IN THE HUT

*After a pause we hear a muffled roll of drums and then the opening bars of 'Land
    of Hope and Glory' played by an organ, but coming apparently from a dis-
    tance. As the lights gradually come on we find that a large magic-lantern
    screen has been lowered, on which is a photograph of* LAWRENCE *in spotlessly
    white Arab dress, with a large, curved, ornamental dagger around his waist.*

*He is lying on the ground, a rifle by his side, gazing thoughtfully into space. A camel squats sleepily behind him. The desert background looks decidedly unreal and the whole effect is phony and posed. In front of the screen is a lecturer (FRANKS) in dinner-jacket.*

FRANKS. This is the man. The Colonel himself—perhaps the most legendary figure of modern times—the scholar-soldier—the uncrowned King of the Desert—wearing, as you see (*he points to* LAWRENCE'S *dagger*) the insignia of a Prince of Mecca—an honour awarded him by Prince Abdullah—

*He breaks off and speaks testily to the unseen R.A.F. hut.*

FRANKS. Surely this is what you always wanted—?

LAWRENCE'S VOICE. (*Actual, not recorded.*) Not now. Now I only want you to tell them the truth.

FRANKS. But what is the truth? Does anyone know? Ah—Field-Marshal.

*A man whom we are later to meet as* ALLENBY *appears from the darkness beside* FRANKS.

What was your view of Lawrence?

ALLENBY. Well, I was never too sure how much of a charlatan he was. Quite a bit, I should think. Still, there's no disputing the greatness of what he did.

FRANKS *turns to the other side of the stage where another figure, a civilian in tropical clothes, has become visible.*

FRANKS. And you, Mr. Storrs?

STORRS. I think the importance of what he did has perhaps been exaggerated—by the press, by people like you and—to be fair—by himself. It's in what he was that he was great—in my view, probably the greatest Englishman of his time.

*A British Brigadier-General (*BARRINGTON*) in tropical uniform appears on the opposite side of the stage.*

FRANKS. Ah. General. You knew Lawrence, didn't you?

BARRINGTON. Oh, very well. Couldn't bear him. Awful little show-off—quite a bit of a sadist, too. Cold-blooded. No feelings. Doubt if his private life would bear much looking into, either. As for what he did—well, a lot of chaps did just as well, but didn't get the publicity.

*The splendidly dressed figure of* AUDA ABU TAYI *stalks on to the stage, shouldering* BARRINGTON *contemptuously out of the way.*

AUDA. (*Thunderously.*) Tell them in England what I—Auda Abu Tayi—say of el Aurans. Of Manhood—the man. Of Freedom—free. A spirit without equal. I see no flaw in him.

LAWRENCE. (*From the darkness, agonizedly.*) No flaw?

AUDA. I see no flaw in him.

*He stalks away into the darkness. A man in the uniform of a Turkish General approaches the screen, but remains silent, looking towards the hut.*

FRANKS. You see how difficult it is. Where is the truth? They can't all be right, can they? I really think it's safe to stick to the simple story—that boy scout epic of yours. You're a legend, you see—and I mustn't spoil it for the public. They want Lawrence—not Ross. They want a world-hero, not a fever-stricken recruit, sick of life, sick of himself, on the threshold of self-ending. (*To the* TURKISH GENERAL.) Who are you? Are you part of the great Lawrence story?

GENERAL. Not of the legend. But I'm part of the truth. (*Behind* LAWRENCE'S *bed, looking down.*) But don't worry, my friend. I won't tell. I never have and I never will.

LAWRENCE. (*Off.*) One day I will.

GENERAL. (*Politely.*) Will you indeed? I never denied your bravery. But that would really be *very* brave

*The* GENERAL *goes into the darkness.*

FRANKS. (*Relieved.*) That's enough of that unsavoury nonsense. Next slide, please.

*A large map of the Middle Fast (pre-1914 war) is flashed on to the screen.*

In 1916 the whole of this vast area (*he points*) was under the domination of the Turkish Empire, with which the Allies were at war. (*He points again.*) The Turks were menacing the Suez Canal, and the British were too weak to attempt a counter-offensive. The great battle of the Somme had just cost them nearly half a million casualties, with no result. The whole vast war had bogged down in a morass of blood—and there seemed no way for either side to win. However, on June the fifth, 1916, an event occurred down here (*he points to Mecca*) on which the newspapers barely deigned to comment, although it was later to change the world's history. The Sherif of Mecca revolted against the Turks, captured their garrisons at Mecca and Jeddah, and with his sons the Princes Feisal and Abdullah challenged the might of the vast Turkish Empire with his tiny force of Bedouin tribesmen. Disaster, of course, would have followed, but on October the sixteenth, 1916, there landed at Jeddah (*he points*) two Englishmen—one a mature, clever and farseeing diplomat—Ronald Storrs—and the other—next slide, please

*A photograph of* LAWRENCE *is flashed on to the screen. He is in Army uniform* (CAPTAIN) *looking sternly and soulfully straight into the camera lens.*

A young man—filled with an implacable devotion to the cause of Arab unity, and a stern sense of duty to his own country—

*From the darkness there is a gentle laugh.*

What's the matter?

LAWRENCE. (*Off.*) You make it all sound so dull.

FRANKS. Dull?

LAWRENCE. (*Off.*) Yes. It wasn't like that at all. Not in the beginning. It was fun.

FRANKS. (*Sternly.*) Fun, Aircraftman Ross?

LAWRENCE. (*Off.*) Yes. In the beginning—

THE LIGHTS FADE

*There is the sound of Arab martial music, jaunty and barbaric, but not at all stern and military. Interposed are the sounds of shouting and laughter.*

SCENE 4

SCENE: *The interior of an Arab tent. As the lights come on* LAWRENCE *is being helped into an imposing-looking white Arab gown by a ferocious-looking, plainly disapproving Arab servant* (HAMED). *Another servant* (RASHID), *younger and gentler-seeming than the first, holds a mirror for* LAWRENCE *to look into. One of the men we have seen with* FRANKS (STORRS) *sits on a stool, smoking a cigar. The Arab music continues.*

LAWRENCE. (*Surveying himself.*) Storrs, how do I look?

STORRS. The most Anglo-Saxon Arab I ever saw.

LAWRENCE. That's all right. In Syria, before the war—when on archaeological jaunts—I used to pass as a Circassian.

STORRS. May I remind you we're about a thousand miles south of Damascus. Have you ever heard of a Circassian in the Hejaz?

LAWRENCE. (*Still distracted by his appearance.*) No. I can't say I have. Still, *one* might have wandered—

*The noise of martial music subsides.*

The parade must be over. I told Abdullah his men were shooting off far too many bullets that should be kept for the Turks. If I can't say Circassian, what *shall* I say?

STORRS. If I were you I'd say you were an English Intelligence Captain on leave from Cairo, going on an unauthorized visit to Prince Feisal's headquarters, through country that no Christian has ever crossed before. They can't possibly believe you and so all they may do is to make a small incision in your skull to let the devil of madness out. It hurts quite a lot, I believe—but at least there's a chance of survival—

LAWRENCE. Don't you think I need something round the waist?

STORRS. What sort of something?

LAWRENCE. I don't know. Some sort of ornament. A dagger for instance. I'm supposed to be dressed as a great lord of the desert, you see. Abdullah thinks that the more conspicuous I look, the less attention I'll cause, which is rather sensible—don't you think? (*To* HAMED.) Go to the Lord Abdullah and beg him in the name of Allah to lend to his servant Captain Lawrence a dagger that would befit a Prince of Mecca.

HAMED *stares angrily at him for a moment, then turns and goes.*

He seems to do what I tell him, which is a comfort. I hope the others do—

STORRS. What others?

LAWRENCE. Abdullah also wants me to take some of his own men to reinforce his brother—

STORRS. Now I put your chance of survival at zero. The minute they're out of sight of Abdullah's camp they'll slit your infidel throat.

LAWRENCE. That's what Abdullah thinks too.

*He begins to walk up and down.*

A sheik walks differently from ordinary mortals.

STORRS. (*Unhappily.*) I ought to stop you from going.

LAWRENCE. You can't, and well you know it. I don't come under you.

STORRS. Seriously, T.E., the risks are out of all proportion to any good you
    think you can do. Oh yes—I know it'll be fun for you if you get back to
    Cairo to infuriate the senior officers by telling them that they've got their
    facts all wrong—that you've inspected the situation at first hand and
    *know.* But I honestly don't think you will get back to Cairo—

LAWRENCE. When I was an undergraduate I wanted to write a thesis on Cru-
    sader Castles. So I went to Syria alone, without money, in the height of
    summer, and walked twelve hundred miles in three months. I was com-
    pletely dependent on the Arab laws of hospitality. People said then they
    didn't think I'd get back to Oxford—

STORRS. (*Impatiently.*) This isn't Syria. This is their Holy Land. Down here
    the Arab laws of hospitality don't extend to Christians. It's their religious
    duty to kill you—

LAWRENCE. Ah—but I have a bodyguard—don't forget.

STORRS. A bodyguard? You mean that thug over there—and his murderous-
    looking friend—

LAWRENCE. Oh, I don't think Rashid is a thug. I even got him to speak to
    me. He spat afterwards, of course, to clean his mouth, but in quite a polite
    way. I admit I haven't yet had the same success with Hamed, but I won't
    give up trying.

STORRS *gets up suddenly and goes up to* LAWRENCE.

STORRS. (*Touching his arm.*) T.E. (LAWRENCE *withdraws his arm quickly.*) You
    might easily get killed.

LAWRENCE. I might easily get run over by a staff motor in Cairo.

STORRS. Why are you really doing this? (*As* LAWRENCE *opens his mouth.*) Don't
    tell me any more about that mysterious kinship you feel with the Arab
    race. I don't believe it. You don't love the Arabs. You happen to speak
    their language and get on with them, but you're not a mystic like Burton
    or Doughty. You're doing this for some very personal reason. What is it?

LAWRENCE. (*After a pause and speaking with far more weight than his words.*) I
    need air.

*Before* STORRS *can reply* HAMED *comes in with an ornamental belt and dagger
    which he brusquely hands to* LAWRENCE.

(*With a winning smile.*) May Allah bless you, Hamed, friend of my heart
    and guardian of my life—

HAMED *turns his back and walks away with great dignity to stand beside* RASHID.
    (*Shrugging.*) Oh well. Everything takes time. (*Showing* STORRS *the dag-
    ger.*) I say, Storrs—look at this. Isn't this splendid? (*He begins to put it
    on, with apparent glee.*) Rashid, hold the mirror up again. (RASHID *does
    so.*) By jove, yes. With this I shall really be one of the lords of the desert—

*Another man we have seen with* FRANKS (BARRINGTON) *comes into the tent, dressed in tropical uniform. He looks hot and bad-tempered.*

BARRINGTON. Storrs?

STORRS *has got up with alacrity.* LAWRENCE *has glanced quickly over his shoulder at the new arrival, and then reverts to his image in the mirror.*

STORRS. Ah, Colonel. It's good to see you again.

BARRINGTON. I'm sorry I wasn't on the quay to meet you. The message from H.Q. about your arrival came late. How did you find your way to Abdullah's camp?

STORRS. Captain Lawrence found some man to guide us—

BARRINGTON. But that's very dangerous, you know, out here—strictly against regulations, too. And who's Captain Lawrence?

STORRS. (*Helplessly.*) He's over there.

LAWRENCE. (*Turning, affably.*) How do you do. You're Colonel Barrington, aren't you, our representative in Jeddah.

BARRINGTON. Yes, I am.

LAWRENCE. Tell me, what do you think of Abdullah?

BARRINGTON. (*Bewildered.*) What do I think of His Highness? Well, I think he's an exceptionally able and gifted person—

LAWRENCE. Exactly. He's too able and gifted to see anything except defeat. I don't blame him for that, but I don't think he's really our man—do you? I'm putting my money on Feisal.

BARRINGTON. Are you?

LAWRENCE. Ah. You probably see Feisal as a fool because he thinks he can win, and, of course, if he merely *thinks* that, then, I agree, he is a fool. But if—just by some strange chance—he happened to believe it, then— well, he'd be our man, wouldn't he? It seems to me worth a trip, anyway. Excuse me, but I really must make use of as much daylight as possible. Hamed, Rashid, tell the men to make ready and mount.

HAMED *and* RASHID *disappear silently.* LAWRENCE *turns to* STORRS.

Well, good-bye, Storrs. I'll see you in about a month.

BARRINGTON. Are you intending to ride to Feisal? Is that the meaning of this rig-out?

LAWRENCE. It is a bit peculiar, isn't it? At first Abdullah wanted to disguise me as a woman, with a yashmak, but I thought that was going a bit too far. Also—sort of cheating too, don't you think?

BARRINGTON. Do you happen to realize the risks involved?

LAWRENCE. Oh yes. We've been into all that.

BARRINGTON. But do you know anything about the sort of country between here and the Wadi Safru?

LAWRENCE. A bit rough, I'm told.

BARRINGTON. Are you? Well, this is what *I'm* told. Bare desert without any shelter at all, for three days. Then four days climbing a virtually impassable range of mountains, another two days climbing down it, and then another three days across an even worse desert. Then— (*He breaks off.*

LAWRENCE *is counting up on his fingers.*) What are you doing?

LAWRENCE. You've already made it twelve days. Quite frankly, Colonel, I'll be disappointed if we don't do it in six—

*He goes out.*

BARRINGTON. Who on earth is that awful little pip-squeak?

STORRS. Lawrence? My super-cerebral little companion? He's from the Arab Bureau in Cairo—

BARRINGTON. Ah, he's one of *that* menagerie, is he? Why was he sent out here?

STORRS. He wasn't. He just came.

BARRINGTON. Good Lord. Unauthorized?

STORRS *nods.*

What's his job in the Arab Bureau?

STORRS. Making maps.

BARRINGTON. Fine lot of use that's going to be to him.

STORRS. I don't know. His maps are very good.

BARRINGTON. Very artistic, I've no doubt—with the desert a tasteful yellow, and the mountains a pretty shade of mauve. (*Angrily.*) Listen, Storrs—I don't want to have anything to do with this business. I know nothing about it whatever—do you understand?

STORRS. Yes. Very clearly.

BARRINGTON. From now on Captain precious Lawrence of the Arab Bureau is entirely on his own—

STORRS. Yes, I think he'd prefer it that way.

THE LIGHTS FADE

*We hear the sound of a man singing an Arab song, quietly, from a distance.*

SCENE 5

SCENE: *A desert place. There is no feature except a rock against which* LAWRENCE *reclines, writing in a notebook. The rest is sky and burning sun.*

*Beside* LAWRENCE *lies* RASHID, *flat on his back.* HAMED *is asleep, some distance away.*

LAWRENCE. What music is that, Rashid?

RASHID. It is the music of an Howeitat song, el Aurans, in praise of Auda Abu Tayi.

*He spits surreptitiously.*

LAWRENCE. A noble man. They do well to honour him.

RASHID. (*Surprised.*) Even in Cairo they know of Auda?

*He spits again.*

LAWRENCE. Even in Cairo I know of Auda. Seventy-five blood enemies killed by his own hand, and all his tribesmen wounded in his service at least

once. Assuredly the greatest warrior in all Arabia. (*Wistfully.*) What an
ally he would make to Feisal!

RASHID. The Turks pay him too much money. He is a great man but he loves
money. How is it you know so much about our country and our people, el Aurans?

*He spits again.*

LAWRENCE. (*Mildly.*) Rashid, for the last five days I have wondered much
whether Allah might not forgive you if, in conversation with me, you
saved everything up for just one great spit at the end?

RASHID. Don't tell Hamed or he will beat me. He is angry that I speak to
you at all.

LAWRENCE. Your guilty secret will be safe, I swear.

RASHID. Answer my question, then, el Aurans.

LAWRENCE. How do I know so much about your country and your people?
Because I have made it my business to learn.

RASHID. Why do you, an Englishman and a Christian, seek to serve our cause?

LAWRENCE. Because in serving your country I also serve my own. Because in
serving your cause I serve the cause of freedom. And in serving you I
serve myself.

RASHID. The last I don't understand.

LAWRENCE. I don't quite understand it myself. (*He gets to his feet.*) The hour
is nearly finished. In ten minutes you must rouse the others.

RASHID. (*Groaning.*) Oh no, el Aurans. The sun is still too high—

LAWRENCE. We must reach Prince Feisal's camp tonight.

RASHID. You will kill us all. For five days we have had no rest. Look at Hamed
there. (*He points to the sleeping bodyguard.*) Never have I known him so
weary. And I, I am a dying man, el Aurans.

LAWRENCE. Resurrect yourself, then, corpse.

*He playfully prods him with his rifle.* RASHID, *smiling, staggers to his feet, over-
playing his weariness.*

Are you, Bedouins of the desert, to be put to shame by a man who, until
a week ago, had spent two years of his life astride an office stool in Cairo?
I am ashamed to lead so weak and effeminate a band—

RASHID. (*With a giggle.*) Who was it who yesterday had to hold you on your
camel—to save you from falling down that ravine through weariness?

LAWRENCE. It was you, Rashid, and I thank you. But I would not have fallen.

RASHID. Allah would not have saved you.

LAWRENCE. No.

RASHID. Who then?

LAWRENCE. The only god I worship. (*He taps his head.*) It lives up here in
this malformed temple and it is called—the will. (*Looking at* HAMED.)
Surely Hamed will kill me for bringing him from such a happy dream.

RASHID. Let him dream on, el Aurans. And let me join him.

*He sinks to the ground in pretended exhaustion.*

LAWRENCE. (*Gently.*) You are with him in everything else, Rashid. I think at least you should allow him the solitude of his own dream. And it can only last another seven minutes.

RASHID. (*Pleadingly.*) El Aurans, why not wait until the evening? What do five hours matter?

LAWRENCE. They can make the difference between winning and losing a war.

RASHID. A war? (*Pityingly.*) Forgive me, el Aurans, but I am an Arab and you are an Englishman and you do not understand. For five days I have heard you talk of an Arab war, but there is no war. We fight the Turks because we hate them, and we kill them when we can and where we can, and then when we have killed we go home. You speak of the Arab nation— but there is no Arab nation. My tribe is the Harif, and our neighbours are the Masruh. We are blood enemies. If I kill a Turk when I might have killed a man of the Masruh, I commit a crime against my tribe and my blood. And are the Harif and the Masruh the only blood enemies in Arabia? How then can we be a nation, and have an army? And without an army, how can we fight a war against the Turks? When you speak of the Arab war you dream foolish dreams, el Aurans—

LAWRENCE. Very well. I dream foolish dreams. (*Looking at his watch.*) Five minutes and we leave.

RASHID. (*Disgusted.*) To give Prince Feisal these few men when with a thousand times their number he could not storm the Turkish guns that face him at Medina. Is that the only purpose of this mad gallop that is killing us all?

LAWRENCE. No. Not to give Feisal a few men to help him storm Medina, but to give him one who will stop him from trying to storm it at all.

RASHID. Yourself?

LAWRENCE *nods.*

You will not persuade him. He believes in his madness he can drive the Turkish armies from all of the Hejaz.

LAWRENCE. And so do I, Rashid, and I am not mad.

RASHID. By Allah I think you are madder. How can he drive the Turks from the Hejaz and not attack their fortresses?

LAWRENCE. Precisely by not attacking their fortresses, Rashid.

RASHID. And so he will win his battles by not fighting them?

LAWRENCE. Yes. And his war too—by not waging it.

RASHID. It is a splendid riddle, el Aurans.

LAWRENCE. The answer is easy, Rashid. It lies all around you. You have only to look. (*He points to the horizon.*) What do you see?

RASHID. Empty space.

LAWRENCE. (*Pointing again.*) And there—what do you see?

RASHID. (*Shrugging.*) Our camels.

LAWRENCE. Desert and camels. Two weapons that are mightier than the mightiest guns in all the Turkish armies. The two weapons that can win

Feisal his war—if only we are in time to stop him destroying his army and his own faith and courage against the guns of Medina.

*He breaks off at the sound of a shot, followed by confused shouting, coming from close at hand.*

See what that is. Tell the men to save their energies for the ride, and their ammunition for the Turks. Get them mounted.

RASHID *runs off in the direction of the sound of angry voices which still continues.*

(*Pushing* HAMED *with his foot.*) Leave your dreams, Hamed. It is time to go.

HAMED *looks up at* LAWRENCE *bewildered, and then. quickly jumps to his feet. He picks up* LAWRENCE'S *pistol.* LAWRENCE *takes the pistol from him and inspects it.*

LAWRENCE. If this pistol could speak it would surely say: 'See how my guardian reveres me. He keeps me spotless and gleaming, and ready for my master's use.'

*Pause.*

Is that not so, Hamed?

HAMED *makes no reply.*

(*Sighing.*) May Allah give us a short war and not a long one, or your lack of conversation may grow oppressive by the end.

HAMED *looks quickly at him.*

(*Cheerfully.*) Yes, Hamed. By the end. I mean to ask Prince Feisal to appoint you and Rashid permanently as my personal bodyguards. So the only way you will ever gain your freedom from my service will be to ask me for it, and without a spit to follow it.

HAMED *appears to pay no attention to news that is plainly unwelcome. He picks up a cartridge belt that Rashid had left behind.*

He is safe, Hamed. I sent him on an errand—

*The sound of voices off grows loud again.* RASHID *runs on quickly. He looks startled.*

Well?

RASHID. (*Breathlessly.*) Mahmoud the Moroccan has killed Salem of the Ageyli. Salem had insulted Mahmoud's tribe, and Mahmoud took his rifle and shot him when he lay asleep. Now the men of the Ageyli have bound Mahmoud and will leave him here for the vultures when we go.

LAWRENCE. (*Quickly.*) And the other Moroccans? Where are they?

RASHID. Guarded by the Ageyli, each with a rifle to his back. They can do nothing, el Aurans. There are two Ageyli to each one of them.

LAWRENCE. And the others?

RASHID. They say it is no concern of theirs. Perhaps they will listen to you, el Aurans, but they would not hear me.

*There is a pause.* LAWRENCE *looks at the ground in thought.*

LAWRENCE. (*At length, quietly.*) Yes, Rashid. They must listen to me. I am their leader.

HAMED *smiles.* LAWRENCE'S *eyes meet his.*

(*Raising his voice slightly and speaking to* HAMED.) They are soldiers in the
field, and I lead them. If Mahmoud has committed murder then he must
be killed. But— (*after evident difficulty in forcing the thought into speech*)
by me—and not by them.

RASHID. They will not allow that, el Aurans. The Ageyli must kill him themselves, or their honour will not be avenged.

LAWRENCE. And the honour of the other Moroccans who fight for Feisal? How
will that be avenged when they no longer have Ageyli rifles in their backs?
You know well enough, Rashid, and so do I. And then another Moroccan will die. And another Ageyli. No. *One* life for *one* life.

*He looks at his pistol and abstractedly fingers it.*

If they wish the Moroccans can avenge *their* honour by killing me. Then
it is only a Christian who dies and there will be no blood feud. (*Looking
at his pistol.*) Once with this I could hit a matchbox at twenty yards. I
wonder now if I can kill a man at one.

*He turns to go.* RASHID *and* HAMED *make to follow him.*

No. Stay here. I'll face them without a bodyguard. At least I must try to
make them think I am not afraid.

*He goes out.*


THE LIGHTS FADE


*In the darkness we hear first the sound of confused shouts and cries and, at a
moment, growing much louder. Then there is a quick silence, broken by a
voice crying suddenly, in agonized fear: 'Have pity, el Aurans. Give me mercy.
Let me live!' Then comes a pistol shot followed at uncertain intervals by two
more.*


## SCENE 6


SCENE: *The lights come on to illustrate a large wall map of the Hejaz railway. It
is being studied by two men, one the* TURKISH GENERAL *whom we have previously seen in front of the lecturer's screen, and the other a* TURKISH CAPTAIN.

GENERAL. (*Pointing at the map.*) The latest report then puts him about here.

CAPTAIN. Farther east. Here. Nearer to Wadi Sirhan.

GENERAL. But that's over a hundred miles from the railway. Are you sure that's
correct?

CAPTAIN. It was confirmed by our agents.

GENERAL. When was his last raid on the railway?

CAPTAIN. Ten days ago at kilometre 1121. (*He points to a place on the railway
which is marked in kilometres.*) He blew up the line in three places.

GENERAL. And nothing since then?

CAPTAIN. No. Perhaps our railway patrols are getting too hot for him.

GENERAL. The history of the last few months would hardly support that rather optimistic hypothesis. But why has he gone north-east away from Feisal? (*He turns away from the map. Peremptorily.*) Take this down.

*The* CAPTAIN *picks up a pencil and notebook.*

(*Dictating.*) Proclamation. To all loyal inhabitants of Southern Arabia. For some time past the criminal activities of a British spy, saboteur and train-wrecker, named Lawrence, sometimes known as el Aurans, Laurens Bey or the Emir Dynamite, has been causing severe damage to Arabian property, notably the Holy Railway route from Damascus to Medina. In addition his acts of wanton destruction pose a severe threat to the supplies of our garrison at Medina. A reward, therefore, of ten thousand pounds will be paid—

CAPTAIN. (*Looking up, surprised.*) For a figure like that we'll need authorization from Damascus.

GENERAL. I'll write to them. (*Continuing.*) —will be paid to any person giving information leading to his capture. By order of the Military Governor, District of Deraa.

CAPTAIN. Isn't that rather expensive for a terrorist?

GENERAL. For a terrorist. But not, I think, for Lawrence.

CAPTAIN. What's the difference?

GENERAL. The difference between a nuisance and a menace.

CAPTAIN. Menace? (*Scornfully.*) The Emir Dynamite?

GENERAL. (*Turning to the map.*) The Emir Dynamite seems to be skilled in other things than high explosives. Strategy for instance. I don't think ten thousand is too much for a man who, in a few months, has transformed a local disturbance into a major campaign—who has isolated Medina (*he points to the map*) and who has drawn down (*he points to the area of the Hejaz and Southern Arabia*) into Southern Arabia, reinforcements from all over the Turkish Empire which are needed elsewhere. (*Abstractedly.*) Oh no. For this man I think ten thousand's rather cheap. (*With sudden excitement.*) Nearer to the *Wadi Sirhan?* Isn't that what you said?

CAPTAIN. (*At the map.*) Yes. (*He points.*) Here.

GENERAL. But, of course. Auda?

THE LIGHTS FADE *as the sound of Auda's Battle Song can be heard being sung to Arab musical accompaniment.*

SCENE 7

SCENE: *Outside an Arab tent. The sound of a song is coming from somewhere in the distance.* LAWRENCE, *in Arab clothes, is squatting on the ground with eyelids lowered.* RASHID *comes in quickly and speaks in a low voice.*

RASHID. El Aurans, there is danger.

LAWRENCE *raises his head slowly, as if interrupted in some process of thought.*
Hamed has just heard that the Turks have lately been to this camp and
were received with great friendliness.

LAWRENCE *looks at him vaguely, his thoughts evidently elsewhere.*
(*Desperately.*) El Aurans, all Arabia knows this man loves money and takes
it from the Turks. Hamed says we should leave at once.

LAWRENCE. Then he should come and tell me so himself.

RASHID. You know well he cannot. (*Giggling.*) And now he has made it even
harder to break his silence to you. He has bound himself by the holiest
vow he knows.

LAWRENCE. Well—at least that shows he feels temptation.

RASHID. Oh yes. He is tempted.

LAWRENCE. Hamed's must surely be the most prolonged religious sulk in
world history.

RASHID. (*Urgently.*) We have the camels ready, el Aurans. We can leave now.

LAWRENCE. (*Quietly.*) No, Rashid. Not yet. I will tell you when.

*The* SHEIK AUDA ABU TAYI *appears in the tent opening, studying a map with intense concentration. We have seen him already from the lecturer's screen, but
we now see him more clearly as an old man, of great vigour, with a booming
voice, a handsome, hawk-like face and a natural, unassumed majesty of presence. The latter quality is enhanced by the splendour of his clothes. At a nod
from* LAWRENCE, RASHID *has disappeared.*

AUDA *lowers the map and glares at* LAWRENCE.

LAWRENCE. Well?

AUDA (*At length.*) No. It is impossible.

LAWRENCE. Since when has Auda Abu Tayi been turned back from any venture by the dull bonds of possibility?

AUDA. El Aurans, it is only a few hours that I have known you, but I understand you better than you think I do. You have said to yourself, Auda is
an old man who feeds on flattery. All I need to do to bend him to my
will is to remind him of the great feats of his youth. (*Suddenly shouting.*)
Of course there was a time when I ignored the word impossible. There
was a time, forty years ago, when I led a hundred men across the Southern Desert against ten times that number to avenge an insult to my
tribe—and by the great God, avenged it too. That day I killed seven men
by my own hand.

LAWRENCE. Seven? In the Ballad of Auda it says ten.

AUDA. (*Carelessly.*) No doubt some others died of their wounds. Yes, by
heaven. That feat was impossible. And there were others too— (*He
changes tone.*) But I am no longer twenty and what you suggest is— 
(*Shouting, off, angrily at someone offstage.*) Kerim! Order that man, on pain
of instant decapitation, to stop singing his foolish song. The words are
exaggerated and his voice disturbs our thought. (*He turns back to*
LAWRENCE.) There is a boundary between the possible and the impossible that certain exceptional beings such as myself may leap. But there is

a boundary between the impossible and a madman's dream— (*The song stops abruptly.*) Thank Allah! There are fifty-six verses to that song—each in praise of either one of my battles or one of my wives. By the dispensation of God the numbers are exactly equal.

LAWRENCE. Wouldn't it be supremely fitting to the memory of a great warrior if his wives were outnumbered by just one battle—and that one the greatest of all?

AUDA. (*Passionately.*) El Aurans, I have no great love for the Turks. Feisal is my friend and I would be his ally. But what are you asking? A march in the worst month of the year across the worst desert in Arabia—el Houl—the desolate—that even the jackals and vultures fear—where the sun can beat a man to madness and where day or night a wind of such scorching dryness can blow that a man's skin is stripped from his body. It is a terrible desert—el Houl—and terrible is not a word that comes lightly to the lips of Auda Abu Tayi.

LAWRENCE. (*Mildly.*) I had believed it a word unknown to him.

AUDA. My friend, your flattery will not make wells. And it will not stop the few wells there *are* on the fringe of that desert from being poisoned by the Turks the moment they learn of our objective—as they must—

LAWRENCE. Why must they?

AUDA. Do you think I am unknown in Arabia? Do you think that when Auda rides out at the head of five hundred men the Turks will not ask questions?

LAWRENCE. Indeed they will, but will they get the right answer?

AUDA. They are not fools.

LAWRENCE. No. And that is why the last thing they will look for is an attack across el Houl on the port of Akaba. If such a project seems mad even to Auda, how will it seem to the Turks?

AUDA. (*Chuckling.*) By heaven—there is some wisdom there, el Aurans. They would not even guess at it. No sane man ever could—

LAWRENCE. (*Taking the map.*) But just in case they do, the direction of our march should be north-west at first, to make them believe we are aiming at a raid on the railway.

AUDA. (*Abstractedly interrupting.*) Has Feisal much gold?

LAWRENCE. Alas—he is rich only in promises—and so am I on his behalf.

AUDA. And what would you have promised me if I had consented to this madness?

LAWRENCE. A higher price than the Turks could pay.

AUDA. Then it must be high indeed. What is it?

LAWRENCE. The praise of the whole world for the most brilliant feat of arms in Arabian history.

*Pause.*

AUDA. (*Gazing at the map.*) Akaba! Even your own all-powerful Navy has not dared attack it.

LAWRENCE. Oh yes.

AUDA. And were defeated?

LAWRENCE. Oh no. Our Navy is never defeated.

AUDA. Well?

LAWRENCE. After a successful bombardment they withdrew.

AUDA. Beaten off by the Turkish guns.

LAWRENCE. They are very powerful guns.

AUDA. Have I powerful guns?

LAWRENCE. You have no need of guns.

AUDA. How? No need?

LAWRENCE. There is no gun—however powerful—that can fire backwards.
*Pause.*

AUDA. They all point out to sea?

LAWRENCE. All out to sea.

AUDA. Fixed?

LAWRENCE. Fixed.

*Pause.*

AUDA. How strong are the Turks?

LAWRENCE. About two thousand in the area.

AUDA. Against five hundred?

LAWRENCE. Four to one. Auda's odds.

AUDA. (*Chuckling.*) Auda's odds. Have they made no preparations against an attack from the land?

LAWRENCE. None.

AUDA. They believe it impossible?

LAWRENCE. A madman's dream.

AUDA. (*Chuckling.*) The fools. No fortifications facing the land at all?

LAWRENCE. A few—a very few—but they will be easy to surprise.

AUDA. A camel charge, at night. My battle cry, to panic the idiots from their beds, and then amongst them.

LAWRENCE. They may well surrender at the very sound.

AUDA. (*Genuinely alarmed.*) May Allah forbid! My friend, do you think I am marching across el Houl in the deadliest month of the year, to be rewarded at the end with a tame surrender—?

LAWRENCE. Well—then—perhaps no battle cry—

AUDA. That, too, is unthinkable. Even Turks must know who it is that kills them. A charge in daylight, then—after due warning—

LAWRENCE. Not too long a warning.

AUDA. Not too long and not too short. Akaba! What a gift to make to Feisal—

TURKISH CAPTAIN. (*Off.*) Keep the men mounted—

*The* TURKISH CAPTAIN *walks in, past* LAWRENCE *without glancing at him, and up to* AUDA *who has turned at his tent opening. He salutes.*

CAPTAIN. God be with you, Auda Abu Tayi!

AUDA. And with you, Captain.

LAWRENCE *moves unobtrusively to go, but finds his escape barred by a* TURKISH SOLDIER, *whose back can be seen as he lounges at the entrance.* LAWRENCE *slips to the ground adopting the same squatting attitude in which we first saw him in this scene. He keeps his head lowered.*

CAPTAIN. I bring the greetings and love of my master, the Governor, and the precious gift for which you asked—

*He holds out a small package.* AUDA *snatches it eagerly.*

AUDA. By God, but this has been fast work—

CAPTAIN. His Excellency telegraphed to Damascus and had it sent down by the railway.

AUDA. Ah—this is a noble sight—

*He reveals the contents of the package with a delighted flourish. They are a set of false teeth.*

By Allah, these are surely the false teeth of which all other false teeth are but vile and blaspheming copies. Your master's generous answer to his servant's dire need is a great and splendid thing, and will not be forgotten—

CAPTAIN. I shall tell him of your pleasure—it will add to his own.

AUDA. See how well they are made, and how they gleam in the sun. By the prophet, with these in my mouth, I shall be young again. You must eat with me tonight, Captain—and you shall see them in action—

CAPTAIN. I am afraid that will not be possible. I must start back at once.

AUDA. (*Still admiring the teeth.*) A pity. You must ask your master what gift he would like from me in return—

CAPTAIN. You know the gift.

AUDA. Ah yes, I remember—

*He puts the teeth back in the package a trifle abstractedly.*

Why are you so sure he will come to me?

CAPTAIN. The Governor believes that he'll try to win you to the rebel cause.

AUDA. That would be very foolish.

CAPTAIN. Let us hope he is so foolish, Auda. I know my master would rather you earned the reward than anyone.

AUDA. (*Interested.*) Reward? You said nothing before of a reward.

CAPTAIN. It had not then been authorized.

AUDA. (*Abstractedly.*) How much?

CAPTAIN. Ten thousand pounds.

AUDA. (*With a gasp.*) Ten thousand! By Allah—is this Englishman worth so much?

CAPTAIN. The Governor believes him to be.

AUDA. Ten thousand. (*Suddenly speaking to* LAWRENCE'S *lowered head.*) Do you hear that, my friend?

*Pause.* LAWRENCE *slowly raises his head.*

LAWRENCE. (*Looking up at him.*) Yes, Auda. I hear it.

AUDA. What do you say?

LAWRENCE. That it is indeed a high price for so low a scoundrel.

AUDA. It is indeed a high price. A very high price. Would you like to see me win it?

LAWRENCE. I would rather win it, myself. But if not I, then let it be you. For surely no reward is too great for Auda Abu Tayi.

*Pause. The* CAPTAIN *has glanced at* LAWRENCE *with only mild interest.* AUDA *turns back to him.*

AUDA. He speaks loyally and well.

CAPTAIN. He does. (*Reassuringly.*) We have no fears, Auda. We know that you and all the men about you are loyal. But you must fear this Englishman. He has a glib and flattering tongue and by it has lured good men into treachery.

AUDA. Below medium height?

CAPTAIN. Yes.

AUDA. And dresses usually in white?

CAPTAIN. So it is said.

AUDA. Looking more English than Arab?

CAPTAIN. Yes. But you won't need to recognize him, Auda. He will surely announce himself to you. And then—

AUDA. And then?

CAPTAIN. You know what to do to gain ten thousand pounds.

AUDA. Yes. I know what to do.

CAPTAIN. I shall give your messages to the Governor.

AUDA. (*To* LAWRENCE, *abruptly.*) Escort the Captain—

LAWRENCE *gets to his feet.*

CAPTAIN. Thank you, but there is no need—

AUDA. Do you think we have no manners here?

CAPTAIN. (*Smiling.*) God be with you, Auda.

AUDA. And with you, Captain.

CAPTAIN. (*To* LAWRENCE, *who has stationed himself behind him.*) Oh, thank you—

*He goes out.* AUDA *moves quickly to look after him, looking tense and anxious. We hear the sound of a barked word of command, and of horses' hooves moving away.* AUDA *relaxes and shrugs his shoulders.* LAWRENCE *comes back.*

AUDA. By heaven, el Aurans, what a joke that was! What a joke to remember—

LAWRENCE. (*In a low, uncertain voice.*) It won't be easy to forget.

AUDA. (*Touching his arm.*) My friend, you are trembling.

LAWRENCE. Yes. I am.

AUDA. You were afraid?

LAWRENCE. Yes.

AUDA. Of what? Of a degenerate Turk and his few followers? There are five hundred men in this camp. They could have accounted for them in twenty seconds.

LAWRENCE. Yes. They could. The question is whether they would.

AUDA. By Allah, they would if I had ordered them.

LAWRENCE. Yes. But would you have ordered them?

AUDA. Can you doubt it?

LAWRENCE. With some ease.

AUDA. But, my friend, if I had wanted the reward—

LAWRENCE. Auda, do you believe your thoughts are so hard to read? To betray a guest is a great sin, but ten thousand pounds is ten thousand pounds, and surely worth a spin of the wheel of fate. If the Turk recognizes the foreigner, then the foreigner is not betrayed. But, to be recognized, he must first be made to raise his head and show the Turk his English features and then to stand up to show the Turk his white clothes and his meagre height—

AUDA. (*Chuckling.*) What a fool he was, that Turk! (*To* LAWRENCE.) Of course I knew he was a fool or I would never have taken that risk.

LAWRENCE *looks at him, without replying.*

(*Moving to the tent.*) Come, my friend. We have plans to make.

LAWRENCE *makes no move to follow him.*

Very well. I admit that I was tempted. You offered me honour and they, money. Both I love exceedingly and not the one much more than the other. But I spun the wheel and honour won. There is no going back now.

LAWRENCE. And if they raised my price?

AUDA. Ah. But they will not raise your price until after we have taken Akaba.

LAWRENCE *smiles, shrugs his shoulders and goes slowly towards the tent opening.*

AUDA *has picked up the package and is looking at his precious false teeth. Suddenly he hurls them to the ground, picks up a rifle and smashes the butt on them, again and again. After a moment he stops, stoops and picks up the shattered fragments, looking at them with eyes of tragic longing. Then he throws them carelessly away.*

The path of honour.

*He puts his arm round* LAWRENCE *and escorts him into the tent.*


THE LIGHTS FADE


*In the darkness we hear the sound of 'Tipperary' played on a rather scratchy record.*


SCENE 8


SCENE: A *small hut in a British Army camp near Suez.*

*As the lights come on they focus first on an ancient (to our eyes) gramophone, complete with horn. A man is humming the song to this accompaniment and, as the lights come up more strongly, we see he is a* BRITISH CORPORAL *and is using a disinfectant spray in time to the music. The camp has been abandoned through an outbreak of plague, and the hut bears a dilapidated appearance. A door is open at the back, showing the night sky.* HAMED, *looking ragged and desert-stained, comes into the hut and looks round.*

CORPORAL. (*Gesticulating.*) Yellah! Yellah! Shoo!

HAMED *pays no attention, but walks over to a desk where he has seen a telephone.*
Get out of here, woggie. Go on. Hop it, now—

HAMED *picks up the receiver gingerly—rather as if he expected from it some kind of electric shock.*
Get out, woggie, or I'll have to shoot you, and you wouldn't like that, now, would you? This is British Army property and I'm in charge—see. Shoo! Yellah! Shoo!

HAMED, *still paying no attention to the* CORPORAL, *lifts the receiver rather fearfully to his ear, still evidently expecting to be electrocuted. Reassured by his immunity he listens for a moment, until a voice can be heard asking for a number.*
(*Meanwhile.*) Shoo, shoo, shoo, shoo! Out, woggie, out!

HAMED, *still paying no attention to the* CORPORAL, *but satisfied, apparently, with what he has heard on the telephone, replaces the receiver and walks out.*

*The* CORPORAL, *after a shrug, continues his fumigating. The record comes to an end. He is bending over the gramophone as* LAWRENCE *comes in. He looks as travel-stained and dirty as* HAMED.

CORPORAL. Cripes! Another one. (*Shouting.*) Yellah! Yellah! Yellah! Shoo! (*He uses his spray on* LAWRENCE.) Get to hell out of here, woggie! I nearly shot your chum and I'll shoot you, I swear, if you don't buzz off!

LAWRENCE. (*At telephone.*) Does this telephone work, Corporal?

CORPORAL. (*At length.*) Did you speak?

LAWRENCE. Yes, I asked if this telephone works. I want to ring up Suez—

CORPORAL. (*Beyond his depth.*) I am in charge of this camp, which is Government property, and which has been closed down on account of plague—and no unauthorized person may—

LAWRENCE. (*Into telephone.*) Naval Headquarters. It's urgent. (*To* CORPORAL.) Ah. Plague. So that explains it. For the last half-hour I've been wondering if the British troops on the Suez Canal had got bored with the war and gone home.

CORPORAL. (*Pointing to telephone.*) Listen—I said no unauthorized person—

LAWRENCE. (*Into receiver.*) Hullo, Naval Headquarters? I want your senior chap, whoever he is . . . Admiral Makepeace? Right. Put me through . . . No. I don't want any duty officer. I want the man in charge. . . . Then get him away from dinner. . . . Then you'll have to forget your orders, won't you? . . . My name will mean nothing to you and my rank is unimportant, but I can only tell you that if you fail to get your Admiral to the telephone this instant you will probably face a court martial for having delayed the ending of the war by roughly three months. . . . I see. Just hold on a moment . . .

*He puts his hand over the receiver and turns to the* CORPORAL.
Get me some water from that tap outside, would you, old chap?

CORPORAL. It's not for drinking. Strict orders are to boil all water—

LAWRENCE. The last well I drank from—yesterday morning—had a dead goat in it.

CORPORAL. Yes—er—sir. As you say.

*He goes.*

LAWRENCE. (*Into the telephone, mildly.*) Now, in answer to your question I am not off my bleeding chump. I am speaking the simple truth. At your switchboard you hold in your hands the lives of five hundred Allied soldiers and the possession of the most valuable port in Southern Arabia, in which at the moment those soldiers are victoriously sitting, with nothing whatever to eat except their camels or their prisoners, and if I know them, they'll start on the prisoners. . . . Thank you.

*The* CORPORAL *has come back with a mug of water.* LAWRENCE *takes it from him.* By jove, Corporal, it's worked. I think he still thinks I'm off my rocker, though—

CORPORAL. (*Politely.*) Does he, sir? Fancy.

LAWRENCE *splutters into the mug from which he is avidly drinking. After a moment he puts it down.*

LAWRENCE. I've got some men outside who need food and drink. Would you look after them?

CORPORAL. Yes, sir. I don't speak their lingo, sir.

LAWRENCE. If you smile at them and treat them as if they were human, you'll find them quite easy to handle—

CORPORAL. Yes, sir. I'll do my best.

*He goes out.*

LAWRENCE. (*Into telephone.*) Oh, hullo, Admiral. Sorry to disturb you . . . My name's Lawrence. Captain Lawrence . . . Oh, no. Just Army. Look. I want you to send a destroyer to Akaba . . . Destroyer, that's right, but it doesn't *have* to be a destroyer. As a matter of fact a bigger thing—might be better. It's got to take a lot of stuff, you see—food for five hundred men, about six howitzers, thirty machine-guns, as many grenades and rifles as the Army will let you have—oh—and some armoured cars would come in very handy. Also—most important of all really—about fifty thousand pounds in cash . . . Fifty thousand . . . Oh, I'm sorry. Didn't I tell you . . . Yes, we took it. . . . From the land. Rather a long way round, but it seemed to work all right. . . . No. They didn't appear to expect us. . . . Oh, about five hundred killed and seven hundred prisoners. . . . Ours? Two. Unhappily we lost five more on the march, including one of my bodyguard. You see conditions in the desert were a bit—rough. We had three bad sandstorms, and I'm afraid my compass work wasn't all that good, and we missed a well— . . . No, Admiral, I promise you this isn't a joke. Akaba is ours . . . A rather picturesque fellow called Auda Abu Tayi is holding it, but don't let him sell it to you, because he'll certainly try. Now you will get that boat there tonight, won't you? You see, the Turks are bound to react violently, and mount a counter-offensive in the next few days. Will you please inform Cairo for me? I'm a bit tired. . . . No. I won't be available tomorrow. I shall be asleep tomorrow and probably the next day. If they want to talk to me after that they'll find me in

my old office in Cairo. . . . Making maps. . . . Yes. The C.-in-C. does
know of me. In fact General Murray and I have often exchanged words.
. . . Gone? Gone for good? (*Plainly delighted.*) Oh dear! Who, then . . .
Allenby? No. I've not heard of him. Thank you, sir. Good night.

*He rings off and rests his head on the desk.* HAMED *stalks angrily into the office,
holding a sausage on a fork, keeping it as far away from him as possible.*
LAWRENCE *looks up.*

Yes, Hamed?

HAMED *thrusts the fork angrily at him.* LAWRENCE *takes it.*

Ah, I see. The infidel corporal has not understood the laws of Allah. You
must forgive him.

*He pulls the sausage from the fork and begins to eat it.*

Avert your pious eyes from your master's vile gluttony, Hamed, and remember that he has not eaten since yesterday's dawn. Remember too that
it was to the Faithful that he gave up his rations.

HAMED *lowers his eyes.* LAWRENCE *looks up at him, wearily, without getting up.*
(*Smiling.*) Since Rashid died I have not seen you smile, Hamed. Not
once. But before you had begun to learn the trick. (*Quietly.*) Tell me. Is
it that you blame me?

HAMED *signifies dissent.*

You can tell me if it is true. I shall understand.

HAMED *again signifies dissent.*

You smile, then, at no one? At nothing?

HAMED *signifies agreement.*

Because of your grief, and only because of that?

HAMED *signifies assent.*

I am sorry, Hamed. If there was anything that I could have found to say
to you that might have helped you, I would have found it. But I will
not insult you by trying to tell you that one day you will forget. I know
as well as you that you will not. But, at least, in time you will not remember as fiercely as you do now—and I pray that that time may be
soon. I shall see that the corporal gives you food more fitting to Mos-
lem warriors. I want anyway to say good-bye to you all—

*He gets up showing his utter exhaustion. His back is turned to us as* HAMED *speaks.*

HAMED. (*With certainty.*) You will come back to us, el Aurans.

LAWRENCE *turns slowly to look at him. There is a long pause.*

LAWRENCE. Others will come, Hamed. Many others of my countrymen. That
is certain.

HAMED. There are no others we need, but you.

*There is a pause. The telephone rings.* LAWRENCE *makes no move to pick up the
receiver.*

You must come back to us, el Aurans. It is you that we need.

LAWRENCE. (*Finally picking up receiver.*) Yes . . . Yes, this is Lawrence. . . .
Who? Flag Lieutenant? Hold on a moment.

*He lowers the receiver.*

LAWRENCE. Go to the men, Hamed. I'll join you there. (HAMED *turns to go.*)
And Hamed. (HAMED *turns.*) Thank you for your words. Any words from
you would have been welcome, but those words more welcome than all.
HAMED *goes.*

(*Into receiver.*) I'm sorry . . . To get across the Canal? Well, I thought I'd
get some fellow to row me. . . . The Admiral's barge? I say, how splendid. Thank you. (*He rings off. Sitting at the desk he suddenly raises his head
in fierce and glowing pride. Softly.*) Ross, can you hear me?
*Pause.*

I've done it. Done it. I've captured Akaba. I've done what none of the
professional soldiers could have done. I've captured the key to Southern
Arabia with five hundred inefficient, untrustworthy Arab bandits. Why
don't you enjoy the memory? What makes you so unhappy? Is it that
Moroccan I shot in the desert and couldn't kill cleanly because my hand
was shaking so much? The mangled Turkish bodies in the dynamited
trains? Those men that died in the desert? . . . Rashid? . . . Is it Rashid?
*Pause.*

War is war, after all. The enemy has to be killed and our own men have
to die. And surely, at least I've been more sparing of them than any red-
tabbed superman?
*Pause.*

(*Angrily.*) What is wrong in trying to write my name in history? Lawrence of Akaba—perhaps—who knows?
*Pause.*

Oh Ross—how did I become you?
*He gets up and goes wearily out of the hut.*

CURTAIN

SCENE: *A room in G.H.Q., Cairo. There is an imposing desk, a large wall-map, and comfortable arm-chairs: behind the desk sits* ALLENBY, *a large, heavy man, his appearance rather belying his character.*

*A very decorative A.D.C. steps smartly into the room and comes to parade-ground attention.*

ALLENBY. Are they here?

A.D.C. Yes, sir.

ALLENBY. Show them in.

*The* A.D.C. *turns and goes out. After a moment* STORRS *and* BARRINGTON *come in.*

Good morning, Colonel. Ah, Storrs—good of you to come.

STORRS. Not at all, sir. Even in my lax office a request from the Commander-in-Chief is usually counted as an order.

ALLENBY. (*Not smiling.*) Sit down, gentlemen, please.

*They do so.*

I've called you here because I understand you both know this fellow Lawrence.

*They signify assent.*

I don't want to hear too much of what you think of him as a man. I'm prepared to form my own judgment on that. I'm seeing him later on. I want you to tell me what you think of him as a potential leader. Storrs?

STORRS. Lawrence as a leader? (*Thoughtfully.*) He's pure intellectual, and not by nature a man of action at all. He's strongly introverted, withdrawn and self-conscious, and will never allow anyone to see his true nature. He hides everything behind a manner that's either over-meek, over-arrogant, or over-flippant, whichever is going to disconcert the most. He thinks far too much for the good of his soul and feels far too much for the good of his mind. Consequently he's a highly unstable personality. Finally, he has a sublime contempt for authority—in any form, but chiefly military.

ALLENBY. I see. Not very promising

STORRS. On the contrary, sir. I think he'd make a military leader of the highest class.

ALLENBY. (*Snapping.*) Why?

STORRS. Because I find to my surprise that I've just given a description of most great commanders from Julius Caesar to Napoleon.

ALLENBY. (*Nodding after a moment.*) Barrington?

BARRINGTON. I disagree, sir, I'm afraid. I don't deny his success in Akaba—
though how much luck there was in that, we'll never know. (*Angrily.*)
But give him all credit for Akaba—it still makes no difference. He's ir-
responsible—a useful man, no doubt, to have charging around behind
the enemy lines, with his Bedouins blowing up trains. But in a position
of responsibility—no. Definitely, no. May I ask, sir, what appointment
you had in mind?

ALLENBY. In a report to me he has recommended a plan for general revolt of
all the Arab peoples in the north—to be timed to coincide with my offensive through the Gaza Gap in November. (*To* BARRINGTON.) By the
way, security must be dangerously bad here for him to have known both
the time and the place of my offensive.

BARRINGTON. On the contrary, sir, security here is very good. I didn't know
either time or place and I'm sure Storrs didn't—did you?

STORRS. No.

ALLENBY. Well. then, how on earth did *he*?

*Pause.*

STORRS. (*Mildly.*) A point to me, I think.

BARRINGTON. Guesswork.

STORRS. One of the qualities of a leader, isn't it?

ALLENBY. Possibly. Still, I wish he'd confine his attention to the enemy's plans,
and not to mine. However, he suggests that, to support my offensive,
four separate Arab forces should be organized to operate east of the Hejaz
railway, between Maan and Damascus here— (*he points*) along the Turks'
main line of communication—

*Pause.*

BARRINGTON. (*Ironically, at length.*) A rather ambitious plan, isn't it?

ALLENBY. (*Shortly.*) Highly, but I'm accepting it. In fact, I'm accepting all his
recommendations, except one—that a high-ranking officer be appointed
to direct these operations. I'm thinking of appointing Lawrence himself.

BARRINGTON. (*Pained.*) A captain?

ALLENBY. He was gazetted major this morning. And I've recommended him
for an award.

BARRINGTON. I'm afraid my opinion must remain that it would be a very dangerous appointment. Forgive my frankness, sir.

ALLENBY. (*Dryly.*) It does you credit. Storrs?

STORRS. I'll stick to my opinion too.

ALLENBY. (*Presses a bell on his desk.*) I'm grateful to you both.

*The* A.D.C. *appears.*

Is Major Lawrence here?

A.D.C. He's just arrived, sir.

ALLENBY. Send him in.

*The* A.D.C. *goes.*

ALLENBY. (*To* STORRS.) I'm a bit scared of this meeting. Do you think he'll try to floor me with Baudelaire or something?

STORRS. Very likely, sir.

ALLENBY. I wonder if I could floor him with my pet subject.

BARRINGTON. What's that, sir?

ALLENBY. Flowers.

BARRINGTON *looks startled. A door is opened and* LAWRENCE *comes in. He is dressed in a uniform that was never from Savile Row, but now—after loss of weight in the desert—hardly fits him at all. He sees* STORRS *first.*

LAWRENCE. Oh, hullo, Storrs. I was coming to see you this aft—

*A firm sign from* STORRS *indicates the* COMMANDER-IN-CHIEF.

   Oh, I'm sorry.

*He delivers a rather informal-looking salute. Even* ALLENBY, *determined to be surprised at nothing, has to comment.*

ALLENBY. Good gracious!

LAWRENCE. What's the matter?

ALLENBY. Do you always salute like that?

LAWRENCE. Why, sir? Is it wrong?

ALLENBY. It's a little—individual.

LAWRENCE. I was never taught.

ALLENBY. But you must have done some drill training, surely?

LAWRENCE. Well, no. I was a civilian in the Map Section of the War Office in 1914 and one of my jobs was to take maps along to some old general—and he always used to roar at me that he hated civilians in his office and why the dickens wasn't I in uniform? So, one day, I went out to the Army and Navy Stores and bought a uniform.

ALLENBY. (*Unsmiling.*) You mean that you've never been properly commissioned in the Army?

LAWRENCE. I don't think so, sir. No. I'm sure I'd remember it if I had.

ALLENBY. I see. Well, I'm happy to inform you that you've now been gazetted a major.

LAWRENCE. (*Mildly.*) Oh? Good.

ALLENBY. And I've put in a recommendation for you for the C.B.

LAWRENCE. (*Startled.*) C.B.?

ALLENBY. Companion of the Bath.

LAWRENCE. Oh. Thank you.

ALLENBY. (*To the other two.*) Very well, gentlemen. Thank you very much. *They turn to go.*

LAWRENCE. Oh, Storrs. (*To* ALLENBY.) Excuse me.

ALLENBY *nods.*

   Freddie Strong has dug up something at Luxor which I know you'll go absolutely mad about.

STORRS, *detained by the door, is looking acutely embarrassed.* BARRINGTON *flashes* ALLENBY *his parade-ground salute and goes, his face meaningful.*

(*Apparently oblivious.*) It's a small alabaster perfume jar, exquisite shape, twentieth dynasty I should think, with what seems like a strong Minoan influence—

ALLENBY. (*Quietly.*) Minoan influence in the twentieth dynasty?

LAWRENCE *turns to look at him, apparently seeing him for the first time.*

LAWRENCE. (*At length.*) I suppose it couldn't be, could it? I must have got the dynasty wrong.

ALLENBY. Or the influence.

LAWRENCE. (*Slowly.*) Yes. Or the influence.

ALLENBY. (*With authority.*) Good-bye, Storrs, and thank you.

STORRS. Good-bye, sir.

*He goes with evident relief.*

ALLENBY. Sit down, Lawrence.

LAWRENCE *sits. There is a pause.*

(*Smiling suddenly.*) Tell me—did Freddie Strong really dig up a twentieth-dynasty perfume jar?

*There is a pause while* LAWRENCE *and* ALLENBY *look at each other appraisingly across the large desk.*

LAWRENCE. (*At length—with a good-humoured shrug.*) Well, he does dig things up all the time, you know.

ALLENBY. (*Nodding appreciatively.*) Good. I'm glad we understand each other so soon.

LAWRENCE. (*Without rancour.*) Yes. So am I.

ALLENBY. I was lucky with the Minoan influence. I've just been reading Arthur Evans' book, *The Palace of Minos in Crete.*

LAWRENCE. (*Politely.*) It's pleasant to meet a general who's read anything except Clausewitz.

ALLENBY. Yes. You won't catch me on Clausewitz, although I confess I'm a bit rusty. But please don't try me on the campaigns of Belisarius. I gather that is one of your pet subjects?

LAWRENCE. Yes. How did you know?

ALLENBY. I've made it my business to find out. No doubt you've done the same about me.

LAWRENCE. Flowers?

ALLENBY. Correct.

LAWRENCE Shakespeare. Chippendale, mobile warfare, Chopin and children. Not, of course, necessarily in that order.

ALLENBY. Your spies have done even better than mine.

LAWRENCE. I expect yours had less to find out.

ALLENBY. More, I think—but your talent for self-concealment is greater.

LAWRENCE. Perhaps it needs to be.

ALLENBY. Perhaps.

LAWRENCE. (*Smiling.*) A lesser man would have said: 'Oh no—I'm sure not.'

ALLENBY. I'm not interested in the secrets of your soul, Lawrence. I'm interested in only one thing. Are you the right man for the job?

LAWRENCE. (*Genuinely puzzled.*) What job?

ALLENBY. (*Impatiently holding up Lawrence's report and tapping it.*) This, of course.

LAWRENCE. (*Still puzzled.*) My report?

*He gets up, evidently really disturbed.*

Oh no. Great heavens, no. Not me. That would be disastrous.

*He is plainly agitated.* ALLENBY *looks at him inquiringly, evidently wondering whether this is not just another trick.*

ALLENBY. You echo Colonel Barrington.

LAWRENCE. Even Colonel Barrington can be right once in a war's duration. He is now.

ALLENBY. You surprise me.

LAWRENCE. Why?

ALLENBY. I thought you were an ambitious man.

LAWRENCE. So I am.

ALLENBY. Well, here might be your chance.

LAWRENCE. (*Shaking his head.*) I've had my chance. Akaba and being made a major, and the-what's the thing—C.B.—that's enough, isn't it?

ALLENBY. (*Thoughtfully.*) I wouldn't have thought so—for you. When you were writing this report, did it never occur to you I might consider you for the job?

LAWRENCE. Of course it did. That's why I was so determined to make it plain exactly what qualities your man would need. He must be a man of authority, with the patience to remain cheerful in the face of incompetence, cowardice, greed and treachery. He must have a deep practical knowledge of strategy, and of the principles of irregular warfare. Above all he must know how to lie and flatter and cheat in a cause that is not his own, but in which he must appear to believe. And he must forget that he's ever heard of the Sykes-Picot Agreement.

ALLENBY. What agreement?

LAWRENCE. (*Impatiently.*) The secret treaty partitioning post-war Arabia between the French and us.

ALLENBY. I've never heard of it.

LAWRENCE. No? Nor, for the moment, has Feisal, but if he finds out there'll be hell to pay. So it's vital that he and his people should continually be fed, from now on, the right kind of lies by the right kind of liar. Therefore this man of yours has to be a very senior officer. Then his lies will have real weight.

ALLENBY. I thought you didn't approve of senior officers.

LAWRENCE. I don't approve of the man I've just described. And nor, I suspect, do you. But it's the man you want for the job. Not me, General.

ALLENBY. Possibly. The difficulty is that another man hasn't already operated successfully for months behind the Turkish lines, hasn't already won the trust of the Arab rebels, and hasn't taken Akaba.

LAWRENCE. What does Akaba prove?

ALLENBY. Enough.

LAWRENCE. Do you know why I took Akaba? Do you know why I went off alone into the desert in the first place?

ALLENBY. Escape from an office?

LAWRENCE. A little true.

ALLENBY. Escape from yourself?

LAWRENCE. I'm a Greek scholar. I have a profound belief in the virtues of self-knowledge.

ALLENBY. A man can have a belief without practising it.

LAWRENCE. (*Appreciatively.*) I grant you the point. Escape from myself then. What else?

ALLENBY. Escape from too much thinking?

LAWRENCE. No. You can't escape from that, even in the desert.

ALLENBY. But the desert is a cleaner place to think in than an office.

LAWRENCE. There's nothing clean or dirty but thinking makes it so. And death is dirty, even in the desert. Still, I grant you the point.

ALLENBY. Finally, a burning desire to show off to my predecessor, General Murray?

LAWRENCE. Also true. (*Admiringly.*) I must say you've done pretty well, so far.

ALLENBY. Thank you. (*Politely.*) Well, now, shall we get back to the business on hand?

LAWRENCE. (*Sadly.*) This is the business on hand, I'm afraid. You've diagnosed my motives for Akaba and the rest of it quite accurately—although you left out the most important one of all—a cold-blooded experiment with will-power—but at least you must admit that all these motives have one thing in common. They're all flagrantly selfish.

ALLENBY. Possibly, Does that matter?

LAWRENCE. This job is for a Messiah. For a visionary with real faith—not for an intellectual misfit.

ALLENBY. (*Off-handedly.*) But you like the Arabs, don't you?

LAWRENCE. It's not enough to like them. Your man must believe in them and their destiny.

ALLENBY. What about your own country and *its* destiny?

LAWRENCE. (*Quietly.*) Oh yes. I believe in that. And I grant you that in war my country has a perfect right to demand my life. I doubt if it has the right to demand more.

ALLENBY. Aren't you exaggerating the demands of this job a bit?

LAWRENCE. (*Simply.*) No. You're a trained commander, you see. When you send men out to die, you don't question whether it's right—only whether it's wise. If it's unwise, it's wrong, and only then your conscience pricks. My conscience isn't Sandhurst trained. It's as undrilled as my salute, and so soft it must have the armour-plating of a cause to believe in. (*After a pause.*) How on earth can one *think* oneself into a belief?

*Pause.*

ALLENBY. (*Again off-handedly.*) I suppose one can't. But mightn't it be possible to will oneself into it?

*Pause.*

LAWRENCE. (*Laughing.*) You're a bit of a Mephisto, aren't you?

ALLENBY. I'm flattered to be thought so.

LAWRENCE. Do you know, General—I think you and I might get along very well.

ALLENBY. I'm sure I hope so, Major.

*Pause.*

LAWRENCE. Well, the first thing will be money.

ALLENBY. How much?

LAWRENCE. The Turks are lavish spenders and we shall have to outbid them. Say two hundred thousand.

ALLENBY. (*Doubtfully.*) Hm.

LAWRENCE. (*Cheerfully.*) Thinking of the Treasury? Put it under the head of propaganda. They'll like that. It's fashionable. I shall want it all in gold, of course. The Arabs distrust bits of paper. (*Turning to the map.*) Akaba must be made the main Arab base, instead of Jeddah; and I suggest you put Colonel Joyce in charge of it.

ALLENBY. What about Colonel Barrington?

LAWRENCE. Oh, put him on somebody's staff. Make him a general, I'm sure he's overdue. Now the most important thing of all, and this you *must* do—

ALLENBY. (*Mildly.*) One moment, Major Lawrence. I think I must remind you that I have not yet offered you this appointment.

LAWRENCE. No. Nor you have. And I haven't accepted it, yet either. Still, I might as well give you my views—don't you think—as I'm here. So— proceeding—Feisal must be detached from the forces of the Sherif of Mecca and made Commander-in-Chief of all Arab forces in the field, under the orders of yourself. And—for reasons purely of prestige—a small regular Arab force must be formed and trained to operate frontally at the decisive moment—but, of course, our main and vital effort will continue to lie in irregular operations behind the enemy lines. (*After a moment.*) I think that's all.

ALLENBY. Good.

LAWRENCE. Well. I'd better not take up any more of your time, General. I'm sure you've got a host of important things to do. So I'll be off now, if that's all right.

ALLENBY. That's all right.

LAWRENCE. I've got a few things to turn over in my mind, too. By the way, some time you must convert me about Chippendale. I've always thought he was overrated. But I'm rather a Philistine about furniture. I don't use it much, you see. (*At the door.*) Well, good-bye, sir.

ALLENBY. Good-bye.

LAWRENCE. And I suppose I shall hear from you?

ALLENBY. Yes. You'll hear from me.

LAWRENCE *flashes a smile of farewell, turns to the door, and then turns back, having evidently forgotten something. He produces his eccentric salute.*

One of these days I really must show you how to do that.

LAWRENCE. Yes, sir, when we both have the time.

*He goes out.*

THE LIGHTS FADE

SCENE 2

*A spotlight comes on gradually to illumine the face of the* TURKISH GENERAL. *He is speaking into the mouthpiece of a dictaphone.*

GENERAL. Circular telegram to all centres of Turkish Military Intelligence, Central Arabia. Most secret. Begins. Despite all our endeavours and the raising of the reward for Lawrence's capture to the unprecedented sum of twenty thousand pounds, he remains at large, operating behind our lines.

*The lights have come on to show the room in which the* GENERAL *sits, or rather reclines, for he is on a divan, leaning against pillows. It is a small sitting-room with two doors, one leading to his bedroom, the other to the stairs. The* TURKISH CAPTAIN *sits in an arm-chair in a carelessly informal attitude, looking at an illustrated magazine.*

The elimination of this terrorist has now become of vital concern, not only to the success of our military Operations, but to the very continuance of our dominion in Arabia.

CAPTAIN. You're making him sound too important. You don't want to start a panic, do you?

GENERAL. (*Mildly.*) Don't interrupt. Read your magazine. (*Into mouthpiece.*) Since his return to Arabia six months ago Lawrence has been known to have contacted secret revolutionary groups in places as far apart as Jerusalem, Damascus and Beirut. At present he is reported to be operating in the district of Deraa itself. His aim is, probably, to start a general uprising against us, timed to coincide with a British offensive in Palestine. Meanwhile he continues his guerrilla activities against our lines of communication. All this poses a threat that must on no account be taken lightly.

CAPTAIN. (*Angrily.*) Can you see them taking it lightly? They already think he has supernatural powers.

GENERAL. (*Into mouthpiece.*) Paragraph Two. Certain additional facts on Lawrence have now come to light. One. Despite rumours to the contrary he does not wear female disguise. The recent practice of forcible unveiling of women will therefore cease, as injurious to civilian goodwill. Two. The description of Lawrence as already circulated is accurate and has been vouched for (*with a look at the* CAPTAIN) by an officer of my staff, who once came into close contact with him.

*The* CAPTAIN *has jumped up.*

CAPTAIN. Delete that.

GENERAL. (*Mildly.*) I wasn't going to say which member of my staff.

CAPTAIN. You would if Constantinople asked.

GENERAL. I will, if you don't sit down and keep quiet. (*Into mouthpiece.*) Three. In view of information recently come to hand regarding Lawrence's sexual proclivities, the watch at present being maintained on brothels and similar places may be discontinued—

CAPTAIN. (*Eagerly.*) That's interesting. What information?

GENERAL. I'm sorry to disappoint you. The information was decisively negative.

CAPTAIN. In every way? (*The* GENERAL *nods.*) That doesn't seem likely to me.

GENERAL. (*Genially.*) I'm sure it doesn't, but ascetics do exist, you know.

CAPTAIN. But no one is born an ascetic. Is Lawrence very religious?

GENERAL. His self-denial is self-imposed. It has also a very revealing aspect.

CAPTAIN. What?

GENERAL. He avoids physical contact of any kind. Even shaking hands requires an effort.

CAPTAIN. I can't see what's so revealing about that—

GENERAL. Can't you. (*Into mouthpiece.*) Paragraph Four—

CAPTAIN. (*Sulkily.*) What does it reveal?

GENERAL. (*Patiently.*) A rebellious body, a strong will and a troubled spirit. May I go on?

CAPTAIN. You mean he'd like to, but won't admit he'd like to, and so he doesn't?

GENERAL. You put it very subtly. (*Into mouthpiece.*) Paragraph Four. Most important. It must be brought to the attention of all personnel that the capture of Lawrence alive should now be their primary objective. When captured the criminal will not be interrogated locally, but will be handed over forthwith to the requisite high authority. By Order Military Governor, District of Deraa. Message ends.

*He puts down the mouthpiece and goes over to the table where he pours himself out a glass of wine. The* CAPTAIN *watches him disapprovingly.*

A real French burgundy. Have some?

*The* CAPTAIN *shakes his head.*

You're such a good boy. (*Examining the glass.*) I'm so glad I'm not a Christian. In their religion this isn't a sin—

CAPTAIN. If I capture Lawrence, I shall shoot the swine.

GENERAL. (*Mildly.*) You really are very foolish, aren't you? Your bullet might well lose us Arabia. Can't you see that the man's death, by itself, would solve nothing? The Arabs would go on believing in this myth that he's taught them, Arabia for the Arabs—one race, one land, one nation. For a thousand years out here before he came, that idea was only the harmless dream of a few religious fanatics. But he's shown them the way to turn it into fact. Only half a fact as yet, Allah be praised, but even that half is a grave danger to our Empire. The whole fact? Well, then the world is in danger.

CAPTAIN. (*Carelessly.*) The world can sleep easily, I think.

GENERAL. (*Gravely.*) Feisal has chosen Damascus as his capital.

*The* CAPTAIN *laughs.*

I'd laugh too if I didn't know that the brain that planted that fantasy is as brilliant, ice-cold and ruthless as any revolutionary's in history. Do you really think that a bullet in that brain will turn the Arabs back now?

CAPTAIN. (*Shrugging.*) What will?

*Pause. The* GENERAL *sips his wine.*

GENERAL. Well, I suppose that what a brain can create, the same brain can destroy.

CAPTAIN. Get him to recant, you mean?

GENERAL. It's the traditional method of dealing with heresy.

CAPTAIN. But how do you do it?

GENERAL. (*Shrugging.*) By persuasion, I suppose. (*Looking at him.*) What a pity about this climate. It ruins a fair complexion. It shouldn't have affected yours, though, with your Circassian blood.

CAPTAIN. I have no Circassian blood.

GENERAL. I thought you told me that you had.

CAPTAIN. It was you who told me that I had.

GENERAL. Some time ago, I imagine.

CAPTAIN. I don't think you'll get Lawrence to recant by torture.

GENERAL. Who said anything about torture? Persuasion was the word I used.

CAPTAIN. (*Incredulously.*) You'd argue him into it?

GENERAL. Isn't that the best way of getting someone to admit he's wrong? After all, he is wrong. The Arabs' readiness for statehood is a lie and he knows it. That should give his interrogator a considerable advantage. To get him to admit that it's a lie? Difficult. With a man of faith, a real fanatic—like Feisal—impossible. But with an intellectual Englishman who believes only in his own will—and his own destiny—well, such faiths might be shaken. And another faith too—even more vulnerable—what I hear he calls his bodily integrity. One would probably have to start by teaching him a few of the facts of life.

CAPTAIN. Surely if he's an intellectual he must know the facts of life.

*The* GENERAL *laughs.*

Have I said something stupid?

GENERAL. Don't let it concern you. (*He finishes his glass.*) Yes, it's a strange relationship I have with Lawrence. He doesn't even know of my existence, while I probably already know more about him than he knows about himself. I wish all relationships were so pleasant and uncomplicated.

*He looks at the* CAPTAIN, *who turns away.*

There's one thing I don't know about him. I wonder if he really believes
that all the sacrifice is worth it.

*The* GENERAL *has poured himself another glass of wine.*

CAPTAIN. Sacrifice? Sacrifice of what?

GENERAL. (*Taking a sip of his wine and ruffling the* CAPTAIN'S *hair.*) Oh, of everything that makes life worth living.


THE LIGHTS FADE


SCENE 3


SCENE: *A railway embankment. Reclining against a telegraph pole is* LAWRENCE,
*dressed in inconspicuously ragged Arab clothes. As the lights come on he is work-
ing on a pencil sketch of the railway.* HAMED *comes on, and drops down beside
him. There is a silence as* LAWRENCE *continues to sketch.* HAMED *feels in his clothes
for a chicken bone, which he proceeds to gnaw.*

HAMED. (*At length.*) Bad news.

LAWRENCE. Your face told me.

HAMED. They refused the money, and promised nothing.

LAWRENCE. (*Still sketching.*) Why?

HAMED. (*Between bites.*) Frightened. With good cause. Of the three men you
visited in this town last month, two have been arrested and the other is
in hiding. But they have his family and the families of the other two.

LAWRENCE. (*After a pause.*) Who talked?

HAMED. One of Dakhil's children. It seems you gave him a present—an English halfpenny. He showed it in the market and tried to sell it. The great
el Aurans had given it to him, he said. A policeman heard him.

*Pause.*

LAWRENCE. Is Dakhil arrested?

HAMED. Yes, and Ali. It was Suleiman who escaped.

LAWRENCE. (*Still sketching.*) But they have his family?

HAMED. Yes. Even the old grandmother. Or so they say.

*Pause.*

LAWRENCE. An English halfpenny. It was there with the gold. I don't know
why. Because it was bigger and brighter the child wanted it and I let him
play with it. I meant to get it back from him when I left—but—I forgot. (*With sudden tension in his voice.*) I forgot. (*He resumes his sketching.
In a level voice.*) Have they killed Dakhil and Ali?

HAMED. (*Shrugging.*) Let us hope so.

LAWRENCE. Yes.

HAMED. What are you doing?

LAWRENCE. Drawing a plan of the Deraa airfield. Also that road down there
in the valley, along which our men will march—when the day comes.

HAMED. Will the day come?

LAWRENCE. (*Gently.*) You only ask that to anger me, Hamed. It pleases you sometimes to anger me. You know the day will come.

HAMED. But when?

LAWRENCE. (*After a pause.*) In Allah and Allenby's good time.

HAMED. (*Stretching himself out.*) Sometimes I think both have deserted us.

LAWRENCE. They haven't—but if you talk like that, they may. And so may I.

HAMED. (*Laughing.*) You?

*The thought is plainly only laughable to* HAMED. *He stretches himself out, and belches happily.*

What will happen after we win the war? Will you make Prince Feisal King of all Arabia?

LAWRENCE. It won't be for me to make anybody king of anything, Hamed. Prince Feisal will choose for himself. Who am I to make kings?

HAMED. (*After a pause.*) There was a story in our camp at Azrak last night that the English King and the French President have made an agreement after the war to divide Arabia between them. The English will take all the lands beyond the Jordan and the French will take Syria and the North.

*Pause.*

LAWRENCE. (*With bland unconcern.*) You have a fine ear for a story, Hamed.

HAMED. The Headman of Russia—a great and noble rebel—whose name I don't remember—

LAWRENCE. Lenin.

HAMED. Yes, Lenin. He has told it to the world. It was an agreement made two years ago—before you came to us, el Aurans—

LAWRENCE. (*Interrupting.*) The great and noble rebel lies in his teeth. There is no such agreement. Could there be, and I not know?

HAMED. (*After a pause.*) You could be lying to us. You could have lied to us from the beginning.

*He has said it for fun, hoping to get an irritated response from* LAWRENCE. LAWRENCE, *however, does not answer nor meet his glance.*

(*Rather pathetically, after a pause.*) That was a joke, el Aurans.

LAWRENCE. Yes, Hamed. I know. (*He continues his sketch.*) Whenever you hear this story again, will you remember that you are my friend, and beat the man who tells it?

HAMED. Yes. (*Without moving.*) There is a Turkish soldier walking towards us.

LAWRENCE. (*Also not moving.*) Did he see me sketching?

HAMED. I don't know.

LAWRENCE. Have you anything on you, if you are searched?

HAMED. The gold and the list.

LAWRENCE. Be asleep. We don't know each other. Whatever happens, have nothing to do with me.

HAMED *obediently closes his eyes.* LAWRENCE *placidly continues to sketch as a* TURKISH SERGEANT *comes on. He walks past the two* MEN, *apparently not noticing them. Then he stops and walks back to* LAWRENCE.

SERGEANT. An artist?

LAWRENCE. I get pleasure in this, but I am no artist.

SERGEANT. Let me see.

LAWRENCE. I would not affront your Excellency's eyes.

*He drops the sketch on to his lap.*

SERGEANT. You have a white skin for these parts. What is your race?

LAWRENCE. Circassian.

SERGEANT. Circassian? They are rare here.

LAWRENCE. Yes. We are rare.

SERGEANT. What are you doing in Deraa?

LAWRENCE. My business is lawful.

SERGEANT. What is it?

LAWRENCE. Travelling.

SERGEANT. (*Looking at* HAMED).) Alone?

LAWRENCE. Alone.

SERGEANT. Where to?

LAWRENCE. Damascus.

SERGEANT. On your feet, Circassian.

LAWRENCE *gets up quietly, apparently not alarmed.*

　　　You're lying, aren't you?

LAWRENCE. Why should I lie to your Excellency?

SERGEANT. I think you're a deserter.

LAWRENCE. With respect, we Circassians are exempt from military service—

SERGEANT. Don't argue. You're of military age, and therefore a deserter.

LAWRENCE. The argument has force, but hardly logic. By a special decree—

SERGEANT. (*Smiling.*) You want logic, do you?

*He draws his revolver.*

　　　Well, here it is. (*Quite mildly.*) Now come with me.

LAWRENCE. Where to?

SERGEANT. Why should I tell you?

*He digs him in the ribs with his revolver.* LAWRENCE *drops the sketch, then stoops
　　　to pick it up. He glances at it. Then carelessly crumples it up and throws it
　　　away. It lands close to* HAMED.

LAWRENCE. (*Going.*) Why indeed, your Excellency?

*He goes off with the* SERGEANT. HAMED, *as if in sleep, puts an arm out, and picks
　　　up the drawing.*


THE LIGHTS FADE

SCENE: *The lights come on slowly to reveal the* TURKISH GENERAL *sitting in his room in an attitude and with an expression that denotes considerable nervous tension. He seems too to be straining to hear something, but it is not apparent what; although, at one moment, we hear a shout of harsh laughter, cut off abruptly by the evident closing of a door. After a pause the* CAPTAIN *comes in. The* GENERAL *does not look at him. The* CAPTAIN *sits in his favourite chair, and picks up a magazine.*

CAPTAIN. What in the name of God is going on in the guard room?

*Pause.*

GENERAL. They're beating a deserter.

CAPTAIN. Your orders?

GENERAL. Yes.

CAPTAIN. Why?

GENERAL. (*After a pause.*) He was insolent.

CAPTAIN. I didn't see much. I don't like those sights. But I did see a white skin. At least it *was* white, I suppose?

GENERAL. Yes.

CAPTAIN. A Circassian?

GENERAL. Yes.

CAPTAIN. Do I guess accurately at the form his insolence took?

GENERAL. I expect so.

*Pause.*

CAPTAIN. If it's reported there could be trouble.

GENERAL. I don't think so.

CAPTAIN. You should stop it.

GENERAL. Why?

CAPTAIN. They look as if they might kill him.

GENERAL. He can stop it himself. He can stop it at any second. He has only to say yes.

*Pause.*

CAPTAIN. By the look I caught of him he's not paying you much of a compliment.

GENERAL. No.

*The* CAPTAIN, *after staring at the* GENERAL, *gets up suddenly.*

CAPTAIN. I'm going to stop it.

GENERAL. No.

CAPTAIN. I'm going to. For your sake, as much as his.

*He goes to the door. The* GENERAL *bars his way.*

GENERAL. (*Quietly.*) Now, listen carefully. It will be better for you if you don't go down there.

*The* CAPTAIN, *after staring at him, walks past him and out. The* GENERAL *turns*
*back into the room, and pours himself a glass of wine. He is pouring himself*
*another when the* CAPTAIN *comes back, and stares at him with unbelieving*
*eyes.*

CAPTAIN. (*Violently.*) Do you know who it is?

*He reads his answer in the* GENERAL'S *face.*

So that's why you tried to stop me from going down there—

GENERAL. I told you it would be better for you if you didn't.

CAPTAIN. Is that a threat?

GENERAL. Yes. Did you say anything to the men?

CAPTAIN. No.

GENERAL. (*Strength returning to his voice.*) You will say nothing to anyone,
now or at any time. If you do, I'll have you shot. He's a Circassian deserter, called Mohammed Ibn Dheilan. He comes from Kuneitra. He is
being punished for insolence.

CAPTAIN. (*With disgust.*) Punished? Do you know what they're doing to him
now?

GENERAL. They've stopped beating him?

CAPTAIN. Yes.

GENERAL. I see.

CAPTAIN. (*Hysterically.*) What they're doing to him now—are those your orders too?

*There is no reply from the General.*

I thought you couldn't have known—not even you, I thought, could have
ordered that—

GENERAL. You misjudged me.

CAPTAIN. I hate the man, but this is vile and horrible.

GENERAL. It's vile and horrible to be mangled in a wrecked troop train.

CAPTAIN. So it's revenge

GENERAL. No. If it were I might enjoy it.

CAPTAIN. What about your talk that you'd persuade him to admit he's been
wrong?

GENERAL. What about it?

CAPTAIN. Is this what you meant?

GENERAL. I said, if you remember, that his interrogator might have to start
by teaching him a few of the facts of life.

CAPTAIN. (*Sitting suddenly.*) And this is only the beginning?

GENERAL. It may be the ending too.

CAPTAIN. (*Muttering.*) You mean he may die under it?

GENERAL. No. They have my orders not to kill him. I mean that if my plan
succeeds tonight it will be the end for him. Bodily integrity violated, will
broken, enemy destroyed. (*Sharply.*) There's someone on the stairs.

CAPTAIN. (*At the door.*) They're bringing him up. (*Hysterically.*) I don't want
to see it.

GENERAL. Control yourself.

*The* TURKISH SERGEANT *and another* MAN *appear on the threshold. They are supporting* LAWRENCE *between them. He is half-conscious and his head has fallen on to his chest.*

(*Quietly.*) Very well, Captain. Report to me in the morning.

*The* CAPTAIN *comes automatically to attention. Then he goes out, averting his eyes from the sight of* LAWRENCE *as he passes him.*

(*To* SERGEANT.) Well?

*The* SERGEANT, *with a broad grin, nods slowly.*

He said yes?

*The* SERGEANT *shakes his head, still grinning. The* GENERAL *looks at him questioningly.*

SERGEANT. (*At length.*) He didn't need to say it.

*The* GENERAL, *after a pause, nods quietly.*

He's a strange one, this, General, I'm telling you.

GENERAL. (*Sharply.*) All right. Let him go.

*The two* MEN *release* LAWRENCE *whose knees buckle under him. He slips face downwards and motionless on to the floor.*

GENERAL. Get out.

*The two* MEN *go. The* GENERAL *goes slowly over to* LAWRENCE. *He kneels down and, quite gently, pulls his head back and looks at him.*

(*Quietly.*) You must understand that I know.

*He replaces* LAWRENCE's *head gently on the floor.*

You can hear me, I think. (*Slowly repeating.*) You must understand that I know.

*There is no sign from* LAWRENCE *that he has heard. Throughout the ensuing scene he remains completely motionless. The* GENERAL *pours a glass of wine and takes it over to* LAWRENCE. *He thrusts it in front of his face, but* LAWRENCE *makes no movement. The* GENERAL *puts the glass on the floor beside* LAWRENCE *and then stands near him, looking down.*

I do pity you, you know. You won't ever believe it, but it's true. I know what was revealed to you tonight, and I know what that revelation will have done to you. You can think I mean just a broken will, if you like. That might have destroyed you by itself. But I mean more than that. Far more. (*Angrily.*) But why did you leave yourself so vulnerable? What's the use of learning if it doesn't teach you to know yourself as you really are?

*Pause.*

It's a pity your desert adventure couldn't have ended cleanly, in front of a firing squad. But that's for lesser enemies—not for you.

*He kneels down.*

For you, killing wasn't enough.

*He lifts* LAWRENCE's *head again.*

You had to be—destroyed.

*He lowers* LAWRENCE's *head, and stands up.*

    The door at the bottom of the stairs through there is unlocked. It leads into the street.

*He walks into his bedroom.* LAWRENCE, *at length, waveringly thrusts out a hand towards the glass of wine. He draws it to him and drains it. Then, painfully and slowly, he begins to drag himself across the floor towards the other door.*

THE LIGHTS FADE

## Scene 5

SCENE: *Before the lights come on we hear the sound of a military band playing a jaunty march, and the sound of voices and laughter.*

VOICE. (*From darkness.*) Hold it, General.

*There is a flash from the darkness, and the sound of general laughter.*

*The lights go on to show a room in Allenby's field headquarters.* ALLENBY, STORRS, BARRINGTON, *the* A.D.C., *a war correspondent* (FRANKS, *recognized as the lecturer*) *and a* PHOTOGRAPHER *are all present. Everyone seems very jovial. A band is playing outside.*

*It is* ALLENBY *who has just had his photograph taken.*

FRANKS. I think, if you don't mind, General, just one more. And this time can we, perhaps, have a slightly more triumphant expression?

ALLENBY. What? More triumphant? I thought I'd made myself odiously so in that one.

FRANKS. Forgive me, sir, but you really didn't look as if you'd just won a great battle.

ALLENBY. How does one look as if one had just won a great battle? What do you suggest, Storrs?

STORRS. A rather bored and impassive expression, sir, as if taking Jerusalem was something that happened to you every day.

FRANKS. No, no. Not bored. Impassive, if you like, but stern and unyielding and—well—victorious. Now shall we try again, sir? (*To* PHOTOGRAPHER.) Ready?

*The* PHOTOGRAPHER *nods.*

    Right, sir, if you don't mind.

ALLENBY *does as bidden.*

    Just a little to the left. That's right. Now—can we try that expres-sion?

ALLENBY. (*Muttering.*) Oh God, this is agony.

FRANKS. It won't last very long, sir.

ALLENBY *tries an unyielding expression.*

    No. That isn't quite right.

STORRS. Of course a backcloth of Jerusalem would help. And what about some Turkish prisoners, lying on the floor in chains?

ALLENBY. Careful, Storrs. That appointment isn't official yet.

FRANKS. What appointment is that?

ALLENBY. Military Governor of Jerusalem.

FRANKS. Oh. Good. (*To* STORRS.) We must take a photograph of you.

STORRS. (*Cowering.*) Oh no.

ALLENBY. (*Laughing.*) Oh yes. And get him to look gubernatorial.

FRANKS. (*Patiently.*) Now, sir. Can we try again?

ALLENBY *poses.*

Now think of Jerusalem.

ALLENBY. (*Through his teeth.*) Jerusalem I've got. I'm thinking of Damascus.

BARRINGTON. (*Admiring his expression.*) Very good, sir. That has the real Wellington look.

ALLENBY. Quiet, Brigadier—unless you want to be a colonel again.

BARRINGTON. (*Aggrieved.*) I meant it seriously, sir.

FRANKS. Hold it, General.

*The flashlight is released again and the photograph taken.* ALLENBY *relaxes with relief.*

Perhaps just one more—

ALLENBY. No, certainly not. (*Pointing to a tray of drinks.*) Have a drink, gentlemen, and then leave me to fight my war.

BARRINGTON, STORRS, *and the* A.D.C. *go towards the tray, where the* A.D.C. *pours their drinks. The* PHOTOGRAPHER *begins to pack up his apparatus.*

FRANKS. (*To* ALLENBY, *with notebook now handy.*) There's not very much more of your war left to fight, is there, General?

ALLENBY. (*Sharply.*) There certainly is, and please don't give people at home any other impression. The Turkish Army is by no means beaten. It's suffered a defeat, but it's retiring in good order. There are many more battles to come and they'll become increasingly harder as the Turks shorten their lines of communication.

PHOTOGRAPHER. (*At door.*) Will that be all, Mr. Franks?

FRANKS. Yes. Thank you.

*As* PHOTOGRAPHER *prepares to leave.*

Just a moment. (*To* ALLENBY.) We've rigged up a makeshift studio next door. Is there any hope of enticing you there tomorrow?

ALLENBY. I'm afraid I'm far too busy.

FRANKS. Pity. (*To* PHOTOGRAPHER.) All right.

PHOTOGRAPHER. Good night, gentlemen.

*He goes.*

FRANKS. I've just one last request, sir.

ALLENBY. Come and have a whisky and soda while you make it.

*They join* BARRINGTON *and* STORRS.

FRANKS. My editor is very anxious for me to get an interview with Major Lawrence.

ALLENBY. I've no doubt he is.

FRANKS. Could I have your authority?

ALLENBY. My authority over Lawrence is sketchy, at the best of times. As regards an interview—even with you—I should say it was non-existent. Do you agree, Storrs?

STORRS. I would imagine that it might be rather easier for Mr. Franks to get an interview with the Dalai Lama—

ALLENBY. Besides, when last heard from he was at Deraa, some hundred and fifty miles behind the enemy lines—

BARRINGTON. No, sir. He's here. Didn't you know?

ALLENBY. (*Bewildered.*) Here?

BARRINGTON. Yes, sir. I saw him an hour ago. He was waiting to see you, he said. I'm sorry, sir, I thought you must have been told.

ALLENBY. (*To* A.D.C.) Did you know?

A.D.C. No, Sir.

ALLENBY. Well, go and get him at once.

A.D.C. Yes, sir.

*He goes out.*

ALLENBY. Lawrence waiting? Usually he doesn't even knock. I look up and he's standing facing me. (*To* STORRS.) I'd have thought he'd have let you know, at least.

STORRS. (*Shrugging.*) I've ceased to speculate. It's unfruitful.

ALLENBY. Anyway he's here, which is the main thing, and he couldn't have come at a better time. I suppose he knew exactly when I'd take Jerusalem, although, God knows, I didn't. The man's prescience is satanic.

FRANKS. May I stay, sir, for a moment?

ALLENBY. Yes, if you like. I doubt if it'll be much use to you. Storrs, get me a whisky and soda—

A.D.C. (*Opening door.*) Major Lawrence.

LAWRENCE *comes in, walking with a limp that he is evidently at pains to conceal. He is in Arab clothes.*

ALLENBY. Why didn't you let me know you were here?

LAWRENCE. I understood you were busy with the press.

ALLENBY. (*With a glance at* FRANKS.) Ah. I see. This gentleman is the culprit. Mr. Franks, Major Lawrence.

LAWRENCE. (*Politely.*) How do you do?

ALLENBY. (*Taking his whisky from* STORRS.) Oh, thank you.

STORRS. Hullo, T.E.

LAWRENCE. Hullo.

BARRINGTON. Hullo, Lawrence. Have you hurt yourself? You're limping a bit.

LAWRENCE. An accident with a camel. I got dragged through some barbed wire.

ALLENBY. (*Mischievously.*) I think Mr. Franks has a request to make of you, Lawrence.

LAWRENCE. (*Turning politely to* FRANKS.) Oh really?

FRANKS. (*Nervously.*) Well—Major—we war correspondents have our duty to perform like everyone else—so don't be too harsh with me. But you realize that the public interest about you at home has become pretty intense lately and colourful figures are rare enough in this war, and—

*Glancing nervously at* ALLENBY *and* STORRS, *who are plainly enjoying their anticipation of Lawrence's response.*

Well, I suppose I'd just better come straight out with it. Can I have an interview?

LAWRENCE. When?

FRANKS. Well—tomorrow.

LAWRENCE. What time?

FRANKS. Any time that would suit you. Ten o'clock?

LAWRENCE. Yes. Where?

FRANKS. Well, anywhere, but of course, what would be far the best would be if you would come along to the studio I've rigged up—and then we could get some really beautiful photographs.

LAWRENCE. Where is your studio?

FRANKS. (*Hardly able to believe his luck.*) Next door to here.

ALLENBY. (*Approaching* LAWRENCE *with a slightly worried frown.*) He has back-cloths at his studio.

FRANKS. (*Writing feverishly.*) Oh, General, you go on far too much about those backcloths. A photographic cloth can be quite plain, you know. Would you allow yourself to be photographed in front of a backcloth?

LAWRENCE. Whatever you think best.

FRANKS. Good. Oh, good. Ten o'clock, then?

LAWRENCE *nods.*

You're not going to let me down, are you?

LAWRENCE. No, I'll see you tomorrow.

FRANKS. Thank you, Major. (*To* ALLENBY.) Good night, sir. (*To the others.*) Good night.

*He goes.* STORRS, *conscious of an atmosphere, hastily finishes his whisky.*

STORRS. We'd better leave you too, sir.

ALLENBY. (*Looking at* LAWRENCE.) If you would.

STORRS. (*Casually to* LAWRENCE.) I hope I shall see something of you while you're here.

LAWRENCE. I won't be here long.

STORRS. (*To* ALLENBY.) Well, good-bye, sir.

*He goes.*

BARRINGTON. Could I have just two words with Lawrence, sir? Rather important.

ALLENBY *nods.* BARRINGTON *turns to* LAWRENCE.

I've had a rather sharp inquiry from the Foreign Office regarding the question of so-called atrocities on your front—

LAWRENCE. I have no front.

BARRINGTON. Well, during your raids and ambushes and things. It's been alleged through a neutral embassy that you don't take prisoners.

*He awaits a response from* LAWRENCE. *He remains silent.*

An official denial from you would help enormously.

LAWRENCE. (*Politely.*) Then you shall have it.

BARRINGTON. Good. Would you let me have it tomorrow, in writing?

LAWRENCE. In writing?

BARRINGTON *nods.*

All right.

BARRINGTON. Thank you. (*He turns to go.*)

LAWRENCE. The Arabs have been less demanding. My denials to them on more important issues are confined to the verbal.

BARRINGTON. (*Stopping short.*) You mean the denial would be untrue?

LAWRENCE. Not entirely untrue. Misleading is a better word. We do take prisoners—when we are not being chased, and can spare the men to escort them to Feisal and I've managed to keep some control of the situation. A combination of those contingencies is unhappily rare.

BARRINGTON. But this admission is very serious.

LAWRENCE. (*Raising his voice slightly.*) I agree. Did the neutral embassy have anything to say about the Turkish treatment of Arab prisoners?

BARRINGTON. No, but if there have been reprisals—

LAWRENCE. (*With a sharp laugh.*) Reprisals? The old game of who started it? Who's to say? And does it matter? I can only tell you that for a long time now no wounded Arab soldier has been left on the field for the Turks to take. If we can't move him we shoot him.

BARRINGTON. (*Hotly.*) Listen, Lawrence—the Turk's a clean fighter.

LAWRENCE. I've no doubt, General, but ours isn't a clean war. It's an Asiatic revolution, and a European who tries to direct the course of such a thing is apt to find himself rather out of his depth.

BARRINGTON. But—

ALLENBY. (*Interposing.*) That's enough, Barrington. You can see Lawrence tomorrow.

BARRINGTON. Yes, sir.

*He salutes punctiliously, turns on his heels and goes.*

ALLENBY. Don't worry about that.

LAWRENCE. No, sir. I won't.

ALLENBY. You made it sound pretty grim, I must say.

LAWRENCE. I could have made it sound grimmer.

ALLENBY. Well, you've come at a good time.

LAWRENCE. Yes, sir. Congratulations.

ALLENBY. Thank you. Tell me, how did you get the news?

LAWRENCE. I didn't, until I reached here.

ALLENBY. What did you come for, then?

LAWRENCE. To ask you to find me another job.

*Pause.*

ALLENBY. What other job?

LAWRENCE. Any one at all, providing that it has nothing whatever to do with the Arab Revolt. At a pinch I suppose I could still draw you some quite useful maps.

ALLENBY. (*Nodding, at length.*) I see. Go on.

LAWRENCE. Is my request granted?

ALLENBY. It may be. Go on. Tell me why you wish to relinquish your present post.

LAWRENCE. You're going to make it hard for me, are you?

ALLENBY. (*Quietly.*) I see no reason to make it easy.

LAWRENCE. Yes. I admire you for that. You want my excuses for desertion?

ALLENBY. Your reasons.

LAWRENCE. (*Nodding appreciatively.*) Very well. (*Quietly matter of fact.*) I have come to believe that the Arab Revolt is a fake, founded on deceit and sustained by lies, and I want no further part in it.

ALLENBY. (*Making notes.*) Go on.

LAWRENCE. On the military side I have only failure to report. The bridge at Yarmuk has not been blown and Arab forces have at no time successfully intervened in your campaign to date.

ALLENBY. (*Quietly, continuing writing.*) Yes?

LAWRENCE. To sum up, the whole venture is morally, militarily and financially unjustifiable—a total washout, and should be abandoned. (*After a pause.*) Anyway, I can't go on.

*He looks at* ALLENBY *who makes an impassive final note, laying down his pen.* However, if you don't agree with what I've said about the Arab Revolt and want me to suggest someone to take my place—

ALLENBY. (*Quietly.*) There is no one to take your place. Now, dealing with your points in reverse order and leaving out the last. (*Looking at his notes.*) Your military failure is untrue, even after taking into account your tendency for histrionic exaggeration. I haven't required Arab intervention yet in my campaign, and I don't expect you to succeed in blowing up every damn bridge I ask you to destroy. The Arab Revolt a fake? That's for you to say, but you told me once that you could will yourself into believing it wasn't.

LAWRENCE. I think it was you who told me. Anyway, my will has proved less trustworthy than I thought.

ALLENBY. What's happened, Lawrence?

LAWRENCE. (*Suddenly tired.*) Can't we say battle weariness?

ALLENBY. No. Not for you.

LAWRENCE. Disillusionment, cowardice—?

ALLENBY. No. Something extraordinary happened. What?

LAWRENCE. I had a vision. It happens to people in the desert.

ALLENBY. A vision of what?

LAWRENCE. Of the truth.

ALLENBY. About the Arab Revolt?

LAWRENCE. No. About myself.

ALLENBY. And the truth is (*tapping his notes*), 'I can't go on'?

LAWRENCE. That's part of the truth.

ALLENBY. The most important part, isn't it?

LAWRENCE. No. Only the most relevant.

*Pause.*

ALLENBY. (*Suddenly.*) What a pity! What an awful pity.

LAWRENCE *looks at the floor saying nothing.* ALLENBY *gets up brusquely.*

All right. I'll send you back to England.

LAWRENCE. I haven't asked for that.

ALLENBY. The War Office should be glad to have you. You're due for promotion, so I'll appoint you Lieutenant-Colonel. I've also recommended you—some weeks ago—for the D.S.O. so with that and your C.B. and your wound stripes you should make quite a show there.

*The* SENTRY *appears.*

Yes?

SENTRY. Mr. Storrs has an urgent telegram.

ALLENBY. Send him in.

SENTRY. Yes, sir.

LAWRENCE *gets up to go.*

ALLENBY. No, stay. I want a word with you about your successor.

STORRS *comes in.*

STORRS. (*Handing* ALLENBY *a telegram.*) Downing Street, sir. They want you to make a triumphal entry into Jerusalem on Wednesday.

ALLENBY. What do they think I am? A Roman Emperor?

STORRS. Brass bands, victory marches, beautiful girls hurling flowers at us. I'm looking forward to it. (*To* LAWRENCE.) Your man Hamed is outside. Wants to see you.

LAWRENCE. He should have gone. I ordered him back to Prince Feisal's camp two hours ago.

STORRS. Well, he's determined to talk to you. Seems very agitated. When are you going back, T.E.?

ALLENBY. (*With sudden harshness.*) He's not going back.

STORRS. What?

ALLENBY. He feels he can't go on any more. He's had all that flesh and blood will stand. I see his point. I'm sending him to the War Office.

LAWRENCE. (*Looking at the ground.*) May I go, sir? I'm feeling tired. We can, talk about my—successor some other time.

ALLENBY. (*Carelessly.*) Very well. (*As* LAWRENCE *reaches the door.*) Just one moment. I shall want you to take part in this entry on Wednesday.

LAWRENCE. In what capacity?

ALLENBY. Chief British Liaison Officer to Arab Forces in the field, of course.

LAWRENCE. (*Murmuring.*) No, sir.

ALLENBY. (*Coldly.*) It's an order. You will march directly behind me, and attend all the various ceremonies at my side.

LAWRENCE. (*With a sudden hard laugh.*) Oh yes. Good textbook stuff. (*Indicating the telegram.*) A general should be ready at one instant to exploit any opportunity suddenly laid open to him—

ALLENBY. (*Coldly.*) You seem to think my order is a punishment. It isn't. The honour that is being done to you on Wednesday is an award for your past. If it gives you uncomfortable thoughts about your present that's your affair, and not mine.

LAWRENCE. (*Now suddenly weary.*) And that's from the same textbook, isn't it? How to deal with deserters. I've learnt how to deal with them too—but not from Sandhurst training. From experience. Sad, scared, broken-willed little creatures—you can't persuade them or threaten them or even joke them back into battle. But sometimes you can shame them back. It's surprising how often—if you use the right technique. (*In a voice drained of emotion.*) You know, I think, that I admire you more than any man on earth, and I've never admired you more than I do at this moment. On my way here I had worked out for myself every stratagem you might use to get me to go back, and had planned all my moves to counter them. But, I'm beaten in five minutes. Can I see my bodyguard? Storrs says he's outside.

ALLENBY. (*Calling.*) Sentry!

SENTRY. (*Appearing.*) Sir?

ALLENBY. Get Major Lawrence's Arab servant.

SENTRY. Yes, sir.

*He goes out.*

LAWRENCE. I suppose what I left out of account is the splendid core of cruelty that all great generals should have.

HAMED *comes in.*

Hamed, why are you still in Gaza? You had my strict orders to return to Prince Feisal's Camp. Is that not so?

HAMED. (*Murmuring.*) It is so, el Aurans.

LAWRENCE. Why then have you disobeyed me?

HAMED. My camel has died.

LAWRENCE. (*Gently.*) Has it? She seemed all right this morning.

HAMED. A sudden illness must have struck her, el Aurans.

LAWRENCE. Yes. Very sudden. There was my camel—

HAMED. (*Looking at the ground.*) She has died too.

LAWRENCE. Of the same illness?

HAMED. Assuredly. (*Looking up at* LAWRENCE.) So now I must stay with you, here, el Aurans. There is now no means of leaving, is there?

LAWRENCE. Until you find another camel.

HAMED. In Gaza they are hard to find.

LAWRENCE. By Thursday morning, you must have found two new camels—

HAMED. *Two*—?

LAWRENCE. (*Continuing.*) Two fine, fast camels every bit as good as those you have just got rid of.

HAMED. (*His face lighting up with joy.*) In an hour—

LAWRENCE. Listen. Thursday at the first light of dawn. (*With a look at* ALLENBY.) I have a duty to perform in Jerusalem on Wednesday.

HAMED. This is not a joke?

LAWRENCE. No.

HAMED. But you said—

LAWRENCE. You should not always confuse what I say with what I do.

HAMED *bows suddenly to* LAWRENCE, *takes his hand, kisses it, and then places it on his head, Arab fashion. Then he turns and goes out quickly.*
(*Shrugging his shoulders, facing* ALLENBY.) Well, sir, I told you my will isn't what it was.

ALLENBY. I think it'll mend.

LAWRENCE. No. I'll have to try and find a substitute. (*Turning away.*) But there are just two things I wish you knew.

ALLENBY. What?

LAWRENCE. The kind of deserter you're sending back. And the kind of battle you're sending him back to—

LAWRENCE *goes. There is a pause.*

STORRS. You'd have made as good a diplomat as a soldier.

ALLENBY. I deserve the insult.

STORRS. No insult. But were you right to get him to go back?

ALLENBY. (*Angrily.*) Am I supposed to care about what's right? It was necessary. That's all that concerns me. (*Unhappily.*) All that ought to concern me.

*He gets up and goes to pour himself a drink.*
(*With a sigh.*) Oh God, Storrs, won't it be wonderful when this damned war's over.

THE LIGHTS FADE


SCENE 6

*In the darkness we hear the distant rumble of heavy gunfire.*
SCENE: *Outside* LAWRENCE'S *tent.* LAWRENCE *himself is shaving, using a canvas basin and a mirror hung up on a pole. A young R.A.F. officer* (HIGGINS) *comes out of the tent with some typescript in his hand. The gunfire continues throughout the scene.*

HIGGINS. I've done it, sir. I hope I've got it all right. Would you check it as soon as possible? LAWRENCE. Does your pilot want to take off?

HIGGINS. Well—it's getting a bit late, sir, and the C.-in-C. is waiting for this. Highest priority.

LAWRENCE. Read it to me.

HIGGINS. (*Reading.*) Operations of 25th and 26th September, 1918. I decided to place the main Arab force in the direct path of the Turkish Fourth Army's line of retreat. My staff considered this a hazardous enterprise, in view of the fact that the Fourth Army was retreating intact to cover Damascus. They thought that our untried force, outnumbered by roughly four to one, might prove no match for disciplined troops. I, on the other hand, reckoned that the element of surprise would outweigh this disadvantage. I am glad to report that events have justified my unweary optimism.

LAWRENCE. Unweary? This report has enough hubris in it without your adding to it. I said unwary.

HIGGINS. (*Brightly.*) Oh. Sorry, sir. Unwary. (*He makes a correction.*) And what was the other word you used? Hu—something?

LAWRENCE. Hubris. It's the Greek for showing-off.

HIGGINS. Oh but, sir—I mean—surely you've got something (*indicating report*) to show off about, I'd say.

LAWRENCE. You think so?

HIGGINS. The Turks caught in a trap between our chaps in the south and your chaps up here. I mean it's bloody marvellous, sir.

*There is again no reply.*

Bloody marvellous. (*Continuing to read.*) I am happy to report that the Fourth Turkish Army has, since eleven hundred hours this morning, ceased to exist. A detailed report of the operation follows—

LAWRENCE. (*Interrupting.*) Very well. As I have your sanction for hubris, you might as well add this to the main report. After 'ceased to exist'—

HIGGINS *has his pencil and pad.*

In view of this situation it is my intention to enter the City of Damascus at first light tomorrow, and to hold it in the name and authority of Prince Feisal. I assume this action will meet with your approval—an assumption forced on me by the fact that should it not it will anyway be too late for you to inform me.

HIGGINS. My gosh, I'll be able to write my memoirs after the war. *Lawrence of Arabia and I* by S. R. Higgins.

LAWRENCE. (*Interrupting.*) Did you invent that name?

HIGGINS. What? Higgins?

LAWRENCE. No. The other one.

HIGGINS. Lawrence of Arabia? Good heavens, no, sir. That's what the press have been calling you for months.

LAWRENCE. Have they? I didn't know.

*He sits down on the ground, Arab fashion, his face expressionless, but lost in thought.*

HIGGINS. Shall I read the detailed stuff, sir?

LAWRENCE. No. You'd better take off. Was there anything that seemed wrong to you in it?

HIGGINS. (*Doubtfully.*) No. Well—there was just one thing—

*He stops, looking rather scared.*

LAWRENCE. What's that?

HIGGINS. The night raid on that station.

LAWRENCE. What about it?

HIGGINS. There's something in it. I wonder if it's wise to—I mean it is an official report.

LAWRENCE. Read It.

HIGGINS. (*Reading.*) Operations of September 18th. (*Murmuring.*) In order to complete the encirclement of Deraa—a night assault on the railway—surprise not wholly achieved—ah. Here we are, sir. Ordering the Zaali to give covering fire I went down the embankment with my personal bodyguard and laid charges. These were successfully detonated, and the bridge destroyed, but the enemy now directed his fire at the bridge, my companion being badly hit at the first burst. I attempted to drag him up the embankment but without success and, as the Turks were beginning to issue from their blockhouse, I had no recourse but to leave him, after carrying out the usual practice in such cases. I rejoined the troop, and the retirement was completed without further loss.

*He stops.* LAWRENCE *is still looking at the ground.*

LAWRENCE. (*At length.*) What part specifically do you object to?

HIGGINS. Well, sir, the implication.

LAWRENCE. That I killed the man that was wounded?

HIGGINS. Yes, sir.

LAWRENCE. But I did kill him.

HIGGINS. (*Shocked.*) Oh. Well— (*Defiantly.*) But it's not the kind of thing you say in an official report.

LAWRENCE. Isn't it? I describe later on how we killed four thousand Turks.

HIGGINS. (*Horrified.*) Yes—but they're the enemy and this is one of your own men.

LAWRENCE. Yes.

HIGGINS. Of course, I know he was only an Arab, but still it does sound—do forgive me, sir—a bit—callous.

LAWRENCE. I see. And you'd like me to make it sound less callous?

HIGGINS. I really think you should take it out altogether, sir. I mean, there might be trouble with his wife or something—

LAWRENCE. He didn't have a wife. He once had a friend, but he's dead too.

HIGGINS. (*A little cross at* LAWRENCE'S *lack of imagination.*) Well, I'm sure he must have had someone who'll care about his death—

LAWRENCE. Yes, he did. But I doubt if that person will give much trouble.

HIGGINS. Well, you never know. Anyway, sir—have I your permission to edit the passage a little? I could just say the burst of machine-gun fire missed you but killed him instantly.

LAWRENCE. (*Politely.*) A very happy invention.

HIGGINS. I'll do it when I get to H.Q. Good-bye, sir.

LAWRENCE. (*Getting* up.) Good-bye.

AUDA ABU TAYI *strides on. He looks angry, hot and weary. His clothes are torn and bloodstained.*

AUDA. Who would have thought the day would come when Auda would grow tired of killing Turks? (*He throws down his rifle.*) Old age is a terrible thing.

HIGGINS. (*To* LAWRENCE.) Well, sir. I'll be off.

AUDA. (*Squinting at him venomously.*) By Allah—a Turk. (*He picks up his rifle.*)

LAWRENCE. No. No—British.

AUDA. (*Accusingly.*) I know the British uniform. That is a Turk.

LAWRENCE. No. An officer in King George's Air Force. (*To* HIGGINS.) You'd better clear off. He thinks you're the enemy.

HIGGINS. Oh Lord! —I say—what a scruffy-looking old wog, or is he one of your generals?

LAWRENCE. Yes. That's exactly what he is.

HIGGINS. Gosh! Poor old Higgins. Always putting his foot in it. Well—goodbye, sir.

*He salutes again, turns and meets* AUDA'S *darkly suspicious gaze. Rather nervously he salutes him too, and then goes.*

AUDA. (*Wearily.*) Well, my friend, is it over?

LAWRENCE. Yes.

AUDA. Tomorrow—Damascus?

LAWRENCE. Yes.

AUDA. Our enemy destroyed and the dream of two years fulfilled. Damascus! Allah indeed is good.

LAWRENCE. Allah is good.

*Pause.* AUDA *looks at* LAWRENCE *with thoughtful and sympathetic eyes.*

AUDA. They have told me about Hamed.

LAWRENCE. I would not have told you.

AUDA. I am the one you should have told.

LAWRENCE. It's not a tale that should be told to a friend.

AUDA. Who else but a friend?

LAWRENCE. An enemy—or a stranger. To anyone but a friend.

AUDA. (*Gently.*) Let's speak of other things. Let's speak of yesterday's great battle.

*Pause.*

LAWRENCE. He opened his eyes for a moment when I lifted my revolver. He had them tightly closed until that moment. He was in great pain. But it was the will of Fate that he should open his eyes and see me pointing the revolver at his head. He said, 'Rashid will be angry with you, el Aurans.'

AUDA. I remember Rashid. He died on our march in the desert.

LAWRENCE. Yes. The day I failed with my compass. So then I said, 'Salute Rashid from me', and he smiled. Then the pain came back and he closed his eyes again. Just as I was lifting the revolver once more to his head he said, 'God will give you peace.' Then I fired. The Turks were already coming out of the blockhouse.

*Pause.*

AUDA. The memory of it will not always be so sharp.

LAWRENCE. I once said the same to Hamed. He didn't believe it then and nor do I now.

AUDA. You must think of other things. Think of Damascus and what we must do there.

LAWRENCE. Yes.

AUDA. And all that we must do after Damascus. Only now does our fight truly begin. (*Anxiously.*) You will go on fighting with and for us, el Aurans? For Allah knows we will need you in peace even more than we have in war.

LAWRENCE. Yes. I suppose I must try and make amends—

AUDA. Amends?

LAWRENCE. To the people I've misled.

*Pause.*

AUDA. By Allah, I think your victories have made you mad. Have you misled us all from Mecca to Damascus—a thousand miles and more—against an enemy many times our strength?

LAWRENCE. Forgive me, Auda. It was a feeble joke.

AUDA. You will fight for us in peace as you fought for us in war?

LAWRENCE. Yes. To the limits of my strength. Can I say more?

AUDA. No. For what limits are there to the strength of el Aurans?

LAWRENCE. Some, I think.

AUDA. None, I know. (*He embraces* LAWRENCE.) I have lost many sons—yes, and grandsons—but for none of them did I grieve so much as I did for you—that day when you left us and went to Gaza and we thought you had gone for ever. What time tonight?

LAWRENCE. Midnight. We shall be in Damascus by dawn.

BARRINGTON *comes on hurriedly.*

BARRINGTON. Ah, Lawrence. Good. I'm glad I've found you. You really ought to leave clearer indications about the exact site of your headquarters. You see—

AUDA, *under the stress of an evidently stormy emotion, clutches* BARRINGTON'S *tunic, and pulls him to him.*

AUDA. Who are you?

BARRINGTON. My name's Barrington. General Barrington—G.H.Q.

AUDA. (*Fiercely.*) Tell them, G.H.Q., tell them in England what I Auda Abu Tayi say of el Aurans. Of Manhood (*he shakes* BARRINGTON) the man. Of Freedom (*he shakes him again*) free. A spirit (*he shakes him a third time*) without equal. I see no flaw in him. And if any offal-eating traitor should ever deny the greatness of that man (*pointing* to LAWRENCE) may the curse of Auda fall upon his dung-filled head.

*He shakes* BARRINGTON *a fourth time, then releases him abruptly and strides out.*

BARRINGTON. One of your chaps?

LAWRENCE. Yes.

BARRINGTON. The Bedouin are excitable people. Far too excitable.

LAWRENCE. How did you get up here?

BARRINGTON. By armoured car from Deraa. I was with the Fourth Cavalry

Division when they entered the town this morning. The G.O.C. sent me here to find you and bring you down there to him at once.

LAWRENCE. Oh? Under arrest?

BARRINGTON. (*Impatiently.*) No, of course not, but he's raging—absolutely raging—and God knows—after the sights I saw this morning—I don't blame him. Apparently some of your wogs sneaked into the place last night—

LAWRENCE. May we make our language more official, General? A contingent of Prince Feisal's Arab forces, acting under my orders, last night captured the important road and rail centre of Deraa—

BARRINGTON. Yes. I daresay that's how it'll go down in your report. Listen, I'm a fairly hardened soldier, Lawrence, but in all my life I've never seen anything like it. It's utterly sickening. They've been burning and looting everything Turkish they can find—massacring the garrison—there are only a handful of survivors. We've even had to surround the military hospital. It's a dangerous situation, and, as you seem to be the only person who can control these savages, you've got to come down with me now at once—

LAWRENCE. (*Coldly.*) I'm sorry, but I'm afraid I can't spare the time.

*Pause.*

BARRINGTON. (*Wide-eyed.*) Shall I report that to the G.O.C.?

LAWRENCE. You will anyway, so why ask me? You can also tell the G.O.C. that I suggest he orders his troops out of a town which was captured and is now being securely held by mine. And now—General—if you don't mind, I have an important operation planned for tonight, and I must prepare for it—

*He turns to go.* BARRINGTON *runs to bar his way.*

BARRINGTON. I'm getting pretty tired of these schoolboy jokes of yours, Lawrence.

LAWRENCE. (*Amused.*) Schoolboy jokes! How interesting. I've grown up a bit since we first met at Abdullah's camp. Or hadn't you noticed?

BARRINGTON. Your suggestion is serious?

LAWRENCE *shrugs.*

That Deraa be left in the hands of those savages?

LAWRENCE. (*Quietly.*) It may be that some of those savages come from a village called Tafas. We followed the Turks into it two days ago. Outside the village we saw a child with a bayonet wound in his neck—but he was still alive. When I bent over him, he screamed, 'Don't hit me, Baba.' Then he ran away from us until he fell over and died. That was only the first thing we saw. When we went into the village and saw the bodies of eighteen women, all bayoneted obscenely, two of them pregnant, I said, 'The best of you brings me the most Turkish dead.' I note, General, with interest that my wishes were apparently carried out last night in Deraa. (*A thought striking him.*) In Deraa? How stupid! I hadn't realized. In Deraa? (*He laughs softly.*)

*He makes a move to go.* BARRINGTON *stops him forcibly.*

BARRINGTON. Are you quite lost to all human feeling?

LAWRENCE *laughs again, with now a different note.*

LAWRENCE. Do you know, General, I think you're right. That's exactly what I am.

*His laugh grows louder, with a shade of hysteria in it.*

Quite lost to all human feeling.

BARRINGTON. (*Appalled.*) I think you're a callous, soulless, sadistic little brute.

LAWRENCE. (*Still laughing, eagerly.*) Yes, yes, oh yes. Especially soulless.

BARRINGTON. You sicken me.

*He pushes* LAWRENCE *away violently so that he falls down, still laughing, but weakly now.* BARRINGTON *goes out.*

LAWRENCE. (*Calling after him.*) I sicken myself. That's the joke. Not a school-boy joke. Just—a—joke.

*The laughter is no longer laughter, but the sound continues.*

Lawrence of Arabia—the soulless wonder—

*Suddenly a quiet, clear voice (actual not recorded) cuts through the sound that* LAWRENCE *is making.*

HAMED'S VOICE. God will give you peace.

LAWRENCE. (*Struggling to his feet.*) No, Hamed, never. Never in this life.

*He goes out unsteadily.*

HAMED'S VOICE. (*As* LAWRENCE *disappears.*) God will give you peace.

*The lights fade on the tent. Loud and clear comes a bugle call, playing the reveille.*

THE LIGHTS COME UP ON THE NEXT SCENE

SCENE 7

SCENE: *The* FLIGHT LIEUTENANT'S *office. He is sitting at the desk, looking up in bewilderment at a* R.A.F. CORPORAL.

F/LT. What? But I don't understand. The Group Captain coming to see me? Are you sure?

CPL. On his way, sir.

F/LT. But why didn't he tell me to come and see him?

CPL. Don't know, sir.

F/LT. Well, it's very odd. Thank you.

*He begins hastily to clear up his desk, moving a few documents from the 'In' tray to the 'Out' tray, and emptying an overfull ashtray. There is a peremptory knock.*

(*Nervously.*) Come in.

*The* GROUP CAPTAIN *comes in. He is only half-dressed and looks dishevelled and harassed. The* CORPORAL *springs to attention.*

Why, sir. This is a surprise. I don't often have the honour—

G/C. Corporal, tell the Flight Sergeant of B Flight to report to me here immediately.

CPL. Yes, sir.

*He goes out.*

G/C. (*Hoarsely.*) Do you keep any drink here?

F/LT. A little—er—medicinal, sir.

*He opens a cupboard and takes out half a bottle of whisky and a glass.*

G/C. I need it. My office has become a nightmare. The telephone hasn't stopped since six this morning, when the duty officer woke me with the news. (*Taking the glass.*) Now I'm not at all sure it isn't being tapped. Probably the *Daily Mirror*. They were the first on. Thanks. Cheers. (*He takes another swig and hands the glass back to the bewildered* FLIGHT LIEU-TENANT.)

Now, listen, we've got to get this fellow off the station within an hour—

F/LT. Which fellow?

G/C. (*Impatiently.*) Ross, of course. Air Ministry are most insistent that there aren't any photographs, so I suggest we smuggle him through my private gate. Agreed?

F/LT. Er—excuse me, sir, I'm just the least little bit behind. Do I agree that we smuggle Aircraftman Ross off the station, through your own private gate? That was the question, wasn't it?

G/C. Oh, my God! You don't know? No, I suppose you wouldn't. We're trying to keep it as dark as possible, though everyone will know tonight—

F/LT. (*Patiently.*) Has it anything to do with the charge I put him on for hearing by you this morning?

G/C. You put him on a charge?

F/LT. Yes, sir. Gross insubordination.

G/C. Who to?

F/LT. Me.

*Pause.*

G/C. (*Solicitously.*) I think you'd better have a nip of your own whisky.

F/LT. (*Virtuously.*) Never touch it in the morning.

G/C. Well, I will. (*Muttering.*) A charge? God. If the *Mirror* got hold of that.

*He takes another glass from the* FLIGHT LIEUTENANT.

You know who it was you've charged with insubordination? Lawrence of Arabia.

F/LT. (*After a pause, confidently.*) Oh no. Oh no. That can't be. I mean—

G/C. How exactly was he insubordinate?

F/LT. He was late on pass. I asked him who he'd been with, that night. He said the Archbishop of Canterbury (*his voice begins to falter*), Lord and Lady Astor, and Mr. and Mrs. George Bernard—oh my God!

G/C. (*Holding out the bottle.*) Here.

F/LT. (*Taking it.*) But it's unbelievable. Why has he done it?

G/C. Well, that's the question. It's very difficult to get anything out of him. I had an hour with him, nearly. A bit awkward. I had to ask him to sit, of course.

F/LT. Of course.

G/C. Kept on using the one word, refuge. The R.A.F. was his refuge.

F/LT. From what?

G/C. God knows. From himself and his reputation, he said. He wanted a number, not a name. Very insistent about his number. Lets him lose his identity. One of a mass. Fellow's a bit screwy, if you ask me.

F/LT. (*Excitedly.*) It wouldn't be a public protest about the Arabs being let down at Versailles?

G/C. No. Asked him that.

F/LT. Or the Palestine question?

G/C. No. Welcomes a Jewish State.

*He takes out a piece of paper.*

He fought for—er—yes, here it is. (*Reading.*) He fought for the whole Semitic race, irrespective of religion. He has no grievance at all about either Arabia or Palestine. Churchill's recent settlement of the Middle East has brought us out with clean hands. Those were his exact words.

F/LT. Really? His exact words?

G/C. (*Glowering.*) Yes, but don't you quote them.

F/LT. No, sir.

G/C. Queer little fellow. If he wasn't who he is, you might feel quite sorry for him.

F/LT. What's going to happen to him?

G/C. Air Ministry are turning him out pronto. They're flaming mad. They're being badgered already by foreign embassies. Going to be questions in the House too. Oh no. I mean, you can't have the Service turned into a rest home for war heroes. Army too.

F/LT. Legally *can* they turf him out?

G/C. Oh yes. Entered under false name and false particulars.

*There is a knock on the door.*

F/LT. Come in.

*The* FLIGHT SERGEANT *comes in and salutes.*

F/SGT. Flight Sergeant Thompson, B Flight, reporting, sir.

G/C. Yes, Flight. It's about a man in your Flight. Aircraftman Ross.

F/SGT. Yes, Sir.

G/C. He has to be off this station within an hour.

F/SGT. Yes, sir.

G/C. You knew about it?

F/SGT. He told me, sir.

G/C. Did he tell you why?

F/SGT. Yes, sir.

G/C. Oh, well, don't tell the rest of the Flight.

F/SGT. They all know, sir. I told them.

G/C. Oh God! (*To* FLIGHT LIEUTENANT.) It'll be all round the camp by now—

F/LT. (*To* FLIGHT SERGEANT, *curiously*.) Exactly what did he tell you, Flight?

F/SGT. What the Group Captain said to him, sir. That he was the wrong type for the R.A.F. Didn't fit in. Was too old. Couldn't do the job—so he was being hoof—discharged the Service.

*Pause.*

F/LT. That's all he told you, Flight?

F/SGT. Yes, sir.

G/C. Nothing else at all?

F/SGT. (*Trying to remember*.) No, sir. Except that he didn't know—what he was going to do with himself now.

G/C. That's all right, Flight. (*Dismissing him*.) Thank you.

F/SGT. Leave to speak, sir.

*The* GROUP CAPTAIN *nods.*

I've known this airman ten weeks. He's not an ideal recruit, but then who is? In fact he's not a bad little (*he bites the word off*) chap at all. I think—if you only let him stay, sir—I can see to it that he won't get into no more trouble. And I'm sure, some day, he'll make an airman.

*Pause.*

G/C. I'm sorry, Flight—but it's all settled.

F/LT. (*With a faint smile*.) He doesn't fit in.

F/SGT. Yes, sir. It's just that it takes all sorts, sir—that's what I always say—

G/C. (*Sharply*.) That's enough, Flight. See that he's off the station by nine hundred hours—

F/SGT. Yes, sir.

*He salutes, marches to the door and turns.*

Forgive forthrightness, sir. It's just I don't believe there's anyone in this world who can't be made to fit in somehow—

G/C. Yes, Flight. Thank you.

F/SGT. Trust I have given no offence.

G/C. No offence. It's just that Ross happens to be a special case. (*To* FLIGHT LIEUTENANT.) A very special case.

F/SGT. Yes, sir.

*He salutes and goes.*

THE LIGHTS FADE

SCENE 8

SCENE: *Hut fourteen.* LAWRENCE, *in civilian clothes, is packing a kitbag. He is looking out of the window, whence we hear the sound of a bugle. When it stops he turns back to his task.* EVANS *comes in.*

EVANS. (*Embarrassed, but with false joviality*.) Hullo, Rossie-boy. How's the world?

LAWRENCE. All right. Break on?

EVANS. Yes.

LAWRENCE. No cocoa and biscuits this morning?

EVANS. Not hungry. Rossie—

*He holds out some money.*

LAWRENCE. No. You keep that.

EVANS. Oh, but I couldn't.

*He puts the money on the bed.*

You'll be needing it more than me now, anyway.

LAWRENCE. (*Realizing resistance is useless.*) Thank you. Taff. I must give you back the half-crown.

EVANS. (*As* LAWRENCE *holds it out.*) Keep it, man. No, keep it. It's not much, but it could help out there. What are you going to do?

LAWRENCE. (*Putting the money away.*) No idea, Taff.

EVANS. Got a job to go to?

LAWRENCE. No.

EVANS. It's terrible this unemployment. Terrible. I wouldn't be in this place if it weren't for that, I can tell you. No fear. You got a girl?

LAWRENCE. No.

EVANS. (*Smiling.*) Lucky man.

LAWRENCE. Yes. I suppose so.

EVANS. One comfort—you don't have to tell her you got hoofed. Anyone to tell?

LAWRENCE. No.

EVANS. I'll write to anyone if you'll give me the address. Say what bad luck it was you got on the wrong side of the Station Commander. Just unreasonable, I'll say he was—

PARSONS *comes in quickly.*

PARSONS. Listen—I don't want no noes about this, because I've talked to all the others—except Taff here and he'll say yes like the rest, I know—won't you, Taff?

EVANS. (*Plaintively.*) I don't know what it is, yet.

PARSONS. (*Snarling.*) I'm telling you, aren't I?

EVANS. Sorry.

PARSONS. We're writing a document—quite dignified—most respectful—dear sir—we have the honour—all that cock—and we're all signing it and sending it to the Group Captain—and what we're going to say is that we all think that the way they're treating you is the most dirtiest, bleedingest trick that even those bastards have ever pulled on one of us— and that's saying something.

LAWRENCE. (*Quietly.*) On one of us?

PARSONS. Yes—of course—but what I said just now—we must make it respectful—B Flight suggest there has been some slight misapprehension regarding Airman Ross not fitting in (*warming to his subject*) because if he can fit into B Flight he can bloodywell fit into the R.A.F. or into any other bloody Service you can bloodywell think of—sir. (*Thoughtfully.*) Trouble is, we're really going to need you to write this for us. Got the time?

LAWRENCE. No. Besides you mustn't send it.

PARSONS. Don't worry. We're sending it. Aren't we, Taff?

EVANS. I'm game—if all the others are. Are they really, Sailor?

PARSONS. (*Fiercely.*) What kind of a mug do you think I am? In this sort of lark it's all or no one—see. One single blackleg—just one, and they'll beat us. There aren't no blacklegs on this.

LAWRENCE. Dickinson?

PARSONS. He's in. Thinks it's a joke, mind you, hasn't got no proper social conscience—officer class, you see—but he's in all right and glad to be. So you're in too, Taff—right?

EVANS. Right.

PARSONS. (*To* LAWRENCE.) That's all of us, chum. So it's settled—

LAWRENCE. (*Shaking his head, gently.*) No.

PARSONS. Why not?

LAWRENCE. It can only mean trouble.

PARSONS. (*Contemptuously.*) Nah. What can they do? Hoof the whole Flight and have the papers talk about a mutiny at Uxbridge? Put us all on jankers, and have the story round the whole camp? No. Worst they'll do is collective reprimand. (*In his 'officer' voice.*) 'None of you understand Service ways, my boys. That's your trouble.' (*He makes a face.*) Best they can do is reconsider—

LAWRENCE. They won't do that.

PARSONS. (*Obviously agreeing.*) Well, it's a chance. There's always a chance, as the bishop said to the housemaid.

LAWRENCE. Don't send it until tomorrow.

PARSONS. Well—we thought—the sooner the better—

LAWRENCE. No. Not until tomorrow.

PARSONS. All right. Well, good-bye, Rossie.

LAWRENCE. (*Taking his outstretched hand.*) Good-bye, Sailor.

PARSONS. (*Muttering.*) The bastards! I could bloodywell murder them—I could go up to each and every one of them and collectively or individually screw all their—

*He has disappeared.* EVANS *also puts his hand out.*

EVANS. Good-bye, Rossie.

LAWRENCE. Good-bye, Taff.

EVANS. Good luck for the future.

LAWRENCE. Thank you. The same to you. And thank you for the (*remembering the slang*) half-dollar.

EVANS *makes a deprecating gesture and is going out as the* FLIGHT SERGEANT *comes in.*

F/SGT. What do you think you're doing, young Evans? Think the break lasts all morning?

EVANS. I was talking to Ross.

F/SGT. (*Roaring.*) I don't care if you were talking to the Aga Khan, get back on fatigue—

EVANS. Yes, Flight. Sorry, Flight—

*He flees. The* FLIGHT SERGEANT *comes up to* LAWRENCE.

F/SGT. Ready, boy?

LAWRENCE. Nearly.

*He turns to collect some books. The* FLIGHT SERGEANT, *sitting on the bed, pulls out of the nearly filled kitbag* LAWRENCE'S *ornamental dagger.*

F/SGT. What's this?

LAWRENCE. (*Carelessly.*) Oh—sort of keepsake. Would you like to have it?

F/SGT. Well, thanks. I'll give it to the wife to hang on the wall. She loves stuff like that. I'm telling you, son, you'd have made an airman if the bleeders had only let you be. I told 'em that just now—head bleeder and all.

LAWRENCE. Thank you, Flight, I'm grateful.

F/SGT. Didn't work, though. They got it in for you, proper, son—don't know why. Something to do with your past, shouldn't wonder.

LAWRENCE. Yes. It may be.

F/SGT. Well, listen here, my boy, don't let them get you down. What's past is past, see, and finished and dead. What you got to think about is the future. (*Looking at his watch.*) Well—are you ready now?

LAWRENCE. (*Pulling his kitbag closed and tying it.*) Just about.

F/SGT. What are you going to do? Any idea?

LAWRENCE. (*Head bent over kitbag.*) Yes. I think I have. I'm going to get back into the R.A.F. as soon as I can.

F/SGT. (*Surprised.*) Think you can do that?

LAWRENCE. Well, I'll have to change my name, I suppose. Ross won't do any more.

*He points to the name 'Ross' painted on his kitbag.*

Shaw. I thought of that this morning. How do you like it?

F/SGT. All right.

LAWRENCE. But it's not the name that matters. It's the number.

F/SGT. (*Wonderingly.*) The number? What number?

LAWRENCE. Oh, any number. Just provided it's one of a lot of others—like this.

*He points to the number on his kitbag.*

F/SGT. I don't know what you're talking about. Do you really want another dose of all this?

*He indicates the hut.*

LAWRENCE. More than anything else I can think of.

F/SGT. You're a glutton for punishment, aren't you?

LAWRENCE. (*Smiling.*) It rather looks like it.

F/SGT. I've got to sneak you out through the Group Captain's private entrance. Gawd knows why. I'll get the key. You know his house?

LAWRENCE *nods.*

I'll meet you over there.

*He goes out.* LAWRENCE *finishes tying his kitbag, his head bent over it.*

LAWRENCE. God will give you peace.

*He looks round the hut for the last time and then shouldering his kitbag, he follows the* FLIGHT SERGEANT *out. A distant bugle call is sounding as the* CURTAIN FALLS.

# HEART TO HEART

*A play for Television*

First published 1964
by Hamish Hamilton Ltd

*Characters:*

DAVID MANN
PEGGY MANN
FRANK GODSELL (Producer)
JESSIE WESTON (Production Secretary)
SIR STANLEY JOHNSON
LADY JOHNSON
CONTROLLER OF PROGRAMMES (Mr Stockton)
MISS KNOTT
SIR JOHN DAWSON-BROWN, Q.C.
FLOOR MANAGER (Joe)
TECHNICAL OPERATIONS MANAGER (T.O.M.)
ELECTRICIAN (Mickey)
SOUND ENGINEER (Lou)
PROPERTY MASTER (Tom)
CYRIL BROWNE
DAVID MANN'S CHAUFFEUR
LIFTMAN AT EATON SQUARE (William)
WAITRESS IN CAFÉ
P.P.S. TO SIR ERNEST JOHNSON

Various Studio Personnel

*Heart to Heart* was first broadcast on December 6th, 1962, in the B.B.C. Television service with the following cast:

| | |
|---|---|
| DAVID MANN | Kenneth More |
| SIR STANLEY JOHNSON | Ralph Richardson |
| JESSIE WESTON | Wendy Craig |
| PEGGY MANN | Jean Marsh |
| MISS KNOTT | Angela Baddeley |
| FRANK GODSELL | Peter Sallis |
| CONTROLLER | Jack Gwillim |
| LADY JOHNSON | Megs Jenkins |
| SIR JOHN DAWSON BROWN, Q.C. | Derek Francis |
| CYRIL BROWNE | Martin Wyldeck |
| FLOOR MANAGER | John Matthews |
| ANNOUNCER | Bill Cartwright |
| ELECTRICIAN | Roy Wilson |
| T.O.M. | Stephen Hancock |
| VISION MIXER | Patrick Parnell |
| PROP BOY | Henry Green |
| WILLIAM | John Rae |
| CHAUFFEUR | Stan Hollingsworth |
| PARLIAMENTARY PRIVATE SECRETARY | Alan Howard |
| WAITRESS | Jean Alexander |
| FILM EDITOR | Trader Faulkner |
| TOASTMASTER | Harold H. Dean |
| TUC OFFICIAL | George Betton |
| ANNOUNCER | Anthea Wyndham |
| SOUND ENGINEER | Peter Layton |
| PHOTOGRAPHER | Vincent Harding |
| WARDROBE ASSISTANT | Susan Armstrong |

Produced by ALVIN RAKOFF

Designed by BARRY LEAROYD

# HEART TO HEART

*Before the titles the screen is filled with a large close-up of* DAVID MANN *leaning forward eagerly in his chair.*

SIR JOHN. Yes, I would agree to that, Mr. Mann.

DAVID. (*In an incisive voice.*) Sir John, how does a man fulfil himself in life?

*Another large close-up, this time of* SIR JOHN DAWSON-BROWN, *a distinguished-looking man (he is a famous Q.C.) some twenty years older than* DAVID, *who is thirty-five. His usually unruffled features are now distinctly ruled. His answer is hesitating.*

SIR JOHN. I would say that a man fulfils himself by the knowledge that he has always tried to do what is right rather than what is expedient.

DAVID. Can a man always distinguish between the two?

SIR JOHN. I think so.

DAVID. How?

SIR JOHN. There's a thing called conscience—

DAVID. Consciences vary, don't they? To one man a certain action will seem right, to another wrong.

SIR JOHN. Oh, I agree. I'm not claiming there are absolute standards. But the only certain rule in life is that happiness lies in doing one's duty. And one's duty is to do what seems right to one at the time—even though it may, perhaps, ultimately prove wrong.

DAVID. Or even if it may harm not only yourself but other persons?

SIR JOHN. Oh, yes. There can be no doubt at all about it—in my mind, anyway. A man must always try to do his duty as he sees that duty at the time. I don't think there can be any escape from that, Mr. Mann.

*The camera draws back to show the whole extent of the studio floor, and the voices dim to an inaudible murmur behind the introductory music. The titles appear against the shifting background of cameras, arc lights, microphone booms and other identifiable television paraphernalia. Far in the background we see* DAVID *and* SIR JOHN, *sitting, under strong lights, facing each other and still apparently talking, but their voices drowned by the music until the titles are finished. From now on there will be no need to keep the illusion of a straight television interview. Cameras, either active or inactive, will be shown, with cameramen and stage-hands seen going perfunctorily, if efficiently, through what is plainly a perfectly routine job. Only* SIR JOHN *will still seem under strain.*

DAVID. You have had a long career at the bar, Sir John?

SIR JOHN. Thirty-five years.

DAVID. And in your first year as a barrister how much did you earn?

SIR JOHN. Exactly fifteen pounds.

DAVID. And last year? (*As* SIR JOHN *hesitates*.) Don't worry about the Inspector of Taxes. If he should be looking in you can always say it was a slip of the tongue. (*As* SIR JOHN *still hesitates*.) Might I suggest it was nearer fifteen thousand than fifteen?

SIR JOHN. Yes. I suppose you might suggest that—


*CONTROL ROOM. In a shot to establish the general layout of the place we see, briefly, the monitor screens and the line of intent people (of whom the Producer,* FRANK GODSELL, *and the Production Secretary,* JESSIE, *are the only two whose names we need to know) who are watching them. From the transmission screen we see and hear the interview continuing.*


DAVID. (*Off.*) Then I suppose you consider your life has been a long and successful journey?

JESSIE. (*Into microphone.*) Camera three.

*With the resulting camera change the picture on the transmission screen is shown from a different angle, favouring* SIR JOHN.

SIR JOHN. Long certainly, and successful, if success is to be measured purely by increase of income—

DAVID. Surely that's not an unusual way of measuring success, is it?

FRANK. He's rambling a bit. (*Into microphone.*) Joe, he hasn't looked at his clock, does he know he's only got ninety seconds?

SIR JOHN. (*Meanwhile.*) Not unusual, I agree. But, not in my view, the best way—


*THE FLOOR.* JOE, *the floor manager, crouching out of camera range, gives a speed-up sign to* DAVID.


DAVID. (*Briskly.*) Well, Sir John. I'm afraid our time is running short, and I must come to my last question.

SIR JOHN. (*Smiling.*) I shall try to face it bravely—

DAVID. How does a man fulfil himself in life?

SIR JOHN. (*Surprised.*) But you've just asked me that question—


*CONTROL ROOM.* FRANK *has his hand to his head in horror.*


FRANK. (*Moaning gently.*) Oh, Lord! (*To* JESSIE.) Has he been—?

*He makes a quick gesture of taking a drink.* JESSIE *shrugs placidly, and then nods, as if to say that she has not much evidence, but assumes* FRANK'S *suspicions have good grounds.*

JESSIE. (*Into microphone.*) Four to captions.
*The transmission screen changes to a longer shot.*
    Charley—be ready to cut off sound—


*THE FLOOR.* DAVID *is in the process of making a brave recovery.*

DAVID. I often ask a key question twice, Sir John. Sometimes one gets a different answer the second time. You, as a lawyer, should realize the value, in cross-examining a witness—
SIR JOHN. (*Stiffly.*) In a court of law I am not allowed to repeat a question that has already been answered.
DAVID. (*Blandly.*) But this is not a court of law, Sir John. This is 'Heart to Heart'. And may I say, as our time is up, what a very happy and rewarding experience it has been to have had you, as my fifty-ninth victim, on this programme. Thank you very much indeed.
*He extends his hand, smiling amiably.* SIR JOHN *takes it.*


*CONTROL ROOM.* FRANK *is rubbing his forehead in relief.*

FRANK. I will say he has a sublime gift for recovery—
JESSIE. Sublime. (*Into microphone.*) Cue grams. (*To* FRANK, *placidly: she is a placid girl.*) Well, I mean, it's got to be, hasn't it? (*Into microphone.*) Two. Track in as usual—
FRANK. Super captions. Cue announcer.
ANNOUNCER. You have just seen the fifty-ninth edition of 'Heart to Heart', a British Television Company's presentation.
FRANK. In on victim.
ANNOUNCER. In tonight's 'Heart to Heart', the victim was Sir John Dawson-Brown, Q.C.
FRANK. Cut. In on David. Super his caption.
ANNOUNCER. And your Grand Inquisitor, as always, was David Mann.
FRANK. Take out caption. Cue David.


*THE FLOOR.* DAVID *is speaking directly into the camera that is showing the big close-up we have seen on the screen.*

DAVID. (*With a charming, professionally self-assured smile.*) And so we come to the end of another edition of 'Heart to Heart'. Tomorrow night, at our usual nine-fifteen, we will present our last interview in the present series, and for this special occasion we've chosen a victim who—I know you'll all agree—is a very special victim indeed . . .

*We notice a slightly panic-stricken glint momentarily in his otherwise entirely bland expression.*

	. . . a man whose meteoric career in politics has made him the talk of the nation . . .

*He glances at the* FLOOR MANAGER *with a split second's flash of appeal.*

	. . . appointed only—a few weeks ago—a man whose name is a household word all over the country . . .

## CONTROL ROOM.

FRANK. (*In a panic.*) Joe, he's dried on the name. (*Urgently.*) Get the idiot board. Chalk up 'Johnson'. But quick.

*THE FLOOR.* JOE *frantically seizes a blackboard and does as* FRANK *has ordered.*

DAVID. (*Meanwhile.*) . . . it's a name that when you hear it, ladies and gentlemen, I know you will feel it is an eminently fitting one on which to end our present series—

JOE *has held up the blackboard.* DAVID *flashes a glance at it.*

	(*Blandly.*) . . . and here it is—The Rt. Hon. Sir Stanley Johnson, M.P., the newly appointed Minister of Labour. So tune in tomorrow night to 'Heart to Heart', when once again we will present the truth, the real truth, the truth of the heart.

## CONTROL ROOM.

FRANK. Grams up. Super closing captions. Fade it slowly. And fade me out, too.

*The 'Heart to Heart' credits are faded from the screen. Commercials follow before next programme.*

*STUDIO FLOOR. A monitor in foreground, cameras,* DAVID *and* SIR JOHN *beyond it.*

DAVID. Joe, for heaven's sake! I gave you the sign. Do you have to take all night?

FLOOR MANAGER. That's it, studio—clear. (*To* DAVID.) Sorry, David, but I didn't think even you could fluff on Stan Johnson.

DAVID. (*To* ELECTRICIAN, *also angrily.*) And Mickey, you fry me with that bloody light every evening. Does it have to be as close?

SIR JOHN, *meanwhile, his part for the evening over, has left his seat and is chatting to one of the technicians. The* FLOOR MANAGER *approaches him.*

FLOOR MANAGER. Sir John, can we have you for a moment for a photograph? In your original chair, please. (*Calling.*) David—stills, please.

DAVID *and* SIR JOHN *go to their original chairs while the photographers prepare to take their pictures.*

*CONTROL ROOM.* JESSIE *and* FRANK *to the foreground.* FRANK *still has his head in his hands and is evidently the prey of jangled nerves.* JESSIE, *lighting a cigarette,* looks *at him sympathetically.*

JESSIE. It's all right. The fluff on the name he got away with—touch wood.

FRANK. Where do you find wood in a television control room?

T.O.M. (*From farther down the line.*) At Shepherd's Bush, I expect, Frank. Finest old mahogany—

FRANK. (*Getting up.*) Uncalled for, Fred. The motto of the Fifth Channel is 'Amity to all'.

FRANK *and* JESSIE *go towards the door.*

TECHNICIAN. Even Auntie B.B.C.?

FRANK. They do good work, Bill. Their viewers are very happy, I'm told—all sixteen of them.

*THE FLOOR.* DAVID *and* SIR JOHN *are being photographed.*

SIR JOHN. What did you do before this?

DAVID. I was a lecturer in Political Economy at Oxford.

SIR JOHN. Really? Quite a change from all this, I'd imagine?

DAVID. Quite a change.

FLOOR MANAGER. Thank you, gentlemen. Thank you, Sir John. Ordeal's over.

FRANK *and* JESSIE *have joined them on the set as the* FLOOR MANAGER *and photographers go away.*

SIR JOHN. (*Eagerly.*) Ah, Mr. Godsell. How do you think it went?

FRANK. (*Heartily.*) Very well indeed. May I introduce the production secretary, Mrs. Weston?

SIR JOHN. (*Paying her little attention.*) How do you do? How did it seem to you, Mrs.—er—?

JESSIE. (*Smoothly.*) One of the best shows we've ever had.

*She, too, has been asked this question before and invariably gives the same answer. Her calm, cool voice always, however, carries conviction. It does on this occasion.*

SIR JOHN. (*Nodding to* DAVID.) Mind you, he asked me some pretty tough questions, this young man—

DAVID. That's my job, Sir John. To bring out the truth—

*There is only a faint suggestion of inverted commas, but it is there.*

SIR JOHN. Of course. It's my job, too, of course—

DAVID. (*Quietly.*) Not quite, is it? Yours is surely to bring out only that aspect of the truth that happens to suit your case—

FRANK. (*Interrupting quickly: these post-broadcast brushes have happened before.*) Don't let's get into another 'Heart to Heart', now, please.

*A man has come up, evidently from his clothes and manner fairly high up in the hierarchy of the Fifth Channel. His name is* CYRIL BROWNE.

CYRIL. The Controller would like to see you, Frank.

FRANK. (*Angrily.*) Doesn't he *ever* leave that office? Does he eat and sleep up there?

CYRIL. He just likes watching television—

FRANK. Hasn't he got a set at home?

CYRIL. His wife likes 'Coronation Street'. And she talks.

FRANK. (*With a wealth of meaning.*) To *him*? And when she doesn't *have* to? All right. Would you look after Sir John?

CYRIL. A great pleasure. (*As* FRANK *hurries off, over his shoulder.*) One of your best, Dave.

SIR JOHN. Good-bye, Mr. Mann.

DAVID. Good-bye, Sir John.

SIR JOHN. And thank you for letting me off so lightly.

DAVID *inclines his head, smiling.* CYRIL *and* SIR JOHN *disappear into the shadows.* DAVID *and* JESSIE *are left alone.*

DAVID. Did I?

JESSIE. I wouldn't say so.

DAVID. If I did I was bad. He's a phoney—

JESSIE. That came out.

DAVID. A time-server—

JESSIE. That came out too.

DAVID. With a very odd sex life, I shouldn't wonder.

JESSIE. That didn't come out.

DAVID. Why should it? What's a sex life got to do with the truth of the heart?

JESSIE. Do you want me to answer that?

DAVID. No. (*He sits.*) Just have a drink with me, please, Mrs. Weston—

JESSIE. (*Sitting beside him.*) I'll watch you, if you like.

DAVID. You'll join me. (*Calling.*) Hey, Tom. Can I have a couple of prop glasses?

VOICE. (*From the darkness.*) You'll get me in trouble with the Union, you will—

JESSIE. I'll drink from the flask.

DAVID. (*Calling.*) O.K., Tom. Not wanted. (*Handing her the flask.*) Tough girl, eh?

JESSIE. (*After swallowing a sip.*) Not tough at all. Far too soft, about some things. (*Indicating the flask.*) For instance I should be confiscating this. (*Nevertheless she hands him back the flask.*)

DAVID. I should have you barred from television. (*As an afterthought.*) That's if I'm not barred from it myself after tonight. (*He takes a long swig.*) How bad was it?

JESSIE. Not good, Mr. Mann.

DAVID. Why do you always call me Mr. Mann?

*He pockets the flask and gets up to go. She follows him. For the rest of the scene the camera tracks with them past all the paraphernalia of the deserted and darkened studio.*

JESSIE. Because you always call me Mrs. Weston.

DAVID. I only do that to remind myself that you're married.

*Pause.*

JESSIE. How's Mrs. Mann, by the way?

DAVID. Fine, thanks.

JESSIE. Enjoying the new flat, I suppose.

DAVID. Like mad.

JESSIE. (*Brightly.*) Good.

*A figure appears out of the shadows. He is the prop man* DAVID *called to.*

TOM. Ta-ta, Dave. See you tomorrow.

*He goes.*

DAVID. I suppose there will be a tomorrow. They can't sack me before that, can they?

JESSIE. (*Quietly.*) They *could* refuse your new contract.

DAVID. (*With a sigh.*) So?

JESSIE. I see. This is your night for being the embittered success, is it, Mr. Mann?

DAVID. (*With sudden anger.*) Listen, Mrs. Weston, a thing doesn't stop being true just because it's a cliché, and because it's been written about so badly, so often. Success *can* be hell.

JESSIE. You tell me about it. All I know about is failure, and that's not exactly heaven.

DAVID. I wasn't a failure before this—circus—

JESSIE. (*Seriously.*) No, but you will be after this circus if you go on as you're going now.

DAVID. I've got to have a few drinks before I go before the cameras. I've got to. It's not nerves, or exhaustion, or strain. I could do this job on my head, any night—

JESSIE. One of these nights you will—

DAVID. (*Raising an angry voice.*) Stop this eternal wisecracking, will you? That's part of the whole thing—this eternal wisecracking—

*He puts his head in his hands.* JESSIE *looks at him, concerned but, sagely, silent.* It's as if everyone in this business had to joke about their work—just to keep themselves sane. (*Looking up at her.*) Other people don't joke about their work, do they?

JESSIE. Farmers do. I know. I was brought up in the country.
*Pause.*
DAVID. Why do I drink? Can you tell me that?
JESSIE. I can give you one good reason. Because you can afford to. Farmers usually can't—except on Saturday nights. (*As* DAVID *continues to stare at her.*) That wasn't a wisecrack, Mr. Mann. Just a cliché. Hadn't we better get out of here before they lock us in for the night, and I get fatally compromised?
DAVID. (*After looking at her.*) You might just get strangled.
JESSIE *has risen and is pulling him to his feet. He is now, for the first time, showing visible signs of drink.*
JESSIE. I'd still be compromised.
DAVID. And Mr. Weston wouldn't like that?
*She gets him to his feet.*
JESSIE. No. He'd hate it. And so would Mrs. Mann.
*He begins to walk, a shade unsteadily, towards the door over which the EXIT sign still shines.*
DAVID. (*Apologetically.*) Sorry—it's those last two from the flask—
JESSIE. I'd say it was those first six, from the bottle.
DAVID. Do farmers feel ashamed of their jobs?
JESSIE. (*Levelly.*) What makes you feel ashamed of yours, Mr. Mann?
DAVID. (*After a pause, to gather his thoughts.*) In the first place that it's grossly overpaid—
JESSIE. That's a shame I could bear a fraction of. (*As* DAVID *turns on her angrily.*) All right. That was a wisecrack. Go on. Second place?
DAVID. That it's a job that could be done by any other man of fair intelligence, reasonable general knowledge, a modicum of industry and a quickish brain. There must be thousands upon thousands—
JESSIE. Just leave it at thousands.
DAVID. (*Ignoring her.*) —of men who'd do this happily and well for a tenth of my price—
JESSIE. And some of them might stay sober on it, too—
*She opens the door and propels him gently through it.*


CORRIDOR. *Long, bare, whitewashed, with mysterious lights flashing intermittently and, at the moment, deserted.*

DAVID. (*In full spate.*) But I get myself a flat in Belgravia and a Bentley convertible for one reason-one reason only. That. (*He smiles his professional smile, the one we have seen him use before the cameras.*)
JESSIE. What?
DAVID. (*Pointing to his now set grimace.*) That. Apparently it makes a dimple somewhere, God knows where—

JESSIE. God *and* you, Mr. Mann.

DAVID. And ten million morons go for it. Why?

JESSIE. Don't ask me. I'm not one of the ten million.

DAVID. The first few letters were sort of flattering, the next hundred or so, funny, in a way. Now—they're just insulting. Dammit, I'm one of the best political economists in the country. (*Unhappily.*) Well—used to be. (*Pathetically.*) Aren't I worth more than this?

JESSIE. Three hundred pounds a week more, I'm told—

DAVID. Blast you. Good night.

*He turns abruptly and walks a few steps down the corridor.* JESSIE *runs after him, takes his elbow and guides him to a side door marked 'Emergency Exit'.*

JESSIE. David—hadn't we better go this way?

DAVID *turns back.*

*They are in a yard, full of cars.*

JESSIE. Are you driving yourself?

DAVID. Oh, no. A chauffeur. Brand new. Fourteen pounds a week.

JESSIE. Bad luck!

*Pause.*

DAVID. I suppose I *am* just a self-pitying bore, Jessie?

JESSIE. No, David, not to me.

DAVID. You do see my point?

JESSIE. Of course I do. (*Gently.*) You can always go back to political economy, you know.

DAVID. I can't. You must know I can't. I've burnt my boats—

JESSIE. Then you'll just have to learn to live with that dimple, won't you?

DAVID. A homespun philosopher! You must drive your poor husband round the bend.

JESSIE. Possibly. But not to drink.

DAVID. Very funny. Has he sold a poem recently?

JESSIE. Yes—three weeks ago—to one of these intellectual weeklies. He got all of ten guineas for it.

DAVID. Why doesn't he get a regular job? Journalism, or something? Even TV?

JESSIE. Surrender to the Establishment. (*With faint bitterness.*) Like having babies would be a surrender to bourgeois domesticity.

DAVID. So meanwhile he just lives off you.

JESSIE. (*Cheerfully.*) Why not? A genius has to live off somebody.

*She opens the door of a very battered old Morris Minor.*

Here's my grand convertible. I've given Conway, my chauffeur, the night off. Can you find yours?

DAVID. He's around.

*He waves.* JESSIE *gets into her car.* DAVID *speaks to her through the window.*

*In the background we can see a large new Bentley convertible, chauffeur-driven, silently gliding up.*

Well—one thing—we don't do such a bad job, do we? At least it's the
most honest programme of its kind since 'Face to Face', isn't it? (*Fiercely.*)
Now, don't make a wisecrack about that or I *will* strangle you.

JESSIE. I wasn't going to. I think it is. And I think as long as you're on it and
stay sober enough to articulate it'll go on being it.

DAVID. Thank you, Mrs. Weston. Good night.

JESSIE. Good night, Mr. Mann.

*With an ear-splitting grinding of reluctant gears and a blast from its antique
engine, the car moves off in a series of irregular bursts.* DAVID *turns and climbs
into his, the door held open by the chauffeur. Then he glides smoothly out of
sight.*


*CONTROLLER'S OFFICE. Frank is sitting facing the great man across his desk.*

CONTROLLER. Yes, yes. I grant you his following, and the excellent rating. I
even grant you that probably not more than one viewer in a thousand
tonight noticed that anything was wrong. But that's just the one thou-
sandth viewer I have to think of—

FRANK. He's probably a drinker too. The ones that notice usually are.

CONTROLLER. I don't want you to be facetious about this, Frank. It's serious.

FRANK. Oh, I don't think so. He's not an alcoholic. (*Getting up.*) Still, I will
talk to him, I promise.

CONTROLLER. Tell him that in this business no one man is indispensable.

FRANK. I shall remember those exact words—

CONTROLLER. (*Ignorant of the irony.*) And tell him that his new contract isn't
signed yet.

FRANK. I think he knows that. And mine isn't either, come to that. (*On the
way to the door.*) How did you think the show was, otherwise?

CONTROLLER. (*Doubtfully.*) Well—Frank—since you ask—mind you it's your
show and I don't want to interfere at all—I hope you understand that
clearly—

FRANK'S *expression as he stands near the door shows that what he understands
clearly is precisely the opposite.*

But aren't we getting a bit near the bone? I mean, poor old Johnny
Dawson-Brown was made to seem a pretty fair poop tonight.

FRANK. He is a pretty fair poop.

CONTROLLER. (*Coldly.*) Possibly. But he's also a very distinguished man and,
incidentally, a friend of mine. That's nothing to do with it, of course—

FRANK. Of course.

CONTROLLER. Now tomorrow night we have a Minister of the Crown. So I
think a little easing up would be in order. (*After a pause.*) Don't you?
(FRANK *makes no reply.*) Put it to David Mann, anyway. Only as a suggestion, of course. Not as an order. (*Pointing an accusing finger.*) But the
other thing—the drinking—now that *is* an order, and you have to give

it. After all it's *your* show and it's you who have to carry the can when things go wrong.

FRANK. Yes. And in television no one man is indispensable.

CONTROLLER. (*This time both getting it and facing it.*) That's right. (*Smiling acidly.*) Well, good night, Frank.

FRANK. (*Without a smile.*) Good night, Mr. Stockton.

*He goes. After a moment the* CONTROLLER *bangs a file down with surprising violence on his desk.*

CONTROLLER. (*Muttering.*) Producers!


*SITTING-ROOM, DAVID'S FLAT. It is a penthouse, probably in Eaton Square, and the chief feature, of the room is an immensely long window, of the sliding-panel type—curtained at the moment. Before these curtains, in deep contemplation, stands* PEGGY MANN, DAVID'S *wife. Though not of the conventional, model-girl type, she has large eyes, high cheekbones and radiates strong physical allure. At least to her husband.*

*She was born in Riga, but left it for Oxford at the age of five.*

*Only at moments of emotional stress is there the faintest sign of anything but the most Oxford of accents.*

*As* DAVID *comes in from the hall she does not turn from contemplating the curtains.*


DAVID. Hullo, darling.

PEGGY. (*Without turning.*) Hullo, darling. How did it go?

DAVID. (*Going to the drink tray.*) You didn't see it?

PEGGY. No. I had the Wilkinsons in.

DAVID. (*Hesitating over the whisky and deciding on an orange squash.*) Couldn't you have seen it with them?

PEGGY. They hate television.

DAVID. I see.

PEGGY. (*Decisively.*) No, darling, they just won't do.

DAVID. (*Joining her, with his glass.*) What won't do?

*He nuzzles the nape of her neck amorously.*

PEGGY. These curtains. (*Shaking her head impatiently.*) You're ruffling my hair.

DAVID. There was a time when you liked your hair being ruffled.

PEGGY. In those days it started that way and stayed that way.

DAVID. (*Arm still amorously about her waist.*) I preferred it that way. Why won't the curtains do?

PEGGY. (*Moving away from him to demonstrate her points.*) It's too big an expanse to cover with just one plain colour. They make the room cold and bare. The Wilkinsons hated them.

DAVID. The Wilkinsons seem to hate a lot of things.

PEGGY. They're sweet people.

DAVID. I know you think so.

PEGGY. Darling, they're great friends of Barbara Millchester.

DAVID. So that makes you and Lady Millchester who think they're sweet. Personally I think they're ghastly. In my ideal test team of cracking bores they go in first for England. We can't have any new curtains for this room until these are paid for, and that's flat.

*He sits down, pulls some papers out of a brief-case and begins to study them.* PEGGY *suspiciously eyes his glass. The telephone rings at* DAVID'S *side. He takes the receiver.*

Yes? Yes, William. What is it? . . . What lady?

*LOBBY—NIGHT. In a booth,* WILLIAM, *the night porter, is whispering into a telephone, in the evident desire not to be overheard by a lady of whom we see nothing whatever except her age (indeterminately middle-aged) and a highly spectacular, feminine and unsuitable hat.*

WILLIAM. She says she's got to see you. Matter of life and death . . . No. That's why I kept her here in the front lobby because I knew you always slip in at the back. . . . Well, it's just that they don't usually come as late as this—

*SITTING-ROOM.*

DAVID. Tell her to write in to B.T.V. in the ordinary way, or if she wants something more personal to get her head well down in the scrum outside the studio gates—

PEGGY. (*As he puts receiver down.*) What's that you're drinking?

DAVID. Orange squash.

PEGGY. Why?

DAVID. Because I'm thirsty.

PEGGY. I mean why not a whisky as usual?

DAVID. Because I've had too many whiskies, as usual, already.

PEGGY. You sounded to me just now as if you hadn't had enough.

DAVID. I was lurching about until I had a sandwich and three espressos on the way here. Also I boobed part of the interview and dried on Stanley Johnson's name. Stanley Johnson!

*The moment* DAVID *begins to talk about his work* PEGGY, *while pretending to listen, resumes her contemplation of the curtains.*

Mind you, it's their fault. Why on earth do they think it's right and proper for me, who am supposed to keep a quality of remoteness and dignity, to spout their idiotic plugs for them? Why? I should have refused it. Come to think of it—in the next series—I bloody well will. Are you listening to a word I'm saying?

PEGGY. (*Abstractedly.*) Yes. You're not going to do the new plug for them in the next series. And you're quite right too. (*Indicating the curtains.*) Are you sure these haven't been paid for?

DAVID. Quite sure.

PEGGY. I know we paid for *some* curtains.

DAVID. Yes. The ones in the television room—and as the room's never used it seems rather a waste of money.

PEGGY. You *are* in a bad way tonight. (*She sits on the arm of the sofa.*) Are you sure a little drink wouldn't help?

DAVID. (*Continuing to read but conscious of her proximity.*) Quite sure.

PEGGY. I'll watch tomorrow night, darling.

*Pause.* DAVID *stares up at her, but now with a different expression.*

(*Suspiciously.*) What's the matter?

DAVID. I like looking at you from this angle, that's all.

PEGGY. It's not exactly a new one, is it?

*He pulls her down rather violently on to the sofa. She clutches her hair.*

DAVID. Damn your hair.

PEGGY. Why this all of a sudden?

DAVID. It's not all of a sudden. I've loved you like this for eight years, and you know it.

*He kisses her violently.*

What's more it seems to get worse, not better.

PEGGY. (*Aggrieved.*) You mean better, not worse, don't you?

DAVID. (*Fiercely.*) No. I meant it the way I said it.

*He kisses her again.*

PEGGY. (*Murmuring, at length.*) Maybe I should always ask you for new curtains if it makes you as passionate as this.

DAVID. Listen to me, Margarethe Getznevitch.

PEGGY. Peggy Mann—

DAVID. Margarethe Getznevitch of Riga.

PEGGY. What's Riga got to do with anything? I was only five when we left—

DAVID. Later of 196B Banbury Road, North Oxford— (*Breaking off.*) What did your father pay for those two rooms? Two pounds a week?

PEGGY. Thirty-seven shillings. (*Reminiscently.*) Isn't it extraordinary? He took them in 'thirty-nine on a long rent, you see—and quite often I believe thought of giving them up for somewhere cheaper. Somewhere cheaper! Imagine. Of course, after the war they couldn't turn us out.

*She moves over on the sofa, reclining now, so that her head is on his stomach, facing the ceiling, and he is looking down at her. She is toying with a pattern of curtain material that she has had in her hand since* DAVID *first came in.*

Funny to think of it now. Father a Fellow of New College—

DAVID. And his daughter the wife of David Mann.

PEGGY. Yes. And very proud of it, too.

DAVID. Not proud of it enough to switch his programme on, but let that pass.

*Pause.*

Margarethe Getznevitch—do you remember my first present to you?
*She frowns in concentration, but plainly does not.*

It was a china cat.

PEGGY. Oh, yes, of course. It was lovely.

DAVID. It cost me exactly four and six and you cried.

PEGGY. Of course I cried. It was lovely.

DAVID. Since that time, eight years ago, have you ever asked me for anything and been refused?

*There is a pause while* PEGGY *tries to think of something with which to confute him. She fails.*

PEGGY. (*Murmuring.*) No—

DAVID. So do you honestly think the minute there's enough in the bank to pay for them, that you're *not* going to get your new curtains?

*After the moment it takes for this to sink in,* PEGGY *turns joyfully and kisses him fervently.*

PEGGY. Oh, darling. I *am* the most blessed of wives, aren't I?

DAVID. I think so. But then I also think I'm the most blessed of husbands.

*He kisses her in return, but in a way that shows clearly the form in which his conception of marital blessedness differs from hers.*

PEGGY. (*Emerging, at length, unruffled from his embrace.*) Now these are the patterns, and this is the one that I think you'd like the best—

DAVID. Because you like it the best?

*There is a ring at the front door.*

Expecting anyone? (*She shakes her head.*) Well, you'd better answer it anyway. There's a mad woman on the prowl for me. She may have slipped past William.

PEGGY. (*As she goes. Nervously.*) Do you think she'll scratch my eyes out?

DAVID. (*Calling.*) Why give her the chance? You scratch first. It's your right—

*Through the hall we see* PEGGY *carefully opening the door, and then swinging it wide to admit* FRANK.

FRANK. Hullo, Peggy. (*He kisses her on the cheek.*) David in?

DAVID. (*Calling.*) Come in, Frank.

FRANK. (*Coming into the sitting-room.*) The porter says (*in* WILLIAM'S *voice*) to tell you the lady went, but said it didn't matter as she knew where you'd be tomorrow.

DAVID. Of course she knows where I'll be tomorrow. It's her knowing where I am tonight that bothers me. Peggy, get Frank a drink—

FRANK. I'd better not.

DAVID. Why not? This is your time, isn't it?

FRANK. Well—in view of what I've got to say—

DAVID. (*Nodding.*) I see. Don't be a fool. Peggy—give him a stiff one—he'll need it.

FRANK. I'll help myself, then. Peggy, would you mind awfully—

*He indicates his wish to be alone with* DAVID.

PEGGY. (*Turning to go.*) That's all right. I'm used to that—

DAVID. No, Frank. Let her stay. Stay here, Peggy. Sit down and listen to this.
*She does so, obedient but bewildered.*
It may be good for you to hear it. Go ahead, Frank.

FRANK. Well, it seems you already know what I've got to say—

DAVID. But Peggy doesn't. Say it in front of her, will you?

FRANK. No, David, I won't, if you don't mind.

DAVID. Well, *I* will. Correct me where I go wrong. (*To* PEGGY.) Frank has just
been summoned by the Controller of Programmes because I was drunk
in front of the cameras tonight.

FRANK. (*Quietly.*) That isn't true, Peggy. just a couple of minor slips—

PEGGY. (*Now deeply scared.*) I know. He told me. But surely—

DAVID. (*Continuing remorselessly.*) So the Controller has given Frank the pleasant task of telling me that I don't get my new contract, in fact that I'm
out on my ear in television altogether and for ever, unless I sign the
pledge. Or am I out anyway?

FRANK. No. Nor do you have to sign the pledge.

DAVID. But I have to be a good boy from now on.

FRANK. (*Shrugging.*) That's roughly the message.

DAVID. (*In quotation marks.*) In television no one man is indispensable?

FRANK. He did coin that phrase.

DAVID. How ever did I guess? (*He holds* PEGGY'S *hand comfortingly.*) So get
me a big, stiff drink, Frank.

FRANK *obediently turns back to the drink table.*

PEGGY. (*In alarm.*) My God, no! Are you mad—

DAVID. (*Ignoring her, speaking to* FRANK.) I might as well enjoy my last.

FRANK, *pouring the drink, nods understandingly.*

PEGGY. (*To* FRANK.) But do you mean that there's a chance they mightn't sign
the new contract?

FRANK. No chance, Peggy. No chance at all. (*Handing* DAVID *his drink.*)
Here—

PEGGY. (*To* DAVID.) But why didn't you tell me there'd been this trouble?

DAVID. I tried to, my darling, but you didn't seem particularly interested.

PEGGY. (*To* FRANK.) Listen, Frank, if there's any danger of the new contract
not coming through, you can rely on me. My God, *can* you rely on me!

FRANK. (*After a quick, amused exchange of glances with* DAVID.) I know I can,
Peggy. Thank you very much.

PEGGY. From now on there's not going to be a bottle of alcohol in this flat—

DAVID. (*Coolly enjoying the joke with* FRANK.) That's going to go very well with
your friends. (*To* FRANK.) There's a lady called Caroline Wilkinson and
what *she* can do to a bottle of gin—

PEGGY. (*Suddenly pathetic.*) Don't make fun of me, David, please. (*Avoiding
him.*) It's at times like these I feel most my foreign blood. (*Near tears.*) I
don't understand you, David. You have a few whiskies—some times a
few too many—but so do nearly all your friends. You go off to your

show—all right, I don't watch enough—so perhaps I'm a bad wife—but when I do they seem fine to me, and make me happy I'm married to such a brilliant man. And then you come home, and have a couple more whiskies and there seems nothing wrong and I bother you about new curtains. And now I'm told suddenly you're in trouble—bad trouble—

FRANK. He's not in bad trouble, Peggy—

PEGGY. (*Now in tears.*) I don't just mean with the company. I mean real trouble—whatever it is that makes him drink—and take risks like being drunk in front of the cameras—that's real. And I'm his wife and I'm the last to hear about it. Shouldn't I have been the first?

DAVID. (*Holding her trembling arms as he kisses her gently on the brow.*) Yes, my darling, you should. (*Very gently.*) And, in fact, you were—

PEGGY. (*Furiously.*) When have you ever tried to tell me? When?

DAVID. Constantly—from over a year ago—from the moment I started my present job. And it's only now, when I'm in danger of losing it, that I seem, at last, to have got you to listen.

PEGGY. Why do you drink, then? Because of me?

DAVID. No. Because of me. Because of my job—

PEGGY. Then it is because of me, because I'm the one who made you take the job.

DAVID. I'm a free man, Peggy.

*There is a pause, while they stare at each other, he by his eyes showing the untruth of what he has just said, she her feminine recognition of the untruth.*

PEGGY. (*At length, quietly.*) Let go my arms, David. I won't hit you, or throw anything, and I want to blow my nose.

*He lets her arms go, and she uses her handkerchief.*

So you tried to tell me, and I didn't listen to you? Who else have you told who did?

DAVID. Who else would I want to tell but you?

PEGGY. I didn't ask who else you wanted to tell. I asked who else you told.

DAVID. (*At length.*) No one.

PEGGY. I have an answer to that, brief and sharp, but. I won't use it in front of Frank. Good night, Frank. I expect you boys have things to talk about. Sorry about the scene. That's the last drink now. Frank, that's his last drink tonight.

FRANK. Yes, Peggy. Good night.

PEGGY *goes into the bedroom.*

DAVID. (*Gleefully.*) I broke through. Frank, I really broke through, didn't I?

FRANK. Leave me out of your domestic troubles—

DAVID. You don't leave me out of yours, so why should I leave you out of mine? How is Muriel, by the way?

FRANK. (*With a shudder.*) Don't let's go into that.

DAVID. No. We won't. (*Pointing to the bedroom door, still in glee.*) But what about *that*? Didn't you hear her say it was me—her brilliant husband—that she loved?

*Automatically he is pouring himself another drink.* FRANK'S *hand stops him.*

FRANK. Ah—ah, yes, I heard her *say* it.

DAVID. I don't like that reading. And didn't you get that jealousy? *Jealousy!* From *Peggy!* 'Who else have you told?'

FRANK. (*Quietly.*) Who else *have* you told?

*Pause.*

DAVID. You just heard me say: 'no one'.

FRANK. Yes. I just heard you *say* it.

DAVID. I don't like that reading either.

FRANK. I'm sorry, but that's the way I'm reading them tonight. I'm having another drink. I know it's cruelty, but you'll have to get used to it. (*At the drink tray, his back to* DAVID.) Which one of them *do* you really love?

*Pause.*

DAVID. I suppose if you were a stone lighter I'd ask you to come outside—

FRANK. It would be less exhausting for both of us just to answer the question.

DAVID. (*Pointing to the bedroom door.*) That one, of course.

FRANK. Isn't 'of course' redundant?

DAVID. Yes, you clever producer. (*Pointing again.*) That one. Better? (FRANK *nods.*) Anyway, she's my wife and the other one's got a husband, or do you think that's waste footage, too?

FRANK. Not necessarily. It depends how wide the audience is, and the time of transmission. Anyway there aren't any babies to complicate the issue—

DAVID. I wish there were.

FRANK. Since the first went wrong, she can't—?

DAVID. No. But Frank, there *is* no issue to complicate.

FRANK. No?

DAVID. No. Your first shock question was badly framed. I'm the expert on this, and I know. '*Which* one' is based on a huge false assumption—that a man can't love two women equally at the same time.

FRANK. Equally, but not in the same way.

DAVID. Brilliant. You should do my job.

FRANK. I may have to.

DAVID. You'd be awful.

FRANK. I expect so.

DAVID. And you haven't got a dimple—

FRANK. I could try surgery. You're to let up on Sir Stanley Thingummy tomorrow night—

DAVID. (*In the act of pouring himself an orange squash.*) What did you say?

FRANK. Controller's orders. Minister of the Crown. Not a volunteer—national interest—blah, blah, blah—

DAVID. (*After a pause, bitterly.*) I tell you what, Frank. Just for tomorrow night let's alter our slogan a little. The aim of B.T.V. is to give you the half-truth of the heart. (*Getting angry.*) And if the Controller's going to make this a precedent let's keep it in for the next series.

FRANK. If there is a next series.

DAVID. There'll be a next series.

FRANK *nods, finishes his drink, touches* DAVID *on the shoulder and goes to the door.*

FRANK. Eight-thirty a.m. tomorrow. Here's his address.

DAVID. (*Shuddering.*) Eight-thirty? Why eight-thirty?

FRANK. He's got a Cabinet Meeting at ten.

DAVID. (*Looking at the address, and moaning.*) And Ruislip! Why Ruislip?

FRANK. Perhaps he can't afford Belgravia. Don't be late.

DAVID. Can you see her letting me be late now? She'll be prodding me awake at six—

FRANK. Just as a good wife should. Good night, David.

DAVID. Good night.

FRANK *goes.* DAVID *stares nervously at the bedroom door for a moment, and then automatically turns for a drink. He checks himself then walks into the bedroom.*


*THE BEDROOM.* PEGGY *is sitting up in bed, her large eyes staring at* DAVID *as he moves about the room, sometimes invisible, undressing.*

PEGGY. So you think I'm a terrible wife!

DAVID. No.

PEGGY. You tell me your troubles and I won't listen to them.

DAVID. Not often, but that doesn't make you a terrible wife.

PEGGY. From now on I'm going to listen to every word. Every *word*—

DAVID. Good. I must try and make my conversation interesting.

PEGGY. And I'm going to watch you like a hawk. I'm not going to let you out of my sight for a minute.

DAVID. Even better.

*Half-undressed, he falls across the bed and kisses her.*

PEGGY. (*At length.*) This is all I mean to you, isn't it?

DAVID. (*Kissing her.*) No, not all. But rather a lovely high percentage of all—

*With a disengaged foot he kicks the door so that it swings slowly closed, and we are left in darkness.*


*OUTSIDE SIR STANLEY'S HOUSE. DAY. It is a very unpretentious suburban villa.*

*Almost before we see her, we can hear the sound of* JESSIE'S *car as it chugs and roars unwillingly up the street, and comes to a halt outside the house. She gets out, and looks, in surprise, at* DAVID'S *Bentley. The chauffeur is standing beside it. Two or three newspaper photographers are lurking around. Behind them is the* LADY *of the night before, in another, but equally unsuitable, hat.*

*Facing us now, she is about sixty, of a tough, weather-beaten appearance.*
*She stares at* JESSIE *impassively.*

JESSIE. (*In unbelief.*) Mr. Mann here *already?*

CHAUFFEUR. Been here quarter of an hour, miss.

JESSIE. (*Looking at another car, plainly* FRANK'S.) Oh, my gosh! Then I'm the last.

*She hurries up the steps to the front door and rings the bell. The door is instantly*
*opened by a mild-mannered, rather dowdy, middle-aged woman, whom*
JESSIE, *unused to Cabinet Minister's entourages, takes to be a minion of some*
*kind.*

(*Briskly.*) I have an appointment to see the Minister—

LADY JOHNSON. Oh, yes. You're another of the telly crowd, aren't you? Come
in, dear.

JESSIE *does so.* LADY JOHNSON *picks up a cat and strokes it.*


## HALL. SIR STANLEY'S HOUSE.

LADY JOHNSON. (*To the cat.*) No, Charles. You mustn't go out. (*To* JESSIE.) My
husband's just finishing his breakfast. He won't be a minute. The others
are in here—

JESSIE, *startled, finds herself ushered across the hall towards the sitting-room door.*
(*Whispering.*) And if you *could* get that wonderful Mr. Mann to sign this
(*she hands her an autograph book*) I'd be so grateful. Perhaps with a little
message—

JESSIE. I'm sure if you asked him yourself, Lady Johnson—

LADY JOHNSON. Oh, I'd never dare.

*An angry voice* (SIR STANLEY'S) *can be heard coming from a room across the hall.*

SIR STANLEY. (*Off.*) Mabel! Has my P.P.S. come yet?

LADY JOHNSON. (*Calling back.*) No, dear, not yet—

SIR STANLEY. Well, come here. I want you.

LADY JOHNSON. Yes, dear. (*To the cat, which she lets on to the floor.*) Be a good
boy, now, Charles—

SIR STANLEY. (*Again off.*) Mabel!

LADY JOHNSON. Coming, dear.

*She hurries off, across the hall, as* JESSIE, *who has lingered in the door taking in*
*the surroundings, joins the others in the sitting-room.*


## SIR STANLEY'S SITTING-ROOM. *It is furnished entirely in keeping with*
*the rest of the house. One feels that the home of* DAVID'S *chauffeur would have*
*far more pretensions to taste and comfort.*

*As* JESSIE *comes in,* DAVID, *looking hung-over and unhappy, is poring over the typescript we had seen him studying the night before. His hand, as he holds it, is not very steady.*

FRANK. Morning, Jessie.

JESSIE. Morning, Frank. Good morning, Mr. Mann.

DAVID, *without taking his eyes from the typescript, raises his hand but says nothing.*

Portrait of an inquisitor who hasn't done his homework.

P.P.S. *arrives at front door.*

FRANK. (*To* JESSIE.) What do you make of this set-up?

LADY JOHNSON. (*Off.*) Sir Stanley's waiting for you.

SIR STANLEY. (*Off.*) Oh, there you are . . .

JESSIE. Rather impressive. (*In quotation marks.*) Man of the people, lives as he always has, no side about our new Minister of Labour. Power may corrupt others. It's not going to corrupt our Stanley.

FRANK. Is it on the level?

JESSIE. You say first.

FRANK. I'd say it's a front. A flat in Westminster would suit him better, and he could afford it. This looks better in the papers. Now you.

JESSIE. I'd say it's on the level. A man who'd stick *that* on the wall must be on the level. (*She indicates a reproduction of a Victorian Highland painting.*) What do you say, Mr. Mann?

DAVID. I say what I'd give for just one large brandy!

FRANK *and* JESSIE *both look at him.*

Then I might make some sense of this man—

*The loud, impressive (neither altogether plebeian nor altogether 'educated') voice of* SIR STANLEY *can be heard just outside the door, and, as he opens it, we see that he is addressing a very flustered and nervous young man, holding a briefcase in one hand and an official Ministry box in the other. In contrast to* SIR STANLEY *he is immaculately dressed in short black coat and striped trousers.*

SIR STANLEY. All right, young man. I'll forgive you this once. Perhaps, if I'm in a good mood, even twice. But the third time—I'm telling you this straight, lad—you're out and out for good. (*He takes the Ministry box from him.*) Unpunctuality is just one thing I won't stand.

P.P.S. I'm most terribly sorry, Sir Stanley—but the traffic—

*The closing door cuts off his excuses as* SIR STANLEY *comes into the sitting-room. His appearance and manner are as impressive and blunt as his voice.*

SIR STANLEY. Forgive me, ladies and gentlemen. I'm sorry to have called you here at this ungodly time, but it was all I could manage today. Cabinet meeting this morning, and debate on the new wages policy this afternoon.

*He has made his way to a desk, while speaking, and now sits at it, opening the Ministry box with a key from his watch chain.*

FRANK. (*Nervously,*) It's a great privilege to meet you at any time, Sir Stanley. And may I say, on behalf of B.T.V., how very grateful we all are—

SIR STANLEY *has taken out a document and is studying it.*

SIR STANLEY. Yes. Forgive me, would you, if I look at this? It might be important. Sit down, won't you all?

*He continues to read the document.* DAVID *has his head in his hands.* FRANK *and* JESSIE *look across at him anxiously.* SIR STANLEY *finishes reading the document, puts it back in the box and locks it. Then he looks up amiably.*
Right, ladies and gentlemen. Begin.

FRANK. (*Getting up.*) I'd better introduce myself, sir. I'm Frank Godsell, the producer of 'Heart to Heart'. This lady, Mrs. Weston, is my production secretary, and this gentleman (*indicating* DAVID) is Mr. David Mann.

SIR STANLEY. Ah. The great *man* himself. (FRANK *and* JESSIE *laugh politely.* DAVID *manages a polite smile.*) I've no doubt that's a pun that's been used before.

FRANK. I don't remember it, Sir Stanley. (DAVID *gives him just a quick flash of a glance,* JESSIE *the faintest of smiles, and both are observed by* SIR STANLEY.) Now, before Mr. Mann asks his questions—I'll tell you—

SIR STANLEY. If you're going to tell me what the programme is about you don't need. I hear enough about it from my wife. She watches it every night— mind you I think she's in love with our young friend here— (*Again all smile except* DAVID.) and there's nothing I don't know about the truth, the real truth, the truth of the heart, thank you very much. It's unscripted, unrehearsed, unprepared—what do you call this meeting, by the way?— Well, let that pass—and goes out live. The only show of its kind that does. So just tell me what time I'm to be at the studio tonight, and then leave the rest to my inquisitor here.

FRANK. The show goes on at 9.15 and the Controller of Programmes would be glad if you could have a drink with him at the studio half an hour before the broadcast.

SIR STANLEY. I'd be glad to. Now, Mr. Mann. Ask your questions.

DAVID. I don't really think I need waste your time, Sir Stanley.

SIR STANLEY. There must be some questions—

DAVID. I don't think so, sir. (*Patting the typescript.*) I have everything here. It's all perfectly plain and straightforward.

*Pause.*

SIR STANLEY. (*To* FRANK.) Clever. He's trying to give me stagefright. Thinks I'll arrive in front of the cameras a nervous wreck tonight, wondering just *what* questions he's going to ask me.

DAVID. I shall ask you only questions about your background, your early struggles, and your career to date. They may only be a little dull, and, who knows, perhaps your wife will cease to love me.

*Pause.* SIR STANLEY *is plainly intrigued, puzzled and, to a very percipient observer, perhaps even a shade apprehensive.*

SIR STANLEY. Well—we don't want it *too* dull, you know. I mean you'll give them a few of the 'downs' with the 'ups', I take it?

FRANK. Have there been any 'downs', Sir Stanley?

SIR STANLEY. Have there been any 'downs'? A lot of my life has been one long down, seems to me. What about the Durham by-election which I lost by fifty votes and should have won by five thousand? What about having the Whip taken from me in 'fifty-five because I wouldn't play ball over the wage freeze? What about that Appleton Commission— (*To* DAVID, *with a quick turn of the head.*) You'll ask some questions about that, I take it?

DAVID. Yes, sir. I had planned one or two—

SIR STANLEY. (*Emphatically.*) And I shall be very glad to answer them. Very glad, indeed.

FRANK. Appleton Commission?

SIR STANLEY. In 'fifty-eight. That time one of our dear friends in the Shadow Cabinet said the Board of Trade had given an engineering concession to a certain Brazilian gentleman called Lopez in return for expense accounts, hotel bills, vi—vi—how do you pronounce it?—vicuna coats.

FRANK. Oh, yes, I remember. About three years ago. But were you involved in that, sir?

SIR STANLEY. (*With impressive indignation.*) *Involved in* it? I was the villain in chief,

DAVID. That's not quite true, sir, is it? It was your Minister who was the main subject of investigation—

SIR STANLEY. Yes, but if they'd found against poor old Roger, do you think they'd have let his Parliamentary Secretary go? Not on your life. The talk around the Commons' smoking-room then, let me tell you, was that *I* was the real culprit, because Roger would always do anything I told him, anyway. (*Explosively.*) What did they think I was? His lover boy, or something? (*To* JESSIE.) Excuse me, Mrs. —errhm. (JESSIE, *busy taking notes, bows and smiles graciously.*) Well, I mean to say, old Roger who never let me see one important paper— (*Suddenly breaking off.*) What's that cat doing here?

LADY JOHNSON'S *cat has strolled into the room through the window and has jumped up on to the desk.*

Get it out of here, do you mind? Can't bear touching the things myself.

FRANK *and* JESSIE *between them capture Charles and shove him back through the door.*

(*Meanwhile.*) But Lady Johnson's mad about them. If she had her way, I'm telling you, we'd have cats in this house the way other people have mice.

FRANK *and* JESSIE *laugh,* FRANK *with genuine amusement,* JESSIE. *loudly.* DAVID *again refrains but now with a slight frown.*

(*To* JESSIE.) You liked that one, Mrs.—errhm? Rather enjoyed it myself. That's one of my faults, they say in the House. I enjoy my own jokes too much.

*During the disturbance about the cat,* SIR STANLEY *has got up, gathering briefcase and Ministry box. He extends a hand to* DAVID.

Well, Mr. Mann, go easy with me tonight. You can see for yourself I'm fair game for a bright young intellectual like you. Anti-Establishment on principle, I'd say, aren't you?

DAVID. Not on principle. Sometimes on conviction.

SIR STANLEY. Well, you can make mincemeat of me in front of ten million people tonight I don't doubt—

FRANK. Fifteen million—

SIR STANLEY. (*Pleased.*) Is that the estimate? You don't say. (*To* DAVID.) Now, if the P.M. had wanted a worthy antagonist for you, he'd have put up one of our bright boys, and we've plenty of them. No. In choosing me he knew what he was doing. (*As an aside to* FRANK *and* JESSIE.) He usually does, mind. (*Back to* DAVID.) He doesn't care if his new Cabinet Minister's made a bit of an ass of. I've been making a bit of an ass of myself, anyway, all my life. But he knows too that what I've got churning about here (*he touches his heart*), not here (*he touches his head*), but here (*he touches his heart again*), about the good of our country and the future of our people is likely to make a bigger impression on fifteen million viewers than any dozen of his bright boys with their brilliant intellectuality. So, tonight, lead me in a bit—perhaps at the end—about those ideas, would you?

DAVID. Of course, Sir Stanley. It would be easier, though, if I had some inkling of what those ideas are. (*Patting the typescript.*) This is all factual. Perhaps you've written some articles—

SIR STANLEY. Articles? Me? I can hardly write one word after another, and that's a fact. No, I tell you what. Did you hear my speech at the Mansion House last Thursday?

DAVID. No, I'm afraid not.

SIR STANLEY. Well, it was broadcast, televised, all that. There's bound to be a recording—

DAVID. Frank? (*Getting a nod from* FRANK.) Thank you, Sir Stanley. I'll have it run.

SIR STANLEY. Good. Then if there's anything else you want to know about me after that, come to see me at the Ministry this afternoon. Make the appointment with my P.P.S. (*Opening the door.*) Good-bye. Mustn't be late for my first Cabinet meeting. That'd never do.


*HALL. SIR STANLEY'S HOUSE.* SIR STANLEY *is joined by his P.P.S., to whom he hands his Ministry box.*


P.P.S. There are some press photographers outside, Sir Stanley. They want a shot of you getting into the car.

SIR STANLEY. Oh. (*Calling.*) Mabel!

LADY JOHNSON. (*Emerging, holding the cat.*) Yes, dear?

SIR STANLEY. Come and get your picture in the papers.

LADY JOHNSON. Oh, no. I'm not dressed properly, I've been washing up—

SIR STANLEY. Doesn't matter. (*To the others.*) Don't mind if we go first? If they get you in the picture your fifteen million viewers will be thinking to-night's all a put-up job. (*To* LADY JOHNSON, *who is frantically arranging her hair, impeded in this by the cat, still obstinately perched on her shoulder.*) Come on, Mabel. Don't try and make yourself glamorous, or they'll think it's a mistress I've got, not a wife. And put that damn cat down.

LADY JOHNSON. (*Obediently doing so.*) Yes, dear—

SIR STANLEY. No, on second thoughts, keep it. Cats look good in photographs. Only keep the damn thing away from me.

*The* P.P.S. *has opened the front door and* SIR STANLEY *and* LADY JOHNSON *go out. Through the open door we see the photographers and a very small crowd who have been attracted by them to the scene. Amongst them is the* LADY *with the unsuitable hat. The cameras click away,* SIR STANLEY *waving jovially.*

*The television party are lingering in the hall out of camera range.*

DAVID. (*In an agonized voice.*) Coffee! I need coffee.

JESSIE. (*Peeping through the door.*) There's a place across the street.

DAVID. Does it look the sort of place that would have Espresso?

JESSIE. Frankly, no. But it's called Espresso Continentale—

DAVID. I'm in no mood for your humour this morning, Mrs. Weston.

JESSIE. (*At window.*) All right. He's into his car. Coast's clear.

*They go to door, meeting* LADY JOHNSON *as she comes back.*

FRANK. Good-bye, Lady Johnson.

LADY JOHNSON. Good-bye. (*To* JESSIE.) Did you—? (*She timidly indicates* DAVID.)

JESSIE. Oh, no. I forgot. (*She takes an autograph book from her bag.*) And I nearly stole your autograph book. (*She hands it to her.*) How awful!

LADY JOHNSON. It wouldn't have mattered much. It's got no one really interesting in it. Just the Prime Minister and Lord Boothby. (*Handing the book back to* JESSIE.) Do it for me, would you, dear?

JESSIE. (*To* DAVID.) Lady Johnson would like you to sign her book, Mr. Mann.

LADY JOHNSON. (*Murmuring.*) With a little message—

JESSIE. (*En clair.*) With a little message.

DAVID. How nice. (*To* JESSIE *and* FRANK.) Go across and order me a treble Espresso, would you? (JESSIE *moves away. To* LADY JOHNSON.) What would you like me to say?

LADY JOHNSON. (*Ecstatic.*) Anything that comes into your head, Mr. Mann.

DAVID. (*With a brave smile.*) My head, this morning, is not a receptacle in which I place the greatest trust. However, we'll see—


*OUTSIDE SIR STANLEY'S HOUSE. As* JESSIE *and* FRANK *come out and cross the street to the Espresso Continentale the crowd and the photographers have dispersed. Only the middle-aged* LADY *with the unsuitable hat remains. She watches* JESSIE *and* FRANK *as they go past, but doesn't move. She resumes her fixed stare at the Johnsons' front door.*

*From her eyeline we see* DAVID *finishing his chore, and handing the autograph book back to* LADY JOHNSON *with a polite bow. Then he comes down the steps into the street, walks past the middle-aged* LADY, *crosses the street and goes into the Espresso Continentale.*

*ESPRESSO CONTINENTALE CAFÉ. 'Contemporary' when it opened a few years ago, definitely rather sleazy now. It is partitioned into booths. At this hour it is practically deserted.*

JESSIE *and* FRANK *are sitting in a booth, and have just finished ordering as* DAVID *comes up, and slides exhausted on to the bench beside* FRANK.

JESSIE. What immortal message did you find?

DAVID. 'To Lady Johnson, who also loves the truth.'

JESSIE. It should have been: 'To Lady Johnson, who also loves me.'

DAVID. (*Glancing at her malevolently.*) I can't bear you this morning, Mrs. Weston.

JESSIE. I'm not obsessed by your charms either, Mr. Mann.

*The middle-aged* LADY *with the unsuitable hat comes into the café, and finds herself a seat in a booth opposite the group, but out of sight of them.*

*During the next few lines the camera will apparently concentrate on the group in the foreground, but will show in sharp focus a waitress leaving the group's table and going up to the* LADY *for her order. This she will give first (unheard) and then, indicating* DAVID, *hand the* WAITRESS *an envelope to give to him.*

*The* WAITRESS *will reluctantly take it across at the indicated moment. Meanwhile, at the group's table there has been a pause while they sip their coffee.*

FRANK. (*To* DAVID.) Well?

DAVID. (*Surlily.*) Well, what?

FRANK. How do we go? (*Answering himself,* DAVID *is too busy with his coffee.*) I suppose man of the people is the line. Plain, honest Stan—

JESSIE. Not so honest he doesn't steal from James Thurber.

DAVID. (*Appreciatively.*) You noticed that? (*Changing his tone.*) Then why did you laugh like a ruddy hyena?

JESSIE. Because it's funny. It was funny when Thurber wrote it.

FRANK. All right. I'm the ill-read one. Which crack was that?

DAVID. 'We have cats the way other people have mice.' Mrs. Creeper-Weston, here, split a gut.

JESSIE. When the victim laughs I laugh. That's my policy.

DAVID. (*Finishing his coffee.*) No, Frank. I agree, we've nothing to go on except the front he gave us, and possibly the 'coming man of the Party' angle, and as it's to be an evening of sweetness and light, by order, I don't see there's much else—

*The* WAITRESS *has appeared with the envelope.*

WAITRESS. Lady over there asked me to give you this.

DAVID *takes it, and looks in the direction of the waitress's pointing finger. All* DAVID *can see is the* LADY'S *hand as it reaches for a tea-cup, with the little finger curled.*

DAVID. So kind. Would you thank the lady and say—

MISS KNOTT. (*Off, from the booth. A gruff, not unattractive voice.*) Read it, Mr. Mann. It'll interest you.

DAVID *looks at the others and shrugs his shoulders.*

DAVID. (*Calling, politely.*) Of course I'm going to read it, madam. I'm going to read it this very minute—

*He begins slowly to open the envelope, talking meanwhile.*

Mind you, he's an ambitious character—that stands out a mile—and the 'can't write one word after another' is guff—he got an excellent degree at Liverpool—history and economics, I think.

*He takes out of the envelope a document of a curious shape, the size, shape and stiffness of a large postcard.*

*Continuing for a moment he doesn't look at it.* JESSIE *quietly takes it out of his hand as he continues to speak.*

Well, I presume Mrs. Weston will pay as usual, and chalk up quadruple the amount as expenses, so I'll see you two at—

JESSIE. (*In a very sharp voice.*) Sit down a minute. (DAVID *obediently does so.*) You'd better read this.

*She hands the document to him.*

DAVID. (*Fumbling for his spectacles, with a sigh.*) Need I?

JESSIE. It's addressed to you.

DAVID *has already begun to read. He frowns, at first puzzled, then startled. In the distance, we can see* MISS KNOTT'S *hand stirring tea.* DAVID *gazes at* JESSIE *wide-eyed.*

DAVID. This is a very bad joke, isn't it?

JESSIE. (*Perking her thumb.*) Why don't you ask her?

DAVID. Wait a moment. Wait a moment. If this isn't a joke I don't want to get involved in some cheap blackmailing racket. I'd better tear it up.

JESSIE. Then tear it up.

DAVID. (*Looking at the document again.*) The date fits, but of course that would be easy—

FRANK. Would either of you mind letting me know—

JESSIE. If Mr. Mann is going to tear it up, it's far better we shouldn't either of us let you know.

*Pause.*

DAVID. (*Quietly.*) This is a photostat copy of a hotel bill, Frank—the Mirabeau at Cannes—it's for two hundred and fifty-seven thousand eight hundred and fifty-two francs—before new francs, remember, they haven't slipped up there. At the top is written 'Sir Johnson'—clever touch that—'and Lady Johnson'. There is a receipt stamp—French-style handwriting—they've taken real trouble—

FRANK. (*Irritated and worried.*) What do you mean *they*? And why shouldn't the Johnsons have a holiday in the South of France if they want to?

DAVID. (*Ignoring him.*) Across the bill is a large bold signature. (*He slips it along the table to him.*) How do you make it out?

FRANK. (*Deciphering, with difficulty.*) Manuele Lopez.

DAVID. That's how I made it out too.

*Pause.*

FRANK. That was the chap who—

DAVID. Yes.

FRANK. Where is he now?

DAVID. In Brazil, I suppose. He did a bunk before the balloon went up—

FRANK. Then there *were* some grounds—

DAVID. Grounds? Of course there were grounds. He'd certainly *tried* to bribe somebody at the Board of Trade. The Appleton Commission proved that.

JESSIE, *listening, is also watching the hand of the unseen* LADY, *as it primly stirs her tea.*

FRANK. Was there ever anything at all on Sir Stanley?

DAVID. Nothing at all. He came out of the hearings better than anyone. Loyally covering up for his chief. In fact tonight when dealing with the Lopez case, I'd planned to ask him—

*He breaks off sharply, and looks down in a misery of doubt at the document in his hand. For one moment he really seems to be about to tear it up. Then he smiles suddenly, evidently relieved.*

Good. I've got them. They've made an idiotic mistake. Look, Frank. (*He points to an item on the bill.*) Coiffeur, Dames. Twenty-five thousand seven hundred francs. Twenty pounds odd in nine days on her hair—that one? (*He points across the street, and then gets up.*) All right. Wait for me. This might be a job for the police.

*The camera follows him as he walks across the café to the other booth.*

*The* LADY (MISS KNOTT) *sitting placidly drinking her tea, looks up at* DAVID *with a benign smile as he approaches.*

MISS KNOTT. Ah, Mr. Mann. Do sit down.

DAVID. (*Grimly.*) I don't think so.

MISS KNOTT. Just as you please. But you'll want to know my name, won't you?

DAVID. Not particularly, except possibly to give to the police—

MISS KNOTT. It's Knott—Miss Knott. I live at Hightower Mansions, Leinster Gardens, West Kensington, and I'm in the telephone book. But if Sir Stanley wants to prosecute me, he knows perfectly well where to find me. I haven't changed my address in thirteen years, and for ten of them I was his secretary.

DAVID. (*After a pause.*) Can you prove that?

MISS KNOTT. (*Opening her bag and taking out a letter.*) I have his letter of dismissal—

DAVID. Photostatted?

MISS KNOTT. (*Mildly.*) Oh, no—there was no point in Photostatting this.
*She hands him a letter.*

DAVID. You mean you can't blackmail him on it?

MISS KNOTT. (*Pouring herself some more tea.*) Well, I hadn't thought. I suppose I could, really—as contributory evidence, anyway. (*Watching* DAVID
*as he reads.*) You'll notice the sum he offered me to 'tide me over'—doesn't
he say?—was rather larger than the sum people usually offer their secre-
taries when they sack them. It eases my conscience just a weeny bit to
be able to tell you I sent back the cheque.

DAVID *finishes reading the letter and hands it back to her.*

DAVID. Very well, I'll accept that someone called Miss Knott was his secretary. How do I know—?

MISS KNOTT. (*Anticipating him by pulling a passport from her bag and handing
it to him.*) Not a very flattering photograph, I'm afraid. I had quite the
wrong hat on that day—

DAVID. (*Looks at it and hands it back to her.*) Very well, Miss Knott. Where is
the original of this? (*He taps the photostat bill.*)

MISS KNOTT. In a safe deposit box at my bank.

DAVID. (*Roughly.*) So you admit at least that you stole a document belonging
to your ex-employer-

MISS KNOTT. Oh, no. I don't admit that. I'm a naughty girl in a hundred ways,
but I've never stolen anything in my life. I found it. And only two months
ago.

DAVID. Where?

MISS KNOTT. In a little secret pocket in my suitcase where I never keep anything. I must have put it in there that night—you see I had to think of
the Customs, coming home.

DAVID. Your story is that you were in Cannes with them?

MISS KNOTT. Oh, yes. I always went on those sort of jaunts with them. Sir
Stanley didn't ever want any personal contact with Mr. Lopez, so I was
always used as a sort of glorified messenger girl, running between Mr.
Lopez's yacht and Sir Stanley, usually carrying large dollops of cash, and
sometimes even at night, if Sir Stanley had had a bad time at the Casino. (*Lowering her voice.*) And you know those terrible rough young men
who lounge up and down the Croisette at night, giving the girls those
impertinent stares. Well, sometimes I thought, when one of them was
staring particularly hard at me—isn't it a mercy it's just me he's looking
at, and doesn't know what's in my bag. Once, in Capri—

DAVID. (*Interrupting the flow and tapping the photostat.*) I'm afraid I still think
that this is a forgery. In fact I know it is.

MISS KNOTT. Really? How?

DAVID. You were employed by Sir Ernest for ten years, so you must have
known his wife well—

MISS KNOTT. Oh, yes. Very well. We used to get on like a house on fire.

DAVID. Then how did you or your associates come to make such a ridiculous mistake as to invent this charge, here? (*His finger points.*) Coiffeur, Dames—twenty-five thousand seven hundred.

MISS KNOTT. (*Squinting at the figure.*) But that was rather cheap for her—

DAVID. For Lady Johnson?

MISS KNOTT. (*Laughing.*) Oh. Oh, I see. What a stupid error. I hadn't even noticed it. Lady Johnson. That must have been that charming young cashier leaping to conclusions. But it's all right, Mr. Mann. All that side of it was always perfectly above board. She *always* registered under her own name, and they *always* took separate rooms, usually with a sitting-room between— (*Pointing to the top of the bill.*) You see, they did here.

*Pause.*

DAVID. What was her own name?

MISS KNOTT. Clay. Miss Enid Clay. Rabbity girl, with teeth coming out like this. (*She protrudes her teeth.*) She couldn't act, either.

DAVID. Where is she now?

MISS KNOTT. Oh, when the trouble blew up he got rid of her. I believe she went off to Australia and got married—

DAVID. It's rather convenient for you, isn't it, that all material witnesses seem to have disappeared—Lopez—Clay—

MISS KNOTT. (*Cheerfully.*) Well, *I'm* still here, aren't I?

DAVID. I don't think you're a very reliable witness, Miss Knott. Your testimony wouldn't stand a chance in a court of law—

MISS KNOTT. (*Powdering her nose.*) Oh, I know it wouldn't. Dismissed secretary, turning on her ex-boss. Says nothing for three years, and then turns up with a photostat copy of a bill that isn't her property. Almost certainly jealous. Probably was in love with him—

DAVID. Were you?

MISS KNOTT. Oh, yes, I suppose so.

DAVID. And jealous of this Enid Clay—if she existed?

MISS KNOTT. She existed all right. But I wasn't jealous of her. You couldn't be. She was such a harmless little creature. I just felt awfully sorry for her—tied up to that dreadful man—

DAVID. You thought he was a dreadful man and you say you were in love with him? How do these two statements fit?

MISS KNOTT. Like a glove, I should have thought. Really, what a silly question! What on earth has what you think of a man got to do with what you feel for him?

DAVID, *momentarily nonplussed, is silent. He sees* JESSIE'S *face peering at him round the partition of her booth. She gives him an inquiring look. All he can do is to give her a helpless shrug in return.*

DAVID. Why did you come to me?

MISS KNOTT. I don't want him to go to gaol, or anything. You see, I'm really quite a patriotic woman, you know. When I left him it didn't look as if he was going to get anywhere, now he's in the Cabinet, and people are even saying he's the next but one Prime Minister. (*Brightly.*) Well, we can't have that, can we, Mr. Mann? You've got ideals too—haven't you?

DAVID. (*Remorselessly.*) I want to know why you had this bill photostatted if it wasn't for blackmail?

MISS KNOTT. Oh, but it *was* for blackmail. I sent it to him through the post, registered mail, with a letter.

DAVID. (*Getting up.*) Thank you. I don't think we need talk any more—

MISS KNOTT. (*Holding him by raising her voice.*) But the blackmail wasn't for money, Mr. Mann.

DAVID. What was it for, then? For love?

MISS KNOTT. How unkind. No. For something very simple, and quite easy for him to have done. Funny you haven't guessed it.

DAVID. What?

MISS KNOTT. *Not* to accept his post in the Cabinet.

*Pause.*

DAVID. Ah!

MISS KNOTT. But why is *that so* hard to believe, Mr. Mann? Isn't it exactly what you'd have done in my place?

DAVID. In your place I wouldn't have lied to the Commission—

MISS KNOTT. Oh, I expect you would. We all know you're a man of conscience, but most of us have to compromise a bit from time to time. The only question is—how much do we compromise? With Sir Stanley as a Right Honourable I, personally, have reached my limit. I shall be looking in tonight. (*Playfully prodding him.*) Big sister will be watching you, Mr. Mann. (*Changing her tone to one of sincere entreaty.*) Don't let me down, please. Not just me—us—the whole country. Wham! Bam! The Right Honourable out for the count. That's what I expect to see. That's what I'm sure I will see.

*She walks away, and has nearly got to the street when* DAVID *suddenly realizes he is still holding the photostat, and catches* MISS KNOTT *up just as she gets to the café door.*

DAVID. (*Handing* MISS KNOTT *the photostat.*) You'd better take this.

MISS KNOTT. (*Brushing it airily aside.*) Oh, no. Keep it. I've got plenty more. There's my bus. I must run. Would you give this to the waitress?

*She darts through the door,* DAVID *looking after her, his face expressionless.*


PROJECTION ROOM. *Over the heads of* DAVID *and a* NEWSREEL EDITOR *we find ourselves looking at an Editola screen. Then when* SIR STANLEY *begins his speech the newsreel will entirely fill our screen, so that the impression will be of immediacy and actuality. This impression will be abruptly terminated whenever the* NEWSREEL EDITOR *presses his Editola controls to find another passage, when of course the sonorous voice will become a high-pitched scream and the well-timed gestures will be speeded up to seem like something out of*

*Mack Sennett. These moments will be brief. In the main we shall be seeing and hearing* SIR STANLEY *as he was seen and heard by five hundred guests at a Mansion House dinner.*

EDITOR. O.K. Run it.

DAVID. They do themselves well, don't they?

TOASTMASTER. My Lord Mayor, Your Grace, Your Excellencies, My Lords, ladies and gentlemen. Pray silence for the Right Honourable Sir Stanley Johnson, K.B.E., the Minister of Labour.

SIR STANLEY *gets to his feet to a strong round of applause. One feels he is a popular figure, and there is an anticipatory note in the applause that makes one feel that he is known as a good after-dinner speaker. He is in white tie and tails, with the ribbon and star of a K.B.E.*

SIR STANLEY. My Lord Mayor, Your Grace, Your Excellencies, My Lords, ladies and gentlemen. (*Impressively.*) It has fallen to my lot this year to respond to the toast of Her Majesty's Government. (*After the correctly timed pause.*) That's a silly phrase, isn't it, 'fallen to my lot'? In politics we all know what that means (*looking down the table*), and none better, I dare say, than the Leader of Her Majesty's Opposition down there. It means that someone higher up has said: 'You do it this year, Stan.' (*Laughter.*) 'You're the new boy.' (*Another laugh.*) 'We know you'll do it absolutely splendidly (*imitation of educated accent*) —absolutely spiffing, we're sure— (*reverting to his normal voice*) but if you make the muck-up we expect you to, then we'll ruddy well murder you.'

*There is a very big laugh at this, evidently expected by* SIR STANLEY, *who takes the opportunity of a quick glance at his notes.*

DAVID. How long was the speech?

EDITOR. Forty minutes.

DAVID. A lot more funny stuff?

EDITOR. One coming. A real brute. Shall I cut?

DAVID. Hold.

SIR STANLEY. (*From the screen.*) But it is a high responsibility, My Lord Mayor, for a man of my limited attainments—

EDITOR. Humble bit. He's good at this.

SIR STANLEY. (*From the screen.*) —to be granted the task of speaking for Her Majesty's Government to an assemblage as distinguished as this, and I would like, if I may, to strike a very serious note at once. (*Turning rather dramatically.*) My Lord Mayor, I must confess I am most deeply disturbed to observe that despite the economic crises you have seen fit to serve an even richer sauce on your sole bonne femme than last year. (*Dramatically.*) This is naked inflation—

*There is a big laugh.* DAVID'S *voice cuts across it.*

EDITOR. Shall we try a bit in the middle?

DAVID. Yes, somewhere where he talks sense.

*He operates a switch. After the speeding-up process described above, the camera once more rests on* SIR STANLEY, *waiting for a laugh to finish, at ease and plainly in command. His speech has been going well.*

SIR STANLEY. At a gathering of this kind, party politics are quite out of order, and I know that my Right Honourable Friend (*he bows towards the end of the table*) opposite, sitting for once, I notice, without his feet on the table—

DAVID. No. He's going to be funny again.

*There is another whirring of sound and vision as the* NEWSREEL EDITOR *presses the control.*

EDITOR. (*As it runs.*) But he's good, you know. This homey 'chaps together' style worked a fair treat, I can tell you. Highest rating of all yet. I tell you, he's got my money for P.M.

DAVID *reacts.*

*Again we see* SIR STANLEY, *very poised, very serious.*

SIR STANLEY. But let there be no mistake about it. This is a tremendous challenge, and when has this great country—I don't hesitate to use that unfashionable epithet—when has this *great* country of ours ever failed to respond to a challenge? When? We may be divided in our politics but in our ideals we remain, as we always have throughout our history, united.

DAVID. (*Through this.*) Ah. Ideals. Keep it running.

EDITOR. Not much more. A bit about God, I think. He usually ends on God.

SIR STANLEY. Well, My Lord Mayor, the challenge as I see it is this—and perhaps because I haven't the educational advantages of so many who are listening to me—

EDITOR. Humble Stan again—

SIR STANLEY. —and perhaps because I am a very simple—

EDITOR. My foot.

SIR STANLEY. —ordinary and—I hope I can say—honest man—

DAVID *turns and looks at his neighbour at this. There is no reaction.*

I can see more clearly to the heart of this challenge than the experts and intellectuals who have been plaguing us recently with all their commissions and reports—

EDITOR. The intellectuals always get it from Stan—

SIR STANLEY. (*Who has paused for effect.*) And what is at the heart of the challenge? For me, it is this. And I hope you will not laugh at me for my crass over-simplification. Is this age so irretrievably corrupt and materialistic—and we are often told that it is—that men and women will no longer work for anything but their own gainful good, or can they be led to return to some of the ideals and standards of their fathers, and for the eternal question: 'What's in it for me?' Can they substitute the more honourable plural: 'What's in it for us—for me and for my fellow-men, and for my country?' I have faith that, with God's help and the guidance of their elected leaders, they can—and they will.

*He sits down to applause. The screen is darkened as the* NEWSREEL EDITOR *switches off. Then lights* flood *the projection room.*

EDITOR. Well, that's our Stan for you. Up to form, didn't you think?

DAVID. I don't know the form.

*He moves to the door.*


## *SIR STANLEY'S OFFICE AT THE MINISTRY OF LABOUR.*

*It is a large and imposing office. There is a vast desk at which* SIR STANLEY *is not sitting, and many leather armchairs, in one of which he is, ending an interview with three Trade Union leaders who look as if they have been warmed and impressed by* SIR STANLEY'S *bonhomie and charm.*

SIR STANLEY. Well, gentlemen, I think that just about winds it up. And I can only conclude by saying how very much I've appreciated the spirit of moderation and tact which you have shown. (*He gets up, smiling.*) I can assure you that not all your colleagues in the T.U.C. would have shown half— (*To* P.P.S., *who has just entered.*) Yes?

P.P.S. Mr. David Mann, by appointment.

SIR STANLEY. (*Conspiratorially, to his guests.*) Ah. The Telly. Can't keep him waiting. Will you forgive me, gentlemen? (*To* P.P.S.) Send him in.

VISITOR. Of course, you're on that show tonight, aren't you? I'll make a point of looking in.

SIR STANLEY. (*Shaking hands all round.*) Oh, I wouldn't. I'm not an interesting enough character to be stripped bare. (*To* DAVID, *who has come in.*) Sit down, young fellow. (*To the others.*) Good-bye, then, gentlemen. I shall have that agreement sketched out in writing for your approval.

*The three visitors are ushered out by the* P.P.S. SIR STANLEY *turns to* DAVID.

Well, did you get what you wanted from that speech?

DAVID. Yes, sir, I think so.

SIR STANLEY. Mind you, on an occasion like that you can't get too serious, you know, but I hope you've got some notion now of these ideas and ideals of mine I was talking about—

DAVID. (*Interrupting firmly.*) Sir Stanley, it's my duty to show you this.

*He hands him the photostat.* SIR STANLEY *studies it without noticeable concern.*

SIR STANLEY. Oh, she's been at you, has she? Do you know, I had an idea she might. She's tried to give this to about everyone in the country, some time or another. The papers—they wouldn't touch it, of course, I wish they would. I could do with those damages—the Leader of the Opposition—he tried to get her arrested, only I stopped him—and even the P.M.—

DAVID. What did he say?

SIR STANLEY. Took it quite seriously. Had the gall to ask me if it was true. Care for a cigar?

DAVID. No, thank you. And how did you answer?

SIR STANLEY. (*Lighting a cigar.*) That I had been at the Mirabeau on those dates,

that I had spent that sum, or something like it—that, in fact, it probably is my bill, but that the signature across it is a forgery.

DAVID. (*Mildly.*) Is it a forgery? It looks rather close to me.

SIR STANLEY. (*Laughing.*) You've been sleuthing, have you. Where did you find
Lopez's signature?

DAVID. There was a copy of a signed letter in the Appleton Report.

SIR STANLEY. Ah, yes, of course. But the man was so uneducated he could
hardly spell his name, much less sign it. No two signatures of his were
ever alike—

DAVID. How do you know?

SIR STANLEY. (*Genially.*) Am I being cross-examined in my own office? Because I saw the Lopez papers, of course. I had to. I was involved—

DAVID. Yes. Of course you were.

SIR STANLEY. Now can we turn to less idiotic matters?

*He puts the photostat away in his breast pocket.*

The sort of question I thought you might ask me tonight—

DAVID. (*Quietly.*) Can I have that back, please?

SIR STANLEY. (*Puzzled.*) What? Oh, that.

*He takes the photostat from his pocket and slides it across the desk to* DAVID.

Of course, if you want it as a souvenir—

DAVID. Not as a souvenir. (*He pockets it.*) Before we pass to less idiotic subjects may I ask if either the Prime Minister, the Leader of the Opposition
or any of the newspapers took the trouble to ring up the cashier at the
Mirabeau?

*Pause. For the first time* SIR STANLEY'S *eyes are giving him away, although his
voice remains steady.*

SIR STANLEY. Meaning you have?

DAVID. Yes.

SIR STANLEY. What did he say?

DAVID. That Mr. Lopez signed the bill in person. You and the lady were leaving that night, and the cashier accepted the signature as payment. He
knew Lopez well, of course. When you came down and saw the bill you
were very angry with your secretary, Miss Knott, and blamed her for care-
lessness. She said it wasn't her fault, that Mr. Lopez must have done it
on his own, and that she'd collected the cash from him earlier to pay the
bill. She wanted to tear up the bill with the signature on it, and have
another made out for cash but you wouldn't let her. You said: 'The more
fool him'—I think that was the phrase, but I have it all on tape anyway—
you put the cash in your pocket and you left. Miss Knott took the bill.

*Pause.*

SIR STANLEY. (*Who has been smoking placidly.*) Really? And he remembers all
that after three years?

DAVID. Apparently.

SIR STANLEY. A remarkable memory.

DAVID. It was a remarkable incident.

SIR STANLEY. Would he come to this country and say the same thing on oath in a court of law?

DAVID. He offered me a sworn statement to use as I like.

SIR STANLEY. (*His manner abruptly changed.*) I can stop that, all right, never you fear. A word from me to the French Foreign Minister—or to our Ambassador over there—

DAVID *laughs, abruptly and harshly.* SIR STANLEY *looks at him, confused, aware now that he has given himself away:*

(*Hardly even trying.*) I mean I can stop this phoney blackmailing racket.

DAVID. That's not what you meant at all. And for your comfort, the cashier refused to make a sworn statement. But thank you, all the same, Sir Stanley. You've removed all my fears. Miss Knott might have been mad, the cashier might have been a liar, but from you, at last, I've got the truth.

SIR STANLEY. (*Smiling, and relighting his cigar.*) The real truth? The truth of the heart?

DAVID. Yes.

SIR STANLEY. Thinking of using it tonight, by any chance?

DAVID. Yes.

SIR STANLEY. You and the Governors of the Fifth Channel and the Director-General of the B.T.V. are going to look a fine bunch of boobies in that dock at the Old Bailey. For criminal slander you get quite a long stretch—

DAVID. You seem to forget how my programme is shaped, Sir Stanley. I don't make statements. I merely ask questions.

SIR STANLEY. A question can be slanderous, too, you know.

DAVID. When did you stop beating your wife? Yes, I know that hazard. My questions tonight won't be slanderous, Sir Stanley. Every single one will give you a chance of replying that the whole thing is a malicious invention, and that you really *are* a simple, ordinary and honest man who believes in the destiny of his country and in the standards and ideals of our fathers, and that you never had a hotel bill paid for by Manuele Lopez—

*Pause.*

SIR STANLEY. Are you going to use that tape?

DAVID. There is no tape. I've never taped a telephone conversation in my life. I wouldn't know how.

*Another pause.*

SIR STANLEY. (*Meditatively.*) Then you've got no evidence at all, have you?

DAVID. (*Tapping his pocket.*) Only this.

SIR STANLEY. I've told you. That's no evidence.

DAVID. Not in court.

*Pause.*

SIR STANLEY. There's a question of ethics here, isn't there? Are you a law-abiding citizen, believing in the paramountcy of the law of the land?

DAVID. Yes.

SIR STANLEY. Then do you approve of trial by television?

DAVID. No, I don't. Most emphatically I don't.

SIR STANLEY. (*Gently shrugging.*) Well, then—?

DAVID. Except in one case. When I know a truth which the law can't reveal—
and to reveal the truth is in the public good.

*Pause.*

SIR STANLEY. (*Still gently.*) *Pro bono publico*, eh? Just you and me, then—in
the ring together tonight.

DAVID. Yes, Sir Stanley. Just you and me.

SIR STANLEY. Well, I enjoy a fight. Always have.

DAVID. Me too.

SIR STANLEY. And this one should be fun.

DAVID. Yes. It should.

SIR STANLEY. No holds barred, of course?

DAVID. No holds barred.

SIR STANLEY. Would you like a drink?

DAVID. No, thank you. I'm off it.

SIR STANLEY. Are you really? That's new, isn't it?

*Pause.* DAVID, *at the door, looks at his antagonist with wary respect. The first of
the 'barred holds' have been shown.*

DAVID. Yes, Sir Stanley. Quite new.

*He goes out. Immediately* SIR STANLEY *reaches for the telephone.*

SIR STANLEY. Get me the British Television Company, Fifth Channel. I want
to speak to a Mr. Stockton.

*CONTROLLER'S OFFICE. A very angry and masterful* MR. STOCKTON *is clos-
eted with his assistant,* CYRIL BROWNE, *who seems very flustered.*

CONTROLLER. (*Shouting.*) I know it's short notice. Is it my fault if the man
goes mad or gets drunk within a few hours of the broadcast and starts
blackmailing Cabinet Ministers? (*The telephone rings.*)

VOICE. (*On telephone.*) Mr. Mann is here, sir.

CONTROLLER. Yes? . . . Good. Send him in. (*Angrily to* CYRIL). But *not* a cartoon. Anything but a cartoon.

CYRIL. (*Sadly.*) It's that travelogue, then. (*In pain.*) At nine-fifteen a travelogue!
Can't you hear that sound of all those sets being switched to other chan-
nels now?

CONTROLLER. Don't panic, man. Listen. Take my assurance for this. (*Forcefully.*) You won't have to use your alternative programme. There's not a
chance of it. But in dealing with an hysterical type like David Mann, I
have to be forearmed.

*He begins to talk to* CYRIL *with a complete change of tone for the benefit of* DAVID
*who, as he enters, hears what appears to be a very controlled* CONTROLLER
*giving very controlled* CONTROLLER'S *instructions to his assistant.*

So that's settled, then, Cyril. If the necessity should arise— (*To* DAVID.) Hullo, David. I won't be a moment— (*To* CYRIL.) If the necessity should arise we have the announcement of Mr. Mann's indisposition made at half-hourly intervals—from seven p.m. onwards, and at nine-fifteen we run that film you suggested. Thank you, Cyril. That's all understood?

CYRIL. Perfectly. Good-bye.

*He goes out.* DAVID, *standing at the window, in his overcoat, looking out, speaks at the sound of the closing door.*

DAVID. Why *my* indisposition and not Sir Stanley Johnson's?

CONTROLLER. (*Smoothly.*) Because the indisposition will be yours and not his. Better take your coat off and sit down—

DAVID. I'd rather stand. (*Quietly.*) At nine-fifteen I won't be indisposed, Mr. Stockton. I shall be on stage five, changed and ready to face the cameras. If Sir Stanley is not, then we must presume he has been taken very suddenly, very curiously and, to my suspicious mind, very revealingly ill, and I would like *that* fact announced tonight, and not some damaging lie about myself.

CONTROLLER. (*Also quietly.*) Listen, David—we'd better not fight about this. We don't have to, you know. Can I see that photostat?

DAVID *takes it from his pocket and hands it to him.*

(*Chuckling.*) Yes. Gosh! She's done a good job, all right. Must give her credit. I can quite see how even a brilliant brain like yours could have been taken in—

DAVID. You have a brilliant brain yourself, Mr. Stockton. Why isn't yours taken in?

CONTROLLER. Because I know Stan Johnson, and you don't. (*He hands back the photostat.*) He's incapable of that kind of fraud. (*As* DAVID *opens his mouth.*) Oh, yes. I know about your call to the cashier. You see, David, there you are. He didn't have to tell me about that, did he? He could have denied any knowledge whatever about the whole ridiculous affair. But far from it. In his telephone conversation with me he went out of his way to justify you completely—

DAVID. Didn't he, perhaps, give you a faint hint that I might have had rather a good lunch?

CONTROLLER. (*Snapping suddenly.*) Wasn't that natural, with your record?

DAVID. How did he know about my record? (*Before the* CONTROLLER *can answer.*) Of course. You know him and I don't. What did he say about the cashier?

CONTROLLER. That he remembers the cashier, now, very well—

DAVID. On retrospection.

CONTROLLER. Yes. It was some boy who had conceived a violent passion for Enid Clay—

DAVID. You knew about Enid Clay?

CONTROLLER. Of course. Who didn't?

DAVID. I didn't.

CONTROLLER. (*With an amused, sophisticated shrug.*) It's a model girl now. (*Gently smiling.*) Politicians are human, David—

DAVID. It's surprising how often that word is misused.

CONTROLLER. Anyway his sex life is hardly in your brief, is it?

DAVID. No. But that cashier is. He was in love with Enid Clay?

CONTROLLER. Yes, and so of course was wildly jealous of her protector. Sir Stanley says he remembers all sorts of trouble with the boy—and he's quite sure he'd say or do anything in the world to injure him. It's a pity you rang that cashier, David.

DAVID. Yes, it is, isn't it? But I did, and I believed every word he told me. And I still do. What's more I'll be believing it at nine-fifteen and despising Sir Stanley Johnson even more for telling you a lot of stupid lies. So, what do you suggest we do?

*Pause.*

CONTROLLER. (*Quietly.*) I don't *suggest* anything. It's not my programme and suggestions from me are out of place. I'll just state some facts. Fact one. I have given Sir Stanley my word that if the interview takes place tonight the Appleton Report will not be referred to at all; that the name Lopez will not be mentioned, and that the document in your pocket will be surrendered to him before the show. Fact two. That the general tenor of the interview will be friendly and constructive, and will show him to the viewers in a favourable light. Fact three—

DAVID. We don't need fact three. On those conditions I don't do the interview.

*He turns to go.*

CONTROLLER. (*Quietly.*) I think we need fact three. It's that if the 'Heart to Heart' programme does not go on tonight as advertised, my report to the Directors will be forced to refer to the known unreliability of the present Grand Inquisitor.

DAVID. 'Will be forced to' is good.

CONTROLLER. (*Angrily.*) It's good because it's the truth. Dammit, do you think I want to lose you from the next series? Who else will do it half as well? There's been no word from me to the Directors about last night, and there won't be, either, provided—

DAVID. Provided I play ball?

CONTROLLER. Provided you don't force my hand.

DAVID *nods and turns once more to open the door.*

Call me before six forty-five, and tell me what you've decided.

DAVID. (*Without looking at him.*) I've told you what I've decided.

CONTROLLER. (*Amiably.*) Call me, anyway.

DAVID *goes. The* CONTROLLER *switches on his desk telephone. A voice replies.*

VOICE. Yes, Mr. Stockton?

CONTROLLER. Get a message through to Sir Stanley Johnson at the House of Commons. Tell him I have every reason to suppose that tonight's interview is on.

VOICE. Yes, Mr. Stockton.

CONTROLLER. And after that get me Mrs. David Mann.

VOICE. (*Faintly surprised.*) *Mrs.* David Mann?

CONTROLLER. Yes.

*He switches off, and sits, musing quietly. His expression is not unduly troubled.*


*DAVID'S SITTING-ROOM. Night.* DAVID *enters from hall.* PEGGY *says nothing as he slips off his overcoat, and throws it on to a chair. Then he kisses her gently.*

*She does not respond, but stands stiff and still, her arms at her sides.* DAVID *plainly realizes at once that something is wrong.*

DAVID. (*At length.*) Someone's told you, it seems. Who was it? Frank?

PEGGY *does not reply.* DAVID *goes over to the drink tray.*

PEGGY. It wasn't Frank.

DAVID. (*Pouring himself a large whisky.*) I didn't think it was. Who was it, then? Not Jessie. Surely not Jessie.

PEGGY. (*Tense and angry.*) What are you doing?

DAVID. Pouring myself a drink—

PEGGY *takes a couple of quick strides and knocks the glass out of his hand.* DAVID *stares at her, for a moment, before speaking.*

Whoever's told it to you, hasn't apparently told it to you right. I'm not doing the show tonight, Peggy—so, if I want to—I can get quite drunk.

*He bends down to pick up the glass, which has not broken.*

They always say whisky doesn't stain—but perhaps—a rag—

*As he straightens himself* PEGGY *takes the glass from his hand and puts it on the tray.*

PEGGY. The rag can wait. Sit here, darling. I'm sorry about that, but at least it shows you how much I care, doesn't it?

*She smiles at him, hysteria still simmering just below the surface, but the surface is now in process of being carefully composed to allure, flatter and persuade. He stares at her, still puzzled, for a moment, and then realization dawns.*

DAVID. Stockton! Of course. (*More amused than angry.*) Well, well, well. No holds barred.

PEGGY. (*Still smiling.*) What's that?

DAVID. A metaphor from wrestling. It means a licence to kick your opponent where it's going to hurt him the most.

PEGGY. Isn't it me that's going to be hurt?

DAVID. That's just what I mean.

PEGGY. I'm not going to argue with you. It's never any good arguing with you. A girl can't win. I'm just going to say that you must do whatever you think is right, and whatever you do I shall love you and go on loving you for ever.

*Pause.*

DAVID. (*With a faint smile.*) Can't a girl win?

*He gets up and goes to the drink tray.*

I'm getting a drink.

PEGGY. (*Rising, sharply.*) No, David.

DAVID. (*Mildly.*) I dropped a whisky on the carpet a moment ago, darling—remember—and I want to fill my glass.

PEGGY. You'd better have it straight from the shoulder, David. That's from boxing, isn't it?

DAVID. Yes.

PEGGY. If you lose the job you lose me.

*Pause.* DAVID *smiles.*

DAVID. But you'll still love me, and go on loving me for ever?

PEGGY. (*Sincerely.*) Yes, I will.

DAVID. From whose bed?

PEGGY. Does it matter?

DAVID. John Wilkinson's bed is already occupied.

PEGGY. He wants a divorce.

DAVID. (*Miserably.*) I'm not surprised.

*He turns to the drink tray, with slightly unsteady hands, pours himself a whisky.*

PEGGY. (*Curiously.*) How long have you known about it?

DAVID. Since June 30th, 1959. The date's in my diary. It was during that weekend at that awful place of theirs at Henley. Caroline didn't notice. I did.

PEGGY. Why have you never said anything?

DAVID. (*Looking at his whisky and not drinking it.*) Because I was afraid I might lose you.

PEGGY *takes a step towards him.*

(*Sharply.*) Don't come any nearer, do you mind?

*She stops, but looks at him with honest compassion as he continues to stare into his glass.*

And it wasn't happening so very often. I figured it at about once every two months. Was that an underestimate?

PEGGY. No, over, if anything.

DAVID. And then again I knew it was his world you really wanted, not him. Lady Millchester. (*He takes his first gulp.*) I met her once. A charming lady. She'd even heard of the name—David Mann. (*He takes another long gulp.*) I'm not going to give you a divorce—

PEGGY. Why should you?

DAVID. (*Finishing the drink.*) Only one reason I can think of. So that I can marry Caroline Wilkinson—

PEGGY. Not Jessie Weston?

DAVID. She's married. And how long have you known about that?

PEGGY. Do you think I'm blind?

DAVID. We haven't slept together, you know.

PEGGY. (*With a faint laugh.*) Do I need to be told that? I'm not giving you up without a fight, you know. Do you think any girl in her senses would willingly exchange you for John Wilkinson?

*Pause.*

DAVID. Shall I tell you something, Peggy? It's taken me eight years to get the courage to say it to you, but I can say it now. I despise you.

PEGGY. (*Smiles. She is now mistress of the situation and knows it.*) But I despise myself, darling. You know that. I love money, and flats in Eaton Square, and convertible Bentleys with chauffeurs. I like fur coats and Balmain dresses, too—

DAVID. Did he give you a fur coat?

PEGGY. No. How could he?

DAVID. But that black dress, with the long sleeves and the—

PEGGY. Yes. That's Balmain.

DAVID. Harrods' sale, you said, I think?

*She nods.*

When you were in Paris, that time?

PEGGY. Yes.

*Pause.*

So go on despising me. That's all right. Nice girls don't behave like me, or admit they want the things I want. But not many nice girls faced starvation when they were five, or had to dress themselves in other professors' daughters' thrown-out clothes when they were eighteen. Nice girls love their husbands, and respect their husbands' principles. They didn't have to go through what my father made me go through for *his* principles. (*With sudden ferocity.*) If he'd stayed on in Riga, after the Russians came, do you know that as a Professor of Physics he'd be getting three times— *three* times as much money now as he's getting at New College?

DAVID. I don't doubt it. He might even have had a new sputnik named after him—

PEGGY. Is that so bad?

DAVID. No. It's very good. (*Hopelessly.*) Only—if he'd stayed in Riga—you and I would never have met.

PEGGY. No. And you'd have been free to have married Jessie Weston—

DAVID. Yes. I suppose I would.

PEGGY. And lived happily ever after—

DAVID. (*Hopelessly.*) Not necessarily. But *lived*, anyway.

PEGGY. (*Smiling at him. She is now in complete command of herself. Her victory is won.*) With Jessie, would it have been—living?

*Pause.*

DAVID. As they say in the quiz shows, it depends what you mean by living.

PEGGY. (*With a light laugh.*) I know what you mean by living. Who better? (*She comes closer to him.*) It's what I mean too, you know. Of course you know. Who better?

*She smiles at him. Pause.*

DAVID. This is all very corny. Vamping scenes went out with silent pictures— and anyway you need a tiger rug and the right lighting. I want a drink.

PEGGY. (*Her hand on his, gently.*) Of course you must have another. I'll pour it for you.

*She does so, measuring the amount of whisky with myopic intensity. It is a small amount.*

DAVID. Do you call *that* a drink?

PEGGY. Yes, darling, I call that a drink.

*Pause.*

Now let's talk about plans. If we're going to part for ever, we've got a lot of plans to talk about, haven't we?

DAVID. Corny! It's—so corny—

PEGGY. (*Turning to stare at him.*) Your eyes look a bit red. Have you been crying?

DAVID. Yes.

PEGGY. When?

DAVID. About half an hour ago. At the studio in a gents—

PEGGY. (*Worriedly staring.*) It's all right. It won't show under the lights.

*She pulls him gently down on to the sofa.*

What was it made you cry, darling?

*Pause.*

DAVID. I hate you, you know. I really hate you.

PEGGY. (*Smiling.*) Of course you do. I hate myself.

DAVID. But you don't hate yourself for the same reasons that I hate you.

PEGGY. What are they?

DAVID. The chief one is . . .

PEGGY. (*Quietly.*) What?

*He buries his face in her breast.* PEGGY, *sure anyway of her victory, looks down at him with a hint of compassion.* DAVID *neither answers nor stirs.*

What is it, darling?

*Again* DAVID *makes no response. He could, conceivably, be crying, but no sound comes from him.* PEGGY *looks at her watch, and, having coolly taken in the information it conveys, bends her head lovingly over him.*

Darling, now let's be sensible. After all, we do have an awful lot to discuss—

*A TELEVISION SCREEN. A commercial is just finishing. A time signal sounds and then an announcer's voice.*

VOICE. Eight forty-five. Channel Five.

*The screen shows a very beautiful, highly photogenic, female* ANNOUNCER.

ANNOUNCER. (*With a set smile, but in tones of passionate expectation.*) At nine-fifteen tonight the sixtieth edition of 'Heart to Heart' will bring to you our Grand Inquisitor, David Mann, versus the new Minister of Labour, Sir Stanley Johnson—

*A still of* DAVID *and* SIR STANLEY, *looking jovial but statesmanlike.*

—in a fifteen-minute all-out fight. Don't fail to keep tuned—

*CONTROLLER'S OFFICE. The* CONTROLLER, JESSIE *and* FRANK *are present. Through the soundproof windows that overlook the floor, we see a concourse of about twenty guests drinking on the set.* DAVID *is not among them, but* SIR STANLEY *is.*

CONTROLLER. (*To* FRANK.) All right. Now you've got that clear, have you?

FRANK. Quite clear.

CONTROLLER. At any reference to the Appleton Report, or any reference to Lopez, or any reference to anything that seems to you dangerous you are to cut off sound instantaneously.

FRANK *nods.*

Mrs.—er—you have that clear, too, haven't you?

JESSIE, *having been taking notes, nods over her shorthand book.*

It may be a question of split seconds—you understand—

JESSIE. But I thought he'd given his word.

CONTROLLER. Well, strictly speaking, he's given nothing. It was his wife who called to say the interview was on.

JESSIE. Under your conditions?

CONTROLLER. Obviously that was the understanding. Both she and he knew what my conditions are, and in agreeing to do the interview at all, he presumably has accepted them. But with this man we have also a drink problem to face— (*Breaking off, to* FRANK.) I'm sorry. I shouldn't have said that in front of Mrs.—er—

FRANK. No, you shouldn't.

CONTROLLER. (*To* JESSIE.) Forget I said that, please, Mrs.—er—Weston. It's not a problem that need concern you.

JESSIE. No.

CONTROLLER. (*To* FRANK.) I shall have an open line anyway to the Technical Operations Manager here in the Control Room, so that if either of you *should* slip up—and I'm sure you won't—but if you should, I can have the sound cut like that. (*He snaps his fingers decisively.*) Vision can remain on until the 'Normal transmission will be resumed as soon as possible' notice. Then, I suggest, we make an apology—

DAVID *comes in.*

—about the technical failure—hullo, David—and a vague promise about the interview being done at a later date. (*To* DAVID, *very pleasantly.*) Don't

let this make you nervous. It's just in case of a technical hitch. There won't
be one, I know.

DAVID *nods politely. He smiles at* FRANK, *and then catches* JESSIE'S *eye, which is
firmly and unwaveringly fixed on his face.*

DAVID. Hullo, Frank. Hullo, Jessie.

*They murmur their hullos in return.*

CONTROLLER. (*To* DAVID.) Was there anything you wanted to say to me?

DAVID. No, Mr. Stockton. Nothing at all.

CONTROLLER. Good. Then let's go down to the party. (*Looking through the
window.*) He seems quite happy. Cyril's looking after him.

DAVID. Could I have one word with Mrs. Weston? A technical matter—

CONTROLLER. Of course. Come on, Frank.

*He leads the way down the stairs to the floor.* JESSIE *and* DAVID *are left alone.*

DAVID. What am I to do?

JESSIE. Haven't you already done it?

DAVID. (*Angrily.*) I've promised nothing.

JESSIE. Your wife has.

DAVID. Does that bind *me*?

JESSIE. If you heard her telephoning and didn't stop her or contradict her,
I'd say it did. (*Briskly.*) And now you're here, and sober, too, I see. (*She
gets up.*) I don't think there's anything more of this technical matter to
discuss, is there, Mr. Mann?

DAVID. (*Pleadingly.*) Don't give me the bright, hard stuff now, Jessie.

JESSIE. (*Facing him.*) What do you want me to give you?

DAVID. Nothing, except . . .

*Pause.*

JESSIE. Except what?

DAVID. I need you. I love you, Jessie.

*Another pause.*

JESSIE. My God! How unfair can you get?

DAVID. Jessie, if I go through with this I can't do it alone. I must know that
you, at least, are behind me.

JESSIE. 'At least.' Damn you, David—why can't you leave me out of this?

DAVID. Can't you help me?

JESSIE. (*Having recovered herself.*) How? It's all set, isn't it? My orders anyway
are clear. If you mention the Appleton Report I'm to cut off sound. So
what're you going to do?

DAVID. I'm going to get the sound cut off.

JESSIE. What the hell good do you think that will do?

DAVID. I don't know. I wanted you to tell me.

JESSIE. All right, I will. No one watching tonight will be one whit the wiser
about our new Minister of Labour. Honest Stan down there will continue to flourish, and honest David will be out on his ear in television
for life.

DAVID. What you don't know is that if I do what I'm planning to do tonight,

I shall be without a wife.

JESSIE. And that'd be tough for you, I'd imagine.

DAVID. Oh, yes. Very tough indeed. But I could survive it, I think—I just could—if— (*He stops. The* CONTROLLER *is waving at him from the floor. To* JESSIE.) We'd better go down—

JESSIE. *If,* you said. If what? If—like I left my husband?

DAVID. You don't even like him.

JESSIE. I'm an eccentric, you see, David. I happen to believe that when you marry a man you marry him. So now that's cleared up—and for good. (DAVID *turns away.*) David, give it to Sir Stan tonight, give it to him good. Let's go down.


*STAIRS AND STUDIO FLOOR.* DAVID *and* JESSIE *come down the stairs.*


DAVID. Which won't be heard by anyone—

JESSIE. Yes, it'll be heard by Mr. Stockton. By Sir Stan, too. By me, if it comes to that—

DAVID. But it won't do any good.

JESSIE. And that matters?

DAVID. Yes, it matters. I only know I need some help, and more help than just the Production Secretary's moral support from the Control Room—

JESSIE. Who said you had the Production Secretary's moral support? You have Jessie Weston's best wishes. You'll always have those, Mr. Mann. But what the Production Secretary always likes best is a nice smooth show, without technical hitches. I'm sorry, David—but you're on your own. So let's go.

*They move towards the party, the sounds of which have been heard in the background throughout this scene.*

*Some people have gone, for it is getting late, but the noise of amiable, if vacuous, conversation is loud. The* CONTROLLER *is standing near the door, with* PEGGY. *Both turn as* JESSIE *and* DAVID *come in.*

PEGGY. (*Warmly and affectionately.*) Why, hullo, Jessie.

JESSIE. Hullo, Mrs. Mann.

PEGGY. You look so smart. I'm not used to seeing you in evening dress. It's new, isn't it?

JESSIE. New enough. Five years old, that's all. Excuse me. I have to talk to Frank.

*She smiles amiably at* PEGGY *and merges into the crowd.*

CONTROLLER. (*Meanwhile.*) Well, David, feeling in form?

DAVID. Oh, yes.

CONTROLLER. Technical problems all ironed out?

DAVID. Completely.

CONTROLLER. (*Touching* SIR STANLEY *on the back.*) Stanley, your inquisitor is here.

SIR STANLEY. (*Turning. He looks jovial and relaxed.*) Oh, hullo. (*He offers his hand to* DAVID, *who, after a slight pause, takes it.*) Where are the photographers?

*The* CONTROLLER *signals up two photographers who have been taking publicity snapshots of the party.*

Better get this one, now, don't you think, while we can, I mean. (*Holding his pose with* DAVID.) Afterwards all they might get is me cuffing our young friend over the ear-hole.

*There is a polite laugh from the people in the vicinity.*

(*To* DAVID.) Well, smile—young feller. Even heavyweight boxers smile at the weigh-in. That's right. Give us the famous dimple.

PHOTOGRAPHER. Smile, please, Mr. Mann.

*The shot is taken before* DAVID *has the chance to eliminate the dimple.* PEGGY *affectionately takes his arm.*

PEGGY. Oh, darling. I do love you so much—

SIR STANLEY. (*Nudging* DAVID'S *elbow.*) Talk about luck. (*Indicating* PEGGY.) Having a wife who looks like that. Why isn't she on television?

DAVID. I don't think she can act very well.

SIR STANLEY. How do you know until you've seen her?

DAVID. I've seen her.

PEGGY. (*Hugging his arm fondly.*) He's so silly. It's a private joke, Sir Stanley. I've never acted in my life—

SIR STANLEY. Well, you should try. You should get him to send you for a term or two to one of those drama schools—like R.A.D.A.—

DAVID. Is that where Enid Clay went?

*The* CONTROLLER *comes up. He has not heard this exchange.*

FLOOR MANAGER. Five minutes, studio, five minutes!

CONTROLLER. (*To* SIR STANLEY *and* DAVID.) Floor Manager's just called the five minutes. We're clearing the set. Good luck to you both. I know it's going to be a fine show.

GIRL. The viewing-room is this way, Lady Johnson.

*The* CONTROLLER *goes off. In the background we see him politely shooing the guests away as cameramen begin to take up their places and technicians to make their preliminary arrangements for the show.* LADY JOHNSON *comes up and takes her husband's arm.*

LADY JOHNSON. Good luck, dear.

SIR STANLEY. (*To* DAVID.) Birmingham Rep.

DAVID. (*Who has been watching* PEGGY.) What was that?

SIR STANLEY. Enid Clay. You were asking about Enid Clay, weren't you? Well, she went to Birmingham Rep.

LADY JOHNSON *looks at her husband with an expression that proclaims to* DAVID *her evident knowledge of the name's significance, and her pain at its mention at this moment. On the other hand her expression shows no surprise at all.*

DAVID. Well, thank you for the information.

SIR STANLEY. Not at all. If you think of anything else to ask me before the interview, you won't hesitate, will you?

DAVID. No, Sir Stanley. Of course I won't. But I think I'm already pretty well briefed—

FLOOR MANAGER. (*Shouting.*) Four minutes! Opening positions! (*Approaching* SIR STANLEY.) Sir Stanley—this way, please.

PEGGY *comes up to* DAVID *and kisses him.*

PEGGY. Good luck, darling. Tonight, at least, I will be watching.

DAVID *says nothing.* PEGGY *smiles and drifts away.*

DAVID *goes to his allotted seat opposite* SIR STANLEY. *Cameras, lights and microphone booms are being moved around in an atmosphere of utterly relaxed confusion.*

FLOOR MANAGER. Three minutes, everyone! Three minutes!


*CONTROL ROOM. The same group as the night before are in the same positions. Here, too, the atmosphere seems calm, although the expression on* JESSIE'S *and* FRANK'S *faces might betray something very different in a close-up.*


JESSIE. (*Into microphone.*) Can we have a sound test, please?


*FLOOR. The* FLOOR MANAGER *comes up to* DAVID.


FLOOR MANAGER. Ready for a sound test, Charley?

CHARLEY'S VOICE. O.K.

FLOOR MANAGER. David.

DAVID. One, two, three, four, five, six. Tell me, Sir Stanley, have you been reading anything interesting lately?

SIR STANLEY. Yes. I've read one or two things that have interested me quite a lot. Quite a lot.

DAVID. Such as?

SIR STANLEY. Oh, documents and things you know—

DAVID. And have you had any good holidays—?


*CONTROL ROOM.* FRANK *has his head in his hands.*


FRANK. Oh, no!

SIR STANLEY'S VOICE. (*From the monitor screen.*) Oh, yes. I like an occasional holiday, you know—

JESSIE. (*Into microphone.*) O.K., sound. Thank you. Number one, usual track in, number two close on Sir Stanley after titles. (*To* FRANK.) What?

FRANK. You heard.

JESSIE. When that microphone is live, then you can start groaning—

*A telephone rings. The* TECHNICAL OPERATIONS MANAGER *answers it.*

T.O.M. Hullo . . . Oh, yes, Mr. Stockton.


*CONTROLLER'S OFFICE. The* CONTROLLER *is on the telephone, and in the background is a television set, on which, at the moment, a newscast is showing, with the volume turned down.*

CONTROLLER. T.O.M.? . . . Right. I'm keeping this line open to you throughout the entire transmission. Understood?


*CONTROL ROOM.*

T.O.M. Yes, Mr. Stockton . . . Yes, I'll hold on throughout . . . Yes—of course, Mr. Stockton. At a word from you . . . Yes, that's understood—

JESSIE. (*To* FRANK.) Could it be that we're not being altogether trusted? (*Into microphone.*) Ninety seconds, Joe. Give Sir Stanley the opening drill, will you?

FLOOR MANAGER. O.K.


*FLOOR. Cameras and lights are still being moved around, as* DAVID *and* SIR STANLEY *face each other in their assigned positions.*

SIR STANLEY. All right if I smoke?

DAVID. Yes. Good for the nerves. You should.

*The* FLOOR MANAGER *comes up.*

FLOOR MANAGER. Sir Stanley—

SIR STANLEY. (*Waving him away, while he fixes* DAVID *with a firm look.*) Just a moment. Can I have that document, please?

DAVID. What document, Sir Stanley?

SIR STANLEY. You know blooming well what document.

DAVID. Ah, yes. Now where did I put it? I had it here, somewhere. (*To* FLOOR MANAGER.) Go ahead, Joe. Give him the drill—

SIR STANLEY. I want that document—

FLOOR MANAGER. Stand by, studio—one minute.

DAVID. (*Fumbling relaxedly in his pockets.*) You'll have it, Sir Stanley. I've got it somewhere. I think you should listen to the Floor Manager. We've less than a minute to go. Go ahead, Joe.

FLOOR MANAGER. Yes, David. (*To* SIR STANLEY.) Sir Stanley, when I drop my arm we're on vision, which means the cameras are on but sound is off.

That's when the programme titles are on the screen. They're superimposed over pictures of you and Mr. Mann. So we'll be able to see you but we can't hear you speak. Then I'll give a second cue, when the sound goes on, and the viewers can hear you. At the start, as Mr. Mann's probably told you, you should be smiling at each other.

DAVID. No. I'd forgotten that. In the opening shots we must be seen smiling at each other, Sir Stanley—you know—like heavyweight boxers at the weigh-in—

SIR STANLEY. Give me that bill—

DAVID. Of course. It's just a question of finding where I put it.

FLOOR MANAGER. You've got the idea, Sir Stanley? First cue is for vision, second is for sound. After the titles fade, that light will shine (*pointing*) and you're on the air.

SIR STANLEY. (*To* DAVID.) I'm not on the air without that bill in my pocket— I'm telling you that. Give me that bill.

DAVID. You shall have it when I find it. Excuse me. (*Into microphone.*) Jessie?

JESSIE. Yes, David.

DAVID. I shall want that insert close-up on cue.

JESSIE. What insert close-up?

DAVID. That still we had taken of a photostatted hotel bill.

FLOOR MANAGER. Twenty seconds.

JESSIE. (*Quickly.*) O.K., David.

DAVID. And I shall want that tape-recorded telephone conversation ready to run.

JESSIE. As you say, David. Ten seconds, Joe.

FLOOR MANAGER. Ten seconds.

DAVID. You remember the cue all right?

FLOOR MANAGER. Eight seconds.

JESSIE'S VOICE. Six seconds.

SIR STANLEY. What's this about an insert close-up?

FLOOR MANAGER. Four seconds.

SIR STANLEY. And a tape-recording. You said you didn't have. . .

FLOOR MANAGER. Two seconds.

SIR STANLEY. . . . a tape of that talk with the cashier.

DAVID. (*Still smiling.*) Yes. I suppose I did say that.

SIR STANLEY. What was the idea in telling me that dirty lie?

DAVID. (*Laughing gently as if* SIR STANLEY *has made a joke.*) Just to get you sitting in that chair facing me, with fifteen million people watching you. (SIR STANLEY *turns sharply to look at the camera light which is on*). Yes, the camera is on us, Sir Stanley, but don't look at it because that's bad. You're supposed to look at me. (SIR STANLEY *does so.*) Say, one, two, three, four and I'll laugh as if you made the most wonderfully funny, bluff, hearty, honest joke. Sound isn't on yet, you see. Go on. Say one, two, three, four.

SIR STANLEY. One, two, three, four. You're a double-crossing bastard.

DAVID. (*Roaring with laughter.*) Oh, but that's brilliant, Sir Stanley. How do you think of them?

FRANK. (*At control panel.*) Super second caption. Cue announcer.

ANNOUNCER. B.T.V. presents the sixtieth edition of 'Heart to Heart'. Tonight's victim is the Right Honourable Sir Stanley Johnson, M.P., Minister of Labour, and your Grand Inquisitor, as always, is David Mann.

SIR STANLEY. (*Smiling.*) I'm pretty sure you're still lying anyway. I don't believe you've got a tape, and I don't believe you've got a shot of that photostat—

DAVID. (*Smiling.*) Well, you'll find that out, won't you? In fifteen seconds we'll be on sound too.

SIR STANLEY. (*Smiling.*) How much?

DAVID. (*Smiling.*) Your resignation.

SIR STANLEY. (*This time genuinely laughing.*) You've got a nerve.

DAVID. (*Laughing uproariously back.*) Yes, haven't I just?

*On the transmission screen all that is coming through is the sound of the title-music to 'Heart to Heart' and the announcement. Visually the shots are as before, of* DAVID *and* SIR STANLEY *laughing happily at each other's jokes.*

JESSIE. (*Into microphone.*) Sound on.

FRANK. Cue David.

DAVID. Sir Stanley, may I begin by welcoming you to this programme, and by saying how very grateful I am to have this opportunity of asking you a few questions?

SIR STANLEY. Delighted to answer them, I'm sure—if they're questions I can answer, that is—

DAVID. (*Laughing.*) Does that mean there are some questions you feel you can't answer, Sir Stanley?

*CONTROLLER'S OFFICE. The* CONTROLLER, *telephone receiver to his ear, is intently watching the television screen.*

CONTROLLER. (*Into receiver.*) You're there, T.O.M.?

T.O.M.'S VOICE. Yes, Mr. Stockton

SIR STANLEY. (*From the television screen, smiling back amiably.*) I can see I've got to watch my step a bit with you, young feller. I nearly fell into that, didn't I? No. You can ask me any damn question you like—can we say that on television? Well, I've said it now, haven't I?—and I'll give you as straight an answer as I can.

DAVID. (*From the television screen.*) And from your reputation, Sir Stanley, we all know how straight those answers will be. Now I was privileged to hear the speech you made, at the Mansion House last Thursday afternoon—

CONTROLLER. (*Into receiver.*) All right so far. Still there, T.O.M.?

CONTROL ROOM. *The routine atmosphere is still present, but is noticeably diminished by the tension generated by* FRANK, *who is lighting one cigarette from the stub of another, while refusing to look at the transmission screen, and by the* T.O.M., *who is answering the,* CONTROLLER.

T.O.M. Yes, Mr. Stockton, I'm still here.

FRANK. Get camera two ready.

JESSIE. (*Quietly, into microphone.*) Number two. Close on Mann.

*The transmission screen changes to show* DAVID'S *face only.*

DAVID. (*From transmission screen.*) Now, Sir Stanley, when you talked about corruption—I think that was the word you used—the corruption of our age, that was it, wasn't it—corruption?

FRANK. Three change lens.

JESSIE. (*Into microphone.*) Three. Close on victim.

*The transmission screen changes to show* SIR STANLEY'S *face only.*

SIR STANLEY. (*From transmission screen.*) Yes. It was the exact word I used.

DAVID. (*From transmission screen, out of shot.*) What form of corruption did you have in mind?

FLOOR. DAVID *is smiling easily at* SIR STANLEY, *whose smile is also still present, but has now become a trifle set. He is sweating a little, too.*

SIR STANLEY. Well—there's corruption all round, isn't there?

DAVID. Yes. All round.

SIR STANLEY. I mean, this is the age of affluence, isn't it? The age of 'I'm all right, Jack' and 'What's in it for me?'

DAVID. Yes. (*Casually he takes out the Photostatted bill from his pocket and looks down at it, as if studying a note.*) What's in it for me? I remember you did use that phrase—

CONTROLLER'S OFFICE.

(*From the screen.*) What's in it for me? And to you, that phrase sums up the spirit of this age?

CONTROLLER. (*Into receiver.*) What's that piece of paper he's looking at?

CONTROL ROOM.

T.O.M. (*To* JESSIE.) Controller wants to know what this piece of paper is he's looking at.

FRANK. (*Shouting.*) How do I know what the piece of paper is? (*Into microphone.*) Four. Two-shot. Medium close—

T.O.M. (*Into receiver.*) Just a piece of paper, sir.

SIR STANLEY. (*Meanwhile, from the transmission screen.*) Yes, that does sum up
the spirit of the age, and you know it very well. For instance—take your
job, young man—

*FLOOR.* SIR STANLEY'S *smile has now faded completely and his sweating is more
pronounced.*

DAVID. (*Gently.*) Yes, Sir Stanley. Take my job.

SIR STANLEY. Well, I doubt if you do it for nothing, do you?

DAVID. Oh, no. For money. But I'd willingly give up both the job and the
money— (*with a charmingly dimpled smile*) who knows, one day I may
have to—rather than conduct an interview—corruptly.

SIR STANLEY. (*Trying to laugh.*) You mean, if someone came to you and said—
look, young feller, it's worth—say—five thousand pounds to me, not to
tell what you know about something or other—well, let's put it higher—
let's say ten thousand—

DAVID. No need to go higher. I'd spit in his eye.

SIR STANLEY. (*Laughing.*) On television? Before fifteen million viewers?

DAVID. (*Laughing back.*) I might wait until after the broadcast.

SIR STANLEY. Then we can take it that at least you're not corrupt, I suppose.

DAVID. Oh, but I'm not all that honest, either. I just have a few principles,
that's all, one of which I'm not prepared to betray. (*Gently.*) But, Sir
Stanley, this interview is not about me. It's about you. Can we get back
to the subject of corruption? (*He looks down at the photostat.*) Now I have
one particular question—

SIR STANLEY *suddenly turns and looks directly into the camera—the play camera—not a dummy.*

SIR STANLEY. Which of these cameras is on us? Is it this one?

CONTROLLER'S *OFFICE. The television screen shows* SIR STANLEY *now looking away from the camera.*

SIR STANLEY. (*From the screen.*) Or is it this one?

CONTROLLER. (*Into receiver.*) Prepare to black out.

DAVID. (*Still seen.*) It's the one with the red light.

CONTROLLER. (*Into receiver, in an angry shout.*) Hold it, hold it. I'll tell you
when. Hold it now.

SIR STANLEY. (*From the screen, meanwhile.*) I see. (*He turns, and again looks
full into the camera.*) Can I have it in close, please? Just me. I don't think
we need to show this young feller any more. I'm fairly sure I'm speaking
for each one of you when I say we're all getting pretty tired of this 'trial
by television'. Mind you, he's so artful, this one, that I don't suppose you
knew it was a trial. But it was—believe me.

*Confusion reigns as everyone in the Control Room gazes at each other and then at* FRANK.

TECHNICIAN. (*This line overlaps the above.*) Frank—what in hell do we do?

FRANK. (*In an even* voice.) Three, track in on victim—full close-up.

SIR STANLEY'S *face now fills the screen.*

SIR STANLEY. Is it on me, now? (*Someone, presumably the* FLOOR MANAGER, *gives him the sign.*) And it's this one, is it? (*Again he presumably gets the sign.*) Good. Now, ladies and gentlemen, I'm sorry for this. It's not what you expected—and to be frank and honest, it's not what I expected either. I am quite frank and honest, you know, in spite of what this young man would have told you to the contrary, if I'd let him go on with this interview. It's still on me, isn't it?

FLOOR MANAGER. (*Unseen.*) Yes, Sir Stanley.

SIR STANLEY. Good. And sound is on too, isn't it? Because I want everyone to hear this—


*CONTROLLER'S OFFICE.*


CONTROLLER. (*Into receiver, in a high passion of excitement.*) Cancel that. Cancel that order. Keep sound on—and get the camera in closer.

*On the screen we get an even closer picture of* SIR STANLEY, *wiping his brow.*

SIR STANLEY. (*Smiling easily.*) It's a bit hot under these lights. Excuse me. Well, ladies and gentlemen, you see the situation is quite simple, but it has to be explained, and explained by me, because from him—

*He jerks his thumb at the unseen* DAVID.

If I'd let him go on the way he was going, you'd have got something a bit distorted, a bit twisted around, a bit—well, you know—intellectual-like—


*CONTROLLER'S OFFICE. On the screen we see* SIR STANLEY *mopping his brow again.*

(*Smiling.*) That's not a guilty conscience, you know. It's just that these lights are blooming hot. And for an old geezer like me who doesn't usually say no to the odd pint of beer—well, it's ruddy uncomfortable, to say the least. Well, now—sorry about not making all this sound a bit more graceful and eloquent—you know—the way you're used to seeing and hearing politicians on the telly screen, but this is the kind of chap I am, and you'll just have to take me or leave me. Well, you'll probably leave me—because I've got a confession to make—and it's not a very nice one, I grant—but before I make it I'd better tell you this. I'm handing in my resignation as Minister of Labour to the Prime Minister tomorrow morning, and it'll be up to him to accept it or reject it, whatever he feels is right. And you can pretty well bet that what he feels is right, is what you'll feel is right.

*Watching the large screen amongst other guests are* LADY JOHNSON *and* PEGGY. SIR STANLEY *still features in large closeup on the screen.*

Well, here goes. This young man here, whom I hope you can't see, because I never want to see him again, I'll tell you that, has got hold of a document—a photostat of a hotel bill—the Mirabeau in Cannes—that's in the South of France—where the wife and I had ourselves a bit of a spree together four years ago. She was a bit run-down and needed the rest and I—well—with me what the wife says usually goes. Now the point is this, ladies and gentlemen. That bill is signed Manuele Lopez. You won't remember that name, but he was rather the villain of the piece in something called the Appleton Commission, which was about how we'd all taken bribes at the Board of Trade, or something. (*He wipes his brow again.*) I'm looking forward to that pint, I'm telling you. Well, of course, we hadn't taken bribes—any of us—that was all proved at the time, but I'm afraid I made a bit of a boob of myself—well, you might think it something a good deal worse, and I wouldn't blame you if you did— and so might the Prime Minister—but I accepted this chap Lopez's offer of a bit of extra foreign currency. I didn't know the first thing about him, mind you, or any connection between him and the Board of Trade— well, I mean, can you see me falling for that old one?—but I *did* know that in accepting his signature on my bill, and paying him back in sterling, I was technically contravening the currency restrictions that were in force at that time—and therefore breaking the law. Yes—I broke the law. I'm a Cabinet Minister and I broke the law. And that's what this young man had against me—

*CONTROL ROOM.*

FRANK. Let's take a reaction shot of David. Four, you've got a good close-up.
JESSIE. Stand by, four.
T.O.M. Controller's orders. Stay on victim.
FRANK. When was Stockton made producer of this show? O.K. Forget it.
JESSIE. Forget it, four. Forget it. We're staying on two.
SIR STANLEY. (*Meanwhile.*) —and which he was planning to reveal to you by showing you a close-up of this. (*He picks up the bill.*) This is the bill, signed by Lopez.
JESSIE. How could he have fallen for that?
FRANK. (*Into microphone.*) Four, get in closer. Try and pick up the signature on that bill.
SIR STANLEY. (*From the screen.*) Can you see it? I don't expect you can, but

anyway that's the signature—Manuele Lopez—and it's genuine. Of course I *could* have said it was a forgery, and tried to bluff it out—but that's not quite my form. If I've done something wrong—and this *was* wrong—the fact that at that time it was being done every day by thousands of people doesn't make it any the less wrong—then I'll admit it freely, as I have tonight, and just take the consequences.

FRANK. Four. Leave the paper in his hand and up on his face, as close as possible.

JESSIE. You can't get right inside, can you?

FRANK. No, but that sweat could just help.

JESSIE. No. It's 'Honest Stan's' honest pint coming out.

FRANK. So? Even that makes good television. (*Slapping her on shoulder.*) And this is great television, lady, great.

SIR STANLEY. (*Meanwhile, from the transmission screen.*) All I'd say in my own defence—and there's not all that much to be said—is that the wife *did* need that holiday, you know. She really *did* need it, and needed it badly, because—well, some of you may have seen a picture in tonight's paper of the two of us with our cat—James. Well, we love James, the wife and I—I like dogs too, of course—but cats are what my dear wife really worships, and so do I. In our house we have cats, you know, the way other people have mice. Well, James's mother—Elizabeth the Third—

FRANK. Now he's gone too far.

JESSIE. He hasn't, you know.

SIR STANLEY. (*Meanwhile.*) —had been run over—a really horrible accident— the poor thing lingered on for—well, I musn't talk about it because my wife might be listening and it would upset her too much—


*PROJECTION ROOM.* LADY JOHNSON *is staring at the screen, without apparent emotion.* PEGGY *is looking at her, curiously.*


LADY JOHNSON. (*Murmuring.*) Elizabeth the Third is rather a nice name for a cat. I must remember that—

SIR STANLEY. (*Meanwhile.*) Anyway, she needed that holiday—and needed it real bad. Still, that doesn't excuse me for what I did, and I don't mean it to. I broke the law, and must take the consequences. From tomorrow on I'm just plain Stan Johnson—not Minister of Labour—perhaps not even an M.P. if my constituency chucks me out—which they have every right to do, mind—just common old Stan, who once made a bloomer and four years later had to pay the price.

LADY JOHNSON. (*To* PEGGY, *with a sigh.*) I think he should do more television—

SIR STANLEY. Well, that's about all, ladies and gentlemen. Sorry it's had to end this way, but there it is . . . So, in conclusion—

*CONTROL ROOM.*

FRANK. Joe, the second he ends his speech, we go to final caption. No closing drill. No going to David for a plug. No nothing. Got that?

*From the door we see the* FLOOR MANAGER *turn and give a plainly bewildered
thumbs up.*

JESSIE. The timing's gone to bothery, and the whole affair is an immortal fid-
dle-de-dee—

FRANK. That's my can to carry, not yours.

SIR STANLEY. (*From the transmission screen, meanwhile.*) I'd like to say that old
Stan here feels pretty damn badly about having let you down, and only
begs for a chance, if one day you'll forgive him, to serve you again, in
whatever capacity might seem good to you. But if you don't forgive him—
and, mind you, he doesn't think you should—well, then, he'll take his
medicine, and you'll hear nothing more from him. He'll blame no one
at all—except himself—otherwise no one—and least of all his Grand
Inquisitor, Mr. David Mann, and this great fine truthful show, 'Heart
to Heart'. Good night, ladies and gentlemen.

SIR STANLEY *hands the photostat back to* DAVID.

FRANK. A plug, yet. If they kick him out of politics we could use this character on the show—

JESSIE. (*Into microphone.*) Cut, sound. Start titles. One, track in on usual two-
shot. Cue grams.

*On the transmission screen we see a silent shot of* SIR STANLEY *and* DAVID *shaking
hands.*

(*To* FRANK.) Kick *him* out of politics?

FRANK. You think he's got away with it?

JESSIE. Why are you a producer and me just a menial?

FRANK. Cue announcer. What about David?

JESSIE. Well—that's a question more worth asking. Give me a cigarette. (FRANK
*does so.*) About even money? (FRANK *shrugs.*) Tonight's show will make
the front page of every newspaper all over the world. Even Stockton will
have to coin some such immortal phrase as 'We made television history'.
In on victim.

ANNOUNCER. (*Overlaps last three lines.*) You have just seen the sixtieth edition of 'Heart to Heart', a British Television Company presentation. In
tonight's 'Heart to Heart' the victim was the Right Honourable Sir
Stanley Johnson, M.P., the Minister of Labour. And your Grand Inquisitor, as always, was David Mann. Tonight's edition was the last of the
current series. But we shall return to your screens in six weeks' time with
a new series, starring your Grand Inquisitor, David Mann.

SIR STANLEY. Are those bloody cameras still on us?

DAVID. Yes. I'll tell you when they're off.

SIR STANLEY. You oughtn't to be smiling at me, ought you? Won't it all look a
put-up job?

DAVID. (*Smiling.*) You would like me to register facially my disapproval of a man who once contravened the currency regulations in order to console his wife for the loss of her cat, Elizabeth the Third, mother of her present cat, Charles.

SIR STANLEY. Charles! Dammit. Well, there aren't many who know its real name. Cameras off?

FLOOR MANAGER. Off you, studio.

DAVID. Yes, Sir Stanley. They're off.

FLOOR MANAGER. Thank you, chaps. There was a bit of a muck-up somewhere but not our fault.

SIR STANLEY. Thank the Lord!

*He gets up and stretches himself.*

(*Amiably.*) Well. Who would you say won?

DAVID. (*Wearily, still sitting.*) Won?

SIR STANLEY. The fight.

DAVID. Fight?

SIR STANLEY. Between you and me.

DAVID. (*Looking at him with bleared eyes; we can see now the full physical effects of the strain he has just been through.*) Oh—that fight; you won. You won it hands down.

SIR STANLEY. Was there another fight?

DAVID. (*Getting up, a shade unsteadily.*) Yes. Not between us. Between me and me. (*Hysterically, covering his face with his hands.*) I think I won it. I think I won it—me and me—one of us has got to win, haven't we?

SIR STANLEY. You cuckoo or something? Did you have that slide and that tape?

DAVID. Of course I didn't.

SIR STANLEY. I was pretty sure you didn't. Still, I couldn't take the chance—now—could I?

FRANK *and* JESSIE *come up.* DAVID, *recovering himself, looks up at them.*

DAVID. I suppose the viewers are phoning in like mad?

JESSIE. (*Briskly, referring to a note.*) Just checked. Two hundred and eighty-four in already. Out of those two hundred and eighty-four—

DAVID. Yes?

JESSIE. —two hundred and seventy-two say that Sir Stanley mustn't, on any account, resign.

FRANK. And of the other twelve, five said that the whole thing was plainly a put-up job—

SIR STANLEY. (*To* DAVID, *a shade put out.*) What did I tell you? It was that smiling after—

FRANK. —and four have said that they hope we took a tape of the broadcast, because they would like a repeat tomorrow night—so as to make up their minds.

*Pause.*

DAVID. That still leaves three.

FRANK. Yes. They think Sir Stanley should resign.

*The* CONTROLLER *and* PEGGY *come, up. The* CONTROLLER *is beaming. He looks as if he has just been congratulated by someone even higher in the hierarchy than himself—and so he has.* PEGGY, *until referred to by the* CONTROLLER, *stands in the background placidly looking around.*

CONTROLLER. (*Jovially.*) Well, well, well. That was a bit of a mix-up, wasn't it?

FRANK. Yes. I'm sorry.

CONTROLLER. Don't be sorry—we made television history. (FRANK *and* JESSIE *exchange a glance. The* CONTROLLER *turns to* SIR STANLEY.) Stanley, it's going to be all right. You heard how the calls are running?

SIR STANLEY. Yes. Very gratifying.

CONTROLLER. I've made it my business to see that that information gets the fullest publicity by tomorrow. From a certain feeler I've just had from a certain quarter, I don't think a certain very important person can possibly ignore the expressed and declared will of the people.

SIR STANLEY. Well, in a democracy it is that which in the long run must decide, mustn't it? Mind you—my resignation still goes in tonight—

CONTROLLER. Of course. Now let me take you off for that pint—

SIR STANLEY. Pint? Beer's for the cameras. You know what I want? A quadruple brandy— (*To* LADY JOHNSON.) Well, dear? What did you think?

LADY JOHNSON. (*After a long pause.*) I felt so ashamed. There was a little tear in your waistcoat pocket, and I had spotted it this morning and—

SIR STANLEY. Yes, dear. (*To* CONTROLLER.) I need that brandy.

CONTROLLER. You'll get it. (*Going and turning back.*) Oh, David—

DAVID. Yes?

*Pause.*

CONTROLLER. I've brought Peggy down. (*He pushes her forward. She is smiling.*)

DAVID. Yes. I see you have.

DAVID *looks at her. She is still smiling.*

CONTROLLER. And she has a bit of news I gave her that she wants to pass on to you. Better from her than from me, I thought.

DAVID. (*Looking at her.*) Thank you, Mr. Stockton. It was thoughtful of you.

CONTROLLER. Well, good night. (*He goes on to* FRANK) Well, well—good show, Frank. You handled it wonderfully. So did you, Mrs.—er—Mrs. Weston.

*Waving to the stage hands, cameramen, etc., who through this scene have dispassionately been going about their business.*

Good night, boys. It was a great show you did out there tonight. Great. And I thank you all from my heart.

*There is a vague murmur from the shadows.*

You may not know it, but tonight—we made television history.

*Again the murmur is so vague as to amount, virtually, to the deadest of silence. He departs.* PEGGY *comes forward and kisses* DAVID *on the cheek.*

PEGGY. Oh, darling—darling. I'm so excited that I can't say much more than that. Here—feel my heart. (*She takes his hand and puts it to his breast.*)

JESSIE. (*Briskly.*) Frank—I haven't got my car—so could you drop me?

DAVID. (*Still holding* PEGGY.) Come home, to me.

JESSIE. (*Looking at her watch.*) I can't. He'll be waiting—

DAVID. Frank?

FRANK. You bet. I need a drink. I need ten, I think.

DAVID. Then you take Peggy, will you? I'll drop Jessie.

PEGGY. (*After a glance—rather amused glance—at* JESSIE.) David, darling—I've got some very exciting news for you, you know, that the Controller told me to—

DAVID. It can wait till I get home. Go with Frank.

PEGGY. (*Gaily.*) Of course.

*She kisses* DAVID *again, this time perhaps a shade more proprietorially.*

Well done. I'm proud of you. (*Going, with* FRANK) You must have been having heart failure, weren't you—up in that Control Room? What I was going through in that projection room—can you imagine?

FRANK. Yes. Oh, yes, Peggy. I can.

DAVID *and* JESSIE *are left alone on the now empty and nearly blacked-out studio floor. As they move slowly towards the exit the camera work should quietly remind us of the scene they had together in the same spot at the same time the night before.*

DAVID. So I failed, didn't I?

JESSIE. (*In 'television' tones.*) It depends what you mean by 'fail', Mr. Mann.

DAVID. (*In real agony of spirit.*) Don't.

*They have reached the 'Western' set.* DAVID *sits on the same rock.*

I hate failure.

JESSIE. Even more than you hate success? (*He looks at her.*) You didn't fail.

DAVID. I did. Three against—what—two hundred and eighty-six.

JESSIE. A bit over one in a hundred. How many voters are there in this country, Mr. Mann?

DAVID. (*Still miserable.*) You tell me. You're bound to know.

JESSIE. I don't. I only know that these three tonight are going to mean three thousand tomorrow, then three hundred thousand the day after, then—hell, why not?—three million on the day it really matters.

DAVID. (*Looking up at her.*) Women always exaggerate so absurdly. And your arithmetic is absurd.

JESSIE. Sure. But absurd or not, it'll stop Sir honest Stan ever becoming Prime Minister of this country. I'll tell you that. And that's no woman's exaggeration, Mr. Mann. Your name will, one day, appear as a footnote in the political history of England in 1962.

DAVID. Who wants to be a bloody footnote?

JESSIE. You do. (*She pulls him up.*) Come on.

DAVID. (*Holding her.*) Jessie, I haven't lied to you. I do love you. I do need you. Things like tonight I can't face on my own.

JESSIE. Well, you did.

DAVID. I wasn't on my own.

JESSIE. No. (*Taking his hand.*) Let's go. This is a bad set for a love scene.

DAVID. Who said it was a love scene?

JESSIE. (*As they walk on.*) You did. You said love. When a man says that to a woman (*indicating the set*) in the far West, he means 'love', dammit.

DAVID *turns to kiss her. Again she pushes him away.*

No. We're off the set, now.

*They walk in silence up to the door.*

DAVID. I would have done it, Jessie. You believe that, don't you? I *was* going to expose that rat. They could have cut me off, and fired me, but I *was* going to do it, and I'd have lost my job and my flat, and my Bentley, and my wife— You believe that, don't you?

*There is no answer from* JESSIE *as she looks at him.*

JESSIE. (*Softly, at length.*) Your wife came rather low on that list, didn't she?

BOY. (*Coming up to* DAVID.) Dave—excuse me, Mrs. Weston—my little sister's mad about you. She asked me to get your autograph.

JESSIE *walks on.*

DAVID. You do believe it, don't you?

JESSIE. If I didn't, I wouldn't love you, would I?

*He stares at her, until the expression in her eyes makes him relax his grasp.*

Good night, David.

DAVID. I'm dropping you.

JESSIE. No. I'm taking the bus back home.

DAVID. Let me drop you.

JESSIE. No.

DAVID. I didn't mean—

JESSIE. (*This time very quietly, and smiling.*) I know exactly what you didn't mean.

*Pause.*

DAVID. (*Quietly.*) Damn. It would be nice if things could be different, wouldn't it? (*After a pause, defiantly.*) All right. Say it. 'It depends what you mean by nice.'

JESSIE. No. It depends what you mean by different. Go home, David.

*Pause.*

DAVID. Three out of two hundred and eighty-four.

JESSIE. That's right.

DAVID. Well, I'd like to meet those three.

JESSIE. Go home and dream about them.

DAVID. They must be interesting people.

JESSIE. Yes. And I'll go home and dream of the man who made them interesting.

DAVID. Good night, Mrs. Weston.

JESSIE. Good night, Mr. Mann.

*The camera tracks back to* JESSIE. *Then, over her shoulder, we see* DAVID *as he gets into his car. It drives off, past a roadside sign—'Vision of the Future'.*

*As the lights fade,* JESSIE *is walking off in the direction of the sign.*

PREFACE
*by*
B. A. YOUNG

(This Preface appeared in Volume Four of
the Hamish Hamilton edition of 1978)

Terence Rattigan was an unbending romantic. Sometimes he was purely romantic and nothing else, dealing with that most derided but most profitable theme, the love affairs of the upper middle classes. Sometimes he pretended that he was dealing with great affairs of state, such as the conquest of the world by Alexander the Great or the command of the Fleet at Trafalgar. In these cases he homed in at once on the central figures to demonstrate that they had done what they had done not out of any concern with fame or profit or duty, but at the prompting of more familiar feelings—feelings about love and friendship and honour. They were, in fact, honorary members of the British middle class.

In making such an approach to his characters he was working on a purely Shakespearian principle. Shakespeare's Richard III and Henry V were not supposed to be biographically accurate portraits of these monarchs, nor were their dramatic exploits closely matched with available history. Shakespeare peopled his plays with figures that would be familiar, and therefore easily comprehensible, to his audiences. So did Rattigan. In any discussion, both sides must speak in the same language, and Rattigan decided early in his career that the language he would use was to be the language of the West End theatregoer.

Here is what he says in the introduction to the first volume of his collected plays: "'The thraldom of middle-class vernacular.' Such a phrase, from myself, must seem patently insincere. The merest glance at any of the five plays in this volume will show how very little I resent such servitude . . . I believe, with Chekhov's Trigorin, that everybody must write as he pleases and as best he may. I 'please to write' in the naturalistic convention and the 'best I may' would quickly become the worst if I denied myself my gift for telling a story and delineating character in the terms of everyday speech."

Everyday speech and the thraldom of middle-class vernacular are however only the outward and visible signs of an inward and intellectual problem. Everyday thought and middle-class attitudes are also a vital part of Rattigan's equipment, and either he could not or he would not operate outside their bounds. "I've lost my copy of Homer," Alexander says as his army packs up to start a march into India. Alexander in *Adventure Story* would not have looked out of place in the Eton cricket XI, or commanding a squadron of

Eleventh Hussars in the Western Desert. Because we can see him against
such backgrounds in our minds, we can the more easily appreciate his
thoughts and his actions as Rattigan presents them to us. His copy of Homer
would have been a paper-back: and why not? Shakespeare's Brutus takes a
book from the pocket of his gown on a similar occasion. "Is not the leaf
turned down where I left reading?" he muses, lest we should expect his book
to be a roll of papyrus. A hundred years earlier, an author treating the events
of *Adventure Story* for the stage would have filled Alexander's mouth with
lines like "What ho, Perdiccus! Lo, the dawn awakes," and the character
would have remained us unknowable as in Callisthenes or Aristobulus.

The Rattigan method works excellently so long as he is dealing with characters from the equivalent of his own social circle. Outside those barriers,
he is less successful. The Romanian financier Antonescu in *Man and Boy*
remains a two-dimensional figure, both dimensions being English. Working-class characters, usually servants, are made of accepted clichés, offering
at best what I still think of as Kathleen Harrison humour, though it was
Priscilla Morgan who said "I shouldn't have the cold pie if I were you. I saw
what went into it" in *Separate Tables*. In *Table by the Window*, John is told in
a stage-direction to speak with a slight north-country accent; but basically
he is the prosperous post-Wildean Englishman that inhabits most of the
Rattigan world. Only in the last play of all, *Cause Célèbre*, does a working-
class character have anything like a fully-rounded part—Wood, the houseboy
tried with Mrs. Rattenbury for the murder of her husband.

To say that Rattigan is "less successful" in writing characters from stock
is a subjective judgment. In my notice of the 1976 revival of *The Browning
Version*, I wrote: "Apart from the schoolmaster Crocker-Harris and perhaps
the boy Taplow, the characters are stereotypes. Much of the dialogue—'We're
finished, Millie, you and I'—is cast in terms of romantic cliché. Yet so ably
are these puppets handled that the point where the boy gives the master his
copy of the *Agamemnon* in Browning's translation is one of the great moments of pathos in our contemporary drama."

I had supper with the author a few days later. He was not at all put out
by what I had written; on the contrary, I had put my finger exactly on what
he had intended to do. Why should we be interested in anything the assistant master Frank Hunter does besides having a brief fling with
Crocker-Harris's wife and being friendly with Taplow? Why should we be
interested in the private lives of the Gilberts? Their function is to fill in the
background against which Crocker-Harris is drawn.

I suspect, incidentally, that this deliberate use of flat characters is the reason why film versions of Rattigan's plays are seldom as moving as their stage
originals. By the time the stories are "opened out" to split the ears of the
filmgoers, the necessary concentration on the principal characters is lost.
Rattigan writes with more economy than is immediately apparent, when he
is writing for the theatre. In writing for the films, economy is a virtue less in
demand.

Rattigan deliberately aimed his plays at the kind of audience he encapsulated in that notional aunt whose name I decline to pronounce. Even when the rumblings at the Royal Court signified the arrival of a new kind of theatre, he still visualised the house full of matinée-haunting ladies, whose taste he has analysed with much understanding. Irving Wardle, in *The Theatres of George Devine*, reports a conversation in 1956 between Rattigan and that great director.

"Driving back from Stratford to London, Terence Rattigan spent two and a half hours telling Devine why the play could not be a success. 'Well it is,' Devine kept repeating, 'and it's going to make the Royal Court possible.' 'Then I know nothing about plays,' Rattigan eventually answered. 'You know everything about plays, but you don't know a fucking thing about *Look Back in Anger*.'" Rattigan could not believe that there was an audience for the social outcry of the new generation of the underprivileged. He came to admire some of the writers of the new wave, Harold Pinter and Joe Orton particularly; but he did not see them as part of the mainstream of theatre, and indeed a look at the record on Shaftesbury Avenue suggests that, for his own time at any rate, he was not altogether wrong.

Within the confines of his chosen medium, Rattigan is capable of accomplished manipulation of the emotions. When Sir Robert Morton in *The Winslow Boy* says "The boy is plainly innocent. I will accept the brief", he is in the same territory as Hamlet's "O my prophetic soul! My uncle!" Rattigan has even been described as the poet of middle-class English, but of course this is wrong. He was not a poet of any kind. (Indeed, when he needed a parody of "modern" verse in his television play *The Final Test* he asked his friend Paul Dehn to write it for him.) His English is sometimes positively clumsy. A sentence like "He has sat two steps down from his mother who seems bent on stroking his hair and whom he is never averse from having do so" would give a perfectionist like Graham Greene a heart attack. All right, it is only a stage direction, but language of this kind creeps into the dialogue too. Here is Lady Hamilton in *A Bequest to the Nation*: "If you'd gone on trying to catch your death of cold hiding from me outside at night, I could have nursed you later—as I did in Naples—and meanwhile learnt solitaire."

Rattigan made no pretence to be a literary stylist. Using the tools at hand—his fluent deployment of "middle-class vernacular", his close understanding of the minds of his contemporaries, his pliable dramatic technique—he was able over a period of forty years to offer his chosen audiences the plays they wanted. He tells with coy pride a story of a French master at Harrow who, marking a youthful Rattigan drama written as a French exercise, wrote on it "French execrable; theatre sense first class." Looking back on a score of subsequent dramas we can say, not unjustly, "English moderate; theatre sense first class."

He was singularly free from outside influences. His obvious ancestor was Somerset Maugham, by way of writers like Frederick Lonsdale. His early plays are full of peers, these being the kind of character West End audiences had come to expect over the past half-century—Lord Haybrook, the Earl of Harpenden, the Earl of Binfield. (The Stag and Hounds at Binfield was the inn to which Rattigan used to repair when he needed solitude for writing.)

Accepted English comedy was the natural springboard from which any ambitious young writer of the thirties would take off. What is interesting is that Rattigan's style changed so little over the years, for two important events happened during his writing career. The first was the outbreak of poetic plays that began—as far as the West End public was concerned—with Christopher Fry's *The Lady's Not for Burning* in 1948 and T. S. Eliot's *The Cocktail Party* in 1949. This phenomenon passed him by, for verse was, as I have said, outside his range; he was content to admire but not to emulate. The second, much more important, was the new wave of drama that sprang from the Royal Court when the English Stage Company began work in 1956. This not only widened the bounds of what was generally accepted as practical dramatic material; it also laid a delayed-action mine under the offices of the West End managers. Love among the middle classes, and glosses on romantic historical figures like Richard of Bordeaux and Katherine Howard were, it seemed, under sentence of death.

Rattigan's last play when this broke out had been the double-bill *Separate Tables* in 1954. He was aware of the new wave but, as we have seen, suspicious of it. He was not himself interested in writing political drama (though his own political convictions belonged, at any rate in theory, to the left); and the new freedom of expression that led ultimately to the withdrawal of the Lord Chamberlain's powers of censorship did not affect him. He had learnt to disguise taboo subjects under acceptable masks; the unhappy Major Pollock in *Table Number Seven*, the second piece in *Separate Tables*, was guilty in the author's mind of groping boys in the cinema, though in production it had to be women and the play loses nothing through the sex-change. He was not personally averse to taboo subjects; he admired Joe Orton, the first truly successful writer in our age of "black comedy", and even had an investment in Orton's *Entertaining Mr. Sloane*, by way of encouragement rather than in any hope of profit.

But there was little reason why he should adopt a new style while the old style remained successful. In the six years between 1948 and 1954 he had written eight plays, *The Browning Version, Harlequinade, Adventure Story, Who is Sylvia?, The Deep Blue Sea, The Sleeping Prince* and the *Separate Tables* pair. After *Separate Tables* there came a gap of four years, with the Royal Court explosion in the middle of it. The playwrights people were now talking about were Pinter, Osborne, Arden, Wesker. What would the next Rattigan be like?

The next Rattigan was *Variation on a Theme*, almost a gesture of defiance with its tale of romance among the trendy rich in the South of France. By that time the critics had been swept along with the new drama. Among the plays that opened in the same month as *Variation on a Theme*, May 1958, were *Birthday Party, Expresso Bongo* and a piece called *Quaint Honour*, a plea for homosexuality among schoolboys. A typical notice of *Variation on a Theme*, from the normally kind Eric Keown in Punch, said that the play "falls far below Mr. Rattigan's usual level." It had a short run. Only once more did Rattigan write a straightforward piece about life among the bourgeoisie, and this was in response to his distress at the early death from leukaemia of Kay Kendall—*After Lydia*, the longer play in the double bill *In Praise of Love*. (*After Lydia* was itself renamed *In Praise of Love*, and is called so in this volume. Rattigan's original script was much cut in John Dexter's production so that with *Before Dawn*, the curtain-raiser sending up Sardou's *La Tosca*, it might comfortably fill an evening. Afterwards the cuts were restored and the piece played on its own. The script as printed here conforms precisely neither to that used in the London production at the Duchess nor that acted the following year at the Morosco in New York).

*Variation on a Theme* may have been below Mr Rattigan's usual level, but it is of critical interest, for with the exception of *Cause Célèbre*, which I will come to later, it expresses more clearly than in any of his other plays the theme that runs so persistently through his work—the dominance of the weak over the strong, "the worst form of tyranny the world has ever known," as Oscar Wilde called it.

Once Rattigan had found a true individual voice, this idea is to be found in play after play. It is in *The Browning Version*, where the schoolboy's gesture breaks the master's self-control. It is the mainspring of *The Deep Blue Sea* and of *Table by the Window*. It is the whole basis of *Variation on a Theme*. It is detectable in *Man and Boy* and in *A Bequest to the Nation*, where boys with no power but their youthful sentiments influence the decisions of their seniors; and it is presented nakedly in *Cause Célèbre*. T. C. Worsley, reviewing *Man and Boy* in *The Financial Times*, distilled the essence of the matter: "Its subject is humiliation, which has indeed been the subject of all Mr. Rattigan's plays . . . the weak have a terrible clinging strength . . . they will always come back to haunt and weaken the strong with their misguided devotion."

At the end of Act One of *Variation on a Theme*, young Ron the up-and-coming dancer who thinks himself in love with the *grande cocotte* Rose née Fisch sprains his ankle one evening when Rose is due to dine with her next rich lover. Rose asks her confidante Hettie to cancel the appointment:

HETTIE: Shall I tell him what's happened?
ROSE: No.
HETTIE: Then what shall I tell him?
ROSE: Whatever you think best, in the circumstances.
HETTIE: What are the circumstances?
ROSE: I'm needed by Ron.

I happened to be staying at Rattigan's house one week-end while the play was gestating (while it was still possible that it might be called *Heart and Soul*, or *Rose Fisch*, or *This Same Flower*, or *Finish, Good Lady*) and he was most emphatic about the importance of this curtain line. To be needed was what Rose required, not to be loved. This was, of course, precisely the emotion that stimulated the author in his own life, and accounted for some of the associations that his friends thought so unsatisfactory. *Sub specie aeternitatis*, we can see that they were not so wholly unsatisfactory, no more so than Shakespeare's associations with the Earl of Southampton and the Dark Lady, for they gave him dramatic energy. The apparently irrational behaviour of Hester in *The Deep Blue Sea*, for instance, makes perfect sense if you see her as the willing victim of the humiliation courted to an almost masochistic degree by Rattigan's characters.

In *Cause Célèbre*, Rattigan's last play, the principle is taken to an extreme point. The play is based on the actual case of Mrs. Rattenbury, who murdered her husband so that she might the better pursue an affair with her 18-year-old houseboy. This case occurred in 1935, but Rattigan has said that it so fascinated him that he always intended to write about it. The play, written originally for radio and not, to my mind, quite adequately adapted for stage production (Rattigan made at least three scripts in consultation with the director, Robin Midgley, but he was already seriously ill, and writing was painful to him), presents the young-old relationship with all its facets laid out plain. Here is Mrs. Rattenbury, a mature, thrice-married woman on the one hand. Here is George Wood on the other, a naive and somewhat overgrown 17-year-old. Sex is of course the detonator that sets their relationship off; but the relationship takes on the typical Rattigan pattern. By providing her friend with unaccustomed luxuries, Alma Rattenbury had ensured his dependence on her. It was a dependence that outstayed its welcome:

JUDGE: Now I am not sure that I have followed this. You say you tried to break the affair with Wood but were unable to—one of the reasons being the difference in your ages. Surely that very thing would make it easier?

ALMA: No, my lord. Sorry, but it makes it harder.

JUDGE: But surely the older party must be the dominant party?

ALMA: Excuse me, my lord, but to me it's the other way round. Anyway it was with me and George. I think it must be with many people.

*Cause Célèbre* was the last of five plays that Rattigan wrote after *Variation on a Theme* had come to grief on the trip-wire of the new drama. Ironically, it might have begun a new wave in Rattigan's writing, for there are qualities in it that suggest a broadening of landscape. It is, for example, his only play where the principals could by no stretch of the imagination be equated with the members of his own circle. Then a single set is required to stand for two sitting-rooms, Court No. 1 at the Old Bailey, a prison cell and some other places, the swift radio-style flicking from scene to scene being effected solely by the lighting. If Rattigan had lived, he might well have realised that there were production techniques in use which would free him from his long-standing preference for the standing set and the long developing scene. If anyone had suggested to him in 1948 that *The Browning Version* might be played on a fit-up stage at the back of a pub, he would have been pretty sceptical; yet in 1976 such a production occurred, and he was well pleased with it.

On the whole, however, there is little evidence in these late plays of any intention to challenge the new wave at its own game. *Ross* and *A Bequest to the Nation* go back, in their different ways, to the model of *Adventure Story*; *Man and Boy* may be compared with *The Winslow Boy* in its fictionalised account of a public affair; *In Praise of Love* is a domestic tragi-comedy.

What all of them display is Rattigan's lasting conviction that the West End audience seeks entertainment rather than instruction. Even Bernard Shaw, who devoted his whole playwriting career to telling audiences the facts of political life, was aware of this simple principle, and concealed the pills of his instruction in copious quantities of the high-quality jam of amusement. Rattigan was not in fact at all concerned with administering pills. He was never didactic or satirical. It is doubtful if he had any message to deliver to the world except that people might be a little more tolerant of one another's weaknesses—a virtue, incidentally, that he practised to extremes in his own life. No socially committed director a century hence will be able to produce *Flare Path* as if it were anti-war propaganda or *The Sleeping Prince* as a diatribe against monarchy. To suggest that his plays might have been "better" if he had been more socially conscious would be pointless; they would not be the same plays. You might as well criticise Mendelssohn for not being Wagner.

Rattigan's long suit was romance, and it was the essence of everything he wrote. Alexander the Great and Lawrence of Arabia, seen through his eyes, become the perfect romantic heroes of his time, figures that might have been invented by Major Charles Gilson or Herbert Strang for the pages of *Chums* and the *B.O.P.* They are not diminished by such treatment, any more than Henry VI is diminished when Shakespeare makes him muse on the repose of a shepherd's life. The story of *Man and Boy* is not only about how Antonescu used his estranged son in an attempt to evade justice; it is about how evading justice brought a reconciliation between Antonescu and his son.

It is a characteristic of the British public that they see events, great and small, in terms of romance. The assassination of a president suggests a weeping widow before it suggests a political upheaval. This may be a fault, but it is a fact, and it is a fact that Rattigan kept firmly in mind whatever he chose to write about. Even the second world war, in which he served with distinction as an air-gunner, appears in his stage work only as the comedy of *While the Sun Shines* and the sentiment of *Flare Path*. Occupied territory was for him occupied Ingrid Bergman and her yellow Rolls-Royce—though it's amusing to note that the operations command vehicle of 7th Armoured Division, the Desert Rats, went into the Normandy campaign and on to Berlin labelled on the front bumper with the name of Mabel Crum, the heroine of *While the Sun Shines*.

There seems to have been a slight withdrawal from this principle after *Variation on a Theme*. West End managements were temporising with "modern" plays; Rattigan's own management, H. M. Tennent, who had presented most of his plays since *Flare Path*, were producing new writers like Robert Bolt, Peter Shaffer, even the American Arthur Kopit. *Ross*, with its hint of sexual malpractice, was a step in the direction of the new realism; but Lawrence's adventures in the desert, his relationships with Auda Abu Tayi and his Arab companions Hamed and Rashid are obstinately romantic.

Then, after a pause of three years, came *Man and Boy*. In this there is an overtly homosexual sub-plot, and the main plot concerns international finance: clearly we were edging towards the theatre of fact. But *Man and Boy* can hardly be accounted either an artistic or a commercial success. Horses for courses is as wise a rule on the stage as on the turf, and Rattigan was straying into what was for him comparatively uncharted territory. Though it received some handsome reviews (Bernard Levin said firmly that it was "Rattigan's best play"), *Man and Boy* did not have much of a run. Significantly, Rattigan then withdrew from the stage altogether for seven years and confined himself to the writing of film-scripts.

*A Bequest to the Nation*, originally a television play, ended the silence with an engagement to romance as committed as *Variation on a Theme* twelve years previously. Though the characters include Nelson and Lady Hamilton, besides Lady Nelson and the First Lord of the Admiralty and Captain Hardy, the plot concerns an old-fashioned "triangle". The angles are not occupied by Nelson, Emma Hamilton and Lady, Nelson, but by Nelson, Emma Hamilton and the command of the Fleet; but the play is an old-fashioned triangle none the less. And if there were not enough romance in that, Rattigan has introduced a sub-plot in which a teenage schoolboy, acting out of gentlemanly regard for Lady Nelson, who is his aunt, contrives to get himself dramatically humiliated by Nelson—and then "comes back to haunt and weaken the strong with his misguided devotion", compelling his hero to make him a profound apology.

Having thus brought himself home to familiar ground, from which by an odd chance his departure was marked by a play about a soldier and his return by a play about a sailor, he once more had the confidence to write a straightforward domestic romance about the kind of people he knew and liked. *In Praise of Love* was inspired by the death of Kay Kendall, whose company he had always enjoyed. It is one of his best works, a play in the class of *The Winslow Boy*, *The Browning Version* and *The Deep Blue Sea*.

A touching feature in it is the quiet bravery with which both Lydia and her husband Sebastian face Lydia's inevitable death. When he wrote the play, Rattigan was himself in the early stages of the same illness, and he too faced it with remarkable composure. I met him one day on one of his rare visits to the Garrick Club for luncheon. "I expect you've been asked to 'do' me," he said.

"I've already done you," I told him.

"Flatteringly, I hope," he said.

The next time I saw him was after the revival of *The Browning Version*. I had supper with him at Claridge's and we watched television, a political broadcast and the skating at the Olympic Games. "What do you think of this?" he asked suddenly, crossing the room and passing me a piece of paper from a drawer.

It was a doctor's diagnosis of his illness—a sentence of death. He treated it as light-heartedly as if it were a cutting from a gossip-column.

MAN AND BOY

First published 1964
by Hamish Hamilton Ltd

To
MICHAEL WEIGHT

*Characters:*

CAROL PENN
BASIL ANTHONY
GREGOR ANTONESCU
SVEN JOHNSON
MARK HERRIES
DAVID BEESTON
COUNTESS ANTONESCU

The action of the play takes place in a basement apartment in Greenwich Village, New York, and is continuous, roughly between 6 p.m. and 8.30 p.m. on a July night in 1934. There will be two intervals.

*Man and Boy* was first produced at the Queen's Theatre, London, on September 4th, 1963, with the following cast:

| | |
|---|---|
| CAROL PENN | Alice Kennedy Turner |
| BASIL ANTHONY | Barry Justice |
| GREGOR ANTONESCU | Charles Boyer |
| SVEN JOHNSON | Geoffrey Keen |
| MARK HERRIES | Austin Willis |
| DAVID BEESTON | William Smithers |
| COUNTESS ANTONESCU | Jane Downs |

Directed by MICHAEL BENTHALL

Setting by RALPH ALSWANG

# ACT I

SCENE: *Basil Anthony's basement apartment in Greenwich Village. Whatever else the designer may choose to show us, in order to give a visual impression of a rather sleazy neighbourhood, on a summer evening in 1934 (about 6 p.m.), two rooms only are necessary for the action, namely the barely furnished living-room with a screened-off kitchenette and into which the front door directly opens, and the adjoining bedroom, which has another door leading to a shower and lavatory.*

*Before the rise of the curtain music (Guy Lombardo) is coming from a radio. The curtain rises on darkness, and the music, after growing louder for a moment, fades to a time signal.*

ANNOUNCER. (*From the darkness.*) Six p.m. B.U.L.O.V.A. Bulova Watch Time. Every hour on the hour the *New York Times* brings you important news bulletins.

*The lights begin to come on very gradually. A boy (BASIL ANTHONY) half-dressed in a stiff shirt and evening trousers has been lying on the bed. As the announcer begins his news story he swings his legs off the bed and listens intently. It is plain the news is important to him, although evidently not heard for the first time.*

All day sensational rumours regarding the impending collapse of the financial empire of Gregor Antonescu, the half-legendary, Rumanian-born radio and oil king, have been coming in minute by minute. It has been hard to separate fact from fiction, but this much is known. The crisis began late last night when first reports that a merger planned between one of Antonescu's concerns, Manson Radios, with the great combine American Electric, had failed, hit Wall Street with the force of a hurricane. Today a wave of selling has flooded the market, and stock-markets all over the world have reported panic unloading Of all Antonescu shares. On Wall Street the ticker-tape fell, at times, over forty minutes behind.

BASIL *has moved into the sitting-room and is listening intently.*

The crash, if it should come, will be much the biggest in financial history. President Roosevelt at a press conference today stated that he had no exact information regarding the crisis as yet but that, quote, 'the country's economy in this third year of our Administration is now sound enough to weather any storm, no matter from what quarter it may come'.

*There has been the sound of a shower, which now stops. The lights should by now be fully on.*

The international banker, Mr. J. P. Morgan, said an hour ago that Antonescu had undoubtedly over-extended himself with his loans to many European countries, and that the failure of Antonescu's merger with American Electric was merely the last straw—

*A girl* (CAROL PENN) *comes out of the shower with a bath-towel round her.*

ANNOUNCER. —a straw that not only has shown which way the wind is blowing but has also, perhaps, broken the camel's back—

CAROL. (*Calling into sitting-room.*) He's mixing his metaphors a bit, isn't he? Hey, where's that bathrobe?

BASIL *doesn't reply. His attention is on the radio.*

ANNOUNCER. Of the financier himself, Gregor Antonescu, so-called Saviour and mystery roan of Europe—

CAROL. (*Louder.*) Where's that bathrobe?

BASIL. (*Tensely.*) Bathrobe?

CAROL. The usual.

BASIL. Hanging up.

ANNOUNCER. (*Through this.*) Nothing has been heard since he was photographed leaving his Long Island mansion this morning, supposedly for the Antonescu Building on Wall Street. But there have been several rumours as to his whereabouts—none of them confirmed—

BASIL *turns off the radio abruptly.* CAROL *has gone back into the shower.*

CAROL. (*From the shower.*) Why cut off the rumours? I like them.

*There is no answer from* BASIL, *who pours himself a drink.*

(*Emerging from the shower.*) I said why cut off the rumours? They're the best part—

*She comes into the sitting-room and sees him with his drink.*

Sure. That's my Basil.

BASIL. It's my whisky if I want to drink it.

CAROL. Sure. It's your life too if you want to shorten it.

BASIL. You exaggerate abominably.

CAROL. (*Delightedly mimicking.*) Exaggerate abominably. Gee, I go for that English accent.

BASIL. I'm not English. I've told you a hundred times—

CAROL. (*Soothingly.*) Sure, you're American. All of two months American. But you *were* English. (BASIL *doesn't reply.*) *You* can't fool me. I can tell an English accent. I see Ronald Colman pictures.

BASIL. (*Moodily sipping his drink.*) O.K. So I was English then. It's not true, but if it suits you—

*Pause.*

CAROL. I see. We're in one of those moods, are we?

BASIL. I don't know about you, but I've had rather a good afternoon.

CAROL. No. No complaints about that. I mean the 'why are we all living—what is the purpose of it all?' mood.

BASIL. I'm sorry. I just feel a bit low, that's all. I had some bad news—

CAROL. You wouldn't care to tell me what, I suppose? (BASIL *is silent.*) No. You wouldn't. In six months when have you ever told me anything about yourself? (BASIL *is still silent.*) You haven't been fired, have you?

BASIL. No. As a matter of fact I've got a raise.

CAROL. No kidding.

BASIL. I'm up to twenty-six dollars a week. I play at a dinner session now—

CAROL. I wondered why you were in your working-clothes so early. Honey, isn't *that* something you could have told me?

BASIL. I didn't think of it.

CAROL. That's what I mean. I'd think of it if the Federal Theatre raised *me* two dollars. Fine chance of that. (BASIL *has gone to pour himself another drink.*) I think you've had enough, haven't you? You've been at it all afternoon—

BASIL. (*Pouring himself another drink.*) We're not married yet.

CAROL. (*Steadily.*) No, we're not, but I still think you've had enough to drink.

BASIL *carefully pours out a far smaller whisky than his previous one—holding it up for her to see.*

(*Nodding.*) Looks like I got influence. Not a lot, maybe yet—but some—

*She goes into the bedroom, slipping out of her bathrobe. The telephone rings.* BASIL *has picked up a newspaper, already obviously read, with blazing headlines of which the words 'Antonescu Crisis' are visible.*

(*From the bedroom.*) Shall I answer it?

BASIL. (*Deep in the papers.*) Thanks.

CAROL. (*Picking up receiver.*) Hello. Yes, he's here. Who wants him? (*The telephone goes dead.*) Hey— (*She stares at the receiver.*) Some guy asked for you and hung up. (BASIL *seems not to have heard.* CAROL *struggles into her dress.*) Come do me up, would you?

BASIL *throws the paper away and goes into the bedroom. He begins to do up her dress, then suddenly embraces her.*

BASIL. I'm sorry. I love you very much. I don't show it enough, I know—

CAROL. Yes, you show it. Sometimes by not showing it, you show it. (*She kisses him.*) I love you too, and I do show it. Unwomanly perhaps, but honest.

*She turns round and he resumes his fastening up.*

When you said 'yet' just now—we're not married *yet*—does that mean you haven't finally turned me down?

BASIL. (*Murmuring.*) We haven't enough money to get married. How can I keep a family on twenty-four a week?

CAROL. Twenty-six. And I'm earning too.

BASIL. This week.

CAROL. There'll be another part. Come the end of the Depression and I'll be keeping you. Thanks.

*She sits on the bed to put on shoes and stockings.*

BASIL. (*Bitterly.*) Come the end of the Depression!

CAROL. Yeah. Today's news won't help any, I guess. You know about these things. If this guy crashes it could be real serious, couldn't it?

BASIL. Yes.

CAROL. He's the tops, isn't he? Not like the Insulls and the Staviskys. The real tops?

BASIL. Yes.

CAROL. Advises the Treasury, his word his bond, saved the pound sterling—

BASIL. No.

CAROL. He saved some currency—

BASIL. The franc in 1926—

*There is a knock at the door.*

That may be Joe. He said he might drop by.

CAROL. (*As he goes.*) I suppose you're delighted.

BASIL *turns at the door.*

BASIL. (*With a faint suspicion of a stammer.*) D-delighted?

CAROL. You want the Capitalist System to crash, don't you?

BASIL. (*Carefully.*) Not necessarily *want* it to crash. I just know it's going to, that's all, and probably very soon. Certainly before the thirties are out. And, when it does, there'll be a better system to take its place.

*There is another imperious knock.*

Coming.

CAROL. (*From the bedroom door.*) You doggone bolshie!

BASIL. O.K. So I'm a doggone bolshie—

CAROL *goes into the shower, where we see her repairing her make-up.* BASIL *opens the door, and then, after a slight pause, steps back quickly into the room, staring at his visitor. It is* GREGOR ANTONESCU.

GREGOR'S *age is indeterminate, is officially given as 43, but is certainly more. He is wearing a black hat, slightly lowered over his face, and a light over-coat, with the collar turned up. He carries gloves and an umbrella. The hat he now takes off, and lowers the collar of his overcoat. We now see a face that is perfectly smooth and relaxed, if it shows signs of fatigue it is the fatigue of an athlete rather than of a man on the verge of losing a billion-dollar empire.*

GREGOR. Ah, mon chéri, comme je suis ému de te revoir. (*He comes forward and embraces him, kissing hint on both cheeks.* BASIL *shrinks from the embrace but receives it in silence.* GREGOR *stands back from him, his hands on* BASIL'S *shoulders, looking at him.*) Mon dieu, ça fait plus de cinq ans que je ne t'ai vu. Tu as un peu maigri, non?

BASIL. (*Speaking with difficulty and stammering badly.*) Qu'est-ce q-q-que to f-f-fais ici?

GREGOR. Mais, je suis venu pour to revoir, mon chéri.

BASIL. Ce n'est pas v-v-vrai. Tu es a N-N-New York depuis j-j-janvier—(*Suddenly and loudly.*) Why are we speaking French?

GREGOR. We always did speak French.

BASIL. Now we speak English.

GREGOR. Roumanian, if you like.

BASIL. (*Angrily.*) English! It's not true you've come here to see me. (*His voice stronger and clearer.*) You've been in New York since January and made no effort—

GREGOR. Ah, my dear boy, the pressures of business—

BASIL. And you've been in New York at least t-ten times in the last five years, and you've n-never even tried to get in touch with me.

GREGOR. Nor have you with me, carissimo mio.

BASIL. That's different. You know why.

GREGOR. (*Sadly.*) Ah, yes, I know why.

BASIL. So why suddenly now?

GREGOR. Shall we say—circumstances alter cases. As you know, I detest businessmen's clichés, but they are sometimes true, unhappily. Or, in this altered case, happily. Very happily.

CAROL *comes in and stops short at sight of a stranger. As* GREGOR *turns politely towards her, her eyes widen.*

BASIL. How did you know this address?

CAROL. My name is Carol Penn.

GREGOR. (*Shaking hands.*) How do you do, Miss Penn. And my name is Gregor Antonescu.

CAROL. Yes, I know.

GREGOR. (*Indicating newspaper.*) Yes, my poor dull face has been rather overexposed in the press lately, I'm afraid. I blush every time I see those photographs. Especially that old one of me getting onto a train somewhere. It looks so furtive and sinister—as if I was fleeing from some desperate doom—

BASIL. How did you know the address?

GREGOR. But my dearest child, how does one know anything?

BASIL. How long have you known?

GREGOR. Since you moved down here from West Ninety-Second Street. A good move. Greenwich Village is a much smarter address.

CAROL. So it was you who called just now?

GREGOR. Yes. From a telephone booth in Washington Square. I had been sitting there on a bench and I saw this telephone booth and I said to myself, I wonder if I can work this thing. I never have, you see, but I had to find out if Vassily was at home—

CAROL. (*Murmuring.*) Vassily?

GREGOR. (*Continuing.*) —and I felt that all it needed was the right coin and some courage.

CAROL. You—on a bench in Washington Square—

GREGOR. (*Rather proudly.*) And feeding the pigeons. But, my dear Miss Penn, you have no idea how I have been hounded, all day. These journalists have become ravening monsters. Well, I could not even go to a friend's apartment. They are all being watched. Not that I have so many friends in New York. Only some ladies—very few, of course, at my age—but they are all known too. So the streets and Washington Square became my easiest refuge. And I am so tired, Miss Penn. For three nights now I have not slept—because of this little breeze. Telephone, telephone, telephone. I shall sit down. (*To* BASIL, *who doesn't reply.*) May I, dearest boy? (*He slips his coat off and hands it to* CAROL.) I am so sorry to have hung up—that is correct?—to have hung up in your face, but I thought I was speaking to a stranger, you see. Naturally if I had known it was you—

BASIL. You knew about Carol?

GREGOR. But of course. And now that I meet her in the flesh I can only congratulate you, most warmly, dearest boy.

BASIL. (*Furiously.*) The Antonescu Intelligence System!

GREGOR. The dossier department still functions. (*To* CAROL.) A necessary evil, Miss Penn. I do business with a great many people, all over the world, and some facts about them are often useful. But to call it an 'Intelligence System', as the press do, and Vassily just has, is ridiculous. I employ a few clerks to collect and file important private information—

BASIL. You don't do business with me, do you?

GREGOR. No.

BASIL. Then why do I have a dossier?

GREGOR. Because you're my son.

BASIL. (*Involuntarily.*) No.

GREGOR. (*Gently.*) Ah, but yes. You may have become an American citizen, carissimo, and had your name changed. By the way I was most flattered to learn how very slight that change was, but you are still my son, mon chou. And isn't it natural for a father to try to keep track of his son?

BASIL. (*Brutally.*) Natural!

GREGOR. Of my natural son—agreed.

BASIL. I meant—you—natural?

GREGOR. I knew that was what you meant, and I made a poor joke in return. But my excuse is that I am very tired.

CAROL. (*Looking at* BASIL.) Basil Anthony—Vassily Antonescu?

GREGOR. (*Nodding.*) Not a very startling change of name, you will agree, for a son who has disowned his father for five years.

CAROL. No. Rather close, Why Antonescu, if he's illegitimate?

GREGOR. I gave him the name when I adopted him and made him my heir—

CAROL. Your *heir?* Heir to that empire—

BASIL *laughs.* GREGOR *glances at* him.

GREGOR. How right you are, dear Vassily. The empire *has* slightly shrunk in the last few hours—

BASIL. (*To* CAROL.) But he'll come through all right. He always comes through.

GREGOR. Thank you, dear boy. May I have a glass of wine?

BASIL. I haven't any wine here.

GREGOR. Perhaps some Vermouth?

BASIL. No. I've only Bourbon and gin.

GREGOR. Unimpeachably American. But for you and Greenwich Village I would have thought a little bourgeois. I would like a little Bourbon with no water and a little ice.

BASIL *doesn't move. It is* CAROL *who goes to the table to get it.*

GREGOR. Thank you, Miss Penn.

CAROL. Can I ask you just a couple more questions, Mr. Antonescu?

GREGOR. Of course.

CAROL. Your son isn't the most informative person in the world, you know.

GREGOR. Yes, I know.

CAROL. He disowned you?

GREGOR. Correct.

CAROL. Five years ago?

GREGOR. Correct.

CAROL. Why?

GREGOR. (*Shrugging.*) Thank you, Miss Penn. On his coming-of-age party— in Roumania a son comes of age at eighteen—we had words.

CAROL. They must have been important words.

GREGOR. (*Looking at* BASIL.) They were.

CAROL. What were they about?

GREGOR. (*Still looking at* BASIL.) Truth and falsehood. (*To* CAROL.) Are there any words more important than those?

CAROL. I shouldn't say so—

BASIL. (*Quietly.*) Why don't you tell her I tried to kill you?

*Pause.*

GREGOR. (*Equally quietly.*) For a very simple reason, cheri. You didn't.

BASIL. I fired—

GREGOR. (*Interrupting coldly but with authority.*) And missed. (*To* CAROL.) Any further questions, Miss Penn?

CAROL. Who was his mother?

GREGOR. He never knew her. She died when he was two. She was a dancer in Berlin.

BASIL. A strip-tease dancer—

GREGOR. (*Gently.*) Dear boy—in nineteen eleven? (*To* CAROL.) A flame dancer, Miss Penn. She finished her days in great comfort on an estate I gave her in East Prussia. Enough questions, don't you think, for the moment? (*To* BASIL.) I have asked Sven Johnson here at six-fifteen. You remember him, of course?

BASIL. What about the bodyguard?

GREGOR. William and Sergei?

BASIL. Guarding the street with their tommy guns?

GREGOR. No. They are not with me tonight. (*To* CAROL.) Vassily is so melo-dramatic. William and Sergei are two close friends of mine whose duty it is to look after me. They do carry revolvers, it is true—but after all, there have been attempts on my life, you know. Quite a few as it hap-

pens. Only a few months ago, in New York, there was a very clever attempt to run me down with a truck, did you know that? And in Berlin
one night someone threw a bomb through my bedroom window. Happily I wasn't there at the time. I was out—visiting. These are ordinary
hazards of running rather a large enterprise entirely on one's own. (*To*
BASIL, *after a sip.*) Delicious.

*He finishes the glass and hands it to* CAROL *without looking at her. Obediently
she takes the glass and puts it back. Meanwhile, to* BASIL:

William and Sergei have been promoted since your time. William is President of two companies and Sergei is Chairman of a Bank. Where is your
telephone?

BASIL. In the bedroom.

GREGOR. I shall need to use it. Some international calls, and many local ones.

BASIL. All right. I won't be here.

GREGOR. My dearest boy, there's no need—

BASIL. And if you want to stay the night here you may. I'll find a bed somewhere else.

GREGOR. But carissimo, do you think I would dream of turning you out of
your own apartment?

BASIL. (*Obviously wrought up.*) I don't know whether you would or you
wouldn't. I only know I'm not staying—

GREGOR. (*Murmuring.*) How hurtful you can be sometimes, mon petit—

BASIL *turns his back quickly.* CAROL *steps forward to* GREGOR.

CAROL. Look, Mr. Antonescu, I'm going now, so if you want to talk to your
son—

BASIL. (*Turning on her.*) No. Don't go yet.

CAROL. I've got to get to the theatre.

BASIL. You've got plenty of time. Don't leave me alone. Please don't. I've got
to finish dressing and go to the club—

GREGOR. So soon? I thought you only played at the Green Hat at eleven and
one.

BASIL. I've got a dinner session now. Isn't that in the dossier?

GREGOR. No. I don't think it is. (*To* CAROL.) Miss Penn, another Bourbon,
please, but smaller and with no more ice.

CAROL. Sure.

*She turns to the table, where* BASIL *is already pouring himself a drink.*

GREGOR. But don't think Vassily has inherited his drinking habits from me.
For me this is very rare. A sign, I'm afraid, of exhaustion.

BASIL. My drinking habits are in the dossier?

GREGOR. It's been known to me for sometime that you, drink too much. And
never get drunk either, which is a bad sign.

BASIL. I'm going to change. (*Stiffly and formally.*) Forgive me.

GREGOR. Of course.

BASIL, *holding his drink, goes into the bedroom where, after closing the door, he falls on the bed, face down. In the sitting-room* CAROL *brings* GREGOR *his drink.*

CAROL. Shall I taste it first to show you I haven't poisoned it?

GREGOR. Hardly necessary, I think.

*He swallows it in a gulp and hands it back to her. She takes it.*

CAROL. Another?

GREGOR. No. Tonight of all nights I must keep a clear head.

CAROL *puts the glass back on the table.*

CAROL. Well, then—do you mind if—

*She points to the bedroom door.*

GREGOR. No, no. Don't concern yourself about me. I shall just sit here and concentrate. And believe me, Miss Penn, tonight I have much to concentrate on.

CAROL. (*At bedroom door.*) Gee, I feel kinda lost. I only wish I could help—some way.

GREGOR. Thank you, Miss Penn. That is most kind. But at the moment I really don't need help.

*And from the way he smiles at her we can almost believe him.* CAROL *smiles back, plainly taken. Then she goes into the bedroom. As soon as she has gone* GREGOR'S *smile is replaced by a slight frown of deep concentration. During the ensuing scene he will take out a notebook and make some quick notes—plainly of figures, from the lightning speed with which they are written.*

*In the bedroom,* BASIL, *on* CAROL'S *entrance, has sat up quickly, his back to us. We don't therefore see his expression but* CAROL *does.*

CAROL. (*Kneeling beside him.*) You could have told me.

BASIL. I couldn't tell you.

CAROL. Hell, I can be trusted. (BASIL *doesn't reply.* CAROL *looks at his face with concern.*) Not with everything. Not with who Laura Bligh's sleeping with—things like that. But with this I could have been. Did you really try to kill him?

*Pause.*

BASIL. You heard what he said. I missed—

CAROL. What really happened that night?

BASIL. In six months I haven't told you my true name. Do you think I'm going to tell you now what really happened that night?

CAROL. (*Helping him on with his jacket, quietly.*) No, I don't. But I think somehow it would help you if you did.

BASIL. Yes, it would somehow, but I can't. I can't ever. Get it? (CAROL *nods.*) Look all right?

CAROL. Yes, O.K. Are you quite determined to run out on him?

BASIL. (*His back to her.*) I've got the dinner session—

CAROL. One call would fix that.

BASIL. (*Attending to his eyes.*) Saying?

CAROL. Saying something like—well—how about this? Look, Joe, my father has turned up at my apartment rather unexpectedly, I haven't seen him in five years, he seems to be in a bit of trouble, and I'd rather like a few hours with him—so would you do my dinner spot tonight, and I'll do your morning spot tomorrow?

*Pause.*

BASIL. (*His back still to her.*) Damn you.

CAROL. (*Going to him.*) Honey—you do what you think right. Hell, he's your father, not mine.

BASIL *turns and buries his face on her shoulder.*

BASIL. (*His voice muffled.*) If you knew. If only you knew—

CAROL. (*In a firm, matter-of-fact voice.*) No. I don't. And, as you're not going to tell me, I never will. So stop making those eyes red. (*He turns from her into the shower.*) Have you got any eye-wash?

BASIL. (*From the shower.*) Yes. Some place. (*He finds it, and we can see him applying towel and eye-bath.*)

CAROL. (*Still matter-of-fact.*) Who's the Countess Antonescu?

BASIL. (*From the shower.*) His wife.

CAROL. Ever met her?

BASIL. Since my time. I gather she was a typist from the London pool.

CAROL. Why the title?

BASIL. He bought it for her. Holy Roman—

CAROL. Doesn't that make him a 'Count'?

BASIL. (*Applying eye-bath.*) He won't use it for himself. He says the name Gregor Antonescu needs no appendage, and shall I tell you something? He's right. Better now?

CAROL. (*Inspecting his eyes.*) Yes. You can duck out with dignity now.

BASIL. Duck out?

CAROL. That's what I said.

BASIL. (*Now without emotion.*) *Duck* out? (*He sits on the bed.*) Yes. I should have seen it. Ducking out is just what he expects of me. The little boy who was scared of horses, and wouldn't learn to swim and ran away from everything. Always ran away. Even from him. (*He reaches for the telephone and begins to dial.*) O.K., you win.

CAROL. I said, do what you think right.

BASIL. I think this is right. (*Into telephone.*) Hullo, Sam. Is Joe in the club . . . upstairs? Well, get him for me, will you? . . . Sure, I'll hold on.

CAROL *sits beside him and takes his hand. He kisses her gently.*

*In the other room* SVEN JOHNSON *has knocked at the open door at about the same moment as* BASIL *has begun to talk on the telephone and, in response to* GREGOR'S *'Come in', has walked into the sitting-room. He is dressed much like Gregor, and also carries a black hat and an umbrella, but wears no coat.*

GREGOR. You are five minutes late.

SVEN. I'm sorry, G.A. The traffic in Wall Street—

GREGOR. Minutes are precious tonight. You have arranged the meeting with Herries?

SVEN. Yes. Seven p.m. here. He is coming straight from his office.

GREGOR. Did he seem surprised at the address?

SVEN. Not particularly. He understood why you couldn't meet him at the Antonescu Building, or go to him at American Electric.

GREGOR. (*Urgently.*) But this address? A basement apartment in the seamier side of Greenwich Village? Did you give him no explanation at all?

SVEN. I couldn't think of one to give him.

GREGOR. You should have. The President of the second biggest company in America summoned without explanation to meet *me* in *this* place. (*He looks around in distaste.*) A park bench in Washington Square would have been better.

SVEN. I'm very sorry, G.A.

GREGOR. I shall have to think of something before he comes. You stopped him issuing the statement?

SVEN. Yes—but he would only postpone it. Three hours. It has to catch the morning press.

GREGOR. Did he give you a copy?

SVEN. No, but I have it from one of the typists. It only cost a thousand dollars—

GREGOR *nods approvingly and takes the document which* SVEN *gives him. While he is studying it, without expression,* BASIL *speaks on the telephone.*

BASIL. Joe? Basil. I can't make the dinner session. Something important . . . No, *really* important. Vital, even. Can you do it for me, and I'll do yours tomorrow? . . . Thanks, pal. Thanks a lot.

CAROL *pats his hand approvingly.* BASIL *stands up, but, at the door, again shows the same hesitation about going in. Meanwhile in the sitting-room* GREGOR *hands back the document to* SVEN.

SVEN. Bad reading?

GREGOR. Not to me. And no one else will read it. Have you arranged the call to London?

SVEN. It is timed for six-forty-five.

BASIL *comes in, at last. Neither pays him any attention.*

GREGOR. And the calls to Rome and Paris?

SVEN. They have all been booked from this number—but for no specific time. I didn't know how long the meeting with Herries will last.

GREGOR. Not too long, I think. Longer, perhaps, though, than Herries thinks. (*Seeing* BASIL.) Ah, carissimo, so elegant you look, in your dinner-jacket. You remember Sven Johnson?

SVEN. Why, Vassily, how you have changed! So thin!

GREGOR. Ah, to vois? C'est ce que je lui disais. Il est trop maigre—et si pâle—

BASIL. (*Taking* SVEN'S *outstretched hand.*) Hullo, Sven.

SVEN. And this will be Miss Carol Penn.

BASIL *stares at him angrily.*

CAROL. That's right. (*She shakes hands with him.*)

BASIL. (*Shortly.*) Father, I've put off my dinner session.

GREGOR. (*Absently.*) Have you, dear boy? Why?

BASIL. To be with you—

GREGOR. (*Catching himself up hastily.*) But, my dearest child, how very kind. How very, very kind. What happiness you give me with such a gesture—

BASIL *abruptly turns to the drink table, pouring himself out a drink, and watched solicitously by* CAROL.

(*To* SVEN, *in a level voice.*) I believe I have thought of an excuse for Herries. A good one.

SVEN. The truth?

GREGOR. The truth could have its virtues with some American financiers. Not I think with this one. No. Something rather more useful. Two birds with one single stone—

BASIL. (*Turning.*) Father, can I get you some food?

GREGOR. Dearest boy, no. I have reached a stage of exhaustion where the effort of eating would only exhaust me further—

BASIL. Shouldn't you lie down in there?

GREGOR. Yes. Later I will and perhaps even sleep for an hour or two. But now I must carry on a little longer.

BASIL. You l-look very tired, Father.

GREGOR. I am very tired, carissimo. Tired even unto death. How good of you to care. (*To* SVEN, *in a strong, level voice.*) I forgot to ask you. Did you get in touch with my wife?

SVEN. Yes. I found her still at the Plaza Hotel. She has been waiting there for over an hour.

GREGOR. Why?

SVEN. You called her from Long Island on Friday and made a date there for dinner.

GREGOR. Did I? How odd! Anyway, she should have realized from today's papers, at least, that I could hardly have kept it. I suppose the reporters have been at her apartment all day?

SVEN *nods.*

Did she say anything?

SVEN. She says not. But they followed her to the Plaza, and when I spoke to her they were still there. Two of them were at the call-box, trying to listen.

GREGOR. She probably repeated this address in a loud—clear voice—

SVEN. No. I stopped her. She wrote it down.

GREGOR. On a piece of paper which she no doubt dropped in the lobby?

SVEN. (*Smiling.*) Let us hope not.

GREGOR. (*Remembering* BASIL's *presence.*) I have taken the liberty of asking your—er—well, stepmother, shall we call her?—to come here tonight. It is important for a particular reason. I hope you don't mind.

BASIL. No, of course not.

GREGOR. You will get on very well with her. She is adorable. (*To* SVEN.) How have you arranged for her to arrive here without being followed?

SVEN. Sergei is looking after it. He believes the reporters don't know about the stairs to the apartment below. If she uses that and takes the subway—

GREGOR. Subway? It is hard to imagine a more conspicuous sight than Florence on a subway.

CAROL, *as if to assert her presence in the apartment, turns on the radio.*

SVEN. Sergei said he would see that she was suitably dressed.

GREGOR. A raincoat with a ruby and diamond belt, I expect. It's a big risk but I need her here tonight.

*The music begins.* CAROL *twiddles the dial to another station, also music.* (*Flicking his fingers imperiously.*) Please turn that off. (*He turns his head to see that it is* CAROL *who has turned it* on, *and is now turning it off.*) I'm so sorry, Miss Penn. Music hath charms but destroys concentration.

CAROL. I thought you might like to hear the news—

GREGOR. Why should I? I know the news, and I hate hearing it distorted. Not only by the announcer but by that frightful radio. (*To* BASIL.) It's one of ours, I noticed, and not American Electric. Thank you for your loyalty, cheri, but you really must get a newer model—

BASIL. I bought it second-hand. I didn't know it was yours, Father.

GREGOR. Ah. Manson Radios are since your time, of course. You use my fountain pens, too, I see. Now *that* you must have known about, dearest boy. 'Kenway Pens' were going when you were still—with us. How much did you pay for the radio?

BASIL. Twenty-three dollars.

GREGOR. Too much. We have a new model for twenty dollars that is twice as good. You were grossly cheated, mon petit.

*The telephone rings in the bedroom.*

SVEN. (*Looking at his watch.*) This may be London. (*He goes quickly towards the bedroom door and then remembers his manners. To* BASIL.) I have your permission, dear Vassily?

BASIL. Of course.

SVEN *goes into the bedroom. He picks up the receiver and repeats the Gramercy number. Then after a moment we hear him say:* Transatlantic? Yes . . . Yes . . . Yes, I'll hold on.

CAROL. (*In the sitting-room, meanwhile.*) Mr. Antonescu?

GREGOR. Yes, Miss Penn?

CAROL. When you said just now that you didn't like hearing the news distorted by the radio announcer, do you mean that the news isn't as bad as it seems?

GREGOR. Well, Miss Penn, it would be ridiculous for me to claim that panic selling of all my shares on all exchanges in the world, makes the real news exactly joyful. But if you have any money to invest I think you would help yourself to a fairly agreeable profit if you buy Antonescu shares early tomorrow morning. Manson Radios would be best, although any will do. But be early. Later in the day they won't be easy to buy. (*Offhandedly.*) You do that, too, Vassily, or does your new social conscience forbid it?

BASIL. Is my new social conscience in the dossier too?

GREGOR. (*Amused.*) My dearest boy, I have always known how strong your conscience is. That it should now incline more to Karl Marx than to God the Father could possibly have been guessed.

BASIL. I'm not a Marxist.

GREGOR. What are you?

BASIL. A socialist.

GREGOR. I never quite know the difference, except that with Stalin I can do business and with Ramsay MacDonald I can't. At least I couldn't when he *was* a socialist. As a matter of fact, if he'd accepted my help in 1931 I might just have saved him from committing political suicide. But Stalin—now there is a man after my own heart. I find him a very level-headed businessman—

BASIL. What about the labour camps?

GREGOR. (*Shrugging.*) Capitalist propaganda. (*To* CAROL.) So buy those shares, Miss Penn—I implore you.

CAROL. I haven't any money to invest.

GREGOR. What a pity.

CAROL. But if I had I don't know if—I mean, forgive me, Mr. Antonescu, but it does seem—as of this moment—like you've got a pretty serious crisis on your hands.

GREGOR. Oh, yes. I have. As of this moment. That is a good phrase. American idiom?

CAROL *nods.*

I must remember it. As of this moment, Miss Penn, I have got a serious crisis, yes. A crisis of confidence and of liquidity—exactly the same crisis as our world economy is passing through today. But *passing* through, I'm happy to say—thanks to your great President. I'm going to pass through mine, and by tomorrow morning I shall have.

CAROL. What is liquidity?

*In the bedroom* SVEN *speaks on the telephone.*

SVEN. Lord Thornton? . . . Johnson here. The *Alan* wants a word with you . . . Yes 'The Man' himself . . . I knew you would be pleased. Hold on.

*He has got up and walked to the sitting-room door. He enters the sitting-room as* CAROL *asks her question.*

GREGOR. Liquidity?

SVEN. London is on the line.

GREGOR. (*Ignoring him.*) A short definition is ready access to cash. Liquidity and confidence are really the same problem. You have some money in that charming handbag?

CAROL. A dollar, fifty—

GREGOR. (*Smiling.*) I didn't ask how much. But since you have been kind enough to tell me we can say that, as far as your fare home tonight is concerned, you are enviably liquid.

CAROL. First time I've ever been envied for what's in my bag—

GREGOR. But supposing you had occasion to go immediately to Baltimore—

CAROL. I can't think why I should.

GREGOR. Something to do with your work?

CAROL. Like an audition or something?

GREGOR. Yes. An audition for a part. Excellent—

SVEN. (*Raising his voice a little.*) Lord Thornton is on the line from London, G. A.

GREGOR. (*Again ignoring him.*) So you have occasion to go to Baltimore immediately, now. It will mean this part with much money. Fifty—a hundred dollars a week—

CAROL. (*Touching wood.*) Say fifty.

GREGOR. The fare to Baltimore is how much?

CAROL. Gee, I don't know. Say ten dollars.

GREGOR. You have a dollar fifty in your bag. Your bank is closed. No place to cash a cheque down here. Even the pawnshops are closed, for your wrist-watch and that delightful brooch would certainly raise good money. You have the cash at home, no doubt, but no time to get there. The train leaves in ten minutes. What do you do?

CAROL. Borrow it off Basil—Vassily.

GREGOR. And suppose by some mischance he didn't have it? Perhaps his tailors have been dunning him for that dinner-jacket, and he's had to pay them all his cash for this week. What then?

CAROL. Well, I guess I lose the part.

GREGOR. And the world is the poorer. And so, incidentally, are you. And so is Vassily, to whom I am sure you would have given a handsome present to celebrate your success. Liquidity is the life blood of our economy, Miss Penn. Since 'twenty-nine our financial arteries have hardened and the blood no longer circulates nearly as freely as it should. The whole capitalist system is in danger of arteriosclerosis—sick unto death some say. Many say. Well, Miss Penn, I don't. I am an optimist—perhaps the only one—in my position, left in the whole, wide world. I believe the crisis is past.

CAROL. What about your own crisis?

GREGOR. Exactly the same as the world's. And exactly the same as your imaginary one with that emergency trip to Baltimore. Now, like everyone else in the world I have been hit by the depression. My enemies realize it—they are known as bears—those beasts who thrive on human misery—and lately they have been closing in for the kill. Two days ago a merger between my radio company and American Electric seemed likely to fail. If it had succeeded it would have netted me seventy-five million dollars cash—which is my fare to Baltimore—Baltimore, in this case, being certain pressing debts and the chance of a highly advantageous loan to Mussolini in return for some trading concessions. My enemies, the bears, saw that I looked like being stranded at Grand Central Station and took advantage of it. As simple as that.

CAROL. O.K. So I couldn't get to Baltimore just now. So how do you?

GREGOR. I intend to raise the fare. And to raise it before the stock market opens in the morning, which is when my train to Baltimore must leave.

CAROL. With you on it?

GREGOR. (*Smiling confidently.*) With me on it.

*He goes to the bedroom door, where* SVEN *is still awaiting him.*

You must get Vassily to explain to you what liquidity really means—in rather less childish terms. Vassily has a very good financial brain—

*He goes into the bedroom beckoning* SVEN *in and closing the door.*

Before Herries arrives the girl must go.

SVEN. (*Looking at his watch.*) She will be leaving anyway in a few moments. To get to her theatre by subway she will need at least half an hour. It is an eight o'clock curtain and understudies have to report by seven-thirty. I checked on that.

GREGOR *lies on the bed. It is a moment before he picks up the receiver. During this moment* BASIL, *in the sitting-room, has finished his glass and turned to the drink bottle.*

CAROL. (*Taking glass from his hand.*) No more of that. I'll make you some coffee. You need it. Hell, we both need it.

*She disappears into the kitchenette.*

GREGOR. (*Picking up receiver at length.*) My dear Thornton . . . How good to hear your voice. Forgive me dear fellow, I will be with you in one minute. Keep the line open please, and have the balance sheet of Manson Radios ready, if you would be so kind.

*He puts the receiver on the floor and stretches out fully on the bed, in an utterly relaxed attitude.*

We will make it two minutes, I think. Wake me, if I sleep. (*He closes his eyes.*)

SVEN. What about the boy? Shouldn't I get rid of him before Herries arrives?

GREGOR. (*Murmuring.*) No.

SVEN. Won't he be a nuisance?

GREGOR. (*Sleepily.*) No.

*He lies absolutely still. It is impossible to tell if he is asleep or awake.* SVEN *sits down, watching over him.*

*In the sitting-room* CAROL, *having filled the kettle and lit the stove comes back into the room.* BASIL *is sitting, staring into space.* CAROL, *sits on the arm of his chair and strokes his head.*

CAROL. (*Affectionately.*) Well, tough guy—

BASIL. (*Bitterly.*) Tough guy.

CAROL. To up and leave that father? Does anything come tougher than that? Wow, what a charmer. (*Judiciously.*) Of course he has to be—I see that—

he couldn't be what he is without it. But you don't see the charm being switched on and off, like with some actor. It just is on, or it is off. You don't spot the trick. I guess he's a kind of genius.

BASIL. I guess he is.

CAROL. With you he's different, in a funny way. Of course I can see right through all that carissimo, cheri stuff—

BASIL. And what do you see?

CAROL. I don't know. Whatever it is could be genuine.

BASIL. (*Eagerly.*) Do you really think so?

CAROL. I didn't say genuine *what*. I just said genuine.

BASIL. Like—contempt?

CAROL. I shouldn't say so. That's what you like to think he feels, because you feel it yourself about yourself. (*Fondly.*) I know you fairly well, Vassily Antonescu.

BASIL. Basil Anthony.

CAROL. Sure. Basil Anthony. Still my Basil. Tougher than I knew, but still my Basil.

BASIL. Like hate, then?

CAROL. Could be. Or love. Or both. Or neither. Or something else I've missed and you certainly have. Is that kettle boiling? (*She looks.*) No. (*Coming back.*) He sees through you O.K.—that's for sure.

BASIL. You mean he looks through me—as if I weren't there—

CAROL. Oh, no. For him you're there all right. I meant he sees through you—

BASIL. Sees what?

CAROL. (*Quietly.*) How you worship him.

*Pause.* BASIL *stares at her, frowning.*

BASIL. (*Equally quiet.*) I haven't seen my father for five years. I could have called him at any time and been welcomed back with open arms, and with carissimos and chéris and champagne parties, and a huge allowance and, probably been reinstated as his heir. But I haven't, have I? I've lived in Greenwich Village as an indifferent piano-player on twenty to twenty-six dollars a week, and on Sundays I've sometimes waved a red flag and shouted slogans which, when interpreted, can only mean 'down with Gregor Antonescu'. Now, how, to a balanced, objective, rational judge, can that add up to worship?

CAROL. (*Shrugging.*) Perhaps the balanced, objective, rational judge hasn't seen the way you look at him when he's in the same room. And that is the kettle boiling.

*She goes behind the screen into the kitchenette. In the bedroom* SVEN *has gently touched* GREGOR. *If* GREGOR *was asleep he is perfectly controlled and alert as he nods to* SVEN *and picks up the receiver from the floor.*

GREGOR. (*Into receiver.*) My dear Thornton, so sorry to have kept you waiting. You, and my other London associates would have had, I imagine, an anxious day . . . I? My dear fellow, I am so much more accustomed to these little disturbances. 'Thirty-one was just as bad, you know, and 'twenty-nine was even worse . . . Oh, no. Please believe me. No real cause for concern at all . . . Yes, that is correct . . . quite correct, dear Thornton. You have an exceptionally acute financial brain . . . Yes, my dear Viscount. (*Chuckling.*) How very right you are. With the recent loans to Hungary and Jugoslavia I was vulnerable to an attack from the naughty 'bears'. J. P. Morgan has just said exactly the same thing . . . Yes, great minds do indeed think alike . . . (*To* SVEN.) Thornton must go . . . Yes. Twenty-three per cent off . . . yes, undoubtedly serious, dear old chap but what you don't know, and none of you know, are three things. First, I have a very large sum standing to my account at the Berliner Bank . . . The Berliner Bank . . . My dear fellow, an old-fashioned, most trustworthy German bank. I am most surprised that you—vice-chairman, as you are, of the City of London Bank, have not heard of it . . . Yes. I am on the board of directors of the Berliner Bank. So are the ex-Crown Prince and Hermann Goering. I have a sum standing in their account to the tune of over two hundred million dollars . . . No, I am sorry. I cannot authorize them to give you the exact figure, because my promise, even to that nasty little guttersnipe, Hitler, is binding . . . Yes . . . Yes, exactly, you have hit upon it, dear boy. It was a secret loan made in 1933 and now partly repaid. Now. Second point, the Antonescu Foundation, of which as you know, my wife is the President, is ready at any moment to make me a substantial loan . . . A charitable concern, of course, but a loan is perfectly legal, and don't you believe, dear old fellow, that charity begins at home? So that brings my immediately realizable assets to something in the nature of half a billion . . . I have held it all back for a very simple reason, dear chap—I don't want my enemies to know that I have it. It's a 'masse de manoeuvre' that I intend to launch against them at the very crisis of the battle . . . A 'masse de manoeuvre'. It means a force in reserve, . . . You are quite right. It is not a banking term, dearest old fellow, it is a military metaphor . . . (*To* SVEN.) He really must go. (*Into receiver.*) Now, the third and last, and most important of all. The merger of Manson Radios with American Electric has not failed . . . I repeat, *has not failed,* and will, after all, go through. Herries is coming to see me in fifteen minutes . . . Yes it will go through. You have my word, dearest fellow . . . (*Icily.*) Well, if you really prefer some wild Wall Street rumours to my own word, your best course would be for you and my other London associates to sell all your Antonescu holdings at once. I suggest, however, that a more profitable course would be to hold on to them and to see that the news I have just given you reaches the London Stock Exchange very early tomorrow morning . . . (*Still icily.*) I am glad that you weren't doubting my word. (*More warmly.*) But of course things have looked black—and no doubt even blacker from three thousand miles away—but never forget, dearest Thornton: 'The darkest hour is just before the dawn.' (*To* SVEN.) Forgive me, but I *have* to speak his language . . . (*Into receiver.*) Happier now? I am so glad . . .

Yes. The merger would transform the whole situation, but I don't care for your conditional tense, Thornton. The merger will transform the whole situation . . . Yes. Good. (*Briskly.*) Now, dearest Viscount, will you please read over to me the balance sheet, of June the first, 1934, of Manson Radios . . . No. There is no need to go slowly. I am not writing it down . . . (*For the first time showing anger.*) I am not writing it down, Thornton. Don't you know me well enough by now. Begin, please.

*He puts his unoccupied hand over his eyes and listens to a distant voice reciting, audibly but indistinctly, row upon row of figures. Very occasionally he will interrupt with some such request as:*

Give me the undistributed profit again.

*or*

Preferred ordinary interim, please, once more. The figure seems excessive . . . Yes. I see. Of course. I had forgotten.

*But in the main he lies quite still, hand over eyes concentrating on the figures as they are read to him.*

*In the sitting-room* CAROL *has come out some moments before with a tray on which are two cups, a jug of cream, a bowl of sugar, and a pot of coffee. Putting it down on the table, she has poured* BASIL *a cup. She plainly knows exactly how he likes it, creaming and sugaring it herself. Then she hands it to him.*

BASIL. Your girlish intuition has led you astray. I don't worship him now—

CAROL. (*Pouring out her own coffee.*) That 'now' is meaningful—

BASIL. (*Fiercely.*) Why? A man can change can't he?

CAROL. Not that man, I wouldn't think. How has he changed?

BASIL. Well—it's the system that's changed him—

CAROL. (*Placidly sipping.*) Oh. The system.

BASIL. (*Fiercely again.*) Yes. The system. The system does pervert and destroy human character. That's not just a slogan. It's the truth. (*Agitatedly striding up and down, watched solicitously by* CAROL.) You'd better know a story about him—about him as a child. In Bucharest he starved—I mean literally starved—not just going short, like our poor here—N.R.A. and soup kitchens and Buddy Can You Spare A Dime? I mean a child with a belly swollen from hunger, sitting in the gutter of Bucharest, begging for a crust of bread. His father drank and beat him. His mother hated him. He was the fifth child, and they couldn't hope to feed four, let alone five. But he was the one who did the begging because, at three or four, his sores were so repulsive, and his face so thin, and his eyes so huge that people—rich people—did sometimes press a coin into his hand—always being careful to look the other way—

CAROL. (*For a warm-hearted girl, curiously unimpressed.*) How do you know all this?

BASIL. It's in all the biographies. You've only got to go to the public library—

CAROL. (*Placidly finishing her coffee.* BASIL *has gone back to his.*) I bet they didn't look the other way.

BASIL. What do you mean?

CAROL. I bet they chose him because he was the prettiest. And, now having met him, I should think he painted those sores on himself, and in the most provocative places—

BASIL. (*In genuine anguish.*) Don't make a joke of it. Carol, don't!

CAROL. (*Going to him instantly.*) Darling, I'm sorry. (*She embraces him.*) Hit me, or something, but forgive me.

BASIL. It's all right. It's only it's important to me, to remember sometimes—

CAROL. (*Maternally.*) Of course it is. That man in there is your business, not mine. You're my business, and I didn't mean to hurt you. God knows I didn't. It seems like you've been hurt enough as it is. (*Looking at her watch.*) I've got to get going. Darling, if there's anything I can do to help tonight—

BASIL. Come back if you can.

CAROL. I'll damn well see I can.

*There is a moment's silence while they are in each other's arms.*

GREGOR. (*In the bedroom.*) Thank you, Thornton . . . Yes. I have all I need. Good night. And sleep soundly, dear old fellow. And tell all the others to sleep soundly too. (*He rings off. To* SVEN.) Quel imbecile!

CAROL. (*Kissing* BASIL *on the mouth.*) I *do* love you, you know. More than ever now, I think.

BASIL. (*Murmuring.*) I love you, too. Remember that, won't you? Whatever happens, remember that.

GREGOR *comes in, followed by* SVEN. *He watches the spectacle of his son kissing* CAROL *with seemingly paternal benevolence. It is a moment before* BASIL *sees him, and then he breaks away from* CAROL, *almost as if he had been caught in a guilty act.*

GREGOR. Goodness, I am sorry. You must please forgive me. (*To* SVEN.) That small one there, please. There (*Pointing to a corner of the sofa.*) is where Herries sits.

SVEN, *under his instructions, re-arranges an arm-chair to face the sofa.*

(*To* BASIL.) Si je comprends bien, to vas épouser cette charmante jeune fille?

CAROL. (*To* BASIL.) Épouser?

BASIL. Marry.

CAROL. (*Boldly to* GREGOR.) The subject has been broached, Mr. Antonescu, but more by me than by your son. I must go. (*She begins to collect her things.*)

GREGOR. Too bad. (*To* SVEN.) No. Not so close.

SVEN *alters the position.*

About three inches, more. (*To* BASIL.) Mais, mon petit, pourquoi ne pas vous marier? Je la trouve ravissante. Vous vous connaissez depuis longtemps?

BASIL. (*His stammer becoming painful.*) Nous n-nous c-c-connaissons d-depuis s-s—

*His father waits patiently, the benign smile never fading.*

—six mois. (*With a bit of hysteria.*) We've known each other six months. I told you to speak English.

GREGOR. I'm so sorry. I forgot. Six months? Well, in these frank days I am quite sure you have discovered all there is to know about each other.

BASIL. Yes, Father.

GREGOR. So what is the impediment, dearest boy?

CAROL. I don't think he can answer that.

GREGOR. You can?

CAROL. I couldn't before this evening. Now I have a glimmering of an idea. (*To* BASIL.) Good-bye, darling.

*She holds out her arms to him as if almost commanding him to come and kiss her in front of his father. This* BASIL *does.* GREGOR *abruptly turns to* SVEN.

GREGOR. (*To* SVEN.) Now—that light out, I think.

SVEN *turns it out.*

No, that is not right. Perhaps if you bring up that lamp a little further—

SVEN *does so.*

then I will be in shadow—

BASIL. (*To* CAROL.) I'll walk with you to the subway.

GREGOR. (*Without looking at him, but sharply.*) No.

BASIL. Why not, Father?

GREGOR. I want you here. You can help.

BASIL. How?

GREGOR. By making yourself agreeable. Dearest boy—this is *your* apartment— and so Mr. Herries, the President of American Electric Incorporated is, strictly speaking, *your* guest. (*To* SVEN.) I see now. That light is still too strong. The—is it bulb or globe in this Continent?

SVEN. Globe.

GREGOR. Change that globe from that lamp to this.

SVEN *does so.* GREGOR *is now paying no attention to* CAROL *and* BASIL.

BASIL. (*Kissing her.*) Well, good night, then.

CAROL. No, not good night, I'll call back. We could go out some place, maybe. (*To* GREGOR.) Good-bye, Mr. Antonescu.

GREGOR. Good-bye—Miss—er— (*To* SVEN.) That is much better, Sven. Well done.

CAROL *goes,* BASIL *holding door open for her.*

(*Looking at his watch.*) Five minutes. (*As* BASIL *comes back into the room he looks at him appraisingly with a slight frown.*) Dearest boy—would you do me a favour? Would you divest yourself of that frightful dinner-jacket?

BASIL. (*Self-consciously.*) I know it must look terrible. I bought it for nine dollars. Still that's a lot for working-clothes. (*He goes to the bedroom door.*) What shall I put on?

GREGOR. Have you got a good suit?

BASIL. Nothing you would call good. I mean they are all over five years old and hang on me a bit.

GREGOR. (*Considering him.*) Yes, they would. What do you usually wear then?

424                            MAN AND BOY

BASIL. Down here in the Village, usually slacks and a sweater or a shirt. Sandals too, I'm afraid.

GREGOR. Well, Mr. Herries is a snob but he is also known to have literary
leanings. I'm sure he would rather have written Gray's Elegy than have
captured America—which financially speaking one might say he almost
has. Something Bohemian, then. May I come and advise?

BASIL. Yes, Father.

*He leads the way into the bedroom and opens a cupboard* for GREGOR'S *inspection. There is a knock at the front door.*

BASIL. (*In alarm.*) There he is.

GREGOR. (*Unalarmed.*) Two minutes early. (*Pulling down a pair of trousers.*)
These are rather chic.

BASIL. They're really for the beach.

GREGOR. It doesn't matter, dear boy. They look expensive.

BASIL. They're not.

GREGOR. In such things looks are all that count. Now, where are your shirts?

BASIL. (*Undressing.*) Over there—middle drawer—

GREGOR *opens the indicated drawers and begins an inspection.*

SVEN *meanwhile has gone to the front door—unhurriedly because he too
knows that* HERRIES *is early and that* GREGOR *is occupied. He opens it now.*
MARK HERRIES, *a smooth, highly prosperous-looking man, in the early
fifties, comes in. He is followed by* DAVID BEESTON, *who looks what he is—
an accountant.*

*He is in the middle thirties, earnest and sincere. Also more than a little awed
both by the occasion and by* MR. HERRIES, *who went to Harvard, knows only
the very best people, and doesn't usually consort with accountants outside office
hours.*

HERRIES. Good evening, Johnson.

SVEN. Good evening, Mr. Herries. It's very good of you to be here so
promptly.

HERRIES. Not at all. I fully realize the immense importance of the occasion.
I've brought Mr. Beeston with me. He was our accountant who inspected
those books in Bucharest, and unearthed that little—discrepancy. (*In-
troducing.*) Mr. Beeston, Mr. Sven Johnson, The Crown Prince of the
Antonescu empire. (*To* SVEN.) You don't mind that appellation?

SVEN. I'm very flattered. But my succession, if it comes, is a very distant prospect. Won't you both sit down.

HERRIES. Thank you.

SVEN *tries to manoeuvre* HERRIES *on to the sofa, but fails.* HERRIES *firmly sits in
the chair.* BEESTON *perches on a window seat.*

GREGOR. (*In the bedroom, turning with a rather brightly coloured silk shirt. He
has taken his time over the inspection of the shirts, calmly having considered
two or three before finally making his selection.*) This one, I think.

BASIL. Yes, that one *was* expensive, I should think. A Christmas present. But
I've never worn it. It's too chi-chi for me.

GREGOR. Ah, mais non, pas du tout. It should suit you very well and go well with those slacks too—

*In the sitting-room, through this,* SVEN *has been speaking to* HERRIES.

SVEN. I think you'll find the sofa more comfortable.

HERRIES. I'm very happy in this chair, thank you.

SVEN. I'll just tell G. A. you're here.

HERRIES. How is he?

SVEN. You'll see for yourself in a moment. Excuse me.

*He slips into the bedroom before* GREGOR *speaks his last line, and closes the door.*

He's brought that accountant.

GREGOR. Good. That's what I hoped.

SVEN. And Herries is sitting in your chair.

GREGOR. Trust him. (*To* BASIL, *who has pulled on his slacks sometime before and is now busily tucking his shirt in.*) Very smart. Perhaps the hair needs a little attention—

BASIL. Yes, Father.

*He goes into the shower.* GREGOR *closes the door after him.*

GREGOR. Our private information on Herries is correct, isn't it?

SVEN. His part in the Medworth deal?

GREGOR. No. Private information.

SVEN. Yes. I understand. (*Looking at* GREGOR *admiringly.*) Yes. *That* information—quite correct.

GREGOR. Anything concrete?

SVEN. Someone called— (*He puts his hand to his head in an effort to remember.*)

GREGOR. (*Speaking with a hitherto unheard intensity.*) Someone called what?

SVEN *shakes his head.*

What?

SVEN *still shakes his head.*

Remember! You must remember—

SVEN. (*Suddenly.*) Larter. Mike Larter.

GREGOR. How old?

SVEN. Early twenties.

GREGOR. Recently?

SVEN. Last year.

GREGOR. Trouble?

SVEN. He died of an overdose of sleeping-pills.

GREGOR. (*Pointing at the sitting-room.*) Involved?

SVEN. Not directly. The inquest may have been fixed. But Larter had no job, left no money, and it was an expensive apartment.

GREGOR. Where?

SVEN. Park Avenue, I think.

GREGOR. (*Intensely.*) Don't think. Be sure!

BASIL *comes out of the shower.* GREGOR *instantly relaxes the tone of his voice.*

So you can't be quite certain of that, Sven?

SVEN. *Almost* certain—

GREGOR *nods mildly, then turns to* BASIL.

GREGOR. Bravo, mon petit. Very neat. Very tidy. I think your father needs a little sprucing up, too. Have you a face-cloth?

BASIL. Yes. On the wash-basin—

GREGOR. (*Going towards the shower.*) A little hot water under the eyes, I think. A trick I learnt in the Far East. Three nights without sleep mustn't be shown—

*He goes into the shower. In the sitting-room* HERRIES, *who has been looking around him with keen interest, breaks a silence.*

HERRIES. Extraordinary place for G. A. to choose for a conference. Some kind of hide-out, I suppose.

BEESTON. Yes, Mr. Herries. It certainly looks like it.

HERRIES. The appearances are, in short, that our friend is a rather desperate man. You've brought all the—er—documentary evidence?

BEESTON. Yes, Mr. Herries.

HERRIES. And, of course, the press statement for nine o'clock?

BEESTON. (*Tapping his brief-case.*) I have it all here.

HERRIES. Good.

*He resumes his contemplation o f the room.* GREGOR *comes out of the shower, dabbing his eyes with a towel.* BASIL, *meanwhile, has been putting on a pair of sandals.*

GREGOR. Well, dear boy—now a rather decisive meeting, perhaps the most decisive of my life. (*He smiles.*) As a good socialist I know you must hope it fails. As my son, it would help me to have your blessing.

BASIL. You have my blessing, Father.

GREGOR. Thank you, chéri. Come in only when I open the door. Oh—and better not call me Father. Our friend is a little—straight-laced about such things.

BASIL. Yes, Father.

GREGOR. So you remain Basil Anthony. Right.

BASIL. Right.

GREGOR *finishes drying his eyes, and still smiling fondly, hands the towel to* BASIL. *Then he inspects himself carefully in the mirror.*

HERRIES. (*Looking round the sitting-room again.*) Yes. Extraordinary. Quite extraordinary.

GREGOR. (*Straightening himself, to* SVEN.) Sit facing the accountant.

HERRIES. (*From the other room.*) I'm afraid it does look a little, doesn't it, Beeston, like a cornered rat?

GREGOR *moves towards the sitting-room door, with* SVEN *following.*
*The lights fade.*

END OF ACT I

## ACT II

*In the sitting-room* GREGOR *is advancing on* HERRIES *with an affable outstretched hand, and an entirely relaxed smile.* SVEN *has followed him in.* HERRIES *and* BEESTON *both get up.*

GREGOR. My dear Mark, how very good of you to come to my little down-town dump—and at such an hour.

HERRIES. Oh, it's not a dump, G. A. It's—er—a very unusual and decorative little—hideout—

GREGOR. (*Smiling.*) Not exactly a *hideout*, Mark. If I should ever, in the future, have need of such a thing, I have better ones than this, I assure you. No, this is just a little—place I—use from time to time. Do sit down.

*He has stood in such a position that* HERRIES *has no option, without being openly rude, but to take the indicated place.* SVEN *rather more abruptly ushers* BEESTON *into the seat planned for him.* GREGOR *has not, at the moment, even glanced at* BEESTON, *who sits, in a designedly uncomfortable chair, clutching his brief-case and trying to look firm.*

You understand why I had to postpone our meeting at a more appropriate place this afternoon?

HERRIES. You've been pretty well hounded today, I should imagine.

GREGOR. (*With an amused shrug.*) Twenty-three per cent off the value of all my shares in one day has apparently made the press photographers even more anxious to get close-up photographs of my dull face. Eventually if they'd gone on flashing long enough they might have got one photograph of me looking haggard, drawn and anxious, flashlights do that to one anyway, don't you find—and my shares would have dropped another twenty-three per cent tomorrow.

HERRIES. I'm so sorry, G. A.

GREGOR. (*Interrupting hastily.*) Dear Mark—these things happen. (*With a smile.*) Not perhaps to American Electric—but anyway to me. I'm not a solid and respectable president of a vast, solid and respectable corporation like you. I'm a speculator—and known to be, and, worst of all, an optimist at a time of slump. So—when a vague rumour hits Wall Street that a merger has failed—

HERRIES. (*Grimly.*) Hardly a rumour, G. A. Our merger *has* failed. And Beeston and I are here tonight, I'm afraid, to tell you so. (*Looking at* BEESTON.) Oh, forgive me. May I introduce—

GREGOR. (*Raising his head, politely, to stop* HERRIES.) Just one moment. (*Nodding at* BEESTON, *the first time he has looked at him.*) Forgive me, dear fellow. (*To* HERRIES.) Just—as they say over here—for the record—a rumour is still a rumour even if, as in this case, it tells the truth.

HERRIES. (*Nodding.*) I stand—or rather sit—corrected. Now this is Mr. Beeston.

GREGOR *gets up to greet* BEESTON, *who shakes hands nervously.*

GREGOR. Good of you to come.

BEESTON. Not at all, Mr. Antonescu.

HERRIES. Mr. Beeston is the accountant who—

GREGOR. (*Amiably, as he resumes his seat.*) Ah. The villain of the piece.

HERRIES. (*Smiling.*) Yes. The villain of the piece . . .

GREGOR. (*Smiling at* BEESTON.) I am very happy to meet a young man whose command of figures and understanding of balance sheets can wreck a great merger and cause a full-scale panic on Wall Street. Do either of you smoke?

HERRIES. (*After getting a shake of the head from* BEESTON.) No, G. A.

GREGOR. Just as well, perhaps. I doubt if this 'dump'—as you called it—holds any cigarettes. Certainly no cigars.

HERRIES. I don't think I called it a dump, G. A. I think you did.

GREGOR. (*Shrugging.*) Does it matter who called it what? It is a dump, and it has no cigarettes or cigars. It doesn't—as you may have guessed—belong to me.

HERRIES. (*Looking round.*) I didn't really think so. Who does it belong to?

GREGOR *smiles quietly and with a nice hint of embarrassment. The shrug gives a faint suggestion that* HERRIES'S *question was in bad taste.*

GREGOR. (*Gently.*) Well, shall we get to business?

HERRIES. (*Hit on his sensitive, Harvard-Club solar plexus.*) I'm sorry. By all means. By all means. Beeston, will you hand Mr. Antonescu a copy of the statement we propose to issue this evening.

GREGOR *has adopted his usual business pose—a hand held to one cheek, concealing that part of his face nearest to his adversary—in this case, of course,* HERRIES—*for* GREGOR *has already discounted* BEESTON. *The latter produces a document from his pocket and hands it to* GREGOR, *who waves it aside.*

GREGOR. Would you read it out, please? You very young people are so lucky in possessing eyes that don't need glasses—

BEESTON. I'm not *very* young, Mr. Antonescu.

GREGOR *waves to him to read.*

(*Reading.*) The President and Board of Directors of American Electric Incorporated announce that the projected merger of certain of their interests with Manson Radios will not now takes place.

GREGOR. (*Behind his hand.*) It sounds a little as if you and I had had a tiff at the altar, Mark.

HERRIES. (*Enjoying the joke.*) I rather agree. (*To* BEESTON.) Would you re-word it to sound a little less like a broken engagement—

BEESTON. (*Already a shade flustered.*) I could say—'has collapsed'—

GREGOR. (*Amused.*) 'Collapse' is not perhaps the most fortunate of terms to

apply to a concern of mine at this precise moment in world history. You
have read tonight's newspapers, Mr.—er—

SVEN. (*Prompting.*) Beeston.

GREGOR. (*Nodding acknowledgement.*) I'm so sorry. Surely a name of all names
I should remember. (To HERRIES.) No doubt when I die you will find
Beeston engraved on my heart. How is it spelt? B E A S T ?

HERRIES. (*Smiling. He does not much like* BEESTON *either.*) No. B double E,
I'm afraid.

GREGOR. A pity. (*To* BEESTON.) I'm so sorry, dear fellow. A very poor joke.
Please go on.

BEESTON. Shall I say 'has failed'?

GREGOR. (*Gently, after a pause.*) I think perhaps you should leave the precise
phrasing to Mr. Herries. I'm sure you'll find a Harvard education adequate to the task.

HERRIES *bows his agreement.* BEESTON'S *nerve gets closer to its eventual breaking
point.*

Please read from there.

BEESTON. (*Muttering.*) 'not now take place—'

GREGOR. (*Smiling at* HERRIES.) Yes. From there. What immortal phrase have
you found to describe the cause of my ruptured romance with Mr.
Herries?

BEESTON. (*Ploughing ahead bravely.*) Information received by the President
and Board following the visit to Bucharest of Mr. David Beeston, accountant to the—

GREGOR. (*Bowing to* BEESTON.) Quite right. Credit where credit is due—young
fellow—

SVEN, *taking his cue from* GREGOR, *laughs quickly. In fact, during the whole
of this scene,* SVEN *takes all cues from* GREGOR—*almost—at times anticipating them. One should see how often the two have worked together at such
meetings, and how invaluable to* GREGOR *is the silent member of the
partnership.*

HERRIES. (*Now impatient with* BEESTON.) Just say—'of one of the corporation's
accountants'—it's quite enough.

BEESTON. (*Making the correction obediently.*) Yes, Mr. Herries. (*Picking up the
thread again.*) —'visit to Bucharest of one of the corporation's accountants, have convinced them' (*To* GREGOR.)—that's the President and
Board—

GREGOR. (*With a shade of impatience.*) I had gathered that, Mr. Beeston.

BEESTON. (*Doggedly, but his voice growing a little shrill.*) —'convinced them
that the state of the finances of certain of the foreign subsidiaries of
Manson Radios—'

GREGOR. (*To* HERRIES.) Rather a lot of 'ofs' there. (*To* BEESTON, *amiably.*) It
doesn't matter, at all, my dear fellow. Mr. Herries and I can work on the
syntax later.

*He waves him on.*

BEESTON. (*Becoming angry. This is what* GREGOR *wants.*) Can I just give you the sense, Mr. Antonescu, and forget the syntax?

GREGOR. (*After a quick eyebrow-raising at* HERRIES.) Dear fellow—your sense has been painfully clear to me, ever since Mr. Herries informed me last week that you seemed to have discovered some flaw in our accounting—

BEESTON. (*Hotly.*) Flaw seems to me a pretty mild word for what I found over there—

GREGOR. (*As if he really wanted to know.*) Did you enjoy Bucharest?

BEESTON. I didn't have much time to enjoy anything, Mr. Antonescu—and what I discovered in your books—

GREGOR. Surely Pavlovski showed you some of the pleasures of my birthplace, Mr. Beeston? I hope he took you to one particular little joint—my favourite—

BEESTON. Pavlovski? Who's Pavlovski?

GREGOR. (*Puzzled.*) Our chief accountant in Bucharest, of course.

BEESTON. I spent all my time with a guy called Andreiev—it was he who showed me the books. He didn't say he wasn't chief—

GREGOR. (*To* SVEN.) Andreiev? Who is he?

SVEN. One of the pool of accountants.

GREGOR. I hadn't heard of him. (*To* BEESTON.) It was this—

SVEN. (*Prompting.*) Andreiev—

GREGOR. Andreiev who looked after you in Bucharest?

BEESTON *nods.*

(*To* SVEN, *mildly.*) Should a minor accountant have been given so important an assignment?

SVEN. (*Humbly.*) I'm very sorry, G. A., It was my mistake. Pavlovski was on holiday, and so were both his assistants. I had no idea that Mr.— (*Looking at him.*) Beeston here, wished to make so full an examination. I thought he was merely looking for information on certain minor matters relating to the projected merger. Andreiev seemed perfectly competent for that—

BEESTON. (*Plaintively.*) But these discrepancies I found *were* relating to the merger. After all—an entry on Manson's Roumanian subsidiary listed as 'Cash in hand and in banks' and amounting to over twelve million dollars—

GREGOR. (*Very quietly.*) Eleven million, three hundred and seventy-six thousand, nine hundred—

BEESTON. Well, I have the figure here. (*He pulls out a document and reads.*) Eleven million, three hundred and seventy-six thousand, nine hundred. (*Confused.*) I was speaking from memory—

HERRIES. (*Rather amused.*) So was Mr. Antonescu.

GREGOR. (*Politely.*) You were saying?

BEESTON. (*Becoming flustered and angry.*) An item—whatever the exact

amount—listed here as 'Cash in hand and in banks' turns out, on examination in Bucharest, to be 'Cash, bankings and on deposit'—that is
the literal translation from the Roumanian—

GREGOR. Felicitari pentru Romineasca dumneavoastra excelenta.

BEESTON. I beg your pardon?

GREGOR. I'm sorry. What I said was—congratulations on your excellent Roumanian.

BEESTON. (*Now really heated.*) Listen, Mr. Antonescu—I didn't need to learn
Roumanian. Figures are the same in any language.

GREGOR. Of course. Not necessarily methods of accounting—

BEESTON. (*Loudly.*) The amount you told Mr. Herries and his Board here as
standing to the credit of Manson Radio Roumanian subsidiary is short
by six million dollars—

GREGOR *opens his mouth to speak.*

O.K. Go on. Tell me the exact figure down to the last cent. I've heard of
that trick, and it's a great one, and I'm sure it's impressed a lot of people
in your time—but six million dollars is a mighty large error in book-
keeping—and you don't get me—in front of Mr. Herries—to—

GREGOR. (*Tapping his knee, gently, to stop the flood.*) Dear fellow, dear fellow,
dear fellow.

*The flood subsides.*

Gracious, how you do go on. I was only going to ask if either of you
would like a little refreshment. (*To* HERRIES.) I am afraid there is only
Bourbon and gin—which is all the young man keeps here—

HERRIES *takes the information in, but without comment.*

Would you care—?

HERRIES. No, thank you. Perhaps Beeston—

GREGOR. (*With a gentle smile.*) You think it might loosen his tongue, perhaps?

HERRIES *quietly enjoys the joke against* BEESTON. *Then he looks round the room
with rather more curiosity than before, while* GREGOR *turns to the now
totally discomfited* BEESTON.

GREGOR. Mr. Beeston?

BEESTON. No, thank you. I'm sorry, Mr. Antonescu. You must please forgive
me—I had no right to speak that way.

GREGOR. (*Jovially.*) But, my dear fellow, what more natural than that you
should show some signs of strain? Anyone who has caused a major world
financial crisis—off his own—bat—isn't that the expression—? has surely
the right to be a little—tetchy. (*Very kindly.*) Dear Mr. Beeston, I am
here to be questioned. You are here to question me. So question me.

BEESTON. Well, Mr. Antonescu, these six million dollars I found listed on
your balance sheet as on deposit, I later discovered, after a very difficult
investigation, had, in fact, been debited to Antonescu Holdings—and
the collateral—

GREGOR. (*To* SVEN.) Does this—Andreiev—does he speak English?

SVEN. Hardly at all.

GREGOR. That explains a great deal.

BEESTON. (*Growing angry again.*) Andreiev could make himself understood well enough—

GREGOR. (*Jovially.*) And if he couldn't, the figures could, eh? Even though the words beside them were written in Roumanian—

BEESTON. O.K. So I don't speak Roumanian. We settled that, didn't we? But figures are the same in any language. We settled that too, didn't we? And the figures I found in Bucharest didn't just speak—they really shouted. Here they are, Mr. Antonescu. I suggest you look at them.

*He takes out a document and hands it to* GREGOR. GREGOR *brushes it gently away, as if it were a rather displeasing object that had settled on his knee.*

GREGOR. (*To* HERRIES, *who is looking round the room.*) The boy has quite good taste, don't you think?

*Pause.* HERRIES, *taking in the operative word, looks round the room.*

HERRIES. Well—I don't go for modern myself, but it's interesting.

GREGOR. I don't go for modern either. And 'interesting' covers a multitude of horrors, these days—like those curtains. (*Lowering his voice slightly.*) But in certain matters one has occasionally to be a little—indulgent. You agree?

HERRIES. (*Interested and puzzled, but uncomfortable.*) Sure.

GREGOR. Besides, the Village is not exactly—Park Avenue, is it, Mark?

HERRIES. (*Stiffly.*) No.

GREGOR. That was a very different apartment.

HERRIES. Whose apartment?

GREGOR. (*Lightly.*) Mike Larter's. (*To* BEESTON.) I'm so sorry, Mr. Beeston, I interrupted you. You wanted me to look at some figures, didn't you?

*He takes the document from* BEESTON, *puts on his spectacles with something of a ceremony, and begins to study it.* HERRIES *has risen.*

HERRIES. May I change my mind, G. A.?

GREGOR. (*Deep in the document.*) Of course. (*With a wave.*) Sven—

HERRIES. (*To* SVEN, *who is instantly on his feet, waiting on him.*) Thank you. Perhaps a Bourbon on the rocks.

SVEN. I don't know whether there's any ice. (*Finding some.*) Ah, yes. He keeps it here.

HERRIES. (*Murmuring—with studied unconcern.*) You don't know this apartment, Johnson?

SVEN. (*Murmuring back, with a faintly suggestive smile.*) Of its existence, yes. I'm the only one. But even I have never before been invited inside. You and I are very privileged. Of course it is a rather special occasion tonight. (*Raising his voice just a fraction, so as to carry to* GREGOR.) It's the—er— young owner-occupier's birthday. I don't know much—I'm not allowed to—but I do know where G. A. can invariably be reached on the evening of July the thirteenth.

*He gives* HERRIES *his Bourbon, and with it a tiny wink.* HERRIES *nods slowly—but still plainly a very puzzled man.*

BEESTON. (*Prodding the document with his finger.*) There it is, Mr. Antonescu! There! In black and white. And not in Roumanian, either. Six million dollars, listed here as cash in hand—actually debited to Antonescu Holdings. Explain that away, if you can.

HERRIES. (*Sharply.*) Beeston—please! Do try and remember your manners.

BEESTON. I'm sorry, Mr. Herries. But a deficiency of six million dollars is—

HERRIES. A deficiency of six million dollars. I know. But there are ways of expressing these things.

GREGOR. (*Stretching himself lazily.*) It's actually a surplus of one million dollars, but Mr. Beeston could hardly be expected to see that—

HERRIES. How, G. A.?

GREGOR. The six million on loan to Antonescu Holdings has been used to buy up a radio concern in France—I think I told you that the other day—or did I forget?

HERRIES. No. You told me. But I had had a rough meeting with the Board. They were furious about Beeston's bombshell. I wasn't, perhaps, listening with as much concentration as I should. On what collateral is the loan secured?

GREGOR. Italian Bonds worth, at present valuation, seven million five hundred and seventy thousand—

BEESTON. (*Frantically searching among his documents.*) Wait a minute. Wait a minute. Those are not at all my figures—

GREGOR. (*Ignoring him totally.*) So I should have said a profit of a million and a half. But, I am, as you know, rather conservative about estimated profits—

HERRIES. Tell me again which French radio company. I forget—

GREGOR. Matthieu Thibault et Compagnie. On April the third this year, when the purchase was made, its assets were seven million one hundred and sixty-three thousand seven hundred and twenty-five dollars. (*After a second's thought.*) Now, was that the figure? (*Reassuring himself.*) Yes, I think that was the figure. (*Joining* HERRIES *at the drink tray.*) I believe I'll join you in a Bourbon, Mark. (*He holds the bottle up.*) Not much left. (*To* SVEN.) Rather looks as if carissimo had been punishing it a little. Ah, well. On anniversaries all things are permitted. (*Raising his glass.*) Down the hatch.

BEESTON *is still frantically searching among his documents.* GREGOR, SVEN *and* HERRIES *are now totally ignoring him.*

HERRIES. (*Murmuring.*) I had heard this was a rather special occasion—

GREGOR. Sven, that was naughty of you.

SVEN. I'm sorry.

GREGOR. There *are* certain things we all like to keep dark. Some things, perhaps, darker than others. It's not for nothing I've got the press title of 'mystery man'. Mind you, Mark—you're not so bad as a mystery man yourself. You know—if it hadn't been for that evening I was taken to that apartment—

HERRIES. I'd no idea you knew Mike Larter. No idea at all.

GREGOR. Oh, I hardly did know him, Mark. I would have liked to have known him very well indeed, but—

*His shrug is quietly suggestive of* HERRIES'S *proprietorial rights.*

HERRIES. But Mike would have told me—

GREGOR. (*Smiling.*) I went as Mr. Gregory. Not very original—

HERRIES. Who brought you?

GREGOR. Oh, a young friend. I forget his name. What a tragic business that was about Mike—

HERRIES. (*Quickly.*) It was an accident, you know—

GREGOR. Oh, of course

HERRIES. The foolish boy would take those damnable pills. I couldn't stop him—and then the drink as well—

GREGOR. My dear Mark, I felt for you most deeply at the time, I couldn't— of course—tell you.

BEESTON. (*With a triumphant shout.*) I've got it.

*He gets up, brandishing a sheet of paper, to be met by three pairs of hostile eyes. He quails a trifle under* HERRIES'S *gaze.*

I'm so sorry, Mr. Herries. May I interrupt?

HERRIES. Yes? What is it, Beeston?

BEESTON. The real value of the Italian Bonds used by Mr. Antonescu as collateral for his loan to his own company is, according to our reckoning, (*Reading.*) four million, seven hundred thousand, five hundred and so that leaves a deficit of—

GREGOR. (*Amused.*) You got those figures from the Wall Street Journal! Dear boy. Do me a favour. And I think Mr. Herries a favour—because this merger would not have been wholly unprofitable to American Electric. Go home and put through a long-distance call to the Finance Minister in Mussolini's Government. Just ask him at what price he values these bonds, as of this moment. (*Repeating the phrase, rather pleased to have remembered it so aptly.*) As of this moment, dear boy. Do that and tell Mr. Herries the result tomorrow. It won't affect the deal which you have killed. But I think the Minister's reply will interest Mr. Herries and his Board. (*To* HERRIES.) Mark—have another. (*To* SVEN.) Sven, remind me to send the boy a case of Bourbon tomorrow—

BEESTON. Listen—you know goddam well I've as much chance of getting through on the telephone to the Italian Finance Minister—as I have of getting through to Signor Mussolini—

GREGOR. (*Gently.*) But you could very easily get through to Signor Mussolini if you cared to use my name—

HERRIES. Why don't you do just that, Beeston?

*He has, of course, not meant it seriously, but he knows that* GREGOR'S *suggestion is by no means an idle boast. And he secretly appreciates* BEESTON'S *discomfiture. There is a pause.*

BEESTON. (*Now finally speechless.*) Jesus!

HERRIES. (*Sternly.*) What did you say, Beeston?

BEESTON. (*Suddenly thrusting a sheaf of documents at* HERRIES.) You'd better take these, Mr. Herries. I can see there's nothing more I can do here—

HERRIES. Don't be hysterical, man! It happens to be true that Mr. Antonescu's name will get you access to almost any Head of State in Europe.

GREGOR. (*Lightly.*) Are you leaving out the White House, Mark?

HERRIES. Yes. I hear he consults you now and then. (*Smiling.*) Don't much care for some of the advice you seem to have been giving him—

GREGOR. (*Shrugging, smiling.*) Desperate times demand desperate remedies—

HERRIES. (*Making a face and then turning back.*) But Beeston, you couldn't think I meant seriously that you should call Signor Mussolini in the middle of the night?

BEESTON. I don't know whether you did or you didn't, Mr. Herries. I guess I'm a little out of my depth here. All I know is—because it's my job to know it—and because you pay me good money to find it out, and because I'm a loyal servant of American Electric—

HERRIES. Who ever said you weren't?

GREGOR. Your loyalty, Mr. Beeston, is the sole quality of yours that none of us have ever questioned.

BEESTON. Jesus!

HERRIES. I wish you wouldn't use that particular expletive, Beeston. It's not very seemly on an occasion like this. But go on. All you know is—?

BEESTON. That this guy here (*Pointing to* GREGOR.) has tried to snitch six million dollars from American Electric, and falsified his books in Bucharest to cover it up—

GREGOR. (*To* HERRIES, *most amused.* SVEN *has laughed on cue as well.*) Snitch? (*To* SVEN.) Please remember that for me, would you? Snitch.

HERRIES. (*Very seriously, to* BEESTON.) I'm afraid I really think you *had* better go, Beeston.

BEESTON. Jesus, I told you—I'm— (*He remembers who his boss is.*) I've already told you, Mr. Herries, I'm going.

GREGOR. You won't have a night-cap, dear fellow?

BEESTON *looks at all three, in silence, then turns and strides towards the front door.*

(*Sharply.*) Sven—

SVEN *goes quickly to open the front door, before* BEESTON *gets there.*

SVEN. (*To* BEESTON.) Oh—perhaps you had better leave behind that copy of the press statement—the one Mr. Herries and G. A. were going to alter the syntax of a little—

BEESTON *plunges his hand into his brief-case and pulls out the required document.*

Thank you so much. Good night.

GREGOR. (*Calling.*) Good night, dear fellow.

BEESTON *goes.* SVEN *hands the document to* GREGOR, *who puts it very openly on the table. For* HERRIES'S *eyes are on him.*

GREGOR. Isn't he very young to be your chief accountant, Mark?

HERRIES, Well—as it happens—he's not actually our *chief* accountant. But he's a good, bright boy, G. A.—

GREGOR. Plainly as bright as a button. The only cause I have for wonder— forgive me, dear fellow—is how you came to entrust this particular bright boy with the whole future of world finance. Another Bourbon? There's just one left, I think.

HERRIES. Thanks.

GREGOR *pours.*

Isn't that putting it a bit high, G. A.?

GREGOR. (*Indifferently.*) I don't think so, Mark. You saw what the mere rumour of our merger's failure did to Wall Street today. When that (*He points to* BEESTON'S *statement.*) is published tomorrow my whole group could easily be wiped out. (*Chuckling amiably.*) In fact, I've already told Sven here that in a few weeks I fully expect to be left with nothing more than a few houses, office buildings, furniture, pictures and a couple of oil wells at Ploesti—

HERRIES. Well, G. A., I'm very glad to hear that whatever happens, your personal fortune won't be affected—

GREGOR. (*Carelessly.*) My personal fortune? How much is it? I don't know. It's the one figure I've never bothered either to count or to remember. Three or four million—perhaps a little more—but quite insufficient, for instance, to help the Austrians defeat the new run on their currency as I had promised Dollfuss—

HERRIES. You shouldn't *promise*, G. A. Your trouble is simple. You've spread yourself out too wide—far too wide, G. A.—

GREGOR. (*Suddenly with fervent intensity.*) Of course I have. And why? Because I am a fighter, and I know my enemy. So do you. It's the Depression. The rest of you have been watching me these last five years, clucking your disapproval, saying, to each other, 'That fellow is riding for a fall.' Well, as you now know, so he was. (*Shrugging.*) Tant pis! But what have you all been doing since 'twenty-nine? Squatting on your stagnant businesses, mouthing idiotic platitudes about 'prosperity being just around the corner', and 'we've only got to wait'. Wait? Wait for what? For a miracle? Well, I don't believe in miracles. In finance man makes his own miracles. For five years I made mine. And—without that—(*He points to the document.*) I could have made miracles for another five. By then I might have proved to you all how the slump *can* be beaten—I

really believe I would have done that, Mark, and so does Maynard
Keynes, incidentally.

HERRIES. Keynes? The English economist?

GREGOR. In my view the greatest alive. You've read him, of course.

HERRIES. (*Who has not.*) Oh, sure.

GREGOR. Liquidity and confidence, that's all the crisis is about. But liquidity
first. A free, unrestricted supply of cheap money and the 'big bad wolf'
will no longer be there to be 'afraid' of. He'll be dead. (*Passionately.*) Aren't
those my own ideas? What else have I fought for all my life? Who gave
roads to Jugoslavia and electricity to Hungary? And what will the unemployment figure reach in America when my group crashes? (*Mildly,
after a sigh.*) Yes, Mark. I've spread myself out too wide. Are you sure
you don't smoke?

HERRIES. No. Never have.

GREGOR'S *eloquence has not gone without effect on* HERRIES, *but, as he opens his
mouth to speak, he has not yet the look of a converted man.*

I have never denied, G. A., that there is much sense in your fiscal ideas—
and I have always admired your courage—but there is, in my view, a basic
unsoundness in inflationary financing—

GREGOR, *realizing instantly that his battle is not yet over, has made a convincing show of not wanting to listen to* HERRIES. *He is smiling as he stops the
measured words.*

GREGOR. Yes, yes, yes. Dear fellow, don't let's argue finance. (*Pointing to the
document.*) My battle is over and lost, anyway. No point in wasting
breath—

HERRIES. G. A., I don't want you to think that that (*Also pointing to the document.*) has been in any way my personal fault. It was by a unanimous
decision of the Board—

GREGOR. (*With a gentle smile.*) Yes, yes, dear Mark. My own boards, where
unpleasant decisions have to be made, are also always unanimous. Now
I think it's time you met our host.

*He opens the door into the bedroom and calls:*

Carissimo. You can come out, now. Our business is finished.

BASIL, *who through all this has been sitting patiently on his bed, his back to us,
gets up and nervously walks into the living-room. His father puts his arm
affectionately around his shoulder.*

I want you to meet a very good friend of mine, called Mark. Mark, this
is Basil.

*They shake hands.*

Not too bored, waiting, I hope?

BASIL. No, I thought you'd be much longer. I thought business conferences
always went on all night.

GREGOR. Some do. But not this one. The issue has been decided against me
before it began. I was given no chance to fight.

HERRIES. (*Who has been looking at* BASIL.) That's a little unfair, G. A.

GREGOR. (*His hand on* BASIL'S *shoulder, with a smile.*) Well, then—give me a chance to fight. Let me come to your Board tomorrow and explain this mysterious sum that I've tried to—

*He stops and clicks his fingers.*

Sven?

SVEN. Snitch.

GREGOR. Snitch from American Electric—

HERRIES. (*Sincerely.*) G. A., I'm sorry about that. Really sorry. I guess Beeston just lost his head, that's all. And yet he's supposed to be a level-headed enough young man.

GREGOR. Is he? (*Bitterly.*) I'm glad I haven't got a head so level that it can throw another million or more out of work because of a minor confusion between American and Roumanian accounting practices.

*To* BASIL, *whom he is gently holding.*

Do you approve of that sort of level head, dear boy?

BASIL. No. Certainly not.

GREGOR. (*Fondly, to* HERRIES.) Basil has a strong social conscience. (*To* BASIL.) I like the shirt. Is it in honour of Mr. Herries?

*Pause.* BASIL *is not yet beginning to suspect the part he is playing. All he knows is that he is supposed to be playing some part, and that it is important he should be polite to his father's adversary.*

BASIL. (*Smiling.*) Yes, of course. In your honour too.

GREGOR. (*Releasing* BASIL *and walking away.*) I'm flattered. I hope you are, Mark.

HERRIES. Very honoured indeed.

*He goes to* BASIL *and inspects the shirt at close quarters, fingering the material.*

Where did you get it?

BASIL. A present—

HERRIES. (*Looking at* GREGOR.) Ah. I see. Very fetching indeed. It suits you, if I may borrow an expression off our English cousins, a fair treat. You *are* English, aren't you?

BASIL. No. Just brought up there.

GREGOR. He's a hundred per cent, red-blooded American boy, Mark. Don't let his Oxford accent fool you.

HERRIES. (*His snob instincts now also aroused.*) Oxford, eh? Which college?

BASIL. Christ Church.

HERRIES. The 'House'? (*As* BASIL *is silent.*) Isn't that what it's called?

BASIL. Yes. By some people.

HERRIES. I don't know about your social conscience, but I notice you chose yourself a pretty 'posh' (*Pronouncing it English.*) college there.

GREGOR. (*Quietly.*) Perhaps the choice wasn't entirely his *own.*

HERRIES. Ah. I get you. (*To* BASIL.) Gee, Basil—I almost forgot to wish you many happy returns—

*This is a moment of danger for* GREGOR. SVEN *has overstepped the mark, and not foreseen this possibility.* GREGOR *steps in smoothly, as* BASIL *looks blankly at* HERRIES.

GREGOR. You don't think it's his *birthday*, do you, Mark? Even Basil has only *one* birthday a year—March the twelfth—right, Basil?

BASIL. Yes.

HERRIES. (*Pointing to* SVEN.) But he said—

GREGOR. There are things I keep even from Sven—for instance the very special significance of this date.

HERRIES. (*Puzzled.*) But, G. A., *you* said—

GREGOR. *I* said 'anniversary'. I don't think we'd better go on about it, Mark, or we'll embarrass poor Basil. (*To* BASIL.) Basil, mon cher petit, we seem to have polished off your whisky. I'm so sorry. Would you be an angel and get another from the local drug store?

*A pause. A glimmer of the truth is just beginning to get home.* BASIL *turns, in silence, and goes back to the door.* GREGOR *gently calls him back.*

Just a moment, dear boy.

BASIL *returns.* GREGOR *turns to* SVEN.

(*With a quick gesture to his breast pocket.*) Sven, please.

SVEN, *understanding the gesture instantly, slips out his wallet and hands it to* GREGOR, *who takes out a bill from it, seemingly at random. The bill he hands to* BASIL, *and the wallet he throws back to* SVEN. BASIL *holds the bill, looking at his father with troubled inquiry and still not able quite to believe his mounting suspicions. There is no answer for him from* GREGOR'S *eyes. They are quite expressionless and quite blank.* BASIL *turns to the door.*

HERRIES. But he may not get change for a hundred dollars down here—

GREGOR. But he'll still get the whisky. Liquidity and confidence, eh, Mark?

BASIL, *at the door, turns back again, now deeply disturbed, to stare at his father. But he only sees his back. He goes.*

HERRIES. Well, well, well.

GREGOR. Poor dear Basil. Always so shy with strangers. Especially, of course, with the famous Mark Herries—

HERRIES. I wonder—G. A.—I wonder if— (*He glances at* SVEN.)

GREGOR. Sven, be a good fellow, and leave us alone a moment.

SVEN *nods and goes into the bedroom. There is a pause after he has gone.* HERRIES *is longing to ask a lot of questions, but* GREGOR *is determined not to help him too much. He patiently awaits the first question.*

HERRIES. (*At length.*) G. A.—I'm afraid I can't phrase it any better than this— forgive the bluntness—but—is—well is—what I am thinking true?

GREGOR. (*Fondly.*) Dear Mark—always so direct. How do I know what you are thinking? That Basil's my son?

HERRIES. No, no. Although you did have a son, didn't you? I remember you telling me he died five years ago.

GREGOR *nods.*

Very sad for you. No. I wasn't thinking *quite* of a son— (*He flounders into silence.*)

GREGOR. (*Touching his shoulder, very fondly now.*) Dear, dear Mark—let me put you out of your doubts and suspicions at once. I asked you here because you are one of the very few men in New York I would trust with the truth. (*Simply.*) So now you have the truth.

HERRIES. I'm staggered, G. A. Absolutely staggered. Jesus—(*Catching himself up.*) that's that dreadful Beeston's expletive. I'm sorry—but gosh, G. A.—those mistresses. Gosh—you have the most highly publicized mistresses of any man in the world—also a beautiful young wife—come to think of it—even more publicized—

GREGOR. Dear Mark, what is for public show is not always for private pleasure. About Beeston and his expletives—could I ask you a favour?

HERRIES. (*Absently.*) Sure.

GREGOR. When I come tomorrow to meet your Board and explain this— I've forgotten the word again—ah, yes 'snitching'—could I, please, be spared the presence of Mr. Beeston?

HERRIES. Well, most unhappily, Beeston is the man who personally inspected those books. He's the only one with all the relevant facts. I really think we ought to have him there—

GREGOR. (*With a wide gesture.*) Then I don't come. I'm sorry, Mark. I just don't come—

HERRIES. I'll get him to apologize to you personally—

GREGOR. No, no. I'm sorry, Mark. It's not just that word, for heaven's sake. Tonight isn't the first time I've had criminal slanders of that kind flung at my head. I've always laughed at them—you know that. (*Suddenly intensely serious.*) It's *hysteria*. Mark—in matters of high finance I hate dealing with *hysterics*—

HERRIES. Beeston? Before tonight there's never been a sign—

GREGOR. Dear Mark, the indications are obvious. Those eyes. Haven't you ever noticed the pupils?

HERRIES. No. I can't say I have. You can't mean you think he might be—

GREGOR. I don't mean anything, Mark. I am sure you have checked up on his private life. (*Firmly.*) I just mean I can't stand hysterics.

HERRIES. All right. I'll get Broadbent. He's senior, and I expect he'll be briefed on the facts. But tomorrow? Did we say tomorrow?

GREGOR. That's what I thought you said.

HERRIES. I can't convene my whole Board tomorrow, G. A.

GREGOR. (*With a smile.*) And, of course, you never make any decision without a Board, do you, Mark? (*Carelessly.*) Make it Wednesday, then, and I'll bring *my* Board too. We'll both of us have to sleep patiently through hours and hours of our vice-president and directors showing you or me how indispensable they are to us both—but if that's how you want it— (*He shrugs and looks at a picture.*) I wonder when the boy bought this— he is acquiring quite a taste for pictures, I'm glad to see—

HERRIES. (*Not listening.*) It could be a waste of time at that.

GREGOR *turns, waiting patiently.*

If we meet alone I'll need *two* accountants.

GREGOR. After tonight's experience it might be advisable.

HERRIES. You can bring two of yours.

GREGOR. Thank you. I'll come alone.

HERRIES. (*Nodding resignedly.*) What time tomorrow? Would three suit?

GREGOR. Admirably.

*He picks up the statement from the table and, smiling at* HERRIES, *tears it up slowly.*

HERRIES. (*Smiling.*) Don't count chickens, G. A.

GREGOR. I never do. (*Looking at the picture again.*) I'm glad I seem to be teaching him something. I'm able to see so very little of him. He gets lonely, I'm afraid. It would be very good of you, Mark, if sometime, perhaps—

HERRIES. I'd be delighted, G. A. Delighted.

GREGOR. (*Carelessly.*) Oh—that statement. I wish I hadn't torn it up.

HERRIES. Why?

GREGOR. Well, the press have been told to expect a statement and after what happened on Wall Street today I think we have to say *something*. (*Calling.*) Sven—

HERRIES. Well—it's difficult now to know just what *to* say.

SVEN *has appeared.*

GREGOR. How about this? Sven—take this down, would you?

SVEN *nods, and whips out a notebook.*

Mr. Mark Herries—President of American Electric Incorporated— (*Genially.*) we'll leave out your Board this time shall we, Mark?

BASIL *comes back with a bottle of Bourbon.*

Ah. Good boy. Pour out a drink for Mr. Herries, would you?

HERRIES. (*Looking at* BASIL.) Just a very small one—

BASIL *nods and goes to the drink tray.*

GREGOR. (*To* SVEN.) 'Mr. Mark Herries, etc., wishes to state that the rumours at present circulating Wall Street and other Stock Exchanges regarding the failure of the projected merger with Manson Radios Incorporated have no foundation whatever in fact'—

BASIL *turns, startled.*

HERRIES. (*Also startled.*) Now listen—that's equivalent to saying the merger is going through. You must use your own phrase—'as of this moment'—

GREGOR. (*Smoothly.*) And that's equivalent to saying the merger is *not* going through. Let's just add this. 'Negotiations are still actively proceeding between the respective heads of the two concerns, and it is confidently expected that a conclusive result will be reached tomorrow when a further statement will be issued.' That's vague enough for you, isn't it, Mark?

HERRIES. (*Who has been looking at* BASIL.) It seems to meet the case, G. A.

GREGOR. (*Nodding to* SVEN *peremptorily.*) Good.

SVEN *goes into the bedroom and once inside, with the door closed, runs to the telephone, where he feverishly dials a number.*

SVEN. (*In bedroom, murmuring urgently.*) William?—get this down . . . For

God's sake, man, don't waste time—every second is vital. Right. Are you ready?. . . 'Mr. Mark Herries, President of American Electric Incorporated, wishes to state that the rumours at present circulating Wall Street regarding the failure of the projected merger with Manson Radios Incorporated have no foundation whatever in fact. Negotiations are still actively proceeding between the respective heads of the two concerns and it is confidently expected that a conclusive result'—wait William—omit conclusive—insert favourable . . . favourable result . . . No, but my memory isn't so good these days. Get me? . . . I agree. Conclusive could mean favourable, but favourable *does* mean favourable. No. He won't remember. If he does, it's my fault, not 'The Man's'. All right, William? Ready to go on?—'favourable result will be reached today—July fourteenth—when a further statement will be issued' . . . All right. Got it? Read it over . . . Yes, William. Like Pearl White, saved in the nick of time . . . Yes, William. Back on top of the world. Control your exuberation a little, would you, dear fellow, and read me that statement over?

*Not much of this will be, nor need be, heard. For meanwhile, in the living-room,* HERRIES *on* SVEN'S *exit into the bedroom, has turned politely to* BASIL, *visibly (but not obviously) exuding well-bred charm.*

HERRIES. Basil—I may call you that, mayn't I?—I did just now—and if it isn't too rude a question—have you an occupation of any kind?

*He gives a glance at* GREGOR, *who considerately turns his back.*

I know, of course, you don't need one—

BASIL. (*In a strained voice.*) I play the piano in a club on Twelfth Street.

HERRIES. Really? Was it there you met . . . ? (*He nods at* GREGOR. BASIL, *clasping his hands tight, does not reply.* HERRIES *chuckles.*) Discretion. Good boy. You've plainly learnt some valuable lessons from the mystery-man of Europe.

BASIL. Yes.

HERRIES. You must be proud—very proud—to have such a great man as your particular friend.

GREGOR. (*Quickly, his back still to them.*) Don't flatter me too much, Mark. Basil won't like it. Remember his social conscience.

HERRIES. (*Chuckling.*) I've made that note, G. A. (*To* BASIL.) What is the name of this club?

*There is a considerable pause before* BASIL *answers. He is trying, almost beseechingly, to catch his father's eye, but* GREGOR'S *back is still turned to him.*

BASIL. (*At length.*) The Green Hat.

HERRIES. (*Noting it down.*) The Green Hat. On Twelfth Street. Thank you. (*Still writing.*) Basil—what is the surname?

*Again a pause. This time* GREGOR *turns and meets* BASIL'S *gaze with a look that is quietly indifferent—as much as to say 'dear boy—if you want to betray me now—and throw another million people out of work, I am in your hands.'* BASIL *lowers his eyes.*

BASIL. (*Murmuring.*) Anthony.

HERRIES. (*Writing it down.*) Basil Anthony. Telephone?

BASIL. Gramercy 7-3961.

HERRIES. Good. (*He closes his notebook.*) I'll call you, if I may, after G. A. has gone to Europe? Here is my card. (*He hands him one.*) We might fix an evening?

BASIL. (*Staring at the card and suddenly stammering.*) I w-w-work—very late— Mr. Herries—

GREGOR *is instantly at his side, his arm protectively and affectionately round his shoulder.*

GREGOR. Basil's stammer only appears on very special occasions, Mark. I think you should be flattered.

GREGOR'S *hand on* BASIL'S *shoulder is now a firm grip.* HERRIES *finishes his drink.*

HERRIES. Flattered? Don't give me ideas, G. A. Remember I'm fifty-five—

GREGOR. No one would think it, Mark. Would they, Basil?

BASIL. (*Only just able to say it.*) N-n-no.

HERRIES. Well, good-bye, G. A. Three p.m. tomorrow?

GREGOR. You surrounded with accountants. I, poor little lost boy, all alone to face my accusers. (*In threatening tones and quotation marks.*) 'When did you last see your father?' Couldn't you do with *one* less accountant, Mark?

HERRIES. Well, maybe. Just Broadbent, huh?

GREGOR. Broadbent's a very sound man. I get on very well with Broadbent.

HERRIES. (*Genially.*) Sure. That's what I'm afraid of. (*Holding out his hand.*) O.K. It's a promise. Thanks, G. A. (*Glancing at* BASIL, *who is still held by his father.*) It's been a great occasion.

GREGOR. (*Giving* BASIL *a friendly push.*) See your honoured guest off, Basil. Got your car, Mark?

HERRIES. (*At the door.*) Yes. Good night, G. A. (*To* BASIL, *who has opened the door.*) Oh, how very kind of you, dear boy—

GREGOR. Good night, Mark. Pleasant dreams.

HERRIES *goes out,* BASIL *following. Left alone* GREGOR'S *face undergoes a complete transformation. The bland, gentle mask is dropped and, as he raises his hands to heaven, or to whatever gods he worships, there is in his expression a victorious defiance of the fates which had threatened to overwhelm him, and which he now believes—and with good cause—to have worsted.* SVEN, *having finished his telephoning comes in at this precise moment of naked triumph.* GREGOR, *unashamed, turns to him, his arms still held victoriously aloft.* SVEN, *laughing, runs to him, copying his pose.* GREGOR *now begins to laugh too, and they embrace—dissolving into mutual (and to* GREGOR'S *case, exhausted and hysterical) paroxysms of joyful laughter. At the climax of the exhibition,* BASIL *re-enters, unnoticed or ignored by both. Standing by the door he watches in silence.*

SVEN. (*At length.*) Man! Man! Never in your whole life—

GREGOR. (*Still laughing.*) Don't say any more. I deserve it all. Oh, my God—

*He falls, utterly exhausted, on to a sofa.*

(*Weakly.*) I didn't know how tired I was. One more second of that silly, pink-faced, old—what is the American expression for it, Sven—there is one very expressive one—not the English one—

SVEN *shakes his head.*

GREGOR. (*Hand over eyes.*) You fail me sometimes, Sven. You fail me. I've got it . . . fairy! That silly, pink-faced old fairy—

BASIL, *after staring at his father, runs into the bedroom, slamming the door.* (*Sleepily.*) What was that?

SVEN. Vassily—going into his bedroom.

*Pause.* GREGOR, *hand still over eyes, seems asleep. Meanwhile we see* BASIL *pull off his silk shirt and tear it in half, hurling the pieces into a corner of the room. He then runs into the shower, slamming the door.*

GREGOR. (*At length, murmuring sleepily.*) Better watch him.

SVEN *goes into the bedroom and knocks on the door of the shower.*

SVEN. Vassily? . . . Vassily? Vassily, dear boy, are you all right? . . .

*There is still no reply. He comes back into the living-room.*

He's locked himself in the shower.

*Long pause.* GREGOR *might well be asleep.*

GREGOR. (*At length.*) Of course.

*He makes an effort, visibly difficult, to rouse himself, and then sits up, blinking and swaying with exhaustion, but smiling.*

Get to work. Transmit to all confidential centres the news that the merger is through—

SVEN. (*Murmuring.*) Safe?

GREGOR. Care to bet some of that seven hundred thousand dollars you 'snitched'—from the Polish deal, and keep tucked away in the Guaranty Trust?

SVEN. (*After a pause.*) No.

GREGOR. I thought not. Dear Sven, has there ever been anything safer? (*With a jubilant laugh.*) My fare to Baltimore! That curious little girl. Not un-attractive though. I wonder why she wants to marry Vassily of all people? Oh, well.

BASIL *comes out of the bathroom.*

Now, where was I? Yes. All centres, this message—

BASIL *enters the living-room. He stands facing his father, who, from under his hand, returns his gaze, while still talking to* SVEN.

The merger will go through tomorrow and thus realize for my immedi-ate use the cash sum of seventy-five million dollars. The crisis therefore, is past. All payments can and will be met. There is no longer any single Antonescu enterprise anywhere in the world in any danger at all. To all my stock-market agents just one word: 'Buy'. Add another phrase—'And keep on buying'.

*He waves him away, then summons him back. He is still looking at his son, un-waveringly.*

And, Sven—I'm not boastful, as you know, but I think it might not be bad for morale to preface all messages with some reference to me—by my code name, of course. Perhaps: 'The Man is still the Man'. Do you like that?

SVEN. Excellent.

GREGOR. Mon petit Vassily, tu as été absolument parfait. I'm sorry I had to pass you off as un petit pédéraste in front of Mr. Herries, but I had no choice. I hope you are not too cross with me.

*There is a pause.* BASIL *is plainly having a struggle with himself not to attack his father physically.* SVEN *watches him guardedly, realizing it.* GREGOR *realizes it too, but continues to smile fondly at his son.*

BASIL. (*At length, with quiet intensity.*) You are *nothing*. You live and breathe and have being and you are my father—but you are *nothing*.

GREGOR *does not reply. He stares up amusedly at his son.* BASIL *turns quickly and runs out of the front door, slamming it after him.*

SVEN. Vassily, come back. Vassily—

GREGOR. Let him go.

SVEN. I'm going after him.

GREGOR. Why?

SVEN. Because it's too dangerous to let him roam around New York in that mood. It's too dangerous, G. A.

GREGOR. He can do no harm.

SVEN. He can talk.

GREGOR. (*Relaxing again.*) He won't.

SVEN. (*Still anxious.*) A word from him to Herries could kill the deal. If there's one thing the Herries type hates it's being made a fool of—

GREGOR. (*Murmuring sleepily.*) There won't *be* a word from Vassily.

SVEN. You can't be sure.

GREGOR. (*Murmuring sleepily.*) I can. He had his chance to finish me five years ago. He didn't take it then. He won't take it now. In this world there are those who do and those who don't, Sven. Call them the strong and the weak, if you like. By now you should know on which side dear Vassily lies.

SVEN. (*After a pause.*) What did he know, five years ago?

GREGOR. (*After another pause.*) Too much.

SVEN. Why did you tell him too much?

GREGOR. He was my son. A son has to be taught the facts of life.

SVEN. Not a son that hates you.

GREGOR. Oh, dear Sven, how stupid you can be, sometimes. (*He struggles into a sitting position.*) I mustn't sleep. I shall have to talk personally to Rome later. Can I have two more of those pills?

SVEN *takes out a bottle, shakes two pills into his palm, and hands them to* GREGOR *reluctantly.*

SVEN. Too many of these are dangerous.

GREGOR. Any more dangerous than letting Vassily wander around New York

with Mark Herries's private number in his pocket? Vassily won't harm
me, and nor will these pills.

SVEN. How was I stupid? I think you forget I once saw him try to kill you.

GREGOR. On the night he left me? Dear, dear Sven. One bullet in a chande-
lier six feet over my head doesn't argue a very serious attempt to kill. The
revolver was mine, anyway. I handed it to him ten minutes earlier, and
invited patricide. But—even supposing the bullet had been meant for
my heart, and his aim had been genuinely wild—a possibility, I suppose,
with these hysterical types—what on earth has killing to do with hatred?

*Pause.* SVEN *shrugs his shoulders.*

SVEN. You used to do your best to *make* him hate you.

GREGOR. Did I? Yes, I suppose I did.

SVEN. And tonight too.

GREGOR. Tonight? (*He shrugs.*) Perhaps. But if so it was unconscious. Vassily
was useful to me tonight. That was all, I think.

SVEN. Well, you certainly took a big risk not to warn him of the part he was
supposed to play.

GREGOR. I know I did, I had to. A far bigger risk than handing him that revolver five years ago and daring him to shoot me. (*With relish.*) But, Sven,
how much more fun! What I did tonight I did alone—without an ac-
complice—and that was important to me. A moment ago I asked you
to boost my subordinates' morale. What about my own? Do you think
I've enjoyed being on the run all day, sitting on a park bench in Washington Square with my coat collar turned up, trying to remember which
tramp steamer Insull took refuge on, thinking of Kreuger lying on that
bed in Paris with that little hole through his heart, Loewenstein jumping from that plane? (*As an afterthought.*) By the way—there's an
interesting idea I had for a development scheme in Washington Square.
Remind me of it sometime, would you?

*He has got up and is now striding round the room with gusto.*

No. Tonight—in this little, downtown dump—it was I who once again
controlled events. I alone, you could say, who perhaps changed the face
of the world again—I can be megalomaniac in front of you—and after
all Mussolini will get his loan now—and so may even Dollfuss, if affairs
go right—and such things can change the course of history. My God,
Sven—do you really think for all that I wanted to have to thank Vassily?
Vassily? Of all people?

SVEN. Why did you try to make him hate you?

*Pause.* GREGOR *suddenly puts his hand to his head, as though bewildered.*

GREGOR. You change the subject rather quickly, Sven. We were talking about
me—weren't we?

SVEN. Before, we were talking about Vassily.

GREGOR. (*Holding his head.*) Why did I try to get Vassily to hate me? That
was your question, wasn't it?

SVEN. Yes. Don't answer it if you don't want to.

GREGOR. (*Angrily.*) I'll answer any question put to me by anyone in the world. (*He continues to hold his head.*) Those pills are working too fast, or something worse is happening. I'm losing concentration.

SVEN. (*Instantly on his feet by* GREGOR'S *side.*) G. A.—you should sleep on that bed for at least two hours—

GREGOR. (*Pushing him away.*) I'm not sleepy. But I mustn't lose concentration. God—if that happened—let me think of that balance sheet. (*After a pause.*) Yes. All right. (*Speaking now in a normal voice; there had been a hint of panic.*) The point is, of course, I never have been able to think very clearly about Vassily. After three nights of no sleep it makes it no easier—

SVEN. Don't bother about Vassily—

GREGOR. No. You asked me a question and I must answer it. Try to, at least. (*After a pause.*) It shouldn't have been a son, of course. That's obvious. I think I could have endured a daughter loving me— Yes. A girl *might* have been different. But I doubt it. (*After a pause of intense concentration.*) It was all right when Vassily was a child. Even more than all right, remember?

SVEN. Very clearly.

GREGOR. I suppose I felt I could have let him love me then without danger.

SVEN. What danger?

GREGOR. Danger to me, to my way of life, to my universe. The whole world can hero-worship me, and some of it does, and there is no danger. But to be loved and worshipped by one's own boy—and by this boy above all . . . Oh, no. No. I will take almost any risk—you know that, Sven— but not the risk of being so close to the pure in heart. 'And virtue entered into him'—isn't that from the Bible?

SVEN. The New Testament.

GREGOR. I prefer the Old. Yes. Then here's your answer. It's perfectly clear. It shouldn't have taken me so long to see it. If I wanted to make my son hate me instead of loving me it's because I can, at least, understand hatred. I don't feel it, for anyone or anything, but I can understand it, and even relish it. And surely a good father should always try to understand his own son.

*There is a pause.* GREGOR *looks at* SVEN, *wondering if he has shocked him.*

Perhaps these pills make the brain too clear. Was that a bad thing to say?

SVEN. Most fathers would think so.

GREGOR. Do you like your two boys?

SVEN. Oh, yes.

GREGOR. And they love you?

SVEN. From time to time.

GREGOR. And you enjoy it?

SVEN. Oh, yes. (*Repeating* GREGOR'S *words with slight emphasis.*) I *relish* it.

GREGOR. (*Sitting again.*) I wonder if I am a very bad man.

SVEN. Oh, no. To be bad you must at least have some idea of what badness
   is.

GREGOR. (*Interested.*) And I don't? Perhaps not. And yet I have a conscience.
   I must have, or I wouldn't have tried so hard to drive it away.

SVEN. (*Smiling.*) When did you have a conscience?

GREGOR. (*Shrugging.*) It came in human shape. And I did drive it away—
   five years ago.

*There is a knock at the front door.* SVEN *is on his feet quickly.*

   Am I what Vassily called me, Sven? Am I—nothing?

SVEN. You're Gregor Antonescu. And being so I think you had better get out
   of the line of sight of this door before I open it.

GREGOR. In God's name why? An hour ago, yes. But not now. (*He faces the
   door.*) Here I stand—ready and happy to face the whole world—

SVEN *has opened the door to reveal the shapely form of* FLORENCE, *Countess
   Antonescu. She is not dressed in the predicted manner, but in a very smart
   evening-dress. Only the jewels are as foreseen. She is in the late twenties, and
   spectacularly beautiful.*

   (*In a flat voice.*) Oh, it's you. (*He walks forward to greet her.*)

*The lights fade.*


END OF ACT II

# ACT III

GREGOR *is walking forward to greet his wife.*

FLORENCE. Well, what's all this about?

*In her three years as the Countess Antonescu her accent has acquired some cosmopolitan flourishes, but is still basically English plebeian.*

GREGOR. (*Kissing her.*) How are you, my love?

FLORENCE. Worried to death, since you ask. Do you know what I just heard from John? That you'd been arrested by the F.B.I. and carted off to gaol. Imagine my feelings.

GREGOR. I'm happy to show you, in person, that it isn't true.

FLORENCE. Yes, but imagine my feelings hearing a thing like that. And then there was another one John heard—that you'd disguised yourself as a steward and gone off on the Aquitania—

GREGOR. (*To* SVEN.) Who is John?

SVEN. The Countess's chauffeur.

GREGOR. Personal, or from the pool?

FLORENCE. (*Slighted.*) Personal. You said I could have one personal—and I told you the one I was getting.

GREGOR. So you did. Well, my dear, if he alarms you with these sorts of rumours you'll have to fire him.

FLORENCE. I can't very well fire him—

GREGOR. Ah, yes. You told me that, too.

FLORENCE. I wish you'd tell me now what's going on?

GREGOR. I gather you didn't come by subway?

FLORENCE. No. I wouldn't. I told Sergei if he was going to get me into a subway he'd have to knock me unconscious first—

GREGOR. And he didn't?

FLORENCE. (*Ignoring him, talking to* SVEN.) Well, I mean, it was so silly. Disguising myself as someone ordinary and going down secret staircases—it was all tout ce qu'il y est de plus Warner Brothers. N'est ce pas, Sven?

SVEN. Vous êtes ici, Comtesse. C'est là l'important. (*He kisses her hand.*)

FLORENCE. Merci, mon cher. (*Looking round.*) Well, what kind of a place is this, when it's at home?

GREGOR. It's a basement apartment in Greenwich Village. Rather a smart thing to have these days. Sven, would you give the Countess that cheque for her to sign.

FLORENCE. *Another* cheque?

GREGOR. It is necessary.

FLORENCE. (*As* SVEN *hands her a cheque and a pen.*) Blank, as usual. I've signed about twenty of these in the last three weeks. Just how much *are* you snitching from the Foundation?

SVEN *and* GREGOR *laugh.*

Why are you laughing?

GREGOR. The word 'snitch' has a certain amusing association.

FLORENCE. Well, I hope there's enough left for my Maternity Centre.

GREGOR. Never fear, my dear. A cause so near your heart must not suffer. You may have to wait a few weeks to settle some bills, no more—Sven, would you add your signature?

FLORENCE. (*Alarmed.*) But the sub-Committee has promised the contractors a cheque by the week-end.

GREGOR. Go to Paris, then, my dear, before the week-end, and don't answer overseas calls. Sven, would you send those cables?

SVEN. In cypher?

GREGOR *nods.*

It'll take some time to encypher them.

GREGOR. I can't risk 'en clair'.

FLORENCE. Listen, you're not involving me in anything fishy, are you?

GREGOR. Fishy? The Antonescu Foundation? The greatest charitable organization in the world? And you, the world's greatest philanthropist? How could you think such a thing, my dear? (*To* SVEN.) Give me that file on the Mussolini loan.

SVEN *hands him a file, and then goes into the bedroom where, throughout the ensuing scene, he will be busy with pen, paper and a code book.* GREGOR *politely turns back to* FLORENCE, *kisses her absently as he passes her, goes to a chair, and begins to study the file. During the whole of this scene he never subsequently takes his eyes from it except at the moment indicated. But though he is plainly concentrating hard on matters relating to the Mussolini loan, his answers to* FLORENCE *are perfectly alert and made without pauses. One should feel that, of his immense faculty of concentration, he has relegated to* FLORENCE'S *conversation roughly one per cent, and that that percentage is proving perfectly sufficient.*

FLORENCE. (*Looking round.*) Well, which one does this apartment belong to?

GREGOR. Which one?

FLORENCE. (*Impatiently.*) Which girl friend?

GREGOR. No girl friend, my dear. If anything you might call it a boy friend—

FLORENCE. (*Scornfully.*) Don't give me that. They say a lot of things about you—and most of them are true—but that's one thing they *can't* say. Come on. Come clean, for once.

GREGOR. I always come clean with you, my love—

FLORENCE. Like hell you do. (*Growing angry.*) I'm your lawfully wedded wife, aren't I?

GREGOR. Indeed you are.

FLORENCE. O.K. Then tell me who this place belongs to.

GREGOR. A young man whom I happen to know very well. You don't at all, and very likely never will. There is no reason whatever for you to concern yourself about him or for me to give you his name.

FLORENCE. Yes. That's the sort of answer I've got used to these last three years. Well, here's another question for you—and this time I'd like a proper answer, please.

GREGOR. If I can give it to you, I will.

FLORENCE. You wouldn't like to look at me while I ask it, I suppose?

GREGOR. (*Politely.*) Of course, my dear. (*He puts a finger nail on the exact spot in the file his concentration had reached, and looks up at her.*) I should have asked you anyway to forgive my bad manners in studying these figures while talking to you, but time is rather important to me tonight.

FLORENCE. Oh, yes. We all know about the famous powers of concentration. Read a balance sheet, dictate to a secretary, speak on the telephone, and make love to your wife—all at the same time—

GREGOR. (*After a pause, very quietly.*) What is your question, my love?

FLORENCE. It's the same one I ask most Mondays. Who spent the week-end with you at Long Island?

GREGOR. Sven, his wife and children, William and Sergei, of course—and then a lot of people were coming and going from New York. There's been rather a big crisis on, you see. (*Politely.*) You allow me, now?

*He returns his gaze to the file, and removes his finger from the page.*

FLORENCE. Crisis? I'll say there's a crisis. Do you think I enjoyed having photographers on the penthouse terrace this morning—peeping through my bedroom windows?

GREGOR. I'm sure any photographs they took of you were delightful, and equally sure they were only of you.

FLORENCE. Fat lot you'd care if they weren't.

GREGOR. I'd care a great deal.

FLORENCE. Only because of the publicity.

GREGOR. (*Looking up voluntarily.*) I'd care a great deal.

*He stares at her quietly and gravely, for a moment, and then looks down at his file again.*

FLORENCE. Here we go again—switching everything round on to me. Well— there was no one in my bedroom this morning—get that—and there hasn't been the whole month we've been in New York.

GREGOR. Except, I presume, John.

FLORENCE. (*Furiously.*) He doesn't stay all night.

GREGOR. I'm delighted to hear it.

FLORENCE. I'm not having my maids catch me with him. I've a good deal more savoir-faire than that.

GREGOR. I'm quite sure you have, my dear.

FLORENCE. I'm getting side-tracked again. I know why they call you a genius. It's a genius for side-tracking people—nothing else—

GREGOR. —with the addition of a lucky aptitude for memorizing figures—

FLORENCE. Which of the girls went down for the weekend?

GREGOR. No girl, my dear.

FLORENCE. I expect it was the one who went last weekend. That Follies girl. She seems the current head of the New York harem.

GREGOR. If there were a New York harem—if there were a London, Paris or Bucharest harem—if there were indeed any harem at all—it would always be you who would be the head of it, my dear.

FLORENCE. Yes. Thank you very much. That just about sums up my position. Head of the Antonescu harem. And why am I head? Because I'm the one with the ring and the title. I'm only the something head. What's the word?

GREGOR. (*Glancing at her.*) Titular.

FLORENCE. Titular head. That's all I am. All I'm really good for is sex and signatures, isn't that right?

GREGOR. Oh, no. Your conversation is often very stimulating indeed, my dear.

FLORENCE. But I'm not head because you like me best of the bunch, I know that.

GREGOR. But I do like you the best of the bunch, dear heart.

FLORENCE. Well, why a wife? Do you ever treat me like a wife?

GREGOR'S *head is bent again over his file.*

A real wife, not just poor old Flo, the ex-typist—the London lay—carted round the world, dressed up to kill and calling herself Countess, because three years ago you decided to have yourself a good laugh by waving your magic wand and making all her silly dreams come true—plus giving her the name so you could use it for your Foundation—

*Pause*

GREGOR. (*Turning a page.*) I am speculating about our reasons for choosing this precise moment in world history to plough this rather familiar furrow.

FLORENCE. World history. There's your answer. World history. Look at me again, Gregor.

GREGOR *puts his finger precisely on the file and looks up politely.*

I'm the wife of the greatest financier in the world, yes?

GREGOR. Since there is no other financier present to hear me—yes.

FLORENCE. Well, imagine my feelings these last few days—

GREGOR. (*Still looking at her.*) You have already asked me to do that tonight, my dear, twice—

FLORENCE. Don't give me the sarcasm. This is serious. How do you think I've been feeling stuck up in that dreary penthouse reading those great blazing headlines, and not even able to talk to you? 'Antonescu faces crisis.' 'Will Antonescu crash?' Oh, yes—and here's one I remember— 'Antonescu's empire totters'—I remember that because if you're an emperor I'm bloody well an empress, and if your throne is tottering so is mine.

GREGOR. Yes.

*Patiently he puts down his file, having marked a place in pencil, gets up and goes over to her.*

FLORENCE. And then there was another one.

*Her voice subsides in trepidation as she watches him approach. He puts his hands in an affectionate gesture on her shoulders and kisses the top of her head.*

GREGOR. I am happy to tell you that neither my throne nor yours is tottering any longer—

FLORENCE. (*Looking up at him.*) No kidding?

GREGOR. No kidding. The crisis is over.

FLORENCE. Well, I'm not surprised. I knew you'd come through it.

GREGOR. You did?

FLORENCE. Well, everyone I spoke to who knows you said you would. (*Plaintively.*) But you do see I had the right to be worried—

GREGOR. Every right in the world.

FLORENCE. (*Seriously.*) No. Just a wife's right.

*She gets up and faces him.*

I wasn't being jealous just now when I asked you which one came down for the week-end. Well, not jealous in the usual way. I just felt that if you were in trouble it ought to be *my* shoulder you cried on, and not one of the others.

GREGOR. As it happens I cried on none.

FLORENCE. I didn't mean that literally, dear. To see you crying—that'll be the day. I meant you might be wanting a bit of comfort—

GREGOR. (*Fondling her.*) I asked you to come here tonight.

FLORENCE. (*Not angrily.*) Don't give me that. I know why you asked me here tonight. Just that signature. Sergei gave it away.

GREGOR. Naughty Sergei.

FLORENCE. Gregor—I *could* love you, if you gave me the chance.

GREGOR. I shall give you the chance, my dear, if you care to stay, (*He looks at his watch.*) in about an hour's time. Forgive me now.

*He walks away from her back to his chair, where he picks up his file and methodically resumes reading it at the point he left off.*

FLORENCE. (*Plaintively, as he goes.*) I didn't *mean* that kind of love.

*She sits down again, staring at his bent head in baffled frustration. There is a pause.*

(*At length, resignedly, and realizing she is really speaking only to herself, although her husband will listen to every word.*) There was another news story I remember. It was in one of the columns. It said: 'Antonescu, the lonely genius of finance, fights his biggest battle.' Lonely genius. You must admit that's a bit of a laugh.

GREGOR. If I am expected to laugh at 'genius', I do it readily. If at 'lonely'— I can manage to keep my face straight.

FLORENCE. Lonely? *Lonely?* You?

*There is no reply from* GREGOR.

What about the Follies girl? What about that Italian—Oh, hell—the list's
too long even to start—

GREGOR. (*In his usual, even voice.*) I don't think you can measure loneliness
by the dimensions of a bed—

FLORENCE. Well—that's what I mean. That's all I've been saying. You need
someone in your life who—

*The front door is thrown open to reveal* BASIL. GREGOR *looks up at him from his
file, keeping his finger on the point he has reached, and smiles his satisfaction at seeing him.* BASIL'S *face is a mask. He is holding two papers (New
York Daily Mirror and New York Daily News, early editions) under his arm.
He stands for a long moment facing his father, his back to us, and unfolds
the first paper slowly, so that* GREGOR *can read the headline.* GREGOR'S *own
face now becomes a mask.* BASIL *puts the paper down on the floor beside*
GREGOR, *folding it up neatly, and then displays the other one. Then, this too
he folds, and lays beside* GREGOR. *Then he turns abruptly to pour himself a
drink.* FLORENCE *has also seen the headlines.*

No. Oh, no

*She makes a move to pick up the papers, but* GREGOR'S *icy voice stops her.*

GREGOR. Would you ask Sven to come in, please?

FLORENCE *goes to the bedroom door.*

FLORENCE. Sven—come in quick—something awful—he wants you—

SVEN *runs into the sitting-room.*

GREGOR. (*Quietly, to* SVEN.) Vassily has just brought in two papers. I imagine
they are early editions of the tabloids. One headline seems to read
'Antonescu—Indictment sought'. Another says 'Antonescu. Arrest Im-
minent'—with a question mark I think. Would you read the stories please
and tell me what they mean?

SVEN *snatches up the papers.*

SVEN. (*As he reads, savagely, to* BASIL.) Is this you?

BASIL. How could it be? I've only been gone half an hour, and haven't been
out of a bar except to buy those.

GREGOR. (*Gently.*) But of course it isn't Basil.

SVEN *continues to read the stories, his eyes darting down each column.* GREGOR
*watches him without apparent emotion, but he can be seen to be gripping
the arms of his chair tightly, and the mask of impassivity—which he will
try to keep as long as his physical strength allows—is already beginning to
crack.*

SVEN. (*At length.*) The Bank of the City of London has applied to Scotland
Yard for a warrant for your arrest.

GREGOR. The Bank of the City of London?

SVEN. If they succeed there will have to be extradition proceedings over here—

GREGOR. The Bank of the City Of London?

SVEN. (*Reading.*) The Bank issued no details but it is understood the charges
will relate to certain securities deposited by Antonescu as collateral for a
loan in 1929.

*He looks up at* GREGOR *inquiringly.* GREGOR *stares back at him blankly.*

What securities are those, G. A.?

*There is no reply.* GREGOR *continues to stare at* SVEN *blankly.*

(*Urgently.*) G. A.—what securities did you deposit at the Bank in 1929?

*Another pause.*

G.A.—

GREGOR. (*Smiling.*) Nothing.

SVEN. (*Loudly.*) G. A.—you did raise a loan from that Bank in 1929. I remember it. It was for over six million pounds and it was to finance the Czechoslovakian Loan.

*He waits for* GREGOR *to reply, but he continues to sit staring blankly at him.*

So you must have pledged some collateral. What was it?

GREGOR. Nothing.

SVEN *turns hopelessly away.*

GREGOR. Wait. Wait. (*In a perfectly normal voice.*) So sorry, Sven—dear fellow. Forgive me. I was talking nonsense. It's so hard sometimes to remember, and when one can't think . . . and after what Vassily said earlier . . . (*Suddenly.*) Six million one hundred and twenty-six thousand—

SVEN. That was the *amount* of the loan, G. A. What did you *pledge* for it?

GREGOR. (*After a pause.*) Some bonds. I'll remember in a moment, dear boy. (*Plaintively.*) Don't plague me—

SVEN. G. A.—we must get through to London tonight. But before we do, there is one thing I must know. Were these securities you pledged to the Bank of the City of London, five years ago, Polish bonds?

GREGOR. Yes. That is correct. They were Polish bonds.

SVEN. Were they forged?

*There is a pause during which* GREGOR *remains utterly still.*

GREGOR. (*Speaking with difficulty.*) If I could move I wouldn't sit still in this chair to receive insults. I would go to my bed and leave you. But—you see . . . I can't move.

SVEN. (*Briskly.*) Vassily—help me—

SVEN *has gone quickly to the chair and is trying to raise* GREGOR *from it.* BASIL *joins him.*

Take his other arm.

BASIL *does so.*

That's right. It's easier if we get him on his feet—

BASIL. Has this happened before?

SVEN. Yes. A few times.

BASIL. Should I get a doctor?

SVEN. No.

*They succeed in getting* GREGOR *on his feet. He is conscious but apparently oblivious of his surroundings. Supported by* BASIL, *and* SVEN *he walks with difficulty, but without resisting his helpers, towards the bedroom.*

FLORENCE. I didn't know this happened. I've never seen him like this. (*Hys-*

*terically*.) We must get a doctor—*now*. Where's the telephone? I'll call Doctor Thompson—

SVEN. No, Countess. Not yet. We may have to take the risk later, but not yet.

FLORENCE. You mean—if the police are looking for him . . . But Doctor Thompson wouldn't tell—

SVEN. (*To* BASIL.) Open the door. I'll hold him.

BASIL *does so.*

Now take his arm again. That's right.

*They move into the bedroom.*

(*To* FLORENCE.) He can recover from these things very quickly. No need yet to take an unnecessary risk.

*As* GREGOR *reaches the bed he suddenly pushes* SVEN *and* BASIL *away.*

GREGOR. Put them through, please, Sven.

SVEN. Lie down on the bed, G. A.

GREGOR. The telephone is ringing. It will be Rome. I want to speak to them, please.

BASIL. (*Holding him.*) Later, Father. Lie down now.

GREGOR *turns and stares at* BASIL *with a mildly puzzled frown.*

GREGOR. (*At length, gently.*) Vassily, dear boy—I know something has happened to me, but I have to speak to Rome. I have all the figures in my mind. The initial payment of five hundred million lire will be made on August 31st of this year. This sum will be partly raised out of the proceeds of the American Electric merger remaining to me after payment of debts amounting in all to eight million seven hundred and thirty thousand dollars, leaving a residue of sixteen million two hundred and seventy thousand dollars; and partly out of the issue of debentures by Antonescu Holdings of fifteen million dollars at six per cent—six and a half per cent— (*He holds his head, and then turns pleadingly to* BASIL.) Vassily—six or six and a half?

BASIL. (*Gently, but firmly.*) Father—you are ill. You must please lie down and rest—

GREGOR. But if Rome is on the line—

BASIL. There's no one on the line, Father.

GREGOR. No one? I thought the telephone— (*He points.*)

BASIL. No. It didn't ring.

GREGOR. How foolish of me. (*To* BASIL.) Are you quite sure—mon enfant? Tu ne mens pas à ton papa?

BASIL. (*Quietly and firmly.*) No, Father. I'm not lying to you. I'm quite sure the telephone didn't ring.

GREGOR *nods slowly and then, assisted by* SVEN *and* BASIL, *lies on the bed.*

GREGOR. Six and a *half* per cent. Sven—I'm all right. The figures are still quite clear.

SVEN. Yes, G. A. Just lie there for a moment. Can you sleep?

GREGOR. I expect so. What's Vassily doing here?

SVEN. This is his apartment, G. A. You're lying on his bed.

GREGOR. Oh, yes, of course. How foolish. (*To* BASIL.) Mon petit Vassily, to es très gentil de prêter ton lit à ton papa—

BASIL. (*With the same quiet, firm voice he had used earlier.*) I'm turning out the light, Father. You must try and sleep.

*He turns the lights out in the bedroom.*

GREGOR. (*Murmuring from the dark.*) Oui, mon petit.

SVEN, *after a look at* GREGOR, *goes back into the living-room, where* FLORENCE *has been sitting, looking frightened, since* GREGOR *was taken into the bedroom.*

FLORENCE. How is he?

SVEN *shrugs, picks up the newspapers from where he had dropped them, and continues to read them.*

I'm sorry I wasn't more help, but I can't bear illness. You do understand that, don't you? Sven, mon cher, il y a des gens qui ne peuvent pas supporter la maladie—

SVEN. (*Without looking up from his paper.*) Oui, Comtesse. Je comprends très bien.

*In the bedroom* BASIL *has approached the darkened bed, looking down at his father, who is lying on his back, still and apparently asleep.*

GREGOR. (*Suddenly, speaking quite clearly.*) What a sweet revenge for you— dearest boy.

BASIL *moves away from the bed, out of* GREGOR'S *sight, and watches him a moment from there. There is no further sound or sign of life from* GREGOR. BASIL *goes quickly into the living-room. He is plainly in a state of deep distress. He looks at* SVEN, *who has glanced up at him from the paper he is reading.*

BASIL. (*Speaking carefully.*) A man came in the bar with those papers—I saw the headlines and went out and bought them. After all, I *have* a right to be interested—haven't I?

SVEN, *still reading, nods.*

I brought them in because I thought at least he ought to be warned.

SVEN. Quite right.

BASIL. I wasn't to know—was I?

SVEN. No. Of course not.

BASIL. Five years ago he was healthy—much healthier than me.

SVEN. (*Gently.*) Dear boy, you weren't to know. And he would have learnt the news anyway.

BASIL. But not from me. Not from me holding up the headlines.

SVEN, *for the first time interested in what he is saying, looks up at him.*

I was mad as hell at him, you know that—and I was a bit drunk too. After—well, you saw what happened—I went out and I was going to get a bed and never come back and never see him again—not this time— not ever, ever, ever. But I did come back and I came back with those goddam papers—and no one, no one had told me that I could give him a stroke—

SVEN. (*At length, puzzled and rather amused by his outburst.*) The strokes he has had lately have been very minor ones. I'm sure he'll be perfectly all right in a few hours.

BASIL. He says it's revenge—

SVEN. Of course he does.

BASIL. Do you?

SVEN. I really hadn't bothered to think about it. Now that you force me to, I'd say merely that if it wasn't revenge, it should have been.

BASIL. (*Fiercely.*) But *was* it?

SVEN. What an extraordinary boy you are. I begin to see why G. A. found you such a handful. Why, I wonder, were you born to *him*, of all people? How many other fathers would have *relished* you.

*He gets up and leads* FLORENCE *forward.*

Of course you haven't been introduced, have you?

BASIL. I'm sorry. I knew who you were. I've seen photographs.

FLORENCE. Vassily? Not the—son, Vassily?

BASIL. Yes.

FLORENCE. Did you have a brother?

BASIL. No.

FLORENCE. Then you must be the one he said died five years ago.

BASIL. He said that?

FLORENCE. Yes. Not only to me. To everyone—

BASIL. Well, I suppose—to him—I did die—five years ago.

FLORENCE. You ran away?

BASIL. Yes. I did. Excuse me. (*He turns to* SVEN.) There's no point in reading those. They won't tell you anything. What he pledged to the Bank of the City of London for his six million pounds was exactly what he said—nothing.

SVEN. There must have been collateral.

BASIL. (*Hopelessly.*) Yes. A receipt from the International Bank of Liechtenstein for some bonds held to the credit of Antonescu Holdings.

SVEN. International Bank of Liechtenstein. That's a new one for me.

BASIL. I'm surprised.

SVEN. He never told me everything, you know.

BASIL. He told me. He told me especially at my coming-of-age party. You were there later, Sven.

SVEN. Oh, yes, I knocked you out.

BASIL. You needn't have done. I was safe with that gun. He knew it. Who were you going to talk to in London?

SVEN. One of our agents there who has friends at Scotland Yard—

BASIL. It's no good, Sven, it's gone too far for that.

SVEN. This Bank at Liechtenstein—it's the usual thing?

BASIL. Yes. Like all the four hundred other Antonescu Banks. A set of portable books, a board of directors who don't know what they're directing but accept because it's Antonescu who's asked them, and a local crooked accountant, paid a hundred dollars a week—or has the salary gone up since my time—?

SVEN. Oh, trebled, quadrupled—

BASIL. Blackmail is expensive.

SVEN. Why didn't you make your fortune, dear boy—while there was still time?

BASIL. The way you have?

SVEN. (*Genially.*) Perfectly permissible if said to me. But unwise if said to the police.

BASIL *says nothing.*

FLORENCE. (*Looking in bewilderment from one to the other.*) But what's he done? I don't understand.

SVEN. (*Firmly.*) Countess, I realize this is all very distressing for you, but what Vassily and I are saying to each other now is very important to your husband, and it'll be easier for us to concentrate without interruption. Why don't you go in there and watch over him as a good wife should.

FLORENCE *goes reluctantly to the bedroom door.*

BASIL. Sven, how has he got away with it for so long?

SVEN. (*Shrugging.*) Confidence.

FLORENCE. (*Having opened the door, peeped in and closed the door again.*) He's asleep. (*Meeting* BASIL'S *eyes, apologetically.*) I can't bear illness.

*She goes over to a chair in the corner.*

I'll sit here. I won't disturb you.

BASIL. (*Hopelessly.*) 'Liquidity and confidence'.

SVEN. Liquidity dried up with the Depression. But confidence still remained—well, until yesterday, when at least the Bank of the City of London evidently felt it time to inspect the Antonescu account rather more closely. Other banks too, I'm afraid, will be doing the same thing. How many other transactions of this kind do you know of?

BASIL. Dozens. And since nineteen-thirty you must know of dozens more.

SVEN. Oh, no. I never knew of anything actually—criminal. (*Spreading his hands.*) Obviously, I couldn't have, could I—and stayed with him?

*There is a pause while* BASIL *stares at* SVEN.

BASIL. Don't desert him, Sven. Don't you desert him.

SVEN. My dear Vassily, you must know that I have always served your father with the deepest and truest devotion.

BASIL. (*Pleadingly.*) So go on. Please go on. Miracles must have happened these last five years to let him get away with what he has. Can't you and I make another miracle for him now?

SVEN. In finance miracles are made by man himself. That's one of your father's sayings. He meant, of course, by *the* man himself. Whatever happens, he used to say to me, I'll at least, go down to history as the greatest confidence trickster of all time.

BASIL. But that's not the way he must go down to history. That's not a crook, in there. Not a common swindler, Sven. That's—that's— (*With difficulty.*) A great man.

*Pause.* SVEN *looks at* BASIL *with faint amusement, but greater sympathy.*

SVEN. (*At length.*) Poor Vassily.

BASIL. Don't say that. Don't look at me like father. I mean that what he's tried to do is great—and what he's succeeded in doing. Of course he's not great in himself. How could he be when it's all—founded on—on (*Bravely.*) fraud. But he hasn't done it to enrich himself. It's to enrich the world. However dis-dis-honestly they were got, the loans he has given out to poor countries are real. Who gave—

SVEN. (*Interrupting gently.*)—roads to Jugoslavia and electricity to Hungary? Your father, of course.

FLORENCE *is fiddling with the radio, trying to get a news broadcast.*

BASIL. (*Realizing he is being laughed at.*) Well, he did, and much more besides. What's so wrong in getting money to circulate freely from rich countries to poor countries—?

SVEN. I'd measure it at about fifteen years' hard labour.

BASIL. But it's the system that should be on trial, not father.

SVEN. Yes, yes. The system.

FLORENCE. (*At radio.*) Ah, I've, got something.

BASIL. (*Passionately.*) Have you heard about his childhood in Bucharest?

SVEN. Oh, yes. Many times

FLORENCE. (*Turning up the radio's volume.*) Quiet. I've got some news.

RADIO ANNOUNCER. (*Loudly.*) . . . one of the biggest financial scandals of all time, dwarfing the recent Stavisky affair in Paris, and the crash and flight to Greece of Samuel Insull last year. The warrant held by the F.B.I. for the arrest of Gregor Antonescu—

FLORENCE. ⎫ (*Simultaneously.*) Warrant?
BASIL. ⎭ Oh, God.

RADIO. —will be executed as soon as the missing financier, who is believed now to be still in hiding somewhere on Manhattan Island, is located and captured. All ports, airfields and frontier posts are being watched. F.B.I. Headquarters state they are confident the arrest will be made either tonight, or early this morning . . . An automobile accident at the junction of—

BASIL *has signed to* FLORENCE *to switch it off. He goes to the front door and locks it.*

*Meanwhile, in the bedroom,* GREGOR, *at a moment just before the broadcast, which he plainly does not hear, has stirred from his lying position and is now sitting on the bed, swaying his head slowly from side to side, as if trying to clear his brain. After a time he stops, and stares at the floor, still sitting, but motionless.*

BASIL. (*Turning anxiously to* SVEN) Herries has given them this address.

SVEN. No. Oh, no. Herries wouldn't want to be implicated. (*With a faint smile.*) Besides he'd hardly give them *this* address.

BASIL. (*Turning to* FLORENCE.) Did you come here by car?

FLORENCE. Yes. But we drove very fast, and way out somewhere by Jersey City. I know we'd shaken them off before I got here.

BASIL. So they *did* follow—anyway for a time?

FLORENCE. Yes, but they were only reporters—I mean they weren't police-men—

BASIL. (*Having turned back to* SVEN.) That's how they know he's in New York.

SVEN. I imagine.

BASIL. We can't be sure at least one didn't follow her here. They said Man-hattan Island. We'll have to get him out of here at once.

SVEN. Where?

BASIL. Carol Penn. She lives on West Twenty-third Street. Let me think. A taxi's no good. He might be recognized. I'll borrow Fred's car. It's an old coupe—so if we have to try and get him into Mexico it might be better to use it instead of anything you, Sergei or William can organize for him. I'll have to drive him, but that's all right. How much cash has he on him?

SVEN. He never carries any. (*He pulls out a wallet and throws it to* BASIL.) There's over a thousand there.

BASIL. What about you?

SVEN. Thank you. I'm provided for.

BASIL *goes into the bedroom.* GREGOR *looks up at him from his sitting position.*

BASIL. You're feeling better?

GREGOR *nods.*

Shouldn't you be lying down?

GREGOR *shakes his head.* BASIL *arranges pillows behind his head.*

BASIL. (*Quietly.*) Father, I'm sorry, but this news has to be given to you sud-denly. Can you hear and understand what I am saying? And are you strong enough to hear it?

GREGOR *nods slowly. It is plain that he does hear and understand.*

We've just heard on the radio that the F.B.I. have a warrant out for your arrest.

GREGOR *nods again, slowly, but quite calmly, still evidently understanding.*

We think they may know of this place, and so I'm going out now to get a car and move you to another apartment. It belongs to Carol Penn, the girl you met earlier tonight—

GREGOR *nods again and then, lifting his head, speaks very softly.*

GREGOR. Does she know that it's an offence in law to harbour a wanted crimi-nal?

*Pause.* GREGOR *continues to look up at* BASIL *quietly and gravely.* BASIL *smiles at his father, suddenly, and for the first time that evening.*

BASIL. Yes, Father. She knows and I know. We both know.

*He turns and goes to the living-room door.*

GREGOR. (*Quietly.*) Would you ask Sven to come in?

BASIL *nods and goes.*

*During his absence from the living-room, the following colloquy has quietly taken place, leaving a silence to cover the moment of* BASIL'S *announcement of the news to* GREGOR *and the subsequent passages.*

FLORENCE. Do I have to stay?

SVEN. He might need you.

FLORENCE. I don't know for what. There's nothing I can do to help here—

SVEN *shrugs and the silence continues until* BASIL'S *reentrance.*

BASIL. (*To* SVEN.) He wants to see you.

SVEN *nods and goes towards the bedroom.*

FLORENCE. How is he?

BASIL. (*Going to the front door.*) Better. We'll get him into the car O.K.

FLORENCE. (*With ingenuous curiosity.*) Why did you leave him?

BASIL. (*At door, with a shrug.*) He made me.

*He goes out. In the bedroom* GREGOR *is looking up at* SVEN *from the bed with a faint, wry smile.*

GREGOR. What the boy said is true? There's a warrant out for me over here?

SVEN *nods.*

   Yes, of course, Vassily doesn't lie.

SVEN. He's taking you to his girl tonight in a borrowed two-seater, and to-morrow he's going to try and drive you down to the Mexican frontier—

GREGOR. (*With a faint laugh.*) Mexican frontier? Vassily always did suffer from an over-romantic mind.

SVEN. Have you ever made plans to meet this emergency?

GREGOR. Yes. But they don't involve escape.

*There is a pause.* GREGOR *looks down at the floor and shivers slightly.*

   Is it cold in here?

SVEN. It's a warm night—

GREGOR. Put something over my shoulders, would you—there's a good fel-low.

SVEN *puts* BASIL'S *dinner jacket round* GREGOR'S *shoulders. He nods gratefully.*

   I've left you the controlling interest in Manson Radios. If I were you, I'd hold on. For a couple of years they'll be worthless, but things will pick up one day and there's a patent on a new television process that could be valuable.

SVEN. Won't you at least let Vassily try?

GREGOR. How long would it take him to drive me to the Mexican border?

SVEN. (*Shrugging.*) Five or six days.

GREGOR. (*Smiling gently up at* SVEN.) Five or six days alone in a two-seater with my conscience? No. As the expression is, I'd rather die.

*Despite his covering, he shivers again.*

   Where is Sergei, at this moment?

SVEN. At his apartment.

GREGOR. Gramercy Place? (SVEN *nods.*) Conveniently close.

SVEN. (*After a pause.*) Convenient for what?

GREGOR. (*Quietly.*) For you to go there and borrow a gun.

SVEN *is silent. Pause.*

Will you do that for me, please?

SVEN *is still silent.* GREGOR *looks up at him.*

(*With a flash of authority.*) Do that for me, please, Sven.

SVEN *still makes no move to go.*

Neither you nor Sergei will be involved in any way. I shall leave the usual note.

SVEN *still makes no move.*

(*More gently.*) I don't really need it, you know—there are other ways. But it would be a great favour to let me have it tonight.

SVEN. (*At length.*) I'll do what you say—

*He goes into the living-room, picks up his hat, and goes to the front door.* FLORENCE, *alarmed at this apparent desertion, is on her feet quickly.*

FLORENCE. You're not leaving?

SVEN. I have something to do.

FLORENCE. Do I have to stay?

SVEN. You're his wife.

*He goes out quickly.* FLORENCE *subsides gloomily into a chair. In the bedroom* GREGOR *is staring at the floor.*

GREGOR. Florence? Florence? Are you still here?

*He gets off the bed and staggers to the living-room door.* FLORENCE, *in the living-room, has risen, startled at the sound from the next room. She is cowering in a corner as* GREGOR *comes in and sees her.*

(*At length, almost laughing with relief.*) I thought you'd gone.

FLORENCE. They told me to stay.

GREGOR. I'm glad. I'm very glad.

*He holds out his arms to her.*

Come here—

*Timidly* FLORENCE *approaches him. He embraces her.*

My darling, I'm so happy you stayed. Earlier tonight, didn't you say you wanted to be a wife—a real wife?

FLORENCE. Yes.

GREGOR. Even the wife of a hunted man?

FLORENCE. What have you done, Gregor?

GREGOR. It would be a little complicated to explain. I must sit down. Do you mind?

*He flops on to the chair.* FLORENCE *stands, staring at him cautiously.*

You came here by car, didn't you?

FLORENCE. (*Letting her hand be grasped, but not responding.*) Yes. The Lincoln.

GREGOR. Is it still there?

FLORENCE. I expect so.

GREGOR. Have a look.

FLORENCE *goes to the front door.*

If it's there see if there are any people hanging around—or if there's a policeman—

FLORENCE. (*At door, startled.*) Policemen? They won't be after *me?*

GREGOR. (*Patiently.*) No, my dear. Only after me.

FLORENCE *opens the front door, walks up a few steps and peers out down the street.*

FLORENCE. (*Returning.*) Yes. John's still there. And there's no one about—

GREGOR *nods and attempts to get to his feet.* FLORENCE *does not assist him in his struggle. Finally he flops back, exhausted.*

GREGOR. It's no good. Later you'll have to get him to come here and help me in—

FLORENCE. You're not going to use my car for a getaway? You said yourself it'd be known—

GREGOR. (*Still exhausted.*) No, my dear. Not for a getaway. At least only from this place—

FLORENCE. What for, then?

GREGOR. To drive me to some place. Perhaps to Washington Square. We could sit on a bench for a few moments together, and then, perhaps, you could still be with me when— (*He stops.*)

*Pause.* FLORENCE *stares at him in horror.*

FLORENCE. When what? When what? When you kill yourself? Is that what you mean?

GREGOR. I'm not going to be arrested. I decided that years ago. (*Kissing her.*) Thank you for caring.

FLORENCE. (*In horror.*) And you want me there? There, when you actually do it?

*Pause.*

GREGOR. Perhaps that was not a good idea. (*With sudden anguish.*) I just crave for some human being to be with me for the next hour, that's all.

FLORENCE. There's Vassily.

GREGOR. (*Fiercely.*) Not Vassily.

FLORENCE. But he's your son—

GREGOR. (*More loudly.*) Not Vassily—

FLORENCE. But he loves you—even that snapshot he's kept of you over there shows he loves you.

*Pause.* GREGOR *says nothing.*

He's the one you want with you tonight. Not me. I don't know why you should suddenly want it to be *me.*

GREGOR. (*In a harsh voice.*) Because you're here—because you're my wife—because that dress you're wearing and those jewels and that Lincoln and the chauffeur are all mine—because even your title is mine—bought and paid for by me—and because I think you owe me in return one hour of my last night on earth.

FLORENCE. But it *should* be Vassily.

GREGOR. No! Poor Vassily. Whatever happens to me tonight I won't ask him to hold my hand and lend me a shoulder to cry on. (*After a pause.*) You said that, didn't you, earlier? Something about a shoulder to cry on? Didn't you say it should be yours?

FLORENCE. Yes. I suppose I did.

GREGOR. Well?

FLORENCE. (*Plaintively.*) I don't want to get involved, Gregor.

*Pause.*

GREGOR. (*At length.*) I see.

FLORENCE. Don't blame me.

GREGOR. I don't.

FLORENCE. Perhaps it could have been different, if you'd wanted it before. But you never did, did you? Not till now, and now—well—it's just too late, that's all.

*Pause.*

GREGOR. Antonescu-training, I see. (*After a pause, briskly.*) Well, good-bye, then my dear.

FLORENCE. You do understand?

GREGOR. Very clearly. I've left you a cash sum of one million dollars. (*Bitterly.*) Whatever happens, that, at least, can't be involved. Sven knows where it is.

FLORENCE. (*Quickly.*) Sven? Was it wise to trust Sven? Personally I wouldn't trust him further than I can throw him.

GREGOR *looks at her, with a faint smile.*

It's not just the money. You know that. It's just that I wouldn't like to see him get away with anything.

GREGOR. I understand perfectly, my dear.

FLORENCE *stands above him looking down on him.*

FLORENCE. Good-bye, then.

GREGOR. (*Without looking at her.*) Good-bye, my dear.

FLORENCE *comes round the chair to offer a farewell kiss.*

Don't kiss me, please.

FLORENCE *straightens herself and wanders forlornly to the front door.*

FLORENCE. (*At door.*) I'm sorry, Gregor. Really, I'm sorry. You see—

*She can find no words for her explanation.* GREGOR *sitting stiff and still, says nothing, merely looking at her.* FLORENCE *goes, leaving the door open.*

GREGOR, *left alone, begins to shiver. Then he rises and crosses with difficulty to the drinks tray, where he pours himself out one. As he drinks,* BASIL *returns.*

BASIL. Well done.

GREGOR. Dear boy.

BASIL. Ready to go?

GREGOR. No, I'm not going. At least not with you, dearest Vassily.

BASIL. But I've got the car.

GREGOR. I'm most deeply touched at all you've tried to do for me. Believe it. But Sven has organized something, perhaps a little more—secure. A private aeroplane.

BASIL. (*Deeply disappointed.*) Tonight?

GREGOR. Oh, of course tonight. Now, in fact. I was just waiting for you—to say good-bye and thank you—before getting on my way.

BASIL. Are you fit enough to travel tonight?

GREGOR. My dearest boy—I am perfectly well.

BASIL. Can I come with you?

GREGOR. No.

BASIL. Can't I help at all?

GREGOR. (*Gently.*) No.

BASIL. I really want to, you know.

GREGOR. Yes. I do know. Why do you drink? Is it because of me?

BASIL. No. I think it's because of me. No strength of will. Do you remember, Father? The weak go to the wall?

GREGOR. (*Gravely.*) And the strong—fly to Mexico.

BASIL. I didn't mean that.

GREGOR. I know you didn't. How much harm have I done you, Vassily?

BASIL. (*Murmuring.*) Not much.

GREGOR. Be truthful with me, please. Have I ruined your life?

BASIL. No. I am what you've always said I am—soft, that's all. I'll get by. When you get to Mexico where will you go?

GREGOR. Sven has made plans.

BASIL. Wherever you end up, will you remember that I'm always here to help you?

GREGOR. Yes. I will.

BASIL. But this is one—contact—they won't trace. Basil Anthony—piano player and song-writer—

GREGOR. Do you write good songs?

BASIL. I think so. The publishers don't.

GREGOR. I think you will write good songs.

BASIL. Thank you, Father. (*Takes* GREGOR'S *glass and goes to drinks tray.*)

GREGOR. Don't you want a drink?

BASIL. No.

GREGOR. Interesting.

BASIL. (*Pouring* GREGOR'S *drink.*) Why?

GREGOR. Our roles are becoming reversed. Who is now the strong and who the weak?

BASIL. I'm not strong. I could never be.

*He hands him his glass.*

GREGOR. I don't know. But something tells me you won't find it too hard, in the future, to give up the bottle. Tell me, how much joy will there be in the Socialist ranks at my downfall?

BASIL. Not too much. You've done your best. If you fail it will be because the system has failed, not you. And if you rose to be the greatest monopoly capitalist of all time, it was because, instinctively, you had to get your revenge on society—

GREGOR. (*Mildly.*) Why? Whatever had society done to me?

BASIL. Starved you in Bucharest. Sent you out, as a child, to beg in the streets—

GREGOR. Did I tell you that?

BASIL. I don't remember. It's in every book about you—

GREGOR. Is it? Plainly no one has bothered to check up. Now, I imagine, they will. How amusing.

*Pause.* BASIL, *in sudden panic, bounds from his chair, and goes to pour himself a drink.*

(*Gently.*) Yes, have that. But let it be your last, dearest Vassily. I have no further illusions to break for you. I have never had to beg for anything in my life.

BASIL. (*His back still to* GREGOR.) That must be a lie.

GREGOR. Why, at this moment, should I tell you a lie?

BASIL. (*Like a small boy, still with his back to* GREGOR.) Because you always have told me lies—

GREGOR. Oh, no, it's the truth I've always told you, and it's the truth I'm telling you now. Your political beliefs are a fraud, dear Vassily—

BASIL. Don't destroy them—

GREGOR. (*Continuing remorselessly.*) A far greater fraud than any of mine. I at least knew what I was doing. But when you wave your red flag, all you are doing is to try and find an excuse for your father. But there is no excuse for your father, Vassily. He is a swindler simply because that is what he chose to be, and that is all—

BASIL. (*Indistinctly.*) God damn you! God damn you!

GREGOR. Poor Vassily! Always so easy to make you cry.

SVEN *opens the door abruptly and stands watching the two.* GREGOR *looks at him inquiringly,* SVEN *nods.*

(*Gently.*) You must go now, dearest boy. Sven is here and we have plans to make.

BASIL. But can't I stay and help?

GREGOR. (*Gently.*) Better not.

BASIL. I had hoped— (*He stops uncertainly.*) I had hoped you might allow me to come with you.

*There is a pause.* GREGOR *motions* SVEN *with his head to leave the bedroom, indicating his wish to be left alone.* SVEN *goes in, carrying his brief-case, and closes the door quietly.* GREGOR *stares at his son in silence for a moment.*

GREGOR. (*Sighing gently.*) Dear God, what a boy! Isn't there anything I can do to kill it?

BASIL. No. Not anything. But why do you have to try?

GREGOR. I don't know. (*Shrugging.*) Perhaps, because—having had to live all my life without a conscience it would be rather—unmanly—to acquire one now, don't you think? Go and return that two-seater to its owner.

*Pause.*

BASIL. (*Desperately.*) Isn't there *any* way—isn't there any way at all, Father—
I can be of use to you at this moment?

GREGOR. No. (*Gravely looking at him.*) I wish there were.

*He holds out an arm to him.* BASIL *walks slowly to him and* GREGOR *embraces
him. The contrast with the other paternal embraces which we have seen is
very marked, it is the face of a deeply anguished man who stares at us,
sightlessly, from over* BASIL'S *shoulder. Then* GREGOR, *with a brisk change of
tone, pats him on the back.*

Marry that girl. (*He propels him gently towards the door and opens it for
him.*) And give up that tiresome habit of drinking, it's really a very foolish one, dear boy.

BASIL. Yes, Father. I know.

*He turns abruptly to go, to prevent his father seeing his emotion.*

GREGOR. Oh—and—Vassily—

BASIL, *his foot on the step, turns back.*

GREGOR. (*Gently.*) Whatever happens never, in the future, let the truth make
you cry.

BASIL. I won't—not any more.

GREGOR. Good!

BASIL. Good luck! You'll come through, Father, you always do.

GREGOR. Thank you, dear boy.

BASIL *goes.* GREGOR *closes the door after him. Then he walks into the bedroom
where* SVEN *is standing by the window.*

You've brought it?

SVEN. Yes.

GREGOR. Let me have it, please.

*He sits on the bed.* SVEN *does not move.* GREGOR *looks up at him sharply.*

Give it to me, Sven.

SVEN. One moment, G. A.

*He goes quickly into the living-room, goes to the desk and pulls out a piece of
paper and a pen.*

*Then, about to return to the bedroom, his attention is caught by a small, framed
snapshot. He picks it up, examines it a moment, and then slips it into his
pocket. He returns to the bedroom, where* GREGOR *is still sitting on the bed,
shivering at moments.* SVEN *methodically picks up a telephone book, pushes*
GREGOR'S *knees together, lays a sheet of paper on the telephone book and hands*
GREGOR *a pen.*

(*In a tone of new authority.*) Can you write with that on your knee?

GREGOR *stares at him, then laughs.*

GREGOR. Ah, Antonescu-training too.

*He props the book on his knee with the paper on it. Then he unscrews the pen.*

(*Wearily.*) Who to?

SVEN. (*Firmly.*) To me.

GREGOR. Correctly it should be to Florence.

SVEN. I'm your best friend.

GREGOR. (*Quietly, after a pause.*) And you have the gun.

*He begins to write.*

'Dear Sven'— (*Looking up at him.*) Can I avoid the cliché of 'This is the only way out'? (*After a moment's thought.*) Why not? It's true. (*He writes.*) Would you get that coat of mine from the other room and put it round my shoulders? I don't know why, but I still feel cold.

SVEN *puts the overcoat round his shoulders. After a pause:*

I have written: 'Dear Sven, this is the only way out. I took this revolver earlier tonight from Sergei's apartment when neither of you were looking, with the intention of shooting myself. I am sorry to leave affairs in such a hopeless mess. Good-bye, my dearest friend.'

SVEN. Have you signed it?

GREGOR. Yes. ' Gregor.'

SVEN. Then would you please add this PS.

GREGOR *obediently takes up his pen.*

'You will be appalled to hear of the many criminal transactions—'

GREGOR *looks up at him at this and laughs, harshly and sharply. But he continues to write.*

'—which, during my life, I have perpetrated—'

GREGOR. May I say 'done?'

SVEN. Of course.

GREGOR. (*Continuing to write.*) Thank you. After all it will be published—

SVEN. In every single one of these transactions—

GREGOR. (*Writing.*) In every single one of—*them.* Better?

SVEN. You have been the innocent dupe.

GREGOR. (*Writing.*) You, my dearest, dearest Sven—a little touch of sentiment never hurts—have been the innocent dupe.

*He hands the paper to* SVEN.

SVEN. (*Quietly.*) You might just put your signature to it, would you?

GREGOR. (*Doing so.*) It's not usual with a PS. (*Handing the paper to him again.*) Don't you think it might look at little—forced?

SVEN. Better than looking forged.

*He puts the note in his pocket.*

GREGOR. Yes. Perfectly correct. (*Pointing to the note.*) How will you explain your getting that?

SVEN. It came through the post too late for me to do anything. (*He thinks of something.*) Oh. Perhaps you'd better add the date.

*He hands the letter back to* GREGOR.

GREGOR. What is the date?

SVEN. Just put Monday night.

GREGOR *adds the two words.* SVEN *takes it from him. Then he pulls a revolver from his pocket and hands it silently to* GREGOR.

GREGOR. Is it loaded?

SVEN. Yes. (*Pointing.*) You cock it here.

GREGOR. I see.

SVEN. I'll do it for you.

*He puts it on a bedside table.*

GREGOR. The mouth is best, isn't it?

SVEN. So they say.

GREGOR. Kreuger shot himself through the heart. But I think he was lucky. There are some chances not even I will take. (*After a pause.*) On the other hand I don't like to be beaten by Kreuger.

*He shivers again.* SVEN *is moving towards the door.*

Are you leaving, dear fellow?

SVEN. Surely it's better—

GREGOR. I had hoped— (*He looks up at him.*) I had hoped you might stay with me—

SVEN. Oh, no. Oh, no, G. A. You must see, I can't be involved. And with this letter—

GREGOR. (*With difficulty.*) Yes. Yes, of course. Good-bye, then.

SVEN *makes a move towards him.*

Don't touch me, do you mind? (*Smiling at him.*) It nearly worked, didn't it? Another twenty-four hours and we'd have done it again.

SVEN *nods. As a sudden thought he takes out of his pocket the snapshot he has removed from the desk and hands it to* GREGOR.

SVEN. I found this on the desk.

GREGOR. What is it? I can't see without my glasses.

SVEN. It's a snapshot of you and Vassily on a beach somewhere. He must have been about eight or nine, I think.

GREGOR. (*Peering.*) Eight or nine? Yes, I remember. It was at Biarritz. There's something written on it. What is it?

SVEN. 'To Vassily, from his father, with love.' I thought you wouldn't want it found by the police.

GREGOR. The police won't find anything *here*.

SVEN. I see. I didn't know.

GREGOR. How careless of him, though! How typical! He calls himself Basil Anthony, American citizen, denies his father and keeps a photograph of him—

SVEN. What shall I do with it?

GREGOR. Put it back, I suppose. It seems to have some value to him—

SVEN *nods and goes into the living-room. He throws the snapshot back on to the desk.*

(*Calling.*) Turn on the radio, would you?

SVEN. Do you want the news?

GREGOR. I'd like to know if they have any idea where I am.

SVEN. They know you're on Manhattan Island.

*He turns on the radio, and after he has twiddled the dials for a moment, we hear an* ANNOUNCER'S *voice.*

ANNOUNCER. —the switch of programmes due to the Antonescu news. It is a crisis that will affect each and every one of us, either directly or indirectly, and we are devoting the next fifteen minutes—

SVEN. Is that loud enough?

GREGOR. Yes.

ANNOUNCER. (*Continuing.*) —to an assessment of the man described as the greatest monopoly capitalist of all time, and who is now a hunted criminal—

SVEN *appears at the bedroom door.*

GREGOR. (*Without turning.*) Go away, dearest fellow, if you're going.

SVEN *picks up his hat, gloves and umbrella and goes out, slamming the door. The sound of it reaches* GREGOR, *who looks up from the revolver he is fingering with a faint smile.* GREGOR *gets up and moves into the sitting-room, turning out the bedroom light as he goes. He crosses to desk and puts out the light on it.*

ANNOUNCER. Wherever he may be tonight, and latest rumours put him in Buenos Aires—it is certain that this suave, cool, elegant and utterly charming personality is showing the same unruffled front that he has always shown to the world, through every crisis that has beset him.

GREGOR *has been struggling into his overcoat. He smiles at the radio announcer's prediction, and then goes to pour himself a drink.*

(*Meanwhile.*) The question that is being asked all over the world is a simple one. Why did a man who, by 1929, had achieved every ambition that any great financier could hope for, a man who was already acclaimed as the Saviour of Europe, whose advice was sought by Presidents, Ministers, and Kings, who, in a financial sense, ruled the whole world—why did this man descend to what may be common swindling and to what is certainly total ruin—both for himself and for millions of those who trusted him? What is certain is that it was not for personal gain. By 1929 it is estimated that his personal fortune was well over fifty millions.

GREGOR *nods in agreement.*

Someone once said that absolute power corrupts absolutely. But is this true? Is it not perhaps truer to say, as Professor Hall of Yale has already stated a few minutes ago, on this very station, this very evening and on this very subject, that to be absolutely powerful a man must first corrupt *himself* absolutely.

GREGOR, *sipping his drink, again nods approvingly.*

GREGOR. (*Raising his glass and murmuring.*) Professor Hall—

ANNOUNCER. To answer these intriguing questions we have invited to our microphone at this time a world-famous industrialist, the man whose suspicions of Antonescu precipitated his crash, the President of American Electric—Mr. Mark Herries.

GREGOR *puts his glass down and goes to the front door, switching off the lights there. As he does so the curtain falls. The radio continues to play . . .*

A BEQUEST TO THE NATION

First published 1970
by Hamish Hamilton Ltd

FOR
M. J. F.

*Speaking Parts*

GEORGE MATCHAM SENIOR
FOOTMAN
KATHERINE MATCHAM
BETSY
GEORGE MATCHAM JUNIOR
EMILY
FRANCES NELSON
LORD BARHAM NELSON
FRANCESCA
EMMA HAMILTON
LORD MINTO
CAPTAIN HARDY
REV. WILLIAM NELSON
CAPTAIN BLACKWOOD
MIDSHIPMAN

*A Bequest to the Nation* was first produced at the Theatre Royal, Haymarket, London, on September 23rd, 1970, with the following cast:

*Characters in order of their appearance*

| | |
|---|---|
| GEORGE MATCHAM SNR | Ewan Roberts |
| KATHERINE MATCHAM | Jean Harvey |
| BETSY | Deborah Watling |
| GEORGE MATCHAM JNR | Michael Wardle |
| EMILY | Una Brandon Jones |
| FRANCES, LADY NELSON | Leueen MacGrath |
| NELSON | Ian Holm |
| LORD BARHAM | A. J. Brown |
| EMMA HAMILTON | Zoe Caldwell |
| FRANCESCA | Marisa Merlini |
| LORD MINTO | Michael Aldridge |
| CAPTAIN HARDY | Brian Glover |
| REV. WILLIAM NELSON | Geoffrey Edwards |
| SARAH NELSON | Eira Griffiths |
| HORATIO | Stuart Knee |
| CAPTAIN BLACKWOOD | Geoffrey Beevers |
| MIDSHIPMAN | Stuart Knee |
| FOOTMEN, SAILORS, MAIDS | Stanley Lloyd |
| | Conrad Asquith |
| | Graham Edwards |
| | Chris Carbis |
| | Deborah Watling |
| | Alison Coleridge |

Directed by PETER GLENVILLE

## NARRATIVE

The main action of the play covers the twenty-five days between Nelson's return to England on August 10th and his departure for Cadiz on September 13th, 1805. The "Naval Action fought off Cape Trafalgar" was on October 21st of that year, and the final scene of the play would have taken place some days after the news reached London, on November 5th.

## SETTING

The play is set in a permanent and open architectural structure which will include a staircase and different levels for the various acting areas. Neither doors nor windows will be shown although both are sometimes referred to in the text. The reader therefore, might find it more convenient to visualize their existence.

Nevertheless the sets are not naturalistic, and the scene changes are indicated more by the use of lighting than by physical transformations.

There are four backcloths to represent, in order, Bath, London, Merton and Trafalgar.

# ACT ONE

## SCENE I

*The lights come on. We are in a part of the Matchams' house in Bath, comprising a morning room and a glimpse of a staircase.* GEORGE MATCHAM *is completing the packing of some hand luggage. A trunk is in process of being carried down the staircase by a footman. The footman slips and curses.*

MATCHAM. Be careful with that. It has brandy for Lady Hamilton.

FOOTMAN. Sure it hasn't some cannon for his Lordship?

MATCHAM. Well, get Tom to help you.

FOOTMAN. He's helping Mrs. Matcham close t'other.

MATCHAM. Two trunks?

*The* FOOTMAN *disappears.* MATCHAM *calls up the stairs.*

MATCHAM. (*Calling.*) Kitty, why two trunks?

KATHERINE. (*Off.*) We need two.

*The second trunk is descending the stairs on a second footman's back. A maid (*BETSY*) comes down the stairs behind, carrying a vanity case and some hat boxes.*

(*Appearing.*) Careful, Bob. There's my lavender in that. (*Calling in sudden panic.*) Betsy—Betsy—did I forget my jewel case?

BETSY. It's in this hat box, Ma'am. You packed it there special.

KATHERINE. Of course. Just make sure, though.

GEORGE MATCHAM JNR. *comes in. He is a schoolboy of sixteen. He carries a newspaper.*

GEORGE. (*Excitedly.*) We're in the Bath *Gazette*—all three of us.

MATCHAM. Indeed?

BETSY. (*Having made sure.*) It's here, Ma'am.

*She goes out.*

MATCHAM. Why do you have a jewel case if you keep it in a hat box?

KATHERINE. In case of highwaymen.

MATCHAM. Madam, there has been no highwayman apprehended on the Bath to London Road for some twenty-five years.

KATHERINE. You never know. (*To* GEORGE.) Shouldn't you be at school?

GEORGE. Not for half an hour. Mother, I said we're in the *Gazette*.

KATHERINE. Being in the *Gazette* is no new thing to us, George. Nor in *The Times* of London either.

GEORGE. But this time I'm in it—

KATHERINE. Are you, dear? (*To* MATCHAM.) When should we leave?

MATCHAM. Very shortly. The coach seats are booked, but I made no mention of two trunks.

GEORGE. May I read what it says about me? (*Finding the place excitedly.*) Their eldest son, George Matcham, junior—

KATHERINE. (*Sipping coffee.*) Perhaps you had better begin just a little earlier, dear.

GEORGE. Oh, sorry.

*He takes a Bath bun and begins to eat it.*

(*Reading fast.*) It is not yet known whether Lord Nelson's unexpected return to these shores has been commanded by the Admiralty in order that he should enjoy the rest that is undoubtedly due to him following his unremitting labours—etcetera—West Indies etcetera, etcetera but—

KATHERINE. Don't read with your mouth full. And I said 'a *little* earlier'

GEORGE. Well it leads on. Here it is. (*Reading.*) There is some confirmation of this view in the undoubted fact that Lord Nelson has already invited to visit him at his newly completed house at Merton, Surrey, almost every single close member of his family—

MATCHAM. (*Sharply.*) Almost?

GEORGE. Yes, father.

KATHERINE. They probably meant nothing.

MATCHAM. They never mean nothing. Go on, George.

GEORGE. (*Reading.*) and three residents of Bath so honoured are His Lordship's sister, Mrs. Matcham, Mr. George Matcham, the well-known financier, and (*Giving it point.*) their son, George Matcham, junior, who—

*He is stopped by an imperious gesture from his mother.*

KATHERINE. Financier I don't care for. It sounds—it sounds as if—

MATCHAM. I dealt in finance. I do.

KATHERINE. But as if you did so as a business.

MATCHAM. I do so as a business. (*Growing angry.*) There seems to be this growing assumption that since your brother has become a demi-god, you have become a demi-goddess—and that you have therefore married quite beneath you. When you were at Burnham Rectory you were glad enough to land a business-man, Madam—

KATHERINE. (*With dignity, to* GEORGE.) You were saying, George—their son, George Matcham, Junior?

GEORGE. (*Reading to* MATCHAM.)—who is at school near Bath and who will also be journeying to Merton in a week's time when his term is finished. Indeed (*To* MATCHAM.) listen to this—indeed young George Matcham must surely account himself the luckiest schoolboy in all of England.

KATHERINE. I hope you do, George.

GEORGE. (*With a fervour missed by both his parents.*) I do.

MATCHAM *takes the paper from him and, rather sulkily, begins to read it.* GEORGE *goes to his satchel and busies himself with what is evidently his homework.*

KATHERINE. (*To* MATCHAM.) Anything about the rest of the family?

MATCHAM. Your brother William. They call him Dean.

KATHERINE. That is very proper.

MATCHAM. If not in the least accurate.

KATHERINE. Is there much about our dear Emma?

MATCHAM *glances over the newspaper quickly.*

MATCHAM. Much the usual.

KATHERINE. Nothing, I trust—out of place?

MATCHAM. Dammit, Madam, what, in this case, is in place?

KATHERINE. If it is written of with delicacy—

MATCHAM. It sounds far worse. Listen (*Reading.*) Lady H. has been reported as flitting constantly between her house in Clarges Street and her temporary abode at Merton—

KATHERINE. 'Temporary's' perfectly delicate—

MATCHAM. (*Continuing.*)—where she will no doubt be pleased to enact once more that role of honorary hostess to the House of Nelson, which befits Her Ladyship as gracefully in her widowhood—

KATHERINE. If only he could have lasted a year or two longer.

MATCHAM. Yes. It was indelicate of him to die. (*Reading.*)—as gracefully in her widowhood as ever it did in former times when Sir William, Lord Nelson and Her Ladyship were all three joined together in bonds of perfect and mutual amity—tria juncta in uno—three joined in one—

GEORGE. (*Deep in his homework.*) Sounds like a real old rough and tumble.

*Pause.*

KATHERINE. (*At length, outraged.*) George!

GEORGE. (*Turning.*) Oh, it's all right, mother. Of course I know it wasn't anything like that really. Sir William must have upped anchor when Uncle Horatio sailed in—and who can blame him? But 'tria juncta in uno' does make it sound a bit—well—Roman.

KATHERINE. It is the motto of your uncle and Sir William's order of the Bath.

GEORGE. (*Laughing.*) That makes it worse. Did she get one too? A bath, I mean? All three together?

*And now he laughs helplessly—a schoolboy's laugh at a schoolboy's joke.*

KATHERINE. George, I am appalled. Utterly appalled. Stop laughing at once! (*To* MATCHAM.) Oh, do something.

MATCHAM. Stop laughing, sir, this instant!

GEORGE. Yes, Father.

*And, apart from a faint splutter or two, he does.*

KATHERINE. I can't think what they teach boys at school these days.

MATCHAM. Roman history.

KATHERINE. But it's monstrous that a boy of his age should ever imagine such terrible and unnatural things about his uncle—it's nothing but the rankest disloyalty—

GEORGE. (*Facing her quietly.*) I couldn't be disloyal about him, mother. To me he is simply the greatest man on earth.

KATHERINE. But you said—

GEORGE. If I made a joke, I'm sorry, but it's one that all England makes, and there's no harm—

MATCHAM. How came you by this intimate knowledge of all England, sir?

GEORGE. Father, I'm not a child.

MATCHAM. (*Losing the argument.*) You are a child, sir.

GEORGE. (*Winning it.*) If you say so, father. But, after all, now that I'm going to stay with Uncle Horatio and Lady Hamilton in their house—

KATHERINE. *His* house.

MATCHAM. *My* house, until he repays the mortgage—

GEORGE. Well, Lady Hamilton's going to be my honorary hostess, isn't she? It says that in the *Gazette.* So what am I supposed to suppose, mother?

KATHERINE. (*Harassed, but firm.*) That she's a very close and dear friend of Lord Nelson's who—who—

MATCHAM. Helps with the housekeeping.

*She gives her husband a look and begins to gather some impedimenta.*

KATHERINE. You are far too young to understand such a lofty and noble relationship between two exalted human beings.

GEORGE. (*Sincerely.*) No, mother, I don't think I am—especially when one of them is Uncle Horatio and the other, they say, is one of the most beautiful and gracious ladies who ever lived. The only thing I can't understand is that 'three in one' business. What on earth did people think that time when they all lived together?

*Pause.* BETSY *appears in the stairway with an old woman* (EMILY) *to whom she points out the morning-room before disappearing herself upstairs.* EMILY *waits on the threshold nervously.*

MATCHAM. (*Looking at his watch.*) My dearest Kitty, your reply to that, which I'm sure would have been a model of refinement and sensibility, had better be deferred to a later and more convenient—

EMILY *has had the courage to enter the morning-room.* MATCHAM *sees her and starts. Pause.*

Why, Emily, what a surprise. How pleasant to see you. How are you, these days?

EMILY. Quite well, thank you, Mr. Matcham. (*Bobbing.*) Mrs. Matcham.

KATHERINE *nods.*

Why, Master George, how you've grown.

GEORGE. Have I?

EMILY. Oh yes. (*To* MATCHAM *and* KATHERINE.) Lady Nelson's compliments to you both and might she have two words with you. She's waiting outside.

KATHERINE. Outside this house?

EMILY. Yes, Ma'am.

KATHERINE. At six in the morning?

EMILY. She wanted to see you before the coach left.

KATHERINE. Well, quite aside from the propriety of that, she has left it rather too late—

EMILY. No, Ma'am. The coach has been delayed half an hour for despatches.

She went to the Coach Yard to see you and found out. So she had to come here.

KATHERINE. And is waiting in this street?

EMILY. Yes, Ma'am. In her chaise.

*There is a pause.* MATCHAM *looks at his wife in uneasy enquiry, and receives a steely negative.*

MATCHAM. I'm afraid it's still too late, Emily. We have so much to attend to.

EMILY. Just two words, Her Ladyship said. She has read by the papers how you were both going to Merton House today, and she's most anxious to see you.

KATHERINE. And why?

EMILY. I don't know for sure, Mrs. Matcham, but I'd fancy it might be a message for his Lordship.

KATHERINE. What kind of message?

EMILY. I suppose the kind of message a wife could send to a husband she hasn't seen since over four years. Meaning, of course, Madam, no disrespect.

KATHERINE. You may tell your mistress, Emily, that there is no point whatever in our seeing her at the present time and in the present circumstances, and that she should know much, much better than to ask such a thing at all, and that my husband and I confess ourselves extremely surprised at such unrefined behaviour. You may quote those very words, Emily— in full.

EMILY. Very good. Mrs. Matcham. I told her it was no good. I told her not to try—

KATHERINE. She should have listened to you. (*Graciously.*) We bear you personally, Emily, no ill-will at all.

EMILY. Very kind, Ma'am, I'm sure.

*She bobs and goes.*

KATHERINE. (*Outraged.*) Well. The insensibility of it! What a cold, hard, conniving bitch! George, you did not hear that.

GEORGE. (*Grinning in his coffee.*) I did.

KATHERINE. Oh wait till I tell Horatio of this latest exploit of Tom Tit. (*To* MATCHAM.) Do you know what I think she's going to do now? I think she's going to blockade us in here, so that we can't possibly go to our carriage without passing her chaise and talking. (*Picking up objects with determination.*) Well, if she thinks that, she's in for a very big surprise. (*To* MATCHAM.) Come.

MATCHAM. Should we? I confess, I have no great stomach for an armed sortie against an enemy in force.

GEORGE. (*Grinning.*) That from a Nelson.

MATCHAM. Don't be impertinent, sir. And I am not a Nelson.

KATHERINE. Well, I am, and to walk past that chaise and give that woman one of my special looks will not dismay me at all. I shall, in fact, relish it keenly.

*She goes.*

MATCHAM. (*Embracing* GEORGE.) Goodbye, George. When I see you at Merton in a week's time I expect a good report from your Headmaster.

GEORGE. I hope I'll give you one, sir.

MATCHAM. (*Benignly—he is fond of his son.*) Even if you have to write it yourself, eh?

*He goes out.*

KATHERINE. (*Off.*) We are leaving, Bob.

BOB *appears and gathers up some hat-boxes.*

MATCHAM. (*Off.*) Kitty, we could easily send Betsy to tell the carriage to come to the back door.

KATHERINE. (*Off, outraged.*) The back door? To avoid Tom Tit? What kind of man are you?

MATCHAM. (*Off.*) A man civilised enough to wish to avoid causing hurt to a member of his family.

GEORGE *has sat down again at his homework.* BETSY *appears and approaches* GEORGE *as if she has been waiting for this moment.*

BETSY. Master George, next week, when you go to see your Uncle Horatio, would you take something from me? I couldn't ask your mother, you know what she'd have said. It's in my room, all wrapped up and ready.

GEORGE. What is it, Betsy?

BETSY. Something against the ague. I read he gets these attacks.

GEORGE. A medicine?

BETSY. No. Something for him to wear against the skin.

GEORGE. Did you buy it?

BETSY. Didn't steal it.

GEORGE. You shouldn't have spent your money—

BETSY. Why not? It might work. Will you give it him?

GEORGE. Of course. And I'll tell him who it's from, too.

BETSY. Oh, you don't need to do that. Just give it to him, that's all. And tell him to wear it.

*There is the sound of a bell.*

That's the post. You won't forget now, will you?

GEORGE. Of course I won't. I hope you didn't pay too much for it.

BETSY. What if I did? Think where we'd all be now without him.

BETSY *goes.* GEORGE *goes back to his homework.*

*After a moment,* BETSY, *looking startled, reappears followed by* FRANCES, LADY NELSON. *She is the same age as her husband* (46). *Her face was never beautiful, but it has a composure and a gentle dignity that gives it distinction.* BETSY *indicates the morning-room, and then flees.*

FRANCES. Good morning, George.

GEORGE *is deeply alarmed, but flight is impossible. He gives her, at length, a stiff formal bow.*

GEORGE. Your Ladyship.

FRANCES. (*Returning the bow.*) Am I no longer Aunt Frances?

GEORGE. (*Bowing again.*) Aunt Frances.

FRANCES. Emily was right. You have grown. You're too tall for those breeches. Who buys your clothes for you now?

GEORGE. My mother.

FRANCES. I did rather better when I used to buy your clothes. Kitty never did understand how quickly boys grow out of things.

*There is a pause during which we see that* FRANCES *is quite as nervous as her nephew.*

(*Timidly proffering a packet.*) Do you still like toffees? I've bought some at Hathertons for you.

GEORGE. (*His voice growing squeaky with embarrassment.*) I thank your Ladyship, I have already eaten breakfast, and a Bath bun.

FRANCES. I should have thought of that. (*Holding out the packet.*) Take them anyway.

GEORGE. (*Declining.*) No thank you.

FRANCES. Oh dear. I've made things worse, haven't I? Emily said I would.

GEORGE. (*Making a decisive movement.*) I must go to my class, so, if your Ladyship will forgive me—

FRANCES. (*With some edge.*) Her Ladyship will not forgive you. Nor will your Aunt Frances, who knows perfectly well what time your classes start. Sit down, George.

GEORGE *involuntarily obeys the voice of authority and sits.*

You are going to Merton next week?

GEORGE. Yes.

FRANCES. On what day?

GEORGE. Thursday.

FRANCES. I am going to London on Tuesday—to my house in Somerset Street. I shall be there several weeks.

*Pause.* GEORGE *says nothing. There seems, indeed nothing for him to say. But* FRANCES *had hoped that he would say something, for she is plainly searching for words, and her brief access of aunty authority has not dissipated her extreme nervousness.*

Is this coffee still hot?

GEORGE. I'll order some more.

FRANCES. This will do. There's an extra cup. It's almost as if they expected me to breakfast. Your mother delivers a cut so badly, George. You should look through your victim, not over her head. And your father—(*she laughs, then tries to pull herself together*) Oh George, forgive me. The truth is you make me so nervous that I can't speak—

GEORGE. I make you nervous?

FRANCES. Look at my hand.

*She puts the coffee cup down. It has indeed been impossible for her to get it into her mouth.*

Isn't it silly?

GEORGE. Yes, it is. If you're like this with me, I can't think what you'd have been like with mother and father, if they'd let you come in.

FRANCES. Oh, not nervous at all. It's they whose hands would have been shaking, not mine. It's guilt makes people's hands shake, George. Conscience making cowards of us—like you bowing to the ground and saying 'Ladyship' to an aunt you used once to call your favourite.

GEORGE. Why have you a conscience about me?

FRANCES. Because of something I'm going to ask you to do for me—something my conscience says I shouldn't.

GEORGE. What is it?

FRANCES. Take a letter to Merton.

GEORGE. To him?

FRANCES. To my husband.

*Pause.* GEORGE *frowns as he tries to think of ways in which his conscience might be persuaded to say no.*

GEORGE. What kind of letter?

FRANCES. An ordinary letter.

GEORGE. Does it say anything beastly—like calling Lady Hamilton a whore?

FRANCES. It doesn't mention Lady Hamilton. If it did there would be little point in reminding him of the profession she is reputed to have once followed.

GEORGE. (*Angrily.*) You're not trying to get me to believe Lady Hamilton really was a whore?

FRANCES. (*Smiling.*) Of course not, George. I'm merely observing that in the matter of preserving her original country-bred chastity, appearances do seem to have been somewhat against her. (*Opening her reticule.*) Now here is the letter. As you see, the covering is blank, and I haven't used the seal.

GEORGE. Why?

FRANCES. My handwriting and seal are both well known to your hostess.

GEORGE. But if I take it myself—

FRANCES. You'll have a servant to clean your room. Several probably—I'm told Lady Hamilton is very lavish with staff—and must surely pay them all very well—

GEORGE. (*Laughing.*) Aren't you being too suspicious?

FRANCES. No. If you take that, keep it under lock and key.

GEORGE. (*Still laughing.*) You mean she'd burn it, or something?

FRANCES. No. She would probably do what she did with my last letter to him—the one I was stupid enough to send to him by the post. It was returned to me, and the covering had a message written on it. 'Opened by mistake by Lord Nelson, but not read'.

GEORGE. In her handwriting?

FRANCES. No. Mr. Davidson's.

GEORGE. Uncle Horatio's agent?

FRANCES *nods.*

> She made him do that?

FRANCES. It would seem so.

GEORGE. But Mr. Davidson used to be a great friend of yours.

FRANCES. So did a lot of people.

GEORGE. (*A shade shamefacedly.*) Yes, I suppose so.

FRANCES. (*Affectionately.*) Dear George, you look so grown up now—

GEORGE. But I can't believe anyone would behave like that. And Mr. Davidson—it's such a bad thing to do to Lord Nelson—of all people—to make him seem dishonourable. Surely Mr. Davidson would be the very last person—look, Aunt Frances—I'm not being rude but you know what people say about you in the family, these days?

FRANCES. About the mischief-making Tom Tit?

GEORGE. Well, both mother and father say you do make things up about the present situation.

FRANCES. Why do I need to make things up?

GEORGE. Well, to get pity and so on.

FRANCES. I hate pity. I can't bear it.

GEORGE. Well you can't deny you must feel pretty hostile to Lady Hamilton.

FRANCES. No, I can't deny that. But what I told you about that letter is true. Look.

*She takes the letter out of her reticule and removes the outer covering showing him the enclosure.*

GEORGE. (*Spelling with difficulty.*) 'Opened by mistake by Lord Nelson, but not read. A. Davidson.'

FRANCES *nods.*

> It is the same letter?

FRANCES. Yes.

GEORGE. When was it written?

FRANCES. On December eighteenth, 1801.

GEORGE. A Christmas letter?

FRANCES. Is that what shocks you?

GEORGE. Well, it's bad at any time I agree. But Christmas! Well, perhaps I'm sentimental.

FRANCES. So am I—but I hadn't, until now, connected that rejected letter of mine with any special season.

GEORGE. (*Gravely.*) You will swear that there's nothing in it that will upset him or make him angry?

FRANCES. How can I swear that? How do I know, after four years, what will upset him or make him angry?

GEORGE. But is there anything in the letter itself?

FRANCES. There is nothing in the letter itself that a wife might not write to a husband who has deserted her and whom she still most deeply loves.

GEORGE. (*Uncomfortably.*) But do you? They all say—

FRANCES. (*Shortly.*) I know what they all say. (*Brightly.*) Your mother looks well, George. I saw her and your father at the Pump Room, the other night—together with your Uncle William and Aunt Sarah. Quite an assembly of in-laws, I must say. Of course I fled. Poor things. It is difficult for them all my being in Bath. In London, of course, things are different. I so seldom go out there. Are you going to give him that?

GEORGE. Yes.

FRANCES. To him personally?

GEORGE. Oh, of course.

FRANCES. You're not scared?

GEORGE. Of him? Of Uncle Horatio? Of course not. He's the kindest soul alive.

FRANCES. Yes he is. (*There is no irony.*) There's not a midshipman sails with him who doesn't worship him. (*She gets up with difficulty.*) Is that a promise, George?

GEORGE. Yes. A promise.

FRANCES. And, of course, you must not tell your mother—

GEORGE. (*Laughing.*) Is that likely?

FRANCES. (*Fumbling in her purse.*) I haven't seen you for three Christmases.

GEORGE. (*Indignantly.*) I don't need bribing.

FRANCES. No. I'm sorry. (*She picks up the bag of toffee.*) Not even these?

GEORGE. Well, those are different. (*He takes the bag.*) Thanks awfully, Aunt Frances.

FRANCES. (*Timidly.*) Of course, if you could let slip that I am returned to Somerset Street—and would be overjoyed to—set eyes on him again just once, alone, for a few brief moments—no one need ever know he'd been to see me—or if he'd just give me some inkling where I could go to see him—not to talk, George, if it displeases him—or at least only about such trivial things as whether his eye still hurts him and if he is still wearing his green shade—or just if he'd let me sit in a room with him alone, not speaking at all, just looking—I'm sorry—I forget how I began the sentence. A bad habit. You had better tell him none of these things. They would only irritate him. (*Brightly again.*) Just tell him you were waylaid by Tom Tit in your own home and that she gave you that letter. Oh, do explain, George, why am I now called Tom Tit?

GEORGE. Don't you know?

FRANCES. No.

GEORGE. Weren't you called that before—I mean in the old days?

FRANCES. No, I don't think so.

GEORGE. You really want to know?

FRANCES. Yes, please.

GEORGE. You won't mind?

FRANCES. Of course not.

GEORGE. It's the way you walk.

FRANCES. The way I walk?

GEORGE. Yes, like a bird. (*Politely.*) At least that's what they say—

FRANCES. Of course. With my rheumaticky legs, it must seem most bird-like. I see.

*They are both smiling,* GEORGE *rather embarrassedly,* FRANCES *as if enjoying a joke.*

And does Lord Nelson call me that too?

GEORGE. Oh, yes.

FRANCES. You've heard him.

GEORGE. Oh yes. (*Hastily.*) It's not unkind.

FRANCES. No, of course it's not unkind—

*The tears that have never been far away during the scene now come out in sudden, ugly racking sobs.* GEORGE *stands helpless, watching her.*

GEORGE. Shall I get Emily?

FRANCES. No.

GEORGE *watches her unhappily while she struggles to recover herself.*

(*At length.*) Oh, dear Heavens, I'm so sorry—

GEORGE. (*Sitting opposite her.*) I don't understand.

FRANCES. What don't you understand?

GEORGE. What you did to make them all so against you.

FRANCES. What do your mother and father say I did?

GEORGE. They won't tell me, but they're always hinting it was very bad—

FRANCES. Perhaps it was.

GEORGE. What was it?

FRANCES. In the end I told him he had to choose.

GEORGE. But that's not bad.

FRANCES. It was for him.

GEORGE. But is that all?

FRANCES. I think so.

*She gets up.* GEORGE *tries to help her.*

I'm all right now, thank you, George. Yes, I've often wondered how else I've offended.

GEORGE. But why did the whole family turn against you?

FRANCES. (*In a hard voice.*) Why does your Reverend Uncle William now hold a stall at Canterbury, when he can't read so much as a Morning Collect? Why is your cousin Tom Bolton a Knight before he is even twenty? Why is—oh, it doesn't matter. Lord Nelson is deservedly a man of great and powerful influence in England, and he is very good to his family.

GEORGE. You said 'why is' and stopped. Were you going to say why is my father now a Director of the East India Company? Because, if you were, I know the answer. Lord Liverpool spoke for him.

FRANCES. And who spoke for him to Lord Liverpool?

*Pause.* GEORGE *has no answer and knows he can never find one, except in tears and hopeless rage both of which he forbears.*

GEORGE. You say he has actually bribed my father to turn against you?

FRANCES. I said no such thing. You did.

GEORGE. But why does Uncle Horatio hate you so much?

FRANCES. I don't know, George. I'm sure, knowing him, there must be a good reason. I wish I knew what it was.

*She turns to go as the lights fade and the sound of a naval band is heard, together with the noise and cheers of a crowd. The music and cheering will continue into and through the beginning of the next scene.*

## Scene II

*The figure of* NELSON *is looking much as our imaginations have always pictured him—in full dress uniform, with four glittering stars, a black patch over his right eye and the empty sleeve of his right arm tucked into his tunic. He is apparently staring out of a window, facing the auditorium.*

LORD BARHAM, *First Lord of the Admiralty, is at his desk.*

BARHAM *is eighty, and recently appointed, but is scared neither of* NELSON *whom he has never met, nor of his formidable post, in this year of threatened invasion.*

BARHAM. (*He indicates.*) Perhaps you would care to sit down, Lord Nelson— the sight of you at that window seems to excite the crowd that has been attracted here by your visit.

NELSON. Did I attract them, Lord Barham?

BARHAM. Undoubtedly. The name is pronounced Barham.

*He uses the short A.*

NELSON. I'm so sorry. A junior Vice-Admiral should at least know how to pronounce the name of the First Lord.

BARHAM. I see no reason. It's a very new title, and a very new appointment.

*He motions* NELSON *to a seat.*

NELSON. You have my heartiest congratulations on both.

BARHAM. Thank you. May we get to business? (*He picks up a document.*) Now, I have been instructed by their Lordships to speak to you regarding your recent operations in the following terms.

NELSON. (*Quietly.*) Please, don't trouble yourself to tell me what you were instructed to say to me. I mean no disrespect to their Lordships, but we both know that their judgement of naval operations can be coloured by circumstances. Tell me, not as First Lord but as—what was it?—Admiral Middleton?

BARHAM *nods.*

Tell me then as Admiral, did I do right to chase Villeneuve to the West Indies and back, and leave England unguarded?

BARHAM. Not quite unguarded. I made certain Naval dispositions.

NELSON. But unguarded enough to have risked giving Napoleon that eight

hours command of the Channel he says he needs for his invasion. Did I
do right?

BARHAM. In the event—

NELSON. In the event Villeneuve's courage failed him but that doesn't answer my question.

BARHAM. Perhaps it does. Villeneuve's courage failed him precisely because
he learnt that it was you who was chasing him. Another Admiral chasing him and his courage would not have failed.

NELSON. I was hardly to know that—

BARHAM. You might have guessed it.

NELSON. I might. (*Grinning.*) I did. Yes, to be honest, I knew my name to
be worth the addition of a frigate or two to our Naval forces in the dis-
comforting of an enemy.

BARHAM. About five battle ships, my lord. That is my own estimation. Some
would put it higher.

NELSON. I can hardly dispute the estimation of a First Lord.

BARHAM. I thought it was to an Admiral you wished to speak.

*Pause.* NELSON *laughs.*

NELSON. By God, I like you. I was told I wouldn't, but I do.

BARHAM. Thank you, Lord Nelson. Now, is your question what I would have
done, had I been in Command at Toulon and Villeneuve had slipped
me and sailed for the Atlantic?

NELSON *nods.*

I would not have done as you did, my Lord.

NELSON. I like you the more.

BARHAM. With Napoleon's whole army at Boulogne and only pitchforks to
throw against him if he landed, I wouldn't have given chase half across
the world. My mind would have been only on defence. But then my
name was only Middleton.

*Pause.* NELSON *laughs, unconstrainedly pleased.*

NELSON. I have never received a more graceful and inspiring appraisal of an
agonising and most hazardous decision. You see now why I asked you
not to read me that testimonial. Their Lordships would not have said a
tenth as much in a hundredth part the length. You do me great honour,
Lord Barham.

BARHAM. I am back to First Lord again?

NELSON. (*Laughing.*) By Heavens you are, and with great honour to your
office. (*Changing tone.*) Oh but the agony of that chase—

BARHAM. I can guess it.

NELSON. To have been forced to gamble so wildly—so recklessly—on the
merest whiff of intuition—and with such a stake—

BARHAM. Your reputation is indeed a great stake, my Lord.

NELSON. (*Suddenly quiet.*) Oh, God! Did you think I meant that?

BARHAM. I'm sorry. Your country, of course, is a greater one.

NELSON. A greater one? I love my reputation, and the cheers from those good people outside, don't as you've noticed, entirely displease me. But how can you measure one man's reputation against the safety of England? You talk like Charles James Fox.

BARHAM. Mr. Fox's speeches are becoming something more patriotic. His love of England keeps pace with the diminishing ardour of his infatuation with the Emperor Napoleon as a revolutionary.

NELSON. (*Sincerely.*) I don't understand how a man's love of England can keep pace with anything except just England. You don't love England as you love a person or a thing or an idea. You don't even love it because it's your country. You love it because it's England, and if you don't love it, you are damned. Voilà tout, as the enemy might say. I don't doubt but that Mr. Fox would make mincemeat of that argument—

BARHAM. A statement of faith is hardly arguable, my Lord.

NELSON. Well, back to business. You believe then, as I do, that we must attack to survive.

BARHAM. The boldest measures are always the safest. Your own saying, is it not, Lord Nelson?

NELSON. Well, you don't fight a war except to win it, do you?

BARHAM. Not all agree with you. Some feel that just by holding out in this island we may achieve a peace.

NELSON. Peace, with Napoleon?

BARHAM. Some think it possible.

NELSON. Peace? Now that he has crowned himself Emperor of the World—

BARHAM. Not quite 'of the world', my Lord. 'Of the French', is the title, I believe.

NELSON. And that is already 'of Europe', and tomorrow it will be of the world. I tell you Lord Barham, this new Caesar means to conquer the entire globe. He has said so. Peace with such a man? How is it possible?

BARHAM. Some think that, if we stand the long siege, he may grow tired, and leave us alone.

NELSON. (*Contemptuously.*) Or he may exhaust himself in the embraces of his Empress, and take up gardening at the Tuileries. My Lord, we speak of the man who means to be master of the world. He makes no secret of it. He may speak in the holy names of Liberty, Equality, Fraternity— but do you seriously think he even knows what those words mean? (*Anxiously.*) I do trust that Mr. Pitt pays proper study to the public speeches of Napoleon?

BARHAM. Your Lordships trust is not, I believe, misplaced.

NELSON. Good. Well, then to master the world, the man must first destroy this island. This island must therefore destroy the man. That, too, is hardly arguable, is it?

BARHAM. As your Lordship puts it, no. But what might merit debate is exactly how this island is to manage the job.

NELSON. Not by skulking behind a ditch, waiting for him to cross it. By crossing it ourselves and attacking him. Not with pitchforks either, but with an expeditionary force armed with the best weapons our factories can make.

BARHAM. Where do we land it?

NELSON. Anywhere. Europe's coast line is three thousand miles long. Even Napoleon can't be everywhere at once. But I would advise Mr. Pitt to look closely at the Kingdom of Naples, where our troops were recently engaged, and which has proved to be Napoleon's Achilles' heel. (*Carelessly.*) I don't say that on grounds of personal attachment, just in case you think I do.

BARHAM. (*Carefully.*) I had heard of your Lordship's strong friendship for the exiled King and Queen of Naples.

NELSON. (*Having fun.*) And not for the widow of our late Ambassador there?

BARHAM. I read my newspapers.

NELSON. And perhaps find a moment to glance at the cartoonists in St. James's Street?

BARHAM. (*Stiffly.*) Seldom, my lord.

NELSON. You should more often. Some are very witty, I assure you—although they are apt to portray Lady Hamilton as somewhat too large and myself as somewhat too small. But one doesn't expect to find the exact truth in cartoons. Where were we?

BARHAM. Attacking Napoleon at Naples.

NELSON. Ah, but not only Naples. In Portugal and Spain, for instance. Another expeditionary force landed, say at Lisbon—

BARHAM. (*Abruptly.*) Pardon my interruption, Lord Nelson, but this is the Admiralty, and not the War Office. How can we attack anywhere on the continent of Europe without full and unchallenged command of the seas?

NELSON. Well, of course, we must have that.

BARHAM. (*Barking.*) How?

NELSON. By annihilation.

BARHAM. Such words are easy.

NELSON. The matter is easy. Now that the combined enemy fleets have locked themselves up in Cadiz, from which they must mean to emerge soon and fight—for Cadiz can't supply so vast an Armada for long—

BARHAM. Who told you that?

NELSON. (*Gently.*) My Lord, I learnt the capacities of Cadiz as a supply base at my mother's knee.

BARHAM. (*Raising his voice.*) I meant who told you that the combined fleets were now at Cadiz?

NELSON. Captain Blackwood of the Frigate Euryalus. He had despatches from Admiral Collingwood off Cadiz.

BARHAM. Those despatches were addressed to me.

NELSON. And my house lies on the Portsmouth Road.

BARHAM. But not even Mr. Pitt has read those despatches yet.

NELSON. Gracious me! I hope you have used a fast runner to Downing Street. For plainly what Mr. Pitt should do now—

BARHAM. Excuse me, but perhaps your Lordship would be good enough to inform me first what I should do now.

NELSON. Most gladly. You must reinforce Collingwood immediately with everything that you have. Within weeks the enemy must come out from Cadiz and we must then destroy him. Annihilate is a better word. This chance may never come again.

BARHAM. May I be blunt? Does 'everything that I have' include Nelson?

NELSON. No.

*Pause.*

BARHAM. You don't feel capable—

NELSON. Capable? (*He nearly raises to the bait but restrains himself.*) I must remind your Lordship that I am on sick leave. I am indeed a very sick man.

BARHAM. Too sick to go out again, my Lord?

NELSON. Too sick to be capable of going out again, my Lord.

BARHAM. It will grieve Mr. Pitt. He will certainly want it. So, of course, will the country.

NELSON. The country and Mr. Pitt expect too much of me. (*Angrily now.*) Lord Barham, I am crippled, blind, infirm and nearly dead with service of Mr. Pitt and my country. And I am not now needed. The ships and the men and the commander for the battle will be the best that we have, and when they come on the enemy the plan of battle is already laid out—

BARHAM. Your plan, my Lord?

NELSON. (*Shrugging.*) If Collingwood uses it it will be his. And he will use it, I'm sure. For complete annihilation it is the only one.

BARHAM. I would be interested to hear it?

NELSON. Perhaps another time. I am keeping a certain lady waiting.

*He gets up.*

BARHAM. (*Rather stiffly.*) I am sorry, my Lord. Perhaps, at your convenience, you would draft it for me as a memorandum?

NELSON. I would be happy. May I take my leave?

BARHAM *says nothing. There is a tense pause.*

NELSON *suddenly changes his tone to one of desperate pleading.*

   Oh for the sake of Heaven, Barham, show some humanity! Don't you understand how I am placed?

BARHAM. Your Lordship has made it clear—

NELSON. Not clear enough it seems. You disapprove—I can see it all over your face—and I am childish enough to hate any man's disapproval— let alone a First Lord's. Barham, when were you last in love?

BARHAM. When I was a junior captain, I think.

NELSON. So was I, when I was a junior captain. Or was I? It doesn't matter. But to be in love as an Admiral—at my age, a crippled forty-six—there is a folly, perhaps—but a bliss and an agony together that demands, if not sympathy, at least some understanding. I haven't seen her for *two years*. Two years in a cabin, never a foot on shore, often ague-ridden, sometimes sea-sick, always racked with doubts and jealousies—(*Hastily.*) although no need, of course—by God there are many people I might sue for slander if I had a mind—but the fevers of the middle-aged lover know no reason—they grow to an obsession—

BARHAM *is looking at his desk. It is hard for him to look anywhere else.*

but enough of that. It was not what I meant to speak of. You may regard it as a simple case—of a man who hasn't seen his much-beloved mistress for two years, and very little of her for five—for since I was relieved of my command at Naples their Lordships have been most diligent in keeping Lady Hamilton and me apart. No, Barham for the love of Jesus, try to see my case!

BARHAM. I see your case, my Lord, and am indeed most sorry for it.

NELSON. Then you will take that look of disapproval from your face?

BARHAM. My face can hardly express what I do not feel. A case such as yours is not one to be either approved or disapproved. It is simply to be accepted.

NELSON. With understanding and compassion?

BARHAM. With compassion.

NELSON. I am rebuked.

BARHAM. No, my Lord. I rebuke myself. I have too dull and prosaic a soul to attempt understanding of such gothick and extravagant matters as the fevers of a middle-aged obsession. (*Proffering a document.*) Would you care to keep this?

NELSON. What is it?

BARHAM. The Lords of the Admiralty's testimonial on your recent operations in the Atlantic. It is quite worth reading, and would only intrude an hour or two on your Lordship's well-earned leisure.

*Pause.* NELSON *looks at* BARHAM *and still reads that mark of official disapproval in* BARHAM'S *face. He takes the testimonial.*

NELSON. (*Bowing.*) Your servant. . .

BARHAM. (*Rising.*) Lord Nelson.

NELSON *walks briskly out of the room, watched by* BARHAM. *Again we hear the band this time playing a gay and popular theme of the time.*

*The lights fade, and once more we hear the distant sounds of cheering.*

*A light comes up on a painting of Emma Hamilton, done in her extreme youth. Then another light shows us a very rumpled bed, with only its occupant's hair showing. Finally all necessary lights come on to show us the bedroom and bou- doir of* EMMA HAMILTON *in Clarges Street, London. A screen in the bedroom area masks the powder room.*

FRANCESCA, EMMA'S *personal maid, a middle-aged Neapolitan of peasant extraction whom Emma has imported into England from Naples some years before, but who has resolutely refused to learn more than the barest minimum of English, is ushering in young* GEORGE MATCHAM *into the boudoir. He looks intensely nervous and is plainly determined to be on his very best behaviour in such an exalted place.*

FRANCESCA. (*Gesturing.*) I tell. You stay.

*She goes into the bedroom area, leaving* GEORGE *staring at the painting.*
    FRANCESCA *shakes her Ladyship's shoulder.*)
        Eccelenza—

EMMA. (*Not stirring.*) Fart off.

FRANCESCA. Eccelenza, il Signorino Matcham sta qua.

EMMA. (*Rolling over.*) You're mad, Francesca. It's the middle of the night.

FRANCESCA. Vi piacerebbe, non e vero? Quante volte stanotte?

*She disappears behind the screen.*

EMMA. (*Calling after her.*) Stai zitta, cretina.

EMMA *sits up. Her hair tousled from sleep and her eyes heavy from lack of it, she doesn't naturally, look at her best-and her best, in her fortieth year is by no means what* GEORGE *in the boudoir, is currently gazing at. She blinks, yawns and stretches herself.* FRANCESCA *comes back with a tankard into which she is pouring porter. She hands it to* EMMA.

EMMA. Con Cognac?

FRANCESCA. Naturalmente.

EMMA. Not naturalmente at all. It just happens that this morning I happen to need it laced. (*She takes a swig and puts her other hand up to indicate the number seven.*)

FRANCESCA. Eccelenza?

EMMA. I'm answering your question.

FRANCESCA. Sette? Ancora un anno a mare è—Pouff!

*She hands* EMMA *a mirror and a comb, and places a vanity box beside her.*

EMMA. You're an impertinent cow and I wonder why I keep you.

FRANCESCA. Pouff! Un nodi vostra eccelenza e sarebbe la vittoria di Napoleone.

EMMA. (*Busy on her hair.*) Me say no?

FRANCESCA. Qualche volta è necessario.

EMMA. Mai.

FRANCESCA. Ne anche per fare Merton piu bello?

EMMA. I can build two Mertons anyway, if I choose. It's not in my nature to say no, Francesca—not to anyone—but least of all to my Nelson, my hero, my beloved, great Jupiter himself—the Lord of Olympus—

*In making a heroic gesture the mirror flies out of her hand across the room.*

Oh farting arses! Did I break my shiting glass? That means seven years bad luck, if I did.

FRANCESCA. No, no, eccellenza. Non e successo niente.

EMMA. I didn't much like what I saw in it anyway. Let's have another look.

FRANCESCA *hands it to her.*

It's worse. (*She goes on with her hair.*) What's this young Matcham like?

FRANCESCA. Un ragazzo qualunque.

EMMA. No nephew of Nelson's can be an ordinary little boy. How do I look.

FRANCESCA. Bellissima Emma Hamilton, come sempre.

EMMA. Bitch. (*Making a face at her.*) Bring him in. And then get me another porter.

FRANCESCA. Con cognac?

EMMA. Pochlssimo, pochissimo.

FRANCESCA. Mangiare dopo? Far este meglio.

EMMA. My stomach wouldn't take food this morning. Well—perhaps I'll toy with a piece of cold mutton in my bath—

FRANCESCA *approaches* GEORGE *who is stood, fidgeting with his hat.*

FRANCESCA. Sua eccelenza vi aspetta.

GEORGE *not understanding, stands nervously.* FRANCESCA *summons him with a gesture.*

Venite. Venite.

GEORGE *frantically nervous, gives a last look at the picture and then follows* FRANCESCA *into the bedroom area, and up to the bed. As* EMMA *turns her head to welcome him he stops uncertainly, plainly wondering if there hasn't been some mistake.* FRANCESCA *continues on into the powder room.*

EMMA. (*Holding out her arms.*) My dearest little George Matcham. Come here and let me kiss you.

*It is noticeable that whenever* EMMA *is not talking to an intimate, as* FRANCESCA *plainly is, and is in control of herself, as she is now, that she can readily adopt a manner that does not confound belief that she was once the British Ambassadress in Naples. (Although even here a figure of fun to visiting English gentry.) She has a fairly strong accent (Lincolnshire, to be pedantically precise) and a coarseness of expression that comes from an honest refusal to pretend that her origins were anything but the most humble and obscure; but with all that we can see the lady who has presided at Sir William's elegant and expansive dinner-tables, and who has been on terms of intimacy—extreme intimacy in many cases—with the greatest in the land.*

You must forgive me, little George, for receiving you in my bed, but this morning, for some reason, I am afflicted with the plaguiest migraine ever.

FRANCESCA *arrives with the tankard refilled.*

(*To* GEORGE.) Recommended by my doctor for just such occasions.

GEORGE. I'm so sorry, Lady Hamilton.

EMMA. It will soon pass, I assure you.

*She toasts him and takes a gigantic swig, followed by an ill-suppressed belch. She squeezes his arm.*

Well, dear young George, aren't you excited to be here and coming down to Merton?

GEORGE. Oh yes, of course I am.

*During the ensuing few lines a procession of* SERVANTS *march through the bedroom towards the powder room. First comes a* FOOTMAN *carrying a hip-bath, then a series of* MAIDS *with towels and peignoirs, then more* FOOTMEN *carrying huge ewers of steaming water and finally the* HEAD HOUSEMAID *who is there simply to direct operations.*

EMMA. (*Looking at him.*) Yes—I could have told you were a Matcham. Isn't it such splendid news, your father being made so important in the city?

GEORGE *nods unhappily.*

Oh, my Nelson had to work hard for him, I tell you. I kept him to it. We can't have any member of our family not looked to. So you're young nephew George? The last of all the Nelsons to be welcomed to Clarges Street and Merton. (*Fondling him again and making him more nervous.*) Oh, we have had such a houseful at Merton this last week, all of the family, and such coming and going of Ministers and Princes of the Blood, but them I don't give a fart for, and that's the truth, George, it's my Nelson's family only that I love—as I love everything that is shared between me and him. His family is now mine, George. You know that, don't you?

GEORGE. Yes, my Lady.

EMMA. Don't call me my Lady.

GEORGE. What shall I call you?

EMMA. Aunt, of course, what else? Aunt Emma. (*Glancing at him.*) You favour your father I see, with perhaps a touch of my Nelson about the eyes—

GEORGE. (*Eagerly.*) Oh, do you really think so?

EMMA. That you favour your father?

GEORGE. No. That I have my uncle's eyes?

EMMA. His poor eyes. (*Continuing to make herself up.*) Yes, you have, George. You're proud of that?

GEORGE *makes no answer to so obvious a question.*

Of course you are. To be Jove's nephew gives you a place on Olympus too. I call him great Jove sometimes to tease him, but it's not far from the truth—my opinion. (*Striking an attitude, although not yet an 'Attitude', by flourishing her glass.*) Great Jove, immortal of all immortals. (*She nearly spills her porter.*) Oh, frig it! All over the poxy bed—

FRANCESCA *comes in.*

FRANCESCA. Quello di taffeta verde?

EMMA. Jesu Maria, no. There'll be a crowd outside. I don't want to look like a curate's prick. I'd better come and choose. Here (*To* GEORGE.) hold this. (*She hands him the tankard and climbs out of bed.*) Yes, George, your uncle is the perfect pattern of a hero, to stand before this age and any other. A man both great and good, and how rare that is in this wicked world.

*She totters a little as* FRANCESCA *helps her into a peignoir.*

Hold me up, you silly cow. (*Seeing* GEORGE'S *face.*) It's my migraine, George. And my Lord and I were a trifle late last night too-

GEORGE. At Court? I read there was a ball—

*The procession of* SERVANTS *emerges from behind the screen during the following speech, and walk out, their duty done.* EMMA, *exhausted, flops into a chair.*

EMMA. (*Shortly.*) No, not a Court. His Lordship and I—well, we don't frequent the Court. Not this one, anyway. Naples of course was different. The Queen of Naples—I count as perhaps my dearest friend in all the world. How I miss her. You know, George, so close was Her dear Majesty of Naples and me that we would sometimes, when she was lonely or scared of those devilish Jacobins who murdered her poor sister, Marie—the martyred Antoinette—we would sometimes sleep all night together in the very same bed. And the King, he would do everything to honour me too, but not, of course, quite in the same way. But this old English absurdity and his German Frau, they're—well they're not really royal in my opinion.

*A* FOOTMAN *comes in with a card on a salver. He hands it to* EMMA, *who is engaged in swigging her porter.*

(*Indicating card.*) Lord Minto—an old friend of my Nelson's, indeed of us both—but I haven't seen him for some time. (*To* FOOTMAN.) Show him in here. He lives in Scotland—or somewhere. Quite in the wilderness—nowadays—although he was our Ambassador in Vienna, when me and my Nelson visited there—(*To* FRANCESCA.) Will the water keep hot?

FRANCESCA. Ci stanno due brocche ancora piene.

EMMA. (*To* GEORGE.) He's coming down with us to Merton.

FRANCESCA. L'Ambasciatore Minto.

MINTO *comes in. He is middle-aged, very elegant in appearance and urbane in manner.*

MINTO. (*Bowing low over her hand.*) Dear Lady Hamilton, what an exquisite pleasure, after so long.

EMMA. I don't know that I'm speaking to you, Minto. Since Vienna you've avoided me like the pox.

MINTO. Dear Lady, since Vienna I've avoided everyone like the—plague who doesn't happen to live in Roxburghshire.

EMMA. That's not true, and I know it. You've been reported at Court many times.

MINTO. (*Shrugging.*) Ah. At Court. But nowhere else.

EMMA. You were at that ball last night, I'll wager.

MINTO. Oh yes. I looked for you and Lord Nelson.

EMMA. We weren't asked, and well you know it.

MINTO. An oversight, surely?

EMMA. Oversight my arse. They won't have us, at any price. I don't mind for myself, but I do mind for him. Two years away, the West Indies saved and then—not so much as a coffee at the Palace. No more of that. I can only say, Minto, it doesn't take you long to leave your beloved Roxburghshire when you hear my Nelson's back in England. Not that I'm not glad to see you, of course.

MINTO. I had some business in town.

EMMA. You didn't have some business in town when it was to see me, did you? Only to see my Nelson. (*To* GEORGE.) Lord Minto is loved by Lord Nelson best of all persons in the world—second only to me, of course. Isn't that true, Minto?

MINTO. I would be happy to think so, my Lady. But you should have added that I run you a very poor second, for the competition provided by your Ladyship is, to say the very least, large.

EMMA. (*Covering up that part of her body to which his eyes has momentarily strayed.*) Large?

MINTO. I meant that I unhappily possessed neither the figure nor the gender to compete in such a race—

EMMA. Every word you say makes it worse, you beast. This is young George Matcham, my Nelson's nephew.

MINTO. Master Matcham.

GEORGE. Lord Minto.

*For the rest of the scene both* EMMA *and* MINTO *continue to ignore him.* GEORGE *sits unhappily on the bed where he has been pushed by* EMMA, *holding the tankard from which* EMMA *takes an occasional sip.* FRANCESCA *has gone back into the powder room.*

MINTO. (*To* EMMA.) I assure your Ladyship that my compliments to you, clumsy as they are, bear no illusion whatever to your most handsome embonpoint—which suits you, as always, quite admirably.

EMMA. If you did possess my gender, I'd just call you bitch and have done. Oh well, it's happiness makes me fat—and, let me tell you, Minto, I've heard no objections about that from the only source that matters. Anyway, when my Nelson goes to sea again next year, I'll pine away to a shadow, see if I don't.

MINTO. Next year?

EMMA. (*Savagely.*) Is he not due a year's rest?

MINTO. (*Shrugging.*) He's due a lifetime.

EMMA. A lifetime wouldn't last him long if you and your politician friends had your way. But you won't have your way—none of you. He's given me his word on that—and that's not lightly given.

MINTO. I know it isn't.

EMMA. Nor lightly broken, neither. (*Wagging an admonishing finger at* MINTO.) So I want no meddling, Minto—from you or anyone else. See?

MINTO. Meddling?

*They are on opposite sides of the bed, talking over* GEORGE'S *head.*

EMMA. I know you. Like all his fine friends you want the two of us separate—by a thousand leagues of sea if you can. You can't bear the thought of what might lose your party a few boroughs at the next election. Nelson living with a woman not his wife? Oh no—we can't have the electors hear such wicked, malicious, scandalous things about the man whose reputation keeps Mr. Pitt in Downing Street.

MINTO. I might perhaps remind your Ladyship that I am a Whig, and that the House of Lords has anyway no need to woo electors. I personally am therefore absolved from your Ladyship's suspicions.

EMMA. Oh no you're not. Whig and Tory, Commoner and Peer, King and Queen, you're all alike. You need your Nelson, and you need him pure. There's not one of you doesn't want to split us, and wouldn't say afterwards it was done for England, not for yourselves. Perish the thought! Well, let me tell you, Minto, what England wants. England wants a live and happy Nelson, not a Nelson broken and sick, and half dead with longing. And as for me you don't care that—(*Flicking her fingers.*) any of you. Nelson dead and I'm thrown on to the dust-heap. Do you think I don't know that, Minto? So—on this visit—no meddling, do you hear?

*Pause.*

MINTO. The epithet 'bitch' I could perhaps agree to be saddled with, my Lady, saving my gender, but 'meddler' never. So, may it just be 'bitch'?

EMMA. (*With a rough, sincere laugh.*) I could like you, Minto, if you'd ever let me.

FRANCESCA. (*Appearing.*) Il bagno di vostra eccelenza si sta raffredando.

EMMA *nods, and gets up, now with less difficulty.*

EMMA. I got angry with what you said about 'large'. Yes, you caught me there, I'll grant. Still, would you have me a flagpole? (*Laughing again.*) Perhaps you think my Nelson would, so that he could more easily run up his flag? But his flag does well enough as it is, thank you very much.

*She takes a large swig of her tankard, from* GEORGE, *while* MINTO *joins in her laughter.*

Last night it was nailed to the mast, at 'no surrender' and with the signals all at 'close action'.

*She laughs again, and handing the tankard back stops at the sight of* GEORGE.

George, into the next room with you. You too, Minto.

GEORGE. (*Keen to go.*) Yes, Lady Hamilton.

EMMA. Aunt Emma.

GEORGE. Sorry. Aunt Emma.

GEORGE *goes into the boudoir.* EMMA *stops* MINTO *from joining him.*

EMMA. Did he understand that?

MINTO. At that age they understand most things, and enjoy them just as keenly as your Ladyship.

EMMA *appears at the entrance to the boudoir. She sees* GEORGE *studying the painting again.*

EMMA. Not more interested in the dead painting than in the live model, George?

GEORGE. Oh no, most assuredly not—

EMMA. Assuredly? If I could have spoken like that at his age I might have ended a duchess.

MINTO. (*Entering the boudoir.*) You may yet end a duchess.

EMMA. Emma, Duchess of Bronte, Viscountess Nelson? There's a certain much to be hoped for event that has to take place first might I remind you. But they do say the winters at Bath aren't too healthy for the rheumatical.

MINTO. They have indeed reported a certain malignancy of vapours there.

EMMA. (*Raising her tankard.*) Good luck to the vapours, say I, and don't let them spare any Toms, or any Tits. By which I don't mean something vulgar, Minto—like what you've been staring at this last five minutes. (*Calling to* GEORGE.) George, talk to Lord Minto now, but don't listen to a word he says about me, because he hates me like the pox—which is nothing, of course, save the greatest jealousy.

MINTO. Who now, my Lady, is the bitch?

EMMA, *on her way towards the powder room laughs, finishes her tankard and disappears behind the screen.* MINTO *in the boudoir, approaches* GEORGE. (*Breaking a pause.*) Do I need to tell you that what our hostess just said is a joke?

GEORGE *discomforted and bewildered, is silent. It seems safest.* MINTO *pours himself out some wine from a tray of drinks on a table.*
   Will you join me?

GEORGE. No, thank you.

MINTO. Not allowed it?

GEORGE. Oh, I'm allowed it.

MINTO. Then have some. (*He pours a glass and hands it to* GEORGE.) It might help to remove that look.

GEORGE. What look?

MINTO. To meet Lady Hamilton, for the first time, can, I know, be rather a shock to a juvenile sensibility. Never, I dare say, more than to a nephew of Lord Nelson's. Your look is one of surprise, Master Matcham. Remove it. It will not be popular at Merton. Your good health, sir.

GEORGE. (*Sipping.*) My Lord.

MINTO. (*Appreciatively.*) She keeps a good wine. I wonder who pays for it. Not your uncle, I trust. He has not prize money enough for even a pipe of this. (*Appreciatively again.*) Excellent.

GEORGE. I thought Lady Hamilton was rich.

MINTO. Rich in everything but money. Sir William left her only his debts. But we were commanded not to talk of her. Do you go to school?

GEORGE. Oh yes.

*He has turned to look at the portrait again. Pause.*

MINTO. Where?

GEORGE. Bath.

MINTO. And do you enjoy it?

GEORGE. (*Listlessly.*) Oh yes.

MINTO. I'm so glad.

*Pause.* GEORGE *is plainly disinclined for conversation, at least on these terms.* (*Indicating painting.*) As Ariadne. She was then I believe, sixteen. A rather mature sixteen.

GEORGE. (*Turning slowly.*) Are you fond of Lady Hamilton?

MINTO. You seem, Master Matcham, to have inherited your uncle's flair for surprise attacks.

GEORGE. I'm sorry.

MINTO. Don't be. I always tell the truth, except when I have need to tell a lie. I am fond of Emma Hamilton. She's a very generous and good-hearted lady—loyal, passionate, and kind.

GEORGE. Kind?

MINTO. Very kind. Except of course, to her enemies—but as they are mainly Neapolitan revolutionaries—

GEORGE. I was thinking of an enemy nearer home.

MINTO. (*Frowning.*) Ah. But why fret about her either?

GEORGE. She's my aunt.

MINTO. An aunt, superseded by events. You now have an Aunt Emma. You had better have some more of this. You still have that look.

GEORGE. No, thank you. (*Pointing to the picture.*) If you could only explain— (*He stops.*)

MINTO. Explain what?

GEORGE. It doesn't matter. I shouldn't ask.

MINTO. I don't think you should, Master Matcham. (*Raising his hand to stop* GEORGE'S *apology.*) not because the question is likely to be improper but because it is likely to be unanswerable. What does Lord Nelson see in her? Is that what you want explained?

GEORGE *nods.*

What does one person see in another person? That question has been asked since the beginning of time and will be asked to the end of it— and there is very rarely any answer, Master Matcham.

GEORGE. But he's a great man. (*Passionately.*) You *do* believe that, don't you?

MINTO. Oh yes.

GEORGE. Great because of what he has done or because of what he is?

MINTO. I think you should defer that question to Captain Hardy, his Flag

Captain. He can speak for him in both capacities better than I. I can only speak for him as a man in love.

*Pause.*

GEORGE. Above all things I don't understand how he could allow her to treat his wife the way she does.

MINTO. Your ex-Aunt Frances? In what way does she treat her? Does she send poisoned pork pies to Bath?

GEORGE. (*Angrily.*) She's bribed his whole family to desert her.

MINTO. (*Shrugging.*) They've deserted her readily enough, and I'd say that any bribes have been his, not hers.

GEORGE. (*Stiff with rage.*) Oh no! That's a lie.

*Pause.*

MINTO. Master Matcham, you are not quite old enough yet to challenge and not quite young enough to put across my knee. I really think you must withdraw that observation.

GEORGE. I'm sorry—I'm very sorry, my Lord—but it can't be Lord Nelson. It just can't be—That's all I meant—

*Pause.* MINTO *looks at him thoughtfully.*

MINTO. (*Shrugging.*) Very likely not. It hardly matters, anyway, as the wife in question is, I hear, perfectly content with her two thousand a year, and her reflected glory in the society of Bath.

GEORGE. That isn't true—

MINTO. (*Smiling.*) Again, sir?

GEORGE. I mean I *know that* isn't true. I've seen her recently and she's very—well . . . upset.

MINTO. Really? Tears? You'll learn one day that the tears of a neglected but comfortably pensioned-off grass widow aren't always very real.

GEORGE. Hers were real.

MINTO. When did you last see her?

GEORGE. A week ago, and she gave me a letter to deliver to her husband.

*Pause.*

MINTO. You must, of course, on no account, deliver it.

GEORGE. My Lord, I must.

MINTO. Must?

GEORGE. I gave my word.

MINTO. Oh God, deliver me from a schoolboy's honour! Do you want to destroy your uncle's peace of mind?

GEORGE. Oh no! Oh Heaven, no!

MINTO. Then give me that letter and let me tear it up. Or, better still, return it to her unread.

GEORGE. It's already been returned to her opened and unread. That's why I'm taking it down, so that this time he'll receive it at least.

*Pause.* MINTO *has entirely lost his urbanity. Of the two he is now the one to seem shocked.*

MINTO. Who returned it?

GEORGE. Mr. Davidson.

MINTO. By whose command did Davidson return an opened letter?

GEORGE. Well, on the cover it says by Lord Nelson. It actually reads: 'opened by mistake by Lord Nelson but not read'—but, my Lord, it stands to reason—

MINTO. Nothing, sir, in Lord Nelson's present life, stands to reason. *Pause.*

GEORGE. Oh no. That I'll not believe.

MINTO. I'll forgive you this third time, sir, since I'll not believe it either. *After a pause.*

But Davidson doesn't take his orders from Lady Hamilton.

GEORGE. Still she must have opened it, and told him it was a bad, vile letter, full of abuse and that he mustn't read it. Then she must have got him to order Davidson to send it back. That's how I've worked it out.

MINTO. (*Thoughtfully.*) You have worked it out most ingeniously, Master Matcham. A very reasonable solution.

GEORGE. You're not still hinting—

MINTO. I'm hinting nothing, except that I want that letter kept from Lord Nelson, and I want you to give it to me now.

GEORGE. No.

MINTO. I am a pacific man and deplore violence, but it has suddenly occurred to me that I am, for once, in the position of facing defiance from someone who is rather smaller than myself. (*Menacingly.*) You will give me that letter at once, sir.

GEORGE. It's under lock and key.

MINTO. You have the key on you?

GEORGE. No. (*With squeaky bravado.*) You can put your sword to my throat, my Lord, but I'll give that letter to only one man; the man to whom it was addressed.

*Pause.*

MINTO. You have been seeing Master Betty on the stage recently.

GEORGE. I saw him at Bath.

MINTO. I don't happen to be wearing a sword, nor indeed have I these twenty years. This is no matter for boyish heroics, sir, I beg. You have a charge of gunpowder under lock and key and you apparently intend to ignite it in your uncle's face. Believe me it will explode as hurtfully to you as to him. And all because a jealous wife squeezed out some easy tears into your lap.

GEORGE. (*After a pause, quietly.*) She cried the way I've never seen anyone cry before in my whole life—or at least not a grown-up. She cried from deep, deep down in herself, as if she were ill. It was terrible. I'll never forget it as long as I live.

MINTO. You must try.

GEORGE. I can't. And I never will.

MINTO. Then at least keep it to yourself. He'll not thank you, I promise, for having seen Tom Tit in tears.

GEORGE. Why should what's happened make him turn so much against his wife?

MINTO. I don't know, and nor does anyone else. But I must earnestly beg you not to deliver to him that letter.

GEORGE *shakes his head.*

(*Urgently.*) You can at least postpone delivery until tomorrow night?

GEORGE. Well, perhaps, just for twenty-four hours.

MINTO. In the meantime, I see I shall have to speak to Lady Nelson myself, which will put me in the unlikely role of trying to put out a fire in a powder magazine. I have no doubt but that I'll be blown to pieces, with no posthumous medal for gallantry to console my family.

EMMA *flies out of the powder room struggling into her peignoir, and runs across the bedroom into the boudoir.*

EMMA. He's brought the biggest crowd yet. I was looking out of the closet window.

MINTO. Was that quite wise, my Lady?

EMMA. Oh, you're such a prude. The crowd have often seen me with nothing on. They like it.

MINTO. I'm sure, but—

EMMA. (*Interrupting.*) They were holding up babies for him to bless. (*Hugging* GEORGE.) Oh George, aren't you proud?

GEORGE. Yes, Lady Hamilton.

EMMA. Aunt Emma. I nearly huzzaed myself out of the window.

MINTO. That would have pleased the Cartoonists—

EMMA. The Cartoonists? Those buggers aren't worth my piss—

NELSON *comes in. He is dressed as when we last saw him, having come from the Admiralty. He looks only at her, ignoring* MINTO *and* GEORGE.

You kept your promise?

NELSON. Did you doubt me? (*He embraces her ardently.*)

EMMA. In that poxy Admiralty I always doubt you. Those people in there could get you to go out tomorrow. Did you ask for a year.

NELSON. I didn't specify.

EMMA. (*Angrily.*) You promised—

NELSON. I just told him I wasn't going out now, to Cadiz—and insisted my refusal be accepted. But it'll be a year, my heart, never fear. A whole year— I promise.

EMMA. (*Kissing him.*) Oh I do fear, Nelson.

NELSON. Don't. (*He gives her a long, possessive embrace.*)

EMMA. (*Breaking away.*) We have company.

NELSON *sees the other two. Plainly he has difficulty with his eyesight.*

NELSON. Why, Minto—you have obeyed your summons! By God, I'm most heartily flattered (*he embraces him*) and more happy to see you than I can properly tell you. You've grown thin up north. We'll alter that at Merton. Emma is the most perfect housekeeper in the world—if a thought extravagant in these days of high prices.

EMMA. Enough of that, Nelson. All's done for you and no one else. (*Pointing to* GEORGE.) This is Master—

NELSON. (*Warmly embracing* GEORGE.) I know who this is. Dear nephew George! My dearest, dearest boy! How good to see you! But you have grown so much I had pains to recognize you. By God, you look older than I did when I was first made a Captain, doesn't he, Emma?

EMMA. How do I know? When you were first made a captain we hadn't met.

NELSON. (*Smiling at her.*) Perhaps that is just as well.

EMMA. Nelson!

NELSON. (*Hastily.*) For the Navy's sake, I mean, not my own.

EMMA. But that's worse. Do you want young George to think that his Aunt Emma's influence on Nelson has been bad for the Country?

NELSON. (*To* GEORGE, *quietly.*) All I meant, George, was that to have met Lady Hamilton as a youth might—to the detriment of my later service—have made me chary of risking a life suddenly grown too precious to lose.

EMMA. That's better. He can turn quite a phrase for a sailor, can't he?

NELSON. (*Suddenly noticing.*) Emma, why are you undressed before these men?

EMMA. Oh, they're not really men, Nelson—I mean one's a boy and the other's a—well, he's from Roxburgh.

*A* FOOTMAN *comes in with a card on silver salver.*

(*Reading it.*) Captain Hardy. Show him up.

*The* FOOTMAN *goes.*

Hardy, I'll agree, does count as a man. What's more he thinks I'm the whore of Babylon even when I'm in my winter woollies. I'll not be long.

NELSON. May I come in with you?

EMMA. You'd best receive you precious Hardy here first, hadn't you?

NELSON. I'm not anxious to. You of all people know why.

EMMA. Coward! Scared of his own Flag-Captain! What a hero! You tell him now and get it over.

*She kisses him and then goes out into the bedroom, where* FRANCESCA *is waiting, and they both disappear behind the screen.*

NELSON. The crowd seemed even bigger than after Copenhagen. It's surprising after two years. Oh, how I long sometimes to walk in London unrecognised. But how can I do it?

GEORGE. (*Taking it literally.*) Perhaps, Uncle Horatio, if you didn't wear all your stars and decorations—

NELSON. (*After a faint pause, good-humouredly.*) You're quite right George. It's my vanity that betrays me.

GEORGE. Oh, I didn't mean that.

NELSON. (*To* MINTO.) The boy's right, Minto. Even for an interview with the

First Lord, I could wear a plain suit. I am on leave. (*Touching his four stars with a smile.*) But damme, I like people to know what I've done! (*To* MINTO.) I suppose, Minto, that you'd call that babyish.

MINTO. Will you never forgive me for that unfortunate remark?

NELSON. No, by God, I won't. (*To* GEORGE.) He once told me that ashore I was a babe in arms, while at sea—well, no matter—

MINTO. At sea, an Alexander.

NELSON. Was it Alexander? Well, George, in both he exaggerated deeply—

FOOTMAN. (*Entering.*) Captain Hardy.

HARDY *comes in. He is a veteran sailor, at home in my company in the world, except, possibly, where he finds himself now.* NELSON *embraces him without a word, and then turns to introduce* GEORGE.

NELSON. My nephew, George Matcham.

HARDY *bows.*

And Lord Minto, whom I expect you know—

HARDY. (*Shaking hands.*) Why yes. It's a great pleasure.

MINTO. Mine too, Captain.

*There is an uneasy pause.* NELSON *is plainly nervous.*

HARDY. Her Ladyship?

NELSON. Is getting ready. I think perhaps—if you'll excuse me—(*He goes towards the bedroom.*)

HARDY. Before you go—I take it you've seen the First Lord?

NELSON *nods.*

Has he news where Villeneuve's gone?

*Pause. This is moment* NELSON *has dreaded.*

NELSON. Yes, Hardy—he has.

HARDY. Where? North?

NELSON. No, South. In fact, Cadiz.

HARDY. (*Excitedly.*) Cadiz? Cadiz? He can't stay there long.

NELSON. No.

HARDY. Cadiz! That's the best news ever. We'll catch him, then. How many ships?

NELSON. Something over thirty.

HARDY. And how many can we muster?

NELSON. Enough.

HARDY. As many as theirs?

NELSON. Who wants as many as theirs, Hardy? I said enough.

HARDY *laughs delightedly, and clutches* NELSON'S *arm.*

HARDY. That's good. That can go in the press when the news is out. So when does the Victory sail?

*Pause.*

NELSON. (*Speaking carefully.*) It must be soon—for it's sure that they'll need every ship they can spare.

*Pause.* NELSON *plainly hates the look of growing disappointment he sees in* HARDY'S *expression.*

HARDY. Every ship?

NELSON. (*Smiling.*) And every Captain, too.

*There is another pause.* HARDY *says nothing.*

I don't doubt you'll have your orders to sail the Victory south in a few days.

HARDY. (*At long length.*) Yes, my lord.

NELSON. She's still a good enough ship for the kind of pell-mell battle this is likely to be. Perhaps Collingwood will choose to fly his flag in her rather than the Royal Sovereign. I know I would, if I had my choice, in spite of the Royal Sovereign's new copper and the Victory's barnacles of two years—(*with a slightly embarrassed bow.*) Captain Hardy.

HARDY. (*Equally embarrassed.*) Lord Nelson.

NELSON *goes into the bedroom and sits on the bed, staring at the floor, quite motionless.*

(*In the boudoir at length.*) I need some rum.

MINTO. I don't think she keeps it.

HARDY. (*Fiercely.*) Not keep rum? What kind of an Admiral's Lady is she—

MINTO. In some things—unsuitable.

HARDY. In some things?

MINTO. There's good wine, Captain. And brandy, of course.

HARDY. French muck. (*Angrily.*) There's nothing here that's English at all. Yes there is. (*He holds up a bottle.*) Gin. A whore's drink. Well, I'll have it. This is suitable wouldn't you say, my Lord?

MINTO. (*Gently.*) He has been away for two years, Captain.

HARDY. Yes. And so have I. Your health. (*To* GEORGE.) Sir.

*He downs the drink in one, replenishes, and then sits down in morose abstraction.* MINTO *glances from* GEORGE *to* HARDY *and then back again—two figures both showing clear traces of shock and disillusion.*

MINTO. (*After a pause, with a hint of mischief.*) You may settle a point for our young friend, Captain. He asked me earlier if your Admiral is accounted a great man for what he has done, or for what he is. I told him to refer that question to you.

HARDY. (*After a pause, gruffly.*) He is great in both. How could he have done what he's done without being what he is?

MINTO. (*To* GEORGE.) You are well answered.

GEORGE. You mean he wouldn't have won his battles without genius?

HARDY. Genius? Genius is nothing at sea. Nothing much, anyway. It's keeping to windward of the enemy line and attacking it at the right place and the right time—That's part of his genius. I meant something much more than that. I meant having the right ships and the right men to attack with.

GEORGE. (*Puzzled.*) Our ships and seamen are surely much better than the French—

HARDY. That's what you read. Man to man and ship to ship, I'm not so sure, myself. But if they are the best who made 'em so?

*In the bedroom* NELSON *suddenly gets up from the bed, his depression apparently over. He walks behind the screen into the powder room.*

(*Fiercely.*) Do you know the kind of man a British seaman is, Master Matcham? 'Hearts of oak are our men'? Don't you believe it! Pressed into service, as like as not—four-fifths of them are—and pressed means kidnapped in Chatham or Portsmouth, knocked on the head and thrown into a life as brutal and slavish as any in the world. In Newgate gaol they get better to eat than maggoty biscuit, and they don't get two hundred lashes of the cat-o'-nine-tails for a back answer to their gaoler. Two hundred multiplied by nine? That's a lot of bloody flesh off any man's back, Master Matcham, and the threat of it keeps 'em servile enough—as it'd keep you too—and Lord Minto I don't doubt. And a bumper tot of rum would make you both drunk enough to fight a battle. But would you care overmuch who won it? I ask you that straight, both of you? If you were British seamen would you break your hearts if the revolutionaries won their war against us or the guillotine were set up in Piccadilly? And would you raise that bumper tot of rum to the health of your Admiral?

GEORGE. (*Quickly.*) Before the battle of the Nile the men did drink to Nelson.

HARDY. Yes, sir. To Nelson. That's your answer. *I* don't raise this whore's drink to him now—feeling as I do at the present—but those men do drink their rum to Nelson. They beg to serve in any Squadron he commands and cry like women when they hear he's wounded. Don't ask me how he's done it, but if it's not by a miracle, and it isn't, then it must be by being the kind of man he is. (*Looking at his glass.*) Do you know I'm not sure even this gin isn't foreign—

MINTO. They do make a passable gin in Naples.

HARDY. I wish to Heaven he'd never seen that God-forsaken place. (*Morosely.*) And if you two gentlemen care to repeat that remark I'll bear the consequences like a man.

EMMA *comes out of the powder room, followed by* NELSON. *She is dressed for the drive to Merton. She is walking to the boudoir, but* NELSON *pulls her back and embraces her.*

MINTO. They could be heavy.

HARDY. They couldn't be much heavier than now. Collingwood's flag in the Victory? I'll shoot it down myself.

EMMA *enters the boudoir with* NELSON *behind her.*

EMMA. Captain Hardy, what honour you do me!

HARDY. It is I who have the honour, your Ladyship.

EMMA. The crowd is now quite immense. (*To* HARDY.) Did they give you a cheer, Captain, when you came to the doorstep?

HARDY. I am hardly known to them, my Lady.

EMMA. (*Graciously.*) You should be, and, one day, you will be, I'm sure. (*With a wide gesture.*) One day everyone about my Nelson will be known.

Minto, you are to come in the carriage with us. My Lord thinks it more proper—

NELSON. (*Mildly.*) The word I used was seemly, Emma. Propriety was not in my thoughts.

EMMA. Nor ever will be, I trust.

FRANCESCA *hurries from the bedroom and hands* EMMA *a flask which she whisks into her reticule. Minto notices it.*

It's a long journey, Minto, and you might be glad of it. George, you and Captain Hardy are to follow in the second carriage. You may tell the good people out there, if they ask, who you are. They'll know, of course, where you're going.

NELSON. (*Looking at him.*) By Heaven, George, you have grown! You must tell your mother to get you new breeches. And jacket too. When Fanny bought the children's clothes—

EMMA. (*Warningly*). Nelson, are you going to say something in praise of Tom Tit?

NELSON. (*Lightly.*) Nothing ever in praise of Tom Tit. It's hardly praise to say she had a gift for buying children's clothes—

EMMA. I'll buy George several new suits before he goes—at the best tailors. That's a promise.

NELSON. And most Emma-like in its extravagance. (*Kissing her.*) Perhaps just one new suit.

EMMA. And new boots to go with them. (*She sweeps out.*)

NELSON. (*To* MINTO.) I'm glad you're travelling with us. We have a little matter of business to discuss. The question of a loan to be raised at my bankers—(*Mischievously.*) and in such matters I am, as you know a very great baby indeed.

MINTO. I'll not deny it.

*They follow* EMMA.

And as regards babies, I haven't yet asked about Horatia—

*By now they are out of the room.*

NELSON. (*Off.*) Oh, Minto, she is such an exquisite little creature now. I'm so proud of her. And so is Emma—

MINTO. (*Off.*) She would be five, or thereabouts—

NELSON. (*Off.*) Four and five months exactly.

GEORGE. (*To* HARDY.) Can't we go down?

HARDY. No. Let them get their huzzas! We'll be anonymous, and follow later.

GEORGE. I'll go and watch at the door.

*He disappears.* HARDY, *left alone, stares broodingly into his glass, and then up at the portrait of* EMMA. *Suddenly, with a violent gesture, he hurls the contents of his glass at it. He is pouring himself another gin when* GEORGE *returns, looking bewildered.*

HARDY. Well? Did they cheer heartily?

GEORGE. Yes. Oh yes. But—

HARDY. But what?

GEORGE. Some of them laughed.

HARDY. Did they?

GEORGE. (*Utterly appalled.*) They laughed at *Nelson!*

HARDY *gulps his drink down and gives* GEORGE *a friendly pat.*

HARDY. With Lady Hamilton.

*The lights fade. The cheers, which have started a little earlier, grow to a crescendo and we hear the sound of a string orchestra playing some genteel melody that is no doubt a great favourite at the Pump Room at Bath.*

## SCENE IV

*The lights come on to show a small area representing a downstairs room in Lady Nelson's London house.* MINTO *is rising from a chair.* FRANCES *stands nearby. There is a portrait of the young* NELSON *prominently placed. In this scene* LADY NELSON *uses a stick.*

MINTO. It seems then, that my visit has achieved nothing.

FRANCES. Oh but yes. It's given me the chance of seeing you again, after all these years. I forgot to ask you. Are your wife and family well?

MINTO. Never better.

FRANCES. I'm so glad.

MINTO. You won't relent?

FRANCES. That is an odd word to choose—I mean in the general circumstances. If my nephew George cares to break his promise, that's his own affair, and you may tell him from me that I won't be angry.

MINTO. If I tell him that it will bind him even more strongly to his word of honour.

MINTO *speaks the phrase as if it had quotation marks.* FRANCES' *quiet response pointedly leaves them out.*

FRANCES. Yes. He's an honourable boy, my nephew George.

MINTO. You realise that your honourable nephew may well be seriously blamed for his part in the delivery of this letter?

FRANCES. Why? He has an honourable uncle.

*Pause.* MINTO *finds himself beaten.*

MINTO. Goodbye, my Lady.

FRANCES. I would see you to the door, but I don't walk so well these days. Rather birdlike, as you may have heard.

MINTO *bows and turns.*

One moment. Your visit has at least succeeded in one thing. It has stirred my conscience. You have a notebook with you, I know. Would you write something in it from me for my nephew and let me sign it?

MINTO. Most gladly.

*He takes a notebook and pencil from his pocket.*

FRANCES. But tell me one thing first. You blame me for choosing my school-boy nephew as a go-between. Would you like to tell me, Lord Minto, what other member of my family I might have chosen?

MINTO *is silent.*

Or mutual friend? Would you yourself?

MINTO *makes an impatient gesture.*

Or anyone else you can think of? The post, I have discovered, is liable to interception.

MINTO. Why not the Admiralty?

FRANCES. You think the Admiralty any more reliable than the post? How many friends do you think I have at the Admiralty now?

MINTO. There are a host there who would heartily wish Lady Hamilton dead.

FRANCES. But she isn't, is she? Well, this is for George. You can phrase it as you wish. (*Dictating.*) Dear George, Lord Minto thinks you should not show my husband the letter I gave you, and he may well be right. I must leave it to you to decide, and in order to help that decision you have my permission to read the letter yourself. Should you think that there is anything in it at all which will cause my husband any distress whatever, then it is your duty and my wish that you burn it.

MINTO *has been scribbling.*

Your lawyer's mind will no doubt find a better way of expressing that. So long as you have the main points taken down, I'll sign a blank page.

MINTO. I have taken down exactly what you dictated, and I would prefer that you signed that.

FRANCES. Very well.

*He hands her the notebook and she signs it.*

I only wished to show you that I trusted you.

MINTO. In this matter I'm not sure that I can trust myself.

FRANCES. Why are you so apprehensive?

MINTO. I am not a very brave man, and I am afraid I can already hear the thunder of an approaching battle royal.

FRANCES. (*In her mildest tones yet.*) Oh dear! I am indeed sorry to be the cause of such melodramatics, in your quiet little family circle.

MINTO, *putting away his notebook, smiles for the first time.*

MINTO. I must confess, Lady Nelson, that I most truly admire your spirit.

FRANCES. Thank you. I have some need of it these days.

MINTO. I don't doubt it.

FRANCES. You are going back to Merton?

MINTO. (*Looking at his watch.*) In time for dinner. It's being taken early and I am most strictly commanded not to be late.

FRANCES. Her Ladyship is to give you one of her Attitudes, perhaps?

MINTO. No doubt some beguilement of the kind. He picks up his hat and stick.

FRANCES. I trust you were wise enough not to come here in your own carriage?

MINTO. I have no carriage in London. If I had, would it have been unwise to have used it to come here to Somerset Street?

FRANCES. House number seven, to the north of the street and house number fifty-one, to the south. They are both usually on the alert.

MINTO. There are melodramatics, then, in Somerset Street?

FRANCES. Oh, window-watching isn't melodramatic. It's important to her to know who comes to see me. I perfectly understand why.

*Pause.*

MINTO. Well—

FRANCES. (*Quickly.*) It's wrong to detain you—but I have no one to tell me these things now. I must rely on the newspapers—and they leave out so much. His good eye—is it troubling him?

MINTO. A little, I think.

FRANCES. He will strain it. He must always wear that eye-shield when he works at his desk. Always. Tell him that.

MINTO. Yes, my Lady.

FRANCES. (*Trying to smile.*) But not, of course, as coming from me—

MINTO. (*Not smiling.*) No.

FRANCES. Tell Lady Hamilton that it must be always left near at hand—otherwise he forgets it. And Lord Minto—if you could—I don't say it would be easy for you—but if you could ever get him to understand that I am not his enemy, but his ever-loving wife who, if she's given the chance, will do anything in the world for his good—

*As* MINTO *stays silent.*

But what's the use? You're his friend, now, not mine. I don't blame you. With number seven to the north and number fifty-one to the south, who can now stay friends with both? I realise that it is the situation that is to blame.

MINTO. Do you? Do you, for instance, realise that there is not one of your husband's friends or family that would really wish the situation as it is? That some of them—myself am one—would give nearly all they had to change it.

FRANCES. Why then don't you try to?

MINTO. Because it cannot be changed. Nothing will change it, ever. Ever, my Lady—from now to Doomsday. Do you understand that?

FRANCES. (*In a low voice.*) I understand that he is now gone from me for good. Yes I understand that. (*With a faint return of spirit.*) But I also understand that he is gone from me to a woman who can do his reputation nothing but harm—and has already done so. Is that not true?

MINTO. It is the woman he has chosen. The woman he now loves and who loves him. The woman he will never leave.

FRANCES. I accept that.

MINTO. But do you? Or do you not still hope?

FRANCES. I must sometimes—hope—

MINTO. Don't. Please, Lady Nelson—I most urgently beg you—don't. For you, hope can only mean despair, and if you could kill the one you could also kill the other.

FRANCES. I must then try to kill hope.

MINTO. It really is the best—and I speak only for your own good.

FRANCES. I'm not so much concerned with my own good, Lord Minto, as I am with his. Do you believe that?

MINTO. Yes, I do.

FRANCES. (*Suddenly, fiercely.*) But if I give up hope so then must they. They must cease to picture me as the 'Invalid of Bath.' I am not in a decline. I am not going to die. I will do anything for my husband's pleasure, except to cease from living. That, if you care to, you may tell him—and as coming from me.

MINTO *says nothing, as she struggles with tears that are plainly not so far distant, but succeeds with a visible effort in overcoming them. Then, with the aid of her stick, she manages a very passable curtsey.*

Lord Minto.

*She rises again, her back straight and her head held high.*

MINTO. (*Bowing.*) Lady Nelson.

*He goes.* FRANCES *stands motionless, her back to the portrait of the young Nelson. As the lights fade on the scene the portrait still glows brightly—until that too fades into darkness.*

END OF ACT ONE

## ACT TWO

### Scene I

*The lights come on to show the central acting area which will represent the drawing-room and the dining-room at Merton. This time the rooms are not directly connecting and anyone going from one room to the other will be seen making a rather circuitous journey before entering either room from the back. Beyond the dining-room area there lies a staircase leading to the bedrooms.*

*At the moment it is the drawing-room—the larger of the two areas—on which we will be concentrating, for* EMMA *is in the midst of an Attitude and the lighting, at the beginning of the scene, will be almost entirely on her, as she stands with right arm upraised, expression borrowed, probably, from Mrs. Siddons, and clothed in classical costume.*

EMMA. And so the great hero fell and all the nation mourned him! But of all who mourned him, none mourned him more piteously than the woman who had borne his child, the woman whom he had chosen of all women to love and to keep, and the woman who had cherished him in her bosom and loved him more than very life—Andromache of Troy!

*By now we can see her audience. It consists of the* GEORGE MATCHAMS, *Senior and Junior,* KATHERINE MATCHAM, *the* REV. WILLIAM NELSON (*elder brother by a year to* NELSON), *his wife* SARAH, *his son* HORATIO (GEORGE'S *age*), MINTO, HARDY *and another Captain—*BLACKWOOD, *who brought the Cadiz despatches.* NELSON *sits rather apart from the others, on a kind of throne. Much of* EMMA'S *performance is inevitably directed at him. There are also some senior servants present, while* FRANCESCA *acts as a kind of Stage-Manageress.* KATHERINE MATCHAM *provides background on a harpsichord, and is not as sure of her cues as is* FRANCESCA, *or as* EMMA *would like.*

EMMA. But she knew not yet what had befallen her great husband. . .

HARDY. (*Murmuring to* MINTO.) Who was her great husband?

EMMA. (*Before* MINTO *can reply, transfixing* HARDY *with a furious glance.*) Only that Hector had gone forth to battle—Hector, son of the King of Troy—(*This though indisputably accurate, is an improvisation for* HARDY, *who nods, satisfied.*) and Andromache sat in her dwelling wearing a purple mantle fringed with flowers—

*This is* FRANCESCA'S *cue to drape* EMMA'S *shoulders with a purple mantle, and for* EMMA *to recline on a couch in a graceful mime of happy expectation.*

and she bade her maidens make ready a bath for her husband when he returned from battle.

*She does this, too, in mime.* KATHERINE'S *trilling music, indicative of maidens*

*preparing a bath, is interrupted by her nervous difficulty in turning over a*
*page, and she gets a very sharp glance from* EMMA.

But suddenly a great cry goes up from the walls of Troy and Andromache
bounds from her couch—

EMMA *manages the bounding from the couch with a little deft assistance from*
FRANCESCA.

FRANCESCA. Attenzione.

EMMA. —and runs towards the ramparts. What does she see? Oh, most heavy
sight! Not Hector slain! (*To* FRANCESCA.) Oh say he is not dead! Not dead?
Not dead?

FRANCESCA. (*Firmly.*) È, morto.

*She adjusts the purple mantle more becomingly on her mistress's shoulders.*

EMMA. Ah, say not so! Is my life, my love, my all, now only dust?

FRANCESCA. E polvere.

*She joins the audience, her duties now performed.*

EMMA. Ah! Aah! Aaah!

*Three long cries of tragic grief.*

Has Hector gone and am I now alone?

*She speaks this quietly and with feeling. For one brief moment we might feel
that she could have had some talent as a professional actress. But, in an instant, she has thrown her arms to Heaven and is well back into the 'heroic'
style.*

Then death, takest thou me too! Ah, my maidens—come quickly all my
maidens, and prepare my funeral pyre! For I must die with him—

*There is a certain amount of gesturing to imaginary maidens after which* EMMA,
*unaided this time, lies on the couch in an attitude of tragic despair, care-
fully once more arranging her mantle to fall in the correctly classical folds.*

MINTO. (*Meanwhile, whispering to* MATCHAM SR.) Did Andromache kill herself?

MATCHAM. (*Whispering back.*) In Emma's version, anyway—

EMMA. (*Still arranging her folds.*) Ah most lugubrious and heavy woe! Ah,
day of misery! Ah, noxious and lamentable fate!

MINTO. (*Whispering to* NELSON.) Who wrote the words?

NELSON. (*Indicating the* REVEREND WILLIAM.) My brother William—

EMMA. Ah my maidens, my maidens! Most wretched of all mortals am I now!
Andromache weeps for her dead hero, the beloved of his country and
the Gods.

*The* REVEREND WILLIAM *had heard* NELSON *and is inclining his head to what he
assumes is* MINTO'S *approbation of his literary skills.*

The crown o' the earth doth melt, and withered is the garland of the war!
The odds is gone, and there is nothing left remarkable beneath the visiting moon.

MINTO. (*To* NELSON.) Brother William?

*He has spoken a shade too loudly.* EMMA *gives him a glare, and brother* WILLIAM
*is distinctly put out.* NELSON *smiles, a shade nervously.*

NELSON. Sometimes a little of another William—

EMMA. (*Loudly.*) The soldier's pole is fall'n. Young girls and boys are level now with men. Great Hector's gone, and the mind boggles with simple disbelief. The great defender of our native home is slain, and all the nation bewail him—

KATHERINE *has slipped into the Dead March from Saul.*

Husband I come! Now to that name my courage prove my title! I am fire and air! I come, I come. Poor, poor Andromache! Husband—ah, my husband!

*She stabs herself and falls back on the couch.*

*The rest is silence.*

*She dies. There is loud applause. It must here be noted that eye-witness reports of* EMMA HAMILTON'S *Attitudes almost unanimously ascribe to her a singular talent for heroic acting, a pleasing soprano voice and a marked predilection for going a mile too far. All these qualities will have been noticeable in the performance she has just given, and any slurring of speech or unhappy impromptus—the excerpts from Antony and Cleopatra were not in Brother* WILLIAM'S *script—could on this occasion, be well excused by the fact that it is quite late in the evening and that she has had a fairly full complement of brandy and champagne. It is noticeable that, after taking a gracious bow and, while still curtseying to* NELSON, *she takes a glass that* FRANCESCA *has just filled for her, and sips it thirstily; and if we are observant we will notice that what she is sipping is indeed champagne liberally spiked with brandy.*

NELSON. Bravo, Emma! Bravo!

*He kisses her.*

You were never better, on my life.

MINTO. (*To* EMMA.) Magnificent as always, dearest lady. It is not a piece I had heard from you, before.

EMMA. It's a favourite. Tonight I was as nervous as a pregnant nun—(*To* REVEREND WILLIAM.) saving your cloth, Reverend.

*The* REVEREND *saves his cloth with a smirk.*

MINTO. The very bravura of the performance makes that hard to believe.

REV. WILLIAM. You were splendidly lifelike. (*To* MINTO.) Those words from the other William were not my doing, my Lord. Lady Hamilton is some-times pleased to make certain additions—

EMMA. Emma, brother! What's this 'Lady Hamilton'? Shall I call you 'Dean Nelson?'

REV. WILLIAM. (*The most sycophantic of an unhappily sycophantic family.*) Oh, Heaven forbid! (*To* MINTO.) Dearest Emma, I was saying, is sometimes inclined to insert certain passages of her own finding, and Shakespeare's Cleopatra, it seems, is one of her favourite heroines.

MINTO. Of course.

EMMA. What do you mean by that, Minto?

MINTO. Of course Emma Hamilton would have as her favourite that other 'lass unparallel'd'.

EMMA. Lass unparallel'd? Well I'll accept 'unparallel'd' at any hour and at ten in the evening I'll even believe in 'lass'.

*The audience has broken up into groups.* MINTO *and* EMMA *are alone.*

(*Admiringly.*) You think quick, Minto. If you'd said something about 'this dotage of our Admiral' you'd have had this in you face.

*Turning to* BLACKWOOD.

Captain Blackwood, you are new to this house, and so new to my little entertainments—

BLACKWOOD. (*Who has a stammer, increased by his present nervousness.*) At N-Naples once I had the p-p-privilege—

EMMA. Of course, at Naples. Your frigate was in the Bay and Sir William and I came aboard.

BLACKWOOD. (*Miserably trying to remember.*) It was—oh dear—something cl-classical.

EMMA. Of course. But what?

BLACKWOOD. Oh dear. It was something—r-rather happier than the perform-ance you have just given, I meant j-j-jollier—

*His nervousness is increased by* NELSON'S *genial presence at his elbow.*

I meant it wasn't a l-lady m-mourning for her l-lover's death or anything l-like that—

EMMA. (*Unhelpfully.*) Husband's death—

BLACKWOOD. Oh, husband's death. Yes. In Naples you gave us a j-j-jolly lady—

EMMA. My thoughts in Naples were perhaps something jollier, Captain. You don't remember the lady's name?

BLACKWOOD. (*Excitedly.*) She was a B-B-Bachante—that's what she was—of course—and you made her most abandoned and true to life.

EMMA. But my performance this evening—less jolly, I agree—how did you find that?

BLACKWOOD. Oh, quite pitiful.

*Unhappily this is about the one word that has come out straight and clear.* BLACKWOOD *is instantly confused.*

I mean—

NELSON. (*Stepping in to the rescue.*) The word you used to me about the per-formance, Blackwood, was affecting.

BLACKWOOD. Oh yes. Aff-affecting was what I meant. I was most deeply aff-aff-affected by the whole thing.

EMMA. I am flattered. It takes much, I am sure, to affect the gallant captain of the Euryalus.

*To* NELSON, *hand over mouth.*

Oh! Have I made one?

NELSON. No, my love. The name was most nobly remembered. It is in fact, Blackwood's Euryalus that lately brought us the news from Cadiz about Villeneuve.

EMMA. Oh, of course. And he goes back in her tomorrow, you said?

*She takes another glass of champagne and brandy from* FRANCESCA, *whose continued presence in the room—the other servants having left—seems designed
solely for this purpose. The* NELSON *family is grouped together in a corner of
the room, standing rather formally, their faces smirking obsequiously, as if
in the presence of Royalty.* HARDY *the only one of the important guests not to
have congratulated* EMMA, *wanders from the room, and we see him walking
through the hall area at the back towards the dining-room, which eventually he enters. A map has been laid out on the table and it would appear
that* NELSON *had been giving his captains a rough briefing of the battle to
come.* HARDY *studies the map and begins to move some objects on the dining
table.* EMMA *has been most conscious of his exit from the sitting-room.*

(*To* BLACKWOOD.) You see, dear Captain, how well rehearsed I am in all
matters concerning Nelson's fleet.

NELSON. (*Smiling.*) Collingwood's fleet.

EMMA. Well, it would be my Nelson's if he were there.

BLACKWOOD. No doubt of that, my Lady.

NELSON. But he is not there. He is here—

EMMA. (*Sharply.*)—and most happily here—

NELSON. Indeed outrageously happily here—so it remains Collingwood's
fleet, and it's Collingwood's fleet he sets sail to rejoin tomorrow.

EMMA. (*Raising her glass.*) I wish you a fair wind, Captain.

BLACKWOOD *bows. To* NELSON.

I suppose when Collingwood fights your battle they'll make him an Earl.

NELSON. Do you grudge it to him?

EMMA. I wouldn't grudge Old Coll. being made Arse-licker in Ordinary to
His Majesty—saving your cloth again, Reverend.

WILLIAM *saves his cloth again with a smirk and a bow.*

—So I could keep my Nelson here with me.

*Her arm is lovingly around him, and from a glance around, she evidently wishes
HARDY were there.*

What was it—in my Andromache—affected you most, Captain
Blackwood?

FRANCESCA *at a gesture, replaces* EMMA'S *glass with yet another.*

BLACKWOOD. (*Who had hoped himself out of gunshot.*) Ah. That is a qu-ques-
tion. Well, Lady Hamilton, when you spoke of H-Hector, I was made
to think of another even greater d-defender of his country—

EMMA. Not too much so, I hope. This defender is alive and so I mean to
keep him—despite the underhand work of some who call him their
friend.

*Again she looks towards the sitting-room entrance, but* HARDY *is still in the dining-room, intent on his battle.* EMMA *polishes of her champagne and puts
down the glass, striking an heroic Attitude.*

But still Europe's great defender! Let me see, let me see. How does it go?

*She raises* NELSON'S *arm.* HARDY *goes out of the dining-room.*

Yes. His legs bestrid—but why past tense?—His legs bestride the ocean—

in whose livery walks crown and crownets—realms and islands are as plates dropped from his pockets—

HARDY *comes in.*

NELSON. Emma, dearest—

EMMA. I was quoting a speech of Cleopatra's. (*At* HARDY.) Moll-Cleopatra—as some officers in your fleet call me, I hear.

NELSON. (*Following her glance.*) A very pitiful joke, my love.

EMMA. But those words are Shakespeare's—and they're as true of you as they were of that silly old antique Roman when spoken by his strumpet gypsy. Captain—are you listening?

HARDY *shakes his head politely.* NELSON *realising from experience all the signs of an incipient scene, speaks quickly and lightly.*

NELSON. In that scene her Ladyship of Egypt was something exaggerating, I think.

EMMA. (*Loudly.*) This Ladyship of England exaggerates nothing. When I see my pillar of the world I see great Jove himself—

HARDY. (*To* MINTO, *quite audibly.*) It's a wonder she can see anything at all.

EMMA *wheels on him, evidently meaning to let go with some of the 'gutter language' for which she is famed. But, more dangerously, if less uncomfortably, for all, she decides to speak quietly.*

EMMA. I heard that, Captain Hardy. This is my house, and if I should choose to toast the guest who does such honour to this roof in what to your puritan mind might seem a glass too many of brandy and champagne, that I think should be my affair and not yours, don't you?

HARDY. I do, my Lady, indeed. It was only that my puritan mind hadn't perhaps quite grasped the fact that this was your Ladyship's house.

HARDY *seems happy to answer a broadside with a broadside.* NELSON *quickly interposes himself to stop what could be, for him, the most disastrous battle of all.*

NELSON. Merton is *our* house, Hardy—*your* house, *everyone's* house who comes to visit it. And most certainly it is Emma's. Emma, my dearest, Captain Hardy is anxious to talk to me on the matter of these despatches that Blackwood takes tomorrow to Collingwood—and, as he leaves us early in the morning—

EMMA. (*Impatiently pushing* NELSON *aside.*) You haven't yet spoken of my performance, Captain. I am afraid you were most heartily bored by my drunken posturings.

NELSON. Emma—

HARDY. Not bored, Lady Hamilton. Far from bored. Nor did they seem so drunken. I had heard much of your Ladyship's famous Attitudes and can now, with my description of this lady you have just so formidably personated, most happily entertain my brother officers in the Victory. In their passage to Cadiz to join Admiral Collingwood's fleet they may, perhaps, need some entertainment.

EMMA. You may tell them, if their classical education should want as much as yours seems to, that the lady I so formidably personated was called Andromache, and that she was—in the classical sense, but not the puritan—the true and loyal *wife* of her hero, Hector—and that therefore the house she lived in with him, was hers as much as his—

NELSON. (*Now severe.*) Emma, I must beg you to stop this stupidity. All that Hardy meant was—

*He sees rightly that* EMMA *is on the verge of losing all control, and he is still trying to smile. The family meanwhile are being hastily pushed by brother* WILLIAM *out of the room. Only* GEORGE *contrives to stay—watching the scene with deep distress.* MINTO *attentive and bored simultaneously, has picked up a book.*

EMMA. (*Pushing* NELSON *aside.*) I know well all that Captain Hardy meant, and so does he. He meant that I'm not your wife, Nelson—not by virtue of Mother Church. Well, Captain—a pox on Mother Church! I am, by everything that is just and honest in this world, the true and only wife of this man here—the father of my child, Horatia Nelson—

NELSON. (*Warningly.*) Emma, please stop this now—

EMMA. (*Too far gone in her tantrum to stop anything now.*) To all people in this house, Captain—to my Lord's family, to my Lord's friends, to my Lord's servants even—I am Lord Nelson's wife. To the whole of England I am his wife—and a pox on that old man madman of Windsor and his German bitch of a Queen!

*She drinks her glass and throws it over her shoulder.*

There's my loyal toast, Captain Hardy! To the whole of the rest of England, I, Emma Hamilton, am the true wife of Lord Nelson.

HARDY. Excepting, I would suppose, to Lady Nelson.

*Pause, broken before* EMMA *can break it more violently, by* NELSON.

NELSON. Hardy, that was unforgivable.

HARDY. I shall leave.

NELSON. No.

*As* HARDY *still moves away we hear the sudden rasp of authority in* NELSON'S *voice.*

You will stay here, Hardy. I command it.

HARDY *stops. That is a voice he can never disobey. But* EMMA *is continuing.*

EMMA. Tell the bugger to get out of this house now, and never come back. Nelson *I* command *you*—

NELSON. You command me in most things, Emma, but not in that.

EMMA. Oh, indeed? Then perhaps I should leave your Lordships house. Francesca—have my carriage brought round at once—

FRANCESCA. Subito, eccelenza, subito.

NELSON. Francesca, you will pay no attention to that, and you will leave this room at once. Your mistress will ring for you when she has need.

FRANCESCA *frightened too by the sound of* NELSON'S *seldom heard voice of command, bobs, and looks uncertainly at her mistress.*

*Pause.*

FRANCESCA. (*Finally, with a deep curtsey to the conqueror of Naples.*) A vostro ordine, signoria. (*Crossing herself as she hurries out.*) Jesu! Jesu!

NELSON. (*Turning to* EMMA.) Emma, you will apologise to Captain Hardy for what you have just said about the King and Queen. Also to Captain Blackwood.

EMMA. Apologise? Are you mad?

NELSON. They are serving Naval Officers of his Majesty the King who must not ever be spoken of in such terms in their hearing. Never. Understand me?

EMMA. Because they've sworn a vow of loyalty to his old lunacy?

NELSON. Yes.

EMMA. And vows are such sacred things, aren't they?

NELSON. Yes.

EMMA. More sacred, I don't doubt, than vows sworn by certain person in the bed-chamber.

NELSON. (*Quietly.*) All vows are equally sacred, Emma. Some that are made unwillingly in church may have to be broken, but there's no happiness in that—

EMMA. Oh—no happiness. That's good. So that's where we are now, is it? More happily in Tom Tit's bed-chamber than in mine? Why don't you go back to it then, if that's how you feel?

NELSON. (*Not raising his voice.*) Emma, you are making yourself a spectacle to strangers—and above all things else in the world I hate that. If you will apologise to the Captains, we will forget it all.

EMMA. (*Scornfully.*) And you'll love me after? You'll vow that?

NELSON. I will love you always. That needs no vow. You know it.

EMMA. I don't know it. If I did there might be no need for apologies now.

NELSON. (*Sharply.*) Do it, please, Emma—for my sake.

*There is a pause.* EMMA *finishes her drink.*

EMMA. I'll do better than you ask. To show them I meant no real disrespect, I'll sing them the National Anthem. Can I do fairer than that?

*Going to the harpsichord.*

And isn't it the proper way to round off a performance? Kitty? Where's Kitty.

GEORGE. I'll get her. (*Calling.*) Mother, mother! Come quickly! You're wanted at the harpsichord to play 'God Save the King'.

KATHERINE *flies in breathlessly.*

EMMA. Kitty, I want you to play the National Anthem, while I sing it.

KATHERINE. Oh, most gladly.

*She sits at the harpsichord and strikes up. The rest of the family, evidently believing that the storm is over, come back.* EMMA *waits—for them before beginning to sing. Then she turns to* NELSON *and sings straight to him.*

EMMA. (*Singing.*)

Join we great Nelson's name,

First on the rolls of Fame,
Him let us sing.
Spread we his fame around,
Honour of British ground,
Who made Nile's shores resound,
God save my King.

*And with a deep curtsey she makes perfectly plain exactly whom she means as 'her King.'*

(*Abruptly.*) That is the only verse I know—or care to learn.

*All look at* NELSON *to see how they should take* EMMA'S *'apology'. He applauds politely.*

NELSON. Well sung, indeed, dear Emma. I am, as always, most deeply flattered by those words.

*Turning from her abruptly.*

Hardy, shall we talk in the dining-room? The weather seems to have put my garden quarter-deck out of the question. Blackwood, will you join us? You carry that despatch on you for details?

BLACKWOOD. Ay, ay, my Lord.

NELSON. If the rest of you should happen to be going to your beds—

*It is a royal command and there is a general hasty murmur of assent.*

then I'll bid you all a collective good night, and a most pleasant rest until tomorrow.

CHORUS OF VOICES. Goodnight, brother, brother-in-law, uncle, etc.

NELSON *bows, and then quietly ushers* HARDY *and* BLACKWOOD *out of the room. We see the three men making their way to the dining-room.* EMMA, *now at the harpsichord, strumming some notes gently, laughs.*

EMMA. (*To the departing family.*) Your loving aunt, sister, sister-in-law and (*To* MINTO.) fellow guest—echoes those sentiments. A pleasant rest above all. Above all, that. A pleasant rest indeed!

*The family murmuring politely, go out. They file past the dining-room entrance before they disappear up the stairs.* EMMA, *still plainly in a fury, slams down the lid of the harpsichord and goes to pour herself another drink.* MINTO *is the last to leave the room.*

MINTO. Good night, my Lady.

EMMA. Minto, you stay.

MINTO. It *is* rather late.

EMMA. When have you ever found ten past eleven late?

MINTO. Well, I have some papers—

EMMA. Minto, Minto! I know you think me a vulgar, drunken slut, and wish me dead like a million others, but don't desert me in my distress? Do you want me to face the thunder of mighty Jove's wrath alone?

*Pause.* MINTO *shrugging decides to stay.*

MINTO. I have a thought that mighty Jove's thunder may quickly turn into a baby's drum once your Ladyship has applied the right arts.

EMMA. The right arts? What are they?

MINTO. Your Ladyship should know them by now.

EMMA. Oh yes. Her Ladyship does. But so does his Lordship—and that's the trouble.

*In the dining-room, we see the two captains and* NELSON *in conference. Once again the table silver is being moved about.*

Or beginning to be.

MINTO. (*In mock wonderment.*) When those arts fail the world will end.

EMMA. It will, for me.

MINTO. And for him.

EMMA. True. And for him. So they mustn't fail, must they?

MINTO. They won't.

EMMA. At this time of night I'll agree with you. Tomorrow morning, when Francesca brings in my morning tankard, I'll think different, and begin again to wonder. Oh, Minto, you knew me five years ago. Was I quite such a vulgar, drunken slut?

*Turning to him.*

Oh no. You won't answer that, so I'll answer it for you. Vulgar? Yes. Your Ladyship was always vulgar. Being a blacksmith's daughter shows—it always must.

MINTO. No.

EMMA. (*Scornfully.*) There speaks your humbug English Whiggery. (*Imitating a political speech.*) An honest blacksmith's honest daughter can, in our blessed land of the free, rise to the most exalted station in life—such as even Ambassador's wife in Naples—and retain never a trace of her humble beginnings. (*Raising an imaginary quizzing glass.*) A blacksmith's daughter? Pon my soul, you'd hardly know it, save for her inelegant bearing, her coarse mode of expression and her large feet—

MINTO. (*Protestingly.*) Your Ladyship's feet—

EMMA. Are large and crushed so into small slippers they give me hell. But still—if I'm vulgar it's not just because I'm a blacksmith's daughter, but because I'm plain vulgar—and would be if I were the daughter of a duke—which, to a couple of Dukes I could mention, I almost have been—and God save us all from incestuous thoughts! Jesu Maria! Do you think I couldn't have made myself into a genteel English lady under old Sir Willum if I'd set my mind to it? But God, who'd want to be as refined as, say Kitty Matcham? What a death in life! (*She drinks.*) So—vulgar I always was, and vulgar I'll always remain—and for choice. But slut? What of that, Minto?

MINTO. Your Ladyship's generosity is known to be prodigious. Why should it have stopped short of the bed?

EMMA. (*Thoughtfully.*) Yes, I've been generous enough. I didn't ever take money except in my teens. And old Sir Willum—he had no cause for complaint. He didn't want much—poor old love—although what with my standing stark naked for hours on a plinth in draughty rooms, while he—pottered about in his special fashion—I caught a plaguy

lot of colds. Poor old Sir Willum! Well, I was an honest wife to him in
my own way.

*As* MINTO *raises his eyebrows.*

Oh, yes—that was Sir Willum's way too. Cuckolded by England's greatest hero? It kept the old boy alive. To be honest—a bit too long for
propriety's sake. Oh, what a boon we all were then to the Cartoonists—
with Sir Willum beaming from a box at Drury Lane—and me beside
him, eight months gone with Horatia—and Nelson on the other side,
saluted from the stage with music and drums and patriotic tableaux, and
Tom Tit tucked in there into the bargain—

MINTO. Where would she sit?

EMMA. Behind us, of course. She knew her place, even then. But getting all
the sympathy, the bitch! That gentle, resigned look, that smile of infinite understanding and forgiveness. Oh, I could have strangled her!

*After a pause.*

Oh, Minto—yes—I know what you're thinking. What a human monster she is, this Emma Hamilton, to hate the woman she's dispossessed
and humiliated! Well, I do—and that's that. And I don't hate easily. But
I'm scared of Tom Tit and I hate what scares me.

MINTO. She's no threat. Why does she scare you?

EMMA. I don't know. (*She shivers.*) Perhaps because she's there alive and waiting.

MINTO. Not for him—

EMMA. I don't know. But she's waiting—and making him feel guilty and miserable with all those principles he learnt from his father, the Rector. You
can't blame her. That's her revenge.

MINTO. (*Smiling.*) As an Avenging Fury she is rather overparted.

EMMA. Overparted my arsehole! Do you think an Avenging Fury has to be a
witch on a broomstick. A genteel and rheumatic English lady with a refined sense of decorum, the book of Common Prayer on her lap and
the law on her side does much better, I tell you. Get me another drink,
love. It's good for forgetting fear.

MINTO. (*Replenishing her glass.*) I might remind your Ladyship that it's also
good for becoming drunk.

EMMA. Oh yes. I've learnt that too. Well, Minto, there's 'vulgar' and 'slut'.
Now 'drunken'. How do you compare that to five years ago?

MINTO. (*Handing her a glass.*) Your Ladyship has never seemed averse from
fortifying by artificial aids a vivacity already richly endowed by nature.

EMMA. Jesus! (*She takes along drink.*)

MINTO. (*Seriously.*) I think you drink more now, and get less drunk.

*Pause.*

EMMA. Yes. You're a sharp one, Minto. Nothing much escapes you, does it?
I drink from morning until night, and no longer for enjoyment. Mine
or anyone else's, it seems. Still Hardy was a cheeky bastard to have said

what he did. I'm scared of Hardy too—and he knows it. What do you think they're plotting in the dining-room.

MINTO. A battle.

EMMA. To be fought by Collingwood.

MINTO. (*Piously.*) And—let us pray for England's sake—to be won by him.

EMMA. Oh it will be. It's Nelson's plan. (*Striding about in sudden agitation.*) I'm scared he's trying to shame Nelson into going out again himself. He's foxy, that Hardy. He knows what the muttering of a few words like 'Duty', 'Honour', 'England', will do to my Nelson. He's muttering them in there now—never fear. And I do fear. I fear that my arts—as you called them—might by sunk by Captain Hardy's hornpipe.

MINTO. (*Seriously.*) I don't think so.

EMMA. (*Eagerly.*) You don't? I still look well enough, do I?

MINTO. (*Politely.*) As desirable as when you sat for Romney.

EMMA. (*Shadily.*) Don't say that! I can eat flattery, God knows, but if you mention Romney, than I'll know you're lying.

MINTO. (*Quietly.*) I didn't say beautiful. I said desirable.

EMMA. By candle-light, to a man half-blind? (*She dabs at her eyes.*) Brandy tears.

MINTO. You must know that by candle-light or daylight, half-blind or with both eyes clear, Nelson will always see you as Romney saw you—as his Divine Lady.

EMMA. But how do I see myself? Answer me that. When I get up in the mornings and look at myself in my glass, don't you think I don't say to myself—but he can't love that! Not that! It's too absurd. So Francesca fills me up with a few tankards of porter and brandy at breakfast, and by evening I'm the Divine Lady again and I'm saying—but, of course Nelson loves me, and he's damn lucky to have me. But tonight's different, I don't know why. (*She dabs her eyes again and puts the handkerchief away.*) Oh, my Nelson—I do love him!

MINTO. I think you do.

EMMA. Only think, Minto? By heaven, I love my Nelson more than I love life. (*Catching herself in a dramatic posture.*) No that's an Attitude and I mustn't attitudinise about my feelings for Nelson. Well, I suppose the truth is that I love Nelson because he sees me in the only way I can ever bear to be seen by any lover now—(*With sudden anger.*) He's been in there long enough.

*She goes to the harpsichord.*

Shall I see if my arts still work?

*She opens the harpsichord and begins to strum some notes again.*

We have a signal. An absolute signal. The day he fails to answer it I am lost. Mind you—after the way I've behaved tonight . . . Well, we'll see.

*She plays the verse of Rule Britannia, not loudly and heroically, but rather gently and prettily.*

NELSON, *in the dining-room looks up, evidently hearing. Then he goes back to work.*

I'm nervous.

MINTO. Perhaps the refrain itself is more commanding?

EMMA. Oh no. We never get to the Rule Britannia bit. He thinks it vulgar.

*She continues to play but nothing appears to happen. What in fact does happen is that* NELSON *walks quickly out of the dining-room.*

(*In alarm.*) Minto, did I behave so badly tonight that he'll never forgive me?

*The question is answered for her as* NELSON *walks in.* EMMA *rises from the harpsichord and goes to* NELSON. *They kiss.*

(*At length.*) Minto, you told me you had some papers to read.

MINTO. (*At the door.*) I am already appending my notes.

*He goes out. Left alone,* EMMA *sinks gracefully on to one knee, bending her head in submission.*

EMMA. Nelson, the culprit begs forgiveness.

NELSON. (*Trying to lift her.*) Emma, Emma—

EMMA. Oh, my Lord—I have most grievously offended, and I hereby submit myself to your Lordship's great will.

NELSON. (*Laughing at her.*) You know what my will is, Emma. Whether it's great is another matter—but it's unquenchable—that's certain.

*He tries to lift her.*

EMMA. No—I must first have your gracious pardon and on my knee I beg it.

NELSON. Must we behave like this? There's no one here.

EMMA. (*Faintly irritated.*) I thought you'd like to see me on my knee before you, admitting my fault and craving humble indulgence.

NELSON. I like to see you in any position before me, but not now in an Attitude.

EMMA. You don't like my Attitudes?

NELSON. (*Succeeding in lifting her.*) You know I adore them as I adore you—but not always, dearest Emma. Not when we are alone.

*He kisses her passionately now—and she responds.*

EMMA. I was very bad, wasn't I?

NELSON. It's forgotten.

EMMA. Didn't I call him a bugger?

NELSON. Yes, but let us hope, inaccurately.

EMMA. I shamed you in front of all. Why do you put up with me?

NELSON. Don't you know yet?

*He kisses her greedily now, fondling her.*

EMMA. Have you finished talking to your Captains?

NELSON. Another five minutes.

EMMA. I'll go straight up.

NELSON. Please—

EMMA. I'll make it so good tonight—

NELSON. You don't need to make it anything but what it always is—and that is bliss enough.

EMMA. Who's attitudinising now?

NELSON. Oh, it's not an Attitude, my dearest, dearest heart. If you could only know the joy—the wonder—you see my hand is trembling—

EMMA. And that's not all. Come up very soon. When I do shame you, it's only out of love, and fear of losing you—

NELSON. How could you ever lose me?

KATHERINE *appears at the entrance. Neither* NELSON *nor* EMMA *trouble to move.*

EMMA. Come in, Kitty.

KATHERINE *comes in, and takes in the scene with pleasure, but little surprise.*

KATHERINE. Forgive me, dear brother, dear Emma—

NELSON. (*Still holding* EMMA.) Come in, Kitty. What is it?

KATHERINE. Young George—it's his last night. He leaves very early in the morning and may not see you, and he does so want to say goodbye.

EMMA. Send him in. I like young George. Five years older, I could make you jealous of young George—

KATHERINE. (*Smirking.*) Dearest Emma—always so generous about the family—

*Going to the door.*

And he has some special message he wants to deliver to Horatio—

EMMA. (*Smiling.*) And not to me?

KATHERINE. (*Beckoning.*) I don't think so. He's very secretive about it. Come in, dear.

GEORGE *comes in, very frightened, still and grave faced.*

(*To* GEORGE.) Don't be scared. And please say all the right things to your great and gracious host and hostess.

*She goes out.* NELSON *and* EMMA, *who have remained locked until this moment, separate and smile at* GEORGE *warmly.*

GEORGE. I want to thank you both for the most memorable four days of my life.

EMMA. (*Kissing him fondly.*) Dearest George, I have loved having you as my guest at Merton and I promise I'll make sure that it won't be long before you return.

GEORGE. (*Bowing.*) I am most grateful, my Lady.

EMMA. What's this my Lady again?

GEORGE. I'm sorry. Aunt Emma.

EMMA. (*To* NELSON.) Don't be long. And you tell your Captain Hardy I'm sorry for having called him a bugger—

*Blowing a kiss to* GEORGE *she goes out.* GEORGE, *left alone with* NELSON, *is plainly nervous, but equally plainly conscious of a duty to be performed.* NELSON *is gazing after* EMMA, *hardly conscious of* GEORGE. GEORGE *fumbles in his pockets.*

GEORGE. I have this to give you, Uncle Horatio.

*He produces an object wrapped in paper.*

NELSON. (*Unwraps it.*) What is it?

GEORGE. It's supposed to be against the ague. I was asked to give it to you by our maid at Bath.

NELSON. Very kind.

GEORGE. I told her you had hundreds of such things sent you through the post, but she insisted I give it to you personally and be sure to tell you it came from our Betsy.

NELSON. (*Smiling.*) I must remember to write to her.

*Picking up his brief case which he has carried in from the dining-room.*

Well—why don't I do it now, and you may deliver it to her? I hope she will forgive a pencil?

GEORGE. Oh, but you shouldn't bother—

NELSON. (*Writing.*) Of course I should. Betsy—you say?

GEORGE. Yes.

*After a pause, while* NELSON *writes.*

But you shouldn't strain your eyes, Uncle—especially with writing letters that aren't important—

NELSON. Oh, but a letter of thanks for a kindly thought is important, George. Very important. Whatever they say of me, they mustn't ever say that I have forgotten my manners . . . your most grateful servant, Nelson and Bronte.

*He hands* GEORGE *the letter.*

GEORGE. She'll be—I don't know what she'll be. I hope she doesn't sell it, that's all.

NELSON. Let her, But not for too small a price.

*Coming from the desk to shake hands.*

You have been a most pleasant guest, George, and are growing into a fine young man. As her Ladyship says, you will always be welcome at Merton.

GEORGE. Thank you.

*As Nelson has stepped away.*

There's just one other thing.

NELSON *stops and turns.*

You may be angry—

NELSON. With you? Never.

GEORGE. I've brought a letter to you from your wife.

GEORGE *takes it out of his pocket.* NELSON *makes no move to take it. There is a pause.*

NELSON. (*Quietly.*) That you should never have done.

GEORGE. I gave a promise.

NELSON. That, too, you should not have done. To whom did you give this promise?

GEORGE. To Aunt Frances.

NELSON. (*Angrily.*) Don't call her that! (*Controlling himself.*) Where did you meet Lady Nelson?

GEORGE. In Bath, by accident.

NELSON. Where were your mother and father?

GEORGE. They had just gone on the London coach.

NELSON. And you were alone?

GEORGE. Yes.

NELSON. (*Bitterly.*) By accident!

*He snatches the letter from* GEORGE, *but doesn't attempt to open it.*

   This is not her handwriting.

GEORGE. No, it's mine.

NELSON. Why is it yours?

GEORGE. The other covering was written on already. You see, it's a letter she wrote to you some time ago, and it went—astray. You never read it, she's sure, and she's very anxious for you to read it now.

NELSON. Went astray? How?

GEORGE. I—er—don't quite know.

NELSON. Very well. You've fulfilled your promise.

*He throws it unopened onto a table.*

   And never make such a promise again.

GEORGE. No, Uncle Horatio.

NELSON. Well, (*Patting his shoulder.*) it's not you who are to blame I suppose. Go to bed.

GEORGE. There's just one thing else. I promised her you would read it.

*Pause.*

NELSON. (*With quiet rage.*) How did you dare do that?

GEORGE. I didn't know how you felt, then. But I thought whatever's happened, a husband can surely still read a letter from his wife. Especially you—

NELSON. Especially me?

GEORGE. Especially, when the husband is you—of all people in the world.

NELSON. Thank you for the compliment, but this is a husband of all husbands in the world who happens to prefer to think his wife is no longer alive.

GEORGE. (*With spirit.*) But she is alive, isn't she, Uncle Horatio? As alive, anyway, as our maid Betsy. I mean—didn't you speak, just now, about manners?

*There is a pause.* NELSON *clenches and unclenches his fist, like a man whose patience is very strained. Then he abruptly picks up the letter, opens the covering, and pulls out the enclosure. He has only read a couple of sentences when he screws the letter up and hurls it to the floor.*

NELSON. (*Now in open rage.*) You double-dealing, traitorous dog! It's a plot! I'll have you kicked out of this house tonight, and never come back!

*At the hall door, shouting.*

   Kitty! Kitty! Come here at once! And Matcham too! Come down! (*To* GEORGE.) I'll make you regret this trick you've played on me for the rest of your life—

GEORGE. But I played no trick, Uncle—

NELSON. To bring me a letter of such vileness that I had to return it to her three years ago—

GEORGE. Vileness? How can you say that about it? (KATHERINE *has appeared breathlessly*.)

KATHERINE. What is it, Horatio?

NELSON *ignores her. He is staring at the boy.* MATCHAM, *in a dressing-gown appears behind* KATHERINE.

NELSON. (*To* GEORGE.) You've read this letter?

GEORGE. Yes.

NELSON. She gave it to you to read?

GEORGE. She said I could just to make sure it wasn't what you've just called it. (*Boldly.*) And it wasn't, it wasn't vile. Oh God, Uncle, I wish I could see it was, oh God, I do—

KATHERINE. (*Murmuring.*) Don't blaspheme—

GEORGE. (*Picking up the letter.*) But I can't see that it's a letter that any man should have sent back to his wife, with such a cruel message on it—

NELSON. (*Very quietly.*) Least of all me?

EMMA *comes into the room, pushing aside the frightened* MATCHAMS.

EMMA. What's this?

NELSON. It has nothing to do with you, Emma.

EMMA. Nothing to do with me? You, shouting in a rage all over the house, and now shaking like you had the palsy—and it's nothing to do with me? Tell me this instance.

NELSON. I won't speak of it now—or probably ever. Just—take this boy away from me, please.

EMMA. (*To* KATHERINE.) What has he done?

KATHERINE. (*Murmuring unhappily.*) I don't know—but I think he's brought some letter from Tom Tit—

EMMA. (*Appalled, to* GEORGE.) Is that true?

GEORGE *is too distraught with what he seems to have done to* NELSON *to answer her.*

You answer me, then, Nelson. Is that true?

NELSON. I tell you—it is none of your business.

EMMA. (*Thunderstruck.*) A secret letter from Tom Tit to you not my business?

NELSON. (*Raising his voice.*) Leave me be. I must go out.

EMMA. Go out in this weather? Are you mad?

NELSON. Matcham—light me a lantern, please.

MATCHAM *goes to the hall area.* NELSON *is following him when* EMMA *interposes herself.*

EMMA. You are certainly not going out in this weather, Nelson—and you are not leaving this room until I have a proper explanation.

NELSON. (*With his suddenly commanding voice.*) Make way, if you please.

MATCHAM *comes in, lighting a lantern.*

EMMA. Don't give him that.

NELSON. The lantern please, Matcham.

MATCHAM. But Lady Hamilton has just said—

NELSON. This is my house and not yet Lady Hamilton's, although she is sometimes pleased to think that it is otherwise. If I wish to leave it for my
garden, I do so without her permission. Give me that lantern.

MATCHAM *hands him the lantern.* EMMA *still bars the way.*

EMMA. (*Still interposing herself.*) Nelson, I'll not endure this. I'm coming with
you.

NELSON. (*Coldly.*) No. I go alone. (*As* EMMA *still bars his way.*) By your leave,
My Lady.

EMMA. (*Taking a step back.*) My Lady?

NELSON *walks past her, finds a cloak, wraps it around him and turns.*

NELSON. (*To* MATCHAM.) You will please get your boy to his room—

EMMA. To his room? We'll whip the hide off him.

NELSON. (*His voice coldly cutting across hers.*) No, he will not be harmed in
any way at all. Anyone who dares to do so—or orders it done—(*Looking at* EMMA.) anyone at all—will leave my house tonight. (*To the*
MATCHAMS.) You will take him to his room, Matcham. He leaves early
anyway. I should have remembered that. I am truly sorry to have disturbed you both. Good night, again.

*He goes out.* EMMA *runs after him.*

EMMA. (*Shouting.*) Nelson. (*Then more pleadingly.*) Nelson . . .

NELSON *walks away from her without looking back.*

*The lights fade to a complete blackout. During it we hear, at first, some music
indicative of inner turmoil, and then the sound of wind and rain, inter-
mingled at a moment by a peal of thunder.*

## Scene II

*When the lights come on again it is to show the dining-room where* HARDY, *still
and wide-awake, and* BLACKWOOD, *asleep, are waiting. After several moments*
NELSON *appears as from the front door. His cloak is now dripping wet. He makes
his way quietly towards the stairs, sees candles still alight in the dining-room and
goes towards it.* HARDY *stands up as* NELSON *enters.*

NELSON. (*Standing at the entrance.*) I fear you have had a long watch.

HARDY. Oh, I had company.

BLACKWOOD *stumbles to his feet at the sound of* NELSON'S *voice.*

BLACKWOOD. My Lord—you are s-s-safe returned?

NELSON. (*Smiling.*) That safety can only be measured by the state of my health
in the morning.

*He takes off his dripping cloak and lays it across a chair. Then he rubs his hand
under his stump.*

BLACKWOOD. Hardy and I—we I-I-looked everywhere for you.

NELSON. Didn't Hardy guess where I was?

HARDY. (*To* BLACKWOOD.) Captain Blackwood, it is time for your bunk. You leave for Portsmouth at dawn—which is in rather less than two hours.

BLACKWOOD. Ay, ay, Captain. (*Bowing, naval fashion.*) Lord Nelson, I confess I am most h-h-heartily relieved to see you s-s-standing here before me. I had so much f-feared—we had all so much f-feared—Her Ladyship has even s-sent search parties out—

NELSON. (*To* HARDY.) Where is she?

HARDY. In bed at last.

NELSON. (*To* BLACKWOOD.). Good night, Captain Blackwood—or what remains of this night. I am most sorry to have disturbed the larger part of it.

BLACKWOOD. Oh, My Lord, that was n-n-nothing. (*Bowing.*) My Lord.

*He goes and we see him mounting the stairs to bed.*

NELSON. (*To* HARDY.) Didn't you guess where I was?

HARDY. Yes, of course—but as you had plainly hidden yourself away on that particular crow's nest of yours, and as it is so very private—even if a little unsheltered on such a night—I knew you had no wish to be disturbed there—even by me. (*He feels his cloak.*) You should take a double tot of grog, I think.

NELSON. (*Pretending to be outraged.*) Grog, Hardy? My best French brandy?

*He allows* HARDY *to fill a glass and pour some drops down his throat.*

But I suppose it would hardly be called a hero's death to die of a chill contracted on the roof of a folly in my garden, after a tiff with my mistress.

HARDY. By all accounts it was something more than a tiff.

NELSON. Yes, it was, I suppose. Was there great uproar afterwards?

HARDY. Not many turned in before three, I think. Her Ladyship even later.

NELSON. (*Smiling.*) And she sent out search parties?

HARDY. Yes, but surprisingly refused at all times to go out herself.

NELSON. Oh no. She would never go out herself.

HARDY. A matter of pride or of weather?

NELSON. Pride. I must always go to her. And go I will, when I have rid myself of this shivering. (*He pours another small glass.*) Where is the boy?

HARDY. In his room.

NELSON. He has not been beaten?

HARDY. No. You had forbidden it.

NELSON. And the letter? With what spirited version did she oblige you all of that occurrence?

HARDY. That the boy brought you a written message from your wife so vile that you could only throw it back in his face, and order him out of the house, never to be seen or spoken to again, and that then—for some mad reason that she cannot for the life of her fathom—you turned on her and insulted her and called her 'Her Ladyship', and went rushing off into

the night—after saying of all wicked things, in the world, it was none of
her poxy business. Am I well briefed?

NELSON. She has added some colour, but you're briefed well enough. (*Anxiously*.) This letter? Did she read it?

HARDY. No. The boy has locked it up, and hidden the key. There has been, as your Lordship might imagine, something of a hue and cry—

NELSON. Has he talked?

HARDY. No.

NELSON. Not a word?

HARDY. Not that I know of.

NELSON. Not even that he read the letter himself?

HARDY. His mother heard him say that to you.

NELSON. Yes, I suppose she did. And she heard, and has no doubt informed you all, of his description of it—as the kind of letter that no honourable man would ever send back to his wife?

HARDY. No one, of course, will believe that.

NELSON. And why not, Hardy? Why in God's name not? Isn't it all of a piece with what's known of the case. A faithful loving wife, most foully wronged by her husband and living now in loneliness and despair because that very villain who has thrown her off so cruelly has bribed his family and threatened his friends to make them desert her too? A pitiful, mistreated wretch, flying her flag with genteel dignity in Bath, while her besotted husband rollicks away his honour and reputation in drunkenness and lechery with the mother of his bastard child. That's how that boy now sees it, Hardy. Why shouldn't the world see it too, through his eyes?

HARDY. The world is not your nephew, my Lord.

NELSON. I'm not at all so sure my nephew is not the world.

HARDY. Well—young eyes usually see the truth of things in a distorting mirror—and so does the world, I suppose.

NELSON. But how is this truth distorted?

HARDY. How can I answer that without facts?

NELSON. You have the facts.

HARDY. (*Losing patience*.) I have the fact that you have wronged your wife. What you have never told me is how your wife has wronged you. I only know that she has.

NELSON. How do you know?

HARDY. Because I'm your friend and I know as a simple truth that you— Lord Nelson—could never behave as you have and as you do to that lady unless she had first done you some most grievous wrong.

*After a pause.*

She has, has she not?

NELSON. Yes.

HARDY. Most grievous?

NELSON. Yes.

HARDY. I don't ask how. I only ask, how if the true facts are not known, how can the world pass true judgement?

NELSON *rises abruptly.*

NELSON. Oh God, how easy compassion is! You don't understand it at all, Hardy—

HARDY. I said if I knew the true facts—

NELSON. (*In mounting fury.*) You know the true facts. Six years ago, in Naples, I wittingly and of my own free will, deserted a loving and loyal wife for the embraces of a notorious charmer. How much did you all laugh in the wardroom of the Vanguard when you saw that happening? 'Not leaving his wife for that woman,' did you say? 'Not for the one who displayed herself naked for show at fourteen in Vauxhall Gardens, who was sold by Greville to Hamilton as payment for a bad debt, and has been bedded by half the nobility and gentry of England before becoming Sir William's wife? Not leaving his wife for her! Not for Emma Hamilton!' Do you think I never imagined how loud that laughter must have been?

*Pause.*

HARDY. My Lord, the wardroom could not have guessed that you were so aware. I did not guess it myself, until this minute. You pretend very well, you see.

NELSON. Oh God, Hardy—how do you think I can keep my sanity and not be aware?

*Pause. He turns his face from* HARDY.

My Divine Lady? God in Heaven, Hardy, when Emma throws a glass of champagne, after an insult to my King, don't you think I see exactly what you see, a drunken, middle-aged woman making a fool of herself and of me. Do you think I relish the gutter-talk, don't wince at the vulgarity, and have lost the capacity to smell liquor on the breath? Do you think I don't feel blasted with shame nearly every day that I spend at Emma's side?

*Pause.*

HARDY. Then why have you so long endured such days?

NELSON. (*Facing him.*) Because after the days there are the nights.

*Pause.* NELSON *smiles.*

And now of course, you are asking yourself the question how can any love be respected that begins and ends in the bed?

HARDY. Yes. How can it?

NELSON. To me, very easily. To the forty-year-old Admiral who had never known or enjoyed what most other men have enjoyed and long since forgotten—that in the release of the bed there lies an ecstacy so strong and a satisfaction so profound that it seems that it is everything that life can offer a man, the very purpose of his existence on earth—well to that poor crass innocent of an Admiral in Naples Bay the question was not so easy—oh no, Hardy, not easy at all. You must remember, you see, that, even at that age, I was still the rector's son who, from the cradle, had been preached the abomination of carnal love, and the ineffable joys of holy wedlock. But when at last I surrendered to Emma, I found— why should I be ashamed to say it?—that carnal love concerns the soul quite as much as it concerns the body. For the body is still the soul and the soul is still the body. At least they are for me. You must understand that there is nothing in Emma I would change, Hardy. I love her and I want her exactly as she is—because I am obsessed and I want her absolutely.

*Pause.*

HARDY. I don't think this love of yours does begin and end in the bed, My Lord.

NELSON. You are right. And yet without the bed what would it be? Nothing. But that other love—that ineffable bliss of wedlock—the one so blessed by my father and thought by all the world so fitting for a national hero; the tight brave smile, the rigid body the—'if this makes my beloved husband happy then I'll do it, even if the messy business quite disgusts my well-bred sensibilities'. Oh Hardy, that was a hell of humiliation—a hell—but a hell from which I am now so very happily escaped—

*He covers his face. Then he rises, nods to* HARDY *and goes out to the stairs.*

We should get some rest.

HARDY *follows him.*

HARDY. (*On the stairs.*) Did you say happily, My Lord.

NELSON. (*Continuing up the stairs.*) Find another word if you like. Satisfyingly?

HARDY. Is it so satisfying to be laughed at in Clarges Street?

NELSON *stops short.*

NELSON. That was nothing. A few brutish boors, probably hired by my enemies.

HARDY. Has your Lordship any enemies, apart from the French? I doubt if Napoleon would hire spies to risk jeering you into going out again to sea.

NELSON *turns violently and stares down at* HARDY.

NELSON. God damn you, Hardy, but you fight foul! (*Looks down at him.*) I'll not go out to Cadiz, do you hear?

HARDY. I hear.

NELSON *makes his way brusquely down the stairs and into the sitting-room.* HARDY *follows him. In the sitting-room* NELSON *picks up his brief case.*

NELSON. (*Loudly, not knowing* HARDY *has followed him.*) It's all you've thought about since that morning in Clarges Street. 'I don't care how sacred a vow is', you've said, 'I don't care what it may cost him in spirit and health and love. I'll get him to go out again.' Well, Hardy, you won't and that's an end of it. Let them laugh and guffaw at me in the streets, and let them cheer Collingwood as their new hero—

HARDY. (*At his elbow, quietly.*) No. That they'll not do.

NELSON. Of course they will, when he wins his battle.

HARDY. He won't win it. Mind you I don't say he'll lose it either. A couple of prizes, perhaps, and some damage to their flagship. Perhaps some damage to one or two of ours, but which must happen when two lines of warships sail in parallel, exchanging broadsides—

NELSON. In parallel? Are you mad? Go back to the dining-room and study my plan.

HARDY. I had many hours tonight to study it, My Lord. Laid out with all your silver, it looks very pretty.

NELSON. God damn it, Hardy, where in blazes on that table are two parallel lines of battle? Are you mad or drunk, sir? The two British lines of battle point at right angles to the enemy line, one at his heart, the other at his liver. The very genius of the plan is to reverse completely all the rules by which naval battles until now have been fought, and to abolish parallel lines altogether, with their formal cannonading and their couple or three of prizes and some damage to a flagship. This is annihilation, Hardy.

HARDY. (*Politely.*) Yes, My Lord, I have often heard you say so.

NELSON. After this battle the French and Spanish fleets must never put to sea again. Not a single ship among them. God damn your eyes, Hardy, if my plan means anything at all, it means victory so complete and absolute that we will rule the seas and oceans for perhaps a hundred years—

HARDY. Oh yes, it is a very pretty plan.

NELSON. (*Beside himself.*) Pretty? Pretty? By God, Hardy, if I had two arms I would throttle you for that.

HARDY. I only meant that it looks pretty on your dining-table, My Lord. I also meant that your dining-table was not the Atlantic ocean.

*Pause.*

NELSON. I've thought of everything, haven't I?

HARDY. Nearly everything.

NELSON. What have I left out?

HARDY. Yourself.

*Pause.* NELSON *laughs.*

NELSON. Do you think I can be caught by so foolish and obvious a trap? Collingwood is a great commander.

HARDY. Not great. Say good—

NELSON. Good enough to win the battle with this plan.

HARDY. If he uses it.

NELSON. Why should he not use it? When I last saw him he agreed to it in every detail—

HARDY. I've no doubt. But when, in a few weeks' time, he sees thirty or more French and Spanish sail, in line of battle, on his horizon—and it will be quite an awesome sight—five miles or more of broadsides facing him and his outnumbered fleet—which does your Lordship really believe he'll follow—your plan or the training of a lifetime?

*Pause.*

NELSON. My plan.

HARDY. May you be right. Myself I believe that no Admiral in the world would risk losing his entire fleet in a single afternoon by following a revolutionary plan of battle, never tried before, and conceived by a genius who has decided to be absent from the action.

NELSON *is silent, unable to answer. The figure of George can be seen stealthily descending the stairs and making for the front door. He is carrying a bag.* (*During this.*) Well—My Lord—have I your leave to go to bed? The thought of it is infinitely inviting.

NELSON. (*Sharply.*) Who is that in the hall?

HARDY *goes quickly out of the dining-room and confronts* GEORGE *who, startled, tries to go back up the stairs.* NELSON *has followed* HARDY *to the dining-room entrance.*

Is it young George?

HARDY. Yes, My Lord.

NELSON. Come in here, George. (*As* GEORGE *hesitates, commandingly.*) Come in here. (*To* HARDY.) Good-night, Captain Hardy.

HARDY. (*Bowing.*) Your Lordship.

*He goes up the stairs.* GEORGE *appears in the dining-room, reluctantly.*

NELSON. Where are you going at this hour? You're not due to leave until eight—and then with your father and mother.

GEORGE. Yes.

*Pause.*

NELSON. Where were you intending to walk to tonight?

GEORGE. London, I think.

NELSON. Nineteen miles, in the rain?

GEORGE. It's stopped raining.

NELSON. Give me that. (*He takes the bag.*) Sit down.

GEORGE *sits awkwardly.*

You're running away?

GEORGE *nods.*

From me and Lady Hamilton? Well, that I understand. But why from your father and mother?

GEORGE *doesn't answer.*

Did you think you were going to be beaten?

GEORGE. I wouldn't have minded.

NELSON. What is it then?

GEORGE. I want to leave this house, that's all.

NELSON. You are leaving this house, in three hours—with your parents.

GEORGE. I don't want them talking to me. They'll ask questions that I can't answer. Please, I don't want to talk to you either. May I go?

NELSON. No. (*He pours out a glass of wine.*) You look as if you'd been crying. Have you?

GEORGE. Not much.

NELSON. You'd better drink this.

GEORGE. I don't want it.

NELSON. It'll make you feel better.

GEORGE. Nothing will make me feel better. Nothing as long as I live.

NELSON. Drink it.

GEORGE *takes it obediently, sips a mouthful and hands it back hastily.*

You take things too hard. I called you some names, and said some things I didn't mean.

GEORGE. You didn't say anything bad.

NELSON. Well, whatever it was I said that upset you, you must forget it.

GEORGE. I'll try. May I go?

NELSON. George—what have I done?

GEORGE. Nothing.

NELSON. (*Pointing to the bag.*) You have that letter in there?

GEORGE. Yes.

NELSON. You're going to return it to her?

GEORGE. No, of course not. If I see her I'll just say I delivered it, as I promised, and that you read it.

NELSON. And called it vile?

GEORGE. No, never.

NELSON. Why are you keeping it?

GEORGE. To read again.

NELSON. Why?

GEORGE. I might understand.

NELSON. Might you? I don't think you will.

GEORGE. Nor do I.

NELSON. Will you promise never to show it to anyone else in the world?

GEORGE. What kind of person do you think I am?

*Pause.* NELSON *pours himself another brandy.*

NELSON. A very good, brave and most honourable boy. A nephew I am proud to have.

GEORGE *makes a sound.*

Don't laugh. Too many people laugh at me these days. Despise me, if you like, but don't laugh. What I just said was true.

*He finishes the brandy, and faces* GEORGE.

Very well, George. Here it is. Now you may begin your lesson in the understanding of adult emotions. (*Quietly and without the faintest effort of memory.*) 'The eighteenth of December eighteen hundred and one. My dearest husband, it is some time that I have written to you. The silence you have imposed is more than my affection will allow me—

GEORGE *stares at him with wide eyes.*

'and in this instance I hope you will forgive me for not obeying you. One thing I omitted in my letter of July which I now have to offer for your accommodation—a comfortable warm house.'

GEORGE, *understanding that* NELSON *has not only read the letter, but in fact knows it by heart, drops his head in misery.*

(*Continuing gently but remorselessly.*) 'Do, my dear husband, let us live together. I can never be happy until such an event takes place. I assure you again, I have but one wish in the world, to please you. Let everything be buried in oblivion, it will pass away like a dream.'

GEORGE *makes a gesture for him to stop.*

Hear it out. A few more tears tonight won't hurt. 'I can only entreat you to believe I am most sincerely and affectionately your wife, Frances H. Nelson.'

*He pours himself another brandy.*

You see that you and she need have had no fears that I didn't read it.

GEORGE. (*At length.*) And sent it back—with that message?

NELSON. (*Nodding.*) I, of all people in the world—

GEORGE. What did she do to you to make you do that? It must have been something really dreadful—

NELSON. It was.

GEORGE. What was it?

NELSON. She wrote me that letter.

*Pause.*

GEORGE. But it's a kind and loving letter.

NELSON. It's brutal.

GEORGE. It isn't—

NELSON. Many brutal acts are done out of love and kindness, George. Perhaps most. (*Seeing his blank face.*) Oh dear God, must I explain? Is this so important to you?

GEORGE. (*Simply.*) The most important thing on earth.

NELSON. It won't save my honour, which you seem so to cherish.

GEORGE. If it's true, it will.

NELSON. It's true.

*He sits beside him, and speaks very quietly.*

George, when one has done wrong to someone—an open wrong, a shameful and humiliating wrong, a wrong on an epic scale, to be forgiven for it is the very hell.

*He drinks.* GEORGE *stares at him in silence.*

I shock you, of course. You're my Reverend father's grandson and to answer forgiveness by hatred must seem unchristian at the least. But is it? Jesus told us how to answer a blow on the cheek, but he never told us how to answer a kiss. I haven't always been a bad Christian, George. I've even managed sometimes, to love my enemies a little. Not too much, mind you. Moderation in all things. But I do try to save them from drowning, even at risk to our ships, and no one can say I ever treated a prisoner-of-war other than with honour and gentleness. But George—

*He seems to find it hard to continue.* GEORGE'S *eyes are unwaveringly fixed on his, and they are the eyes of his own conscience.*

George—what about an enemy who won't retaliate? Who answers every broadside with a signal gently fluttering at the mast which says: 'Whatever you do to me, my dearest husband, I will always forgive you and go on loving you for ever.' What about that enemy, George? In this matter of loving enemies my dearest wife has beat me in the chase. What is there, then, left for me but to hate?

*He finishes his glass and goes back to the table, looking down on the pretended battle. There is a long pause.*

That ends your opening lesson in a long and difficult course. Human love and human hate. It's a perplexing study for anyone.

*He pours himself another brandy, watched, in silence by* GEORGE. MINTO, *in a dressing gown is descending the stairs.*

(*After drinking.*) For anyone in the world. And I never went to school. Not your kind of school. An eleven-year-old midshipman may learn many things if he is diligent—but not very much about life.

MINTO, *having heard voices, makes a discreet appearance at the door. He is plainly surprised to see* GEORGE, *but masks it with the ease of an accomplished ambassador.*

MINTO. I trust I don't interrupt?

NELSON. George and I were discussing certain metaphysical matters. I have been trying to unravel a puzzle for him. (*To* GEORGE.) Have you understood, even a little.

GEORGE. No.

NELSON. Well, you're in good company. (*He leads him to the hall.*) Go back to your room, now. (*Trying to be inaudible to* MINTO.) No more of this nonsense of running away. It's cowardly to run away, didn't you know that? (GEORGE *nods.*) Well, then, back to your bed.

*He pushes him towards the stairs and watches him as he mounts them.*

Good night, George.

GEORGE *continues on his way for a few steps before stopping.*

GEORGE. Good night—Uncle Horatio. (*He continues to go up.*) Thank you for the port.

NELSON *turns quickly and goes into the dining-room, where he finds* MINTO *sipping a glass of brandy.*

MINTO. (*Indicating the glass.*) Either a little too early or else a little too late. It is difficult to know. I grant it is not the first time in my life that I have been similarly confused. I have a message for you.

NELSON. I can guess it.

MINTO. I have no doubt. My Lord, but may I satisfy my conscience by delivering it. (*He finishes his brandy.*) Both too early and too late. Her Ladyship has just paid me the delightful compliment of rousing me from my sleep. It appears that she heard your and Hardy's voices on the stairs some moments ago. They awakened her, in fact.

NELSON. (*Wearily.*) And I am commanded to go to her at once.

MINTO. No, My Lord.

NELSON. No?

MINTO. My message is the reverse. Her Ladyship feels herself so mortified by the events of tonight that she has found herself in honour bound

(*Yawning*.) forgive me—to lock and bolt the doors of her bedroom and she wishes me categorically to affirm that no knock or entreaties, however loud and piteous, will induce her to open them before mid-day (*Yawning again*.)—oh dear—when she has ordered her carriage to take her on a round of visits to various gentlemen with whom she feels she will be a more welcome guest than under your Lordship's roof. Now I trust I have delivered her correctly. I was particularly to remember the part about the roof. So, if your Lordship will forgive me, I will return to my bed and pray to be allowed to sleep reasonably undisturbed by the ensuing commotions.

NELSON. You may sleep soundly. There will be no knocks or entreaties. As for the round of visits tomorrow—well mid-day is still many hours away, and, who knows, the various gentlemen may even yet be disappointed.

*He has accompanied* MINTO *into the hall.* MINTO *begins to mount the stairs, then notices that* NELSON *is moving back towards the dining-room.*

MINTO. Where will you sleep?

NELSON. Oh, I'll find somewhere. Who knows, Minto? It is always possible, don't you think, that those bolts may not hold?

*Emotion suddenly seems to overcome him. It is with difficulty that he manages a smile on these last words.*

They should, by now, have grown a trifle rusty.

*He puts his hand to his face and, turning his back on* MINTO, *goes back quickly into the dining-room, where he collapses into a chair, his whole body suddenly shaken with an access of dry, soundless sobs. On the stairs* MINTO *hesitates, seriously considering whether he should go to him or not. He decides, rightly, against, and disappears.*

*In the dining-room* NELSON *reaches a trembling hand for some brandy, pours it with difficulty and drinks it. We have been witnessing not only the pent-up emotional outburst of a deeply distressed man, but also one of those celebrated ague fits for which Betsy of Bath has hoped to provide the remedy. It is some time before he has recovered himself enough to rest his head on his hand outstretched on the table—no longer ague-ridden and sobbing, but utterly exhausted.*

*After a few moments* EMMA *appears at the head of the staircase. She is in a peignoir. She comes down the stairs with extreme timidity—at one moment even apparently considering a return to her room. Then she makes up her mind and walks to the dining-room entrance. She looks at* NELSON *for a moment then slides into the chair next to his, and rests her head on his shoulder.*

EMMA. Oh Nelson, forgive me!

NELSON *looks up. For a moment he seems so dazed as not to take in her presence.*

NELSON. (*At length*.) For what, my dearest?

EMMA. For whatever I did.

NELSON. What was it?

EMMA. I thought you'd tell me.

NELSON. I can't, Emma, I don't know.

EMMA. I expect you'll remember. And I'm sure it was something dreadful I did to you.

NELSON. You did nothing dreadful to me, my dearest. You never have and you never could. (*Feeling her hand.*) You're cold.

EMMA. Sleeping alone can freeze a lady—

NELSON. Well—that at least can be rectified.

*He gets up and stretches himself.* EMMA *puts her head on his breast again, lovingly and timidly.*

EMMA. I've been so scared.

NELSON. What of?

EMMA. That you'd left me.

NELSON. I'll never leave you, Emma. Not until death.

EMMA. Have you been drinking brandy?

NELSON. Rather a lot, it seems.

EMMA. Learning from me, eh?

NELSON. I haven't quite your own regal capacity for the stuff.

EMMA. (*Holding up the decanter.*) Well, you're not doing too badly for a beginner. Shall we have one now? Together.

NELSON. Why not?

EMMA *pours for both.*

EMMA. What shall we drink to?

NELSON. To Emma—and her Nelson. What else?

NELSON *looks down at the plan, and with a brusque gesture disarranges it suddenly from a neat pattern to chaos.*

EMMA. You've spoiled your pretty plan.

NELSON. Yes . . . Did you too think it pretty?

EMMA. Very pretty—and I'd have kept this table laid out just this way—to show to visitors exactly how Nelson won his battle off Cadiz.

NELSON. (*Gently.*) Exactly how Collingwood won Nelson's battle off Cadiz.

EMMA. I said how Nelson won it.

*Pause.*

NELSON. Emma—I have not asked you—

EMMA. No, but you were going to.

NELSON. No, my dearest, you are wrong. I would never, never, have asked.

EMMA. But you might have called me 'my Lady' a little more, and shown a greater fancy for going out alone in the rain as the time of Collingwood's battle approached? I love my Nelson—But I love all of him. I don't want him only half a man, with the better half pining to be out at sea.

NELSON. Has Hardy talked with you tonight?

EMMA. That b—that person? I wouldn't soil my lips.

NELSON. (*Embracing her.*) Oh Emma, my darling!

EMMA. It wasn't only that thought, Nelson. If you'd gone on trying to catch your death of cold hiding from me outside at night, I could have nursed you later—as I did in Naples—and meanwhile learnt solitaire. No, it wasn't only that—to be really truthful—

NELSON. You always are really truthful.

EMMA. Well, I can exaggerate a bit, like paying a round of visits to various gentlemen. (*They both laugh, holding hands.*) I wouldn't want to be thought of as a woman who kept you from going out when the country needed you. It is my country, too, you know.

NELSON. You, too, think I'm needed?

EMMA. There's only one Nelson in the world. But he's mine. Mine alone.

NELSON. Truly only yours.

EMMA. Mine to keep—and mine to give too. (*She is near tears.*) Only—one thing, my darling—this time take care. (*She can't go on.*)

NELSON. Yes, my heart.

EMMA. Don't leave your Emma alone and deserted.

NELSON. I won't.

EMMA. Swear it properly. Swear that this time you'll do all that lies in your power, not to get yourself killed.

NELSON. (*Gravely.*) I will do all that lies in my power not to leave my Emma alone and deserted, and that I do most solemnly swear to, before God.

EMMA. Well, you're good with vows, and you do your best to keep them. You'd have kept the one about not going out, you say?

NELSON. (*Kissing her hand.*) Yes, I do. Oh my Emma, I love you so deeply.

EMMA. (*Getting up.*) No, Nelson. That won't do at all. I want something more memorable. Something I can quote to my friends. I've thought of something—

NELSON. I would expect that you might have.

EMMA. I wrote it down in my journal in bed.

*As* NELSON *looks at her.*

Oh yes. You didn't need to risk any agues in a wet garden. I'd have told you this last night in bed—but I wanted you to know I was giving you—not having you filched from me by an underhand, contriving prick of a Flag-Captain. Now let me remember. I know. 'Dear Emma, brave Emma. If there were more Emmas in the world there'd be more Nelson's.' How do you like that?

NELSON. (*Staring at her.*) I like it very much. I like it because it's absolutely true.

EMMA. Not really. Nelson's are born, not made.

NELSON. They can sometimes be reborn.

*He begins to arrange the table again.*

My pretty battle. Well, we shall see.

EMMA. (*Watching him.*) Just tell me one thing, love. It will be another victory, won't it?

NELSON. I think so.

EMMA. A big one?

NELSON. Yes. Very big.

EMMA. It needs to be.

NELSON. (*Eagerly.*) Yes, it does. The strategic situation—

EMMA. (*Laughing.*) Do you think I talk strategies? It has to be big, my darling, because, since the crowds in the streets have taken to laughing at
us—

NELSON. Laughing?

EMMA. You heard them in Clarges Street.

NELSON. I heard nothing but cheers.

EMMA. (*Holding his arm.*) You heard laughter and you knew who it was they
laughed at. Well, I am grown a little laughable I suppose, these days. I
should fast a little, take off weight. And drink less, of course.

*Absent-mindedly, she takes a gulp of brandy.* NELSON *smiles affectionately. She
takes his hand.*

Oh my darling, to afford an Emma Hamilton, you need a very big victory indeed. Then you'll find they won't laugh any more. It'll be 'huzza,
brave Nelson!' again and, perhaps even, 'huzza, brave Emma!' too. A
likely thought! (*Picking up two sauce-boats.*) What are these?

NELSON. The lead ships of our two attacking lines—

EMMA. One of them now the Victory, I suppose?

NELSON. Well, it may be. The other certainly the Royal Sovereign. They'll
need to be heavy ships, you see, to lead the two prongs of our attack.

EMMA. (*Scornfully.*) I know you think I'm half-witted on naval matters and
don't attend at all when you talk about them—(*Accusingly.*) but, how
often, at this table, have I heard you say to those sailors that these two
ships (*She flourishes the sauce-boats.*) will have to bear so heavy a weight
of cannon that they might well be sunk before they can even fire back a
shot.

NELSON. They'll not be sunk, Emma.

EMMA. But all those broadsides at them, from their biggest ships! (*Angrily.*)
Why haven't they designed a warship that can fire forwards, instead of
always these eternal broadsides?

NELSON. (*Busy on the table.*) One day they may.

EMMA. But they haven't yet, and for an hour or more in this position, you'll
be pacing your quarter-deck, fired at by most of the enemy fleet. (*She
indicates.*) and being head on, with not a chance of firing as much as a
single shot in return.

NELSON. Half an hour. Less even than that, with a stiff breeze.

EMMA. Why do you have to be in the Victory?

NELSON. (*Smoothly.*) But I don't have to be in the Victory. I recommended
to Collingwood to fly his flag in a frigate somewhere to the rear—the
better to control the action.

EMMA. Oh yes! I can just see you flying your flag in a frigate—somewhere to
the rear!

NELSON. There's no shame in that.

EMMA. (*Near tears again.*) No shame to Collingwood, perhaps. But your flag? Oh Nelson, how you lie to me sometimes!

NELSON. (*Piously, while rearranging his battle.*) Heaven forbid, dearest Emma!

EMMA. Nelson, do you remember what you have just vowed to me?

NELSON. Very clearly.

EMMA. Then vow another one. Vow about this.

*She picks up a sauce-boat, and puts it carefully to the rear.*

NELSON. My dear, you have put poor Victory on direct collision course with H.M.S. Agamemnon, H.M.S. Ajax and H.M.S. Orion. (*He picks up the sauce-boat and holds it.*) I think, dearest Emma, you should allow me to make my own dispositions. They may not be perfect, but at least they may avoid sinking four of my own battleships before contact with the enemy.

EMMA. Well at least swear one thing—

NELSON. Two vows in one morning, is a little too much for the Almighty, don't you think? Especially when the one will so absolutely cover the other.

EMMA. Will it?

NELSON. You know it must.

EMMA. (*Embracing him.*) Then leave your battle for tonight. Let's go up. Time's short.

NELSON. Most, most gladly.

EMMA. Now do you remember your little speech? She goes to the entrance.

NELSON. My speech?

*He replaces the sauce-boat exactly where it was.* EMMA *has reached the stairs.*

EMMA. The one I wrote in my journal.

NELSON. Oh yes.

*He goes. She is waiting for him.*

Now, let me see. Brave, dear Emma. If there were more women in the world like you—

*He joins her at the stairs.*

EMMA. No, no, no! It's 'dear Emma, brave Emma—if there were more Emmas in the world there'd be more Nelson's.'

NELSON. Oh yes. Dear Emma, brave Emma, if there were more brave Emmas—

*They begin to walk up the stairs.*

EMMA. If there were more Emmas. Try again.

NELSON. Dear Emma, brave Emma. If there were more Emmas—oh dear, I forget what would happen—

EMMA. (*Kissing him.*) There'd be more Nelsons.

*The lights fade and we hear the distant boom of cannon. The hazy murmurs of a melancholy sea shanty comes to our ears as though muffed by the sound of billowing sails in a wind.*

*The lights come up on Nelson's cabin in the Victory. Two* SEAMEN *are carrying in a sea-chest, a small table and a chair. On the table is a document and writing material. The distant gunfire continues through the scene. After a moment* NELSON *walks into his cabin wearing a plain jacket without stars. He nods dismissal to the* SEAMEN, *who go.* NELSON, *left alone, falls to his knees.*

NELSON. May the great God, whom I worship, grant to my country—

HARDY *comes in with* BLACKWOOD, *followed by* HARDY'S ORDERLY (*a midshipman*). NELSON *smiles at them and motions them to be quiet for a moment. They bow their heads.*

—and for the benefit of Europe in general, a great and glorious victory; and may no misconduct in anyone tarnish it; and may humanity after victory be the predominant feature in the British fleet. For myself, individually, I commit my life to Him who made me, and may His blessing light upon my endeavours for serving my country faithfully. To Him I resign myself and the just cause which is entrusted to me to defend. Amen, amen, amen.

*He remains for a few seconds on his knees and then rises alertly. His manner from this point on is quiet, resigned and happy.*

Hardy, Blackwood? It seems that the enemy are being rather wasteful of their shot. Are they falling short?

HARDY. By a cable or so . . . But one went over us.

NELSON. Yes, it will be hotter soon. (*Glancing at his watch.*) It must be some forty minutes at least before we can answer their fire at all. Lady Hamilton has suggested that we design a battle-ship that can fire forwards, I think it rather a good idea, don't you?

HARDY. A ship designed to fire its broadsides forwards might be a shade unseaworthy, my lord. Something like a maritime balloon.

NELSON. No, no. A swivelling turret crammed with cannon could do it. Let's hope our new tactics here will inspire our naval inventors. However, in the absence of swivelling gun turrets, I admit I could have done with a fresher breeze. How goes the Royal Sovereign?

HARDY. Most bravely, my Lord? She'll be in action before us.

NELSON. (*Genially.*) Damn Collingwood with his new copper! And damn poor Victory with her barnacles of two years! Blackwood, you should be getting aboard.

BLACKWOOD. I have waited, my Lord, under s-strict orders.

NELSON. Whose orders?

BLACKWOOD. Y-yours, my Lord. You said l-last night at our general m-meeting that you might be flying your flag in my frigate.

NELSON. I said such a thing?

BLACKWOOD. Well—the other Admirals s-said it but I understood that your L-L-Lordship agreed. After all it was your written r-recommendation that the Commander-in-Chief—

NELSON. Fiddle.

BLACKWOOD. I beg pardon, my Lord?

NELSON. I said 'fiddle'. A frigate was for Collingwood. Go on board yours and carry her well.

BLACKWOOD. Ay, ay, my Lord.

HARDY. (*Detaining* BLACKWOOD.) My Lord, will you please reconsider? The Victory will have the weight of four enemy battleships against her, alone and unsupported.

NELSON. Do you make it four? I make it five.

*Pause.*

HARDY. Will you at least give orders that the Temeraire pass us? She is close on our heels.

NELSON *says nothing.* HARDY *accepts his silence as consent.*

(*To his* MIDSHIPMAN.) Tell the Signals Officer to hail Captain Harvey and order him to sail his ship to lead the line.

MIDSHIPMAN. Ay, ay, sir.

*The* MIDSHIPMAN *goes off.*

NELSON. (*Not listening.*) Yes, yes. Very wise. But first, as you and Blackwood are both conveniently here, will you attest my signature? See, I have signed.

*They bend over the document,* HARDY *taking the pen first.*

It is not necessary for you to read it, but in case we get burnt or sunk, I should tell you the gist, I think. This document most clearly and absolutely leaves Lady Hamilton—well it's too complicated, perhaps to tell. I'll read the last paragraph. (*Reading quickly.*) 'I leave Emma, Lady Hamilton, therefore a Legacy to my King and Country, that they will give her an ample provision to maintain her rank in life.' Will you sign there? I think that will make it all legal.

HARDY *signs.* BLACKWOOD *follows him. The* MIDSHIPMAN *comes back.*

MIDSHIPMAN. Your orders carried out, sir.

NELSON *walks to the extreme limit of the stage and peers as through an imaginary porthole.*

NELSON. What's the damned blackguard Harvey doing with his Temeraire, Hardy? By God—he's trying to pass us, I swear. Hail him at once to keep his proper station.

HARDY. (*Patiently.*) What is his proper station, my Lord?

NELSON. Behind the Victory, of course. Where else?

HARDY. But at your last orders I have had him hailed to the exact contrary.

NELSON. Fiddle.

*Pause.*

HARDY. Yes, my Lord. (*With a sigh, to* MIDSHIPMAN.) Countermand my last order.

MIDSHIPMAN. Ay, ay, Captain. (*He goes out.*)

NELSON. Oh Hardy—did you see that signal I made to amuse the fleet?

HARDY. I did, my Lord.

NELSON. 'England confides this day'

HARDY. There was no signal for 'confides', so the signals officer altered it to 'expects' . . .

NELSON. 'England expects'? It doesn't sound half as good. You've been below—did the fellows hear of it? Did it amuse them?

HARDY. Not much, my Lord. The only comment I heard was an enquiry whether the Admiral had gone off his head. They all know what's to be done, they said, and don't need any signal from you to tell them. Still, as it was from you, they did give it a cheer.

NELSON. A loud cheer?

HARDY. Almost inaudible. But they yelled their heads off at your Lordship's next signal—the one for close action.

NELSON *laughs*.

NELSON. Oh well—I love them all—each and every damned rascal. (*To* BLACKWOOD.) On board, Blackwood!

BLACKWOOD. Ay, ay, my Lord. (*Extending his hand.*) May I wish your Lordship the most complete and crushing victory ever won?

NELSON. Well, if it could be that it would be no more than I have planned. But God will decide all. Goodbye, Blackwood.

BLACKWOOD. And—after the battle—may it be the Eu-Eu-Euryalus that brings the news to London?

NELSON. (*Absently.*) Yes. Hardy, please remember to tell Collingwood that is my wish.

HARDY. It will be you who will give the order, my Lord.

NELSON. Of course. I meant—in case I forget.

BLACKWOOD *goes.* HARDY *looks at the plain uniform.*

HARDY. I'm very glad you have taken my advice about the, plain tunic. To wear the one with all your stars up on the quarter-deck would be simple suicide.

NELSON. Oh, of course.

HARDY. With those sharp-shooters up in their mizzen-masts, if you had been strutting about your quarter-deck with your breast blazing like the sun—

NELSON. I don't strut, Hardy.

HARDY. No, my Lord.

NELSON. (*At the imaginary porthole.*) That damned Temeraire is gaining still. I'll have Harvey court-martialled—see if I don't. Go up and hail him yourself.

HARDY. (*With a sigh.*) Ay, ay, my Lord.

*There is a moment's silence then the men, as if by mutual instinct, embrace awkwardly.*

NELSON. Despite all things, I have not—have I—been too great a sinner?

HARDY. No. my Lord.

NELSON. (*Patting him on the back.*) Well, well. At least they'll not say of me that I haven't clone my duty. And for that, I suppose, I should thank my Maker.

HARDY. You should, I believe, my Lord.

*The sound of gunfire increases, as* HARDY *leaves the cabin. Left alone,* NELSON *goes to the chest and pulls out from it his, familiar bestarred uniform. He clambers into it with some difficulty. Then he polishes the stars with his sleeve, smiling a little. That done, he puts on his cocked hat at a carefully jaunty angle and strolls out of the cabin, up towards the quarter-deck.*

*The lights in the cabin fade quickly, but remain on the Turneresque backcloth whale the gunfire grows even louder. Then, through the gunfire we hear the single tolling of a church bell. The lights on the backcloth fade quickly and the gunfire rumbles into silence. There is the sound of church music.*

SCENE IV

*The bell tolls more loudly. When the lights go on we are in Merton.*

LADY NELSON, *in deep mourning, is standing very still in the sitting-room. The furniture is covered with dust sheets.* FRANCESCA, *in deep distress, comes down the stairs.*

FRANCESCA. Lady Hamilton, vi vuole vedere, eccelenza, ma forse sarebbe.

*As* FRANCES *appears not to understand.*

Lady Hamilton . . . not good . . . is better . . . later.

FRANCES. Well, perhaps if I could leave her a note?

FRANCESCA. Si, si, eccelenza. I fetch paper.

EMMA *can be seen walking, none too steadily, towards the hall area. She is in a nightdress, and is trying unsuccessfully to put on the purple mantle she wore as Andromache.*

EMMA. (*Off.*) Francesca! Francesca! Dove stai, idiota?

FRANCESCA *flies up the stairs to mask* FRANCES *from her.*

FRANCESCA. Se n'è andata-se n' è andatornate a letto.

EMMA. L'ho vista, bugiarda. Her carriage is still outside.

*She pushes* FRANCESCA *out of the way, and goes into the sitting-room where* FRANCES *has risen to greet her. The bell tolls.*

Lady Nelson. (*She curtsies clumsily.*)

FRANCES. Lady Hamilton. (*She returns the curtsey with dignity.*)

EMMA. (*To* FRANCESCA.) Aiutami.

*She indicates the mantle.* FRANCESCA, *near tears, drapes it round her. The bell tolls again.*

(*Meanwhile to* FRANCES.) I've been through my whole wardrobe and found nothing else of mourning. I never could abide black, you see—and I've not been out of my bed for a long, long time. (*To* FRANCESCA.) Stop fumbling. I'll fasten it. Leave us.

FRANCESCA *goes.*

This is a costume I have sometimes worn for one of my little entertainments. Purple is mourning, isn't it? It must be. Anyway it was for Andromache. That was the character I personated in this mantle—the last time I did so was here, in this very room, one night, before—your husband.

*It has been an effort for her to use that phrase. The bell tolls.*

Your visit, Lady Nelson, does me great honour. To what do I attrib-attribute it?

FRANCES. I would never, rest assured, have intruded on your Ladyship's grief without the most urgent of reasons.

EMMA. I do rest assured you would not.

FRANCES. I have news of the greatest importance for yourself, and I judged it best that I should be the one to give it you, rather than that you read it in the newspapers tomorrow.

*The bell tolls again.*

EMMA. I don't read the newspapers any more. (*Looking around.*) I'm sorry you should see the house like this. It was a pretty house—and this room really the prettiest of all. The truth is, my staff has left me—all save Francesca. It was a matter of their wages being overdue. But Your Ladyship would hardly understand such things.

FRANCES. Please, Lady Hamilton, will you hear my news?

EMMA. Your news? Yes, in a moment—a moment. (*She looks around.*) There should be some refreshment for your Ladyship.

FRANCES. Please. I don't need any refreshment.

EMMA. Well, this Ladyship does. Excuse me.

*She takes up a bottle of brandy from the only table not covered and slops some into a tankard.*

A shortage of glassware. There are some glasses in the dining-room, but it's too far to walk. Your Ladyship should see the dining-room before you leave. It is left exactly as he arranged it one night with the glasses and the silverware to show the two fleets as they were to come into action—and as they did come into action—almost exactly so, from all accounts—off Cape Trafalgar. Of course some of the silver has had to go, but there must be enough left still to make the picture. Very pretty it looked, when last I saw it.

*She drinks again. The bell tolls.*

(*Suddenly screaming.*) Oh why don't they stop that bell? We all know Nelson's dead! Wasn't it a victory? The biggest (*Her voice breaks.*) yet—as he vowed it would be. Forgive me, your Ladyship, if I sit down. My legs are rather weak from staying in bed. And, of course, from brandy too. There's no denying the brandy to Your Ladyship.

FRANCES. I should not have come. I see that now.

EMMA. Why not? You've come to gloat, haven't you?

FRANCES. No, no. That's not true. Simply not true. But how can any of us know the real reasons for doing what we sincerely believe to be right?

EMMA. If I'd been in your shoes, I'd have come down here to gloat.

FRANCES. No. I am sure you would not, Lady Hamilton.

EMMA. Oh yes I would. I'd have gloated all right—because that's the kind of woman I am.

FRANCES. I don't believe it. I have heard much about you, as you must appreciate. I have learnt much about you too as you, in my position, would also, surely have done. (EMMA *nods*.) But there is nothing that I have learnt of you that has ever indicated anything but a most wide and generous nature.

*Pause.* EMMA *laughs.*

EMMA. Oh God, how easy are words! Wide and generous. A whore—that's all. A whore who stole your husband.

FRANCES. My husband left my bed for yours. He was bound to have left it, one day, for somebody's. I have understood that—for a long time now. Why need we quarrel because the bed happened to be yours?

EMMA. We quarrel because you were my enemy. My remorseless, implacable enemy. You hated me, didn't you?

FRANCES. (*Quietly.*) Yes, I did. Just as you must have hated me.

EMMA. But I had reason. He was mine. I had him. He was all mine. Mine—absolutely. But you were still there, in the shadows, waiting. Always waiting. Can you deny it?

FRANCES. No.

EMMA. Sitting there waiting—knitting, darning, waiting—Penelope waiting for her Ulysses to come home.

FRANCES. Yes, I waited for my Ulysses. Oh yes. But my Ulysses did not come home. And my waiting for him, Lady Hamilton, all those years, was not in the least an Attitude. Forgive me, please. That was unkind.

EMMA. Well he's returning to you all right. He's in a cask of brandy in the Bay of Biscay now, and he's returning to you, Lady, Viscountess—what are you now—? Countess Nelson. Not returning to me, whom he loved—absolutely. Delivered in a barrel of alcohol. Is that all you were waiting for?

FRANCES. No.

EMMA. (*Laughing.*) You were waiting for him—alive?

FRANCES. Yes, I was. It was foolish, I know, but I confess it now. I was waiting for him to return to me, alive.

EMMA. You. Tom Tit?

FRANCES. I was waiting for his old age. That at least, would have been mine.

*Pause.*

EMMA. (*Raising her glass.*) Oh well. Here's to his old age, then! (*She drinks.*) My doctor says this is going to kill me, you know—and that it mayn't take too long. Well, it had better not. I'm not too happy at the thought of spending the rest of my days on earth in a debtor's prison, which is what I'll be threatened with before long.

FRANCES. There'll be no debtor's prison for you, Lady Hamilton. That is part of what I have come to tell you—

EMMA. You mean—

FRANCES. A document has arrived with other papers. It is signed by Lord Nelson, and duly attested by Captain Blackwood and Commodore Hardy—

EMMA. Oh, Hardy's made Commodore, is he?

FRANCES. Yes.

EMMA. And I called him a bugger. Well, I suppose there's promotion and medals for all. So—what does the will say?

FRANCES. It is the very last known document of my—of Lord Nelson's—life, and it leaves you, Emma, Lady Hamilton, as a Legacy to the Nation.

*There is along pause. The bell tolls.*

*Then* EMMA *throws her head back and literally shouts with laughter.*

EMMA. A Legacy to the Nation? Me? Oh God in Heaven! I think I'll die of this.

*She continues to laugh in high hysterics watched with deep concern by* FRANCES.

Left to the Nation? Me, on a plinth in Westminster Hall, naked like when old Sir Willum was alive, with all those Peers and Commoners up to old Sir Willum's tricks. Or sitting between the King and Queen at Windsor on a throne with a plaque on it saying, left to King and country by Viscount Nelson, here sits Emma Hamilton, the late hero's whore—Oh, my poor, poor Nelson! What a baby he was? But of course—that was his vow that night. Not deserted and not alone. How could I be deserted and alone if I'm left to the Nation? Oh my poor, dear baby! It would take him to think of that—

*The bell tolls.*

FRANCES. Everything possible will be done to see that my Lord's last wishes are met. The Earl himself has agreed—

EMMA. The Earl? What Earl?

FRANCES. Earl Nelson—William Nelson that was, my husband's brother.

EMMA. So he's an Earl now, is he? The arse-licking Dean, who never said a prayer in his life, except perhaps to wish his brother dead in battle and himself made Earl. And what have the rest of that grubby crew of Nelson's got? William's son—he'll be something—

FRANCES. The Viscount Trafalgar.

EMMA. The Viscount Trafalgar? That little snotty-nosed brat? Oh God what a world!

*The bell tolls.*

And I suppose they're all back your way now? I know they've all left me. And Minto? Do you see Minto?

FRANCES *nods*.

Yes. The first to rat, I warrant. Well, quite a triumph for you, isn't it?

FRANCES. If it is, you must not suppose for a single second that it is one I relish.

EMMA. I can't think why you don't.

FRANCES. Because I am not the kind of woman who would. Why else am I here? You don't understand me, Lady Hamilton.

*Pause.*

EMMA. No. I never did. I never understood you at all, I suppose.

*The bell tolls.*

EMMA *comes close to* FRANCES *and stares at her*.

I wonder what it's like to be good.

FRANCES. Trying to be is not always very easy.

EMMA. Did you ever understand me?

FRANCES. No.

EMMA. It's a funny world, isn't it?

FRANCES. I think you should go back to bed, and I'll say goodbye. Shall I call your maid?

EMMA. I'll call her. (*Yelling.*) Francesca! Vieni qui pronto!

FRANCESCA *appears*.

Francesca, accompagna la signora contessa alla sua corrozza.

FRANCES. Look after your mistress. I can find my own way out. (*To* EMMA.) You must believe me, Lady Hamilton, when I say that I myself intend to use any influence that I might have to see that my Lord's last wishes are fully met, and that your debts at least are paid for by Parliament.

EMMA. I believe you. (*She takes a drink.*) But of course you won't succeed. Parliament? (*Laughing.*) They won't even put it to the vote. (*Looking at her mantle.*) Oh withered is the garland of war. Young boys and girls— I can't remember, what young boys and girls did. The usual, I suppose. (*To* FRANCES.) I'm sorry. I put some of Cleopatra in that night. Quite a lot just to annoy Hardy. It didn't of course, because he's too ignorant to know his Shakespeare. Now I've forgot it too. I can only remember— the odds is gone, and there is nothing left remarkable beneath the visiting moon.

FRANCES. Please don't lose hope. I will do all that I can, I promise.

EMMA. You don't need to promise. (*Conversationally.*) I wonder, Lady Nelson, just as a matter of idle interest, which one of us will be better remembered in a hundred years as Nelson's woman. You, I suppose. I'll just be a figure of fun! Well, here's to the figure of fun! (*She takes another swig. The bell tolls. Screaming.*) Oh, why don't they stop that bell!

FRANCES. I'm leaving you now. Francesca, please do look after her. Please! *With her curious hobbling walk, she goes out of the room, but pauses to look back as* FRANCESCA *speaks*.

FRANCESCA. (*Holding Emma.*) E mo, eccelenza, per l'amore di Dio, tornate a letto.

EMMA. No.

*She throws* FRANCESCA *off her and staggers to the harpsichord. She uncovers the keyboard with difficulty and sits down at the stool. Then, with the left finger, she plays the first few bars of the verse of 'Rule Britannia' and looks up expectantly as if waiting for an answer.*

*The bell tolls.*

EMMA'S *head, whether through drink, or despair, crashes on the keyboard, emitting a jangled discord, and the bottle of brandy held in her right hand spills slowly on to the floor.* FRANCESCA *flies to her side.*

FRANCES. (*From the hall, with genuine pity.*) Poor Lady Hamilton!

*She hobbles her birdlike way into darkness.*

CURTAIN

# IN PRAISE OF LOVE

*with a curtain-raiser*
## BEFORE DAWN

First published 1973
by Hamish Hamilton Ltd

FOR
**BINKIE,**
**and JOHN**

*In Praise of Love* was first produced at the Duchess Theatre, London, on September 27th, 1973, with the following cast:

LYDIA CRUTTWELL        Joan Greenwood
SEBASTIAN CRUTTWELL     Donald Sinden
MARK WALTERS        Don Fellows
JOEY CRUTTWELL       Richard Warwick


The cast for *Before Dawn* was

THE BARON         Donald Sinden
THE LACKEY         Don Fellows
THE CAPTAIN        Richard Warwick
THE DIVA         Joan Greenwood


Directed by JOHN DEXTER

Designer: DESMOND HEALEY

## AUTHOR'S NOTE

The plays are published in the order in which they were written, and in the order in which I had intended them to be performed. I was then thinking of *The Browning Version* and *Harlequinade* (*Playbill, 1948*), in which the insubstantial play successfully followed the substantial and an audience, moved by the first, seemed to be reasonably diverted by the second.

During previews of *In Praise of Love* (first intended as a collective title to parallel *Playbill* and *Separate Tables*) we experimented with the order of running, and it was proved to the entire satisfaction of the director, John Dexter, and myself that the insubstantial should, on this particular theatrical occasion, precede the substantial. We both of us liked to think that the impact of the substantial on the audience was even stronger than that of *The Browning Version*. It is certain that they seemed in no mood for any subsequent frivolity, as with *Playbill* they had.

As a result the plays are now being performed in the reverse order, with *Before Dawn* serving purely as a truncated curtain-raiser to the play that was always intended to be the main part of the evening's entertainment and which is now, to avoid confusing our audiences, being performed under the original collective title: *In Praise o f Love.*

*October 1973*                                                      T. R.

IN PRAISE OF LOVE


*Characters*

LYDIA CRUTTWELL
SEBASTIAN CRUTTWELL
MARK WALTERS
JOEY CRUTTWELL


*Setting:* North London
*Time:* The present

# ACT I

*The Cruttwells' flat in Islington. We see a small hall, large living-room and part of a kitchen when the sliding doors are opened. A staircase—probably put in during conversion—runs from the living-room: first, up a few steps, to the kitchen (where the Cruttwells also eat), then turns sharply to lead to the rooms above. No window is needed, nor fireplace. The predominant feature of the room is books, for some of which there is no space but the floor, the book-cases having been stretched to their limit. There is a book-case even in the diminutive hall, and on top of that, looking incongruous, a man's white hat-box which once plainly contained a top hat, and may still. Other prominent objects are a small table on which some ordinary black and white chessmen are set out, plainly for use and not for decoration, a table bearing a tray of drinks, a sofa and various armchairs. The front door and hall are at the back and a door R. leads to* SEBASTIAN's *work-room. From this is coming the sound of a typewriter being very intermittently used, with long pauses between short bouts, usually followed by unmistakable sounds of angry erasure. It is about six o'clock of a spring evening. The time is the present.*

*LYDIA lets herself in with a latch-key. A woman of about 50, very simply dressed, she shows signs of both physical and mental distress. The physical distress takes the form of utter exhaustion. She sits on a chair in the hall before she can find the strength to move into the sitting-room, where she promptly sits again. She has no parcels to carry, and although the flat is two flights up from the street (as we will later learn) the long deep breaths she is taking do not give any impression of someone who has hurried the stairs. Rather the reverse. Her mental stress is shown by the slow unblinking stare which encompasses almost every object in the room, however trivial, and by her expression as, her inspection of the room completed, she stares blankly in front of her while she regains her breath.*

*SEBASTIAN comes out from his work-room, a cigarette between his lips, an empty glass in his hand, and spectacles over his nose.*

SEBASTIAN. Oh good, darling, you're back. The heating has gone wrong.

LYDIA. Has it? It seems all right in here.

*She gets briskly to her feet and feels an ancient radiator.*

Yes, it's on.

SEBASTIAN. (*At the book-case.*) It's icy in my room.

LYDIA *goes through the open door of the work-room.* SEBASTIAN, *left alone, pulls down a book and begins to search for some reference. Vainly. He puts that one on a pile near him and picks another. Same process.* LYDIA *comes out and quietly takes his glass from his hand.*

Oh thank you so much, darling—

*She fills up his glass, a procedure she can carry out in her sleep.*

LYDIA. You hadn't turned it on.

SEBASTIAN. What on?

LYDIA. The heat.

SEBASTIAN. (*Deep in a book.*) Really?

*He says it as if it were a matter of the most breathless interest, a sure sign with him that he hasn't heard a word.*

LYDIA *comes back with his glass.*

Oh thank you, darling. What kept you out so long? Oh, of course, old Doctor Scheister. What did he say?

LYDIA. Schuster. He's very pleased indeed.

SEBASTIAN. What did I tell you? And you got held up by the bus-strike?

LYDIA. Not really. I found a new way on the Tube.

SEBASTIAN. (*Worried.*) Should you have?

LYDIA. Oh, it was quite easy

SEBASTIAN. I meant isn't it a bit like strike-breaking?

LYDIA. Your social conscience would have preferred I walked?

SEBASTIAN. It's not all that far, is it?

LYDIA. About as far as Fleet Street—to which I notice you've had a hire-car the last three days.

SEBASTIAN. A hire-car is different.

LYDIA. Why?

SEBASTIAN. I charge it to the paper, so it's on their conscience not mine. Good. I've got what I'm looking for—which is a wonder. Darling, our books have got in the most terrible mess again.

*He pulls a book out.*

Norman Mailer in the poetry section. Why?

*Seeing something.*

And—I can't believe it—Tarzan of the Apes. How did that get there?

LYDIA. You must have reviewed it, some time.

SEBASTIAN. Don't make tasteless jokes . . . Oh yes. I remember. There was a book on Rousseau called *The Noble Savage,* and I had to research.

*Throwing her the book.*

Well that's for your favourite charity . . . What is it? . . . 'The little Sisters of the Poor', or do you think it might give those nuns ideas?

LYDIA. Hardly give them. Remind them possibly.

SEBASTIAN. (*Pointing to the shelf.*) Darling, it's an awful muddle. Couldn't Mrs. Mackintyre—?

LYDIA. Mrs. Reedy. It hasn't been Mrs. MacKintyre for three months.

SEBASTIAN. I call her Mrs. MacKintyre.

LYDIA. She's noticed that.

SEBASTIAN *pulls out another book, clicking his teeth.* LYDIA *takes it.*

SEBASTIAN. Well couldn't *she*—?

LYDIA. No. She isn't, oddly enough, a trained librarian. She isn't a trained anything, come to that. She comes three times a week for two hours a day, never stops eating and costs a bomb.

SEBASTIAN. Is she worth having then?

LYDIA. Yes.

SEBASTIAN. I mean if she costs a bomb—

LYDIA. (*Loudly.*) She's worth having.

SEBASTIAN. A little tetchy this afternoon, are we?

*He reaches up and grabs another book.*

*Plain Talk About Sex*—next to Peter Pan.

LYDIA. (*Taking it.*) That's mine.

SEBASTIAN. For God's sake, why?

LYDIA. I bought it for a train, sometime.

SEBASTIAN. (*Taking off his spectacles.*) That doesn't answer my question. Darling, I mean, with your early life—

LYDIA. Perhaps it needed a bit of brushing up.

*Pause.*

SEBASTIAN. (*Blowing on his glasses, carefully.*) A criticism?

LYDIA. No. A comment. Where shall I put these books?

SEBASTIAN. In their proper sections. Where I suggest you might have put the Others. You might go through them when you have a little time.

LYDIA. When I have a little time, it will be high on my list.

SEBASTIAN. You're in a stinking mood this evening, aren't you?

LYDIA. Am I?

SEBASTIAN. Was it what I said about your early misadventures?

LYDIA. (*Smiling.*) No, stupid. You of all people have the right to talk about that. I mean thirty years after—nearly thirty—St. George must have occasionally reminded his damsel of the dragon he rescued her from.

SEBASTIAN. (*Embarrassed.*) St. George! Really! Anyway St. George didn't have several ding-dongs with his damsel before he rescued her—

LYDIA. How do you know he didn't?

SEBASTIAN. Well, he wouldn't have been a saint, would he?

LYDIA. I think it was about what you said about 'criticism'. As if I would—

SEBASTIAN. But you said 'comment'.

LYDIA. There can be good comment as well as bad, can't there?

SEBASTIAN. In theory, yes. In fact, no. Remember, darling, that you're speaking to a critic. You meant something a bit harsh by 'comment'. Oh yes. I know. Now, darling you must realise—

LYDIA. You can't be expected to poke an old skeleton. I know.

SEBASTIAN. Darling, really! That wasn't very—tasteful, was it?

LYDIA. It was your taste. You said it.

SEBASTIAN. Then you shouldn't have remembered it. Not the actual *words.*

*Looking at her.*

Did I say skeleton?

LYDIA. Yes, I know. I've put on four pounds in the last four weeks. That's not an invitation just a fact.

SEBASTIAN. (*In 'breathless interest' again.*) Have you? Have you really? Put on four pounds? Well, that's splendid—absolutely splendid. I mean, it's marvellous news, isn't it. Marvellous.

*He is looking at his book.*

LYDIA. You hadn't actually noticed?

SEBASTIAN. (*Looking up from his book.*) Of course I'd noticed. I mean these last few months I've been watching you like a hawk.

*Returning to his book.*

And I am not so ignorant as not to know that putting on weight is a good sign. Conclusive, in a way—

LYDIA. Well, here's something even more conclusive. I was told by Uncle Constantin to show you this.

*She takes a paper from her bag.*

It's the result of my last tests.

SEBASTIAN. Oh? When were they taken?

LYDIA. Two weeks ago. That's about average for these days.

SEBASTIAN. Yes, because under the Tories the Health Service personnel were grossly underpaid and even more grossly overworked, so it is hardly unnatural that—

LYDIA. But we're under the other side now.

SEBASTIAN. I am aware of which side we are under, Madam, but, as you know, in my view there is nothing whatever to choose between either of them.

*Flourishing the paper.*

In a properly organised state-run Health Service—

LYDIA. You'd get the results through by special rocket from the Kremlin, I know. Darling, do read that. It makes nice reading—really it does—

SEBASTIAN. Well, it'll be Greek to me—except that I can read Greek.

LYDIA. (*Pointing, over his shoulder.*) That's my wee-wee test—

SEBASTIAN. Darling, please let's be adult about this. This is your urine test—and this is your faeces test which no doubt you were going you name your 'Ka-Ka' test—

LYDIA. I was. And the others are kidney, liver, heart, etcetera.

*Pointing*

Don't read the figures, just the words

SEBASTIAN. (*Reading.*) Normal, normal, normal, near-normal, normal, normal . . . Sounds like a very dull party—

LYDIA. (*Eagerly.*) And there—under General Remarks—

SEBASTIAN. (*Reading.*) 'Patient's encouraging progress fully maintained. If the results of the biopsy confirm these tests, as early reports suggest, then further monthly tests may be discontinued and the patient may resume her normal life . . .' The Lab. people wrote that?

LYDIA. Of course.

SEBASTIAN. (*Nodding.*) Of course. Oh darling, I *am* glad. Isn't that marvellous for you!—Marvellous.—For me too, of course—

*He kisses the top of her head, absently, and picks up a book.*

I bet old Schuster is pleased.

LYDIA. Delighted. Imagine, no dieting, no waggon, late nights—anything in the world I like—

SEBASTIAN. (*Eyebrows raised.*) Anything?

LYDIA. Practically anything. He wants me to have a holiday, anyway.

SEBASTIAN. Well, where are we now?—April. Well in a couple of months' time I'll take you to Italy, if there isn't a revolution.

LYDIA. I thought that was what you wanted.

SEBASTIAN. (*Deep in his book.*) Wanted what?

LYDIA. Revolution.

SEBASTIAN. (*Tetchily.*) Darling, not an *Italian* one. It'd be so noisy—tenors blasting off the Internationale in every direction . . . I've lost my place now. Here it is. All right, darling. I'll be about half an hour— (*He turns to his door.*)

LYDIA. You won't.

SEBASTIAN. Won't what?

LYDIA. Be about half an hour. Mark's due here five minutes ago.

SEBASTIAN. Mark? Mark Walters?

LYDIA *nods.*

He's in Hong Kong . . . No, that's right. He's back. I spoke to him yesterday—

LYDIA. And asked him to dinner.

SEBASTIAN. On a *Thursday?* My copy day. I couldn't have—

LYDIA. You did. What's more you asked him to be sure and come an hour early.

SEBASTIAN. (*Explosively.*) Damn and blast! Why didn't you stop me? I remember now. I remember perfectly. You just sat there, with your vapid smile on, and did nothing—nothing—there's loyalty—

LYDIA. I thought you must have an easy one this week.

SEBASTIAN. Easy? *Easy?* Two sodding Professors on Shakespeare's imagery taking opposing points of view. Where is Mark?

*He goes to the telephone.*

In that hideous palace of his in Eaton Square—?

LYDIA. No. The workmen are there, adding something. He's at the Savoy.

*Taking the receiver from him.*

It's far too late, darling. With the bus-strike and the traffic he must have started an hour ago.

SEBASTIAN. Oh bugger!

LYDIA. (*Soothingly.*) Leave it to me. When he arrives I'll tell him you've got to meet a deadline. He's a writer too.

SEBASTIAN. Too? A writer is merely a euphemism, but 'too' is an insult.

LYDIA. Why? I wouldn't mind your selling a million copies before your publication date, and the film rights for half a million, sight unseen—

SEBASTIAN. I see. I see. So that's going to be thrown in my face. My novels
sell five thousand and make me about seven hundred pounds in all—

LYDIA. Oh shut up! You don't write novels. I wish you did, but you don't—

SEBASTIAN *opens his mouth to speak.*

Twenty-five years ago you wrote a masterpiece, and followed it up four
years later with another—

SEBASTIAN. No. The second was a mess—

LYDIA. It was as good as the first.

SEBASTIAN. It was a mess.

LYDIA. It was only that they all turned on you for not writing *Out of the Night*
all over again. And so you gave up and joined the enemy. If you can't
beat them, join them, I know, but you did give up a bit soon.

SEBASTIAN. Thank you very much.

LYDIA. My God, if Mark Walters took *his* notices as seriously as you did—

SEBASTIAN. His research staff and his stenographers and the man who writes
the descriptive passages between bashes would all be out of a job. And
Mark would still be a multi-millionaire. Oh God, the injustice of it all!

*He holds out his glass for her to refill. She takes it.*

Just take some power-mad tycoon with a permanent hard-on—

LYDIA. They're not all tycoons. His last one was about a Presidential candidate—

SEBASTIAN. With a permanent hard-on?

LYDIA. Semi-permanent. His son has the permanent one—he whams it up
everything in sight.

SEBASTIAN. A wham a chapter as usual?

LYDIA. Sometimes more, but it averages out. Now the son meets a lion-
tamer—

SEBASTIAN. Don't go on. Being fairly familiar with the author's 'oeuvre' I can
catch the drift.

*He looks towards his work-room.*

I'll have to work late, that's all—and you know what that does to my
bladder.

LYDIA. You finish now. Mark won't mind. I can delay dinner—

SEBASTIAN *nods gloomily and goes towards his door.*

Oh—talking of novels—

SEBASTIAN. We weren't.

LYDIA. I mean *your* novels. Darling are those notes for a new novel I came
on in there the other day?

*Pause.*

SEBASTIAN. 'Came on' is good. 'Came on' is very good. I noticed that they'd
been disturbed.

*Roaring.*

Is there *nothing* I can keep concealed in this house?

LYDIA. Oh—so you *concealed* them, did you? Why?

SEBASTIAN. Because I knew that once you got your X-ray eyes on them you'd be bouncing up and down, clapping your little hands and shouting: 'Oh goody, goody, he's writing a novel!'

LYDIA. Well goody-goody he is.

SEBASTIAN. No. Not necessarily at all. He may well decide to give it up, because it stinks, or decided that he hasn't got time for it anyway.

LYDIA. Oh, time isn't important. You can make that—

SEBASTIAN. What utter balls you do talk sometimes—

*There is a ring at the front door.*

Oh God!

LYDIA. You go in. I'll explain.

SEBASTIAN. No. I'd better say hullo.

LYDIA *opens the front door to* MARK. *He is in the early forties, and physically the exact opposite one would imagine, of any of his power-mad, randy heroes. He has a pleasantly mild expression and a weedy physique. He pants at the mildest physical exertion and is panting now. He carries two parcels under his arm.*

LYDIA. Mark, darling—this is wonderful—

*She throws her arms round his neck.*

MARK. Wonderful for me too. Let me get my breath back. Don't they have elevators in Islington?

SEBASTIAN. No.

MARK. Hell, lifts. As a resident I should remember. Hullo, Sebastian.

*They embrace briefly.*

Still murdering literary reputations?

SEBASTIAN. Yours is safe.

MARK. These days no one gives me notices. Even my friends on the *Cleveland Plain Dealer* who used to find me 'compulsive' now just says 'another Walters!'

SEBASTIAN. (*Snatching a parcel.*) Are these presents?

MARK. You've got Lydia's. This is yours.

LYDIA. Oh Mark, you shouldn't.

SEBASTIAN. Of course he should. It's his duty to redistribute his wealth. Mine rattles.

MARK. (*Snatching it from him.*) Then don't rattle it.

SEBASTIAN. As good as that, eh? I'll open it later, do you mind? I've got a little work to finish off. Lydia forgot it was my copy day—

LYDIA. *He* forgot.

MARK. Look if I'm a nuisance here why don't I take Lydia out for dinner and leave you to work—?

SEBASTIAN. And how do I get dinner?

MARK. Couldn't you scramble yourself some eggs?

SEBASTIAN. Are you mad?

MARK. Yes, I'm mad. For a moment I was thinking you were a normal husband.

SEBASTIAN. Oh—talking of normal. Mark. Do you remember that little scare we had about the old girl when you were last here?—Not really a scare, of course, but she kept on catching colds and things. You remember how her old throat kept on getting sore?

LYDIA. Less of this old please.

SEBASTIAN. Darling, we must face facts.

LYDIA. I'll face the fact that I'm a year younger than you. Right?

SEBASTIAN. No need to get ugly, darling.

*To* LYDIA.

Well her doctor, some refugee friend of hers from Riga—

LYDIA. Tallinn

SEBASTIAN. Put her in rather a flap suddenly. He told her it might be some obscure oriental disease, due to malnutrition—

LYDIA. He didn't say oriental. And he didn't put me in a flap—I was as calm as ice.

SEBASTIAN. Cool as ice, dear. Calm as a mill-pond. And both of them clichés. But malnutrition, Mark—when you think how the old girl tucks it away. Eats like a bloody horse—

LYDIA. I didn't always, you know. We didn't eat like bloody horses in Estonia between '39 and '46.

SEBASTIAN. (*Mildly.*) Darling, not another refugee story—do you mind. I'm sure they bore Mark senseless.

*To* MARK.

Now about this little flap—

MARK. I know about the little flap.

SEBASTIAN. How do you know? You've been in Hong Kong.

LYDIA. There's a postal service even in Hong Kong.

SEBASTIAN. (*Genuinely surprised.*) You write to each other? How extraordinary! Well, anyway, after a time things got better and better and today she's had her final clearance, a piece of paper with 'normal' written all over it. Show it to him, darling.

LYDIA *hands* MARK *the blood-test. While* MARK *is reading:*

What's more she's put on ten pounds.

LYDIA. Four. Three really.

MARK. Well, that's great, Lydia.

*He hands it to her. She puts it on a table.*

SEBASTIAN. You saw that note at the end telling her to piss off and not bother them any more? She shouldn't have written to you, Mark, and bothered you.

MARK. I like being bothered.

SEBASTIAN. I don't write and tell you about my bladder trouble, do I?

MARK. No.
*Politely.*
How is your bladder trouble?
SEBASTIAN. Absolutely terrible. Sometimes I sit in there, screaming.
MARK. Screaming what?
SEBASTIAN. For someone to care. You look terrible.
MARK. I know. I always do.
SEBASTIAN. Why don't you look like your heroes?
MARK. If I did I'd write about heroes who looked like me, and I wouldn't sell.
SEBASTIAN. (*Having laughed.*) I often think if you'd had any education you might actually write.
MARK. If I'd had any education I'd know I couldn't.
SEBASTIAN. (*Kissing his cheek.*) I love you a little, do you know that?
*To* LYDIA.
Darling, fill this up, would you, and then get Mark a drink.
LYDIA *takes his glass again.*
MARK. How's Joey?
LYDIA. (*Eagerly.*) Oh he's doing wonderfully well, Mark.
SEBASTIAN. Wonderfully well? He has an unpaid job at the headquarters of a crypto-fascist political organisation called the Liberal Party.
MARK. Jesus! You mean the party that Gladstone was once head of?
SEBASTIAN. (*Pronouncing correctly, whereas* MARK *pronounced it to rhyme with 'bone'.*) Gladstone. *Gladstone* is the name of a hotel in New York, isn't it?
MARK. No, seriously. That party that got all those votes in the last election— is *that* crypto-fascist?
LYDIA. That was a little joke, Mark.
SEBASTIAN. It was *not* a little joke. The modern Liberal party is a vote-splitting organisation carefully designed to keep the Establishment in power under cosy left-wing labels, and the real Left forever out. And moreover, there is little doubt that the whole movement is clandestinely backed by South African gold—
LYDIA. (*To* MARK *who looks confused.*) That was another little joke . . . Oh Mark, don't you think it's wonderful Joey getting that job all by himself?
SEBASTIAN. Unpaid.
LYDIA. Only now. After the bye-election they're going to pay him.
SEBASTIAN. Thirty pieces of silver, I should think.
MARK. (*Still at* sea.) Bye-election?
*Pause.*
SEBASTIAN. How long have you lived in England, Mark?
MARK. Well, now, let's see. I came over first for the English publication of *The Naked Truth,* or was it *Pride of Possession,* so that would be—
SEBASTIAN. Don't let's see. I should never have brought it up. A bye-election is—

MARK. (*In the nick of time.*) —when a member of Parliament dies and they elect his successor. We have the same thing in the States—

SEBASTIAN. And what do they call them there?

*Pause.*

MARK. Bye-elections, I guess.

SEBASTIAN. (*At length.*) Christ. Do you read nothing but *Terry and the Pirates?*

MARK. It's just that with us bye-elections aren't all that important. Are they here?

SEBASTIAN. In your benighted country you have elections every two years: in our even more benighted one we have ours every five—well, usually that is. With us a bye-election is an authentic indication of what the voters are thinking about government policies.—Take this bye-election at East Worsley, for instance, where my son is currently working for the Liberals.

*The thought of it overcomes him.*

The Liberals, Mark! Helping to split the Left and let the Tories in! . . . My own son, Mark—My own son!

MARK. Too bad. Go on.

SEBASTIAN. Well it's a safe Labour seat. Majority never fallen below ten thousand. But with a *Liberal* candidate canvassed for by Joey and by hundreds of other little Joeys, with their clean hair, winning smiles, fetching little turtle-necks, unstained little leather jackets—No. The thought is too awful to be borne—My own son, Mark—my own son-helping the enemy . . . Perhaps putting a Tory in—

LYDIA. Isn't it awful.

*After a pause—brightly.*

You know he's earned three hundred pounds, Mark, for a television play he's written. Isn't that marvellous?

*She gives* SEBASTIAN *his drink.*

SEBASTIAN. The B.B.C. 2 series for which this piece of pseudo-Kafka crap was written, Mark, happens to be limited to plays by authors under twenty-one—

LYDIA. It's still an achievement—and you ought to be proud.

SEBASTIAN. Oh I am, very.

*He sips his drink.*

A touch too much water, darling.

LYDIA *angrily snatches the drink back.*

MARK. When's this play being done?

LYDIA Tomorrow at 7.30.

MARK. I'll try and get to watch.

SEBASTIAN. (*In a murmur.*) Don't.

LYDIA. You wouldn't come and watch it here with us, would you?

*She brings the drink back to* SEBASTIAN *having added whisky.*

SEBASTIAN. Darling, what a thing to ask the poor man!

LYDIA. It's only he could see Joey too. He's coming up from his bye-election especially to watch it with us. Don't you think that's rather sweet of him, when he could have seen it with his friends?

SEBASTIAN. I think it's wise. He knows we've got to like it.

LYDIA. Damn you, damn you!

*She begins to switch lights on.*

SEBASTIAN. Forgive her, Mark. She's been a bit hysterical lately.

LYDIA. Go and work.

SEBASTIAN. (*Soothingly.*) Yes, darling, I'm just going.

SEBASTIAN *goes to his door.*

LYDIA. Would you, Mark? I know it's an awful thing to ask but Joey would be thrilled out of his mind.

SEBASTIAN. Out of his what?

MARK. I'd love to.

SEBASTIAN. Good God.

*He goes out.*

MARK *faces* LYDIA. *There is a pause.*

MARK. Tell me please that I've come for no reason.

LYDIA. You've come, Marcus, and I'm eternally grateful.

MARK. What you told me in your last letter is true?

LYDIA. Well, while there's life and Marcus Waldt—

*Holding him.*

darling, darling Marcus Waldt—there must be hope—

MARK. You're goddamn right there's hope.

*He studies the tests.*

LYDIA *goes to the drink table. She pours herself a drink.*

LYDIA. I'm going to give myself a drink. First in six months. Sure you won't have one?

MARK. Sure.

*Indicating the papers.*

These reports are phoney. Is that what you're trying to tell me?

LYDIA. Yes.

MARK. How do you know?

LYDIA. I know Uncle Constantin's typewriter. His Ss and Es don't work.

MARK. Uncle Constantin?

LYDIA. The one I wrote you about.

MARK. Oh. And he typed them?

LYDIA. Yes.

MARK. Why?

LYDIA. A kind of reassuring word sent out to a friend in need.

*A shade wearily.*

But not even darling Uncle Constantin could fake or forge the figures on official laboratory paper. Those figures are worse than last month's— and a great deal worse than the month's before.

MARK. How do you know?

LYDIA. Oh, I get to see them.

MARK How do you get to see them?

LYDIA. I pinch them, memorise the figures, and then put them back in Uncle Constantin's desk, exactly as they were.

MARK. I don't believe that.

LYDIA. Don't. It doesn't matter—

MARK. It does.

*Pause.*

LYDIA. I'm sorry, Marcus. Yes, it does. Well, you mustn't forget that in between bouts of concentration camps I did serve a little time in Estonian Resistance—when there *was* any Estonian Resistance—With three invasions, from different sides, it wasn't too easy—

MARK. (*Harshly.*) I know all that. Come to the point.

*Pause.*

LYDIA. I'm sorry. Refugee stories. They bore you senseless—

MARK. They don't and you know it. But please come to the point.

LYDIA. Well, I learnt a little about memorising figures. If you train yourself to do that at eighteen, you don't forget the knack—never mind. You also learn to rifle desks quickly, knowing which are the operative drawers.— Well, Uncle Constantin wouldn't have made a very high rank in the Gestapo—poor lamb—or the K.G.B.—You see each time I go to him I have to spend a penny for a wee-wee—sorry, *urine* test—and I tell him I can't do it with someone in the room, even behind a screen. So he discreetly disappears and I'm into his desk the way I did with that Russian General, remember, I told you.

MARK. Yes. Go on.

LYDIA. There's nothing to go on about. You see I know what they've all been looking for these last six months—

MARK. How?

LYDIA. By listening—Mainly to student doctors. They're always around at these tests, with their young eager, pretty faces—Well, not always pretty— but eager anyway. I'd address them in fluent Estonian which somehow seemed to give them the idea that I didn't speak English. So they, sometimes, did between themselves. And that particular word came to stick-out.

MARK. Poly-Arteritis?

MARK. Darling Marcus—you really must care a bit! You've even learnt the word.

MARK. Don't be coy.

*He takes out a notebook and begins comparing the figures in the tests sheets which he is holding with others in his notebook.*

LYDIA. That hurt.—Yes, I *am* being. I'm sorry. I'm getting myself another drink

MARK. (*Sharply.*) Allowed it?

LYDIA. Encouraged, Marcus, encouraged.

*She takes a sip.*

Oh God, how horrible American Vodka is!—Still it's better than prune juice.

*After another sip.*

*Just* better—What are you doing?

MARK. The minute I read your letter I put my best researcher on to—

LYDIA. Oh Marcus, I do love you.

MARK. (*Absently.*) And I love you too. Do you happen to know your blood pressure?

LYDIA. With my resistance training, do you think I can't read upside down?

MARK. What is it?

LYDIA. High.

MARK. How high?

LYDIA. Very.

MARK. How long has it stayed that way?

*Pause.*

LYDIA. Your researcher's done his work well, hasn't he? Well I've done some researching too. For far too long to give me any kind of a chance.

MARK. (*Violently.*) Don't talk that way!

LYDIA. (*Quietly.*) I will, if I want to. To you, anyway. That's what you're here for, Marcus. Cheers!

MARK. Lydia, if you have got this thing, it's bad. It's even very bad. But— look—it's not necessarily fatal—

*Pause.*

LYDIA. Your researcher and I seem to have been reading different books. Of course it takes time. It could even take two years.

*She finishes her vodka.*

Hell—it doesn't even taste like vodka. Still—who's caring what it tastes like?

*She pours another.*

It's what it does that matters. And what it does is good. So here's to two years—

MARK. Listen. This I do know. There can be no certain diagnosis until there's been a biopsy. You know that, don't you?

LYDIA. Yes.

*After drinking.*

There's been a biopsy.

MARK. (*Triumphantly tapping the tests.*) But the result isn't through. It says so here—

LYDIA. It says a lot of things there.

MARK. Is the result through?

LYDIA. No. Not officially.

MARK. Well, then—

LYDIA. Have you forgotten 'Lydia, Heroine of the Glorious Estonian Resist-ance'?—Heroine is funny. Me and two small boys, none of us lasting more than six weeks—But still, who needs the written result when you can get the verbal one more quickly and more easily.—That was in our manual—Uncle Constantin's nurse is Scandinavian, you see. Accent very like mine. So today I call the hospital, get the consultant's secretary, say Doctor Schuster needs a verbal report and couldn't speak himself as the patient's in his consulting-room at that moment—She swallowed it like a nice Scandinavian lamb. Said she'd look it up—

MARK. You called from the doctor's office?

LYDIA. No. In a call-box, scared to death it would sound off too soon. It didn't. She came back. 'Mrs. Lydia Cruttwell. Poly-Arteritis. Positive.' Very brisk voice. Very Swedish—very—health-sounding. So there you are. Now you'll have that drink?

MARK. Yes.

LYDIA *gets it. Pause. He sips his drink.* LYDIA *sits beside him.*

And he doesn't know a thing?

LYDIA. No.

MARK. Shouldn't you have let him know?

LYDIA. No.

*After a Pause.*

How was Hong Kong?

MARK. What I expected.

LYDIA. Susie Wongs everywhere?

MARK. Sammy Wongs more.—Is that funny?

LYDIA. No.

MARK. I'll lose it.

*Toward door.*

He should know.

LYDIA. (*She kisses his cheek.*) And just what do I tell him?

MARK. The truth for Christ's sake! Isn't the truth what you tell your husband?

LYDIA. Not this husband.

MARK. But he'll have to be told sometime.

LYDIA. When the ambulance comes. Not before. Perhaps not even then.

*Pause.*

MARK. Listen, he could *resent* your not telling him, you know that?

LYDIA. Oh yes, he could. He probably will. In fact he certainly will—

MARK. Then why—?

LYDIA. Because I won't bore him, I love him too much for that. Marcus, don't let's fool ourselves—is there any surer way of boring our nearest and dearest than by getting ourselves a long slow terminal illness?

MARK. But isn't that just what our nearest and dearest are for?

LYDIA. You are. And don't you worry—I'll bore *you* good and proper before I'm through—Is that correct idiom 'good and proper'? Or should it be 'well and properly'?

MARK. Good and proper will do.

LYDIA. But Sebastian isn't you—

MARK. You got a point there.

LYDIA. I mean he's so bad at being bored. You must have noticed that—

MARK. I've noticed it.

LYDIA. Of course if I *had* told him he'd have been quite upset—perhaps even very upset—for a week or so, and he'd have remembered his manners too. Manners Makyth Man. That's the motto of his old school, Winchester. 'Don't tire yourself, old girl. Just lie there. I'll get you your tea.'

*She laughs.*

Oh God, just to hear that I sometimes wish I *had* told him. But not for two years, Mark. Two years!

*She touches wood surreptitiously.*

No, Marcus, I've chosen this way, and it's the best way. The best for me, as well as for him. I promise you.

*Pause.*

MARK. God damn it, why do you look so well?

LYDIA. Cortisone! Lashings of cortisone! What Uncle Constantin calls my vitamin pills. Which reminds me.

*She takes a bottle from her bag, and shakes two into her hand.*

Two six times a day now. It was two four times a day.

*She swallows two.*

I don't know whether that's a good sign or a bad sign—Bad, I suppose, but who cares? . . . Cortisone's a marvellous drug, Marcus. It makes one feel sixteen. They dope racehorses with it—

MARK. (*Taking the bottle from her.*) It doesn't say cortisone.

LYDIA. Of course it doesn't. Uncle Constantin's far too cute for that. He as them specially labelled—

MARK. Then how do you know they're cortisone?

LYDIA. Heroine of the Estonian Resistance at English chemist—Heavy Baltic accent—Could you Miss, helping me please? These pills am I finding in old bottle—I am thinking they are aspirin—are they so being? . . . A little wait, then . . . Not aspirin? Cortisone? . . . Powerful drug? Then down the loo-loo am I putting them—instantly . . .

*Her voice is beginning to quaver. She ends the speech in near tears, her head on his chest.*

You're supposed to be laughing—

MARK. I guess so.

LYDIA. Oh Marcus, are you angry with me for pulling you half across the globe just to hear me whining—Not much of a Heroine am I?—The thing is I had to tell someone. It couldn't be Sebastian, so it had to be you—which is a song, I think.

MARK. Want me to sing it?

LYDIA. Later. Oh Marcus, I'm so happy to see you. Thank you for coming.

MARK You said that already.

LYDIA. Yes, I did, didn't I? I don't know why it is that you're the only real friend I've got.

MARK. Nor do I.

LYDIA. It must be something to do with your being Lithuanian—

MARK. I'm not Lithuanian, I'm American. And you're British . . .

LYDIA. I mean, Baltic blood.

MARK. In my case more Jewish than Baltic—

LYDIA. No need to boast. I had a jewish grandfather, remember.

MARK. You didn't even know that until the Nazis came—

LYDIA. I knew it then all right.

*She suppresses a shiver.*

No, the English aren't easy to make friends from—and, of course, as a refugee in 1945 I started off on the wrong foot.

*She laughs reminiscently.*

A few days after I got here, when I was delirious with joy, and loving England and everything English—

MARK. Not their cabbage?

LYDIA. Even their cabbage—Sebastian asked about ten or twelve of his best friends round to meet me.

MARK. Before the wedding?

LYDIA. No, after. We got married in Berlin. I thought you knew that—

*Remembering something.*

No, you didn't, and there's a good reason why you didn't—why nobody does—Back to Sebastian's party. Do you know, Mark, the party started at nine and at eleven there was no one left. No one at all. I'd bored the whole lot out into the night.

MARK. Refugee stories?

LYDIA. (*Indignantly.*) I didn't know they were forbidden! I mean, people that night asked me politely about what it had been like being invaded alternately by the Russians, then by the Germans and then by the Russians again over six years—and like a bloody idiot I went and told them. All of them. Finally, they were round me in a circle, looking at me so politely—you know those polite English looks—Oh God, how I hate polite English looks. . . !

MARK. I hate politeness.

LYDIA. (*Aggressively.*) You don't. You're the politest man I know—

MARK. Yeh, but I don't look it.

LYDIA. True. Sebastian's friends did. Glassy-eyed from boredom, of course, but I didn't see that. Sebastian did and tried to stop me, but I wasn't to be stopped. I told them all about myself—All!

MARK. Even the Russian General?

LYDIA. You bet, the Russian General . . . You see the one thing I was so sure about the English, was that they all had a sense of humour . . . Famous for it . . . So when I told them that a Russian General had selected me from a Labour Camp to be his personal driver because he liked my 'Bodywork', oh how I thought they'd roar—

MARK. Not a titter?

LYDIA. Not a smirk.

MARK. Well there wouldn't be, would there? It's a terrible joke.

LYDIA. (*Indignantly.*) It was the best I could manage in the circumstances—

*A pause.*

Oh, those glassy stares!—Oh God, and how angry Sebastian was!

*Imitating him.*

'You see, my darling girl, it isn't quite done over here to parade your emotions so publicly. We as a race, on the whole prefer to—*understate.* Do you understand, my darting?'—I was guilty of bad form, especially as, I think I did, I cried a bit when I told them . . . Oh damn the English! Sometimes I think that their bad form doesn't just lie in revealing their emotions, it's in having any at all. Do you like the English?

MARK. I don't quite dig them, of course, but who does?

LYDIA. (*Sadly.*) Who does?—Who does?

MARK. Still I like their country, so I live in it rather than mine.

*Indicating his glass.*

May I?

LYDIA. Yes—and get me another vodka.

MARK. (*Doubtfully.*) Should you? After all you've already had—

LYDIA. Why not?

MARK. (*Giving her her drink.*) I can think of reasons.

LYDIA. Don't.

MARK. O.K. I won't.

*Facing her.*

Why didn't I know you got married in Berlin?

*Pause.*

LYDIA. I said I couldn't tell you that.

MARK. But you *can* tell me you're dying.

LYDIA. (*Angrily.*) Who said anything about dying?—Eighteen months to two years—why, it's a life-time.

MARK *laughs.* LYDIA *glares at him angrily.*

Why didn't you stay in Hong Kong?

MARK. Because you asked me to come here.

*Pause.*

LYDIA. What is so important about where I got married?

MARK. I don't know, but if you've kept it a secret from me for twenty-five years, it's important. So I should know. Now, I mean.

*Pause.*

LYDIA. Inquisitor!

MARK. The Grand.

*Pause.*

LYDIA. It's only feminine pride that's stopped me telling you, that's all—

MARK. (*Surprised.*) Bun in the oven?

LYDIA. (*Outraged.*) No! And that's a revolting expression. Wherever did you learn it?

MARK. From a Susie Wong. They all speak English slang—

LYDIA. You lead a shocking life

MARK. I wish it shocked me.

*Pause.*

LYDIA. Sebastian married me in Berlin because that was the only way he could marry me at all. I was still a Russian citizen, Estonia having vanished into Russia. Sebastian was a British Intelligence Officer, with contacts. In fact I'm not at all sure that Marshall Zhukov didn't have a hand in it somewhere.

*Boldly, after a pause.*

Sebastian never took me for better, for worse, Mark—in sickness and in health to love and cherish, till death do us part. He took me for one reason only: to give me a British passport.

*Pause.*

MARK. Other reasons too, surely?

LYDIA. Two, if you like. That night I first met him and later nights too—I made him enjoy going to bed with me—I'd learnt how to by then. You see—even with the visiting Politburo. Besides a British Junior Officer was—was—well quite a change from some of those very Senior Russians—and for the first time I—oh dear—I'd say I enjoyed my work!—Then my funny English made him laugh that night, and other nights, and I think my being a kind of slave—we weren't paid, you know just bed and board—that shocked him, coming from his friends, the Russians. So he decided to rescue me—Poor Sebastian! It was much more of a job than he'd thought, but he sticks to things once he's decided, and I finally ended up with a passport made out to Mrs. Sebastian Cruttwell, with a British Occupation Authority Stamp all over it . . . We must have had some kind of wedding, I suppose, but I can't remember it. I can only remember Sebastian roaring at some British Chaplain that he'd be buggered if he'd say 'Obey'. He thought that was his *line*, you see—

MARK. But I imagine he made no objection when he found out that it was yours?

LYDIA. Asked for a repetition. Our agreement—kind of unspoken—was that once in England we'd get ourselves a divorce. But he was writing a novel then, and I was typing it, and collecting material, and generally making myself useful . . . Too useful to be got rid of—deliberately, Mark, deliberately. You see—well you've always known—I was in love with him—always have been, in spite of—

*Suddenly angry with him.*

All right, I might have gone away with you when you asked me. I didn't lie to you. I nearly did go away with you.

MARK. Not very nearly. I think.

LYDIA. (*Angry again.*) Oh you don't know how nearly. You don't know what being married to a Sebastian is like—

MARK. Happily, I don't.

LYDIA. Then it had been only for three years. Now it's twenty eight. Twenty eight years! Jesus!

MARK. Jesus indeed.

LYDIA. And after Joey appeared, then there was no longer any question . . .

*She stops short.*

Oh damn it! Why did I mention Joey? Now I've gone and made myself cry—

*She sobs quietly on his breast.*

MARK. Does Joey know?

LYDIA. (*Fiercely.*) Of course, he doesn't. And he mustn't. Like Sebastian, he mustn't—oh God. Joey!

*Pause.*

MARK. Yes, I'm glad I'm here. I'm glad you've got somebody around.

*He holds her in a tight embrace.* SEBASTIAN *puts his head round the door.*

SEBASTIAN. Darling, my special reading light doesn't go on.

*Neither* MARK *nor* LYDIA *show any embarrassment at their intimate attitude.*

Darling, I said my special reading light—

LYDIA. I heard you. What's the matter with it?

SEBASTIAN. (*Simply and reasonably.*) It doesn't go on.

LYDIA. Probably the bulb.

*She goes past him into the room.*

SEBASTIAN. Do forgive me, Mark. Just two more sentences. You haven't been too bored, I hope.

MARK. Not at all. What are you writing on this week?

SEBASTIAN. That complacent old burgher of Stratford-on-Avon. God, he's so maddening. With his worship of the Establishment he makes nonsense of everything we write, don't you think?

MARK. *We?*

SEBASTIAN. (*Appalled.*) Are you a *Republican?*

MARK. (*Hastily.*) Gee no. I'm a Democrat—

SEBASTIAN. Well Shakespeare *must* infuriate people like us who passionately believe that no man can write well whose heart isn't in the right place.

MARK. Meaning the left place?

SEBASTIAN. (*Feeling his heart.*) Which is where the heart is. Thank you, Mark. I might use that as my pay-off.

LYDIA *appears.*

Well?

LYDIA, It wasn't plugged in.

SEBASTIAN. Who unplugged it. Mrs. Macreedy?

LYDIA. Mrs. Reedy. Probably she did.

SEBASTIAN. You must speak to her, darling. Set up the chessmen, Mark.

*He goes into his room. There is a pause.*

MARK. Now who on earth is going to look after him, if—

LYDIA. Say 'when', Mark. Get used to it, please.

MARK. (*Stubbornly.*) I'm not saying 'when', Lydia. I'm sorry. Someone's got

to keep a little hope going around here. You seemed to have resigned
yourself to black despair—

LYDIA. Black despair! *Me!* Really, Mark. I left that behind in Bentinck Strasse.
You don't think I'm scared of dying, do you?

MARK. I think you've resigned yourself to it far too soon. You're not fighting,
Lydia—

LYDIA. What is there to fight? If you've got it, it kills you—and that's that.
But if my books are right it kills you quite gently—'To cease upon the
midnight with no pain'. Can't you well-fed, uninvaded Americans understand how many millions of us in Europe during those years longed
for just that—and didn't get it?—Black despair! Me? I'm insulted—

MARK. All right, all right. I'd sooner not talk about it too much, if you don't
mind.

*He pulls one of his parcels out and begins to open it.*

LYDIA. Well, we've got to talk about it a little or you're not going to be much
of a help, are you?

MARK. O.K., but not now. Do you mind?

LYDIA. Just one thing more. You asked a question and I've got to answer it.

MARK *is taking out a set of very beautiful, carved, Chinese chessmen, in red and
white, and is methodically replacing the black and white pieces with them
on the table in the corner.* LYDIA. *obsessed with her problem, has not yet noticed what he is unobtrusively doing.*

Who's going to look after that one

*She thumbs at* SEBASTIAN'S *door.*

when *I* can't any more. Well I've an idea—

MARK. I suppose he couldn't just look after himself?

LYDIA. Are you mad?

MARK. Hasn't he ever *had* to? Surely in the war—

LYDIA. Commission in Army Intelligence at once, and with a batman. Knowing him, probably two. What are you doing over there?

MARK. Don't look yet. How does he reconcile all that with his Marxism?

LYDIA. Surprisingly easily. No, I've got an idea. There's a girl called Prunella
Larkin—a journalist, who's mad about him, and I gather rather his form
too, mentally *and* physically. Anyway he's been seeing an awful lot of
her recently. In fact I think for the last three months they've been having a thing—

MARK. You don't say. How do you know it's a thing?

LYDIA. Well he's not a master of subterfuge. He takes this Larkin out to dinner—a little business chat, you know, darling—and later gets caught in
the rain when there isn't any, and stays the night with his Editor who
sends him a postcard the next day from Tangier. You know the form.

MARK. Who better? Only my wives didn't go to that much trouble. They just
slept around and when I asked who with—it was mental cruelty.

LYDIA. Now the doctor says I must have a holiday. Will you take me away
for ten days?

MARK. Sure. Where?

LYDIA. Brighton's nice—

MARK. Monte Carlo's nicer. What's this to do with Miss Larkin?

LYDIA. Mrs. Larkin, divorced. Well when I tell him I'm going off with you for ten days, he'll say: 'Yes, that's fine for you darling—but who the hell is going to look after *me*?' Wouldn't you say that's likely?

MARK. I'd say it's goddam certain. So?

LYDIA. So I'll say: 'What about that nice girl Prunella you're always talking about—The one that's so intelligent, and bright and admires your writing so much . . . I wonder if *she'd* move in here, and look after you?—or maybe you could move in with her?'—He'll jump at it, of course. So if their ten days together are a success—well, I can make my plans for the future accordingly. I mean I'll have found my replacement, won't I?

*Pause.*

MARK. What exactly would be those plans?

LYDIA. Well, I could maybe fade into the background a bit sooner than I needed—knowing at least that someone is plugging in his reading lamp . . . And I'd be able to put my feet up and read Agatha Christie—

*Another pause.*

Well? Don't you think it's a clever idea?

MARK. I can only repeat what Sebastian so often says to you: you are an extraordinary woman. All right. Now you can look.

*He carries the completed table over to the centre of the room.*

LYDIA *looks in wonder.*

LYDIA. (*Picking up a piece.*) Oh but these are exquisite.

MARK. Chinese. Nothing very grand. Modern.

LYDIA. But they're beautiful. He'll adore them. My God, if his is as good as that, I'm going to open mine.

*She snatches up the remaining parcel and begins furiously to unwrap it.*

MARK. Listen—if that doesn't suit—

LYDIA *has managed to open the parcel which is a box and peers inside, past tissue paper. Then she closes the box.*

LYDIA. No. Take it back.

MARK. Lydia.

LYDIA. Take it back this instant.

*But she holds on to it firmly. There is a pause. Then gathering strength, she whisks out a silver mink wrap. She gazes at it lovingly.*

I said—take it back.

MARK. I heard you.

*He takes the wrap from her and holds it out far her to slip into. She does so.*

LYDIA. I didn't mean a word of what I said just now. I think you're an absolute horror.

MARK. Yes.

LYDIA. Flaunting your wealth, showing girls what they've missed by not divorcing their husbands and marrying you.

*She looks at herself from every angle in the mirror. Then she gives him a passion-*
*ate embrace. Finally she takes his empty glass.*

You can't just say thank you for mink, can you? I'll say it in Estonian. It
sounds better. Tanan vaga. If you think I'm ever going to take this off,
you're crazy. Marcus, don't redistribute your wealth quite so much, please.
If I'd been your wife I wouldn't have let you give mink coats to old lady
friends—

*She gives him his glass.*

MARK. Well, maybe I sensed this was special.

LYDIA. Special it was. Thank you, dear Marcus.

*She embraces him again.* SEBASTIAN *comes in.*

SEBASTIAN. Have you two nothing better to do? You're not even giving the
poor man a chance to smoke.

LYDIA. I haven't seen him for six months.

SEBASTIAN. Nor have I. Nor has anyone. Darling, that lovely patent folding
table of yours doesn't fold—

LYDIA. (*Looking in the room.*) Well, of course, it doesn't if you leave the typewriter on it.

*She flaunts her wrap in front of his eyes, to no effect whatever. Crossly she goes*
*into the work-room.*

SEBASTIAN. (*Very half-heartedly after her.*) Oh darling—do let me—

*He takes half a step to the work-room, and three or four full and determined*
*steps over to the drink tray.*

MARK. Finished?

SEBASTIAN. More or less. I've fixed both the Professors, and the Swan is sunk
in his own Avon without a trace.

MARK. Never to rise again?

SEBASTIAN. Ay. There's the rub. One has to admit that the bloody old hon-
ours-hunting bourgeois could write. William Shakespeare, Gent. Hard
to forgive him for that. It should have stamped him a forgettable non-
entity for the rest of creation. instead of which—

MARK. Didn't you get something?

SEBASTIAN. An O.B.E.

*With rage.*

Lydia forced me into that. She staged a sit-down strike.

MARK. Isn't an O.B.E. what's called an honour?

SEBASTIAN. I would rather not speak of it, if you please.

*He slips into the chair opposite* MARK, *facing him across the chessmen. He picks*
*up a white pawn in one hand, and a red one in the other.*

Now, are you prepared for your usual thrashing?

MARK *taps his left hand.* SEBASTIAN *opens it, revealing a red pawn.*

Good. There is no question at all that I am better playing red than—
Red?

*He picks up his pawn again, feels it lovingly and then stares at the whole board.*

*Then without a word he gets up, crosses to* MARK *and gives him a full, fervent kiss on the mouth.*

I passionately adore you, and am prepared to live with you for the rest of my life.

*He picks up more pieces to feel them.*

What is more I take everything back that I've ever written about your novels.

MARK. You've never written anything about my novels.

SEBASTIAN. Your next one will get my whole three columns—

MARK. I think I'd rather have a kiss.

SEBASTIAN. Nonsense. I can always find something to praise. Your un-put-down-ability . . . rattling good yarn . . . every story tells a picture.

*To himself.*

That's rather good. I must remember that.

MARK *moves a piece.*

Pawn to *Queen* four? What's the matter? You've got bored with pawn to King four?

SEBASTIAN *answers the move appropriately.*

MARK. I've been studying Fischer-Spassky.

SEBASTIAN. You mean you've had your research staff study Fischer-Spassky.

MARK. Touché. You know something. I'd give a million bucks to write one novel a tenth as good as your *Out of the Night.*

SEBASTIAN. So would I. Only I haven't a million bucks.

*Picking up his King and Queen to fondle them.*

These are marvellous. Of course you can't tell the King from the Queen, but when can you these days?

MARK Are you never going to try another novel?

SEBASTIAN. That'd be telling.

MARK. Good. That means yes.

SEBASTIAN. No. You said 'try'. I've got to be *moved,* Mark. The war did move me and that novel was good. It wasn't Tolstoy like some idiots said, but it was good. The Peace didn't stir the juices, and that novel was bad.

MARK No.

SEBASTIAN. (*Belligerently,*) Listen, who's the critic here?

MARK. Sorry.

SEBASTIAN. But I'm not beyond hope about the next—if I do it. Ah.

*Referring to the game.*

The Queen's gambit. I thought you'd grown out of that—

MARK. I've got a new variation—

SEBASTIAN. You'll need it. My reply to the Queen's gambit makes strong men quake—

*He takes a central pawn.*

Queen's gambit—*accepted.*

MARK. You're not supposed to do that.

LYDIA *comes in unobserved.*

SEBASTIAN. Why not?

MARK. It'll weaken your central pawn position later—

SEBASTIAN. (*Complacently.*) Let it. Let it. Meanwhile you're a pawn down.

*To* LYDIA *who is moving about, ostentatiously showing off her wrap.*

Darling, can you leave the ashtrays till later? It's a bit distracting, all that moving about.

LYDIA *stands still with a sigh.*

Oh, by the way—do you see what Mark's given me?

LYDIA. I'm trying to show you what Mark's given me.

SEBASTIAN. (*Looking up at her.*) Oh, what?

*After a pause.*

Oh, that.

*Another pause. To* MARK.

What fur exactly is that?

LYDIA. (*Explosively.*) Don't tell him!

*Savagely.*

Dyed rabbit.

SEBASTIAN. Mink? I see.

*Pause.*

Very nice.

*Pause.*

Isn't that light shade just a bit—forgive me, darling—on the young side—?

*Before he has finished* LYDIA *has slipped the wrap off and has swung it at his head, disturbing several chess pieces. Outraged.*

Darling, really. These are valuable—

*He and* MARK *pick up the pieces.* LYDIA *goes to sit down in a sulk, hand on fist, staring at her husband with hatred.*

I'd just moved pawn to King 3.

*Holding a pawn.*

Superb workmanship.

*He allows* MARK *to re-arrange the board.*

Where did you get them?

MARK. Hong Kong.

SEBASTIAN. Of course.

*A horrifying thought strikes him.*

Oh Mark, I may have to give them back. All that sweated labour—

MARK. Imported from Pekin.

SEBASTIAN. (*With a deep sigh of relief.*) Ah. Good.

MARK. It's all right if they sweat in Pekin?

SEBASTIAN. They don't sweat in Pekin.

MARK. Or they'd be arrested.

SEBASTIAN. Please don't make cheap jokes like that, do you mind? Now. Your move.

*They have re-arranged the board.* LYDIA, *after a questioning glance at* MARK, *fills up her own glass.*

LYDIA. Sebastian, Mark wants to take me down to Monte Carlo for ten days or so—

SEBASTIAN. What for?

LYDIA. A holiday. A rest—like the doctor said—

SEBASTIAN. Well, can't you have a rest here?

LYDIA. Since you ask—no. Unless you go to Monte Carlo instead.

SEBASTIAN. Well that might be an idea. I doubt if my Editor would scream with joy through, seeing he's away too.

LYDIA. In Tangier.

SEBASTIAN. Yes. How did you know? Well, can you get Mrs. Macreedy to come in every day?

LYDIA. Not a chance.

SEBASTIAN. Just as well. It'd be very expensive.

LYDIA. But I've got a better idea. I haven't asked her. but I think I might just get Prunella to look after you.

SEBASTIAN. Prunella? Prunella Larkin?

LYDIA. Yes. Just for that little time.

*Pause.*

SEBASTIAN. There is no such thing as a little time with Prunella Larkin. An hour is an eternity. Ten days—ten *consecutive* days with her and I'd be a gibbering lunatic.

LYDIA. (*Not displeased.*) Oh. It's just that you did seem to have been seeing quite a lot of her recently

*Pause.*

SEBASTIAN. (*Carefully.*) Mrs. Larkin and I do, I grant, have certain interests in common, but they are interests that can usually be shared in well under thirty minutes of fairly *concentrated converse.* If after those brief encounters I should choose not to plod back to Islington but to sleep in my editor's flat, to which I have a key, that is a matter for my conscience but not for your prurient suspicions. If you insist on skipping off on this extravagant jaunt, I shall go to the Savoy and send the bill in to Mark. If he doesn't pay I shall sell these chessmen. Now, does that settle the matter?

LYDIA. (*A shade breathlessly.*) Yes. Oh yes. Oh yes, it does.

SEBASTIAN. Good.

*Gravely.*

Your move, Mark.

LYDIA *suddenly bursts into a peal of slightly drunken laughter and kisses his head.*
Darling, please. This game needs concentration. Bobby Fischer won't have a camera click ten yards away—much less a hyena screeching tipsily in his ear.

LYDIA. Sorry. I was trying to kiss you.

SEBASTIAN. There is a time and a place.

LYDIA. Yes. I know both.

*Trying to be very silent, she puts down her glass, fumbles in her bag and takes out two pills from the familiar bottle. In doing so she knocks a glass over.*

SEBASTIAN. Darling, go and cook dinner.

LYDIA. Yes.

*She swallows the pills with a sip of vodka.* MARK *sees her.*

MARK. (*Sharply.*) You've already had two of those—

LYDIA. Yes, but I missed two after lunch.

SEBASTIAN. What's she had two of?

LYDIA. My tonic pills.

SEBASTIAN. (*Deep in thought.*) Oh yes, those iron things. Very good for her, Mark. Put on eight pounds—

LYDIA. (*Shouting.*) Two!

MARK *castles.*

SEBASTIAN. The move of a coward.

*After a pause.*

How did we get to know each other, Mark? It was in California when I was lecturing at U.C.L.A., but I don't remember exactly how—was it chess?

MARK. No, it was Lydia. I came to hear the new Tolstoy lecture and sat next to the new Tolstoy's wife.

SEBASTIAN. Oh yes, of course. You thought for a moment you were in love with her or something, didn't you?

MARK. (*Looking at* LYDIA.) I think I still am—or something—

SEBASTIAN. (*Deep in the game.*) Extraordinary.

LYDIA *picks up her wrap to have another go, but is warned by* MARK *with a gesture.*

How long ago was it that we had that fantastic scene?

MARK. Twenty-five years—

SEBASTIAN. Pissed as newts in a topless joint in downtown Los Angeles—

MARK. They didn't have topless joints then.

SEBASTIAN. Where was it?

MARK. Just a bar.

SEBASTIAN. It seemed rather topless, but I suppose everything did in those days. Did you ever tell Lydia about it?

LYDIA *has set herself firmly down again. The conversation is interesting her.*

LYDIA. No, he didn't.

SEBASTIAN. Well he should have. It was all very funny, really.

*To* MARK.

Knight to King's Bishop four, Mark.

MARK. (*Savagely.*) I can see—

SEBASTIAN. Well you couldn't see anything that night. I suppose I couldn't either, come to that.

*To* LYDIA.

It was about four in the morning and Mark suddenly threw his arms around me, shattering all the glasses at the bar—

MARK. We were at a table, in a corner—and I shattered no glasses.

SEBASTIAN. (*Sternly.*) We were at the bar, you broke at least six of their best pony glasses, and you startled an elderly hooker almost to death—

MARK. A *topless* elderly hooker, of course. Don't listen to him, Lydia, his memory's going rapidly . . . It's very sad—

SEBASTIAN. (*To* LYDIA.) You get the picture, darling. Mark has thrown his arms around me and the cutlery has gone flying—

LYDIA. Get to the dialogue.

SEBASTIAN. The dialogue . . . Yes. Well, suiting words to his astonishing action, he said: Oh, what a pity it is that I admire you so much more than any writer on earth, and that I love you so very, very passionately . . .

MARK. I never said 'passionately'—

SEBASTIAN. Well whatever the word was, it put that hooker out like a light—

MARK. There was no hooker. He's inventing all this, Lydia . . .

LYDIA. (*Wrapt.*) Go on.

SEBASTIAN. So, naturally, I said: 'Why do you feel it a pity?' and he said: *Imitating a lachrymose drunk.*
Because, whatever I may feel for you, I feel far more for your wife, whom I want to—

MARK. One thing's certain. I never said '*whom*'.

SEBASTIAN. My mistake. You wouldn't have. '*Who* I want to take away from you and live with for the rest of my life. And, what is more, who I intend to get to do just that with . . .' The syntax went a bit at the end . . .

*He waits for an appropriately laughing response from* LYDIA. *But she is merely sitting, chin on hand, staring.*

LYDIA. (*At length.*) Go on.

SEBASTIAN. Well, so I said: 'Are you trying to tell me that you are in love with Lydia?'

*Pause.*

LYDIA. Can I give you the right inflection? 'Are you trying to tell me that you are in love with *Lydia?*'

*Her inflections, undoubtedly the truthful ones, indicate profound amazement, some jocularity, and a vague certainty that* MARK, *in his tipsy state, must certainly have confused her with another woman, probably called 'Mavis'.*

MARK. Good—I've moved, Sebastian. My Knight to Queen's Bishop three—

LYDIA. Let him go on with the story. What happened then?

SEBASTIAN. Well, I thought—here we are in this bar, and it's four o'clock, and we don't really want a brawl do we? Besides I couldn't very well hit an older man, with heart problems, too. So I decided on a course of correct English courtesy. I said: And what pray, leads you so suppose that my wife, a lady of some taste and discernment, would care to spend the rest of *her* life with some hairy old baboon who couldn't write BUM on a wall and who, if he could, would certainly spell it UMB?

LYDIA. The *delicate* approach—

SEBASTIAN. I thought it best to take it lightly. I then settled the bill, paid for the broken Waterford, took him to his dreadful English Tudor mansion in Beverly Hills, undressed him lovingly, and put him to bed. In return for which I received a passionate embrace—

MARK. *Not passionate!* I was never *passionate*—

SEBASTIAN. You were in no condition to judge . . .

*Back to the board.*

Knight to Queen's Bishop three? Interesting—

LYDIA. Is that the end of the story?

SEBASTIAN. (*His back to her.*) Oh yes, of course. How would you have wanted it to end?

*Pause.*

LYDIA. The way it did, of course.

*She finishes her drink, and stares at the two heads, both bent over the chess board.*
How else?

*Pause*

SEBASTIAN. Darling, don't you think it's time you started our dinner?

LYDIA. Yes.

*She goes up a couple of stairs.*

Something tells me it's going tonight to taste a little pecul—peculiarlar.

*She goes into the kitchen. There is a very long pause.* SEBASTIAN *leans back abstractedly, murmuring.*

SEBASTIAN. Ay, but to die and go we know not where;
　　　To lie in cold obstruction and to rot;

MARK *who has been about to make a move stops with his hand on the piece, staring at* SEBASTIAN.

　　　This sensible warm motion to become
　　　A kneaded clod; and the delighted spirit—

Are you making that move?

MARK. I don't know yet. Is that Shakespeare?

SEBASTIAN.

　　　To be imprisoned in the viewless winds,
　　　And blown with restless violence round about
　　　The pendant world!

Can't keep your hand on it for ever, you know—as the Bishop said to the actress—

MARK. O.K. That's my move.

SEBASTIAN. And a bloody silly one too, if I might say so.

*He considers, and them continues softly.*

　　　The weariest and most loathed worldly life
　　　That age, ache, penury and imprisonment

> Can lay on nature, is a paradise
> To what we fear of death.

Yes, Shakespeare. One is forced to admit that he could sometimes sort out the words. Pessimistic old sod!

MARK. I thought he was a complacent old bourgeois.

SEBASTIAN. He was both—that's the trouble.

*He moves.*

This move will lead to your ultimate annihilation.

MARK. The Cruttwell variation? It has interest, if only fleeting.

*He considers the board.*

What made you choose that particular quotation?

SEBASTIAN. Hm?—Oh, it's in my article. The same man that wrote those lines also wrote:

> We are such stuff as dreams are made on,
> And our little life is rounded with a Sleep.

*Angrily.*

Rounded with a sleep! Phooey! It's what we all hope, but do we know? See what I mean about the two Shakespeares? That last one's cosy, middle-class, comforting and commercial. But: 'To be imprison'd in the viewless winds, And blown with restless violence round about The pendant world . . .' Can any of your modern, hippy poets top that?—Fellow wasn't consistent, you see.

MARK. (*making a move.*) Check.

*A key turns in the front door and* JOEY *comes in. His hair is long, but neat: his sweater and slacks are of sober hue. He looks what he is, a Liberal. He carries an overnight bag.*

SEBASTIAN. (*Not seeing him.*) I think you have fallen right into my trap.

JOEY. Hullo, Dad.

*Pause. Neither smiles.*

SEBASTIAN. Are we expecting you?

JOEY. No.

*With warmth.*

Hullo, Mr. Walters.

MARK. (*Getting up and shaking hands.*) Hullo. Joey. You look ten years older than when I last saw you.

JOEY. I feel ten years older. You don't know what canvassing in a bye-election can do to one.

*He puts down his bag.*

SEBASTIAN *contents himself with an abstracted Pah!*

MARK. Congratulations on getting a play done on TV, Joey. That's great.

JOEY. I'm scared to death. Anyway, seven thirty. No one'll see it. No hope of you seeing it, is there?

MARK. Sure. I'm coming here tomorrow just for that.

JOEY. (*Awed.*) Specially to see my play?

MARK. Yep.

JOEY. Jesus—

MARK. I'm sure it'll be great—

SEBASTIAN. (*Loudly.*) Do you mind not yakkety-yakketing with my vote-splitting son? You are playing chess with me.

JOEY. Who's winning?

SEBASTIAN. I have him in a trap. It's only a question of how best to snap together its steel jaws.

JOEY *examines the game.*

JOEY. Looks the other way round to me.

SEBASTIAN. (*Snarling.*) Do you mind?

JOEY. Sorry.

SEBASTIAN *puts his hand on a piece.* JOEY *hisses gently.* SEBASTIAN *withdraws it. Then he put his hand on another piece* JOEY *hisses again.*

SEBASTIAN. Will you kindly cease your imitation of a cobra on heat? Faulty though it may seem to outside observers, I prefer my game to *be* my own.

JOEY. I just didn't want to see you lose your Knight.

SEBASTIAN. (*Who plainly hasn't seen.*) My Knight?

JOEY. Two moves ahead—

SEBASTIAN. (*After a pause.*) Now a Knight sacrifice might well be my plan. How do you know it isn't, eh?

*Nevertheless he withdraws his hand. After a moment he makes another move without hesitation.*

JOEY. That's torn it.

SEBASTIAN. (*Explosively.*) If you're so bloody good, why don't you ever play?

JOEY. I do.

SEBASTIAN. I meant with me.

*Pause.*

JOEY. Two reasons, I suppose. One, you don't ask me. Two, if I did win you'd call me a fascist pig.

SEBASTIAN. Meaning I'm a bad loser?

JOEY. Meaning that anyone who stamps on your ego is always a fascist pig.

SEBASTIAN. Go away, or I'll stamp on something more painful than your ego.

JOEY. I want to watch. You don't mind, do you Mr. Walters?

MARK. Not at all.

SEBASTIAN. (*Calling.*) Lydia! Lydia!

*She comes out of the kitchen.*

The brood is here. Remove it before I do it violence.

LYDIA. (*With a joyous cry.*) Joey!

*She begins to run down the stairs. Thinks better of it and waits half-way down for him to bound up to her. There they have d warm embrace.*

Joey! Oh, how marvellous!

*She embraces him again.*

SEBASTIAN. (*To* MARK.) Forgive her, Mark. She hasn't seen him for five days—

LYDIA. Why didn't you let us know? Have you eaten?

JOEY. Yes. I only knew myself at the lunch break. They don't need me until
Election Day—

LYDIA. Thursday? And I've got you till then?

*Joey nods.* SEBASTIAN *looks up at them.*

SEBASTIAN. I've got him too.

JOEY. Don't bother, Dad. I won't be in *your* way.

SEBASTIAN. Not till Election Day? Ha! That must mean your man's given up.

JOEY. He's got it made, Dad. The latest poll gives him twelve per cent over
all other candidates.

SEBASTIAN. I don't believe it.

*Rising to get a drink.*

The electorate, God knows, can be utterly idiotic, but it's not raving mad.

LYDIA. (*To* JOEY.) Could you get your mother a little sip of vodka, dear?

JOEY. I didn't know you drank vodka.

LYDIA. I've rather taken to it in the last hour.

*She sits carefully on the steps.*

JOEY *comes down into the room to get her her drink.*

SEBASTIAN. How can a strong left-wing constituency suddenly go Liberal? It
doesn't make sense.

JOEY. It makes perfect political sense for today. The electorate's got bored with
the Right and the Left, so they're voting centre.

SEBASTIAN. Don't talk to me as if I were a cretinous ape who only involved
himself in politics yesterday—

JOEY. No. It was quite a long time ago, wasn't it, Dad? When Hitler was the
devil. Stalin was in his heaven and all was right with the world. Times
have changed you know. You old-time Marxists are out of touch.

*He takes the vodka up the stairs to his mother. She strokes his hair.*

SEBASTIAN. Out of touch, are we?

LYDIA. (*To* JOEY.) Careful dear.

*To* SEBASTIAN.

Did you ever have hair as beautiful as this?

SEBASTIAN. Much more beautiful. But I was in an army, fighting Fascism,
and I was made to cut it short. That was for hygiene. Lice.

JOEY. Did you get many lice as an Intelligence Officer in Whitehall?

*He has sat two steps down from his mother who seems bent on stroking his hair
and whom he is never averse from having do so.*

SEBASTIAN. I was speaking figuratively.

JOEY. Figurative lice?

LYDIA. (*Hastily.*) Don't annoy him. You know what'll happen.

JOEY. (*Ignoring her advice.*) Do you know how many votes your Jim Grant's
going to get?

SEBASTIAN. Who's my Jim Grant?

JOEY. You involve yourself in politics but you don't know the name of the
candidates in the most important bye-election of the year?

SEBASTIAN. Well, if there was a Communist candidate—

JOEY. (*Returning to his mother.*) There is. Jim Grant.

LYDIA. (*Whispering in his ear.*) Careful, dear.

SEBASTIAN. Well? How many votes is he going to get?

JOEY. Four hundred, if he's lucky.

SEBASTIAN. That's just a damn lie! In a working-class constituency like East
    Worsley—

JOEY. It isn't any more, Dad—at least the voters aren't bound in a fraternal
    brotherhood of cloth caps to vote against cigar-chewing bosses in top
    hats.

SEBASTIAN. (*Returning to his seat.*) I don't wish to hear any more.
*With dignity.*

    Wait till Thursday, my boy—that's all. Just wait till Thursday.

*To* MARK, *with sudden rage.*

    Are you going to take all night?

MARK. (*Startled.*) Sorry.

*He makes his move.*

JOEY. Mind you, Jim Grant's one of the nicest men and most brilliant speakers
    you're ever likely to meet. Very popular with everyone too. But—he's
    like you, Dad. He's out of touch. It's all talk. He really doesn't want ac-
    tion any more. We Liberals do.

SEBASTIAN. Flashing mirrors in the eyes of South African cricketers?

JOEY. We didn't do that. But we did get the tour stopped. And what did you
    do, Dad? Booked tickets for the London matches.

SEBASTIAN. (*Furiously.*) And a fortune they cost me. Fifty quid down the drain
    because of you and your long-haired layabouts . . . (*Recovering himself.*)
    We mustn't flout the issue. A Centre Party is nothing more nor less than
    gross collaboration with the enemy.

LYDIA. (*Happily sipping.*) Collaboration. That's very bad. We used to get shot
    for that—by both sides.

JOEY. (*Patting her hand.*) Mum, that was a long time ago.

LYDIA. Yes, it was. It sometimes doesn't seem so.

JOEY. (*To* SEBASTIAN.) I suppose by 'the enemy' you mean the status quo.

SEBASTIAN. (*Looking at board.*) What?

*To* JOEY.

    I mean the whole, rotten stinking mess that is Britain as it is today.

JOEY. What, mum?

LYDIA *is whispering in* JOEY'S *ear.*

SEBASTIAN. What's she saying?

JOEY. She says 'Isn't it terrible, but she rather likes Britain as it is today.'

SEBASTIAN. She's pissed.

JOEY. (*Laughing.*) Are you, Mum?

LYDIA. Well, it's not a very nice way of—

*Firmly.*

    Yes, I am.

JOEY. Good for you.

MARK. What about America today? Do you know what the drop-out rate is among young people there now?

LYDIA. What's a drop-out?

MARK. A boy or girl who feels he just can't take our present civilisation and just—well—drops out.

LYDIA. Not—pushed or anything? Just—drops out?

MARK. Sure they're pushed. They're pushed by the squalor and degradation of life in America today.

LYDIA. (*To herself, happily.*) Squalor—and—degradation—

JOEY. (*Getting up from the steps.*) Dad, I'm not denying that all of us today, on both sides of the Atlantic, are living in a nightmare. But we want to do something—

LYDIA. (*To herself.*) Nightmare—

*She titters, still happy.*

SEBASTIAN. Darling, are you going to sit there just repeating everything we say?

LYDIA. (*Defiantly.*) Yes, if I want to.

SEBASTIAN. You don't think a touch of light cooking might be in order?

LYDIA. I like this discussion.

SEBASTIAN. Well you're not making a great contribution to it.

LYDIA. How can I make a contrib—join in your discussion? I don't belong to this country.

JOEY. Mum, you do.

LYDIA. No. I'm an Englishwoman—thanks only to the lucky accident of a British Intelligence Officer having a night-out in the Russian Zone of Berlin, and stopping off at Bentinck Strasse sixteen.

SEBASTIAN. For God's sake, Lydia, Joey mightn't know we met in a—in an establishment.

LYDIA. A 'Maison de Rendezvous' is what I've always called it.

JOEY. (*To* SEBASTIAN.) Don't worry, Dad, I knew where you met Mum.

SEBASTIAN. Good. But it's not a thing to go roaring from all the roof tops in Islington.

LYDIA. I was not roaring it from all the roof tops in Islington. I was simply saying that I belong to where I was born, the Republic of Estonia. A rather small country—about twice the size of Wales, with a slightly better climate than Finland, our neighbour to the North.

*She rises with a little help from the banisters.*

Now I'm afraid I can't tell you gentlemen just how nightmarish Estonia is today, because, you see, there isn't an Estonia. Estonia has ceased to exist. So I have no country at all. None at all. Which I'm quite sure is making all you English and Americans cry like billy-oh.

SEBASTIAN. Darling, you must be careful of your idioms. 'Billy-Oh' is very old-fashioned—

LYDIA. Yes, it must be. I learnt it in school in Tallinn. That's our capital city—was our capital city. So all I'm entitled to say about Britain today is that it has been a rather pleasant place for an Estonian to have lived in. I shall now go and cook.

SEBASTIAN. Yes, darling. Good idea.

*To* MARK, *sotto voce.*

Forgive the refugee bit. She doesn't do it much.

JOEY. (*Smiling.*) To have lived in, Mum? Why? Are you planning to leave?

LYDIA *suddenly clutches* JOEY *in a fierce embrace. He is surprised.* LYDIA *recovers quickly.*

LYDIA. (*In a 'matter of fact' voice.*) I meant up to now, Joey, of course.

*She turns, takes a step or two quite firmly away from him, then sways—not drunken and holds on tight to the banisters, her body suddenly rigid.*

Do you know—I think—perhaps—

JOEY, *puzzled goes towards her.* SEBASTIAN *moves with extraordinary quickness to reach her before* JOEY, *whom he roughly pushes back so that he nearly falls.*

*To* SEBASTIAN.

Bed?

SEBASTIAN. Yes, darling. A very good idea.

*He has his arm firmly supporting her.*

Now just one step in front of the other.

*She manages a couple of steps.*

That's very clever. It's called walking.

LYDIA. Dinner—can Joey—?

SEBASTIAN. Yes, of course he can. Now another two steps.

*She manages them.*

That's it. We're doing fine. You can manage dinner, can't you, Joey?

JOEY. Yes, dad.

LYDIA. I'm pissed, that's all.

SEBASTIAN. Yes, darling. That's exactly what I'd say you are. And as a newt.

*To the* OTHERS.

It's quite a shock, after all these years, to find one has a wife with a drink problem—instead of being just a drunk, like me.

LYDIA. I love you.

*To* JOEY.

And I love you.

*To* MARK.

And you. I love you all—

SEBASTIAN. Yes. darling, that's very nice for us all to know, I'm sure.

LYDIA. And I love England—

*Seeing* MARK.

and America—

*She stares again at* JOEY.

Left, Right and—Centre—

SEBASTIAN. Yes, I'm sure that all parties in England and America will be delighted to hear that. We'll issue a communiqué later. Now if you could just manoeuvre your arse round this bend—that's it.

*To* MARK.

My move would have been Pawn to Queen's Rook three—Now, darling, two tiny little steps—well done. Now a little more of this one foot after the other lark. Who knows? You might even get to like it—

*The lights fade.*

## ACT II

*The lights come on to show the same room. It is the following night, and the television has been pulled out of its corner to a position where it can be clearly seen from any one of four chairs which* JOEY *is in the process of carefully arranging. He is dressed as the evening before, except perhaps for a differently coloured sweater. Finished with his meticulous arrangement of the chairs, he inspects the various dishes evidently prepared by* LYDIA *for the night's occasion.*

JOEY. (*Calling.*) Mum!

LYDIA. (*From the kitchen.*) Yes, darling?

JOEY. What will they all be drinking?

LYDIA. (*From the kitchen.*) Leave that to me.

JOEY. O.K.

*He kneels down and turns on the television. A* VOICE *comes on loudly, fades and then comes on again.*

VOICE. Well, I can only repeat what I've just said. It's the Government's responsibility to govern—that's true, none of us have ever denied it—but a bad law is still a bad law whatever government has passed it—

JOEY *turns the volume control down to silent, and manipulates the other controls.* JOEY'S *tense face is illuminated by the picture that he sees and we don't.*

LYDIA *appears from the kitchen with a tray on which is a bottle of champagne and three glasses.*

LYDIA. This is what they'll be drinking.

JOEY. Oh Mum. That's making too much of it.

LYDIA. You can't make too much of it.

*She has honoured the occasion with a becoming long dress.* JOEY *takes the tray from her.*

Nervous?

JOEY. Petrified. Why only three glasses?

LYDIA. Darling, if you forgive me, I think I'll stick to Vichy water.

*She sits down, exhausted.*

That ought to go in a bucket. There's one in the kitchen. Put quite a lot of ice in it. It's been in the fridge—but it'll look better.

JOEY. Are you feeling better?

LYDIA. Yes. But how dare the Americans try and make vodka? Go and get that ice.

JOEY. And another glass—

LYDIA. All right. Just a sip, in your honour.

JOEY. (*Looking at his watch.*) You don't suppose Dad's forgotten, do you?

LYDIA. Of course not. He's been talking of nothing else all day. Go on.

JOEY. Where is he?

LYDIA. They wanted him at the office. An obituary or something. He'll be well on his way back by now.

JOEY. Did you call him?

LYDIA. Yes. He said he'd be back in plenty of time.

JOEY. Good.

*He runs up the stairs.*

LYDIA. And Joey—

*She makes the correct sign.*

Merde.

JOEY. (*Smiling.*) Thanks.

*He goes into kitchen.*

*The second he has gone* LYDIA *is on her feet, walking quickly and silently towards the telephone. She looks up a number in a private book, then dials with speed.*

LYDIA. (*Into receiver.*) Mrs. Larkin?—Lydia Cruttwell. I'm sorry to be embarrassing, but this is a crisis. Is Sebastian with you?—I see. Well, when did your little chat finish? Over an hour ago. Where was he going?— Please, Mrs. Larkin, this isn't a jealous wife. I'm—not jealous—I'm pleased, really. But this is important, dreadfully important—No clue at all? During your chat did he happen to mention that his son had a television play on this evening?—Yes. B.B.C. 2, 7.30—Thank you—Yes. Only twenty—thank you. Yes, that's the crisis—Something worse? What *could* be worse?—Well, he sometimes goes to his Editor's flat after your chats. Did he say anything?—Meet some friends? Where?—Well, what's his favourite haunt up your way? After your flat, of course—

*Her face grows despairing.*

But I can't ring all those. Please try and help. I've got to find out where he—

*She stops abruptly as* JOEY *appears with the bucket and an extra glass. Laughing gaily.*

Oh, that's terribly sweet of you, darling—angelic of you to ask us, but I know Sebastian can't. He gets so tied up in the evenings—it's when he works you know—

*She smiles happily at Joey.*

I'll get him to call you. He's due in any second. Goodbye.

*To* JOEY.

What a bore that woman is!

JOEY. Who?

LYDIA. No one you know. An old woman called Rhoda Robinson. Always trying to get us out for cocktails—

JOEY. I didn't hear the telephone ring—

LYDIA. That happens to me when *I'm* getting ice.

*The doorbell rings. Distractedly.*

That's Mark. Answer it darling.

JOEY *runs to the door.* MARK *is outside. He has graced the evening with a dinner jacket.*

MARK. (*Shaking hands.*) Well, Joey, here's wishing you everything.

JOEY. Gosh, Mr. Walters, you didn't change for me?

MARK. Of course. Always dress for a premiere. Here's a little sprig of heather for luck—

*The sprig of heather is fairly easily recognisable as a small Cartier box.* MARK *comes into the room and kisses* LYDIA.

Evening, Lydia.

LYDIA. (*Gratefully.*) Marcus.

*They kiss.* JOEY *meanwhile is opening his present. They are cuff-links.*

JOEY. Are these cuff-links?

LYDIA. (*Looking at them.*) No, they're ear-rings, and they're meant for me.

*To* MARK.

What are you trying to do, Mark? Keep the whole Cruttwell family?

MARK. Well, this is a very important occasion—the debut of a brilliant young dramatist.

JOEY. Dramatist—gosh—you don't get called dramatist till you're dead.

LYDIA. He let 'brilliant' pass.

JOEY. No I didn't, Mum. I just closed my ears.

*Engrossed in his cuff-links.*

I don't think I've ever had a present like this.

*Belatedly.*

Of course Mum's given me some smashing things—

LYDIA. (*Arm around him.*) Smashing. Nickel cigarette lighters, plastic Indian beads. Joey's going to look after Sebastian while we're away—

MARK. Where's Sebastian?

*Pointing to the work-room.*

Is he in there?

LYDIA. (*Calmly.*) No.

*Looking at her watch.*

He's been at the office, but he's due back any minute.

*To* JOEY.

Don't you think you should wear those cuff-links—for luck?

JOEY. I haven't got a shirt—I mean for links.

LYDIA. Borrow one of your father's.

JOEY. (*Slightly dismayed.*) Does that mean a tie?

LYDIA. Oh no. Don't betray your convictions.

JOEY *bounds up the stairs and off.* LYDIA *instantly becomes tense.*

Mark, Sebastian's lost. It's a hundred to one he's forgotten—

MARK. Oh God, no—

LYDIA. Go down, do you mind? There's a call-box at the end of the street. Have you got change?

MARK. (*Feeling.*) How much now?

LYDIA. Two p.

MARK. Jesus, this inflation. O.K.

LYDIA. Call this number here. Remember it?

MARK. Of course.

LYDIA. I'll answer.

*She is hustling him towards the door.*

I'll tell Joey you're reparking your car, or something—

MARK. What shall I say?

LYDIA. You don't need to say anything. I'll do the talking. Wait a moment.

*She runs to the desk, takes out an envelope and scribbles on it. Then she gives it to him.*

Is that clear. My hand is so shaking with rage—

MARK. (*Reading.*) 'Sebastian—If after 7.30 go away until well after eight. And then, the first thing you say is "Congratulations, Joey". I'm covering for you.'

LYDIA. Not even *he* can fail to follow that, can he?

*She opens the door, licks the flap of the envelope, and sticks it to the door.*

MARK. He can do some funny things.

LYDIA. You see how I'm laughing in anticipation.

JOEY *comes running down the stairs, wearing a shirt much too large for him, outside his slacks. For* JOEY'S *sake.*

Tell the policeman you're a foreigner, Mark. That always works—wait—here's the latch-key—

*She gives him a key and then closes the door quickly in his face. To* JOEY.

Americans always park their cars in the middle of the street.

JOEY. He won't miss anything?

*He looks at his watch.* LYDIA *coming calmly towards him slaps his hand.*

LYDIA. Plenty of time, dear. Don't fuss. You want me to fix these for you?

JOEY. Yes, please. They're complicated.

LYDIA *attends to fixing the links.*

Your hands are shaking, too.

LYDIA. Well, of course, I'm nervous—

*Pause.*

JOEY. Are you sure Dad hasn't forgotten?

LYDIA. Positive.

JOEY. I hope he's not late. If you miss the beginning it's difficult to follow.

LYDIA. His opinion means a lot to you doesn't it?

JOEY. Well—after all—one of the best critics in the world—

LYDIA. Not *the* best?

JOEY. How do I know? I don't read them all.

*Regarding his links.*

But I'd say that on his day he's about the best I've read.

LYDIA. You *admire* him, then, Joey?

JOEY. (*Impatiently.*) I just said so.

*Referring to his links.*

Gosh, aren't these something?

LYDIA. (*Admiring them.*) Something is certainly what they are, Joey. After what you've just said about Sebastian, now might be the moment to ask you to do me a little favour—

JOEY. (*Guardedly.*) Mum I only said I liked him as a *critic*. I didn't say—

LYDIA. I said: 'Do *me a* favour,' Joey.

JOEY. (*Very defensive.*) Something to do with Dad?

LYDIA. Yes.

JOEY. What?

*Pause.*

LYDIA. You took over very well last night, I hear, after your mother got herself a little—over-excited. You cooked a very good dinner . . .

JOEY. I only finished off what you'd got ready.

LYDIA. Your father said it was very good. And after that, he said, you washed up brilliantly.

JOEY. How can you wash up brilliantly? I mean either you wash up or you don't, and as my seniors were plainly bent on shouting insults at each other over the chess-board until about five in the morning, I thought if I'm going to get to bed at all I'd better wash up, now and alone. That's all, Mum. It's not worth three columns in next week's *Sunday Times*—

LYDIA. Still you did it.

JOEY. (*In deepest suspicion.*) Yes, I did. So?

*Pause.*

LYDIA. Now I told you, didn't I, that I was going of on a little holiday next week?

JOEY. (*Even more suspiciously.*) Yes, Mum.

LYDIA. And that means that for about ten days your father's going to be all on his own.

*After no response from* JOEY.

All on his ownsome, Joey—

JOEY. (*Interrupting shrilly.*) No, Mum. No! No! Not in a thousand years—

LYDIA. But Joey, your father would be so pleased—

JOEY. He'd be round the bend in twenty-four hours, and so would I.

LYDIA. That's not true. Now, let's think, you haven't got anything on for the next ten days, have you?

JOEY. I will have now.

LYDIA. You have to pay Jerry and Sue a pound a night for that room don't you?

JOEY. I'll pay them ten pounds a night for the next ten days. It'd be cheap at the price.

*Pause.*

LYDIA. (*Laughing politely.*) You know, Joey, if you stayed on here for that—very short time—your father would be so awfully—touched—Really—I mean *touched*, Joey.

*She knows it's a phony word as soon as she uttered it.*

JOEY. (*Shrill again.*) Touched? Are you bonkers? *Touched? Father?* He wouldn't be touched if I jumped in front of a bus to save him from getting hit by it. He'd just come back and say:

*Imitating him better than does* LYDIA.

'Extraordinary thing just happened, darling. A bus nearly hit me. I think I'll sue London Transport.' And you'd say: 'Where's Joey?' And he'd say: 'Joey? Now, why isn't he here—Oh yes, I remember . . . He's lying under a bus, somewhere.'—

LYDIA. (*After trying to be angry, has to laugh.*) You seem to have inherited your father's creative talent.

JOEY. (*Looking at his watch.*) Well, that's yet to be proved, isn't it, in about seventeen minutes.

*In alarm.*

Mum, do you think he's going to make it?

LYDIA. (*Bravely.*) Of course, he's going to make it. You know, Joey—I think, somehow, you mean rather a lot to him—

JOEY. Oh Mum, no one means a lot to him, and you know it. Not even you.

LYDIA. Now that's a very bad thing to say.

JOEY. Yes it is, but it's the truth. And one has to tell the truth.

LYDIA. Has one?

JOEY. Honesty, in this life, is just about the only thing that matters.

LYDIA. Is It?

JOEY. We both know that the only person who matters to Dad is Dad. Mum, you've admitted that to me often enough—

LYDIA. As a joke, perhaps.

JOEY. No, Mum, as the truth. Don't be dishonest, Mum, please . . .

*Eagerly.*

Is that him?

*He listens intently.* LYDIA *pretends to.*

LYDIA. No. It's Mr. Jackson upstairs. But he'll come. Don't worry.

JOEY. Oh, I don't worry. If he wants to miss it, let him miss it!

LYDIA. He won't . . . Darling, I think you do mean something rather special to him—

JOEY. A rather special punch-bag—

LYDIA. (*Hotly.*) That's not true. You hit him far more often than he hits you.

JOEY. Yes. Because he still sees me as a tiny little Joeykins, who has to have the great Marxist truth spanked into his little tummy every now and then. He doesn't realise I'm grown up, and I've got my own truth now, which I've learnt myself—and I can sometimes get in a couple of quick left hooks into *his* little tummy before he's squared up—

LYDIA. A bit below the belt, sometimes, aren't they?

JOEY. Well that's where he *should* expect them, as he still sees me *that* high . . .

*He indicates some object about two feet high.*

Mum, his political thinking isn't just out of date—God, did Stalin prove *nothing?*—it's so *dishonest!*

LYDIA. (*Glancing at the telephone, absently.*) Which, in your view, is the greatest crime of all?

JOEY. Yes, it is. Dad only spouts red revolution as a kind of spell to prevent it ever happening. The way some old people talk about death—you know the kind—?

LYDIA. Yes. I sympathise a bit—

JOEY. I think it's utterly squalid and corrupt to spout a theory when you personally would hate it coming true. Imagine Dad being ordered by his State-controlled Sunday paper to say that Evelyn Waugh was a bad writer: or that Orwell was a lackey of the Bourgeoisie? He'd be in a Labour Camp in a week.

LYDIA. These days I believe it's a Mental Home—

JOEY. I'm sorry. I was forgetting about your family.

LYDIA. Don't be. It was a very long time ago. Anyway, at least you grant him some integrity—

JOEY. About literature, yes . . . The highest. But about politics, no . . . The lowest. Ten days of the two of us together alone would be disaster, Mum. Please believe it. Either there'd be parricide or the opposite—what's it called—?

LYDIA. (*Looking at the telephone.*) What's *what* called?

JOEY. The killing of a son by a father?

LYDIA. (*Automatically.*) I don't know. You must ask your father.

JOEY. (*Equally automatically.*) Yes, I will. It's 'felicide', I suppose.

LYDIA. I suppose so . . . So you won't do this for *me*, Joey? For *me*, I asked?

JOEY. Mum, I'll do anything for you. You know that. Anything in the world. But not that. Forgive me.

*Pause.*

LYDIA. You see he did like so much what you did for him last night—

JOEY. (*Laughing.*) Oh, Mum!

*Pause.*

LYDIA. (*Serious.*) And I do kind of hate him being left quite alone—

*Pause.*

JOEY. Do you have to go?

LYDIA. Yes, I do. I can't get out of it—And then I may have to go away again, perhaps even for a bit longer—

JOEY. When?

LYDIA. Oh, not yet. Not soon. But there was this talk about my, perhaps, starting up something of my own sometime—

JOEY. Doing what?

LYDIA. Oh—like going back to Estonia, writing some articles about it—even a book. Joey, your father's so *helpless* alone—

JOEY. Well, whose fault is that?

LYDIA. 'Whose fault' is only an argument, never a reason.

*Pause.*

JOEY. Mum. It will be disastrous, he hasn't changed, he's really a very high old Tory. When there was that revolt in Czechoslovakia and the Russians went in to squash it, I was only fifteen, but I remember listening to Dad and even then I was thinking but that's any old member of the Carlton Club saying: 'By God, sir, send in a few tanks—that'll teach the natives to know their place'. And I bet at the time of Hungary he was shouting; 'Send a gunboat up the Danube'. Wasn't he?

LYDIA *is trying loyally not to laugh but has to give way before she can answer.*

LYDIA. Very likely.

JOEY. Sorry, Mum. Now I'm grown up I'm answering back, and he hates it. It just won't work. I know it won't.

LYDIA. Are politics all that important? Joey, if there's one thing I've learnt from a fairly—hectic—life, it's that things—beliefs, creeds, ideas, theories—are so far, far less important than people. Honestly, Joey—in the end you'll find it's only people who matter at all.

*Pause.*

JOEY. I don't agree, but say you're right. He's a person, so am I. We're people. But we're on different wave lengths—Look, I'll give you this. He has tried to communicate with me. Sometimes, in what he thinks is my language, with words like 'cool' and 'hep' and 'with it' and—oh everything. I know he expects me to answer him in a hippy drawl like, man, like it's real groovy man, like it blew my mind, man—

*Hands over face.*

Oh, Mum, it's so embarrassing! That's the way the over-thirties talk—and he's over fifty.

LYDIA. (*Sharply.*) Only just. How do you under-thirties talk?

JOEY. Well, you've heard me, and Jacky and Sue. We try to talk English—the way he did when he was young. I suppose—a bit less Mandarin, I hope. But English.

LYDIA. If it's just a question of idiom—

JOEY. Mum. I'm sorry. I can't stay on. It just isn't possible.

LYDIA. Joey, sons have always turned against their fathers all through history. Sebastian turned against his—

JOEY. The Bishop?

*He laughs.*

Yes, I feel sorry for the Bishop—

*He bends down to put the television on.*

Just warming it up.

*The telephone rings.* LYDIA *crosses to it, muttering to herself.*

LYDIA. Oh, thank God.

*To* JOEY.

Believe me, Joey, he does love you really, he does.

*Into receiver.*

Oh hullo! Hullo, darling! We were getting worried. Where are you?—You're going to watch it there—with the editor? You mean he's going to watch too?

JOEY. Gosh! Is it colour?

LYDIA. Is it colour, Joey wants to know?—Very latest, of course . . .

JOEY. Will the others be watching it too?

LYDIA. (*Into receiver.*) Will the others be watching it too?
*To* JOEY.

    All the others. Some very important people too.

JOEY. Gosh!—Oh gosh! Oh Jesus!

LYDIA. Hurry back, darling. You mustn't miss the beginning. I gather if you
    do you'll find it rather hard to understand the rest. . . Yes, darling. But
    hurry!
*She rings off.*

    You see, Joey—you see!

JOEY. Surprise, surprise!

LYDIA. I hope now you're ashamed of yourself. You see how much he
    cares?

JOEY. I bet it was your idea. To get his Editor to watch. I bet that was your
    idea—

LYDIA. No, it was entirely his own idea.

JOEY. Ha, ha.

LYDIA. Are you implying I'm a liar?

JOEY. Well—I bet you used pressure.

LYDIA. Now, Joey, what pressure have I ever been able to bring on your
    father to do something he didn't want to do?

JOEY. There you are. You're admitting it.

LYDIA. What?

JOEY. That he's a selfish old beast who thinks only of his own comfort.

LYDIA. (*Sharply.*) Joey, I won't have you talking about your father like that—
    do you understand!

JOEY. Yes, Mum.

LYDIA. Especially after this—very—generous thing he's doing for you tonight.
    Going all that way up to Fleet Street?

JOEY. (*Embracing her.*) Yes, I'm sorry.

LYDIA. (*Still trying to be angry.*) And getting his Editor—

JOEY. Yes, I know, I know. I'm sorry.

*Pause.* LYDIA *looks down at his head, bravely resisting the almost overpowering
instinct to stroke it.*

LYDIA. So shall we take it that you'll do what I've just asked?

*No reply from* JOEY. LYDIA *correctly takes it as a 'yes'.*

    Good. Now I know that during those ten days you're going to find out
    a lot more about him—

JOEY. (*His face on her shoulder.*) Oh God, I hope not.

LYDIA. I mean what he's really like.

JOEY. (*Despondently.*) I know what he's really like.

LYDIA. You don't, and I've just proved to you that you don't. Haven't I?

*Pause.* JOEY *releases himself from* LYDIA.

JOEY. There's some conspiracy on here. I don't know what it is, but I can feel it. I mean Dad *can't* want me to be alone with him for ten days—

LYDIA. Why not?

JOEY. Ten *whole* days? It's not possible.

LYDIA. Anything is possible in this life, Joey.

JOEY. Not that. Every time I open my mouth I enrage him.

LYDIA. Then don't open your mouth.

JOEY. I'll have to, sometimes.

LYDIA. Then think of opening it to say something pleasing—

JOEY. (*Suspiciously.*) Like what?

LYDIA. Like saying that you think he's one of the best critics in the world—
*Pause.*

JOEY. I've tried that, and what always happened? I get my teeth kicked in.

LYDIA. Then slip those teeth in your pocket, talk through pursed lips and pretend you're not hurt.

JOEY. Which is what you've always done?

LYDIA *shrugs.*

But hell, Mum, that's *dishonest.*

LYDIA. Of course.

JOEY. And honesty—

LYDIA. Is just about the only thing in life that matters? I know, but you're wrong, Joey. Honesty between people who love each other, or let's say who should love each other, is the thing that matters least in this life.

JOEY. (*Outraged.*) We should *pretend*, you mean?

LYDIA. Pretend like hell.

JOEY. You mean pretend that some half-assed political theory is a great truth?

LYDIA. Why not—provided *you* know it isn't.

JOEY. Pretend to agree with someone when you don't?

LYDIA. Why not—provided you *don't* agree with him.

JOEY. But—but that's just—politeness.

LYDIA. Anything wrong with that?

JOEY. Oh, a lot, these days. You see, Mum, it's—

LYDIA. Dishonest. Oh God, please let's have a little return to dishonesty! It was such a much happier world when people told us little lies about ourselves.

JOEY. You'll be talking of 'manners' next.

LYDIA. Yes, I will.

JOEY. (*Scornfully.*) Mum, really! Manners Makyth Man!

LYDIA. (*Angrily.*) Yes they do, and they makyth other men feel better. It's what I said earlier. Joey. It's people that count, not things—Look at Mark . . .

*Muttering.*

And where the hell is he? . . . Anyway look at Mark. When a writer of his standing takes the trouble to come out to Islington to see a half-hour first play by a twenty-year-old acquaintance, puts on a black tie, and says something pleasant about the debut of a brilliant young dramatist—to say nothing about those bloody links—doesn't that make you feel well—good? Or is honesty so goddam important to you that you'd rather he'd taken one of his three London blonde tricks to the Talk of the Town and on to bed?

*The door opens and* MARK *comes in, panting.*

LYDIA. (*Brightly.*) Oh hullo. We were just talking about you.

MARK. (*Falling into a chair.*) Nicely, I hope.

LYDIA. (*To* JOEY.) Nicely, Joey?

JOEY. (*Turning away abruptly.*) Mum was saying it. I was just listening—

MARK. But you were agreeing with her, I hope.

JOEY, *at the television set, and plainly disturbed, doesn't answer.*

LYDIA. Were you agreeing with me, Joey?

JOEY. (*Quietly.*) Yes, Mum.

*He fingers the dials.*

LYDIA. Oh Mark, I've found my replacement.

MARK. (*Still panting, muttering.*) Your replacement, your replacement, your—
*Getting it.*

        Oh, your *replacement?*

LYDIA. Joey has very sweetly, and quite off his own bat, *volunteered—*

MARK. Well, isn't that swell?

*As* JOEY *doesn't turn from the TV set, we must assume that he has done just that thing. The volume is down.*

JOEY. Are those faces too green?

MARK. They look just right to me.

*Pause.*

LYDIA. (*Rather loudly.*) Sebastian called while you were out, Mark.

MARK. Did he? Sebastian? Did he indeed?

LYDIA. Yes. He's going to see it on a much better set than this.

MARK. (*Almost too loud.* LYDIA *has to frown at him.*) Oh really? Where?

JOEY. (*Turning, eagerly.*) At his Editor's.

MARK. (*Back to normal.*) Well, now, isn't that something!

LYDIA. You'd better sit here, Mark.

JOEY. No, Mum, I want you to sit there—

*He indicates an armchair.*

        and, Mr. Walters, you there.

*He indicates a rather uncomfortable-looking stool.*

LYDIA. But this is more comfortable—

JOEY. I know. It's for you.

MARK. Ah, I get it. He wants his audience attentive.

LYDIA. Well, I'm his audience.

MARK. (*Sitting in the uncomfortable seat.*) You're his mother.

JOEY. (*From the set.*) Sh!

*He turns the set's volume up.*

ANNOUNCER. On B.B.C. 1, in thirty seconds time, there is Match of the Week—

JOEY. Of course that's what they'll all be watching.

LYDIA. Nonsense.

ANNOUNCER. (*Through this.*) Meanwhile on B.B.C. 2 there follows shortly a new thirty-minute play in the current series: Youth Theatre, entitled 'The Trial of Maxwell Henry Peabody', by Joseph Cruttwell.

*There is music.*

LYDIA. (*Sharply.*) *Joseph!* Why Joseph?

JOEY. It sounds more like a writer.

MARK. Yeah. It's a good name, Lydia. Joey's not too good. Joseph Cruttwell sounds like something—

JOEY. Thank you, Mr. Walters.

*The music stops.*

FIRST VOICE. (*Loudly.*) Maxwell Henry Peabody—come into court.

*There is the sound of marching feet.* LYDIA *and* MARK *are both forward in that attitude of strained attention natural to people watching a TV play under the observant scrutiny of the author, who has chosen a vantage point where he can see both screen and audience.*

*The lights fade very quickly. There is a blackout for only a second before they come on again.* LYDIA, MARK *and* JOEY *are in exactly the same strained attitudes as before. One might think no one has moved even a finger to scratch his or her nose.*

Have you anything to say why sentence should not be passed against you?

SECOND VOICE. But this is ridiculous. I have done nothing, I tell you—nothing, nothing, nothing—

FIRST VOICE. I agree. You have done nothing. Nothing to help your fellow human beings, nothing to save the world from the abyss into which it must soon finally fall, nothing save for your own material advantage—

SECOND VOICE. And my wife's. She's a director of several of my companies.

FIRST VOICE. And what did you do to save your son?

*There is mocking laughter, followed by a blare of music, evidently signalling the end. Credits must follow because* JOEY *kneels by the set, his nose practically touching it, to see his name go by.* LYDIA *crouches with him.*

LYDIA. There. Look how big his name is, Mark. Yes, Joseph is better.

*She embraces him.*

Darling, I'm so proud.

JOEY. (*Impatiently.*) But did you *like* it?

LYDIA. I loved it, Joey—

JOEY. (*Staring at her, puzzled.*) Did it make you cry?

LYDIA. A little. Wasn't it meant to?

JOEY. (*Doubtfully.*) Well it's really supposed to make one angry.

LYDIA. (*Reassuringly.*) Oh it did that too.

MARK. (*Choosing his words.*) Congratulations, young man, on a fine achievement—

*The front door is unlocked.* SEBASTIAN *appears, looking angry, holding in his hand* LYDIA'S *message which he has torn from the door.*

SEBASTIAN. What in hell's this? If after eight-thirty don't come in. I'm covering up—

*He stops at sight of the television set in its prominent position, of* LYDIA *in her smart dress, of* MARK *in a dinner jacket and of* JOEY *in one of his own shirts, all staring at him with varying expressions.*

Oh Christ—

JOEY *looks away from him first.*

JOEY. Good night, Mum. Thanks for watching.

LYDIA. But the champagne—

JOEY. No, thanks. Good night, Mr. Walters. Thanks for coming and for these.

*He indicates the cuff links.*

and for what you said.

MARK. It was good—real good, Joey. I mean it.

JOEY. Thanks.

*In silence he walks up the stairs, hoping evidently to achieve dignity. But coming to the end he hurries his steps in a revealing way.* LYDIA *looks after him.*

SEBASTIAN. Oh Lord—

LYDIA *suddenly swings one fist at him, and then the other. They are hard blows, with real fury behind them, and both connect.* SEBASTIAN, *off balance, and slightly unsteady anyhow, is knocked off his feet and falls, upsetting a table.*

LYDIA. (*With deep hatred.*) You bastard!

*She turns and runs up the stairs after her son.* SEBASTIAN *stays where he is, for a moment, putting his hand to his cheek, and shaking his head.* MARK *helps him to his feet.*

SEBASTIAN. (*Indicating television.*) Was it terrible?

MARK. Pretty terrible.

SEBASTIAN. (*In a chair.*) Get me a drink.

MARK. What is it? Scotch?

SEBASTIAN. (*Angrily.*) Of course Scotch.

*With a deep sigh.*

Oh, my God! I had it written down, I'd tied knots in everything, I'd remembered it at lunch—

*He takes the drink from* MARK.

And then after lunch something happened—

*Pause. He stares into his glass.*

A perfect excuse, I suppose, if I could use it. Perfect. But I can't.

MARK What was it?

SEBASTIAN. I can't tell you either. Except—

*He stares into his glass again.*

I have to anyway—but not as an excuse.

*Loudly.*

I have no excuses. I am as God made me, which is an uncaring shit. Oh damn! Poor little bugger. She'd covered up for me?

MARK. You were watching it with your Editor.

SEBASTIAN. He's in Tangier.

MARK. The kid wouldn't have known that.

SEBASTIAN. Damn silly cover. I suppose it might have worked though. She'd have made it work!—I'm not saying I didn't *deserve* a left hook, I'm just asking if you know why it was particularly savage?

MARK. Really want to know?

SEBASTIAN. Yes.

MARK. She'd just got him to promise to stay here with you those ten days she's away—

SEBASTIAN. Stay here with me? Why?

MARK. She thought—you might need company—

SEBASTIAN. His company? Why?

MARK She just thought you might like it.

*Pause. Quite a long one.*

SEBASTIAN. But *he'd* hate it.

MARK. She'd got him to say yes.

*Another pause.*

SEBASTIAN. (*Covering his face.*) Goddam it.

MARK. Yes.

SEBASTIAN. How has she been otherwise tonight, apart from first attempting to win the Nobel Peace Prize—and then turning into Muhammad Ali?

MARK. Oh, fine, I thought.

SEBASTIAN. Fine, you thought. Did you look at all?

MARK. Sure. She didn't look too well, but I don't suppose she is, after her pass-out last night. Hungover, I'd say.

SEBASTIAN. Yes. Well, you'd better brace yourself, I suppose. Have you got a drink?

*Mark holds his up.*

You're rather fond of this girl, aren't you?

MARK. I love her.

SEBASTIAN. And I suppose you're what might laughingly be called one of my best friends?

*Finishing his drink.*

Fill it up for me, would you?

MARK. Sure.

SEBASTIAN. Are you?

MARK. I think you are what you just said God made you, Sebastian—but maybe I'm not all that choosey about my best friends.

SEBASTIAN. Well I'm not either, or I wouldn't choose an ignorant, illiterate porn-monger—

MARK. (*Returning with the drink.*) O.K. O.K. I'm braced.

SEBASTIAN. That wasn't a pass-out last night—not an ordinary one. It was a small stroke.

*Pause.*

MARK. How do you know?

SEBASTIAN. She's had them before, and these last months they're getting more frequent. It's one of the things I've been told to look out for, you see—and it's one of the things you've got to look out for too when you take her away. I've got a list somewhere—

MARK. Surely the vodka—

SEBASTIAN. It probably helped—that and the cortisone—so don't let her wallow in the stuff as I did last night. She's been off any drink at all for over six months—so go fairly easy out there. Mind you the odd piss-up won't make much difference. Here's that list. Now I've got the doctor's address in Monte Carlo somewhere too—

*He fumbles in his pockets again.*

MARK. (*Quietly.*) Did you say cortisone?

SEBASTIAN. What? Yes. She's been on it six weeks. She doesn't know it, of course. Thinks they're iron pills, or something. Old Conny Schuster—he's her doctor—'Uncle Constantin' she calls him—an ex-Estonian—he's quite a wonder. He can get her to believe anything—where the hell did I put that address? Ah, here it is. Docteur Villoret. Address is on it.

MARK *takes it from him.*

Conny Schuster called him this afternoon, so he'll be wise to the situation, as your horrible phrase goes.

MARK. Could you, perhaps, put me wise too?

*Pause.* SEBASTIAN *looks up at him.*

SEBASTIAN. I suppose so. I've been trying to put it off. I can't put it of any longer, can I?

*Another pause.*

She's in the terminal stages of a disease called poly-arteritis. You've probably never heard of it because it isn't very common. It comes from malnutrition early in life.

*Pause.* SEBASTIAN *gets up and takes* MARK'S *glass to fill, patting his arm as he goes.*

Sorry, I had to tell you, you see, because old Conny Schuster wouldn't have let her go otherwise, unless I was along. I'm well-briefed, you see. What's that dreadful drink you have?

MARK. Bourbon. Did you say terminal?

SEBASTIAN. Yes.

MARK. How long does that mean?

SEBASTIAN. Three or four months. Six at most.

*He hands* MARK *the drink.*

MARK. Are you positive?

SEBASTIAN *laughs.*

SEBASTIAN. That's just the word, I'm afraid.

*He pulls another paper from his pocket and hands it to* MARK.

This came from Conny Schuster by hand to the office this afternoon. He'd had it early this morning from the hospital, but couldn't call me because of Lydia. You see there "Poly-Arteritis". "Acute"—Positive.

MARK *stares at the paper with unseeing eyes. He knows, after all, its contents. Then he hands it back.*

*Pause.*

MARK. (*At length.*) So that's the something that happened to you after lunch.

SEBASTIAN. (*Distracted.*) What?—Yes. That. But I'd expected it. Conny hadn't given me any hope. He hasn't, really, for the last three months.

MARK. Who else has she seen?

SEBASTIAN. The best in the country. She doesn't know it, of course, but every man who looks her over in that hospital is hand-picked. Of course they're casual with her, and don't give their names. But they've all been by courtesy of my kind Sunday paper—and all top boys on this disease.

MARK. There's no cure?

SEBASTIAN. There's this man in Denver, Colorado, who boasts a seventy per cent rate. But he's cagey. He won't take a case as advanced as this—

MARK. How do you know?

SEBASTIAN. I've asked him. I gave him all the facts and figures on the telephone, and got our medical correspondent to talk to him, too. No go, Mark. He won't take her, she's too far gone. (*Bitterly.*) He might spoil his record.

MARK. Isn't there anyone else?

SEBASTIAN. Faith healers galore, and acupuncture hounds. All phoneys. Christ, Mark, I haven't lacked for advice. If there'd been the faintest chance I'd have taken her to Timbuctoo—and told her I was covering Saharan literature. I'd already got my story ready for Denver. I'd induced some wretched little local college to offer me a resident lectureship. Jesus, imagine that! . . . Now, Winnie Slobberwicz, stop groping your neighbour and listen. Balls-ache, as you are pleased to pronounce him, is the name of an important French writer and not an occupational disease—You've seen her alone. Does she have the faintest suspicion I'm concealing something from her?

MARK. No.

SEBASTIAN. Swear?

MARK. Swear.

SEBASTIAN. I'm good about never remembering when she's been to the doctor, getting his name wrong and never noticing when she's feeling ill. Also never on any account saying: 'Look I'll do that, darling. Don't you bother.' Can you imagine anything giving the show away quicker than that?

MARK. Frankly, I can't.

SEBASTIAN. Yes. Being what we both agreed God made me does have its advantages when one's dealing with a dying wife.

*He takes the report that he has shown* MARK *from wherever it has been placed and glances at it.*

I suppose I'd better put this with the others.

MARK. Other what?

SEBASTIAN. Other reports—all of them.

*He wheels out some library steps and places them beside a certain point at the book-shelves: in fact just below the hat-box.*

Say: "Hullo Lydia" very loudly if you see her on the stairs.

*He makes an extension to the library steps, an operation which appears to need some application.*

Yes. Uncle Conny sends me her reports every month. They vary so much you see. This is a disease that seems to go up and down.—Not steadily down like some. A little bit up one month, and one got hope. Then down next month. More down than the last down, and then one lost hope.

*He flourishes the last report, and begins his ascent towards the hat-box.*

MARK. Why do you keep a hat-box up there?

SEBASTIAN. To keep a hat in, you clot. What else?

*He opens the box, takes out a top hat, puts his hand into the hat, removes a sheaf of papers, and then puts the hat on.*

Topper to go to the Palace in for that O.B.E. thing.

MARK. Jesus! Why did you keep those there?

SEBASTIAN. Security. Couldn't keep them at the office. Too many nosey parkers.

*He clips the last report on to the bundle of papers, takes off the hat and shoves the hat and papers into the box.*

MARK. That's ingenious.

SEBASTIAN. Yes. I got the idea from Edgar Allan Poe.

MARK. But wouldn't a drawer with a lock be safer?

SEBASTIAN. I haven't got one—but if I had she'd pick it. Pries into everything, you know. Got her nose into my notes for the new novel yesterday, after I'd carefully hidden them in Gibbon's *Decline and Fall.*

*Descending.*

Dusting, she said. As if anyone would dust Gibbon without criminal intent.

MARK. Mightn't she want to dust up there?

SEBASTIAN. Aha! Without these steps she *can't* dust up there, and I'm the only one who knows how to elongate this contraption.—

*He shoves the extension back. He has spoken the truth: without the elongation* LYDIA *would have no hope of reaching it.*

Even Mrs. MacReedy who is a giantess—if she's the Mrs. MacReedy I think she is—can only just flick it with the very last feather of her duster.

*Pleased with himself.*

Yes. I wasn't in intelligence for nothing, you know.

*He wheels the steps away, and then comes back to join* MARK. *He looks up at the box.*

No point, of course, in keeping anything more now. Not after this biopsy.

MARK. Sebastian, are you quite sure you shouldn't tell her?

SEBASTIAN. Quite sure. For six long years she had nothing to think of, Mark, except the almost certain prospect of facing death, in one of a hundred really horrible ways . . . To the Nazis the Balts were 'untermensch'. They didn't deserve gas chambers. That was a luxury kept for the lucky inmates of Auschwitz and Buchenwald down south—A three star death compared to the 'untermensch' up north—

*He sits down hurriedly, and drinks.*

I send her up a bit for her refugee stories, but you know she doesn't really tell them—not about herself—

*He has his empty glass stretched out.* MARK *takes it automatically.*

Oh, thanks so much . . . No. Up North it was open graves, and machine guns—Not always enough machine guns, so people got buried alive. That didn't matter to the Gauleiter, so long as he could report them dead.

MARK *comes back with his drink.*

Thanks. Lydia *was* reported dead, you know. That's how she managed to stay alive. When the Russians came back she was officially a non-person. Labour Camp material, perhaps, but not worth killing. And you know how she became a non-person? Did she ever tell you?

MARK. No.

SEBASTIAN. No, she wouldn't. She only told me once—one night in Bentinck Strasse—Well the drill was, they'd take them out at dusk into the open country, about a thousand at a time. And then they'd be made to dig this big ditch. It had to be pretty big to take a thousand bodies. Of course, they knew what it was for. No 'You're all going to the baths to be deloused,' as in the gas-chambers. No. The 'untermensch' knew what they were digging.

*He drinks.*

Well, when that was finished to the Commandant's satisfaction they were divided into groups of about a hundred and stripped naked—gold fillings were pulled out, of course . . . That didn't apply to Lydia, who was only eighteen.

*He takes another drink.*

Then floodlights were turned on and each group was lined up facing the ditch and machine-gunned into the ditch . . . There were two gunners at either end of the ditch who sprayed the ones who seemed still to be alive—Then the next lot were lined up . . . Lydia's group was nearly the last—She'd seen the others die so she also saw how the machine-gunners operated . . . She counted the time-lag between the order to fire and the actual firing—half a second . . . At eighteen she was a—she was a very good swimmer, you see—I mean, almost Olympic class, I gather— She was trained to the starting gun. She heard the order 'fire,' and dived into that ditch and landed without a scratch . . . 'Beating the gun' she called it . . . And she crawled under the bodies of her friends, dead or dying, so that the two gunners who both shot at her from each side missed her—maybe killed some of those on top of her . . . Later the bulldozer shovelled the earth on top of the grave, and she lay buried for two hours until she thought it was safe to claw her way through the bodies and the earth into the air . . . Although how she knew it was two hours, without a watch, I'll always question . . . She says she counted second by second, which is possible, I suppose . . . But how did she survive that Baltic winter night, in the forest, naked? . . . Well she did, and a farmer took her in, at risk to his own life, in the morning—and gave her boy's clothes—his son's, I think—and a lift to Tallinn, and a new life—until the Russians came back. But that's another story.

*He gets up himself to pour another drink.* MARK *watches him, concerned.*

So, Mark, I don't think it would be quite—the thing—do you—to tell a lady who survived that kind of nonsense that she's now dying of some bloody silly disease that's been caused by her, as a teenager, not eating enough Kellogg's K with her breakfast. Don't you think I'm right?

*Pause.*

MARK. Yeh. I think you might be right . . .

SEBASTIAN. (*Resuming his seat.*) Another thing, Mark. If she had the slightest inkling about herself, she'd worry herself sick over Joey.

MARK. Not over you?

SEBASTIAN. Over *me?* Why should she worry herself over me? She knows I can look after myself—

MARK. Does she?

SEBASTIAN. Well what with Mrs. MacReedy and maybe Prunella—

MARK. Isn't it just Mrs. Reedy?

SEBASTIAN. It may well be Mrs. Cholmondeley-Johnson-Smythe. Would you kindly not interfere in matters that are no concern of yours?

MARK. I'm sorry.

*Pause.*

About this lady Prunella—didn't you say yesterday that you couldn't bear—

SEBASTIAN. I know exactly what I said yesterday. Again it is no possible concern of yours.

MARK *goes to get himself another drink.*

The Bourbon is on the right, and, what with last night, you have come bloody close to drinking it flat.

MARK. (*Belligerently.*) This is *my* Bourbon. Lydia bought it for *me.*

SEBASTIAN. (*Suddenly close to tears.*) And you've left nothing for her favourite charity— "The Little Sisters of the Poor."

*His back to* MARK, *he believes he has concealed his emotion, but he hasn't.*

MARK. (*At the drink table.*) This Prunella—

SEBASTIAN. Yes?

MARK. I guess she means a bit more to you than you let on last night—

SEBASTIAN. (*Speaking with difficulty.*) Why do you guess that?

MARK. Well, it wasn't so difficult. Jesus, did you play that up for Lydia!

SEBASTIAN. Was it so obvious?

MARK. (*Hastily.*) Lydia didn't get it.

SEBASTIAN. Sure?

MARK. Certain.

SEBASTIAN. Terrible if she had. Yes, Prunella means a bit, I suppose.

MARK. Enough for you to go to her and tell her this afternoon that you'd got a letter from Lydia's doctor.

*Pause.*

SEBASTIAN. Yes. Enough for that.

MARK. Enough for her to make you forget that your son had a television play on tonight at seven thirty.

SEBASTIAN. She didn't make me forget it. If she'd known about it she'd have forced me to be here for it—Prunella's all right, Mark.—She's no Lydia, but she's all right—.

*Fumbling with a handkerchief.*

No Lydia—.

*He begins to cry.*

You've got to put up with this a bit, I'm afraid . . . Self-pity, of course . . . You see the thing is, Mark—the un-crying, unsentimental, un-self-pitying thing is that I didn't begin really to love her until I knew I was losing her.

MARK. (*Not indulging him.*) Yeh. That happens.

SEBASTIAN. Perhaps more to people like me than to people like you. You've always loved her, haven't you?

MARK. I guess so.

SEBASTIAN. While I—I've—only had about six months. Anybody but me would have started twenty-eight years sooner.

*He hands out his drink to be refilled.* MARK *takes it. Murmuring.*

No Lydia—

'She'll come no more.

Never, never, never, never, never.'

Oh damn and blast. I'll never review that bloody man Shakespeare again. I won't review anyone. After all they all make you blub somewhere—if they're good enough. No. I'll write my own blub stuff—that's what I'll do—

MARK. Good idea.

SEBASTIAN. All right. I may not sell the film rights for ten million in advance, like some people—

MARK. Only one million—well, a million and a half—for the new one, but who's counting?

SEBASTIAN. And I may not build palaces from its profits in Eaton Square—
East Seventy eighth Street—Beverly Drive—Tonga—

MARK. (*Affronted.*) I haven't got a palace in Tonga—

SEBASTIAN. You will have. No. I will write the second masterpiece of the twentieth century—

MARK. Which was the first?

SEBASTIAN. Modesty forbids. And you and your pathetic attempt to steal Lydia
will be in it—

MARK. Can't you find a better theme than that?

SEBASTIAN. Oh, you're not the theme. You're just a fringe character—Not as
you are, of course. No one would believe that—

MARK. And Lydia?

SEBASTIAN. Oh no. No, not Lydia. I couldn't write Lydia, and never will. Idiot!

MARK. Well, then, Joey?

SEBASTIAN. (*Suddenly still.*) Yes, Joey, I suppose. Little Liberal Joey. The new
assenting young.

*Suddenly overcome again. The influx of adrenalin about his new novel hasn't
been quite enough.*

Poor little bastard!—Oh, the poor little sod—He worships his mother—
Too much for his psychological balances, I suppose, but you can't quite
blame him, can you?

MARK. No.

SEBASTIAN. And she thought he could put up with me for ten days?

MARK. She's an optimistic girl.

SEBASTIAN. Yes. Well tonight won't have helped her optimism . . . Poor little
bugger . . . ten days without her. I don't like to think of that much.

MARK. Then come too.

SEBASTIAN. No. I could—but I've got to get used to—try to get used to—oh
damn! Did I feel about her like this from the beginning? It's possible.
It's possible. And wouldn't allow myself to? Yes, possible.

*Angrily.*

Do you know what 'le vice Anglais?'—the English vice really is? Not flag-
ellation, not pederasty—whatever the French believe it to be. It's our
refusal to admit to our emotions. We think they demean us, I suppose.

*He covers his face.*

Well I'm being punished now, all right—for a lifetime of vice. Very moral
endings to a Victorian novel. I'm becoming maudlin. But, oh Mark, life
without Lydia will be such unending misery.

*He sees* LYDIA *coming down the stairs.* SEBASTIAN *jumps up from his chair and
turns his back, adroitly transforming emotion into huffiness.* LYDIA *looks at
his back a long time. When* SEBASTIAN *turns to face her he is apparently dry-
eyed, and holding his jaw as if in pain.*

SEBASTIAN. (*With dignity.*) Husband-beater!

LYDIA. I came to say I was sorry.

SEBASTIAN. I shall so inform my solicitors. Good night Mark.

MARK. Oh, am I going?

SEBASTIAN. No, I am.

*He gives another withering glance at* LYDIA, *rubs his cheek and walks towards his work-room, even contriving a limp as he does so.*

LYDIA. Are you going to work? Isn't it too late?

SEBASTIAN. Yes, to the first. No, to the second.

LYDIA. Wouldn't you like some of this food?

SEBASTIAN. It would turn to ashes in my mouth.

*He goes out.*

LYDIA. Did I hurt him?

MARK. Not enough.

LYDIA. I could have hit him much harder, you know. And kicked him too—on the ground. Queensberry Rules my fanny. Is he really working or just sulking?

MARK. Sulking, I'd say. I'm going.

LYDIA. (*Looking anxiously at* SEBASTIAN'S *door.*) Yes, I suppose you'd better.

*She kisses him.*

Thank you so very much. Marcus. He really did appreciate it.

MARK. How is Joey?

LYDIA. He's bad, of course.

*Angrily, at the door.*

How could any human being do a thing like that to his son? How *could* he? What's his excuse?

MARK. He forgot.

LYDIA. I mean his excuse for forgetting?

*Pause.*

MARK. About the best a man could have, I guess.

LYDIA. (*Amazed.*) You take his side.

MARK. Yes, on this.

LYDIA. Well what is his excuse?

MARK. Good night, Lydia.

*He goes to the door, leaving* LYDIA *looking bewildered. Turning.*

Oh Christ! Has anybody ever been in such a spot? Look—

*He points to the hat-box.*

That thing up there. It needs dusting.

LYDIA. The hat-box?

MARK. Yes. You can see the dust from here.

LYDIA. But I can't reach it.

MARK *points to some library steps.* LYDIA, *utterly bewildered, goes to get them.* MARK *takes them from her, and wheels them into place. Then, with intense concentration, he works on the process of elongating them which he has plainly learned from watching* SEBASTIAN. *He finds the catch and pulls them up the necessary extra two or three feet.*

MARK. No. Not now. Tomorrow—when Sebastian's out. After you've dusted it—inside as well as out—you'll just have to play it your way—both of you. And then together or separately—tell me how *I'm* to play mine.

*He restores the steps to their unextended length and puts them away.*

LYDIA. I see. He's hidden something there.

MARK. Yes.

LYDIA. Something he doesn't want me to see.

MARK. You bet.

LYDIA. The wily bastard. Love letters?

MARK. Kind of.

LYDIA. (*Aghast.*) You mean—serious?

MARK. Very serious, I think.

LYDIA. Larkin—I suppose—

MARK. No. Someone else.

LYDIA. Jesus—I wish I *had* kicked him. I wish I'd *killed* him.

*Suddenly loyal.*

And why are you giving him away? You're supposed to be his friend.

MARK. I'm supposed to be yours, too. That's what made my life, these last two days, a little confusing. Call you tomorrow.

*He goes out.* LYDIA, *muttering imprecations, first looks at the hat-box, then firmly decides to resist the temptation. She comes into the sitting-room and sits down demurely. Then she looks at the hat-box again, and the library steps. Then she gets up cautiously and listens at* SEBASTIAN'S *door. She hears him typing, and so do we. She darts to the library steps, rolls them into the hall and pulls down the hat-box, opening it and groping inside. Her fingers find what they are looking for and remove a pile of documents. Hastily she replaces the lid, and puts the hat-box back, leaving the library steps where they are. Then she puts on her glasses and settles herself on to the sofa. She riffles through the papers. They are all of identical size, and have needed no more than a few glances. They are, after all, familiar.*

*After a moment or two her legs give way, and she has to fall back on to the sofa. She has opened her bag to fumble for a handkerchief when* SEBASTIAN *opens his door. It is the matter of a split second for an accomplished document peeper to stuff the papers into her bag and close it. The budding tears are a different matter. She had to brush those away. And she is conscious too of the tell-tale library steps.*

SEBASTIAN. (*Gloomily.*) I've been trying to write him a letter you could shove under his door. But it's no good. My mandarin style gets in the way.

LYDIA. It would.

*She gets up casually to drape herself somewhere near the hall, masking the library steps.*

SEBASTIAN. I suppose I'd better see the little sod.

LYDIA. What little sod?

SEBASTIAN. Are there two in the flat? Where is he?

LYDIA. If you're referring to our son—Joseph Cruttwell, dramatist—he's in bed.

SEBASTIAN. Oh darling, do stop sniffling. You know how I hate it.

LYDIA. I wasn't sniffling.

SEBASTIAN. You were. I could hear you from in there.

*A lie.*

And those things under your eyes are tears, aren't they?

*He peers from a distance.*

I'm not coming in range. I think you should know I once hit a sub-editor and he was off-duty for a week. And he wasn't any smaller than you either. However, enough of that. About Joey. What's done is done, and can by dint of my overwhelming charm, be undone. I shall speak to him personally.

LYDIA. I shouldn't rely on your overwhelming charm.

SEBASTIAN. Thank you.

LYDIA. I mean why not just let him see you once as you really are.

SEBASTIAN. I have no idea what that sibylline utterance is supposed to mean. I think I know a father's duty towards his son without prompting from you, Madam.

LYDIA. I think you do.

SEBASTIAN. I gather you tried to torture him tonight into staying with me while you're off sunning yourself in Monte Carlo.

LYDIA. There was no torture involved. He *volunteered.* He said he'd be happy to do it.

SEBASTIAN. Christ, what an appalling liar you are, sometimes.

LYDIA. I'm not a liar! I'm just—

*She stops.*

SEBASTIAN. What?

LYDIA. An optimist.

SEBASTIAN. Isn't that a liar?

LYDIA. Not necessarily. He'd like to stay with you here for ten days.

*Pause.*

SEBASTIAN. After tonight?

LYDIA. (*Bravely.*) Why not?

*Pause.*

SEBASTIAN. Why are you leaning there like Madame Récamier?

LYDIA. I've been putting books in their right places, under your orders, sir.

SEBASTIAN. Good. That'll be a change. All right. Go and get the little bugger down.

LYDIA. No

SEBASTIAN. No?

LYDIA. You go up.

SEBASTIAN. (*Outraged.*) Go up? Knock timidly at this door and beg leave to enter that room with all those Liberal Posters on the wall—crawl across the carpet like a penitent, abase myself like Henry IV at Canossa, scourge myself—all right, I'll go up.

*He goes to the stairs, climbing reluctantly.*

Why are you looking at me like that?

LYDIA. A cat may look at a King.

SEBASTIAN. Are you pissed again?

LYDIA. Oh yes.

SEBASTIAN. Vodka.

LYDIA. Something—kind of—headier—

SEBASTIAN. Kirsch, or slivovitz or something? My God, darling, you'll end up in an alcoholics' ward.

*He disappears. Immediately* LYDIA *darts into the hall climbs the steps and deposits the papers inside. She has just wheeled the steps back when* SEBASTIAN *reappears.*

I looked in and the little bastard was asleep.

*Relieved.*

Tomorrow, don't you think?

*He scoops some food on to a plate. Plying a fork,*

Hm. This is rather good. Who made it? Joey?

LYDIA, *free now to move, pulls her right fist back.*

Oh *you* did?

LYDIA. It's my crab mousse, and you've had it a million times.

SEBASTIAN. It just seemed better than usual.

JOEY, *in a dressing-gown, is coming downstairs. Both parents watch him as he walks in a dignified manner past his father, cutting him dead, and up to* LYDIA.

JOEY. I'm very sorry, Mum. I left you to clear up alone.

LYDIA. Oh that's all right, darling. I can do that myself.

JOEY. I'll help you.

*He picks up two dishes and carries them up to the kitchen.* SEBASTIAN *exchanges a meaning glance with* LYDIA.

SEBASTIAN. (*Loudly.*) Darling, would you fix that draught for me in there.

LYDIA. Oh, yes, I will.

JOEY *reappears, still walking with dignity.*

SEBASTIAN. I think it's coming from the window.

LYDIA. Yes. I shouldn't be surprised.

*She goes into the work-room.*

SEBASTIAN. Joey, put those things down.

JOEY, *at first, is inclined to disobey.* SEBASTIAN *takes them from him.*

Anyway I'm eating from this one.

JOEY. I'm very sorry. If I'd known I wouldn't have touched it.

SEBASTIAN. You've a perfect right to be as rude to me as you like, and to call me every name you can think of. Tonight I behaved to you as badly as any father has ever behaved to his son. If my father had done that to me when I was your age I'd have walked straight out of his house and never talked to him again.

JOEY. You did, didn't you?

SEBASTIAN. No. I was turned out. I may have told you I walked out, because it sounds better. In fact I was booted. A little trouble with one of the maids. I can only say, Joey, that tonight I behaved like a thoughtless bastard—that's the word your Mum used. To Mark I said 'shit'—'an uncaring shit' and meant it. I am that, sometimes, and I behave like that sometimes. If you like you can say usually. Or even always. It may be true. But tonight was the worst thing I've ever done to anyone, anywhere. I may do some bad things to you, Joey, in the future—if we're still seeing each other—but one thing you must know—I can't ever do anything quite as bad as I did tonight. Not even I can break the world record twice—

JOEY. I don't believe you forgot. I believe you did it deliberately.

SEBASTIAN. I can see you'd rather think that. So would I. It's less damaging to the ego. The plain, sordid fact is that I forgot.

JOEY. How could you, Dad?

SEBASTIAN. I did. And I have no excuse at all. Now listen. What I intend to do is this. I shall get our television man to ask to have it re-run—

JOEY. Oh Dad—this is all talk.

SEBASTIAN. At Television Centre, for me, for him—not for my Editor who's in Tangier—and for anyone else who wants to see it. You, of course, too. And our television critic will review it. I don't know what he'll say, and it'll have to be next week, but he'll mention it in his column, I promise.

JOEY. Is this on the level, or will you forget again?

SEBASTIAN. I said you could insult me, but there's no need to kick me in the crutch. Now if I do that for you will you do something for me?

JOEY. (*Suspiciously.*) What?

SEBASTIAN. Sit in that chair.

*He forces him into one and then brings over the chess table.*

And show me for once how you can justify all that hissing that goes on behind my chair.

JOEY. Dad, it's late.

SEBASTIAN. Only for Liberals. Not for men. Go on. You be white. Fifty pence on it?

JOEY. I'll want a two pawns' handicap.

SEBASTIAN. One.

JOEY. Done.

SEBASTIAN *takes one of his pawns off.* JOEY *moves.* SEBASTIAN *moves.* JOEY *moves.*

SEBASTIAN. That's not in *my* 'Twelve Easy Openings for Beginners'.

SEBASTIAN *moves.* JOEY *thinks.* LYDIA, *who has plainly had her ear glued to the keyhole slips out of the work-room. She watches them for a second.* JOEY *moves.* SEBASTIAN *moves.*

JOEY. (*Rising.*) Right. My game.

SEBASTIAN. What do you mean your game?

JOEY. You moved your King three squares.

SEBASTIAN. I beg your pardon, my Queen.

*Horrified.*

My *King?* Oh blast and bugger that Mark Walters! These pieces are going straight back to Hong Kong. I told him a hundred times—

*He is putting the pieces back on the board again.* JOEY *has stood up.*

JOEY. Fifty pence, please.

SEBASTIAN. Are you mad, boy?

JOEY. The rules say firmly—

LYDIA. You must play the rules, dear.

SEBASTIAN. You keep out of this! Go and do something useful somewhere. Better still, go to bed.

JOEY. Yes, Mum. We'll clear up.

SEBASTIAN. Yes, Joey will clear up.

LYDIA. Give Joey his fifty pence.

SEBASTIAN. Oh bugger you both!

*He forks up.*

LYDIA. Charming loser, isn't he?

SEBASTIAN. Loser my arse! I didn't lose. I made a tiny human error in laying out these monstrosities of chessmen—

JOEY *is going.* SEBASTIAN *catches his sleeve.*

Oh, my boy. Oh no. If you think you're taking that fifty pence of mine to bed, you're making a big mistake. All right. Start again. Double or quits. Same moves, but this time with the right pieces in the right places—

*They move rapidly in silence.* LYDIA *watches them for a moment, putting her arm lightly on* SEBASTIAN'S *shoulder.*

LYDIA. Well, good night.

JOEY *jumps up to kiss his mother.*

SEBASTIAN. (*Irritated.*) Don't do that. It upsets concentration. You could have kissed her sitting down, couldn't you?

*He does exactly that, slapping her playfully on the behind. She goes to the stairs.* SEBASTIAN *concentrates on the board. To* JOEY:

I'm afraid your Liberal Party Headquarters is coming under a little pressure.

JOEY. Your Kremlin doesn't look too happy either, Dad.

LYDIA *turns to look back at them.*

SEBASTIAN. (*To* JOEY.) Yes, I can see you have played before. Well, well, well. Do you know those ten days without her might be quite fun—

*He looks up casually. If we didn't know his secret we might even believe him when he says:*

Oh sorry, darling. Didn't see you were still there.

LYDIA *smiles. In fact, radiantly.*

LYDIA. I know you didn't.

SEBASTIAN. Go on. Move, Joey.
*She goes on slowly up the stairs.*
   We haven't got all night ahead of us.
LYDIA *disappears from sight.*
   Except, I suppose, we have.

CURTAIN

BEFORE DAWN

*Characters*

THE BARON
THE LACKEY
THE CAPTAIN
THE DIVA


*Setting:* Rome
*Time:* The Early Hours of June 17, 1800

# BEFORE DAWN

*A room in the Castel Sant' Angelo. One door is visible (R.) which leads—we will discover—to a bedroom. Steps lead up to it. Another door (L.) is invisible but extremely audible, as it invariably opens (Off.) with a loud clanging of bolts and bars. There is a window at the back. The essential furniture is a desk (L.), a settee and armchairs placed wherever convenient. Also, in a corner, a prie-dieu, with an image of the Virgin, lit by a lamp.*

*Most prominent of all is a supper table, covered with a cloth, on which is a fairly lavish cold collation, with two or three bottles of wine. A* MAN *sits at it, served by a* LACKEY. *The table is lit by candelabra, and so is the desk, but outside these two circles of light the room is shadowy and sinister.*

*In short, if the set bears a strong resemblance to Act IV of Sardou's* TOSCA, (*or to Act II of the opera of the same name) it should not too much surprise us: for the gentleman now gorging himself at the supper table is called the* BARON SCARPIA *and he is the Regent of Police to the Bourbons of Naples whose troops, after driving out the French Revolutionary armies and destroying the short-lived 'People's Roman Republic', are currently occupying Rome, until the arrival of the new Pope Pius VII, recently elected in Austrian-occupied Venice. And* BARON SCARPIA *is, of course, a very famous villain indeed, the prototype of all the nine-teenth century moustache-twirlers and 'proud-beauty trappers' to come. He is being served by a liveried* LACKEY.

SCARPIA. What is the time?

*Even as he speaks he is answered by the thunder of metal on metal. The room must be very close to the clock tower, if not in it. There are two echoing peals before the* LACKEY *can reply.*

LACKEY. Two, your Excellency.

SCARPIA. (*Crossly.*) I know, now. Open that window. The air is stifling.

*The* LACKEY *does so. Other clocks, more distant, are striking all over Rome.*

(*Angrily.*) And now I can smell the Tiber drains—

*The* LACKEY *moves to close the window.*

No.

*The* LACKEY *leaves the window open.*

SCARPIA *finishes his plate and takes a gulp of wine, followed by a pinch of snuff.* The horror of these apartments! If His Sicilian Majesty only knew the conditions under which I slave for him—

LACKEY. He'd make you a Duke at the least, Excellency.

SCARPIA. Duca di Scarpia? The sound is not right. Baron is more frighten-ing; and in my post you have to be frightening or nothing.

LACKEY. His Excellency is not nothing.

SCARPIA. Thank you, Giuseppe. No, it's not a Dukedom I want. It's more money.

*There is a loud knock at the unseen iron door.* SCARPIA *makes a gesture to the* LACKEY *to open it. While he goes to do so,* SCARPIA *pours himself a glass of wine—red this time—from another bottle. There is a clatter of bolts and bars and* SCHIARRONE *comes in. He is in the uniform of a Captain of the Guard, and is a rather breathless young man, easily confused.*

You may leave us, Giuseppe.

GIUSEPPE *bows low and disappears. Again we hear the clanging of the iron door.*

SCHIARRONE. I have doubled the guards all over the city, Excellency, and I have put the whole garrison on instant alert.

SCARPIA. (*Sipping wine.*) I wonder if that was necessary. Everything seems very calm.

SCHIARRONE. Everything is not always what it seems, Excellency.

SCARPIA. (*Eyeing him with disfavour.*) True. Very true. Tell me Schiarrone, how did you get yourself promoted Captain so very young?

SCHIARRONE. The fates have been kind, Excellency.

SCARPIA. So, I would imagine, has someone else.

SCHIARRONE. Your Excellency is pleased to mock my aristocratic connections?

SCARPIA. Oh no. I never mock any connections, aristocratic or popular. You fancy the city to be on the verge of a violent revolution?

SCHIARRONE. When news of the northern battle reaches the people—

SCARPIA. The news won't reach them for two days—and then only in the form in which I choose to give it.

SCHIARRONE. Even your Excellency's well-known skill at doctoring disasters to sound like triumphs can hardly conceal from them the fact that there is nothing now between Bonaparte and Rome—

SCARPIA. Two hundred leagues are not nothing, Schiarrone.

SCHIARRONE. I meant no forces. General Melas' surrender at Marengo—

SCARPIA. You mean there are no Austrian forces. But why do you ignore our own skilled and determined Neapolitan armies?

SCHIARRONE. Excellency, I am an ardent admirer of our southern countrymen and no one is more alive to Sicilian and Neapolitan virtues than I—a simple Roman—

SCARPIA. But you would not put martial ardour very high on the list?

SCHIARRONE. Forgive me, Excellency.

SCARPIA. There is nothing to forgive. I said our armies were skilled and determined. I did not say what they were skilled and determined at. So far in these wars it has been pillaging, looting, raping and running.

SCHIARRONE. (*Helplessly.*) So what *can* stop Bonaparte from taking Rome?

SCARPIA. Let us put our faith in God. As a Cardinal's son I presume you believe in Him.

SCHIARRONE. (*Scandalised.*) Excellency! Oh, Excellency!

SCARPIA. Oh dear! I'm so sorry. Nephew of course. But then he treats you just like a son?

SCHIARRONE *nods.*

Well you must get your—uncle to say a very powerful Mass or two in the next few days.

*Tranquilly he pours out another glass, offering the bottle to* SCHIARRONE, *who shakes his head.*

With these high connections of which you boast, how did you escape guillotining during our late Roman Republic?

SCHIARRONE. It's a long story.

SCARPIA. Tell it.

SCHIARRONE. My mother, who was a dancer, used to know the president of the Revolutionary Tribunal—

SCARPIA. But that's a very short story.

SCHIARRONE. There's much more to tell—

SCARPIA. Not very much, surely? Connections both aristocratic and popular? Well you seem well armoured against almost any eventuality in these troubled times—except possibly an invasion by the Americans. Excellent wine.

*Getting up from the table.*

Well, how is our prisoner? Attending reverently, I trust, to his last moments on earth?

SCHIARRONE. He is in the Chapel with the White Friars of Death. But he has deeply distressed those holy men by refusing to recognise their Order, by denying the right of His Sicilian Majesty to have him executed without trial, and by claiming that he has committed no offence against the people of Rome, but only against their oppressors. The time, he says, is at hand when the sacred ideals of Liberty, Equality and Fraternity—

*He is stopped by a gesture from* SCARPIA.

SCARPIA. Yes, yes. Well fraternity he now has, liberty he soon will have, and everyone is equal in death.

*He chuckles villainously.*

Tell me, was he surprised that we knew his plans so well?

SCHIARRONE. Yes, Excellency. He has been perfectly honest about that. His rising was carefully timed for the eve of Bonaparte's entry into the Papal States, and his orders came directly, via the French agents who are everywhere in Rome, from Fouché himself.

SCARPIA. (*Absently.*) From Fouché?

SCHIARRONE. Yes, Excellency. The head of Bonaparte's secret police—

SCARPIA. (*Interrupting with a bellow.*) Idiot! Do you think I am unaware of who Fouché is? What kind of a secret policeman would *I* make if I didn't know the name of my counterpart in Paris?

*With an undisguised note of respect.*

Indeed the acknowledged head of my profession, Schiarrone. He may well be the best, most terrible and most efficient chief of Secret Police who has ever lived, anywhere, at any time. It is a poor general who does not respect his opponent. So Signor Cavaradossi has no idea at all how I found out all the details of his insurrection?

SCHIARRONE. He knows that somehow you infiltrated his group and that one of his fellow-conspirators is a traitor, but he has no idea which. Just for me, Excellency—in confidence—which one is it?

SCARPIA. The last to be shot, of course. Use your wits, Schiarrone. Well, use something anyway. Cavaradossi goes first, of course. How long is it to dawn?

SCHIARRONE. Under two hours—

SCARPIA. Where is the lady?

SCHIARRONE. In the room your Excellency ordered her to be locked in.

SCARPIA. Has it windows?

SCHIARRONE. A skylight—barred.

SCARPIA. Good. These opera singers can be temperamental, and—well—her suicide would be unfortunate. The Queen adores her, for some reason.

SCHIARRONE. No doubt because she sings so exquisitely.

SCARPIA. Well the Queen also adores Lady Hamilton, who doesn't. There may be some other reason, beyond masculine ken, Schiarrone, and certainly beyond mine as Her Majesty's loyal subject and her husband's Regent of Police. Well, you can bring her in.

*As* SCHIARRONE *salutes to leave.*

Oh, Schiarrone, one most important thing. Goodness I nearly forgot! *While eating.*

Now at some stage in my conversation with the lady I may have occasion to summon you back to give you some perfectly idiotic instructions.

SCHIARRONE. In what way idiotic, Excellency?

SCARPIA. (*Sharply.*) In that they are on no account to be obeyed. I may, for instance, tell you to disarm the firing party and re-arm them with blank ammunition, for Cavaradossi to be warned to feign dead at the fatal volley, and then some nonsense about smuggling him off in a coach with drawn blinds to Milan, or somewhere—

SCHIARRONE. (*Armed with notebook and pencil.*) Er—could I have this in writing, Excellency? It seems a little complicated—

SCARPIA. It is not in the least complicated. Your orders are simple. They are to disobey any orders that I give you in the hearing of the lady. Just that and nothing more.

*Pause.*

SCHIARRONE. Supposing you order me to carry out my first orders?

SCARPIA. (*Impatiently.*) Then you carry out your first orders.

SCHIARRONE. Ah, but that wouldn't be *disobeying* your orders, would it? Please, Excellency, I really think it would be better in writing—

SCARPIA. I can't give it to you in writing, idiot. I don't know the lady's mind yet.

SCHIARRONE. Ah. I begin to see.

SCARPIA. (*Muttering.*) God in heaven!

SCHIARRONE. (*Brightly.*) It would perhaps avoid all confusion if your Excellency, when giving me an order that is to be disobeyed, could manage to give me a little wink?

SCARPIA. (*Spluttering.*) Yes. That would look very convincing, wouldn't it? 'Tell the firing party to disarm their muskets and reload with blanks—'
*He gives a large, operatic wink.*

SCHIARRONE. But please Excellency—some sign. This is plainly a very delicate matter. It seems to concern a lady's honour—also, of course, a man's life. Your Excellency would not wish me to make an utter—fiasco of it. Perhaps a handkerchief dropped—something like that.

SCARPIA. All right. A handkerchief dropped. I shall make my meaning plain, never fear. Fetch the lady!

SCHIARRONE *goes.* SCARPIA *sips. A clock—the clock—thunderously strikes the quarter.* SCARPIA, *looking pleased both with himself and the world, smiles and nods, before finishing his glass of wine. There is a great clattering of bolts and bars and suddenly* LA TOSCA *is standing just inside the room, half in shadow.* SCARPIA *rises slowly. He bows politely. She makes no sign.*
You will want to know where you are, Tosca. You are in the Castel Sant' Angelo. You were brought here secretly with a hood over your face, after my police had arrested Signor Mario Cavaradossi in your cellars. Oh what a stupid hiding-place, Signora! A wanted terrorist with a price on his head, to take refuge in the house of a lady whom all Rome knows he loves. What is more, a lady whose revolutionary sympathies are not exactly unknown to the authorities. Did you not once before have a little trouble with my police for singing the Marseillaise in Italian from the top of the Spanish Steps?

TOSCA. (*In a low voice.*) Where is Mario?

SCARPIA. Now, do you know that I have never heard the Marseillaise sung in Italian? To hear it sung by you must be a sublime experience. You would not, I suppose, care to sing it for me now?

TOSCA (*As before.*) Where is Mario? I demand to ask!

SCARPIA. I hardly think that you are in a position to demand anything, Signora. To harbour a known criminal is itself a crime.

TOSCA. He is not a criminal, and nor am I.

SCARPIA. Well, there might be different opinions on that. By the way would you care for a little wine?

TOSCA *makes a scornful gesture of refusal.*
It's excellent, you know. Genuine French—and a good revolutionary vintage—1792. Does not even the year tempt you?

*She makes another scornful gesture.* SCARPIA *begins to move about. She remains still.*
Pity. Well I suppose a good lawyer might plead on your behalf that you, being an artist, an opera singer and a dreamer, might have been totally unaware of your lover's plan to overthrow the State—

TOSCA. (*Scornfully.*) Overthrow the State? And who says that *that* is a crime?

SCARPIA. Well, oddly enough, the State.

TOSCA. The State? *This* State?—Bah!

*Pause.*

SCARPIA. Do you know that would sound very well sung. Music by—who do you think? Haydn—Mozart—?

TOSCA. Where is Mario?

SCARPIA. He is very close to you indeed—just beyond that wall there—

*Pointing to wall L.*

in the Chapel of the White Friars of Death.

TOSCA. —of Death?

SCARPIA. I fear so, yes. He is due to die in two hours. Here is the warrant for his execution at dawn—today.

*He takes out a document from his pocket, flourishes it briefly and replaces it quickly.*

The news must of course distress you very much. I had hoped to spare you knowledge of it—but then you were so very insistent.

TOSCA. To—die—without even a trial?

*Hitting the desk hard with both hands.*

Oh monstrous! Monstrous! Monstrous! Oh cruel! Unspeakable!

SCARPIA. (*Interrupting rather tetchily.*) Signora, do please stop doing that, or you'll do yourself an injury.

*He pulls her away from the desk.*

Or the desk one.

*He examines the top.*

It is an exquisite piece. Believe it or not, it belonged to the Borgias—

TOSCA. Ah I believe it! To the Borgias, yes! That is what Rome has become now again under these Neapolitan assassins! To execute a man without hearing him speak? Ah, Monstrous!

SCARPIA. Oh, we've heard him speak. At great length, in fact, and without interrupting him once, although every word he uttered was either treason, or blasphemy, or both. And in the course of his eloquence he has freely confessed to everything of which he stands accused.

TOSCA. Who signed that warrant?

SCARPIA. The man under whose orders I work, and whose orders I must obey.

TOSCA. The Military Governor? The Queen will countermand it—

SCARPIA. Yes. No doubt she would have if we had allowed you access to her tonight—

TOSCA. Fiend! Was it for that reason that I have been kept here in that locked room all these hours?

SCARPIA. Oh, not officially. Officially you were brought here to help us in our enquiries. It was, after all, in your house that we discovered the culprit. But you may take it from me, my dearest Diva, that our enquiries are now ended, and you are perfectly free to go.

*Pause.*

TOSCA (*Puzzled.*) Then I will go. Have your servants find me a carriage.

SCARPIA. Our clemency hardly extends to a carriage. If you go now you will have to walk or run.

TOSCA *hesitates,* SCARPIA *laughs.*

Exactly. If you cover the distances required as fast as that runner from Marathon—and you are surely capable of that feat—I fear that you will arrive back here, gasping and panting and flourishing the Queen's reprieve, at least an hour too late—

*The clock strikes the half hour—and a quarter.*

TOSCA. Villain! Perfidious murderer! The Queen will have you hanged for this!

SCARPIA. I rather doubt if the sister of Marie-Antoinette will hang the executioner of a would-be regicide.

TOSCA. Assassin! Oh brutal and most bloody tiger! Ten times accursed fiend!

SCARPIA. Oh Signora, please stop! You really mustn't blame *me,* but the man who signed this warrant.

*Tapping his breast pocket.*

I merely obey his orders. I deplore them, of course, but I must obey them—or else—

*He makes the gesture of his own throat being cut.*

TOSCA. A hypocrite too, as well as all else! Ah God—Without a trial—oh, it is too hard! Too hard!

SCARPIA. Deplorable, as I've agreed. But then, dear Tosca, were *your* friends in the late Roman Revolutionary Republic always so nice about giving *their* victims a trial?

TOSCA. (*Still indignant.*) But they were our enemies. They were trying to overthrow the State—

SCARPIA *smiles mildly at her, allowing her to grasp the inadequacy of her argument, before gently approaching her.*

SCARPIA. You see. It all depends on what is the State, and who are its enemies. In moral terms there is really nothing to choose between us—

TOSCA. Most certainly there is. We are on the side of Liberty, and you are against it. Tyrants, villains, assassins, brutal oppressors of the people—!

SCARPIA. (*Stopping her, this time with authority.*) No, not another aria, please. Believe me the cause of Liberty is not worth it.

TOSCA. Don't speak of sacred Liberty! Your lips sully its name.

SCARPIA. I simply ask myself the question: Will the French be more free under a First Consul than under a King?

TOSCA. Of course they will. Bonaparte is the greatest man who ever lived. He is the personification of the invincible power of World Revolution.

SCARPIA. Is he? Well, I agree that at this precise moment of history he hardly seems very vincible.

TOSCA (*Eagerly.*) You have news of the battle in the north?

SCARPIA. I fear I have. It would appear that our forces have met with a slight reverse at the village of Marengo—

TOSCA. (*With the full force of her lungs.*) Vittoria! Vittoria!

*Those familiar with the opera will know that this famous cry from Act II is sung unaccompanied, in a triumphant crescendo by* MARIO *from offstage.* TOSCA'S *version is perhaps less musical—for she has not yet had the chance of hearing Puccini's opera—but it is loud and full-toned.*

SCARPIA. (*Alarmed.*) I beg your pardon—Oh, I'm so sorry. You were improvising—

TOSCA. My hero has not failed me. Ah, great Bonaparte! Liberty, Equality, Fraternity—You will conquer the world. Little reactionary pig, you have had your day! Turn now and salute the new dawn—before you bow your tyrant's head to its inevitable fate!

*She is pointing to a sky that is still pitch black.*

SCARPIA. The only thing is, Tosca, that this particular dawn, when it comes, is the last thing that you should salute, because it isn't my fate that it looks likely to bring, but someone else's. Well, to business. Now, Signora Tosca, this is the situation. Deeply as I regret this little matter about your lover, Mario Cavaradossi, my orders regarding it are formal and absolute. They can only be disobeyed at the greatest possible risk to my own life. Now that is not a risk that I would ordinarily be expected to take, nor would I think of it, were not you, Tosca, Rome's adored one—and my own adored one—so intimately involved. Do sit down now, take a glass of wine, and discuss with me sensibly, how the two of us can possibly manage to rescue Signor Cavaradossi from his deplorable predicament. Because there must *be* a way. There simply must. And your idol, the First Consul, is too far away from Rome to solve it for us.

*He pours two glasses of wine, not looking at her.*

TOSCA *suddenly strides to the table, and sits down with her right arm outstretched and her left hand clutching a wine glass. She contrives, in doing so, to look very like Sarah Bernhardt, in the famous photograph.*

TOSCA. How much?

*Pause.*

SCARPIA. I beg your pardon?

TOSCA. What is your price?

SCARPIA. Oh I see, my price? The highest, Tosca, that you can pay.

TOSCA. Name it. There is no price too high for Mario's life.

SCARPIA. None?

TOSCA. You can have my house, my jewels, my savings, my furs, my Persian rugs—

SCARPIA. Ha!

TOSCA. Why do you laugh? My Persian rugs are worth a fortune. I collect them and have been well-advised—

SCARPIA. Ha!

TOSCA. What is your price?

SCARPIA. You.

TOSCA. What?

SCARPIA. (*Rising.*) The price is you, Tosca, and I shall have my price.

*He attempts to embrace her, but she is a muscular lady and she repels him without difficulty.*

TOSCA. (*Laughing.*) Imbecile! I would rather jump through that window!

*In the struggle, brief though it has been,* SCARPIA *has been a trifle winded. It is a little time before he can manage to regain himself sufficiently to deliver the following—also immortal—line with the requisite dignity.*

SCARPIA. Jump then! Your lover follows you! I wonder how it will please Signor Cavaradossi to see your shattered body lying there in the courtyard. It will be the last sight of anything in this world that he will have before they put the blindfold over his eyes, and shoot their lead balls into his heart—

*Gasping just a little, he is forced to swallow his glass of wine, with a rather trembling hand.*

TOSCA. Oh, Monster! What is this vile bargain you propose?

*Pause.* SCARPIA, *his calm regained, pours another glass.*

SCARPIA. Really, Signora, the matter is perfectly simple. Say the word yes, and I save your lover. Say the word no, and I kill him. Now I can hardly make myself clearer than that, can I?

*Pause.* TOSCA *gathers a deep, operatic breath.*

TOSCA. Lecherous wretch!—devil incarnate!—brutish beast!—fiend from hell!—lustful spawn of Satan—

SCARPIA. Yes, yes, I know all that, but what we have to decide, fairly soon, is whether—

TOSCA *has not filled her lungs for nothing. She sails straight through him.*

TOSCA. Pig! Monster! Degenerate jackal! From what womb were you ripped? No human one, that's certain. No woman born of man could have suckled such a satyr, nurtured in the noisome swamps of evil, weaned in the wilderness of Satan—

SCARPIA. Oh do stop, Tosca! Time, you know, is running out. Now which is it to be? Yes—or no? A simple question surely deserves a simple answer.

*Pause. She draws more breath.*

TOSCA. I shall call from that window and proclaim your infamy to the whole of Rome.

SCARPIA. Even with your magnificent lungs no one will hear you. And if they did my infamy would hardly be news. Now, yes or no. Which is it to be?

TOSCA. I would rather defile myself with a leper.

SCARPIA. (*Nodding.*) Well, I think we might call that a fairly definitive no.

*He goes to pull the bell-cord.*

TOSCA. (*Suddenly human and pathetic.*) No.

SCARPIA. (*His hand still on the bell-cord.*) Do you mean no, no, or no, yes?

TOSCA. What pleasure can it give you to take to your bed a woman who must hate you will all her heart, despise you will all her mind, and resist you with all her body?

*Pause.*

SCARPIA. A good question.

*He drops his hand from the bell-cord.*

Well, I suppose the answer is this. I don't flatter myself that I am a particularly attractive man, Tosca, but you'd really be surprised how easy it has always been for me to entice women—desirable women too—into my bed. And they come there willingly. Nearly always too willingly. A Chief of Police is rather a marked man in that respect. Of course sometimes he is asked for little favours—a lover released, a husband condemned, a peccadillo of their own overlooked. But a very surprising proportion of them want no favours at all. They find my position rather glamorous, you see, and like to boast afterwards of having been ravished by the brutal Chief of Police in his lair at the Castel Sant'Angelo. But really, you know, it's nearly always I who have been the one to be ravished.

*With a sigh.*

That becomes irksome, you know—

TOSCA. (*A half lung-full.*) Cynical rogue! Decadent lackey of the bourgeoisie! How I loathe your vile boasting—

SCARPIA. (*Excitedly.*) Ah. Now you see—that's just the point. You do loathe me, honestly and genuinely, and if you could only bring yourself to accompany me in there—

*He points to door R.*

you will loathe me even more, perhaps biting me and scratching me and even spitting in my face—

*He is approaching her slowly.*

and shouting out your insults, until suddenly your outraged body ceases to struggle and begins to tremble as it slowly—oh so slowly—becomes part of my own trembling body—and then suddenly, as the climax comes to both of us, your flesh is slave to my flesh, and your pleasure becomes my joy. Your hate and my desire will be a coupling for the gods! Oh Tosca, endure your torture, and give me my bliss!

*He is staring at her from very close. But he does not try to embrace her. In that respect he has learnt his lesson.*

TOSCA. Never! Never in this life!

SCARPIA. (*Pulls the bell-cord.*) A pity.

SCHIARRONE *comes in.*

SCHIARRONE. (*Breathlessly.*) Your Excellency's orders?

SCARPIA. You know them.

SCHIARRONE. Do I?

SCARPIA. (*Savagely.*) Carry out the execution.

TOSCA *goes rigid. But so too does* SCHIARRONE.

SCHIARRONE. That means—?

TOSCA. (*Throwing herself at* SCARPIA's *feet.*) No, no, no! Have pity! Have mercy! See I am at your feet, as a beggar before a King. Is that not enough for you?

SCARPIA. No.

*To* SCHIARRONE.

Carry it out.

*As* SCHIARRONE'S *puzzled face grows more puzzled.*

Well, what are you waiting for?

SCHIARRONE. Has your Excellency, by any chance, dropped something?

SCARPIA. What?

*He follows* SCHIARRONE'S *stare around his feet.*

No, idiot! Your *first* orders. Carry them out!

SCHIARRONE *quickly refers to his notebook. His face clears.*

SCHIARRONE. Yes, Excellency. As your Excellency *first* ordered.

*He turns.*

TOSCA. No, wait.

SCHIARRONE *turns to* SCARPIA *for confirmation.*

SCARPIA. Yes, wait.

SCHIARRONE *promptly marches towards the door. Shouting:*

I said 'wait' fool!

SCHIARRONE. (*Muttering.*) Oh, it's so confusing.

SCARPIA. Speak, Tosca.

SCHIARRONE *has waited.* TOSCA *having noticed nothing, has picked herself up gracefully from* SCARPIA'S *feet. She is going to make the most of her next line, and* takes *her time in arranging to do so. She even fills her lungs, although the line will hardly demand it.*

TOSCA. (*To* SCARPIA, *in a despairing murmur.*) Yes.

SCARPIA. Schiarrone, I have changed my mind. I have further orders for you.

SCHIARRONE. (*Murmuring.*) Oh heavens!

*He takes out his notebook again.*

Yes, Excellency?

SCARPIA. You will not shoot Signor Mario Caravadossi.

SCHIARRONE. (*Obediently.*) Not shoot—

*He looks around at* SCARPIA'S *feet again.*

SCARPIA *understands and begins to feel for a handkerchief.* TOSCA, *happily for both of them, has covered her face with her hands and is silently weeping.*

SCARPIA. That is correct. Now, I'll tell you what you are to do. (*His search has been unavailing.*) You are to fake the execution—

SCHIARRONE. (*Taking it down but still looking for the handkerchief.*) Fake the execution—

SCARPIA. You will order the firing party to remove the live ammunition from the muskets—

SCHIARRONE. (*Still looking for the signal.*) Live ammunition from their muskets—

SCARPIA. And replace them with—Schiarrone, do you happen to have a handkerchief on you?

SCHIARRONE. No, Excellency.

SCARPIA. (*Laughing hollowly.*) Funny—neither of us with a handkerchief!

SCHIARRONE. (*Suspiciously.*) Very funny, Excellency.

TOSCA. (*With a wail.*) Oh, what have I said?

SCARPIA. You've said 'yes', dear.

*To* SCHIARRONE.

I think I must have *dropped* my handkerchief somewhere.

SCHIARRONE. Ah. And if I *had* had one and *had* lent it to your Excellency then your Excellency might well have *dropped* that too?

SCARPIA. We understand each other. Splendid fellow!

SCHIARRONE. (*Bowing, delighted.*) Excellency!

TOSCA. (*From wherever she has been weeping.*) How are you going to save my Mario?

SCARPIA. Well, if you listen you will hear. I have an ingenious plan.

*He nods affably to* SCHIARRONE *to continue his writing, but* SCHIARRONE *has put his notebook away.*

Quite right, Schiarrone. These things are better not written down.

*Of course* SCHIARRONE *has brought his notebook out again.*

Very well. For your own security. The live ammunition is to be removed from the firing-party's muskets, and in their place you will serve them only with powder.

SCHIARRONE. (*Writing vigorously.*) Gun powder?

SCARPIA. (*With a look.*) Gun powder. Now you will warn Signor Cavaradossi that when he hears the volley he must fall to the ground, and appear to be dead. You are then to approach the body—

TOSCA. (*Caught lungless but making a good show.*) Ah—

SCARPIA. (*When he can.*) —of the *live* Signor Cavaradossi, announce him to be dead—or give him a fake coup de grace—whichever you prefer—

SCHIARRONE. As the inspiration takes me, Excellency? I mean things like coups de grace can't really be arranged in advance, can they? It so much depends, doesn't it?

*Looking up and getting* SCARPIA'S *steely glance.*

I mean, even in a *fake* execution.

SCARPIA. Even in a *fake* execution.

SCHIARRONE. Yes, Excellency.

*Hesitantly.*

I still have your meaning, I think.

SCARPIA. I hope so. Now a coach with drawn blinds will be waiting in the courtyard. When the firing party is dismissed you will take Cavaradossi into it, and escort him past the Porta Angelica, using my name and authority. You will give orders for the coach to drive directly to Milan, and arrange suitable changes of horses. Before that, I will have some orders for you regarding a carriage to take Signora Tosca to her home.

SCHIARRONE. When will that be, Excellency?

SCARPIA. Some time before dawn.

SCHIARRONE. Could you be more precise?

SCARPIA. (*Angrily.*) No, I could not.

SCHIARRONE. (*Whispering.*) Oh, I see. When you have taken your pleasure—

SCARPIA. (*Loudly.*) Exactly. Now is all that understood, Schiarrone?

SCHIARRONE. (*Fervently.*) Oh God, I hope so.

SCARPIA. Leave us.

SCHIARRONE *begins to go and then turns in doubt. A furious gesture from* SCARPIA *sends him flying. Bolts and bars rattle again and then there is silence.* TOSCA *is at the window, her back to* SCARPIA. *He approaches her and puts his arm on her shoulder. She shrinks away.* SCARPIA *laughs, with relish.*

My dearest Diva, have I organised it well enough for you?

TOSCA. There is one more thing—

SCARPIA. Yes?

TOSCA. I will want to visit my beloved in Milan.

SCARPIA. Of course you will. Very well. I will write you the necessary document.

*He sits down, his back to her and begins to write.*

TOSCA *very warily approaches the table, prominent on which is a large bread-knife. She takes it up.*

SCARPIA *turns almost at the same moment and* TOSCA *conceals the knife, with a lightning gesture, behind her back.*

Lucky Milan! Now the Scala will have a chance to hear that magnificent organ of yours.

TOSCA. (*Icily.*) You are too kind, Baron.

*He turns to write again. With a bound* TOSCA *is on him, stabbing him in the back with all her might. As she strikes:*

Villain! Bloody, bawdy villain! Remorseless, lecherous, treacherous, kindless villain! Ah, vengeance!

*The knife is driven remorselessly into* SCARPIA'S *back, but seems to have no effect whatever. After he has received about five full-bodied blows,* SCARPIA *gets up and politely hands* TOSCA *a document.*

SCARPIA. Your laisser-passer, Signora. (*He removes his tunic to reveal a leather under-garment reminiscent of a bullet-proof jacket. He studies the tunic carefully.*) This will have to go to the tailor's. The last two ladies hardly scratched the fabric. I congratulate you, Signora, on the power of your thrust.

SCARPIA *takes off his leather vest; then with perfect politeness, opens the door to the bedroom inviting her, with a gesture, inside. Pause.* TOSCA *drops a quick reverence to the Virgin before going to the door.*

(*Smiling.*) I thought, as a good revolutionary, you only believed in the Goddess of Reason?

TOSCA. How can the Goddess of Reason help me now?

*She goes past him into the room.*

SCARPIA. (*Sympathetically.*) I see your point.

*He follows her off.*

*As the lights begin to dim the clock thunders out three. A brief pause in dark-
ness, during which we hear the White Friars of Death chanting a Mass from
the nearby chapel. Then their voices fade and the clock strikes the half.*

*The lights come on. There is a pause.* TOSCA *walks slowly from the bedroom. Her
hair is rather tousled and she holds her earrings in her mouth. Otherwise she
looks much as when we last saw her.* SCARPIA *follows her slowly on. He is
clad now in a dressing-gown with the Baronial arms of* SCARPIA *on the left
breast.*

I repeat, Tosca—it can only be something I ate.

TOSCA. Or perhaps you have been overworking. These late hours.

SCARPIA. Aie, Aie, Aieh! The shame of it, the pain of it!

TOSCA. Pain?

SCARPIA. Here, in the very root of my being.

TOSCA. It could hardly be anywhere else.

SCARPIA. Ah, divine Tosca, I could smother you with my kisses, cover you
with caresses—

TOSCA. You already have. (*Yawns.*) Kindly order me my carriage.

SCARPIA. No.

TOSCA. You are in the mood for conversation?

SCARPIA. A thousand curses!

TOSCA. Or perhaps a game of whist?

SCARPIA. Is it possible, my proud beauty, that you have forgotten that you
are still in my power? I can keep you here for as long as I wish. Oh yes,
Tosca, here in these silent chambers, I can still wreak my will.

TOSCA. Your will? or your wont? Forgive me, Baron, for so poor a joke but
the situation seems to permit some levity. To tell the truth, I feel extremely
sorry for you.

SCARPIA. I don't ask for your pity.

TOSCA. A shame, for it seems it is all I have to offer you, just at this moment. I have left my reticule upon your bed, and would like fully to repair
such damage to my toilette as your recent transports have wreaked. Or
is it wrought? When I return I shall expect to find a carriage waiting to
take me to my home. Baron—

*She makes a slight obeisance and goes out.* SCARPIA *rings the bell savagely. Then
he sits at the desk. There are bangs and clatters at the door.* SCHIARRONE *comes
in.*

SCHIARRONE. Excellency?

SCARPIA. There is a change of plan.

SCHIARRONE. (*Murmuring.*) Ah, this time I have brought a handkerchief.

SCARPIA. (*Loudly.*) We don't need a handkerchief. She isn't in the room—

TOSCA *can be heard off, singing* Vissi d'Arte *quietly to herself.*

SCHIARRONE. Nor she is. Good, it makes life easier. (*Referring to his notes.*)
Now your Excellency will require a carriage for the Signora, having taken
your pleasure of her, as per your dictated note, earlier.

SCARPIA. No, idiot! That's to say—no carriage—yet.

TOSCA *can be heard singing more loudly.*

SCHIARRONE. (*Surprised.*) Not yet?

*He gets what is to him plainly the operative idea.*

(*Admiringly.*) Eh, eh? Encora? Eh, eh, eh—?

SCARPIA. Not encora! Schiarrone, I must tell you something, in the strictest confidence—

SCHIARRONE. Your Excellency does me honour. (*He takes out his notebook.*)

SCARPIA. No notes! Heavens, if such notes were to fall into the hands of a Tribunal of Enquiry—

SCHIARRONE. Completely understood, Excellency. (*Notebook away.*) No names, no garrotting—Excuse me. A Neapolitan Army expression.

TOSCA *is heard even more clearly.*

SCARPIA. The Signora Tosca has become a great danger to the state.

SCHIARRONE *has got lost in the glory of* TOSCA'S *voice.*

(*Sharply.*) Did you hear me, Schiarrone?

SCHIARRONE. Forgive me, Excellency, but what a divine voice the Signora does have. What is she singing about?

SCARPIA. Oh something about how she lived for art, lived for love—

SCHIARRONE. Oh yes. And she has. Oh, how she has—

SCARPIA. Well now she must die.

SCHIARRONE. Die?

SCARPIA. Die.

SCHIARRONE. Why?

SCARPIA. Because she has become possessed of a vital secret of state.

*Pause.*

SCHIARRONE. Classified?

SCARPIA. To the highest degree.

SCHIARRONE. King and Police chief only

SCARPIA. Police chief only.

SCHIARRONE. Mama mia!

SCARPIA. Mama, as you say, Schiarrone, mia! Now remembering that the Signora is a personal friend of the Queen, and a famous opera singer whose absence will be noted—how do we both set about it? Shall I have her shot beside her lover?

SCHIARRONE. Mario Cavaradossi? But isn't he to be shot by blanks?

SCARPIA. Balls, Schiarrone, balls.

SCHIARRONE. Oh yes. I'm so sorry. I have it here. Stupid of me. Real balls. *Not* blanks. See, Excellency, it is underlined—

SCARPIA. Yes. But she *thinks* they will be blanks—

TOSCA *is now into the closing phrases.*

Now supposing I told her that a famous painter was going to sketch the scene for posterity—say David—and how heroic and revolutionary she would look, protecting her lover from the cold lead balls of the Royalist murderers—how about that, eh, Schiarrone.

SCHIARRONE. Magnificent, Excellency. Only how will it be explained to the Queen?

*Pause.*

SCARPIA. As an accident. The firing party got confused between their blanks and their balls—

SCHIARRONE *looks doubtful.*

You don't like it? But, heavens, it could happen. The Queen of Naples must know her own subjects—

SCHIARRONE. I think it might land Your Excellency in some rather difficult explanations. For instance why, in a straight-forward political execution, was blank ammunition ordered to be used anyway?

SCARPIA. Charitable reasons? To teach young Cavaradossi a lesson without actually harming him?

SCHIARRONE. Your Excellency's reputation is outstanding for many virtues— but whether charity is the most notable—

SCARPIA. All right, all right. What other way, then?

SCHIARRONE. Poison?

SCARPIA. In the Borgia apartments? That would not look good, Schiarrone. Not good at all.

SCHIARRONE. This vital secret, Excellency. Is it in her reticule.

SCARPIA. In her head.

SCHIARRONE. She has memorised it?

SCARPIA. Vividly. Or so I would think.

SCHIARRONE. That's bad. And it would, I imagine, be something like the Plans of the Central Fortifications?

SCARPIA. Or the lack of them, Schiarrone—which is far more serious—

SCHIARRONE. Deadly. Could Your Excellency perhaps plead with her better nature not to reveal this damaging inadequacy?

SCARPIA. Am I in a position to appeal to her better nature about anything, Schiarrone?

SCHIARRONE. (*Thoughtfully.*) As her ravisher, you mean?

*Pause.*

SCARPIA. Ravisher is not a good word, Schiarrone. There are many other words for this kind of thing.

SCHIARRONE. (*Carried* away.) Like brutal possessor? Or proud and rampant conqueror?

SCARPIA. A precise definition is unnecessary and time-wasting. The point is simple: after tonight's events I doubt if I can exactly throw myself at the Signora's feet and plead for mercy—what are you grinning at, Schiarrone?

SCHIARRONE. The spectacle, that is all, Excellency—

SCARPIA. There is nothing to grin at, dolt. I deeply fear that La Tosca will have to be disposed of. Is that funny?

SCHIARRONE. A tragedy. (*Listening to her voice.*) Such purity of tone, such delicacy of feeling. You would never think, would you, that only minutes ago she was undergoing a fate that many women believe to be worse than death—

SCARPIA. It evidently takes different women different ways. (*Suddenly roaring.*) Idiot! Fool! Imbecile! Never mind about what's worse than death. Mind about death, and how to save La Tosca from it.

*Pause.*

SCHIARRONE. Would it be possible for you to render this dangerous secret inoperative?

SCARPIA. Inoperative?

SCHIARRONE. Your Excellency implied, just now, that what she has discovered was some structural failing in the Central Fortifications. Now is there perhaps some way in which Your Excellency might persuade her that what seemed to her, at first sight, a weakness was, on second sight, a strength.

*Pause.*

SCARPIA. By God, you may have hit on it, Schiarrone! Schiarrone, you may have the answer! Make it *inoperative*—weakness into strength—? (*He takes a sip of red wine.*) And it may well be done. The night, after all, is yet young. (*He looks at his watch.*) Well, youngish.

TOSCA'S *voice stops.*

She is coming out. Now listen, Schiarrone. Delay the execution by an hour—

SCHIARRONE. That will be well after daybreak, Excellency.

SCARPIA. Splendid. It will give the Firing Party a better chance to hit their target. (*Whispering.*) Or targets—Schiarrone—just in case this scheme of yours fails to work in the time allowed.

SCHIARRONE. (*Anxiously.*) Is the time enough, Excellency? You will surely have to construct a whole new imaginary set of plans—

SCARPIA. Oh, they won't be so imaginary, Schiarrone. I have a fairly solid base to work on . . . Fairly solid . . . I hope. Now before the hour is up I will call for you and give you your instructions.

SCHIARRONE. With a handkerchief?

SCARPIA. That signal has not proved infallible. For this, perhaps, a new one, something simpler. I know—if I am scowling at you, then the trick has not worked, and you will take the Signora down to the execution platform for a last adieu to her lover. Your firing party will then shoot them both. Understood?

SCHIARRONE. (*Writing.*) If they can hit them both.

SCARPIA. But if, as I hope, I am smiling at you, it will mean that all has gone as planned, and you will then have merely to summon a carriage and escort the Signora to her home. Now is that clear?

SCHIARRONE. As clear as crystal, Excellency. There is just one thing. Your Excellency's smile is a rather rare phenomenon. Might I be privileged to see one?

SCARPIA, *with some effort, produces one.* SCHIARRONE *observes it carefully and then makes notes that long outlast the smile.*

(*Putting notebook away.*) I think I have it, Your Excellency. Carriage for smile, platform for scowl—

TOSCA *comes in from the bedroom.*

SCARPIA. (*Taking her hands.*) Dearest Diva, what bliss you have been giving us with that heavenly aria. What was it?

TOSCA. I was improvising—

SCARPIA. Of course. Ah, dear Tosca, you possess a truly magnificent organ.

*Pause. It is only for a moment that* TOSCA'S *eyes lower before meeting his again.*

TOSCA. Thank you, dear Baron. But even I have evenings when it is not quite at its peak. (*To* SCHIARRONE.) My carriage is here, Captain?

SCHIARRONE *looks frantically at* SCARPIA *who gives him a brusque shake of the head.* TOSCA *has gone to the window.*

SCHIARRONE. (*To* TOSCA'S *back.*) Yes, Signora—

SCARPIA. (*Hastily.*) The Captain means no Signora, it isn't here yet but it soon will be. Isn't that so, Captain?

SCHIARRONE. (*In a petulant whisper.*) But she's back in the room now—

SCARPIA *scowls at him.*

Oh, it is difficult. (*To* TOSCA.) Yes, Signora. I made a stupid blunder. Whatever Baron Scarpia said about your carriage is correct. It will be here whenever he says it's here.

SCARPIA. Go!

SCHIARRONE. (*Whispering.*) That means?

SCARPIA. Go! Get out! Leave!

SCHIARRONE. (*Getting the meaning.* ) Ah. So much to do—so little time to do it? I understand. (*Saluting.*) Your Excellency.

SCARPIA. Captain.

SCHIARRONE *goes out.*

SCARPIA *goes up to* TOSCA, *who is still at the window. He tries to slip his arm round her waist.*

Ah, my divine Tosca, what is there that I can say?

TOSCA *adroitly but not impolitely evades the encircling arm.*

TOSCA. In these circumstances surely nothing is always best.

SCARPIA. Always? You mean that such a thing has happened—

TOSCA. (*Interrupting severely.*) The experience is entirely new to me, Baron.

SCARPIA. Of course. How could it be otherwise?

TOSCA. How indeed? Nevertheless there are some ladies of my acquaintance— I move freely in the world as you know—to whom the event—or should I say non-event? Forgive me, Baron—is not wholly novel. There may, of course, be reasons for those misfortunes for which it would ill-become me to venture possible causes. However they all have without exception, told me that in such humiliating circumstances silence is best. Is that a lobster pâté?

SCARPIA. It is, dearest one.

TOSCA. And, dare I conjecture, a pork pie?

SCARPIA. A veal and egg pasty.

TOSCA. It will do. (*She sits down at the supper table, with authority.*)

SCARPIA *busies himself with serving her.*

After the dreadful ordeal to which tonight I have been submitted I feel a trifle weak and faint. A little food will do me good.

SCARPIA. (*Carving the pie.*) Do you, dearest heart, speak English?

TOSCA. No. It is a barbarous language. And they have no operas. Why should I speak it?

SCARPIA. It is just they have an expression—(*He puts a piece of pie before her.*) There. How is that? Now which wine?

TOSCA. A white, naturally, for the lobster. For the pie a drinkable red. I think you told me you had one. You made a bad joke about it being a good revolutionary year—'92—the year of the Terror. Also a very good vintage.

SCARPIA *displays a bottle. She inspects it.*

Yes—that must be the one. What is this expression that the English have?

SCARPIA. That you cannot have the best of two worlds. Either tonight you underwent an unspeakable ordeal, or there happened to you an non-event. Now which was it, because you really can't have it *both* ways?

*There is a pause while* TOSCA *masticates a mouthful of lobster pate.*

TOSCA. (*At length.*) You are very direct, Baron . . . in your language . . . A little more of that white wine, if you would be so good—

SCARPIA *is so good.*

There happened to me tonight a non-event which was also an unspeakable ordeal. The English are quite wrong, you see. One can easily have it both ways, if one tries. (*She laughs gaily.*)

SCARPIA *tries to follow her, and then falls grimly silent.*

SCARPIA. Ah, my Tosca—you see in me a very miserable man. I think the shame of tonight may very well be my end—

TOSCA. My dear Baron, you really must not take it so hard—(*correcting herself*) so much to heart. I am sure it is only a temporary affliction.

SCARPIA. Ah yes. So am I. If I thought otherwise I would hurl myself from that window this moment—

TOSCA. But dear Baron, pray pause for a moment to think. What you are speaking of is, after all, only a part of life—

SCARPIA. In the sense that ninety nine is only part of a hundred.

TOSCA. Surely you haven't forgotten that there is quite another kind of love, and that it is always referred to as the higher kind.

SCARPIA. (*Gloomily.*) I wonder why.

TOSCA. Because it is higher, Baron. Because it ennobles the soul and refreshes the spirit, and without it the whole world would be no more than a dungeon in the Castel Sant 'Angelo.—I think, now, I will try the red—

SCARPIA. (*Pouring.*) Is that the kind of love you have for Mario?

TOSCA *sips the red wine before replying.*

TOSCA. Not precisely, no. (*She sips again.*) I wish it were, but it is not. (*She sips once more.*) This is an excellent vintage. I congratulate you.

SCARPIA. Thank you. I knew you would like it. (*He pours her out a full glass.*)

TOSCA. (*After a pause.*) But it is the kind of love that Mario has for me.

SCARPIA. That amazes me.

TOSCA. Why does it?

SCARPIA. To be loved by the most desired and desirable woman in Rome, and not respond?

TOSCA. A lack of response is a relative term, Baron. As you should know. Mario does respond—in his fashion.

SCARPIA. What is his fashion?

TOSCA. Mario is not as other men. He is an idealist, a revolutionary, a poet— a man who has dedicated his whole life to the making of a better world.

SCARPIA. And does not that better world include a bed for the two of you?

*Pause.*

TOSCA. He confides to me most of his plans, Baron, but by no means all. Security you understand is very strict. I am close to Mario, of course, but in our little revolutionary circle, there are some who are even closer.

SCARPIA. Women?

TOSCA. Oh no. Men, naturally. Notably his very special friend, the young firebrand Angelotti. (*Hand over mouth.*) Oh dear—have I been indiscreet?

SCARPIA. The name is in our files.

TOSCA. I was sure it would be.

SCARPIA. He heads the Revolutionary Committee in Padua.

TOSCA. Really? I thought it was Mantua. But, of course, you would know better. Oh dear! My silly tongue! I really must keep a rein on it. I mean— just suppose—

SCARPIA. Have no fear, Signora. Our information on Angelotti, your Mario's bosom friend, needs no replenishing—(*Nevertheless he makes a brisk note at the desk.*) But I am appalled at this news you give me—that Mario is not as other men—

TOSCA. As most other men—But don't be appalled, Baron. I am not. I willingly accept my fate. I am not the first martyr to the glorious cause of Revolution—

SCARPIA. But, of course, you must have many other lovers, who are less highminded, more—responsive—

TOSCA. Oh? Can you name me one?

*Pause.*

SCARPIA. Goodness, gracious me!

TOSCA. As you say, Baron—goodness, gracious you!

SCARPIA. But you were just singing—I lived for Art, I lived for Love—

TOSCA. A total absurdity. How can you live for both? You live for one, or you live for the other, and you make your choice too early in life to know whether you have chosen well. For an opera singer to have lovers in the sense in which you use the term—excuse me, Baron, but the vulgar sense—will make you late for rehearsals, quarrelsome with your castrati and uncertain in your top Cs. A Mario Cavaradossi, who looks very beautiful, has the noblest ideals and makes no demands upon you of any kind whatever is the only luxury that the disciplines of an opera singer's art can afford.

SCARPIA. Yet you say you love him differently? Physically, you meant—

TOSCA. That is my weakness. After all I am not a complete stranger to the less ascetic forms of love. As you may have noticed I am not actually—

SCARPIA. Yes.

TOSCA. A tenor in Assisi—a composer in Ischia. Both were quite unimportant. Mario has been my only true love—

SCARPIA. But shouldn't *true* love be the blissful conjunction of two souls in one perfect bodily union—(*He breaks off in some confusion*). I agree with you about this wine. It has an interesting maturity, and a certain flavour of the peaty earth—

TOSCA. (*Unkindly.*) Continue with your disquisition on true love, Baron. Coming from such a source it should be spellbinding.

SCARPIA. You are unkind.

TOSCA. Have I not the right to be?

SCARPIA. Yes. That does not make you less unkind.

TOSCA *reaches across the table and gently pats his hand.*

TOSCA. Forgive me. Let us talk of the wine—

SCARPIA. No. I accept the challenge. Disquisition on True Love. By Baron Scarpia—brutal and licentious Chief of Police to the hated Bourbons of Sicily—murderer and libertine. (*He gets up to begin pacing about, deep in thought, but with an occasional glance at his watch.*)

TOSCA. Do we need the introduction?

SCARPIA. Yes, we do. I am not by nature a murderer, nor a seducer. My reputation, which I freely grant, is the foulest in all Italy, is based on a total misconception.

*Pause.*

TOSCA. Baron, to whom are you speaking?

SCARPIA. (*Passionately, on his knees.*) To the woman I revere, above all others, to the only woman I have ever loved.

TOSCA. As for reverence, Baron, you have a peculiar manner of showing it. And surely—although I don't wish to keep harping on the topic, a distinctly individual manner of displaying your love.

SCARPIA. (*On his knees.*) Ah, but don't you see, my beloved Tosca, it was precisely because of my reverence and my love that this evening became so humiliating a fiasco—

TOSCA. Excuse me, Baron, but if you would allow me one free hand?

*He releases one, and she continues to eat her pork pie.*

No harm possibly can come of your fondling the other.

SCARPIA *mutters an indistinct curse.*

Now explain to me the logic in what you have just said?

SCARPIA. Is there logic in love?

TOSCA. (*After reflection.*) Not much, no.

SCARPIA. If there were, would you love Mario Cavaradossi?

TOSCA. (*After reflection.*) No.

SCARPIA. Or would I love you?

TOSCA. (*After reflection.*) That is more difficult to answer. Just a touch more of that delicious Bourgogne, if you would be so kind.

*He is so kind.*

You have been good enough to say you loved and even revered me, and far be it from me to give the lie to a gentleman in his own Castello. But how can our two loves be compared. Mine for Mario is pure—

SCARPIA. And so is mine for you—

TOSCA. So indeed it proved.

SCARPIA. So it is. So it always has been. So it always will be. It was the truth that was proved tonight—(*The clock chimes.* SCARPIA *hastily compares the time with his own, and makes some adjustments.*) Since I first saw you in Cherubini's 'Medea', I have been your worshipping slave, Tosca. Ah God, how I remember those three hours! It was January the twelfth, 1798— and, ah the magic of you on that stage. From that moment on the vision of you as the tormented heroine filled the whole horizon of my life. I could think of nothing else. You became for me a mounting obsession— a maddening, torturing vision of love as it could be, of love as it should be, with all its pains and joys, its tribulations, its sacrifices and its joys

TOSCA. Was it the matinee?

SCARPIA. No, the evening.

TOSCA. January the twelfth, 1798? . . . Ah yes, I remember. They put La Pizzoleta on for the matinee, because King Ferdinand was coming in the evening—

SCARPIA. And I came with him. I was in his box.

TOSCA. (*Very perfunctorily.*) Ferdinand! Brutal oppressor, murderer of the masses, fiend from hell. Did he say anything?

SCARPIA. That you were in splendid voice. But for me, Tosca, you became an ideal of radiance, of purity, of loveliness—just such a vision of woman-hood in all its many-faceted beauty as I had felt might rescue me from the squalor and degradation into which my life was so rapidly sinking—

TOSCA. It's funny he didn't come round.

SCARPIA. Who?

TOSCA. King Ferdinand.

SCARPIA. The brutal oppressor, murderer of the masses—?

TOSCA. Yes, it's funny, that's all. Do go on.

SCARPIA. Well, you altered my whole existence. Until I saw and heard your glorious 'Medea' it is possible that my life might—who knows—have continued on its brutal and licentious path to hell. But after that never-to-be-forgotten night—

TOSCA. What made you such a villain?

SCARPIA. Opportunity, I think.

TOSCA. Without opportunity you would have been a simple, honest, god-fearing man?

SCARPIA. Can you doubt it?

TOSCA. (*Playfully.*) Frankly, Baron, I can.

SCARPIA. (*Passionately kneeling.*) Oh, don't doubt it, my beloved, I implore you. I beg you to believe that if it were not for my accursed office, I would be exactly the same as most other men.

TOSCA. That is rather easier to believe. But it is not at all the same question. Tell me then, Baron what made you seek your accursed office?

SCARPIA. Don't call me Baron. Call me Tonnino.

TOSCA. Why?

SCARPIA. It is my name.

TOSCA. Tonnino Scarpia?—I like it, it doesn't suit you at all, but I like it. (*She strokes his hair playfully.*) Tell me, Tonnino, why did you ever allow yourself to become a Chief of Police?

*Pause.*

SCARPIA. (*Awaiting inspiration.*) To the hated Bourbons of Naples?

TOSCA. Yes.

*Pause.*

SCARPIA. And therefore a murderer and a libertine?

TOSCA. Yes.

*Pause.*

SCARPIA. That is a very good question.

TOSCA. Isn't it?

SCARPIA. The simplest answer I can give, off hand, is that it is an office that has to be filled, and that if I didn't fill it someone else would.

*Pause.*

TOSCA. Who might be an even worse murderer and a more brutal libertine than you?

SCARPIA. Beloved, you have exactly hit it.

TOSCA. I thought I had. (*She restrains belatedly the re-filling of her glass.*) No, please. I have an early rehearsal.

*The clock thunders four.*

How many times was that?

SCARPIA. Only four.

TOSCA. Oh good—Four?

SCARPIA. (*Hastily.*) Beloved, I wish to make reparation to you for the dread-

ful humiliation I have inflicted on you earlier tonight a humiliation which
it would take a lifetime to repay, but which it would take but a few brief
minutes to repair.

*Pause.*

TOSCA. (*Gazing at him.*) What are you talking about?

SCARPIA. Your humiliation—my soul.

*As she still seems forgetful, pointing.*

In there, my dearest heart—

TOSCA *now finally does get it. She covers her face in an unsuccessful attempt to
conceal her gleeful laughter.*

TOSCA. Oh yes—You couldn't do it.

SCARPIA. (*Sternly.*) I have already explained to you, light of my life, that it
was my deep love for yourself as a woman, and my devoted reverence
for you as an artist, that prevented that blissful conjunction between our
twin souls and bodies that was surely ordained for us both by the gods.

*Pause.*

TOSCA. You explained that?

SCARPIA. At some length, beloved.

TOSCA. Did you? Aren't you clever?

SCARPIA. (*With a gesture.*) Come, my heart—

TOSCA. Where?

SCARPIA. In there.

TOSCA. Again?

SCARPIA. Come, oh constellation of my universe—

TOSCA. Do you know, dear Baron—

SCARPIA. Tonnino—

TOSCA. I think on the whole, I prefer Baron, I am not being unfriendly but
it suits you better! I can only observe dear Baron—and this observation
might, of course, be a little mellowed by your excellent red and white—
but I can only observe that, had you made your overtures to me earlier
this evening, in this vein, the outcome might have been much happier
for both of us (*she ruffles his hair*) Tonnino! It's too silly. Would you kindly
hand me my reticule?

SCARPIA *retrieves it from wherever it is and hands it to her. While he is doing so*
TOSCA *is staring at the ceiling.*

TOSCA. There are cupids on your ceiling here, as well as in your bedroom.

SCARPIA. Yes, beloved.

TOSCA. How many are there here?

SCARPIA. Twenty-six.

TOSCA. There are twenty-eight in the bedroom, isn't that correct?

SCARPIA. I have no idea. I have never counted them.

TOSCA. I have, quite a number of times. I am quite sure there are twenty-
eight. Tiens, that is odd—twenty-six here, twenty-eight there. (*Out of
her reticule she takes an elaborate, jewelled engagement book.*) Dear Baron,
I think another visit to that room tonight would be inadvisable for both

of us. I have an early rehearsal, you are as you have admitted not quite yourself, and the night is late. In fact it is no longer night. See (*she points to the window*) where jocund day stands tiptoe on the misty mountain tops . . . Romeo and Juliet . . . I suppose that absurd little farce with Mario and those blank cartridges will soon have to be enacted down there. Now what evening can I possibly fit you in? . . .

*She looks through her engagement book and, not getting an answer from* SCARPIA, *looks up sharply.*

Wasn't it to be at dawn?

SCARPIA. (*Uneasily.*) Dawn or dawn-abouts.

TOSCA. I thought these things were always at dawn.

SCARPIA. There is a little—elasticity—

TOSCA. Well, anyway, Mario goes to Milan today. You have made arrangements for his journey?

SCARPIA. I—er—think everything is in hand—

TOSCA. Only *think?*

SCARPIA. Dear Tosca, I have had so much else on my mind. . . .

TOSCA. Yes, I suppose you have. Well we will make quite sure of all that in a minute. I shall want to talk to that young Captain myself. He seems a type who could rather easily be confused. Don't you agree?

SCARPIA. Fervently.

TOSCA. Now, with Mario gone to Milan I could write you down for next Thursday. That is the night of the great gala at the Opera. 'Medea', as, by a coincidence, it happens—Isn't that nice?

SCARPIA. Nice is hardly the word.

TOSCA. I am invited afterwards to the Royal Palace, and you can be my escort.

SCARPIA. That would be wonderful, beloved, but—dare I confess it—a night at the Royal Palace was not exactly what I had in mind.

TOSCA. What you have in mind, Baron, by tonight's events or even non-events, has been quite firmly implanted in my own. Never fear, caro Tonnino . . . No, I'm afraid it *must* be Baron . . . But never fear, on Thursday evening everything will go quite *swimmingly*. You have my guarantee (*Inspecting her engagement book before putting it away.*) Yes, Thursday is a good evening for me, Baron—for even if Mario had been available he would not have been a persona exactly gratissima at the Royal Palace.

SCARPIA. Seeing that his plan was to blow it up?

*Pause.* TOSCA *momentarily loses her calm.*

TOSCA. Your agents know even that?

SCARPIA. One did.

TOSCA. But that plan was known only to me.

SCARPIA. And one other—

TOSCA. (*Without utter misery.*) Ah! Angelotti? It was Angelotti, then who betrayed him? Oh fiend, Oh devil, Oh thrice-accursed traitor! When Mario hears of this—as he shall—have no fear—

SCARPIA. Angelotti did not betray him.

TOSCA. Oh? He didn't? Well, then who did?

SCARPIA. To what other person did your Mario tell his plot?

TOSCA. No one.

SCARPIA. No one at all?

TOSCA. Well, naturally, to the agents of Fouché—

SCARPIA. Aha!

*Pause.*

TOSCA. (*Aghast.*) What you are suggesting is too vile to be believed—

SCARPIA. Nothing in this world. Tosca, is too vile to be believed. This is the
year 1800, Signora, and we live in a cesspit—a world that has gone
mad—

TOSCA. Not—Fouché—

SCARPIA. Fouché.

TOSCA. Betrayed my Mario?

SCARPIA. And all his accomplices.

TOSCA. The first consul of France shall know of this.

SCARPIA. The first consul of France does know of it.

*He produces a document from his tunic pocket the one he once briefly flourished
as a death warrant.*

Do you read that signature?

TOSCA. (*In a whisper.*) Bonaparte. (*She kisses it passionately.*) Oh Bonaparte!
My idol! My love! My inspiration! (*She kisses it again, then rubs the document with a napkin.*) A touch of lobster pâté. (*Reading.*) A Monsieur le
Baron Scarpia, Chef de Police de Sa Majeste, Le Roi Ferdinand . . . Mon
cher ami . . . (*Appalled.*) Mon cher ami?

SCARPIA. (*Snatching the document back.*) There is much in this that must not
be read, even by you—my beloved—or it will cost both of us our heads.
Here is the relevant part: "Regarding the Jacobin conspirators of whom
my Chief of Police Fouché has afforded you a comprehensive list, by far
the most dangerous is Mario Cavaradossi, a known firebrand and revolutionary, and a suspected homos—" I need not read you that particular
passage—"This Cavaradossi's plan to explode the Royal Palace shows a
wanton disregard for the sacred laws of property which I, as First Consul of Revolutionary France cannot and will not countenance. Apart from
causing irreparable damage to a historic building in which, one day, I
might hope to reside, it could also have destroyed some very valuable
paintings which I still need for my collection. Mario Cavaradossi must
be shot out of hand—and at once."

TOSCA *has appeared about to faint.* SCARPIA *hurries to her side with a glass of
wine.*

TOSCA. Ah, Baron—would that you had ravished my body, rather than my
soul!

SCARPIA. Would that I had too. I mean, I quite agree. I really am most awfully sorry to have had to break it to you this way dear Tosca. Would you care for a little brandy?

TOSCA. Yes.

SCARPIA *goes to get it.*

(*Murmuring.*) 'Oh villain, most perfidious villain! Oh monster among men'.

SCARPIA. (*His back to her.*) Me?

TOSCA. No, Bonaparte.

*He returns with the brandy.*

What, after all, are you but Bonaparte's jackal?

SCARPIA. (*Sitting.*) Well at least that's better than being King Ferdinand's jackal, isn't it?

TOSCA. So you are two jackals—

SCARPIA. Yes but for the price of one. I only get paid by King Ferdinand.

TOSCA. Oh what a terrible life you lead—

SCARPIA. It's a terrible world. All I have done is to take out a little insurance on the future.

TOSCA. My ideals are utterly shattered.

SCARPIA. (*Joining her in a brandy.*) Oh dear! Yes, I suppose they must be.

TOSCA. Poor Mario! what is to become of him?

SCARPIA. Well—that is rather a question, isn't it?

TOSCA. Ring the bell.

SCARPIA. Yes, beloved. (*He does so.*)

TOSCA. But to what purpose is this farce of a mock execution? Mario will surely die anyway.

SCARPIA. Well, of course, with a Neapolitan firing squad, accidents can always happen.

TOSCA. I mean he will die of shame and disillusionment.

SCARPIA. Well, better disillusioned than dead,—that's what I always say. Or don't you agree?

SCHIARRONE *has entered.* SCARPIA *confronts him with the customary scowl. Evidently he has forgotten the new signals.*

Now Schiarrone—listen carefully—

SCHIARRONE. (*After searching* SCARPIA'S *face carefully.*) Yes. The Signora is to be taken down to the platform where she is to bid adieu to her lover—

SCARPIA. (*Murmuring.*) No, Schiarrone—

SCHIARRONE. (*Undeterred.*) While the firing squad level their muskets at them both—

SCARPIA. (*Murmuring again.*) Not exactly, Schiarrone—

SCHIARRONE. And the muskets of course, are to be loaded with blanks, not balls. Never fear, Excellency. I have the whole thing pat.

*He looks pleased with himself.* SCARPIA *does not look pleased with him.*

SCARPIA. (*Now really scowling.*) You have not got it pat, Schiarrone. Not pat at all. I will now try to make it pat—

TOSCA. (*Who has not been listening.*) May I speak to the Captain?

SCARPIA. By all means, dearest one.

TOSCA. Captain, what arrangements have you made for conveying Signor Cavaradossi from this place after the business with the firing squad?

*Pause.*

SCHIARRONE. I had arranged a conveyance, Signora.

TOSCA. What kind of conveyance?

SCHIARRONE. (*After a helpless look at* SCARPIA.) A suitable conveyance.

TOSCA. For a long journey?

SCHIARRONE. Very long.

SCARPIA. The Signora means, will it take him to *Milan?* (*He pulls out a handkerchief with a flourish, and drops it.*) Ah, how careless—

TOSCA *has pounced on the handkerchief in a trice, and uses it to press to her eyes.*

TOSCA. Milan! Milan! and Bonaparte! Accursed fiends! Ah, how my heart breaks, how my eyes swim with the memories of my shattered ideals!

*She puts the handkerchief in her reticule watched by both* SCARPIA *and* SCHIARRONE.

We must not send him to any place within reach of his mortal enemy. And yet Bonaparte bestrides the world. Where then may we send him? (*To* SCHIARRONE.) This conveyance that you have ordered for him? Does it go at a fast pace?

SCHIARRONE. Not—usually—

TOSCA. How fast? Would it, for instance, reach Venice by nightfall?

SCHIARRONE. (*Appalled.*) *Venice?*

SCARPIA. I fancy you have made a small error, haven't you Schiarrone, in your ordering of this conveyance for Signor Cavaradossi?

SCHIARRONE. (*Resigned.*) I wouldn't be at all surprised.

SCARPIA. The conveyance that the Captain has ordered for Mario is I imagine rather cumbersome, and accustomed only to local journeys. Isn't that so, Captain?

SCHIARRONE. (*Almost mutinous.*) And it takes it at a rather funereal pace—if the Signora follows me—

SCARPIA. (*Muttering.*) If she did you'd be dead. (*He pats* SCHIARRONE'S *shoulder.*) Now what we need, Schiarrone, is a vehicle that proceeds at a much more lively pace. Understand? Something that might, for instance, get Signore Cavaradossi—alive and well, Schiarrone, alive and well, remember—to Leghorn before dawn.

TOSCA. Leghorn?

SCARPIA. The British Fleet is there, and Mario as an enemy of Bonaparte, can take refuge on a British warship and be given passage to England.

TOSCA. England? But as a known revolutionary he will be shot by King George.

SCARPIA. Oh no. Far more likely he will be invited to Carlton House, as a guest of the Prince of Wales. (*Affably, to* SCHIARRONE.) Now I trust,

Schiarrone, we have cleared up any little confusion you might still have had about this morning's work?

SCHIARRONE *desperately searches his notes.* SCARPIA *brusquely tears off a page and scribbles something in pencil.*

But just in case we haven't—you did say you wanted it all in writing, didn't you? Safer, I think you said, that way. (*He hands it to* SCHIARRONE.)

SCHIARRONE. (*At great length.*) No—balls?

SCARPIA. (*Smiling.*) Precisely.

SCHIARRONE. No balls at all?

SCARPIA. None at all.

*As* SCHIARRONE *ponders the note* SCARPIA *puts his arm on* SCHIARRONE'S *shoulder again.*

SCARPIA. You realise, I hope, that if you bring this night's work to a successful conclusion, you may well receive promotion?

SCHIARRONE. A Major? Me? But I'd have to grow a moustache.

SCARPIA. I have no doubt that even that is not beyond your capabilities.

*Suddenly we hear a tolling of a bell and the sound of muffled drums.* SCARPIA *dashes to the window.*

Oh my god, they're marching him out already, what is the meaning of this, Schiarrone?

SCHIARRONE. Well, they shouldn't be marching him out, I mean, I'm their Captain, and they ought to have waited for me. The thing is, of course, they're used to shooting people at dawn and if they're late home their wives get jealous—

SCARPIA. Call to them from the window—

TOSCA. (*At the window.*) Ah, there is my Mario! How brave and proud he looks! A King among mortals. A Committee Chairman among his Board—

SCARPIA. Shout to them, Schiarrone.

SCHIARRONE. There is no need to get panicky. Excellency, they are my own men. They can and will do nothing without *me*. (*Shouting from the window.*) My brave men! This is your Captain, Captain Schiarrone—

*He is greeted by a ragged, loud and rather drunken cheer. He doesn't seem to be unpopular—but nor does he seem to have exerted over his brave men an absolutely iron discipline. There are several loud and very coarse comments on the identity of the lady framed in the window with him, and on her reasons for being there.* TOSCA *hasn't helped by calling melodiously to her lover.*

TOSCA. Mario! Mario! Mario!

SCHIARRONE. My gallant children I love you all, as you love me. Think always of the glory and fame of the Kingdom of the Two Sicilies—

*There is a sound that (forty years ago) would have been described as a 'raspberry'.*

And of our beloved King Ferdinand, in whose sacred cause we pledge our lives—

*Dead silence, broken by* TOSCA, *in melodious voice.*

TOSCA. Mario, Mario, Mario!!! Oh, my Mario—why do you not look at me?
*There is instant cheering. The soldiers are evidently uncertain about exactly whom she is shouting to, but delighted that it is not to anyone called Ferdinand.*
SCHIARRONE. (*Shouting through the window.*) Loyal sons of Naples, I your Captain, command you to unload your muskets!
*There is the sound of a volley.*
SCARPIA. Oh my god!
SCHIARRONE. Don't fret, Excellency. That's their way of unloading their muskets, it's just high spirits. No one was hurt—(*Looking down.*) I think. (*Shouting.*) Well done, my brave men. Now I personally, your Captain, will descend to give you your orders. Do nothing whatever until I reach your side.
*There is another raspberry and a crash of muskets to the ground.*
TOSCA. (*Calling plaintively.*) Mario! Mario! He will not even turn his head. And yet he must have recognised my voice. Oh, what has happened?
SCHIARRONE. I think I can explain that, Signora. Signor Cavaradossi has heard that you have spent some hours in the Baron's chambers—
TOSCA. Who has betrayed me?
SCHIARRONE. The White Friars of Death. They are inclined to a little gossip between executions. (*To* SCARPIA.) Excellency, about an hour ago, Signor Cavaradossi told me that he would not purchase his life at the price of Signora Tosca's honour.
SCARPIA *looks at* TOSCA. *Pause.*
SCARPIA. His life is not now at stake.
SCHIARRONE. Oh no, but when it *was*—you know when it was going to be a fake *fake* execution—Your Excellency will understand what I mean—and I gave Cavaradossi his instructions which of course were fake too, then—to fall down at the sound of the volley, I mean—which then wouldn't have been fake at all—are you still with me, Excellency?
SCARPIA. (*Menacingly.*) Ahead of you, Schiarrone.
SCHIARRONE. Well, Signor Cavaradossi told me then that he would *not* fall down at the sound of the volley, and that no one could get him to fall down. He would remain standing, he said, shouting revolutionary slogans, and singing the Marseillaise, until they did shoot him. He was quite insistent.
SCARPIA. Why did you not tell me this before?
SCHIARRONE. Well at the time, the question of whether or not Signor Cavaradossi remained standing seemed of comparatively minor importance. (*He laughs.*) But now, of course, it's different. Oh dear, what are we to do?
SCARPIA. Blindfold the firing party!
TOSCA. (*Intervening calmly.*) No, Baron. Dear Baron, there is only one thing to do. Mario must be told the truth.
SCARPIA. The naked truth?

TOSCA. If that is how it can be described.

SCARPIA. Ah no, Tosca. Not that! Anything but that— (*He kneels at her feet.*) I implore you—save me from this shame, this horror, this degradation— pity me, Tosca—oh pity me!

TOSCA. I do pity you, Baron, as you know—but I cannot allow my Mario to go to his exile under the load of a gross and hideous misunderstanding.

SCARPIA *moans.*

Baron, are you man enough? Are you what I think you might yet be?

SCARPIA *gets to his feet, squares his shoulders and faces* SCHIARRONE.

SCARPIA. Schiarrone, you may assure the prisoner, on the word of Baron Scarpia, that the honour of Signora Tosca is safe, and has been these last two hours.

*Pause.*

SCHIARRONE. Non e vero . . . !

SCARPIA. E vero.

SCHIARRONE. But—Excellency. . . (*He points to* SCARPIA'S *attire.*)

SCARPIA. The Signora was prepared to make the sacrifice, but I did not find myself in a position to accept it.

SCHIARRONE. Your Excellency is just surely having his fun?

SCARPIA. (*Thunderously.*) No, you baboon, he is not having his fun. Nor has he had it—And that is the point—

SCHIARRONE. (*Beginning to giggle.*) Il Barone Scarpia!—Il famoso Monstro di Roma!—Il fabulose Barone Scarpia!—(*He doubles up.*)

SCARPIA. (*Quietly.*) I can very easily organise another firing-party, Schiarrone— this time with grape-shot.

SCHIARRONE. (*Instantly sobering.*) Excellency.

SCARPIA. Go and give that message to Signore Cavaradossi. And then take yourself out of my sight—forever.

SCHIARRONE. But the carriage for La Tosca?

SCARPIA. Yes. Arrange that, and then announce it. But after that I never wish to see your face again. Do you understand?

SCHIARRONE. Your Excellency cannot be so unkind.

TOSCA. (*Coming forward.*) Dearest, it is not the mark of a great soul to impute blame for the waywardness of events to a young and wholly innocent party. Captain, I am grateful for your part in the happenings of the past hours, and I promise you that such influence as I may be able to exert upon the Baron will not be wasted on your behalf.

SCHIARRONE. The Signora is too kind.

TOSCA. Pray go and attend to the execution of my beloved. Oh, and many congratulations on your promotion.

SCHIARRONE. Signora!

TOSCA. (*Thoughtfully.*) Yes. A moustache would suit you very well.

SCHIARRONE. Oh Signora—(*Bowing.*) Your Excellency. (*He goes gravely, but his gravity does not outlast his journey to the door. Before the bolts and bars*

*clang into place we hear a shrill peal of youthful laughter. As he goes.*) Il
Barone Scarpia! Impotente! Non e possibile! Non e vero! Eh, eh, eh!
Impotente! Il Barone Scarpia!

SCARPIA *grimly faces* TOSCA.

TOSCA. You have done most nobly, Baron, and I am proud of you. Now, at
last, you have persuaded me that there is some hope for your spiritual
regeneration.

*Pause.*

SCARPIA. At the hands of a good woman?

TOSCA. How else could it come to so villainous a man?

SCARPIA. How indeed? But what about my physical regeneration?

TOSCA. That too will come.

SCARPIA. Also at the hands of a good woman?

TOSCA. Who knows, Baron? Life after all, has its constant surprises—And,
in life, is there any thing more surprising than love? And the many, many
forms it can take? That, at least, is what I always say—

SCHIARRONE'S *voice can be heard barking orders from the platform below.*
Shall we watch? It should be fun—

*They go to together to the window.*
Ah look. Your Captain is giving my Mario your message—

*There is a sudden, loud, tenor's laugh from outside.*
That was a little vulgar. Not like a true Revolutionary—I must speak to
him—when I get the chance.

*More barked orders from* SCHIARRONE *down below. The drums begin to beat
again.*

MARIO. (*Off, singing in a high tenor.*)
Allons, enfants de la Patrie!
Le jour de gloire est arrivé
Contre nous de la tyrannie
L'étendard sanglant—

*A barked order from* SCHIARRONE.

est levé

L'étendard sanglant est. . . .

*The voice is cruelly cut off—and, it seems, perpetually silenced by a volley of
musket fire. There is dead stillness for a moment, before we hear more barked
orders from* SCHIARRONE, *and the sound of the soldiers retreating.*

TOSCA. Ah, how magnificently he fell! One could have almost sworn it was
real. Don't you agree, Baron?

SCARPIA. (*A shade anxiously.*) One could have almost sworn it.

TOSCA. The Captain is now telling him it is safe to rise.

*There is a long pause.*
What is that on Mario's forehead? Is it, can it be, don't tell me—blood?

SCARPIA. It does look a little like blood.

TOSCA. Ah—Viper, toad, devil! Ten times accursed fiend—

*She brings off one of the most spectacular faints in theatrical history.* SCARPIA *is too preoccupied to do more than throw her prostrate body a glance.*

SCARPIA. Schiarrone—what has gone wrong down there?

SCHIARRONE. (*Off.*) A little accident, Excellency—

SCARPIA. I can see that from up here, idiot—

SCHIARRONE. (*Off.*) I think the prisoner fainted at the sound of the volley and hit his head—ah yes. He is recovering, Excellency. See. (*Evidently to* MARIO.) One, two, three and oops! There we are! No harm done. Now we'll just get you to this coach, because you're off to Leghorn and England—

MARIO. (*Agonised, off.*) Oh no! Not England! Why didn't you kill me!

*Meanwhile* SCARPIA *has run to the inert body of* TOSCA *and has lifted it with some difficulty, placing it tenderly on a couch.*

SCARPIA. (*Patting her face.*) Tosca! . . . Tosca! . . . Come to. All is well.

*But she remains lifeless. Distraught he tears some feathers from her fan, goes to the candle, lights them, and holds them under her nose—burning his fingers in the process, and uttering an oath.* TOSCA *opens her eyes.*

TOSCA. What is that terrible smell?

SCARPIA. Feathers—you fainted—

TOSCA. (*Remembering.*) Ah monster—jackal—spawn of Satan—

SCARPIA. But Mario is not dead. He is safe, beloved—

TOSCA. (*Ruefully.*) But my best fan—

SCARPIA. I shall give you ten others, far better—

*He has found himself in an extremely amorous position. Not to mince words you might say that he is now, physically at least, on top.*

TOSCA. Oh no, not ten. Ten is ridiculous. . . . The name of the shop is Marocchetti, in the Via Boccaccio—

SCARPIA. I shall remember, beloved one.

*He has managed to untie the cord of his dressing-gown.*

TOSCA. And you will not forget either, will you dear Baron, the promises you made me about seeking, in future, only the higher forms of love—

SCARPIA. How could I forget them, my divine Tosca? My life, from now on, will be a model of spirituality and good form—

*His dressing-gown slips off without apparent difficulty. He kisses her passionately. She does not resist. Then gently he begins to undress her.*

TOSCA. (*After a pause.*) Twenty-eight cupids, you say?

SCARPIA. No, beloved. Twenty-six. Twenty-eight in the bedroom—

TOSCA. (*Dreamily.*) I think I prefer twenty-six. (*She has been nearly undressed.*)

SCHIARRONE *strides briskly in. He has on a travelling cloak, and is putting on gloves. For the first time in the whole evening he looks supremely confident. This time he knows he has got it right.*

SCHIARRONE. Your Excellency? . . . (*He looks round the room.*) Your Excellency? . . . I am happy to tell you that the Signora's carriage awaits her.

*Pause.*

SCARPIA. (*From the couch.*) Yes, Schiarrone. That is clever of you. You will now send it away, and instruct it to return at dawn.

SCHIARRONE. (*Aggrieved.*) But it is dawn. . .

SCARPIA. No. It will not be dawn until I make it—

SCHIARRONE. And when will that be, Excellency?

SCARPIA. Quite soon, I think. . . . Perhaps even very soon. . . . But not just yet. Go! I will ring for you.

SCHIARRONE. Yes, Excellency. (*He goes towards the door, then stops, as a thought strikes him. He takes out the inevitable notebook.*) Can Your Excellency give me some idea of how long I shall have to wait?

SCARPIA. (*Looking at* TOSCA.) A lifetime. . . .

SCHIARRONE. (*Taking his note.*) A lifetime? I thank Your Excellency. I have your meaning, I hope.

SCARPIA. I hope I have it myself. Go!

SCHIARRONE *puts his notebook away, salutes and goes.*

TOSCA. (*Muttering.*) Twenty-two, twenty-three, twenty-four, twenty—

*Her lips are closed by* SCARPIA'S *before she has completed the full count.*


THE LIGHTS FADE

# CAUSE CELEBRE

First published 1978
by Hamish Hamilton Ltd

TO
**PEGS**
with love and gratitude

*Cause Célèbre* opened at Her Majesty's Theatre in London on Monday 4th July 1977, presented by John Gale.

The director of the production was Robin Midgley, the designer Adrian Vaux and the cast was:

| | |
|---|---|
| ALMA RATTENBURY | Glynis Johns |
| FRANCIS RATTENBURY | Anthony Pedley |
| CHRISTOPHER | Matthew Ryan *or* Douglas Melbourne |
| IRENE RIGGS | Sheila Grant |
| GEORGE WOOD | Neil Daglish |
| EDITH DAVENPORT | Helen Lindsay |
| JOHN DAVENPORT | Jeremy Hawk |
| TONY DAVENPORT | Adam Richardson |
| STELLA MORRISON | Angela Browne |
| RANDOLPH BROWN | Kevin Hart |
| JUDGE | Patrick Barr |
| O'CONNOR | Kenneth Griffith |
| CROOM-JOHNSON | Bernard Archard |
| CASSWELL | Darryl Forbes-Dawson |
| MONTAGU | Philip Bowen |
| CLERK OF THE COURT | David Glover |
| JOAN WEBSTER | Peggy Aitchison |
| SERGEANT BAGWELL | Anthony Pedley |
| PORTER | Anthony Howard |
| WARDER | David Masterman |
| CORONER | David Glover |

The action of the play takes place in Bournemouth and London in 1934 and 1935.

*This play was inspired by the facts of a well-known case, but the characters attributed to the individuals represented are based on the author's imagination, and are not necessarily factual.*

The stage represents at various times Court Number One at the Old Bailey and other parts of the Central Criminal Court in London, a villa at Bournemouth, the drawing-room of a flat in Kensington and other places. Changes of scene are effected mainly by lighting, the curtain falling only at the end of each of the two acts.

## ACT ONE

*Lights on* ALMA *and* MRS. DAVENPORT. *After a moment, light comes up very dimly on the* CLERK OF THE COURT.

CLERK OF THE COURT. Alma Victoria Rattenbury you are charged with the murder of Francis Mawson Rattenbury on March the twenty eighth 1935. Are you guilty or not guilty?

ALMA. (*Almost inaudibly.*) Not guilty.

*The lights change as the* CLERK OF THE COURT *turns towards* MRS. DAVENPORT.

CLERK OF THE COURT. Edith Amelia Davenport, take the book in your right hand and read what is on this card.

*The light on the* CLERK OF THE COURT *slowly fades out.*

MRS. DAVENPORT. I do solemnly swear by Almighty God that I will well and truly try the issues joined between our sovereign Lord the King and the prisoners at the bar and will give a true verdict according to the evidence.

*The spots fade out on* ALMA *and* MRS. DAVENPORT.

MRS. DAVENPORT *and* STELLA MORRISON *in the sitting-room of the flat in Kensington.* STELLA *is* MRS. DAVENPORT'S *sister, a year or two younger.*

STELLA. A jury summons!—my dear, how too frightful. Let's see.

MRS. DAVENPORT *hands her the official letter.*

(*Reading.*) '. . . present yourself at the . . . jury service . . . for fifteen days . . . and fail not at your peril'—indeed!

MRS. DAVENPORT. (*Smiling.*) Yes, rather scaring that. Peril of what d'you think? Hard labour, or the stocks, or just a ducking?

STELLA. Whopping great fine, I should think. Might almost be worth paying it—I'll get Henry to cough up the necessary if you like.

MRS. DAVENPORT. (*Taking back the letter.*) Certainly not. I'm quite looking forward to it, as it happens.

STELLA. What, a whole fortnight?

MRS. DAVENPORT. Well, I've got the time these days, and who knows, I might do a bit of good for some old soul who's snitched a pair of silk stockings from Barkers.

STELLA. More likely to be indecent exposure.

MRS. DAVENPORT. Oh, they wouldn't have women on those juries, would they?

STELLA. My dear, they have women on everything these days.

MRS. DAVENPORT. Well if it is that, I'll just have to face it like—well, like a man, I suppose. But I'm not going on that date—I'm not going to mess up Tony's Christmas hols. I'll ask for a postponement to May, that should be safe.

STELLA. Is he enjoying himself in Cannes?

MRS. DAVENPORT. Tony? He says so in his postcards, but I expect they're written under John's supervision. Thank Heavens it's the last time.

STELLA. You're still determined on the divorce?

MRS. DAVENPORT. Yes. Quite.

STELLA. Well, you know what I think.

MRS. DAVENPORT. A separation doesn't give me custody.

STELLA. You won't get *complete* custody.

MRS. DAVENPORT. Oh yes I will. John won't defend it. He's too scared of his Under Secretary. It'll all be fixed out of court. If he does defend it, I'll win.

STELLA. There was only that one woman, wasn't there?

MRS. DAVENPORT. Oh, no. In the five years before we separated I've found out now there were at least two others. And now there's this dreadful woman.

STELLA. Still, four in five years? That doesn't really make him Bluebeard, you know. In fact for most husbands with unwilling wives I'd say it was about par for the course.

MRS. DAVENPORT. Are you trying to make it my fault again?

STELLA. Well he was only about forty, wasn't he, when you started having headaches? That is a bit young, darling, for a husband to find himself in the spare room.

MRS. DAVENPORT. I couldn't go on, Stella. I told you. I never did care much for that side of things, as you know, and as he got older he got more and more demanding.

STELLA. That's one thing I could never say about Henry—

MRS. DAVENPORT. He used to say that my reluctance made him want it more. Now you can't say that's normal, Stella.

STELLA. I suppose not—I just wonder if it would work with Henry. . . . How does Tony feel about it all? He always seemed to be quite fond of his father.

MRS. DAVENPORT. Well, he was. Of course now that I've told him the truth— not all of it, of course, just enough—he's beginning to see things my way. Unless he's been led astray these last two weeks. I wouldn't put anything past that man. I really hate him.

FADE OUT

DAVENPORT. There should be a car waiting to pick me up. The name's Davenport—would you put that one down there and come back for the other?

PORTER. Very good, sir! (*He exits.*)

DAVENPORT. Well, Tony, I'm afraid this is goodbye. You had better take the Airport bus to Victoria Air Terminus, and get a taxi to Kensington from there . . . I'm going straight to the Home Office, so—

TONY. (*Quickly.*) I understand. (*Pause.*) Dad, I will be seeing you again, won't I?

DAVENPORT. Well, certainly in court.

TONY. I meant after that?

DAVENPORT. I'm afraid that depends on your mother.

TONY. I see. Can I ask one thing?

DAVENPORT. Yes.

TONY. Mum always talks to me—well sometimes talks to me—about *that* woman, etcetera etcetera!

DAVENPORT. Yes.

TONY. Well—there isn't any *that* woman, is there? I mean, I've been with you two weeks, and I'm not half-witted . . .

DAVENPORT. No, you're not.

TONY. You still love Mum, don't you?

DAVENPORT. Yes, I do.

TONY. Dad—is there any *that* woman?

*Pause.*

PORTER I've found your car, sir; do you want the other one in the boot?

DAVENPORT. No, my son is travelling by the bus, so—

PORTER Yes, sir. I'll get him a place.

TONY. Thank you.

DAVENPORT. I'll do the V.I.P. Well, goodbye, Tony.

TONY. Thank you for a marvellous time.

DAVENPORT. A bit dull, I'm afraid.

TONY. Not Cannes. That was smashing.

DAVENPORT. You didn't like Paris?

TONY. Well, don't think I'm ungrateful, Dad, but you did promise to take me to a—to a—you know—that 'House of all Nations'—

DAVENPORT. Tony I did remember that. It's just that—well, you have to take a passport, you see.

TONY. A passport to a brothel?

DAVENPORT. They're very strict about under age.

TONY. (*Despairing.*) Oh Dad! Even in France? I'll have to try Turkey or somewhere.

DAVENPORT. (*Laughing.*) Why Turkey? Why not here—Jermyn Street?

TONY. I'd thought of that, only I'm a bit—well—

DAVENPORT. I'm not serious. At least, not yet. I should give it another year or two, I think old chap, don't you?

TONY. But Dad I'm seventeen!

DAVENPORT. Yes, but that's still a bit young, don't you think? My first wasn't till I was twenty. But still, when you do go, for God's sake take precautions, won't you?

TONY. What—?

PORTER. I've got your place, sir.

DAVENPORT. Thank you. (*Gives him half a crown.*)

PORTER. Thank you, sir. (*He goes.*)

DAVENPORT. Well—

TONY. Dad, what shall I tell Mum—about *that* woman?

DAVENPORT. Tell her you didn't meet her, but I was always talking to her on
the telephone. It's a question of her pride. Off you go, Tony.

WOOD *crosses the stage to stand outside the* RATTENBURY'S *house, taking off his
bicycle clips.*
*The lights come up to show the hall, sitting-room, stairs.* IRENE RIGGS, *maid and
companion to* ALMA—*dressed more as companion than maid—is entering
the tiny hall.*
IRENE. Yes? What is it?
WOOD. I've come about the advert.
IRENE. You're too old.
WOOD. It says fourteen to eighteen.
IRENE. I know what it says. I wrote it myself. You're too old.
WOOD. I'm seventeen.
IRENE. You're still not what we're wanting. Sorry.
ALMA. (*Calling from upstairs.*) Who is it, Irene?
IRENE. (*Calling back.*) A boy about the advert. He's wrong.
ALMA. (*Calling.*) Why?
IRENE. (*Calling.*) He's too old.
WOOD. (*Making his voice heard aloft.*) I'm not. I'm only seventeen.
IRENE. (*Calling.*) But he looks much older.
ALMA. (*After a pause—calling.*) I'll come down.
IRENE. (*Calling.*) I was sending him away.
ALMA. (*Decisively.*) Keep him.
IRENE (*Annoyed, to* WOOD.) You'd better come in. (*Clicking her tongue.*) You're
not the type at all.
ALMA *has meanwhile swung her legs off the bed.*
ALMA (*Calling.*) I'll just slip into something. I won't be a mo.
*Pulls out a pair of day pyjamas—of a fairly hectic design and colour—from the
wardrobe.*
*Downstairs* WOOD *has come in and is waiting uncertainly in the hall, twisting
his homburg hat.*
(*Calling.*) Tell him to go into the lounge, Irene, and make himself com-
fortable.
IRENE (*Nodding towards the sitting-room.*) You heard her.
WOOD (*On his way in.*) You the maid?
IRENE. Companion.
WOOD. You don't like me, do you?
IRENE. I've nothing against you. You're just not the type, that's all.
WOOD. That'll be for her to say, won't it?
*He nods upstairs.* IRENE *regards him coldly.*
IRENE. (*At length.*) Yes, it will.
*She goes down the passage and disappears.* WOOD *looks round the sitting-room
and perches on a chair. Upstairs* ALMA *has finished her dressing and is ap-
plying lipstick, then patting her hair into place.* WOOD *gets up and goes to a*

*small piano, on the stand of which is a piece of sheet music left open. He examines it.* ALMA *comes rapidly down the stairs in slippered feet and surprises him as she comes in. He starts guiltily away from the piano.*

WOOD. Sorry.

ALMA. (*Laughing.*) That's quite all right. I don't mind anyone reading my music.

WOOD. Oh, I don't read music. Did you say *your* music?

ALMA. Look at the front.

WOOD. (*Awed.*) That's a picture of you.

ALMA. Taken a long time ago, I'm afraid. It's twelve years old, that photograph.

WOOD. 'Dark-Haired Marie' by Lozanne. Is that you—Miss Lozanne?

ALMA. Oh no—that's just my pen-name.

*Seeing* WOOD'S *bewilderment.*

It's just the name I put on my songs. My real name's Alma. What's yours?

WOOD. Wood.

ALMA. Christian name?

WOOD. Perce. Percy really. My Dad calls me Perce—so Perce.

ALMA. What does your Dad do for a living?

WOOD. He's a builder, laid off. I work for him when he's got work—but there's not much of that about these days.

ALMA. Oh I know. It's terrible this slump. I can't sell a song these days—for love nor money.

WOOD. Do you do this for a living, Miss?

ALMA. Oh no. I don't have to, thank heavens, or I'd be on the dole. Mind you they do get done sometimes. That song, for instance, that was done only a year ago, on the B.B.C. A baritone sang it.

WOOD. (*Eagerly.*) The Whispering Baritone?

ALMA. No. Just a baritone. Let me take your cap.

WOOD. Thank you, Miss.

*She takes it from him and puts it on the piano.*

ALMA. By the way, it's Mrs. Mrs. three times over, as it happens—

WOOD. Cor. Divorced?

ALMA. (*Gaily.*) Yes once, the other one died and now seven years gone with old Ratz—Mr. Rattenbury, my present one. I'm giving things away, aren't I? I started very young. I've a boy of thirteen. Almost as old as you.

*She laughs. He smiles politely.*

Yes, well . . . I suppose it's working on building sites that's made you so—developed.

WOOD. I bike a lot too.

ALMA. Yes. That does do wonders for the physique. You look quite what I would call—full-grown.

*Pause.* WOOD *has at last dimly realised the nature of his future mistress's interest in him.*

WOOD. Your—Irene—thought I was too full-grown.

ALMA. Yes. Well you see we concocted that advertisement together, and what *she* had in mind was—well—a rather smaller kind of boy. You'd be under her, really, not me . . . Well I'd better tell you what the wages are. It's one of the reasons we wanted a little boy. I'm afraid my husband will only go to a pound a week.

WOOD. Living in?

ALMA. No, I'm afraid not. We haven't room really. There's only one other room besides Irene's you see, and my two boys—I've another little one, only six—well they're in there, during school holidays that is. Of course if you'd been a little boy like I meant in the advert, you could have slept in with them—I mean, if you'd been a really *little* boy but being as you are, and me and Irene slipping about upstairs with next to nothing on— well it would be rather awkward, wouldn't it? . . . (*Rather breathlessly.*) No, I'm afraid living in's quite out of the question.

WOOD. I was only asking. Where does old Ratz sleep?

ALMA. Oh, you mustn't call him Ratz. You must call him Mr. Rattenbury, like Irene.

WOOD. Yes. Where does he sleep?

*Pause.*

ALMA. Inquisitive, aren't you? That's all right. I like an enquiring nature. Mr. Rattenbury sleeps through there.

*She points to the door off the sitting-room.*

He can't do the stairs any more.

*Pause.*

WOOD. I see.

ALMA. (*Lightly, after another pause.*) Well, is it a go, or isn't it?

WOOD. A quid isn't much.

ALMA. Well, I could slip you a few bob on the side—expenses, you know. Only Ratz—Mr. Rattenbury mustn't know. He's a little strict about money. Do you live close?

WOOD. Other side of Bournemouth. About half hour on my bike. You wouldn't like to say how many bob?

ALMA. (*Patting his arm.*) You must ask when you need it.

WOOD. O.K.

ALMA. Well I'm glad that's settled. Why don't we have a little drinkie on it?

WOOD. I'm afraid I don't drink.

ALMA. I expect that's just what you tell all your employers. Gin and it?

WOOD. I don't know what that is.

ALMA. Fancy anyone not knowing what a 'gin and it' is—

*She is busy pouring herself a drink.*

. . . Won't you just try a sip, just to seal our little arrangement?

WOOD. If you insist.

ALMA. Oh I don't *insist.* I never insist. But just this once—There has to be a first time for everything, doesn't there?

WOOD. Yes.

ALMA. A little of what you fancy's my motto, and a very good one too. This is a lovely world we're in, and we were put into it to enjoy it. Don't you agree?

*She hands him the drink.*

WOOD. I might. I don't think my Dad would. He's religious.

ALMA. Well our dear Lord didn't say we mustn't have fun, did He? He turned water into wine, not wine into water. Just tell that to your Dad next time he gets narky. And He said we must love each other, and I think we should.

*Raising her glass.*

Well, Perce—no I can't call you Perce. Or Percy. Have you got a middle name?

WOOD. George.

ALMA. That's nice. I'm going to call you that. (*Raising her glass again.*) George.

WOOD. (*Raising his.*) Mrs. Rattenbury.

ALMA. Alma . . . Not just now—always . . .

WOOD. Alma.

ALMA. George!

*They drink.* WOOD *makes a face.* ALMA *laughs and takes the glass away from him.* I'm not letting you have any more. I'm not having anyone say I'm leading you astray.

*She drinks* WOOD'S *drink in a single gulp.*

Just like water to me. Do you know what Alma means in Latin? A professor told me once, it means life-giving, bountiful. In olden times they used it about goddesses, like Venus.

*Sipping her drink.*

Well I'm not Venus, God knows—but apparently it also means kind and comforting, and that I am, George, though I say it who shouldn't—

RATTENBURY *comes into the hall.*

Here's Ratz. I'd better warn you. You have to shout.

*She opens the sitting-room door.* RATTENBURY *immediately glances at* WOOD. *Deaf he may be, but certainly not blind.* ALMA *kisses him.*

(*Loudly.*) Had a nice walkie?

RATTENBURY. There was an east wind. You should have told me.

ALMA. Poor thing, did you get chilled?

RATTENBURY. Blasted to buggery.

*Paying no attention to* WOOD, *he sits down in what is evidently his usual armchair—significantly one that has its back to a pair of French windows.*

RATTENBURY. Get me a whiskey, would you?

ALMA. It's a bit early for your whiskey, isn't it?

*She begins to get him a drink.*

RATTENBURY. It's a bit early for your gin.

ALMA. I only meant you don't usually have whiskey in the mornings.

RATTENBURY. I don't usually get blasted to buggery in the morning.
*Showing a paper.*
>    Shares are down again.
ALMA. Oh dear. You're probably wondering who the stranger is.
RATTENBURY. No, I wasn't, but who is he?
ALMA. His name is George Wood, and he's the new help.
RATTENBURY. (*After a moody sip.*) Irene said a boy.
ALMA. Well he is a boy. He's only seventeen.
RATTENBURY. Hm.
*He stares at* WOOD *without overmuch interest.*
>    Has he any references?
WOOD. No, sir. I've never done this kind of work before.
RATTENBURY. What?
ALMA. (*Putting her hand on his shoulder.*) Don't worry dear. We had a nice
>    long interview. I'll vouch for him.
RATTENBURY *looks up at her. He grunts acquiescence and hands her his glass.*
>    That one went down pretty fast.
RATTENBURY. Not as fast as my shares.
*As she passes* WOOD.
>    Does he drive?
WOOD. (*Loudly.*) Yes, sir. I've got a licence.
ALMA. (*Coming back with the whiskey.*) Well isn't that marvellous!
>    (*To* RATTENBURY, *loudly.*) Isn't that handy, dear? We've got ourselves a
>    chauffeur.
RATTENBURY. No uniform.
ALMA. (*Loudly.*) No, of course not. (*To* WOOD, *quietly.*) Well, perhaps a cap
>    and a smart mackintosh. You'd look nice in a cap.
RATTENBURY. What are you saying?
ALMA. I was explaining no uniform, dear. (*To* WOOD.) Better go now. (*Loudly.*)
>    I'm just showing the new help to the front door.
ALMA. (*To* WOOD.) Come on. (*To* RATTENBURY.) Back in a jiffy.
*She and* WOOD *go.*
>    —Well that's settled, thank goodness. It's lovely about your driving. Go
>    and buy yourself a cap. (*She fishes in her bag.*) Here's fifteen shillings.
>    Will that be enough?
WOOD. Should be.
CHRISTOPHER *comes in, wearing his scout's uniform.*
CHRISTOPHER. Mummy, there's a smashing bike outside, with low handlebars.
>    (*Seeing* WOOD.) Oh, is it yours, sir?
WOOD. Yes. A Raleigh.
CHRISTOPHER. I was going to ask if I could ride it.
WOOD. Afraid I'm just going.
ALMA. But he's coming back tomorrow—and every day afterwards. He's go-
>    ing to be one of the family.
CHRISTOPHER. Oh good.

ALMA. I'm sure if you ask him nicely he'll let you ride it.

WOOD. You bet.

CHRISTOPHER. Oh thanks awfully, sir. Mummy, when's lunch?

ALMA. Quite soon, darling.

CHRISTOPHER (*Calling and running off.*) Irene!

CHRISTOPHER *disappears up the stairs.*

ALMA. Sweet, isn't he? (*Sincerely.*) I really am very blessed with my children.

WOOD. (*In awe.*) He called me sir.

ALMA. What? (*Misunderstanding.*) Oh they teach him that at his school. Don't worry. He'll soon be calling you George.

WOOD. I'd rather he went on calling me sir.

ALMA. I'll see he does then.

IRENE *appears from the shadows.*

(*Hastily to* WOOD.) Goodbye then. I'll see you tomorrow.

WOOD. What time?

ALMA. What time, Irene?

*Pause.*

IRENE. (*At length, gloomily.*) Seven. Not a second later.

ALMA. Can you manage seven?

WOOD. Easy . . . Be seeing you.

*He goes out.* ALMA, *left alone with* IRENE, *is uneasy under her steady stare.*

IRENE. (*At length.*) You'll have my notice at the end of the week.

ALMA *laughs and embraces her fondly.*

ALMA. Yes, darling, I'm sure I will.

IRENE. I'm serious.

ALMA. You always are. He can drive, Irene, which is more than any of your little teenies could have done.

IRENE. Yes. There's something else he can do that my little teenies couldn't.

ALMA. Irene . . .

IRENE. Anyway you owe me four weeks' wages.

ALMA. Six pounds?

*She looks in her bag.*

Oh dear. And there's Christopher's new cricket bat. (*Nodding towards sitting-room.*) He's in a bad mood . . . still he's got a couple of whiskies inside him. Think of something for me—

IRENE. I don't know.

ALMA. Pray for me.

IRENE. Yes.

*She goes into the sitting-room.* IRENE *exits.* ALMA *goes up to* RATTENBURY.

ALMA. (*To* RATTENBURY, *brightly.*) Well Ratz, darling. Let me get you another little drinkie. There's time for one before lunch.

*She takes his now empty glass to refill it.*

(*Loudly.*) I've been showing George the car.

RATTENBURY. Who's George?

ALMA. Our new chauffeur, darling . . . (*She brings the drink to him.*) He says it's in spanking condition, except just for one little thing—(*She sits down, smiling lovingly.*)—it needs a new carburettor. He says if we don't have one the car might seize up altogether, and that would mean a new car, darling.

RATTENBURY. Well we'll have to walk then, won't we?

ALMA. (*Laughing merrily.*) Oh you are a scream . . .

RATTENBURY. (*He chokes* on *his drink.*) This is too strong.

ALMA *takes the glass and puts more water in it.*

ALMA. Now after lunch we'll get your cheque book out and write out a cheque.

RATTENBURY. I won't sign it.

*She comes back with the drink, and lays her hand lovingly on his head.*

ALMA. Oh yes you will, dear. You're far too kind and loving a husband not to. (*She kisses the top of his head.*) Oh I do love my darling Ratz.

THE LIGHTS FADE

TONY. Mum! Listen to this—Did you know Mrs. Rattenbury and Wood battered old Rattenbury on the head so hard they completely smashed his skull.

MRS. DAVENPORT. What? Oh you're reading about that awful murder. A few years ago, a case like that wouldn't even have been mentioned in *The Times* . . . be a darling . . .

TONY. That's what makes it so funny it happening in Bournemouth.

MRS. DAVENPORT. I don't see that that's funny.

TONY. On Aunt Stella's doorstep . . . And ours, when we get that house. I wonder what their defence will be. Wood's statement says he was doped on cocaine, and the police say Mrs. Rattenbury was as drunk as a fly.

MRS. DAVENPORT. Tony, I don't want you to talk about it. And you shouldn't be reading it. Haven't you your homework to do?

TONY. Finished. Mum, could I ask you a question?

MRS. DAVENPORT. Of course.

TONY. If you'd found out before you started the divorce that there wasn't another woman at all with Dad, would it have made any difference?

*Pause.*

MRS. DAVENPORT. But there is another woman.

TONY. No, there isn't. I'm sure there isn't. And I honestly think he'd come back, if you asked him.

MRS. DAVENPORT. On his terms . . .

TONY. I don't know what they are.

MRS. DAVENPORT. I can't explain it to you, darling. You're far too young to understand . . .

TONY. (*With unexpected vehemence.*) That isn't true! Please believe me—I understand much more than you know.

*Pause.*

MRS. DAVENPORT. . . . . Is Randolph coming here, or are you going to him?

TONY. He's coming here.

MRS. DAVENPORT. (*She takes a note from her handbag.*) Is ten shillings enough?

TONY. Oh, plenty.

MRS. DAVENPORT. And for the cinema too?

TONY. It's only The Kensington.

MRS. DAVENPORT (*Sharply.*) What's the film?

TONY. I don't remember the title. It's got Irene Dunne—

MRS. DAVENPORT. (*Relieved.*) That should be very nice. You haven't told me yet how you like my new dress.

TONY. Spiffing. Who are you out to impress?

MRS. DAVENPORT. Stella's coming to take me to have dinner with General and Lady Whitworth.

TONY. Oh yes. And they're important because of the new house, or something.

MRS. DAVENPORT. He's Chairman of the Bournemouth Country Club, which owns the whole estate—He's a terrible old snob, according to Stella, so I expect it'll be an excruciating evening. A lot of small talk about gout and cricket, and trouble with the under-gardeners.

TONY. Is it worth it?

MRS. DAVENPORT. Oh yes, darling, it's a lovely little house—quite perfect for just the two of us, so I'll have to be a good girl and say all the right things. They're determined only to let in 'a certain class of person'!

TONY. Not Mrs. Rattenbury! (*He laughs.*) Oops, sorry.

MRS. DAVENPORT *smiles.*

You don't have to worry, Mum, I'm sure you'll manage your grapefruit perfectly.

MRS. DAVENPORT. And not eat peas with a knife?

TONY. Or tell any of those filthy stories of yours.

*He laughs.*

MRS. DAVENPORT. (*Embracing him.*) You're a naughty boy. Your hair needs cutting.

TONY. Tomorrow.

*There is a ring at the front door.*

MRS. DAVENPORT. Just stay and say hullo, and then leave us alone for a moment, will you? (*Off.*) Hello Stella, did you come by car?

*She goes out. We hear the sound of greeting in the hall.* TONY *fishes out the discarded copy of the* Evening News, *folds it up and puts it into his breast pocket.*

STELLA MORRISON *comes in, also wearing evening dress but, because she is rich, probably a real Chanel rather than a fake Molyneux.*

STELLA. (*As she comes in.*) No, I sent the Rolls on ahead and had Phillips pick me up off the train. It wasn't the Belle of course, but it had a perfectly good Pullman—hullo Tony.

TONY. Hullo, Aunt Stella.

*He allows himself to be kissed.*

STELLA. You get handsomer every time I see you. (*To* MRS. DAVENPORT.) Any girls in his life yet?

MRS. DAVENPORT. Oh yes. . . Happily they all live in Hollywood.

STELLA. (*To* TONY.) Wouldn't nearer be better?

MRS. DAVENPORT. (*Sharply.*) He's too young for girls.

STELLA. Darling, I wasn't being serious. My dear, what about this murder case!

TONY. Did you ever meet her, Aunt Stella?

STELLA. Mrs. Rattenbury? Oh no. But the awful thing is I suppose one could have. Your uncle Henry, of course, is going around boasting he *did* meet her—at a cocktail party somewhere—and she sang one of her songs. But you know what a liar he is. By next week he'll have had an affair with her—

TONY. Which wasn't too difficult, I gather.

STELLA. Difficult for Henry—even with Mrs. Rattenbury. I said to him— you'd better be careful, dear. You don't know what the gardener's boy and I get up to when you're up at the Stock Exchange. We might swing a mallet on you any time—

TONY. (*Excitedly.*) Do you think they both swung together, or took it in turns? I mean did Wood hit the old boy first and then she finished him off— or—

STELLA. Oh, they both swung together, of course—like two Etonians. (*Singing.*)
'And we'll both swing together, and swear by the best of—'what? Not 'schools'—'pools' would do. I gather from the Commissioner there was a pool of blood all over the floor, inches deep—and she was dancing the black bottom in it.

TONY. No, really?

STELLA. Stark naked, my dear, and trying to kiss all the policemen—and shouting out, 'I did it, I did it—I bumped him off!'

MRS. DAVENPORT. (*Violently.*) Will you please stop!

STELLA *looks at her uneasily. She knows her sister's temperament.*

TONY. Mum's very shocked by it all.

STELLA. Well, of course she is. Of course we all are. (*To her sister.*) But with a thing as appalling as this—and in the heart of Bournemouth too—the only thing one can do is to make a joke of it. If one starts trying to think of it seriously, one would go mad. I mean, it being with a servant! To me, that's the real horror.

MRS. DAVENPORT. Tony, go to your room.

TONY. Yes, Mum. (*He kisses* STELLA.) Goodbye, Aunt Stella.

MRS. DAVENPORT. Goodnight, darling. (*He kisses her.*) I'll try not to disgrace you with the General.

TONY. You'll be a smashing success, I know. (*He goes out.*)

MRS. DAVENPORT. To me the real horror is the boy's age—exactly the same age as Tony—

STELLA. When he met her perhaps. Now he's a year older. Eighteen. Old enough to hang.

MRS. DAVENPORT. Oh God! The law's unjust. It's the woman who should hang.

STELLA. Oh, she will. No doubt of that, thank heavens. But after all, the boy did kill his employer. He really shouldn't get away with that.

MRS. DAVENPORT. (*Violently.*) I don't know. I only know *she* ought to be lynched!

STELLA. Well, she might be. You should hear what they're saying about her in Bournemouth—

MRS. DAVENPORT. I suppose I'm being silly but whenever I think about that horrible case I think about Tony.

STELLA. Yes. I'm afraid you are being rather silly, darling. I doubt if Tony's going to commit murder for a middle-aged nympho-dipso-song-writer. There can't be many in Bournemouth.

MRS. DAVENPORT. (*Darkly.*) There was a married woman at Dieppe last Christmas, well over thirty, who had an eye on him. French too.

STELLA. Was Tony interested?

MRS. DAVENPORT. I didn't give him a chance to be. I changed hotels.

STELLA. Yes. You would. There are worse ways for a boy to start than with a married woman who knows how to take the right precautions—coupled with a bit of French élan.

MRS. DAVENPORT. Stella!

*There is a ring at the front door.*

—Just a moment—

*She goes out. We hear her voice.*

(*Off.*) Oh hullo, Randolph.

BROWNE. (*Off.*) Hullo, Mrs. Davenport.

MRS. DAVENPORT. (*Off.*) Tony's in his bedroom. You know where that is.

BROWNE. (*Off.*) Yes. Thank you.

*She comes back.*

Tony's best pal at Westminster. Randolph Browne. A Bishop's son—and a very good friend for him . . .

STELLA. Well, shall we go?

MRS. DAVENPORT. There's something I want to ask you. Should I mention tonight about John and . . . ?

STELLA. Not the bed part—

MRS. DAVENPORT. Really! As if I would—

STELLA. . . . Well don't mention the word divorce tonight. Leave it to me. When's the decree absolute?

MRS. DAVENPORT. Not for another couple of months.

STELLA. Well I hope it's not in the *Bournemouth Echo*—

MRS. DAVENPORT. Stella—after all I am the innocent party.

STELLA. My dear in Bournemouth *nobody* in a divorce is ever the innocent party.

MRS. DAVENPORT. Well let them see me as a glamorous divorcée then.

STELLA. (*As she goes.*) Frankly, darling, I don't think that's very likely either.

MRS. DAVENPORT. It's all clear, Tony.

TONY. Thank you. Goodbye.

FADE *on the sitting-room as they go out, and* FADE UP *on the bedroom, where* RANDOLPH BROWNE, *be-spectacled and studious, sits, deep in the* Evening Standard. *Beside him sits* TONY *deep in his rescued* Evening News. *There is a pause.*

BROWNE. (*At length.*) Have you got to the orgy in the Royal Palace Hotel?

TONY. I wonder how many times they did it altogether . . .

BROWNE. From the time he went to live in the house—which was—it's here somewhere—Yes—'Congress first took place a month after he was employed'

TONY. Congress?

BROWNE. Legal for 'it'.

TONY. What about the Congress of Anglican Bishops? (*As he makes his calculation.*) Assuming twice a night for . . .

BROWNE. Why only twice a night? He wasn't in training for anything.

TONY. You mean you could have made it more?

BROWNE. Double—Easily.

TONY. Bollocks—Here it is. At twice a night until the murder, three hundred and fourteen times!

BROWNE. You know when they open that trap-door he'll probably float upwards, not drop downwards.

TONY. I'm not being funny, Browne. I really do almost envy him . . .

BROWNE. Mind you, three hundred and fourteen times—That's nothing in a lifetime, and for him it will be a lifetime, poor sod. I hope to put up a million before I die.

TONY. Not a hope. You'll never get enough girls.

BROWNE. You only need one.

TONY. When you're eighty it'll probably still be Jones Minor.

BROWNE. You're out of date.

TONY. Who is it now?

BROWNE. Shuttleworth.

TONY. I don't know him.

BROWNE. He's in the choir.

TONY. God, you are disgusting! Randy by name, and randy by nature.

BROWNE. That's right. Anyway a chap's got to do something, hasn't he? Or else he'd go raving mad.

*Pause.*

TONY. It's hell, isn't it?

BROWNE. Oh, I don't know. It'll do till something better comes along.

TONY. But when will that be? God, it's frustrating. To be seventeen is hell . . . I mean, seventeen and English and upper-class and living in this century is hell . . . It wasn't always like that. Romeo was only seventeen, Juliet only thirteen.

BROWNE. And a ripe mess they made of things.

TONY. But no one in Shakespeare's time thought they were too *young*, did they? A boy of seventeen and a girl of thirteen? How too utterly disgusting, my dear!

BROWNE. Your mother?

TONY *nods.*

BROWNE. Not a good imitation.

*Doing his own imitation evidently of his father.*

My dear Randolph, should you be troubled with impure thoughts, you will find a cold tub and a brisk trot will work wonders—

TONY. The bishop?

BROWNE. Verbatim.

TONY. I wonder what our parents think we *do* between thirteen and twenty-one.

BROWNE. Solo, I should think, or else have cold tubs and brisk trots.

TONY. It's such damn humbug. Of course they know we're safe—apart from Shuttleworths, which they don't like to think about. You should have heard my mother on this Mrs. Rattenbury. The murder apart, my mother seems to think she's the monster of Glamis, just because she's twenty years older than Wood . . . And why not? Look at her. (*He slaps the paper.*) She's damned attractive.

BROWNE. Not bad at all.

TONY. (*Muttering.*) Three hundred and fourteen times. My God, I've a good mind to—and with Mum out—How much money have you got?

BROWNE. Good mind to what?

TONY. Try it. Tonight.

BROWNE. With Mrs. Rattenbury?

TONY. No, idiot. 'It'.

BROWNE. Oh. (*Counting.*) Seventeen and threepence.

TONY. And I've got ten bob. What do you suppose we could get for one pound seven and threepence?

BROWNE. Both of us?

TONY. Don't you want to?

BROWNE. Not for—thirteen and sevenpence halfpenny, thank you.

TONY. Will you lend it to me then?

BROWNE. Are you serious?

TONY. Yes.

BROWNE. I know nothing about it.

*He hands him fifteen shillings.*

TONY. Why? What can happen to me? She can only say no. (*He goes to the door, and stops nervously.*) You won't come with me?

BROWNE. Davenport, you are speaking to the son of a bishop. When I do it it'll be Jermyn Street, and a fiver. I think I should warn you, my dear child, that it's not going to be Romeo and Juliet—or even Wood and Mrs. Rattenbury . . .

*The lights begin to fade.*

TONY. (*Calling off.*) Be out when Mum gets back.

BROWNE. I'm not staying here!

*The lights now come up to illumine a small cell, at the moment empty. We hear the sound of a metal door being unlocked.*

JOAN. (*Off.*) In there.

ALMA *comes on. As a remand prisoner she is allowed to wear her own clothes, and she has on a simple but smart dress. She is followed by a wardress* (JOAN.), *a gruff-voiced, rather forbidding woman, younger than* ALMA.
Wait.

*She goes across the cell to another unseen door, which we hear opening. Then a murmur of voices. Finally* JOAN *returns.* ALMA *meanwhile sits.*
I didn't say you could sit.

ALMA. Sorry, dear.

*She gets up.*

JOAN. If the lawyers allow you to that is their business. I have to obey prison regulations.

ALMA. Yes, of course. What's your name, dear?

JOAN. Wardress Webster.

ALMA. I mean your Christian name.

JOAN. We are not allowed to use first names.

ALMA. Phyllis did. And she used to call me Alma.

JOAN. Who is Phyllis?

ALMA. The other lady. The one that's gone on leave.

JOAN. Oh, Mrs. Stringer. Well, she should not have.

ALMA. Oh I'm sure it was quite wrong. But she was an awful dear, all the same. (*She laughs.*) She used to tell me about her little son, same age as my youngest—my little John.

*No response from* JOAN.
Poor little John . . . Oh well, he doesn't know yet. Christopher—that's my eldest—he does of course. But in his letters he's quite cheerful.

*No response from* JOAN.
Of course he doesn't quite understand . . .

*Her voice trails off.*
How long do you think my trial will last?

JOAN. I could not say, I'm sure.

ALMA. Mr. Montagu—such a dear, Mr. Montagu, and so good-looking too— he says it'll last five days. What will I be allowed to wear?

JOAN. It will be your privilege to dress exactly as you please.

ALMA. Could I wear my pyjamas?

JOAN. I would think what you are currently wearing would be more suitable.

ALMA. Oh, I wasn't serious. Phyllis would have seen the joke. No, I mean that's what they always write about. 'The female prisoner, wearing a fetching blue ensemble' . . . Well they did at the Magistrates' Court, anyway. I just can't go on wearing a fetching blue ensemble five days running. I mean on the fifth day it'll stop fetching and start carrying . . .

*She laughs gaily.* JOAN *does not crack a smile.*

ALMA. (*After a pause.*) What made you become a wardress, dear? Did you think you were cut out for it?

JOAN. We are not allowed to answer personal questions.

ALMA. Aren't you? Phyllis always told me—

JOAN. Mrs. Stringer may have had other ideas. I prefer to abide by the rules.

ALMA. Yes—

*There is the sound of a metal door opening.*

O'CONNOR. (*Off.*) Thank you, Chief.

JOAN. (*Rapping out the order.*) Prisoner Rattenbury, on your feet.

ALMA. (*A shade plaintively.*) I am on my feet.

O'CONNOR *and* MONTAGU *come in.*

O'CONNOR. (*As they come in.*) I don't know . . . quite frankly we'll have our work cut out whoever we get. If we come up at the end of May, it'll probably be Humphreys. Just so long as it isn't Goddard! . . . All right Wardress, you may leave us.

JOAN. Sir.

*She marches out.*

O'CONNOR. Good morning.

ALMA. Good morning.

O'CONNOR. Sit down, please, Mrs. Rattenbury.

ALMA. Oh thank you—

*She sits down. Both barristers sit at a table facing her.* O'CONNOR *busily arranges papers in front of him.* MONTAGU, *a young man, opens a packet of cigarettes and offers it to her.*

MONTAGU. Mrs. Rattenbury. (*Offering Players cigarettes.*).

ALMA. —Players. My favourites. Oh Mr. Montagu, you are a duck.

*He hands her the packet.*

MONTAGU. Will those keep you for a time?

ALMA. Oh yes.

MONTAGU. Is there anything else I can get you that you need?

ALMA. Well not really things that a man would know about. Kirbygrips and things. Irene will see to those.

MONTAGU. She's still coming to see you?

ALMA. Oh yes. You can't keep her away.

O'CONNOR. Mrs. Rattenbury, do you persist in saying that your various statements to the police regarding the murder are true?

ALMA. Well, I *can't* go back on them, can I?

O'CONNOR. You can very easily go back on them. In fact, Mrs. Rattenbury, to save your life—I repeat that—to save your life, you must.

ALMA. Mr. O'Connor. I'd like to say the things you want me to say, I really would. But I can't.

O'CONNOR. Very well. Let me read to you some of the official statements you made to the police. Late on the night of the murder, after the body had been removed to hospital, you say to Inspector Mills: I was playing cards with my husband when he dared me to kill him as he wanted to die. I picked up a mallet, and he said 'You have not the guts to do it'. I then hit him with the mallet. Did you say that? . . . Mrs. Rattenbury, please pay attention.

ALMA. Yes. I'm sorry. What?

O'CONNOR. Did you say that to Inspector Mills?

ALMA. Yes.

O'CONNOR. You remember saying every word?

ALMA. Yes.

O'CONNOR. In spite of having consumed the best part of a bottle of whiskey?

ALMA. My mind was perfectly clear.

O'CONNOR. Perfectly clear? Half an hour before you signed that you were playing the gramophone full blast, dancing about the room half dressed, and trying to kiss several of the policemen—

ALMA. Oh dear! Was I really? They didn't say that at the Magistrates' Court.

O'CONNOR. No, because it didn't suit their case. But they'll say it at the trial because it'll suit mine.

ALMA. Oh . . . Must you? . . . Dancing about half naked, and—
*She covers her face and shoulders.*
—Oh dear! How could I have!

O'CONNOR. You mean you don't remember doing that?

ALMA. No. Nothing like that at all. Just a lot of noise and people there, and me trying to forget and—oh how awful! Oh, I couldn't have—

O'CONNOR. This has come to you as a complete surprise.

ALMA. Oh yes—

O'CONNOR. And yet you remember *clearly every word* of a statement you made only half an hour later, when according to the police you had had even more to drink? . . . Mrs. Rattenbury!

ALMA *looks up at him, realising she is caught.*

ALMA. (*At length.*) My mind must have cleared.

O'CONNOR. And you'll say that in court?

ALMA. I certainly will.

O'CONNOR. Right. Where did you find this mallet?
*Pause.*

ALMA. Lying about.

O'CONNOR. In the sitting-room?

ALMA. No. It couldn't have been, could it? It must have been in the hall.

O'CONNOR. Did you know that Wood had borrowed it from his father earlier that evening?

ALMA. No.

O'CONNOR. What did you do with the mallet afterwards?

ALMA. I hid it.

O'CONNOR. Why?

ALMA *hesitates.*

   If you were going to confess, why did you hide it?

ALMA. It looked so horrible.

O'CONNOR. More horrible than the body of your husband with his head caved in?

ALMA. (*With a half scream.*) Don't—

O'CONNOR I must. *Where* did you hide it, Mrs. Rattenbury?

ALMA. I can't remember, even now.

O'CONNOR. Why should Wood know where the mallet was, and not you?

ALMA. He didn't know.

O'CONNOR. He did. On his arrest, two days after yours, he described to the police exactly where he had hidden it in the garden. And exactly there they found it—with his fingerprints all over it.

ALMA. Well, they would be. He'd carried it all the way from his father's.

O'CONNOR. And why weren't yours on it?

*Pause.*

ALMA. I wore gloves.

O'CONNOR. Where did you find the gloves?

ALMA. Oh I have them upstairs. Lots of pairs.

*Pause.*

O'CONNOR. Your story then is this: Your husband asks you to kill him. You agree. You go out into the hall to find a suitable implement, and find a gardener's mallet, borrowed that evening by Wood. You leave it there, go upstairs and choose a pair of gloves. You come downstairs, pick up the mallet in your gloved hands and hit your husband three times on the back of the head—the *back* of the head, Mrs. Rattenbury, not the front—

ALMA. Don't—don't—

O'CONNOR. And kill him. You then hide the mallet somewhere in the garden, but you can't remember where, and presumably you put the gloves back in a drawer of your bedroom. You then ring up the police, to whom you give a full confession.

ALMA *is silent. She is trapped and knows it.*

   Mrs. Rattenbury, if I told that story in court, the jury's laughter would drown my voice.

ALMA. (*Indifferent.*) Well, if they don't believe it, that's that.

O'CONNOR. No, it isn't quite that, Mrs. Rattenbury. If I tell that story in court, do you know what the jury will believe, they will believe that it was Wood who killed your husband, with a mallet specially acquired for precisely that purpose, and that he did so with your knowledge and your consent, certainly under your influence, and very probably at your urging. That will make you both equally guilty of murder, and your efforts to shield Wood will have the effect of putting a noose around his neck just as surely as around your own.

ALMA. You're just trying to scare me. If I say I did it alone, how can they find him guilty?

O'CONNOR. They can and they will. Mrs. Rattenbury, would you like to tell us the truth?

ALMA, *struggling to keep her composure, finds it hard to reply. But when she does her voice is firm and unwavering.*

ALMA. I've already told you. I killed Ratz alone and George had nothing to do with it.

*Pause.* O'CONNOR *stares at her steadily, then begins to put his papers together.*

O'CONNOR. Montagu—it seems there is nothing more.

MONTAGU. Mr. O'Connor. Might I—?

O'CONNOR. By all means.

*He continues to gather his papers.* MONTAGU *leans forward with a smile.*

MONTAGU. Mrs. Rattenbury, we've come to know each other quite well in the last few weeks, haven't we?

ALMA. Oh yes, very well.

MONTAGU. During our talks, one of those things I've found out about you is that you're a very affectionate person. I mean, for instance, you told me how much you like that wardress—

ALMA. Phyllis? Oh yes. She's a dear.

MONTAGU. And Irene Riggs.

ALMA. I love Irene.

MONTAGU. Then you've told me often how fond you were of your husband.

ALMA. Old Ratz? (*Sincerely.*) Yes. He was a funny old thing in his way, but I *was* fond of him. Very fond of him really.

MONTAGU. (*Gently.*) Mrs. Rattenbury, how can you possibly expect *me*—to believe that you deliberately hit him with a garden mallet with such force that his blood gushed out on the carpet—

ALMA. Stop . . .

MONTAGU. —at the first stroke, that you shattered his skull with the second—

ALMA. (*Jumping up.*) Stop it, stop it!

MONTAGU. —opening up his head so that his brains were exposed—

ALMA. (*Screaming.*) No, no, no! Stop it!

*She puts her hands over her ears.* MONTAGU *continues inexorably.*

MONTAGU. That you changed the grip on the mallet and hit him on the right side of his head opening up a gash just over the eye from which the blood spurted half across the room, and would have blinded him helplessly if he'd stayed alive—

ALMA *hands to her ears, is now sobbing helplessly.*

—and that you coldly left him there in that chair to die suffocating in his own blood—while you calmly hid the mallet in the garden, and the gloves upstairs.

*Helpless with sobs she has tried now to get away from him as far as she can but he comes up to her.*

How can you expect me to believe that you, of all people, did that to him.

*Moaning, she makes no reply. With a brusque gesture he pulls her hands from her ears.*

Above all how can you go on loving and shielding the man who did?

*She falls into a chair, sobbing. He puts his hand gently on her shoulder.*

*He joins* O'CONNOR, *who has been watching the scene dispassionately, except for a faint annoyance that it was his Junior and not himself that achieved the breakthrough.*

*He presses a bell.*

O'CONNOR. (*In what he plainly thinks is an inaudible murmur.*) Yes. That was quite good work, Montagu.

JOAN *comes in.*

MONTAGU. We're going, wardress.

JOAN. Yes, sir. On your feet, Rattenbury.

MONTAGU. No, no. Let her sit for a moment.

JOAN. (*Understanding the reason.*) Yes, sir.

MONTAGU. Please try and save your life, Mrs. Rattenbury, believe me, I think it's worth saving.

JOAN *goes off with the two lawyers.*

O'CONNOR (*Off.*) But it's just a matter of timing, you see. A breakthrough of that kind is of little moment unless one can follow it up at once. And that of course—after you, my dear fellow—you were quite unable to do.

*We hear a door clang, then* JOAN *comes back.* ALMA'S *tears have nearly stopped, but it is plain that her small handkerchief has become a soggy ball.* JOAN *watches her for a moment in silence then reaches for the 'soggy ball' and substitutes for it a massive but serviceable handkerchief of her own.*

ALMA. (*Seated.*) Ta.

*She wipes her eyes and face, offers the handkerchief back to* JOAN.

JOAN. Keep it.

ALMA. Thank you, love. Thank you, Wardress Webster.

*She stuffs the vast napkin into her bag and stands up.* JOAN *pushes her roughly back again. Then, after a lot of fumbling, she produces a packet of cigarettes and proffers it.*

JOAN. (*At length.*) What is it?

ALMA. Nothing. They're trying to get me to say something and I won't, that's all.

JOAN. They usually know best.

ALMA. Not in this case. In this case I know best. You see, Wardress Webster—

JOAN. Joan

ALMA. Well you see, Joan, they both seemed to think just now that I didn't want to save my life—as if anyone in the world doesn't want to save their life—me above all others. I love life—I always have.

JOAN *nods sympathetically.*

It's just the cost, you see—

*She could be speaking about the price of a length of crepe de chine.* JOAN *nods sympathetically however, as if she understood. The lights fade.*

*The lights come up on the sitting-room.*

STELLA. Is anything the matter, Tony?

TONY. No, nothing!

STELLA. Nervous?

MRS. DAVENPORT. Petrified.

STELLA. I heard on the wireless there's an enormous crowd already, and they're getting out mounted police for tomorrow. 'Fears for the female prisoner's safety' or something . . . I suppose you're sure you'll be in Court Number One?

MRS. DAVENPORT. Yes. 'Fraid so.

STELLA. Have you got your speech ready?

MRS. DAVENPORT. I know what I'm going to say. I can't judge this woman fairly and no power on earth can make me.

STELLA. Are you sure you wouldn't like a coffee?

MRS. DAVENPORT. Oh, all right, yes.

STELLA. It's very sweet of you to have these qualms but if I were you I'd go in there, play noughts and crosses for 4 or 5 days, and then vote guilty with the eleven others.

*She goes out.*

MRS. DAVENPORT. Tony, what's the matter with you?

TONY. Nothing.

*Pause.*

MRS. DAVENPORT. I know what it is.

TONY. (*Startled.*) What?

MRS. DAVENPORT. You've written to Irene Dunne, and she hasn't answered.

TONY *doesn't reply.* MRS. DAVENPORT *gets up to go to the door.*

TONY. Mum—I want to see Dad.

MRS. DAVENPORT. You can't—without my permission.

TONY. I want your permission.

*Pause.*

MRS. DAVENPORT. When?

TONY. Now. Tonight.

MRS. DAVENPORT. Certainly not.

TONY. I have to see him. I have to. It's a matter of life and death—

MRS. DAVENPORT. Don't be absurd.

TONY. I meant that literally Mum. Life and death. What's more, whether I get your permission or not, I'm going to see him—now, if he's in. If he's not I'll wait until he is.

*Pause.*

MRS. DAVENPORT. What happened?

TONY. I can't tell you.

*Pause.*

MRS. DAVENPORT. There's nothing you can't tell me. Whatever it is, Tony, you've got to tell me.

TONY. I'd sooner die.

MRS. DAVENPORT. (*Trying to make light of it.*) And I suppose you mean *that* literally too?

TONY. Yes! I'm sorry, Mum, but it's something that can only be talked about between men.

*Pause.*

MRS. DAVENPORT. When did you become a man?

TONY. Do you remember the evening I was reading about Mrs. Rattenbury and you took the paper away from me?

*Pause.*

MRS. DAVENPORT. Yes. Very clearly. It was the evening you went to the Kensington with Randolph.

TONY. Yes. Only I didn't go to the cinema. I went—somewhere else—on my own—don't blame Randy. He warned me—he didn't want me to go—

MRS. DAVENPORT *is silent and unmoving.*

I'm sorry, but that's all I can tell you.

MRS. DAVENPORT. No, it isn't. A boy should be able to tell his mother *everything.*

TONY. I'm not a boy any longer, Mum. I'm grown up . . . A pretty horrible way to grow up, I know—but it's happened, and there it is . . . I went to a doctor and I know what I've got to face now.

MRS. DAVENPORT. Who is this doctor?

TONY. Oh, anonymous. I'm anonymous too. Someone at St. George's hospital. There's a notice up in lavatories in Tube Stations telling you where to go. I didn't have the courage until today.

MRS. DAVENPORT. You should have seen Doctor Macintyre—

TONY. And have him tell you?

MRS. DAVENPORT. *You've* told me.

TONY. Not the lot. Not the sordid details. Not the things I've got to do in the bathroom twice a day. But not in *this* bathroom—I'm determined on that.

MRS. DAVENPORT. (*Bravely.*) Why *not* this bathroom?

TONY *smiles and shakes his head.*

. . . I won't say a word to you about it. I promise you . . . If it's not serious, if it's just something you'll get over with treatment—

TONY. Mum—twice a day for maybe six weeks, maybe longer, I'll have to lock myself in there—(*He points off.*)—and you'll hear a tap running. Do you honestly think I can hope to come out of there without knowing what you're saying to yourself 'My son has committed a filthy,

disgusting act, and he's been punished for it with a filthy, disgusting
disease and a filthy, disgusting treatment—'

MRS. DAVENPORT (*Roused.*) Well, isn't that true?

TONY. No. What I did that night was silly, if you like, but the act was as natural
as breathing—and a good deal more pleasant. Goodnight, Mum.

MRS. DAVENPORT. Tony, don't you realise what I've got to go through tomorrow? You're not going to him now. I won't allow it.

TONY. What will you do? Get out a warrant? And have me tell the judge about
my adventure in Paddington? I'm sorry, Mum. I am terribly sorry. (*He
goes to the door.*) Don't wait up. If he'll have me, I'll stay the night.

*He goes out.* MRS. DAVENPORT *is motionless for a moment—then suddenly she
shudders—quite violently, as if she were ill.*

STELLA. (*Coming in.*) Where's Tony?

MRS. DAVENPORT (*Incoherently muttering.*) That . . . that . . . woman.

THE LIGHTS FADE.


*Cries of* 'Kill her!' 'Hang her!' *Odd screams of* 'Hanging's too good for her!
Give her the Cat too!' *can also be heard. Interspersed with barked orders
from the police, and over all the sound of an incensed woman* (JOAN) *as she
roars abuse at the crowd.*

JOAN. (*Off.*) Out of the way, you old bitch, or I'll fetch you one in the
crutch— . . . You, you bastard, call yourself a man? Bash 'em, officer!
. . . What's your baton for? Hit that old cow on the conk—that's more
like it! Push, push! Run, dear, run.

*The lights have dimly lit a cell. A woman, seemingly a wardress, runs inside
and cowers in the corner. We do not see her face.*

(*Off.*) Get that door closed, officer!

*A door clangs and there is comparative silence.*

(*Off.*) Bloody morons—the lot of 'em.

*She comes into the cell and turns on the light simultaneously. We see she has made
a gallant attempt to dress as* MRS. RATTENBURY *might be expected to—with
pretty femininity, and a decorative hat. What now spoils the effect is that the
hat is over one eye, her dress is torn nearly off her and she has an incipient
black eye.*

(*Cheerfully.*) Well dear, that worked a treat, didn't it?

*The huddled figure in wardress uniform reveals herself to be a very scared and
bewildered* ALMA.

There's no better weapon than a lady's handbag I always say—

*She drops it on to a table whence it emits a sharp sound.*

Come on now. Get out of that uniform. Your dress is here.

*She throws dress down on table.*

ALMA. They were shouting: 'Kill her!'

JOAN. You mustn't take any notice, dear. There are a lot of ill people in the
world. Far more than anyone knows. Have a cup of coffee.

*Out of the bag* (*which also contains a brick*) *she brings a thermos.*

ALMA. Joan—

JOAN. Yes, dear?

ALMA. Why?

JOAN. God knows. I've seen it often before. Never as bad as this, I grant, but—envy, that's what I think it is—plain envy.

ALMA. How can they envy me now?

JOAN. Well, you in the Old Bailey, centre of attention . . . But of course, now it's hate—mob hate, which is the nastiest, illest, ugliest thing in the whole world . . . Mind you, I'm not the Pope. Let's get changed, dear. I don't want the lawyers to catch us like this.

ALMA. (*Hands to her face.*) Hatred is awful!

JOAN. Forget them! It's a compliment to be hated by them. (*Spreading out the dress.*) There's the dress you wanted—You're going to look a picture in court, I know it—

*The lights fade as they both dress, coming up immediately on the lawyer's robing room. Some lockers and a bench are all that is necessary.* CASSWELL *is finishing robing himself as* O'CONNOR. *comes in.*

O'CONNOR. Ah, Casswell, just the man I want to see. Is the enemy about?

CASSWELL. Croom-Johnson? He's just left to muster his witnesses.

O'CONNOR. And quite a crowd he's got, I gather. Was he looking cocky?

CASSWELL. (*Gloomily.*) He's every reason to, hasn't he?

O'CONNOR. We'll see. How's your lad?

CASSWELL. Wood? I haven't seen him yet today.

O'CONNOR. Very spirited disposition, I hear.

CASSWELL. That's one word for it. I call it cheeky. Cheeky and stubborn.

O'CONNOR. A bad combination. How far are you involving us in the borrowing of the mallet?

CASSWELL. Wood's father is going to say he assumed the boy was borrowing it with your client's knowledge and consent!

O'CONNOR. Assumption is nothing. I can tear that apart. What exactly did he tell the father he was borrowing it for?

CASSWELL. To put up a sun-shelter. In the garden.

O'CONNOR. A sun-shelter? In mid-March, and on one of the coldest days of the year?

CASSWELL. Was it?

O'CONNOR. Yes.

CASSWELL. Should I have known that? Is it important?

O'CONNOR. It is to me.

CASSWELL. Why?

O'CONNOR. Trade secret, dear boy. If I thought it would help you I'd tell you—but it won't.

CASSWELL. (*Suspiciously.*) You look cheerful.

O'CONNOR. I always look cheerful. It's half the battle. You'd better do something about yourself. Try a little rouge or something.

CASSWELL. (*Looking at himself.*) I didn't sleep at all last night.

O'CONNOR. That's a mistake. I had a large dinner at the Garrick, got away from the bloody actors and slept two hours in the smoking room. After that—home and bed. Now listen, Casswell, I don't want to bully, but any suggestion that we wielded that mallet and I shall not hesitate to remind the jury that while we are a poor weak woman who couldn't drive an iron peg into soft peat in under forty whacks, you are a hulking great muscular brute of an ex-builder who can easily knock a man's head off in three.

CASSWELL. (*With resigned sigh.*) Yes. And did.

O'CONNOR. That's right. And did. You're not disputing your statement of confession to the police on the day of your arrest?

CASSWELL. How can I?

O'CONNOR. I don't know. I only know I'm disputing every one of mine. After half an hour in there with the Bournemouth Constabulary those seven separate confessions will be floating down past Croom-Johnson's nose like confetti. I suppose while you were knocking the old man's block in, we were winding up the gramophone and cheering and egging you on—?

CASSWELL. Of course. I'm sorry, O'Connor, but it's my only chance.

O'CONNOR. Of what.

CASSWELL. Of getting a manslaughter.

O'CONNOR *chuckles.*

I'd better warn you I intend to push your evil moral influence and your shameless depravity as hard as I can.

O'CONNOR. Push away, my dear fellow, push away, if it's all you've got, I'm going to push your psycho-pathological rages, your surliness and your fits of sudden violence. You won't mind that, I hope?

CASSWELL. The reverse. It might help me to a guilty but insane.

O'CONNOR. Under Humphreys? Not a hope. He sleeps with the Macnaghten rules under his pillow. Did the murderer know what he was doing at the time that he did it? If he did, did he know that what he was doing was wrong? (*He helps himself into a pair of slippers.*) I'd say that your boy had a teeny inkling of both.

CASSWELL. Do you always wear slippers in court?

O'CONNOR. Always. Because they make us as uncomfortable as they can up here (*He indicates his upper half.*) is no reason why we shouldn't be cosy down here. Anyway, aren't you supposed to have committed the murder under the influence of a lorry load of cocaine?

CASSWELL. Yes, damn it. He would choose the one drug that heightens the perceptions rather than dulling them.

O'CONNOR. Change your drug.

CASSWELL. I can't. Cocaine is what I'm instructed to take, and as a Poor Persons' Defence Act Lawyer, I've got to obey my instructions.

O'CONNOR. (*Sententiously.*) My dear fellow, we all have to obey our instructions. Some of us sometimes manage to get them just a little bit—confused—

CASSWELL. Not a chance here. He won't budge an inch.

O'CONNOR. Where did you get the cocaine from?

CASSWELL. Someone somewhere in London. We can't remember who or where.

O'CONNOR. Good God. And you're stuck with his whole confession?

CASSWELL. No way round it. (*Gloomily swallows two pills.*)

O'CONNOR. Hangover?

CASSWELL. No. Nerves. Does one ever get over them?

O'CONNOR. Never. They get worse with age.

CASSWELL. I've never seen you look even remotely nervous.

O'CONNOR. Ah. That's something we do learn—never to show it. But that carafe I always have in front of me. You don't think that's plain water, do you?

CASSWELL. Gin?

O'CONNOR. Vodka. Safe as houses. Not a whiff from a foot away. Is this your first capital charge?

CASSWELL. No. But with the others I had some chance—

O'CONNOR. My dear boy, while there's life there's hope.

CASSWELL. Our hope—their lives.

*Pause.* O'CONNOR *turns slowly on him.*

O'CONNOR. Do you think there's a single moment I'm unconscious of that?

CASSWELL. No. Well, I'd better have one last shot at getting him to change his drug into something else.

O'CONNOR. Yes. Good luck. (*Suddenly savage.*) But look, Casswell!

CASSWELL *turns.*

If there's the faintest suggestion that he got any drugs from her, I'll be on you like a tiger. That poor bitch has got enough to carry into the court without dope peddling (*His hand on* CASSWELL'S *arm.*) Get him to come off drugs altogether. Use our shameless depravity and pernicious influence. It's much safer. And I can't hit back. That's my honest advice, old man.

CASSWELL. (*With a sigh.*) Well, it would be a very foolish advocate who neglected advice from such a source. Thank you.

O'CONNOR. You're very welcome.

CASSWELL *is on his way out when a thought strikes him.*

CASSWELL. Unless such a source happened to be fighting the same trial with him.

O'CONNOR. As an ally, dear fellow—

CASSWELL. An ally who wouldn't hesitate to slash my throat if he thought it could help his client.

O'CONNOR. Slash your throat, my dear Casswell, I've just given you an open invitation to attack me in my weakest spot, to wit, my deplorable moral character. Now how could that possibly be slashing your throat?

MONTAGU *comes in.*

Ah, Montagu. Good . . . (*With an innocent smile.*) Have you got our friend in all right?

*The lights fade on* O'CONNOR *and* MONTAGU *and stay on* CASSWELL *as he walks unhappily towards a small cell where the lights come on to show* WOOD *sitting patiently.* O'CONNOR *and* MONTAGU—*who is already gowned—disappear from view.*

CASSWELL. (*Calls.*) Warder!

WOOD. (*Chirpily.*) Morning, Mr. Casswell. Did you hear that crowd cheering me when I arrived? Some of them shouted 'Good luck, lad'—and 'we won't let you swing'—things like that . . .

CASSWELL. Mr. Wood, we have only a few minutes before you go on trial for your life. Are you still determined to instruct me that you murdered Rattenbury when under the influence of cocaine?

*Pause.*

WOOD. Perce Wood, the odd job boy, has come a long way, hasn't he, instructing someone dressed up like you . . . Well, I instruct you, Mr. Casswell, I done the old man in when I was crazed from cocaine and not responsible for my actions. And that's what I'm going to tell them.

CASSWELL. You won't have the opportunity. I am not putting you in the witness box.

WOOD. How can you stop me?

CASSWELL. By not calling you.

WOOD. Why not? You've got to!

CASSWELL. I am not putting you into the witness box because I would not like to hear you explaining to Mr. Croom-Johnson, one of the most devastating cross-examiners at the Bar, exactly how you became 'a dope fiend'.

WOOD. But that's my defence!

CASSWELL. What does cocaine look like? Mr. Wood? I mean, what colour is it?

WOOD. Colour? (*After a pause.*) Brown.

CASSWELL. Brown.

WOOD. With black specks.

CASSWELL. With black specks . . . And if you went into the witness box you would tell Mr. Croom-Johnson that?

WOOD. Of course.

CASSWELL. And if he asked you why, in popular parlance, it was called snow, how would you answer him?

WOOD. I don't know—I didn't know it was.

CASSWELL. It is called snow because it is white, Mr. Wood—the purest possible *white.*

*Pause.*

WOOD. Jesus.

CASSWELL. Exactly.

WOOD. But without cocaine where's my defence?

CASSWELL. I've told you—many times.

*Pause.*

WOOD. (*Violently.*) No!

CASSWELL. You are of age to be hanged, Mr. Wood.

WOOD. I know.

CASSWELL. You are disposed then to die?

WOOD. No, I'm not. I want to live—Christ, don't I want to live. But I'm not going to say *she* made me do it. They can tear me apart before they'll get me to say that.

CASSWELL. I don't think you quite understand—

WOOD. (*Violently.*) It's you who don't bloody understand. Alma Rattenbury, sex-mad drunken bloody cow that she is, lying deceitful bitch to come to that—she's the only woman I've ever had, and the only one I've ever loved, and I'm not going to shop her now . . . No, it's you who don't bloody understand, Mr. Casswell, nor the others either.

*Pause.*

CASSWELL. Very likely. I'll see you in court.

CASSWELL *picks up his brief. The lights fade, coming up immediately on the other cell.* ALMA *is now dressed.*

JOAN. Not long now, dear. I said you'd look a treat.

O'CONNOR *and* MONTAGU *come in gowned, and carrying their wigs.*

O'CONNOR. Wardress—bring Mrs. Rattenbury, please.

JOAN. Sir.

MONTAGU. (*To* ALMA.) I hope they didn't upset you too much outside.

ALMA. Well, it came as rather a shock—

O'CONNOR. Mrs. Rattenbury, it is my duty to tell you that there will be deep prejudice against you up there.

ALMA. Oh, I know.

O'CONNOR. Very deep indeed, I'm afraid. You must be prepared to answer some very venomous questions.

ALMA. (*Simply.*) Oh, but I'm not going to answer any questions. I'm not going into the witness box. I told you that, Mr. Montagu.

*Pause.* O'CONNOR *makes a sign to* MONTAGU *who slips out of the room.*

O'CONNOR. I beg you most earnestly to reconsider, Madam.

ALMA. I'm sorry. I can't. I will not go into the witness box. *Not* under oath. *Not* giving George away . . .

O'CONNOR. Because you want him to see you as a tragic heroine? You love him as much as that?

ALMA. Me a heroine to George? . . . That's funny. To him I'm just a drunken sexy lying bitch. He's told me so a million times.

O'CONNOR. Then why in Heaven's name sacrifice yourself for him?

ALMA. Because it's right. I'm *responsible,* and neither you nor anyone . . .

MONTAGU *brings* CHRISTOPHER *in.*

CHRISTOPHER. Hello, Mummy.

ALMA *stands still for a moment, then turns furiously on* O'CONNOR.

ALMA. What kind of a man are you?

O'CONNOR. A humane man, Mrs. Rattenbury. I thought you might like a couple of minutes with your boy before you go into court . . . (*With a curt beckoning nod he ushers* MONTAGU *out, following him.*)

CHRISTOPHER. What's Mr. O'Connor done, Mummy? What's made you angry with him?

ALMA. Never mind. (*She embraces him.*) How are you, Chris?

CHRISTOPHER. Oh all right.

ALMA. They brought you up from school?

CHRISTOPHER. I wanted to come. (*Looking at her.*) You're in an ordinary dress . . .

ALMA. Yes. Do you like it?

CHRISTOPHER. Yes. It's nice. I thought—

ALMA. That I'd be in stripes and arrows? Not yet.

CHRISTOPHER. What's it like in prison?

ALMA. Oh, it's not really prison. And the wardresses—the people I'm with—they're very nice. (*Suddenly clutching him.*) They didn't bring you through those crowds?

CHRISTOPHER. Oh yes—but nobody knew who I was. They were nasty people, though.

ALMA. Did you hear them shouting?

CHRISTOPHER. (*Quickly.*) Oh, I didn't listen, Mummy.

*She clutches him fiercely again, then lets him go.*

ALMA. And how's little John?

CHRISTOPHER. Oh all right. He gets a bit tearful, sometimes.

ALMA. They haven't told him—

CHRISTOPHER. Oh no.

ALMA. He misses me?

CHRISTOPHER. *Misses* you?

*Pause.*

ALMA. (*Trying to steady her voice.*) Well, Chris, what have you been told to say to me?

CHRISTOPHER. (*Bewildered.*) Told to say to you?

ALMA. By Mr. O'Connor?

CHRISTOPHER. Nothing.

ALMA. Really? Nothing?

CHRISTOPHER. Well, the obvious thing, of course.

ALMA. What's that?

CHRISTOPHER. About your not giving George away in court. It was a bit of a shock, because he says the jury may find you guilty: but he put it so nicely though . . .

ALMA. (*Faintly.*) How did he put it?

CHRISTOPHER. Well he said that as a schoolboy I'd understand about not sneaking on a friend . . . Well of course I understand except in this kind of thing . . . I mean in a case of murder—real murder—what they might do—except, of course, they'd never do that to you . . . Oh Mummy! . . .

*He runs to her. She clasps him firmly and allows him to cry on her breast.*

Oh damn! I promised I wouldn't.

ALMA. (*At length.*) What else did Mr. O'Connor put so nicely?

CHRISTOPHER. He said that as I was nearly grown-up I should understand that when a woman has a choice between her lover and her children she's almost bound to put her lover first.

ALMA, *apparently unmoved and unmoving, looks down at his head.*

O'CONNOR *and* MONTAGU *come back.* ALMA *has not moved.*

O'CONNOR. The judge has sent us his signal. (*He puts his arm on* CHRISTOPHER'S *shoulder.*) You should be getting to your seat, young man. A Mr. Watson, outside, will be sitting with you—

ALMA. (*Appalled.*) Christopher's not going to be in court?

O'CONNOR. Of course.

ALMA. Will he be there every day?

O'CONNOR. That depends. Say au revoir to your mother, old chap.

CHRISTOPHER. Goodbye, Mummy. Good luck.

O'CONNOR. Montagu, you take him to Watson—Wardress!

ALMA *lets* CHRISTOPHER *kiss her, patting him absently on the head as he goes. He goes out with* MONTAGU.

ALMA. (*At length.*) Don't think you've won, Mr. O'Connor.

O'CONNOR. Oh I never think that about any case, until the end.

## ACT TWO

*As at the beginning of Act One, the lights come up on* ALMA *and* MRS. DAVEN-
PORT. *A light then comes up on the* JUDGE.

JUDGE. Mrs.—er—Davenport, I understand from the Jury Bailiff that you
wish to be excused from jury service on the grounds of conscience?

MRS. DAVENPORT. Yes. From this particular jury, on this particular case. I will
serve on any other.

JUDGE. You have a conscientious objection to capital punishment?

MRS. DAVENPORT. No, My Lord.

JUDGE. Where then does your conscience enter the matter?

MRS. DAVENPORT. My Lord, I have a deep prejudice against that woman. (*She
acknowledges the dock.*)

JUDGE. The female prisoner?

MRS. DAVENPORT. Yes.

JUDGE. Would the female prisoner please rise?

ALMA *rises. She stares at* MRS. DAVENPORT *without surprise—even with faint understanding.*

Do you know this woman personally?

MRS. DAVENPORT. No, but it's as if I did.

JUDGE. I don't follow, I'm afraid.

MRS. DAVENPORT. I've read about her in the newspapers.

*Pause.*

JUDGE. Is that all?

*The lights come up dimly on the Lawyers.*

MRS. DAVENPORT. My Lord, you are here to see that this woman gets a fair
trial. Isn't that so?

JUDGE. It is, Madam. It is also my duty, as it will be yours, to put out of my
head all of the deplorably wide publicity this case has attracted, and to
allow the facts of the case—

MRS. DAVENPORT. I am sorry, My Lord. I know these arguments. You see I
know about the law. My father was a judge in India—

JUDGE. Mrs.—er—but I don't—

MRS. DAVENPORT (*Passionately.*) I warn you now, and I warn these gentlemen
who are defending her that no matter what oath I am forced to take, I
will not be able to try this woman's case without deep prejudice. My mind
is set against her.

*Pause. Her sincerity has evidently impressed the* JUDGE. *He frowns thoughtfully
and then addresses the* LAWYERS' *bench. As he does so, the lights fade except
on* ALMA *and* MRS. DAVENPORT. *The discussion between the* JUDGE *and the*
LAWYERS *is only dimly heard.*

JUDGE. Mr. O'Connor, you have heard my view. It remains unaltered. However you might have cause for a challenge 'propter affectum'. If you have I am very willing to hear it.

O'CONNOR. If Your Lordship permits?

*The* JUDGE *nods.* O'CONNOR *talks to* MONTAGU *in a low voice, their backs to the Judge.*

MONTAGU. She's an asset.

O'CONNOR. On the question of bias?

MONTAGU. Exactly. You can refer to her in your final address.

*He rises again.*

O'CONNOR. My Lord, we will not challenge.

CASSWELL. No challenge, My Lord. The prejudice does not appear to be directed against my client.

JUDGE. Obviously, Mr. Croom-Johnson, you won't wish to challenge. But do you think I am right?

CROOM-JOHNSON, *prosecuting counsel, gets up.*

CROOM-JOHNSON. I feel Your Lordship's view of the matter is both wise and just.

*The light comes up on the* JUDGE.

JUDGE. Mrs. Davenport, we all find that there are no grounds for your self-disqualification. Will you then take the oath?

CLERK. Take the book in your right hand and repeat the words on the cards.

*The lights fade on the* JUDGE *and the* LAWYERS.

*Now only the* TWO WOMEN *can be seen facing each other across the courtroom.*

MRS. DAVENPORT. (*Solemnly, after a pause, the bible in her right hand, a card in the other.*) I, do solemnly swear by Almighty God that I will well and truly try the issues between our Sovereign Lord the King and the prisoners at the bar and will give a true verdict according to the evidence.

*The lights fade quickly to* BLACKOUT.

*In the sitting-room,* STELLA *is dimly seen reading a newspaper. The lights come up on Court Number One at the Old Bailey. The court is not in session. The lawyers are chatting.*

CASSWELL. (*To* CROOM-JOHNSON.) Congratulations on your opening.

CROOM-JOHNSON. Oh, thank you, Casswell, thank you.

CASSWELL. Admirably fair, I thought.

CROOM-JOHNSON. I'm glad.

O'CONNOR. (*Muttering some distance away, to* MONTAGU.) Fair! If that bloody Croom-Johnson uses the phrase 'Woman and *boy*' once more, I'm going to have him disbarred and demand a re-trial—

MONTAGU. Why don't you tell him?

O'CONNOR. And let him know he's scored? We'll have 'woman and *child*' then . . .

CROOM-JOHNSON *moves near.*

(*Calling.*) Good Opening, Croom-Johnson.

CROOM-JOHNSON. Thank you. It was, fair, I think.

O'CONNOR. Every bit as fair as we've come to expect of you.

CROOM-JOHNSON. How kind. Extraordinary incident that was—that woman juror saying she was prejudiced against your client. Very distressing to hear that kind of thing, you know. I wonder you didn't challenge.

O'CONNOR. Yes. I suppose I should have done—

CROOM-JOHNSON. (*Suspiciously.*) You won't, of course, be able to make any reference to her in your final address—

O'CONNOR. Oh no. That would be most deeply improper.

CROOM-JOHNSON. Well I honestly think my opening will have helped remove some of her prejudices—

O'CONNOR. Yes.

CROOM-JOHNSON. I emphasised that this was in no way a court of morals— and that they were to direct their attention only to the facts of the case.

O'CONNOR. (*Unable to contain himself.*)—brought against 'this woman and this boy'—

CROOM-JOHNSON. Ah. I did notice your uneasiness at the appellation 'boy'. But what else in all honesty could I call him, O'Connor? The jury have only to look at the dock—

O'CONNOR. —and see a hulking young man, old enough to be hanged and a woman young-looking enough to pass herself off successfully as his sister.

CROOM-JOHNSON. But the gap in ages is so much a part of the case. One must steel oneself, must one not, to face facts, however disagreeable. (*He gathers up his papers.*)

O'CONNOR. Bloody man!—Do you know I drew him in the Bar golf tournament, and he wouldn't give me a fourteen inch putt? . . . I missed it too. I've got to beat that bugger—(*He smiles at* CROOM-JOHNSON *as he passes again.*)—if it's the last thing I do.

*As the lawyers leave the court, the lights fade, coming up as* MRS. DAVENPORT *enters wearily.* STELLA, *lying on a sofa, is reading an evening newspaper.*

MRS. DAVENPORT. Has Tony come home?

STELLA. Tony? No.

MRS. DAVENPORT. Oh, God, I won't let John take him away from me, I won't, I won't. (*She sits on sofa.*)

STELLA. Darling, you've had a tiring day. Do you want a cup of tea?

MRS. DAVENPORT. No, but I'd love a drink. A whiskey.

STELLA. That's bold of you. (*She gets up to pour the whiskey.*) So it didn't work this morning?

MRS. DAVENPORT. No. And what's worse the jury has elected me forewoman because I'd let out that father was a judge.

STELLA. My dear, how too splendid. What d'you have in court tomorrow?

MRS. DAVENPORT. The rest of the prosecution witnesses, I think. Oh, Stella, it's all so foul.

*She goes out to the bedroom.* STELLA *picks up her newspaper and crosses to the phone.*

STELLA (*Calling.*) Darling, do you know what odds the bookmakers are laying on Mrs. Rattenbury being convicted?

MRS. DAVENPORT (*Off.*) Odds? How can they be so unfeeling?

STELLA No principles, bookmakers. In the city they're even taking bets on whether she'll hang. Good odds too. But for her being convicted—it's here somewhere. (*She looks in the paper.*) Yes, they're giving three to one.

MRS. DAVENPORT (*Off.*) Only three to one? That woman—it's absurd.

STELLA. Well—if ever I heard a tip straight from the horse's mouth—(*Into receiver.*) Hello—still at the office? There's a good Henry! . . . Look, darling, apparently you can get three to one on Mrs. Rattenbury being convicted—well—(*Lowering her voice.*) Edie's just back from court, and she says that in her view those odds are madly generous . . . Yes, and they've made her forewoman too, so of course she'll have a big say . . . Yes, a real hot snip. Well, put on six hundred for me, would you? . . .

TONY *comes in.*

Thank you, darling . . . I will. Henry sends his love. (*She hangs up.*) Tony!

TONY. Hullo, Aunt Stella.

MRS. DAVENPORT *comes to wearing a dressing gown.*

MRS. DAVENPORT. Tony!

TONY. . . . Hullo, Mum.

MRS. DAVENPORT. Tony, thank God. You've come back.

TONY. No, I haven't. Dad's here.

MRS. DAVENPORT. I won't see him!

DAVENPORT *enters.*

I'm not allowed to see you. The judge said—

DAVENPORT. I remember very well what the judge said. No communication of any kind. Hullo, Stella.

STELLA. Hullo, John.

DAVENPORT. So this letter I've brought is just as wrong as my presence (*He holds out a letter.*)

MRS. DAVENPORT. I won't read it.

DAVENPORT. I thought not, which is why I'm delivering it myself.

STELLA. I'll go.

MRS. DAVENPORT. No don't. Please.

DAVENPORT. I don't mind Stella hearing what I've got to say. Tony, go down and wait in the car, would you?

MRS. DAVENPORT. Are you taking him away?

DAVENPORT. To the cottage.

MRS. DAVENPORT. And I forbid him to go.

DAVENPORT. Go ahead, Tony.

MRS. DAVENPORT. No—

TONY. Sorry, Mum. Really. I'll call you tomorrow. (*He goes.*)

MRS. DAVENPORT. I've only to ring the police—

DAVENPORT. Yes. Then I'd have to give my exact reasons to the judge for taking my son away from here. Of course he'd find the reasons quite
insufficient, and I'd be fined or committed, and Tony would be returned
to you. There'd probably be a little something in the papers, which probably would be read by Tony's headmaster—

MRS. DAVENPORT. This is pure blackmail.

DAVENPORT. Yes it is, I suppose. It's also a truthful forecast of what would
happen, must happen, if you invoke the law.

MRS. DAVENPORT. Exactly what lies have you told his headmaster?

DAVENPORT. I told him the truth. Not all of it, but I said the boy had had a
severe psychological shock, that he'd attempted suicide—

MRS. DAVENPORT. That's a lie!

DAVENPORT. It's not. The night before last he swallowed some sleeping pills.

MRS. DAVENPORT. No—

DAVENPORT. If you don't believe me, go into the bathroom and look for your
sleeping pills. Luckily there were only seven or eight left, and they made
him sick at once.

MRS. DAVENPORT. But I'd have heard if—

DAVENPORT. Tony's a polite boy. He can even vomit quietly enough not to
wake his mother. And then apparently lie on the bathroom floor, sobbing—but into a towel, quietly.

MRS. DAVENPORT. But is this—thing he has as dreadful as that?

DAVENPORT. Medically it's nothing, provided it's treated promptly . . . It's the
psychological shock he won't get over so easily, and he'd never get over it
here . . . unless . . .

*Pause.*

Are you going to read my letter?

MRS. DAVENPORT. Never.

DAVENPORT. Then I'll read it to you. (*He takes the letter and opens* it.) 'My
dearest Edie—for the sake of Tony, and also for our own sakes, I want
you to rescind the decree nisi. It's very easily done, by application to a
judge in chambers.

I must tell you with complete truth that there is no other woman in my
life. No single other woman, that is. The one you know about left me
some months ago, with no regrets on either side. She wasn't important
to me. No woman has ever been important to me except yourself. I admit that I've had occasional affairs, but they were necessary to me—you
know why—always brief, and usually with a mercenary tinge.

Without you, Edie, and without Tony, I have been a very lonely man.
So, I believe, are you lonely without me. Please let me come back into
your life. If you do I promise to behave as well as I can. That doesn't,
I'm afraid, mean as well as you'd want me to. It can never mean that,
Edie my darling, as you know. But if you can only bring yourself to
overlook an occasional late night at the office, or the odd dinner at the

Club with the Permanent Secretary, I swear a solemn oath to you that
you will never otherwise be humiliated. I renounce my conjugal rights
entirely, but I earnestly entreat you to let me once again be your loving
husband.

                                                              John.'

*He puts it back in the envelope and hands it to her. She won't take it. He puts it
on the coffee table.*

MRS. DAVENPORT. Your terms.

DAVENPORT. Yours as well.

MRS. DAVENPORT. The answer is no.

STELLA. Think about it, Edie. For God's sake, think about it.

MRS. DAVENPORT. Stella, how can you? He wants me to—condone adultery?
It's unthinkable and you know it. I will not break the standards by which
I've lived all my life.

DAVENPORT. Those standards could be wrong, you know. They're certainly
becoming a little dated . . . You won't reconsider?

*No reply.*

Well, I'll say goodbye. (*At the door.*) Tell me—this Mrs. Rattenbury, is
she for it?

MRS. DAVENPORT. We're not allowed to talk about it.

DAVENPORT. (*Smiling.*) I don't give much for her chances with you judging
her. I don't know anything about Mrs. Rattenbury, except what I've read
in the papers, but that's enough to tell me that her vices, which I am
sure are deplorable, do add up to some kind of affirmation. Your virtues, Edie, which I know are admirable, add up to precisely nothing.
Goodbye!

*He goes.* MRS. DAVENPORT *picks up the letter, then tears it up decisively. The lights
fade as she goes to her room.* STELLA *picks up the pieces of the letter, then sits.*

*The Old Bailey. The trial is in its second day, and* POLICE SERGEANT BAGWELL *is
being examined by* CROOM-JOHNSON *for the prosecution. The dock is unseen.*

CROOM-JOHNSON. At what time did you receive this call from the hospital?
You may use your notebook, if there is no objection.

CASSWELL *and the* JUDGE *both nod acceptance.* O'CONNOR *is too busy muttering
to* MONTAGU *to notice.*

SERGEANT. The call came through at 2.13 a.m., sir, saying that all attempts
to revive the deceased had failed.

CROOM-JOHNSON. What did you do then?

SERGEANT. Acting on this information, I duly presented myself at the Villa
Madeira, at 2.47 a.m. There was a lot of commotion proceeding from
inside—

CROOM-JOHNSON. What kind of commotion?

*The lights fade to a spot on the* POLICE SERGEANT.

SERGEANT. There was a gramophone playing at full blast, sir—and some female laughter of a shrill nature. There being no answer to the bell I tried the door and found it open. I then entered the sitting-room, and found the female prisoner attired in a nightdress, and two police officers to whom she was making flourishing gestures with her bed jacket—in imitation of bullfighting or some such. I immediately summoned the two officers outside, asked what their business had been, and sent them away. I then proceeded back into the house.

*The lights have come up on the sitting-room of the Villa Madeira where* ALMA, *dressed as described by the* SERGEANT, *is continuing her cavortings to a now empty room. The gramophone is playing loudly. Suddenly she notices.*

ALMA. Oh damn and blast! (*Plaintively.*) Where have you gone? Come back. We're having fun.

*She takes a large swig from an evidently almost empty bottle. The record runs out and she goes to change it. She is very drunk. The* SERGEANT *comes in, knocking politely at the open door.* ALMA, *at the gramophone, has her back to him.*

SERGEANT. Beg pardon for the intrusion, but would you be—

ALMA. (*With a shriek of joy.*) Oh, another lovely policeman! Come in. Come in. We're having a gorgeous time—

*The deafening music has started up again.*

SERGEANT. (*Shouting.*) Would you be Mrs. Francis Rattenbury?

ALMA. Alma to you, dear. Come and dance—

*She puts her arms round his neck. He detaches himself.*

SERGEANT. May we have the music down, please?

ALMA. Why? How can we dance with no music?

*She tries again to get him to dance. Again he eludes.*

SERGEANT. Excuse me, Madam. With your permission?

*He goes to the gramophone and turns it off.*

ALMA. Oh why did you do that? Now it's quiet. I don't like it quiet—

*She goes to the gramophone again. He gently restrains her.*

SERGEANT. I'm sorry, Madam, but you could be disturbing the neighbours.

ALMA. (*Laughing.*) Oh, that's terrible. Disturbing the neighbours is terrible.

SERGEANT. I must ask you again if you are Mrs. Francis Rattenbury?

ALMA. That's right.

SERGEANT. The widow of Francis Rattenbury.

ALMA. Widow?

SERGEANT. You have not been informed of your husband's death?

ALMA. Don't talk about awful things. Let's have some music—

SERGEANT. (*Restraining her.*) I must ask you, Madam, what you know about your husband's death.

ALMA. Everything. I know everything. (*She shudders and covers her face, then emerges brightly smiling.*) I did it, you see. All by myself. All alone. (*Singing and dancing.*) All alone, all alone.

*She goes to the bottle. The* SERGEANT *takes it from her.*

SERGEANT. Who else is in this house?

ALMA. Only Irene.

SERGEANT. Irene?

ALMA. She's my maid. My friend. I sent her up to bed. She knows nothing about it. I want my whiskey—

ALMA *takes the bottle from him. She seems to finish it.*

SERGEANT. And this Irene is the only other person in the house?

ALMA, *in the act of looking for another bottle, stops and turns slowly.*

ALMA. There's George too—

SERGEANT. George?

ALMA. My chauffeur. He's only a boy. He's nothing—just an odd-job-boy—

SERGEANT. Where is he?

ALMA. How would I know? I'm not his mother . . . I expect he's upstairs, asleep. He's very young, you see—

SERGEANT. Madam, I must now caution you. You are not obliged to say anything unless you wish to do so, but whatever you do say will be taken down and may be given in evidence. Do you follow me?

ALMA. Anywhere. Are you married? You've lots of girls I expect—Would you like ten pounds? No, it's a crime to give a policeman money.

SERGEANT. Madam, please.

ALMA. He wanted to die, you see. He said he'd lived too long. He gave me a mallet and dared me to kill him, so I did.

SERGEANT. Where is the mallet?

ALMA. (*Yawning.*) What?

SERGEANT. The mallet? Where is the mallet?

ALMA. Oh, I'll remember in the morning. (*She gets up.*) No, mustn't sleep. I might dream. Let's have that music again—

SERGEANT. (*Closing his notebook.*) Madam, I propose to telephone the police station, using the call-box outside—

ALMA. There's one in there. Better still there's one in the bedroom.

SERGEANT. I shall use the call-box, thank you, Madam.

ALMA. Please yourself, but you don't know what you're missing—

*The* SERGEANT *goes out. As he disappears* ALMA *is going towards the gramophone. After he has left she covers her face, emitting a sob, as reality seems to hit her. Then, swaying, she places the record back on the turntable and the music starts up again, deafeningly loud.*

*The lights fade as she moves in time to the music and come up on the courtroom. The* SERGEANT *is continuing his evidence. The music overlaps until it too fades out.*

CROOM-JOHNSON. A general question, sergeant, about Mrs. Rattenbury's behaviour. Remembering that only a few hours before, her husband had been brutally killed, how did you react in your mind to her attitude that night?

SERGEANT. I was—disgusted, sir.

CROOM-JOHNSON. In one word, how would you describe her behaviour?

SERGEANT. (*After thought.*) Callous. Downright brutal.

CROOM-JOHNSON. Thank you, sergeant.

*He sits down.*

MONTAGU. Look at the press boys scampering out. Imagine the headlines.

O'CONNOR. They should have waited. (*He rises.*) Sergeant, how long have you been in the police force?

SERGEANT. Twenty years, sir.

O'CONNOR. In that time you would, of course, have attended at many grue-some occasions—car accidents and the like?

SERGEANT. Yes, sir. Many.

O'CONNOR. You must then be familiar with the medical phenomenon known as shock?

SERGEANT. I've seen cases of shock, sir.

O'CONNOR. Severe shock?

SERGEANT. Some severe.

O'CONNOR. How do such persons usually behave?

SERGEANT. Well, I'd say, sometimes they're not quite all there.

O'CONNOR. Not quite all there? Not aware of their surroundings, or excited and over-talkative?

SERGEANT. Both, sir.

O'CONNOR. Inclined to fits either of hysterical weeping or, quite as likely, hys-terical laughter—and, generally speaking, inclined to behave entirely out of character?

SERGEANT. Yes, sir.

O'CONNOR. Why then were you so disgusted at Mrs. Rattenbury's behaviour that night?

SERGEANT. I didn't think it was shock, sir. I mean I saw no occasion—

O'CONNOR. You saw no occasion? Can you imagine a greater occasion for shock than the brutal murder of a dearly loved husband in her own home? Can you?

SERGEANT. She didn't seem disturbed, sir. Like I said—she was laughing, and dancing and playing about.

O'CONNOR. (*Forcefully.*) Good God, man—have you never heard of hyste-ria?

JUDGE. Mr. O'Connor.

O'CONNOR. I'm sorry, My Lord. Have you never heard of hysteria, Sergeant?

SERGEANT. Of course, sir.

O'CONNOR. What form does it take?'

SERGEANT. Laughing, sir. But this wasn't hysterical laughing—

O'CONNOR. And who are you to judge?

SERGEANT. I've seen hysteria, sir—

O'CONNOR. You've also seen shock, and you failed to recognise that, didn't you? What is the treatment for shock? (*As* SERGEANT *hesitates.*) Come on. You've read your manual. What does it say?

SERGEANT. One should keep the victim warm, using blankets when obtain-able—

O'CONNOR. This victim was half-dressed, on a night in March. Was there a fire in the grate?

SERGEANT. No, sir.

O'CONNOR. Were the windows open?

SERGEANT. Yes, sir.

O'CONNOR. Do you remember what the temperature was that night in Bournemouth?

SERGEANT. No, sir. Not exactly.

O'CONNOR. Would it surprise you to learn that at two o'clock on the morning of March 25 the temperature on the town hall roof was recorded as 3 degrees below freezing?

SERGEANT. I remember it was a bit chilly, sir. I didn't know it was as cold as that.

O'CONNOR. It was as cold as that. And the windows in the sitting-room were open?

SERGEANT. Yes, sir.

O'CONNOR. Back to the manual. If the victim is not kept warm, what does it say can happen to the victim? What is there a danger of?

SERGEANT. Collapse, sir.

O'CONNOR. What happened to Mrs. Rattenbury later that night?

SERGEANT. She did collapse, sir, and had to be put to bed—but that was the whiskey.

O'CONNOR. Was it, indeed? And how much whiskey did Mrs. Rattenbury have to drink that night?

SERGEANT. I don't know, exactly, sir—she was drinking from the bottle, sir—and emptied it.

O'CONNOR. In front of you, sergeant?

SERGEANT. Yes, sir.

O'CONNOR. And you allowed that?

SERGEANT. I had no option, sir.

O'CONNOR. No option? What does your handbook tell you to prevent the victim taking at all costs?

*Pause.*

SERGEANT. Alcohol, sir.

O'CONNOR. And why, sergeant? Do you remember why?

*Pause.*

SERGEANT. (*Quoting from memory.*) Because the effect of alcohol on a shocked system will greatly increase the symptoms, and will in all respect prove strongly deleterious.

O'CONNOR. And—doesn't it add—sometimes fatal?

SERGEANT. Yes, sir.

O'CONNOR. It may be that you are lucky that in this case it was not. Otherwise you could be facing a very grave charge, sergeant—gross negligence while on duty. That's all.

*He sits down.* CROOM-JOHNSON *rises.*

CROOM-JOHNSON. Sergeant, has a person in a state of shock ever made sexual advances to you?

SERGEANT. Certainly not, sir.

CROOM-JOHNSON. Or attempted to bribe you?

SERGEANT. No, sir.

CROOM-JOHNSON. Thank you, sergeant.

*The* SERGEANT *descends from the box.*

That concludes the case for the Crown, My Lord. (*He sits down.*)

JUDGE. Mr. O'Connor. Are you ready?

O'CONNOR. Yes, My Lord.

O'CONNOR *mutters to* MONTAGU, *then shrugs. He rises.*

May it please Your Lordship, members of the jury, it is my intention to call one witness and one witness only—namely Mrs. Rattenbury. I shall therefore claim the right of the last word—

CROOM-JOHNSON. (*Rising swiftly.*) My Lord, this sudden manoeuvre of my learned friend puts me at a grave disadvantage.

O'CONNOR. My Lord, I have to confess that I do not know—even at this very second, as I stand here to begin Mrs. Rattenbury's defence, whether she will in fact obey my summons to the box or not. If she does not, then it is I who will stand at a grave disadvantage—

CROOM-JOHNSON. My Lord, I think an adjournment at this juncture would be the right—

O'CONNOR. (*Angrily.*) It would be most damnably wrong!—Forgive me, My Lord, but I am not exaggerating when I say that in this moment—this exact moment—lies the hinge of this entire trial. Any delay, even of half an hour, might be fatal to the cause of justice. In my view it is vital that my client goes into the witness box to give evidence on her own behalf, as she has the right and, I have told her, the duty to do. I believe and pray that if called upon now, she will go. With Your Lordship's permission. I therefore call Alma Rattenbury.

*There is a pause.* ALMA *enters, and walking as if in a daze, goes to the witness box. In the box a board is handed to her and a bible.*

CLERK. Take the book in your right hand and repeat the following words after me. I swear by Almighty God.

ALMA. I swear by almighty God.

CLERK. That the evidence I shall give to the court—

ALMA. That the evidence I shall give to the court—

CLERK. Shall be the truth, the whole truth, and nothing but the truth.

ALMA. Shall be the truth, the whole truth, and nothing but the truth.

O'CONNOR. You are Alma Victoria Rattenbury.

ALMA. I am.

O'CONNOR. Mrs. Rattenbury, how long were you married to your husband?

ALMA. Eight years.

O'CONNOR. By him did you have a child?

ALMA. Yes. Little John.

JUDGE. Mrs. Rattenbury, I can't hear you. Speak up, please. And please make sure the jury can hear what you say.

ALMA. I'm sorry. I'm sorry.

O'CONNOR. Mrs. Rattenbury—little John, how old is he?

ALMA. Six—Six (*Louder.*)

O'CONNOR. And you have been married twice before, I think?

ALMA. Yes.

O'CONNOR. By the second husband you had a child, did you not?

ALMA. Yes. Christopher.

O'CONNOR. You are fond of him, I think.

ALMA. Yes.

O'CONNOR. Very fond?

ALMA. . . . Very fond.

O'CONNOR. Now, Mrs. Rattenbury, I want you to tell me about your relationship with your husband. Since the birth of—

ALMA. Er—(*She looks towards the public gallery.*)

O'CONNOR. Mrs. Rattenbury?

ALMA. No, I—

JUDGE. Is something wrong, Mr O'Connor?

O'CONNOR. I'm sorry, My Lord. An oversight on my part. If Your Lordship permits—

*He turns to* MONTAGU, *and murmurs. . . 'get the boy out of court, will you . . .'*

MONTAGU *nods and goes.*

I do apologise, My Lord. Now, Mrs. Rattenbury, would you say your married life was happy? . . . Mrs. Rattenbury!

ALMA. I'm sorry?

ALMA *looks at the court, then . . .*

O'CONNOR. Would you say your married life was happy?

ALMA. Well it was a bit—you know—

*She makes a gesture indicating 'up and down'.*

O'CONNOR. You had some quarrels?

ALMA. Not many. Only little ones, and always about money. He was a bit—well—stingy. I often had to tell him little fibs to get the bills paid.

O'CONNOR. Yes. Well, we'll come back to that.

MONTAGU *returns and nods to* O'CONNOR. ALMA *again looks into the court, but clearly* CHRISTOPHER *has gone.*

O'CONNOR. Mrs. Rattenbury, I want you to tell us now about your relationship with your late husband. Be quite frank, please. Since the birth of little John six years ago did you and Mr. Rattenbury live together as husband and wife?

ALMA. No.

JUDGE. Mrs. Rattenbury, I must ask you to speak much louder please. And please address your replies so the jury may hear them.

ALMA. I'm sorry.

O'CONNOR. Since that time you did not live together as husband and wife at all?

ALMA. No.

JUDGE. Mrs. Rattenbury, you do understand what was meant by the question?

ALMA. Yes.

O'CONNOR. Did your husband have a separate room?

ALMA. Yes.

O'CONNOR. Was that at his suggestion or yours?

ALMA. Oh, his.

O'CONNOR. You would have been ready to continue marital relations with him?

ALMA. Oh yes, of course.

O'CONNOR. But he didn't want it?

ALMA. Well I think it was rather a question of the flesh being willing but the spirit being weak—

O'CONNOR. Er—the other way round I think?

ALMA. I expect so.

O'CONNOR. Now, between the months of November 1934 and March 1935 were you having regular sexual intercourse with Wood?

ALMA. Yes.

*Again she has a quick look into the court.*

O'CONNOR. And what attitude did your husband take to all this?

ALMA. None whatsoever.

JUDGE. You mean he didn't know of it?

ALMA. Oh, I think he must have known of it, My Lord.

JUDGE. Then he must have taken some attitude—even if it was one of tactful silence?

ALMA. I just don't think he gave it a thought.

*The* JUDGE *makes a heavy note.*

O'CONNOR. Now, Mrs. Rattenbury, I am going to take you through the events of the week that led up to your husband's murder and I want you to answer my questions with complete truth. You will, will you not?

ALMA *doesn't reply.*

JUDGE. Mrs. Rattenbury, you are under oath. You must reply fully and truthfully to Counsel's questions.

*Again* ALMA *doesn't reply.*

O'CONNOR. On Monday March 18—that is six days before the murder— did you ask your husband for some money? . . . Mrs. Rattenbury?

JUDGE. One moment please. Mrs. Rattenbury, you do understand, do you not, that having taken the oath to tell the truth, the whole truth, and nothing but the truth, you are in law in duty bound to do so. Do you understand that?

ALMA. Yes, My Lord.

JUDGE. Then be so good as to answer Counsel's question.

O'CONNOR. For how much money did you ask?

*Pause.*

ALMA. Two hundred and fifty pounds.

O'CONNOR. What little fib—to quote your words—did you have to tell him?

ALMA. That I was going up to London to have an operation.

O'CONNOR. And on the following day you went up to London?

ALMA. Yes.

O'CONNOR. And you stayed with Wood at an hotel in Kensington?

ALMA. Yes. The Royal Palace.

O'CONNOR. During that time did you give Wood some presents?

ALMA. Yes. A pair of silk pyjamas, a new suit, and then a ring for him to give to me.

O'CONNOR. Now it has been strongly suggested that there was some very sinister significance in this hotel visit only a few days before the murder. It has in fact been represented as a kind of premature honeymoon. What truth is there in that?

ALMA. Oh, none at all. It wasn't the first time we'd gone to a hotel, and he did love it so. He loved being waited on and called sir—

O'CONNOR. And you wanted to give him that pleasure?

ALMA. Yes.

O'CONNOR. And that was the reason for the presents?

ALMA. Yes.

O'CONNOR. And the ring to yourself?

ALMA. The ring was only a pretence.

O'CONNOR. A pretence of what?

ALMA. Well—like an engaged couple.

O'CONNOR. So this visit was no more than a whim, designed to give Wood pleasure. What about you? Did it give you pleasure too?

ALMA. No. It was terrible.

O'CONNOR. In what way terrible.

ALMA. Oh, rows.

O'CONNOR. Serious rows?

ALMA. Not on the surface. But underneath, of course, they were. You see he knew I was trying to finish it.

O'CONNOR. Finish the relationship?

ALMA. Yes.

O'CONNOR. Why?

ALMA. Well, it had got out of hand.

O'CONNOR. Had you told him that?

ALMA. I tried to often, but the difference in our ages made it so difficult. After we'd got back from London I was determined to say 'finish for good'—and mean it. I'm quite sure he knew that, which is why he was making my life hell . . . I'm sorry, My Lord. Dreadful . . .

JUDGE. Hell will do. Now I am not sure I have followed this. You say you tried to break the affair with Wood but were unable to—one of the reasons being the difference in your ages. Surely that very thing would make it easier?

ALMA. No, My Lord. Sorry, but it makes it harder.

JUDGE. But surely the older party must be the dominant party?

ALMA. Excuse me, My Lord, but to me it's the other way round. Anyway it was with me and George. I think it must be with many people. Of course I don't know.

O'CONNOR. Now, Mrs. Rattenbury—

JUDGE. One moment please, Mr. O'Connor.

*The* JUDGE *finishes writing then. signals* O'CONNOR *to continue.*

O'CONNOR. Mrs. Rattenbury. We come now to your return to the Villa Madeira two nights before the murder. Did your husband ask you any awkward question when you saw him?

ALMA. No. It was as if I'd never been gone.

JUDGE. He must surely have asked you about your operation?

ALMA. No, My Lord.

O'CONNOR. Anyway all was normal at the Villa?

ALMA. Oh yes. Very friendly.

O'CONNOR. How was Wood?

ALMA. Well he was a bit sulky. He'd wanted to stay on at the hotel, you see. But he perked up later.

O'CONNOR. You had intercourse that night?

ALMA. Oh yes, everything normal as you said.

O'CONNOR. Thank you. Now we come to Sunday, the day of the murder.

ALMA. Oh no. No. I can't—I . . .

O'CONNOR. One moment Mrs. Rattenbury, please.

ALMA. But I can't—I can't—

O'CONNOR. Please. Please.

ALMA *is silent.*

My Lord, in view of the obvious difficulties which I see your Lordship has noticed, I would crave your indulgence at this point to embark upon a somewhat unusual course. With Your Lordship's permission, I would like to quote certain passages from the signed statement entered by the prosecution yesterday, which was made by the prisoner Wood on the day of his arrest—Exhibit 27, My Lord.

JUDGE. But that is evidence against Wood. You are asking to use it on Mrs. Rattenbury's behalf?

O'CONNOR. Naturally, My Lord. I would hardly use it against her.

CROOM-JOHNSON. My Lord, I must most strenuously object to any part of the statement being read on behalf of Rattenbury. What cannot in law be used against her, must not in law be used for her. My learned friend should know that very well.

O'CONNOR. I really do not need lessons in law from prosecuting counsel. I do know that it is my duty to my client to use any evidence on her behalf that this court will allow—any evidence, of any kind, and from any source.

CROOM-JOHNSON. But My Lord, there are no precedents for such a—

JUDGE. Yes, yes, Mr. Croom-Johnson. It is plainly a matter for me. You are perfectly correct in saying that this proposed course is highly irregular— but having regard for the undoubted fact that the law always allows, and must allow, the greatest possible latitude to the defence in a capital charge, I will decide in favour of Mr. O'Connor.

O'CONNOR. (*Plainly delighted.*) Thank you, My Lord.

CROOM-JOHNSON *sits, muttering . . . 'dangerous precedent . . .' The lights fade to* O'CONNOR *and more dimly on the* JUDGE.

O'CONNOR. I refer Your Lordship to paragraph three, in which Wood is describing the events of the murder. He says: 'They were up in her bedroom together—' That is, Mr. and Mrs. Rattenbury, My Lord.

JUDGE. I have it, thank you, Mr. O'Connor. *The light on the* JUDGE *fades out. The light fades up on* WOOD, *listening outside the bedroom door.*

O'CONNOR. When I went up with the tea the door was locked. So I listened outside, and then I heard them—kissing noises and 'darling'. And then I heard them doing it. I listened to them right through, then I heard them talking and getting off the bed, so I went into my room and waited for them to come out. . .

*The lights come up on the Villa Madeira.* WOOD *goes to his room. The bedroom door opens and* RATTENBURY *comes out, putting on his jacket.* ALMA *has a dressing-gown on. She helps him down the stairs, which he has to take very gingerly.*

ALMA. Gently does it, Ratz. That's right . . . So I'll tell the Jenks we'll be over tomorrow, shall I?

RATTENBURY. If they'll have us.

WOOD *appears, a menacing figure at the top of the stairs. He is in his shirtsleeves.*

ALMA. (*Gaily.*) Of course they'll have us. They're always asking us to stay. How long shall I say? A couple of days?

RATTENBURY. It's a long way to go for a couple of days. Lot of petrol. Make it a week.

ALMA. All right, dear.

WOOD. (*Calling.*) Alma, I want to see you.

ALMA. (*Looking* up.) Come down then.

WOOD. (*Commandingly.*) Up here. Now.

RATTENBURY. (*Muttering.*) You shouldn't let him talk to you like that, Alma.

ALMA. (*Shrugging.*) He's in one of his moods—back in a jiffy.

*She climbs the stairs.* WOOD, *in a passion, grabs her wrists.*

WOOD. Why was that door locked?

ALMA. Locked? Was it?

WOOD. You lying bitch—

ALMA. (*Laughing.*) George, you *can't* think that me and Ratz—

WOOD *opens the door and looks inside.*

WOOD. Yes. Tidied up the bed now, haven't you? You were at it just now with him, weren't you? I heard.

ALMA. Oh George, you are a scream! Ratz, of all people. Oh, I'll die of laughing—

WOOD *hits her hard.*

(*Angry.*) George, if you ever do that again—

WOOD. You'll what?

ALMA. Tell you to get out of this house and never come back—

WOOD *produces a revolver from his pocket.*

WOOD. I could kill you quite easily.

ALMA. (*Calmly.*) Yes I expect you could, dear, but not with Christopher's water pistol.

*She takes it from him quickly.*

George, are you all right?

WOOD. (*Shouting.*) Why was that door locked?

ALMA. Quiet, dear. Even Ratz could have heard that.

*He hasn't. He is in the sitting-room placidly reading the paper.*

The door was locked because it rattles when the window's open—as you should very well know. (*She strokes his face.*) Silly boy!

*She gives him back the pistol.*

WOOD. Are you going to these people tomorrow?

ALMA. Yes.

WOOD. With me driving?

ALMA. Of course.

WOOD. I see. Where will I sleep?

ALMA. Oh, they've lots of room.

WOOD. In a servant's attic?

ALMA. Well, perhaps, but I'll try and see it's a nice one.

WOOD. And eat in the servants' hall?

ALMA. George, it's only for a week

WOOD. And you and Ratz, with a nice big double bed—?

ALMA. (*Angrily.*) Stop this nonsense at once! At once, do you hear?

WOOD. Yes, Ma'am. Very good, Ma'am. Beg pardon I'm sure Ma'am.

*She turns her back on him and picks up the phone.*

ALMA. (*Into phone.*) Could you give me Bridport 31 please? This is Bournemouth 309.

WOOD. (*To her, and taking the phone out of her hand.*) Listen, you cow. You're to go down there now (*Pointing to the sitting-room.*) and tell him you're not going to the Jenks tomorrow—

ALMA. George, you're going to make me very angry.

WOOD. Because if you don't I'm going to do something very bad. Something very very bad.

ALMA. Put acid in that water pistol and squirt it in my face? (*She takes the telephone. Into phone.*) Hallo? (*To* WOOD.) Go into the kitchen and help Irene with supper, there's a good boy.

*Obediently he goes, half into shadow, and then turns to listen.*

(*Into receiver.*) Hallo. Is that Mrs. Jenks? . . . Alma Rattenbury . . . Ratz and I wondered if we could take you at your word and come over for a few days . . . (*To* WOOD.) Go on, ducky—

WOOD. I'm warning you, Alma. Something really *bad*—

ALMA. (*Into receiver.*) Well I thought tomorrow, if you could have us—Oh, that is nice . . . Yes we'll drive over . . . I've a chauffeur now, you know. Lovely, see you soon. Goodbye.

WOOD *runs out.*

*Fade out except for the spot on* O'CONNOR, *and dimly on the* JUDGE.

O'CONNOR. Wood's statement continues:

*The light on the* JUDGE *fades out.*

I went to my Dad's and borrowed the mallet. Then I went back. I could see them through the French windows, playing cribbage. Then she went up to bed. So I went into the room and hit him three times on the back of the head with the mallet. Then I went into the garden and hid the mallet. Then I went up to bed.

*The light on* O'CONNOR *fades and comes up on the Villa Madeira. In the sitting-room, very dimly seen, is the slumped figure of* RATTENBURY *in the armchair. Upstairs* ALMA *is in bed in pyjamas, reading.*

ALMA. (*Calling.*) George!

WOOD. (*Off.*) Yes.

ALMA. Where have you been all evening?

WOOD. (*Off.*) Out.

ALMA. What are you doing?

WOOD. (*Off.*) Getting undressed.

ALMA. You want to come in?

*Pause.*

WOOD *appears in the passage dressed in silk pyjamas. He goes into* ALMA'S *room, and slips off his pyjamas, letting them drop on the floor.*

ALMA. (*Lovingly.*) That's no way to treat three guinea pyjamas, my lad—

*He climbs into bed. She kisses him. He turns on his back.*

WOOD. I'm in trouble, Alma. Real trouble.

ALMA. Real trouble? There's no such thing, that's what I always say—

*He turns over again, his back to her, and begins to cry.*

This is a lovely world, and we're all meant to enjoy it. Now come on. Look at me—

WOOD. I can't.

ALMA. Well at least then tell me what it is.

WOOD. I can't . . . It's Ratz.

ALMA. What about him?

WOOD. I've—hurt him—

ALMA. You had a fight?

WOOD. Not a fight . . . I wish it had been a fight.

ALMA. Have you hurt him badly?

WOOD. Yes. Very badly.

*Suddenly there is a hoarse sound from* RATTENBURY *whose head falls forward.*

ALMA. (*Rising.*) Was that him?

WOOD. It must have been. I thought I'd killed him.

*She sits up in bed.*

ALMA. What have you done to him?

*There is another sound from below.*

ALMA. (*Calling.*) I'm coming, Ratz, I'm coming, darling.

*She puts on a blue kimono, lying on the end of the bed. He clutches her arm.*

WOOD. Don't go down.

ALMA. I must. If he's hurt badly I must help him—

WOOD. I've done for him, Alma. You won't get him back—

ALMA. (*Running down the stairs.*) I'm coming Ratz, darling. I'm coming.

*She runs into the darkened sitting-room. After a moment she lets out a loud scream.*

WOOD *gets back into his pyjamas and leans over the banisters again.*

IRENE *comes out of her room.*

IRENE (*To* WOOD.) What's the matter?

WOOD. Don't know, I'm sure.

*She gives him a suspicious glance, then runs down the stairs, just as* ALMA *comes out of the sitting-room staggering from shock.*

IRENE. What is it?

ALMA. Ratz. Someone's hurt him Irene—Agh!! . . . Doctor O'Donnell. Run out and get Doctor O'Donnell. Quick—Irene—quick . . . Tell him Ratz may be dying.

IRENE *runs out of the front door. We still don't see* RATTENBURY *clearly, but as* ALMA *approaches the chair his body suddenly slumps out of it on the floor.* ALMA *gives a gasp and runs away. Then she kneels at his side.* WOOD *has come into the room.*

ALMA. Ratz—my darling Ratz—help's coming soon. Stay alive, please stay alive—Ratzie, can you hear me?

WOOD *has approached the body.*

WOOD. It's no good, Alma. I told you upstairs I'd done for him, and I have.

ALMA. Oh no, no—he isn't dead. He can't be. Ratz . . . Ratz . . .

WOOD *pours her a large whiskey, and makes her drink it. It makes her retch.*
        Why did you do this? Why, why.

WOOD. I had to. He was stealing you away from me.

ALMA. Oh God, you little idiot. He wasn't stealing me—he couldn't have . . . Look, oh my God! He's—

*She points to* RATTENBURY'S *trousers, where he has fouled himself. Again* ALMA *retches.*

WOOD. I told you I was going to do something really bad—

ALMA. To *me.* I thought you meant to *me.*

*She takes off her kimono, and covers* RATTENBURY *with it.*
        Oh God, poor Ratz. Why didn't you kill me?

*There is a ring at the front door.*

    Go upstairs. Go to your room. Don't come down here unless you're sent for, and then know nothing about it. Nothing at all, do you understand?

*There is another ring at the front door.*

    Go upstairs.

WOOD *turns to go.*

WOOD. What'll you tell them?

ALMA. I'll think something up. Coming?

O'CONNOR. 'I'll think something up' . . . 'I'll think something up'. And what she thought up was the ludicrous mad story she told the police. Was it the story of a sane, calm, balanced woman? Or was it not a story thought up in panic by a woman in a deep state of shock, aggravated by repeated doses of whiskey, and desperate at all costs to save the life of her lover?

CROOM-JOHNSON. You're addressing the Jury! My Lord, really I must object. Counsel is addressing the Jury.

JUDGE. Yes, I quite agree. Mr. O'Connor, that was highly improper. The time for your address to the jury is not yet, as you very well know. That was really highly improper.

O'CONNOR. I'm so sorry, My Lord, you are of course quite right. I'm afraid I was momentarily carried away. I do apologise to my learned friend, and to you, My Lord.

JUDGE. Have you finished with Wood's statement?

O'CONNOR. Yes, My Lord.

JUDGE. And you propose to continue your examination on more conventional lines?

O'CONNOR. Indeed, My Lord.

JUDGE. Then first I must address a few remarks to the Jury, and try to make certain important matters clear. Ladies and Gentlemen of the Jury, I trust you understand that what you have just heard read to you is a statement made by the prisoner Wood, and cannot be used in any way at all as evidence against the prisoner Rattenbury. If you have heard anything you consider prejudicial to Mrs. Rattenbury, you must put it completely out of your minds. I trust that is clear. Very well, Mr. O'Connor, you may proceed.

O'CONNOR. Thank you, My Lord. Now Mrs. Rattenbury, I'm going to ask you a very important question. Is there any part of that statement of Wood's that is in any way inaccurate or untrue?

JUDGE. Mrs. Rattenbury, you must answer the question.

O'CONNOR. Is there?

ALMA *shakes her head.*

O'CONNOR. Mrs. Rattenbury, is any part of that statement inaccurate or untrue in any way?

ALMA. . . . No.

O'CONNOR. None whatever?

ALMA. No.

O'CONNOR. Thank you. And what you thought up, was the ludicrous mad story that you told the police . . .

CROOM-JOHNSON. Is that a question?

O'CONNOR. It is a question. Mrs. Rattenbury, have you ever in your life suffered a greater shock to your mind, body and spirit than you suffered that night when you found your husband battered to death by your lover?

CASSWELL *and* CROOM-JOHNSON *are both on their feet.*

CASSWELL.
CROOM-JOHNSON. } (*Together.*) My Lord—

O'CONNOR. —*Presumably* by your lover?

ALMA. No. Nothing ever—in all my life.

O'CONNOR. These stories of your dancing semi-nude making advances to policemen, playing the gramophone at full blast—did they or did they not come as a complete surprise to you when they were told to you as late as three weeks ago?

ALMA. Yes, they did.

O'CONNOR. And what was your over-riding emotion on hearing of them?

ALMA. Shame. Deep, deep shame.

*Pause.*

O'CONNOR. Mrs. Rattenbury, three last questions. Did you murder your husband?

ALMA. No.

O'CONNOR. Did you take any part whatever in planning his murder?

ALMA. No.

O'CONNOR. Did you, in fact, know a thing about it until Wood told you, in bed upstairs, that he had done it?

ALMA. No. If I'd known, I'd have prevented it.

O'CONNOR. Thank you. That is all.

*He sits down.* ALMA *starts to leave the box.*

CROOM-JOHNSON. (*Getting up quickly.*) Just a moment, Mrs. Rattenbury, you're not finished yet. I have some questions to ask you. In fact a great many questions.

*The lights fade.*

*The lights come up on* CROOM-JOHNSON'S *cross-examination of* MRS. RATTENBURY, *which has now been in progress for some hours. She is very tired.*

. . . Mrs. Rattenbury, just how old was Wood when you first invited him into the Villa Madeira as your lover?

ALMA. I didn't invite him—not in the way you mean. He insisted on living in—

CROOM-JOHNSON. *Insisted?*

ALMA. Why not?

CROOM-JOHNSON. But surely you could have resisted him easily, a boy of seventeen?

ALMA. Not easily at all. Ever since this case began the one thing I've heard is

how I must have dominated this—boy. Well I can only say that if anyone dominated anyone else, it was George who dominated me—

CROOM-JOHNSON. Very interesting, but let us please stick to the facts. You
have admitted, have you not, cheating your husband out of a considerable sum in order to take your lover up to London. Was that done under
Wood's *domination?*

ALMA. It was his idea.

CROOM-JOHNSON. And the Royal Palace his choice of hotel?

ALMA. No. That was mine.

CROOM-JOHNSON. And whose idea was it buying the engagement ring?

ALMA. It wasn't an engagement ring.

CROOM-JOHNSON. Well, whatever it was, who suggested buying it?

*Pause.*

ALMA. I did.

CROOM-JOHNSON. Indeed. Now let us return once more to the evening of
the murder. This purported conversation—this alleged confession of
Wood's—took place in your bedroom?

ALMA. Yes.

CROOM-JOHNSON. But I understood that your sexual meetings usually occurred in Wood's room?

ALMA. Yes. That was because of little John sleeping in mine.

CROOM-JOHNSON. (*A shade wearily.*) That night then little John was somewhere else?

ALMA. (*Almost equally weary.*) No. He was in my room.

*There is a murmur in court.* CROOM-JOHNSON *instantly perks alive. The* JUDGE
*looks up. Even* O'CONNOR *looks unhappy.*

CROOM-JOHNSON. Little John was in your room?

ALMA. Yes, but sound asleep.

CROOM-JOHNSON. Your lover climbed into your bed with your little son in
the same room?

ALMA. Yes, but he was sound asleep.

CROOM-JOHNSON. Used this to happen often?

ALMA. Well it had to sometimes, when Christopher was home.

CROOM-JOHNSON. Your lover would clamber into bed with you and you would
indulge in sexual congress, with your six-year-old child in the same room?

ALMA. But he's a very sound sleeper.

CROOM-JOHNSON. A little child of no more than six summers—

O'CONNOR. My Lord, I fail to see how any of this is pertinent, unless of course
my learned friend intends to call little John as a witness in rebuttal of
his mother's testimony.

CROOM-JOHNSON. I find that remark in the most appalling taste—

O'CONNOR. And I find these constant references to little John's presence in
that room—a cheeild (*He pronounces it so.*) of no more than six summers—autumns, winters and springs come to that—I find these slurs

on my client's moral character not only in appalling taste, but immoral, unfair, and entirely irrelevant. Who killed Francis Mawson Rattenbury? Isn't that what this court is convened to find out? It is surely not whether an act—or several acts—of sexual congress were committed in the distant presence of a heavily dormant child.

CROOM-JOHNSON. I trust my learned friend will have breath for his final address—

O'CONNOR. You need have no fear of that.

JUDGE. Gentlemen, please. This is becoming more of a cockpit than a court of law. I think Mr. O'Connor is right, Mr. Croom-Johnson. You have asked the witness a question—a perfectly relevant one in my view—and she has answered it. Pray let the matter rest there.

CROOM-JOHNSON. As Your Lordship pleases. Now I want to be absolutely fair to you, Mrs. Rattenbury—

O'CONNOR. (*Muttering.*) Fair?

CROOM-JOHNSON. When Wood, in bed with you, with your little boy in the corner—

O'CONNOR. My Lord.

CROOM-JOHNSON. I have not asked my question yet.

JUDGE. Please ask it, Mr. Croom-Johnson.

CROOM-JOHNSON. When Wood told you that night that he had hit your husband with a mallet, did you believe him?

ALMA. (*Her voice a weary croak.*) Not at first. No.

CROOM-JOHNSON. When you went downstairs and found your husband had indeed been hit on the head, did you believe him then?

ALMA. Well, one naturally would, wouldn't one?

CROOM-JOHNSON. You are here to answer my questions, not to ask them of me, Madam.

ALMA. I see. Well I did believe that he had done it then.

CROOM-JOHNSON. It is my duty to submit to you that you knew Wood had done it because you had encouraged him to do it? (*After a pause.*) Well?

ALMA. I'm sorry. Was that a question?

CROOM-JOHNSON. It was a question, Mrs. Rattenbury, and a very important one.

ALMA. I thought I'd answered it. Still, if you want it again. (*Raising her voice.*) I did not plot my husband's death. It was a great shock to me. I have never, in all my life, harmed a human being.

CROOM-JOHNSON. You have never harmed a human being?

*Pause.*

ALMA. (*On the edge of tears.*) Not meaning to. Not till now.

*The* JUDGE *indicates to* CROOM-JOHNSON *to continue.*

CROOM-JOHNSON. Mrs. Rattenbury, in answer to my learned friend you said that if Wood had told you of his intention to murder your husband you would have prevented it. How would you have done that?

ALMA. I'd have told him not to dare do such a wicked thing.

CROOM-JOHNSON. Would that have been enough?

ALMA. The way I'd have said it it would.

CROOM-JOHNSON. But I thought you said he dominated you?

ALMA *does not reply.*

Well—supposing you had failed to persuade him, what would you have done?

ALMA. Gone to the police, I suppose.

CROOM-JOHNSON. But after the murder the police were all over the house. Why did you not tell them then?

ALMA. That was different.

CROOM-JOHNSON. Why?

ALMA. Well Ratz was dead and I suppose I felt responsible.

CROOM-JOHNSON. I beg your pardon?

ALMA. I said—I suppose I felt responsible.

CROOM-JOHNSON. Responsible. Thank you.

*He sits down.* O'CONNOR *gets to his feet, stifling a yawn—an old trick of his.*

O'CONNOR. (*Languidly.*) Only two questions, Mrs. Rattenbury (*Straight at* CROOM-JOHNSON.)—Only *two*. By the word 'responsible' did you mean criminally responsible for your husband's murder?

ALMA. No.

O'CONNOR. Did you mean morally responsible for your lover's protection?

ALMA. Yes. That's exactly what I meant.

O'CONNOR. Thank you, Mrs. Rattenbury. That is all. That is the case for the defence of the Prisoner Rattenbury, My Lord.

JUDGE. Very well. I think that is a convenient moment to adjourn . . .

ALMA *seems momentarily entirely ignored.*

*The* LAWYERS *rise, stretch, and gather their papers, as the* JUDGE *perfunctorily nods three times, and leaves his chair.* MONTAGU *has seen* ALMA *delaying in the box. He assumes rightly that she has not the physical strength to regain the dock—nor, perhaps, the moral strength either. He goes to the box through his preoccupied colleagues, and offers her his arm.*

MONTAGU. You did very well—very well indeed.

*She seems not to have heard.*

(*Comfortingly.*) Your job is done now.

ALMA. (*In a hoarse whisper.*) Yes.

*Fade out on the Court as* ALMA *and the* LAWYERS *leave.*

*The lights come on in* MRS. DAVENPORT'S *sitting-room.* STELLA *is on the sofa, her head deep in a paper.* MRS. DAVENPORT *comes in.*

MRS. DAVENPORT. Has Tony called yet?

STELLA. Tony? No. He hasn't. Well? How was Mrs. Rattenbury?

MRS. DAVENPORT *stops, but doesn't reply.*

My God—she must have dominated that boy. Did she—

MRS. DAVENPORT *laughs harshly.*

What's so funny?

MRS. DAVENPORT. Yes, I suppose that's how it must seem.

STELLA. (*Appalled.*) Seem? Edie, you're not saying—

MRS. DAVENPORT. I'm not saying anything.

STELLA. Yes, you are. I know you too well. 'That's how it must seem'. Edie—she's an awful, awful, woman. Sleeping with that boy with her baby in the room—

MRS. DAVENPORT. What's that got to do with whether she committed murder?

STELLA. Everything, I should have thought—

MRS. DAVENPORT. Then you don't know the law.

STELLA. It seems as if I don't know you.

MRS. DAVENPORT. Perhaps you don't. It's that word—dominated. All the time, all the time that man was on at her: 'You were twenty years older, Madam. Twenty years older. I put it to you—you dominated that boy.' Do you know what she answered? 'When an older person loves a younger, it's the younger who dominates because the younger has so much more to give.'

*Pause.*

STELLA. And you thought of Tony?

MRS. DAVENPORT. Of course.

STELLA. My God, to think that a murderess could go free just because a jurywoman overloves a son who doesn't give a damn for her.

*Pause.*

I'm sorry. I shouldn't have said that.

MRS. DAVENPORT. You did.

STELLA. Tony rang me, this afternoon. We had a talk. A long one

MRS. DAVENPORT. In which he told you he didn't love me?

STELLA. (*Trying to embrace her.*) Oh my God, darling. I only said that because I was so damn angry with you.

MRS. DAVENPORT. Tell me what he said.

STELLA. Well, his father's got him a hundred per cent. It's a love affair.

MRS. DAVENPORT. What does he want to do?

STELLA. Live with him of course.

MRS. DAVENPORT. For ever?

STELLA. Yes.

MRS. DAVENPORT. Supposing I fight?

STELLA. They'll fight back.

MRS. DAVENPORT. How?

STELLA. Tony will tell the judge he prefers his father to you . . . Do you really want that? Of course he said he'd spend some of his holidays with you.

MRS. DAVENPORT. How kind . . .

STELLA. Darling, I do know how dreadful all this is for you. But you must try and forget about it, at least until this awful trial's over. Now, why don't

you put your feet up, let me get you a drink. Darling, I know it's difficult for you, but you've a big responsibility tomorrow. You're not going
to let this terrible business here cloud your judgement about that woman,
are you?

MRS. DAVENPORT. No. I'm not.

FADE OUT

*Before the lights come on again we hear the voice of* CASSWELL. *Then a spot illu-
minates his face, while another focuses on* ALMA'S.

CASSWELL. . . . when this boy met the woman he was an ordinary innocent
English boy, four months later, what do we find? A confessed adulterer,
a confessed thief, a confessed cocaine addict, utterly under the influence
of an hysterical, lying, drunken woman of abnormal sexual appetites and
apparently of no moral conscience whatever . . .

*The voice merges smoothly into* CROOM-JOHNSON'S.

CROOM-JOHNSON. . . . Can you believe a single word that such a woman
says—self-confessed liar, self-confessed adulteress, self-confessed seducer
of a tender youth of seventeen? . . . A woman who, by her own admission, robs her husband of a considerable sum, in order to indulge herself
in a four-day sexual orgy at the Royal Palace Hotel, with a boy young
enough to be her son . . .

*The voice is merged with that of* O'CONNOR.

O'CONNOR. Ladies and gentlemen. One of your number—I cannot, of course,
mention her name, which would be most improper, but I suppose I can
say that she must be one of the foremost among you, a lady, evidently,
of great moral courage and strength of character—she objected to serving on this case. 'Why?' asked His Lordship. 'Because' she replied, 'I am
so prejudiced against Mrs. Rattenbury's moral character that I cannot
be expected to give her a fair trial'. But how could she not be prejudiced
against this woman? How could any one of you fail to feel disgust and
nausea at the ensnaring and degradation of a helpless youth by a middle-aged woman of licentious and degenerate habits? But that is not the
offence with which she is charged here in this court.

*The voice merges into that of the* JUDGE, *speaking in a matter-of-fact tone to the
jury.*

JUDGE. Well, there it is. That is the woman. It is indeed difficult to find
words in the English language in which you may see fit to describe her.
But, members of the jury—the natural disgust you may feel for this
woman must not—I repeat that—*must not* make you any more ready
to convict her of the crime of murder. In fact it should, if anything, make
you *less* ready to do so. Prejudice, dislike, disapproval, disgust, must have
no part in your verdict. Well, that is all I have to say to you. You will
now retire . . .

*The lights have faded to a blackout. A spot picks up the quiet white face of* ALMA,

*which, during the whole of the foregoing judicial onslaught on her char-*
*acter has shown no sign of emotion whatever. Nor does it now as the lights*
*come up in her cell.* JOAN *is with her.* ALMA *is sitting in a hard chair, im-*
*mobile.*

JOAN. Look, dear, they may be a long time. Would you like to lie down? It'll
   have to be the floor—but I've had two blankets sent in, and a pillow—
   and I can make you quite comfy.

*There is no reply from* ALMA. *It is as if* JOAN *had never spoken.*

JOAN. Or I've brought some cards. How about a little game?

ALMA. (*At length.*) Beg your pardon?

JOAN. (*Showing the cards.*) A little game, dear. We could have much longer
   to wait.

ALMA. No, thank you.

JOAN. Anything at all? Coffee? Tea?

ALMA. No.

JOAN. Not with a drop of something in it?

*Pause.*

*Her stare continues unseeing.*

   Try not to fuss dear. What I always tell my ladies—

MONTAGU *comes in.*

MONTAGU. (*With a cheerfulness he doesn't feel.*) Well, Mrs. Rattenbury—how
   are you feeling?

ALMA *seems unconscious of his presence . . .*

   (*To wardress, in a low voice.*) Is she all right?

JOAN. (*Indignantly.*) How could she be, after all that was said about her upstairs?

MONTAGU. I should have warned her.

*He pulls a chair alongside* ALMA'S *and touches her arm.*

ALMA. (*Quite brightly.*) Oh hullo, Mr. Montagu—

MONTAGU. You must try to understand why Mr. O'Connor had to say those
   things about you. They must have been horrible to hear—

ALMA. Not particularly.

MONTAGU. But you see, both Mr. O'Connor and the Judge, by saying all those
   foul things about you, *forced* the jury to concentrate their minds on only
   one thing—did you or did you not commit murder? Well, as we all know
   you didn't—

ALMA. Do you?

MONTAGU. Of course. So does Mr. O'Connor.

ALMA. And Christopher?

MONTAGU. And Christopher, most certainly.

ALMA. Then it really doesn't matter what the jury think, does it?

*Pause.*

MONTAGU. Mrs. Rattenbury, I have every hope that in a matter of hours—
   or even minutes—you will walk out of this place a free woman. If you
   do, what plans have you made?

ALMA *says nothing.*

JOAN. Her friend Irene Riggs is taking her to her home for a few days—

MONTAGU. Oh. That's good.

JOAN. She'll be all right there—she's fond of Irene.

MONTAGU. And then you must think of taking up your career again—

ALMA. My career?

MONTAGU. As a song-writer.

ALMA. Oh that—

JOAN. (*Eagerly.*) Yes, dear, you must. Just imagine how your songs will sell now.

ALMA *laughs harshly.* MONTAGU *gives* JOAN *a silencing look.*

WARDER. (*Off.*) Jury coming back.

ALMA. Mr. Montagu, I want to thank you—

MONTAGU. Don't. You have, and always will have, my admiration.

ALMA. Oh that's nice. That's the way men used to speak to me.

*As they go out, fade into blackout. In the darkness we hear the sound of the* LAW-YERS *returning to Court. The* CLERK OF THE COURT *enters.*

*The lights come up on* MRS. DAVENPORT *and dimly on the* CLERK OF THE COURT.

CLERK OF THE COURT. Members of the jury, are you agreed upon your verdict?

MRS. DAVENPORT. We are.

*The lights come up on* ALMA *and* WOOD, *standing in the dock.*

CLERK OF THE COURT. Do you find the prisoner Percy George Wood guilty or not guilty of murder?

MRS. DAVENPORT. Guilty, but we should like to add a rider to that. A recommendation to mercy.

CLERK OF THE COURT. Do you find the prisoner Alma Victoria Rattenbury guilty or not guilty of murder?

MRS. DAVENPORT. Not guilty.

*The court hears a storm of booing, hissing and shouts of 'shame!', but we do not hear it. Light fades up on the* JUDGE.

CLERK OF THE COURT. (*Hardly heard.*) And those verdicts are the verdicts of you all?

MRS. DAVENPORT. They are.

*The storm of booing is apparently renewed. The light fades out on* MRS. DAVEN-PORT.

JUDGE. This will not be tolerated.

*The storm subsides.*

CLERK OF THE COURT. Percy George Wood, you stand convicted of murder: have you anything to say why the Court should not pass judgement on you?

WOOD. (*With a smile at* ALMA.) Nothing at all.

JUDGE. Percy George Wood, the jury have convicted you of murder, with a recommendation to mercy. That recommendation will be forwarded by me to the proper quarter, where it will doubtless receive consideration.

*They hear cries from the gallery of 'Don't worry, boy! We won't let them do it!'
etc.*

Meanwhile my duty is to pass upon you the only sentence which the
law knows for the crime of which you have been convicted.

*The black triangle is placed upon the* JUDGE'S *wig by the* CLERK OF THE COURT.
The sentence of the court upon you is that you be taken from this place
to a lawful prison, and thence to a place of execution, and that you there
be hanged by the neck until you are dead, and that your body be afterwards buried within the precincts of the prison in which you shall have
been confined before your execution. And may the Lord have mercy on
your soul.

*The* JUDGE *nods for* WOOD *to be taken down.* ALMA *fiercely grabs his arm as if
she would stop him.*

WOOD. Goodbye, you silly cow.

WOOD *goes off.*

JUDGE. Let Alma Victoria Rattenbury be discharged.

*The light fades out on the* JUDGE.

*The lights fade up on the court.*

O'CONNOR *is warmly shaken by the hand by* MONTAGU, *less warmly by* CASSWELL,
*not warmly at all by* CROOM-JOHNSON. ALMA *stands meanwhile, bewildered,
in the dock.*

ALMA *is approached by* IRENE RIGGS, *her face wreathed in an ecstatic smile. She
too embraces her.*

IRENE. I knew it! I never had a moment's doubt. Now here you are, darling.
(*She unfolds a mackintosh.*) Just slip into this. That's right. Now we'd better
have the scarf.

ALMA *takes it off obediently, to have it replaced with a simple beret.*

Now just till we get home—

*She slips on to* ALMA'S *nose a large pair of horn-rimmed glasses.*

There's a policeman waiting going to show us out of a special door.

O'CONNOR. (*Turning.*) Ah, Mrs. Rattenbury. I'm so very pleased—

IRENE. Come on, dear. That policeman's waiting.

ALMA *and* IRENE *leave the court.*

O'CONNOR. Well, Croom-Johnson, may I congratulate you on an admirable
performance. Of course you had a hopeless case—but you fought it very
well.

CROOM-JOHNSON. Thank you—I must warn you that I intend to raise the
matter elsewhere of your directly appealing to a member of the jury by
name—

O'CONNOR. By name?

CROOM-JOHNSON. Forewoman?

O'CONNOR. Foremost, dear fellow. Foremost. Your hearing's letting you down.

CROOM-JOHNSON. It was, in my view, unpardonable—and I will say so.

O'CONNOR. Really! You mustn't let a little set-back sour you, dear fellow. Been
playing much golf lately?

CROOM-JOHNSON. Not much. Excuse me. (*He goes.*)

O'CONNOR. (*Gleefully.*) Bad loser. I've always said so.

CASSWELL. (*Approaching.*) Well, O'Connor. Magnificent. The boldness of it staggered me.

O'CONNOR. (*Chuckling.*) Yes. I took a risk or two.

CASSWELL. There was a moment when I actually thought you were pleading with the jury to have the woman burned as a witch.

IRENE *has appeared, breathless.*

IRENE. Mr. O'Connor—she's disappeared—Alma's disappeared—

O'CONNOR. (*His mind elsewhere.*) Alma?

IRENE. She suddenly ran right across the street and disappeared—

MONTAGU. What happened?

IRENE. Just now. There was this bus, I thought she was going under it. I shouted to her—but she didn't seem to hear. She just ran and ran.

MONTAGU. She knows your address. She's probably going there.

IRENE. But she doesn't.

MONTAGU. Well, the best thing to do is to go back to where she left you. She's bound to come back when there's no one else around—

IRENE. No one recognised her I'm sure. Shouldn't I tell the police?

MONTAGU. There's not much they can do. I'll come with you.

*They exit.*

O'CONNOR. Really, women of that class do panic so easily.

*The lights come up on* MRS. DAVENPORT'S *flat.* STELLA *is standing belligerently facing the door through which* MRS. DAVENPORT *has just entered.*

STELLA. Well? What happened? Edie?

MRS. DAVENPORT *has gone straight to the drink tray, and poured herself out a large whiskey.*

MRS. DAVENPORT. Didn't you hear it on the news?

STELLA. Come on, Edith. I've only got a few minutes. I mean how did you let it happen? What was the voting?

MRS. DAVENPORT. Let's think . . . I was at the head of the table, which is where they put the forewoman.

STELLA. What's the matter with you? Are you drunk?

MRS. DAVENPORT. Yes, I am a bit. (*She takes a long swig.*) Well, each person spoke up, and I took the votes down. That was my job, you see.

STELLA. The voting. How was the voting?

MRS. DAVENPORT. (*Suddenly brisk.*) Five for guilty, and six for not.

*She replenishes her drink.*

STELLA. So your vote made it six all.

MRS. DAVENPORT. No. My vote made it seven-five. Then all the others gave way.

STELLA. Gave way to you?

MRS. DAVENPORT. Yes.

STELLA. In God's name, why?

MRS. DAVENPORT. Because she was innocent.

STELLA. Innocent?

MRS. DAVENPORT. Of murder.

STELLA. Innocent! Who was it who said that nothing was too bad for that woman, that she deserved lynching?

MRS. DAVENPORT. She may deserve that. She does *not* deserve hanging for a murder she didn't commit.

STELLA. What does that matter, for God's sake?

MRS. DAVENPORT. It matters to me.

STELLA. Well, what price your pretty little house in Bournemouth now.

MRS. DAVENPORT. But—but no-one in Bournemouth knows that I was on the—

STELLA. Oh, of course they did.

MRS. DAVENPORT. I see. Well, I'll have to stay on in this flat.

STELLA. Looks like it.

MRS. DAVENPORT. And I hate it.

STELLA. I know. I must go—(*At the door.*) Poor St. Edith, what's to become of you?

*She goes out. The lights on the flat partially fade, as* MRS. DAVENPORT *pours herself a large neat whiskey and then slowly sits.*

*Meanwhile* ALMA *stumbles to centre stage. She sits, and at length she gets a pencil and a few crumpled envelopes from her pocket.*

*She starts to write.*

*The lights come up on a little* MAN, *sitting at an insignificant desk. He reads quietly from a folder in front of him.*

CORONER. Coroner's report in the matter of Alma Rattenbury deceased. William Mayfield, labourer, of this parish of Christchurch, stated that at about eight thirty p.m. on June 4, he was walking across a meadow through which ran a stream. On the bank of the stream he saw a lady sitting and writing. He crossed the stream by a bridge and went down the bank the other side. As he did so, he looked towards her and saw the lady standing, a knife in her hand. He ran back towards her but before he could reach her she had stabbed herself in the body five or six times, three of the wounds penetrating the heart. When he reached her she was dead, her head lying in one foot of water . . . I do not propose to read all the documents found beside the body. Mostly they appear to be random thoughts scribbled in pencil on the backs of envelopes and such-like—but here is one. It begins: 'I want to make it perfectly clear that no one is responsible for my action. I made up my mind during the trial that if George was sentenced to death I would not survive him—'

*He looks up at an unseen court.*

In this context I might mention as an unhappy chance that had Mrs. Rattenbury lived only a few more days she would have heard of the reprieve accorded to George Wood by the Home Secretary.

*He turns to his folder.*

Now here are what must be her very last words as the paper was found under her body with the pencil still on it.

ALMA. Eight o'clock. After so much running and walking I have got here. I should find myself just at this spot, where George and I once made love. It is beautiful here. What a lovely world we are in, if only we would let ourselves see it. It must be easier to be hanged than to have to do the job oneself. But that's just my bad luck. Pray God nothing stops me. God bless my children and look after them. One has to be bold to do this thing. But it is beautiful here, and I am alone. Thank God for peace at last.

MRS. DAVENPORT *gets up unsteadily carrying her whiskey. We now see she is really very drunk.*

MRS. DAVENPORT. (*Suddenly shouting.*) But I gave you life! . . . I gave you life! . . .

*She sips her drink, shaking her head.*

(*In her most Kensington voice.*) And, might I say, at some considerable cost to my own? . . . Really, there's no justice . . .

*She laughs and drinks.*

ALMA *takes out* CHRISTOPHER'S *scout knife. As she looks at it, the lights fade out.*